D0278696

ROBERT GRAVES

MIRANDA SEYMOUR

ROBERT GRAVES

LIFE ON THE EDGE

Doubleday

LONDON · NEW YORK · TORONTO · SYDNEY · AUCKLAND

TRANSWORLD PUBLISHERS LTD
61–63 Uxbridge Road, London W5 5SA

TRANSWORLD PUBLISHERS (AUSTRALIA) PTY LTD
15–25 Helles Avenue, Moorebank, NSW 2170

TRANSWORLD PUBLISHERS (NZ) LTD
3 William Pickering Drive, Albany, Auckland

DOUBLEDAY CANADA LTD
105 Bond Street, Toronto, Ontario M5B 1Y3

First published 1995 by Doubleday
a division of Transworld Publishers Ltd
Copyright © 1995 by Miranda Seymour

The right of Miranda Seymour to be identified
as author of this work has been asserted in accordance
with sections 77 and 78 of the Copyright Designs and
Patents Act 1988.

A catalogue record for this book is available from the British Library

ISBN 0385 404239

Typeset in 11/13pt Bembo by Hewer Text Composition Services, Edinburgh, Scotland.

Printed in Great Britain by Mackays of Chatham plc, Chatham, Kent.

In memory of
Karl Gay

CONTENTS

LIST OF ILLUSTRATIONS

The historian, Leopold von Ranke. (*Canelluñ*)

A Graves family portrait at Red Branch House, c. 1907. (*Paul Cooper*)

Robert Graves in 1919. (*Francis Guilfoyle*)

Nancy Nicholson and Smuts, 1917. (*Catherine Dalton*)

Nancy and Smuts, 1917. (*Sam Graves*)

RG and Nancy on their honeymoon in Wales, 1918. (*Lucia Graves*)

Siegried Sassoon in 1915. (*Hulton Deutsch Collection*)

Laura Riding, 1934. (*Canelluñ*)

Geoffrey (Phibbs) Taylor, 1934. (*Mrs Mary Taylor*)

A group at the Deyá café. (*Canelluñ*)

Juan Gelat, c. 1935. (*Canelluñ*)

Some Deyá village women with Karl Goldschmidt and RG, 1935. (*Canelluñ*)

RG carrying wood from the field behind Vale House, 1941. (*Hulton Deutsch Collection*)

Catherine, Sam, David and RG at the beach, 1937. (*Canelluñ*)

Basil Liddell Hart and RG in Devon, 1940. (*Canelluñ*)

RG, William, Beryl and their neighbour, Lord Falkland, Devon, 1941. (*Karl Gay*)

RG, Lucia and William at Brixham harbour, 1944. (*Douglas Glass*)

Beryl at Club Nautico, Palma, in 1950 on her wedding day. (*Canelluñ*)

Drawing of RG by Ronald Searle, 1950. (*Ronald Searle*)

RG, Beryl and Jenny (Nicholson) Clifford at Portofino, 1950. (*Wendy Toye*)

Janet de Glanville and Martin Seymour-Smith, attended by James Metcalf on their wedding day, Palma, 1951. (*Canelluñ*)

William, Juan, RG and Judith Bledsoe, Lluch Alcari, 1951. (*Canelluñ*)

Betty and Ricardo Sicre, c. 1948. (*Canelluñ*)

Amy and Clarissa Graves at Erinfa, 1949. (*Canelluñ*)

Jenny (Nicholson) Crosse at Torre Grillo, Rome, 1955. (*Canelluñ*)

RG and Joshua Podro at Posada, 1952. (*Canelluñ*)

Norman Cameron and his third wife, Gretl, at Posada. (*Canelluñ*)

John Aldridge in the late Seventies. (*Lady Mancroft*)

Selwyn and Tania Jepson at Portofino. (*Canelluñ*)

RG and Karl (Goldschmidt) Gay in the Canelluñ study. (*Canelluñ*)

Len Lye and RG in Deyá, c. 1960. (*Canelluñ*)

RG with David Ben-Gurion and his secretary. (*Podro*)

Julie Gay, RG, Ava Gardner, Beryl, Lucia, 1958. (*Canelluñ*)

RG having his hair cut at Canelluñ by Rene Gay. (*Canelluñ*)

RG in his study at Canelluñ. (*Tom Weedon*)

RG on his way down to the *cala* at Deyá. (*Tom Weedon*)

Alastair Reid and RG on the 1958 American lecture tour. (*Canelluñ*)

Idries Shah and RG at Deyá, 1962–3 (*Canelluñ*)

RG and Lucia on her wedding day in Deyá. (*Canelluñ*)

Margot Callas and RG, 1961–2 (*Canelluñ*)

Juli Simon, 1968. (*Canelluñ*)

Ralph Jacobs, RG, Cindy Lee, Beryl, Helen Morningstar, Lucia, at Café Indigo. (*Canelluñ*)

RG at Luggala, Co. Wicklow, 1975. (*Angus Forbes*)

INTRODUCTION

IN TWENTIETH-CENTURY POETRY, ROBERT GRAVES IS TO LOVE
what Philip Larkin is to mortality. The passion of his poetry
reflects a life of extreme intensity. Graves loved women, but only
as incarnations of the Goddess he invented and worshipped. Her
gift was inspiration, and her price for it was pain. Graves lived as
he thought a poet should – on an emotional tightrope. Nothing,
neither his family nor his friends, was allowed to get in the way
of that commitment. It was not only the poet who suffered for
his work.

Graves was born in 1895. A strong streak of puritanism, which his
love of women never entirely overwhelmed, was instilled at an early
age. His mother was religious and high-minded; his father came from
a line of hard-working and public-spirited men. Graves inherited his
interest in Celtic poetry from his father; from his mother, he gained
a lifelong, if unorthodox, fascination with biblical history and a sense
of women as pure beings, not to be associated with sexual thoughts
or deeds.

The event which changed Graves's life was the Great War. He was,
at this stage, more strongly attracted to men than to women, and it

was his harrowing years at the Front which gave him the enduring sense of love as an ordeal, requiring the soldierly qualities of love and resilience. Siegfried Sassoon was his fellow-officer and closest friend; Sassoon's acts of daring strengthened Graves's belief that poets are a singular and heroic breed, set apart from other men. A brush with death in the Somme offensive of 1916 caused him to rethink his life and to dedicate himself to poetry. This, he was convinced, was the purpose for which he had been spared.

Poetry became Graves's substitute for the orthodox religion of his parents. By 1920, shell-shocked and traumatized, he was already responding to the call of 'a drumming muse', and searching for a female-figure to worship instead of the God he had been taught to obey. By 1926, he had found Laura Riding. He was not free to join her; instead, he invited Riding to join him and his wife.

In 1918, anxious to escape from the homosexual circle which he found was slowly enclosing him, Graves had married Nancy Nicholson. Nancy, a strong-minded feminist, encouraged and supported his nascent ideas of a primitive world which had been ruled by women. This was the setting in which Graves placed Riding, a brilliant and self-confident young American poet who identified herself as a prophet and leader. Graves saw a goddess and encouraged Riding to regard herself as one when she joined Nancy and him in England. Their Trinity became 'the Holy Circle' when a handsome young Irish poet came to live with them.

Both Graves and Riding were ardent mythologizers of their own lives; the young Irishman became 'the devil' when he departed to live with Nancy, while Riding's suicide attempt in 1929 became an act of martyrdom. She and Graves left England to live in an isolated village on Mallorca. This, with the exception of Graves's return to England from 1936 to 1946, was his home until his death in 1985.

Graves had many lovable qualities; he was also hugely egocentric. The children of his first marriage never recovered from their sense of abandonment when their father left them and Nancy to live abroad. He did not go to the funerals of his parents or of his oldest daughter, Jenny. He did not go to the help of his second daughter when she believed that her husband had been murdered. He made demands on his second wife, Beryl, which a less understanding woman would have found intolerable.

Graves began his life with Beryl in 1940, when he was still legally married to Nancy. (In 1939 Riding, in a curious episode which belongs more convincingly to the pages of a novel than a biography, had joined an American farmer-poet, Schuyler Jackson, after she, with Graves's connivance, had established that Jackson's wife was a witch.) Three years later, motivated in part by the death in action that year of his first son, David, Graves started to develop the idea of a White Goddess for whom death is a necessary sacrifice. In 1950 he began to search for a more tangible source of inspiration; he announced that the goddess can decide to take up residence in the body of a young woman who, while she commits herself to the poet, acts as his muse. It was no coincidence that he reached this view in 1950, the year of his marriage to Beryl. The prospect of years of gentle domesticity heightened his need for a muse. 'The White Goddess,' he wrote, 'is anti-domestic; she is the perpetual "other woman".'

There was never a shortage of candidates, or a lack of readiness on Graves's part. 'I could fall in love with my big toe if I wanted to,' he told one woman-friend before revealing that she had entered his dreams, a sure sign that she was in line to become a muse. When Graves expressed his love, he always made it clear that this was to be no ordinary affair. The muse was presented, not with a verbal declaration, but with a sheaf of poems which told her that she had already been adopted. Few could resist.

Graves did not believe in discretion. *The Greek Myths* and *The White Goddess*, together with his annual American lecture tours, had made him an almost legendary figure by the 1960s. The muses he celebrated in his poems were discussed in his lectures and interviews. Friends and strangers were invited to share his sense that these were remarkable women and that they, as much as he, were responsible for his work. As justification for his beliefs, he poured out a flood of poems, year after year, in which the story of love, betrayal, and love refound was poignantly unveiled. Facts were doctored by the creation of poetic sequences, with which Graves ensured that the muse would always be seen to have lost her divine power, never simply to have left him for a younger man. He had contrived a myth in which he and the Goddess controlled events.

A series of medical operations, beginning in 1959, affected Graves's brilliant mind. He found it increasingly difficult to separate myth from reality. This, by the time he was seventy and attempting to run off to live in Mexico with a muse, afforded a sad spectacle to the friends who loved him.

I have not, here, given much space to the last ten years of Graves's life in which he existed in the twilight world of the senile, without recognizing the faces of his family and talking, until he lost the power to speak, of the war in which, it now seemed to him, he had acted as a murderer. The sense of guilt had never left him. This, rather than the neglect of his children, was the crime which haunted him and caused him to devise a goddess whose service required him to spend his life as a soldier, bound by his own code of honour to suffer and endure for as long as he was able to create.

Graves's determination to live by his pen was one of his most admirable qualities. His energy was remarkable. Between 1916 and 1975 he produced fifty-five collections of poetry, fifteen novels, ten translations, forty works of non-fiction, an autobiography, and a biography of T. E. Lawrence, a close friend of Graves in the 1920s. The novels, dismissed by their author as potboilers, provided his chief source of income. Two of them, *I, Claudius*, and *Claudius the God*, written in the Thirties, established his international reputation. Among the non-fictional works were the lectures which, when he delivered them at Cambridge and Oxford in the Fifties and Sixties, caused an uproar in the academic world.

Graves delighted in his reputation as an iconoclast. There was little he enjoyed more than taking a bite at the trousers of a revered figure. Virgil and Milton were among his pet hates – typically, he chose to praise the little-known John Skelton as the father of English poetry – and they were closely followed by Saint Paul.

The breadth of Graves's interests was as unusual as his ability to marry them all to his belief in the Goddess. To the large circle of friends who knew and loved him, he was a constant source of knowledge and stimulating ideas. Translators who worked with him spoke of his ability to think himself back into the past and to discover, by intuitive leaps, the facts which they, by slower and more scholarly routes, were able to confirm. Friends talked of his kindness, his loyalty, and his love of gossip. He was always ready to send words of encouragement to a struggling poet, to write an enthusiastic introduction for a friend's book, or to settle down for a discussion about any interesting emotional relationship. Here, too, he was always eager to argue that the Goddess must have been at work.

Talk never interrupted his routine. Every day he took the steep walk from his home down to the sea, outpacing his companions until he was in his seventies with his brisk, military step. Every evening he cleared the dinner-table at ten-thirty and set it again for breakfast, to show that the time for relaxation was over. In his quiet study at the back of the house, surrounded by his books and talismanic objects, Graves put on his heavy spectacles, lit a cigarette and settled down to the careful task of revising his poems.

Graves's character seems, at first, to be contradictory. He celebrated the right of women to be free and independent, but his anger knew no bounds when his muses became attached to other men. Having repudiated the orthodox religion of his parents, he spent some of his most productive years in exploring the historical facts of the Christian story and decoding the Book of Genesis. He wrote about sex in terms of unqualified revulsion, but he also wrote with yearning passion about the physical beauty of his muses. He refused to tolerate bad manners, disliked swearing and showed little patience for writers less disciplined than himself; his hospital records show that he drank more heavily than he admitted and he himself openly spoke of the hallucinogenic drugs he took in order to discover the ancient world's sense of Paradise. He saw himself as an isolated figure who stood outside society. Yet, on his visits to England, he dined with the Spenders and the Day-Lewises; in Mallorca, he entertained filmstars, actors and producers. The Graves who slopped around in shabby corduroys with bare feet was no less authentic than the Graves who wore a brocade waistcoat with 'magic' buttons, or the Graves who swaggered out in later years in a black leather jacket, with a broad-brimmed Cordoban hat crammed down on his white curls. Accent and diction proclaimed him to be a buttoned-up Edwardian Englishman; in his passionate belief in Welsh and Irish literature as the shrine of poetry, he was entirely Celtic.

One of the most problematic aspects of Graves is his hostility to his literary contemporaries and the unveiled contempt he showed for the younger generation of poets. His lifelong scorn of Yeats can be explained by his sense of the older poet as belonging to part of his father's world of the Celtic Renaissance – Graves was never able to acknowledge a debt to his father's love of Welsh and Irish poetry. His contempt for Eliot, Auden, and their heirs is less easy to dismiss. To Graves himself, it was crystal clear. Any poet who did not share his own veneration for the muse was not, in the true sense, a poet. Perversely, he chose to praise a handful of good but minor poets, James Reeves, Norman Cameron, Harry Kemp, and devoted himself to promoting them in the face of literary fashion.

These were men who, he believed, shared his own code of honour; it was his contention that a flaw in a poet's character will invariably reveal itself in his work. Neither Yeats nor Auden seemed to him to have the integrity he considered essential for their vocation.

It was partly as a result of this refusal to accept conventional literary attitudes that Graves achieved his position as an outsider to the mainstream of English poetry. The poets he despised frequently admired and imitated his early and, many would say, his finest works: the poems in which the horror of war was still present and in which he, alone among the poets of the Twenties, attempted to analyze himself and exorcize the past. A later generation was profoundly affected by his 'historical grammar of poetic myth', *The White Goddess*. Ted Hughes, who read it as a student at Cambridge, called it 'the chief holy book of my poetic conscience' and encouraged Sylvia Plath to study it, too. The files at Graves's Mallorcan home are crammed with letters from young poets in the Sixties and Seventies who had chosen him for their mentor and exemplar. The love-poetry which he wrote during these decades had a universal appeal which ensured his position as one of the most widely read and loved poets of the time.

I began this book knowing that the whole story had not been told, and that it was there to be uncovered. Already a devoted admirer of Graves's work, this added to my excitement at being invited to write his life. I was aware, too, that nobody had yet examined his relationships with women in any detail; this was a key which needed to be turned if I was to understand Graves's dedication of himself to the Goddess and her muses. As a novelist, I was fascinated by the idea of a man who invented his own poetic myth and forced his life to fit this imposed image.

For the biographer, part of the addictive interest is that of becoming a detective, examining significant locations for some piece of missed evidence, hunting for elusive witnesses, examining medical records, uncovering contradictions, evasions and lies. Graves, from this point of view alone, has been a richly satisfying quarry. Ten years after his death, knowing that I had the goodwill of the family, many people felt ready to talk on subjects they had not previously discussed. Laura Riding's death in 1993 simplified my task. Previous biographers, of both Graves and Riding, had the painful experience of being compelled by her to rewrite their accounts in order to fit in with Riding's own view of events. This, happily, was not a problem which confronted me. The views expressed here, based on documentary evidence, are my own. The witnesses who were kind enough to discuss their own memories of Riding were able, for the first time, to do so without the troubling sense that they might be made to regret their candour.

Most of Graves's letters are in public collections, but a surprising number of these turned out not to have been previously examined. Others are still in private hands. It has been possible for me to study many of these and even – for Graves's friends have in common an unusual degree of good faith – to take them away with me for more leisurely examination. This has resulted, to take one example, in new light being shed on the tangled relationships of 'the Holy Circle' by letters from the Irish poet, Geoffrey Phibbs, and corroboration provided by his widow, Mary Taylor.

Several of the source documents, previously used as if they were of impeccable accuracy, contradict the evidence provided by letters and diaries, and with the oral accounts of witnesses. I have been obliged to reject the stories told by one of Graves's oldest friends, Lucie Brown, of the poet's promiscuous behaviour in the early Thirties. Lucie was not present at some of the most dramatic events described by her. Her memoir, written at the behest of another of Graves's friends, Tom Matthews, was composed when she was no longer in full possession of her memory. Examination of conflicting statements and records has shown that Lucie tended to confuse one story with another, conflating them to create a memorable, but unpersuasive, image of Graves constantly betraying the vow of celibacy which he had undertaken for Laura Riding. The same judgement applies to Tom Matthews's book, *Under the Influence*, an interesting but misleading account of the poet's personal relationships. Matthews too readily depended on Lucie Brown's version; he further confused the issue in his wish – a very understandable one – to distance himself from the distressing events which took place on his friend Schuyler Jackson's farm in 1939.

There has been a growing inclination to accept Laura Riding's claim to have given Graves the ideas for *The White Goddess*. I have shown that the Goddess was present in Graves's mind long before he met her and that Riding is more likely to have been influenced by his knowledgeable accounts of an early matriarchal civilization, and by his belief that certain women were possessed of a magical power. In 1927 Riding and Graves together wrote an influential book, *The*

Survey of Modernist Poetry; later, Riding claimed that she alone had written the sections which influenced William Empson and the school of New Critics which followed him. A careful reading of Graves's early texts, together with the evidence provided by letters from Empson himself, has made it possible to dismiss Riding's assertions and to establish Graves himself as the principal influence.

My chief concern has been to examine the motives for Graves's behaviour. What made him react so violently against parents who had attempted to help and support him? Why, when he was so closely enmeshed in homosexual circles, did he suddenly decide to marry Nancy Nicholson? Why did he, apparently, subordinate himself to Laura Riding? Why did he need to create the all-powerful figure of the White Goddess? Why did he choose a life of exile? Why, having found Beryl, a woman who truly loved him – and for whom he wrote some of his most moving love-poems – did he put himself through the torment and inevitable humiliation of pursuing young women and turning them into his muses? Was his love for the muses sexual, or was it the metaphysical twinning of souls described in his poems? How much of what Graves wrote did he believe? These are important questions in the life of a man who held that there was a direct connection between what he thought and did and what he wrote.

Today, Graves is better-known as the author of the *Claudius* novels and *The Greek Myths* than as a poet. I have tried to redress the balance in this book. It is as a poet that he has earned himself a place in English literature, but it is, sadly, only by poets and a few enthusiasts that he is still regarded as an original and influential presence. Those who have discovered his poetry for themselves have invariably been dazzled and enthralled. But, until very recently, he has been absent from the bookshop poetry shelves with the exception of a few small representative collections and the last – in my view, disastrous – 1975 collection for which Graves, who was then eighty, and senile, cannot be held responsible.

Graves himself was never troubled by changes in fashion. His poetic reputation, he airily announced, went in fifteen-year cycles. He did not doubt that his moment would come again. He made that statement some twenty-five years ago. The time has come for us to acknowledge him again, not only as the author of some of the most brilliant and original poetry of the Twenties and Thirties, but as the greatest love-poet Britain has produced for over a century.

PART ONE

AMY

CHAPTER ONE

1895–1909

YOUTH

SIDE BY SIDE THEY STAND, THIS VERY PROPER VICTORIAN COUPLE on their honeymoon in Munich in 1891. She is Amalia, or Amy, von Ranke, aged thirty-four, the oldest daughter of a German professor of medicine. He is Alfred Perceval Graves, aged forty-five, the second son of the Irish Bishop of Limerick. Her mother is the Norwegian daughter of the Greenwich astronomer Ludwig Tiarks. His mother is a Cheyne, a Scot from a family tracing its line back to the times of Robert the Bruce.

The Graves family and the von Rankes are alike in being industrious, religious and altruistic. The Graveses are superstitious, poetic and quick-witted; they excel in word games, anagrams, puzzles and rhymes. Alfred's father, a brilliant anagrammatist, is also a leading authority on the ancient Irish alphabet called Ogham, which demonstrates his skill at deciphering codes. The Graves family is also famously absent-minded, careless about finishing sentences and ferociously competitive. Several family members have had nervous breakdowns.

The von Rankes are more disciplined and political. Amy's father started out as a rebellious student who participated in the 1848 risings in Prussia and ended by working to improve the diet and living conditions of the Munich poor. Her great-uncle Leopold, who brought the dignifying 'von' into their family, was one of Germany's greatest historians, the man who wrote that he wanted 'wie es eigentlich war' – to see things as they really are. His marriage to Clarissa Graves, Alfred's aunt, united the two families in the 1840s.

The photograph has been taken while Amy introduces Alfred to her father – he has already met her mother and sisters in London – at Laufzorn, the pretty old hunting-lodge near Munich which her mother's money enabled them to buy and restore. It is called a lodge but is in fact a house of handsome size.

In later life, photographs of Alfred show a trim little man in a frock-coat with a long white beard and neat hands and feet. It is not surprising to learn that he enjoyed dancing a jig. Here, as a hard-pressed widower with five children to be cared for and a demanding job as an inspector of schools, he seems earnest and tired. The drooping walrus moustache gives him the look of an honest, depressed bank manager. We know that he is standing either on tiptoe or on a small box because he is a good inch taller than his wife. In other photographs, even though he stands while his wife sits, it is plain that she towers over him. But it would not, on her honeymoon, be diplomatic to do so.

Amy does not care much for clothes and her taste in them is famously dowdy, but she has made an effort today. Perhaps her sister Lily, who helped arrange the match, has chosen her smart jacket with its black satin bows. Robert, in later years, would be astonished by his physical resemblance to his great-great-uncle Leopold. In his wit, his curiosity, his love of language, his superstitiousness, his truculence and his jerky, eloquent, captivating speech, he was a Graves through and through; in looks, he was a von Ranke. Here, in Amy, we see the same full but closed lips, the direct, slightly dreamy stare, the strong, rounded jaw. Not knowing them well, we might guess that Mr and Mrs Graves will make a congenial couple, but not a romantic one, and that the wife, discreetly, will rule the home. If we are given the additional knowledge that Amy is much wealthier than her husband, we might grow even more certain that this will be the case. And we would be right.

* * *

Robert Graves's feelings about his family background fluctuated according to his mood and interests. As a boy, he was proud of his Irish blood. When he wrote *Goodbye to All That*, in 1929, he was still overcome with guilt at the thought of all his German relations who had died in the war. Then, he wrote that he preferred his German family. By 1957, when he revised the book, his son David had been killed in the Second World War and he had become close enough to several Jews to be ashamed of belonging to the same race as the Nazis. In the 1957 edition, the preference switched to his Irish and Scottish antecedents. Later still, Graves liked to say that, having spent much of his childhood in Wales, he was Welsh by adoption. In his last phase of family interest, he became absorbed by the history of the Scottish Cheynes. For the biographer, however, there can be no doubt that, while Graves had many of the physical characteristics of his mother's family, he was first and foremost the product of his father's.

★   ★   ★

The name Graves derives from *graef*, the Norman word for a quarry, suitable enough for a family who loved delving into the meaning of words. Their arrival in England from France is dated, variously, to the twelfth and the fifteenth century. The first notable Graves was a Roundhead colonel who turned royalist after being put in charge of Charles I at Carisbrooke Castle. Robert, a staunch monarchist, approved of his ancestor's change of heart.

Settled in Co. Kerry, Ireland, the family produced an impressive number of clergymen, many of them with a literary bent, most of them long-lived. The great-uncle after whom young Robert was named had been one of Wordsworth's closest friends; Alfred revered him as a second father.

Janie Cooper, the first Mrs Graves, had been dead for six years when Alfred's sister Lily decided that a busy man whose spare time was entirely taken up with helping to run Irish literary and folk-song societies needed a second wife. After holding discussions with their German cousin Friedhelm and his wife, another Lily, she learned that Lily's sister, Amy von Ranke, might be a suitable candidate.

Amy, as her descendants never wearied of saying, was a very good woman. And, as good women will, she sought to instil her own high standards of rectitude and moral probity in her children. In terms of self-sacrifice, hers was a hard act to follow, something of which her sons and daughters were aware long before she wrote her memoirs. (Robert did not see these until 1967, the year in which he reshaped them into the wonderful story, 'Miss Briton's Lady-Companion', with a few additional imaginative flourishes.[1] But he evidently knew most of the details already, since they appear in his 1929 autobiography, *Goodbye to All That*.)

As a child, Amy fondly recalled, she had been known as the little policeman because of the way she watched over her siblings. It had been no hardship. She was glad to be able to warn them of the angels who thrust their spears into the eyes of wicked children, and of the fate that awaited those who took five currants from a plate when only three were offered.

At the age of eighteen, Amy was sent to London to become the companion to Mrs Tiarks, an elderly relation whose husband had adopted Amy's mother and aunt as orphans. Amy went dutifully, and stayed for sixteen years. Mrs Tiarks's terror of poverty meant that the most rigorous economy was practised; the dining-room and drawing-room were always locked against burglars and every scrap of food was accounted for. Once a year, however, Amy was allowed to return home to Germany as 'dear granny's' companion. She was in Munich for the fancy-dress party to celebrate her sister Clara's wedding. Having no sense of humour, Amy went dressed as Nelson's Column to show her affection for London.[2]

Graves, romantically, claimed that his mother had been sent to England to prevent her marrying the rich, ancient Roman Catholic Prime Minister of Bavaria. The true story showed his mother's conscientious nature in a sharper light. She received the Prime Minister's proposal while she was living in London; she was tempted, but refused him because of her promise not to abandon 'dear granny'.

Mrs Tiarks was a bully but not a monster. Having told Amy that she would inherit two-thirds of her fortune, she was ready to keep her word when it was discovered by Amy's computations that she had a surplus £100,000-worth of untouched investments. But Amy insisted that the money should be fairly shared out among her family. After a year of acting as 'dear granny's' nurse, sleeping on a sofa in the corner of her room and using her weekly day off to sing hymns in a hospital to 'some who were worse off than I', she was released by Mrs Tiarks's death. The money was distributed as she had asked – Amy took for herself only the initial £10,000 which she had been promised, and the use of the house for a year. It was this house, in

Gloucester Terrace, Bayswater to which Alfred Graves came to pay court to Amy in October 1851.

★   ★   ★

Amy's family were enthusiastic about the prospect of marrying her off to rosy-cheeked, red-haired little Alfred, the genial author of that well-known Irish ballad 'Father O'Flynn' (from which, having sold his copyright, Alfred had earned only a few guineas while the composer and music publisher had made small fortunes). Mr Graves was welcomed into the Gloucester Terrace house and urged towards Amy who, he was told, was hoping to play the piano for him. Amy, seeing how smartly her sisters retreated to leave them alone, realized that she had been trapped. She did not ask their guest to sing 'Father O'Flynn' and she did not respond to a flowery message the following day to the effect that he had come, seen and was conquered.

Graves and Amy's family had been playing their cards clumsily. Amy liked her independence and she was not romantic. What she wanted was to be useful: she had been planning to go and do missionary work in India. It was only after she had been introduced to his motherless children, Philip, Molly, Richard, Perceval and Susan, that she began to see a role for herself. Even then, however, her memoirs leave an uncomfortable suggestion of a consent achieved by pressure.

> I did not say No, and perhaps I said Yes . . . Alfred at once told my Mother that it was 'All Right' . . . I felt it hard that all should be settled so suddenly and barely before I knew my own mind. Immediately after breakfast we had a little talk in the breakfast room and then he felt bound to wire news of his engagement to his father and Uncle Robert. Now, I felt, my bridges are burnt and I cannot go back.[3]

They married two months later. On their honeymoon, Alfred admitted that any good woman who was ready to look after the children would have done. Theirs was an affectionate, loyal and, latterly, companionable alliance, but, as Robert told a friend many years later, there had been no love in it.[4]

★   ★   ★

Pregnant in the first year of her marriage, Amy hoped for a boy: she wanted, she told the old Bishop of Limerick, to produce a grandson worthy of his name. But her first two children were daughters and Clarissa, the oldest and most sensitive, suffered for it. Rosaleen, born in 1894 and treated with a good deal more affection, became a more assertive character.

Robert, the first of Amy's three sons, was born on 24 July 1895. This made him – by grace of a day – a Leo, a point which is worth noticing, for Graves was a passionate believer in astrology. Shunning any form of analysis, he preferred to put his faith in the zodiac. Many of his later poems display the poet as a lion hero, favoured by the goddess who keeps him for her chosen beast.

> 'Her ladyship is not at home?'
> 'No, sir.'
> 'She was expecting me. My name is Lion.'[5]

In certain ways, Graves fitted his 'given' character uncommonly well; in others, we have to laugh at him for believing in planetary influences. The Leo character is usually thought to love bright colours, to dominate conversation, to show a tendency to bully and swagger, to be extrovert, noisy, active and vain. Leos are also supposed to be impulsive, proud and strong-willed.

If we take the vanity to be of an intellectual kind, these characteristics fit Graves well, but there are just as many which do not fit and which he chose to ignore. The Leo sign produces, for example, extravagance and an obsession with personal appearance. Graves was a lover of bargains and famously dishevelled: stories of his mismatched socks, rumpled hair, use of ties instead of breast-pocket handkerchiefs, bare feet at interviews, are legion. It would be hard to find a man who cared less about how he looked, and yet he had faith in a horoscope which declared him to be a smart dresser. We learn more about the strength of Graves's superstitious faith from this than about the accuracy of astrology.

His first memories were of the handsome brown brick house in Lauriston Road, Wimbledon, which his mother had helped to design. The family had moved to London from Somerset in 1894, when Alfred took up a new appointment to work in Southwark and Bermondsey. The East London schools for which he was now responsible were on the opposite side of the city to the family home, and the children saw little of their father, most of whose evenings were spent chairing discussions of Gaelic and Celtic literature.

'My Best Christmas', a piece published in Robert Graves's old age, provides a detailed account of life in the Wimbledon house when he was four years old, the age at which he started to retain impressions.[6] Robert's grandfather, the Bishop of Limerick, died in the summer of 1899 and, by December, Red Branch House – Alfred named it after a band of chivalrous Irish knights, the Red Branch Heroes, from whom he claimed descent – was full of family treasures of a weightily impressive kind. Prominent among them were two massive marble bas-reliefs of the late Bishop and his wife Selina, a canteen of silver engraved with the haughty Graves motto 'An eagle does not hunt flies' and, on permanent display to inspire the children, the gold medals which Alfred's father and uncles had won at Trinity College, Dublin, for their erudition and scholarship.

On Christmas Eve the children were sent into the unlit hall where they whispered ghost stories to each other until the drawing-room door was flung open to exhibit the glittering tree, the nativity scene and Amy, head back, foot down, playing 'O Come All Ye Faithful' on the piano to welcome them in. Father Christmas (one of Alfred's brothers) then knocked at the window and requested his customary glass of cherry brandy. He drank alone; Amy, Clarissa and even little Robert had taken the pledge in support of Alfred's renunciation of liquor.

The children had already distributed their gifts, bought for 'Jesus's birthday' with their penny-a-week allowances. Now they were each permitted to go to a separate table on which, under a white cloth, their own presents had been arranged by Amy. Her opinion of their behaviour during the year would become clear in the morning when a lump of coal in the stocking sometimes replaced the usual sugar mice and puzzles. But Robert was never punished, for 'I', he reported more than seventy years later, 'was always as good as Prince Albert'.[7]

Robert's saintliness was put to the test in 1899. His presents were magnificent: a musical box, a painting book, a clockwork horse, a toy helmet and drum, two boxes of soldiers, and a red leather prayer-book. A few weeks later he was taken to hospital with scarlet fever and kept in isolation for two months. When he returned home, only the helmet and drum had been rescued by Rosaleen for her personal use until his return; all the other toys had been burnt in case they should infect the new baby. It was not a good beginning to the relationship between Robert and Charles, his baby brother.

Christmas aside, there was little jollity in Wimbledon. The house was full of books but Amy censored what her children read. There were no outings to pantomimes or concerts; Robert remembered only being taken to the British Museum by his mother and told that it was better to see treasures than to own them: 'We can look at them, admire them, and study them for as long as we like. If we had them back at home, we couldn't do better. Besides, they might get stolen.'[8]

Wimbledon Common lay at the end of Lauriston Road, justifying its name in those days by the two or three houses which stood along it beyond Red Branch. Here, the heathland covered more than a thousand acres of scrub, bracken, ponds and disused saw-pits. The early summer woods were thick with bluebells; not far from Lauriston Road there was Caesar's Camp, a neolithic earthwork; a couple of miles away stood a windmill which had been erected just after the Battle of Waterloo and, abandoned, became a playhouse for local children. But Robert did not go to the heath only to play. Repressed at home, he vented his frustration on any small child who crossed his path when he was out of sight of his good-hearted but stern nanny. In the house he was a model of good behaviour; locally he was regarded as moody and rough. He did not, as he grew older, find many young friends in what was still a remote and unassuming extension of the London suburbs.

Although Graves went to his first three schools in Wimbledon, London made little impact on him. His strongest memories of childhood were associated with Germany and North Wales where he spent the school holidays.

Amy continued to visit Laufzorn and Robert went there five times before Grandfather Heinrich's death in 1909 put an end to Bavarian summers. Schloss Aufsess, where Aunt Agnes lived, was an intimidating medieval castle, but Laufzorn was a cheerful, unpretentious manor-house, with a barn where the children jumped from the rafters down to the hay bales, an orchard to be raided, the clear green River Isar to go swimming in and woods to be explored. Wandering through their grandfather's shady pine forest, the Graves children became a tribe of mycophiles who jeered at the English terror of anything more outlandish than the field mushroom.

Robert's youth equipped him well for his later investigations of the mushroom which poisoned the Emperor Claudius, and of its use in ancient religious rites.

Even in London, Robert could terrify himself into staying awake all night with the monster figures of nursery rhymes and fairy stories; in Bavaria, he found gruesome wayside crucifixes with pictures of helpless sinners writhing in sheets of orange flame to add to his private world of nightmares. He did not see the Munich morgue, but his cousins told him how eminent corpses were dressed in their evening clothes and made to sit up, with their limbs attached by strings to a bell. If life remained, the bell would ring. To a child with Robert's vivid imagination, it was a horrifying image; when his grandfather died and went to the morgue, he joined the world of phantoms, sitting upright and glaring-eyed in his silk hat: 'Trying in a nightmare to be alive; but knowing himself dead.'9

Bavaria gave him a rich cluster of childhood memories and a working knowledge of German; the mountains and moors of North Wales gave him an enduring source of myth and imagery.

Graves's attachment to Wales was profound. So was that of his parents, who are both buried at Harlech. It comes as a surprise to find that the family association with it only began after Robert was born. In 1897 Alfred and Amy took the three youngest children for a Welsh holiday on the recommendation of some friends. They stayed in the little grey village which perched on the hillside in the shadow of the most famous of Edward I's 'iron ring' of castles, built as an English defence against Welsh insurrection. Golf-links and the St David's Hotel had not yet arrived; the view from the hillside was as serene as when the king of Ireland sailed across the Bay of Cardigan to Harlech to ask for the hand of the Welsh princess, Branwen.10 Amy, who had not been charmed by Ireland on her one visit to Alfred's relations, saw everything to Harlech's advantage. It was only a five-hour journey from London. It was religious (Lady Winchelsea's mixed choir had already made a name for itself in the area) and there was not a whisper of bohemianism. The countryside was beautiful enough for her to wish to die there – although it was better to live there first, Alfred pointed out – and the land was cheap. By the end of the holiday she had started negotiating to buy a tract of land above the castle (she purchased a good deal more, including adjacent woodland and cottages, over the next few years) on which to erect a house. An architect was found. In 1898, while Alfred worked on in London, Amy returned with the children to oversee the building.

The house she built, Erinfa, was a rectangular stone-clad block with two protruding bays. A steep ascent brought visitors hard up against its side; seen from a distance, it was a bulky shape behind the trees. The charm of Erinfa, meaning 'towards Ireland,' was that of a much-loved holiday house where a brass gong summoned the children to meals, where Clarissa's water-colour landscapes and flowers were arrayed along the wall by the staircase and Amy's piano stood ready for family concerts at the end of the day. In the hall a row of sandy buckets gave way to walking-sticks and golf clubs as the children grew up.[11]

Erinfa, far more than Red Branch House, was home to the young Graveses, who saw it rise from its foundations. 'It was our holiday heaven,' Graves wrote in later life, 'with a sandy beach, wild hills, blackberries, raspberries, blueberries, flowers, mushrooms, adventures.'[12] The house stood on the hillside and Robert's progress there can be charted as an ascent from shore to summit. As a small child he was most familiar with the Morfa, a hard sandy plain from which the sea had withdrawn, tufted with hillocks for playing hide-and-seek and, in spring, for finding plovers' eggs. Old enough to be free of Nurse Emily Dykes, he spent long afternoons with Rosaleen in the great fortress which dominates the village and landscape. 'Oh, to be a child once more, sprawling at ease / On smooth turf of a ruined castle court!' he wrote in 'Down' in 1921, a poem in which the narrator makes sickening identification with a stone dropped through the vacuum of a courtyard well into burning rivers, 'the flame-axis of this terrible world'.[13] Here, as in all his postwar poems which describe falling sensations and imprisonment, the childhood memory of the empty castle was entwined with later experiences of claustrophobia and panic in the trenches.

'I have worked hard on myself in defining and dispersing my terrors,' he wrote in his autobiography. Heights terrified him. The castle at Harlech challenged his worst fears. Accompanied by Rosaleen, he forced himself to scramble up into the broken turrets and towers, to find footholds in the crumbling stone and lean to look down to the miniature shore.[14] This was his first test in self-discipline.

Above and behind the castle stretched the empty hills and moors where, as they grew older, Robert and Rosaleen spent whole days walking and arguing. Sometimes they stopped to rob a lapwing's nest or observe the neat wheel pattern of a heron's daily catch being laid out on a rock. Peering into the dark mouths of caves, they made up their own histories of the area. Time was irrelevant on the Harlech hills; when Graves returned to tramp across them during the war years, he was searching for a return to the anaesthetizing fantasy of an existence in which time meant nothing.

> Time has never journeyed to this lost land,
> Crakeberry and heather bloom out of date,
> The rocks jut, the streams flow singing on either hand,
> Careless if the season be early or late . . .[15]

★   ★   ★

After a visit from the young Hungarian composer Zoltán Kodály in 1895, Alfred had added a collection of wild Hungarian ballads to the repertoire of family songs. His son never forgot them; he was still able to sing them, word for word, when he visited Hungary for the first time in 1968. It was Kodály, too, who gave Alfred the idea of starting every fantastic story with a 'sneeze'. Kodály's opera, *Háry János*, begins with an orchestral equivalent, just to tell us to believe nothing; so, after the young Hungarian's visit, Alfred's stories for his children would always begin with an old gardener blowing his nose on a red pocket handkerchief.

Most of Alfred's spare time, as before his marriage, was devoted to literature. The literary events which occupied his evenings brought him into contact with some eminent men. (His memoirs bring in Swinburne, Ruskin, Yeats and Tennyson, but in a very marginal way. Alfred's eager pursuit of the larger literary figures of his time is an endearing feature of his correspondence.[16]) In 1902 he was made a bard and began to turn Welsh folk-songs into English. Other translations followed; by the time Robert was seven, Alfred was wholeheartedly involved in the world of Welsh poetry. The older boys had left home; Robert was the chief beneficiary of his father's new passion.

Amy's kind but stiff manner and her exceedingly frugal habits had not found her many friends in the Harlech neighbourhood. Alfred had a more gregarious nature. In London he was laughed at behind his back for the zeal with which he pursued literary prestige; in

Harlech his wish to bring Welsh literature and music to the attention of a wider audience could only gratify. Ceirog Hughes, the Welsh Wordsworth, came to call at Erinfa, as did the booming Arch-Druid. Canon Owen Edwards visited, and taught young Robert the difficult rules of writing in bardic rhyme. A local fishmonger from Criccieth took the little boy on a tour of the mythical topography of the area, showed him the path along which the wizard Gwydion had been chased by a king of Dyfed, and told him about the terrible powers of the lovely flower goddess, Blodeuwedd. On one occasion he was taken by his father to the Caernarfon eisteddfod, where his sharp eyes registered the comic contrast between the flowing druid robes and Sunday walking boots plodding through the puddles. Welsh poetry, in Robert's mind, had more to do with the stories of *The Mabinogion* he had started to read in translation than the bowler-hatted gentlemen who stood on platforms with his father to sing the rallying song of the Celts (it was written by Alfred), of which a sample couplet runs: 'That flower of the free is the heather, the heather! / It springs where the sea and the land strive together.'

★   ★   ★

Being Amy's first-born son did not make life easy; on the contrary, it meant that Robert was a child unusually prone to guilt and aware of the need to excel. The family's gold medals were always on display in the Wimbledon drawing-room to remind him of his duty and Amy offered no relief from the silent weight of expectation. Conscious of being second-best to her husband's beloved first wife, she needed her own children to be, at the least, the equals of Janie's older brood. Her maternal affection was closely related to the level of their moral and intellectual achievements; their success was also hers and their conduct was examined with the same scorching zeal which she applied to her own. Failure was not acceptable. Possessed of a precise sense of right and wrong, Amy did not permit her judgements to be questioned. She saw the heavenly pattern plain before her; her self-appointed task was to shape her sons and daughters to fit God's prepared moulds.

Many children have undergone pressured upbringings and survived without noticeable damage. The problem in this case was with the highly-strung nature of the Graves family. Extreme sensitivity was apparent from an early age in Clarissa, Robert and the youngest boy, John, all of whom suffered forms of mental breakdown before the age of thirty. For this, the unforgivingly high standards of their mother were partly responsible. Robert, in later life, invented a mythical figure who would make the same cruel demands on her favourite son. But she, unlike Amy, was controlled by her creator.

Robert adored his mother and he seemed at first to be everything that Amy could want. He was a sturdy, handsome little boy with wide grey eyes, thick, curly black hair and her own full, soft mouth. He had been brave about going to hospital for his first serious illness; he was an obedient if restless member of her hymn-singing group; by the age of six, he knew his Bible well enough to compare banishment from a hymn session to exile in the tents of ungodliness. Full of religious fervour and terrified by Amy's stories of how sinners suffered for their wickedness, he took prayers seriously and won prizes for divinity; pleading for the legacy of a bicycle, he explained that he only wanted one to enable him to visit his dear mother's grave after her death.[17] He readily accepted Amy's pronouncements on the rewards of working hard and the importance of always speaking the truth.

Robert was, in short, given a splendid education in becoming a prig and delighted Amy in the process. Writing to her father at Laufzorn, she reported that he showed a real wish to do things in the correct way. Such conventionality is not instinctive and, in Robert's case, he was driven by a terror of displeasing his mother. In the short term, Amy's views on the importance of keeping himself pure gave her son a fear of sex which was not allayed when she told him in careful detail, at the age of twelve, of how his grandfather had died of cancer of the prostate. (It was an account which he never forgot.) A sense of honour, inflamed by his mother's zeal, made for a miserable experience at school.

He went, in all, to seven establishments, starting with a local dame school and progressing, for two terms, to the new Wimbledon branch of King's College, until he was removed for using bad language. At Rokeby, another local school, he made his name as a quarrelsome bully and was not missed when Alfred, worried that he was not going to achieve the Winchester scholarship they wanted for him, decided on yet another move. The decision was ill-judged; Robert's new boarding-school was run by a man whose abrupt departure seems to have resulted from the discovery of sexual misbehaviour with some of the boys. Graves, in a late story, asserted that the headmaster was given twenty-four hours by the police to leave the country.[18]

The move had one great benefit. It was at this school near Rugby that Graves learned the plain and forceful style of English which enabled him to appeal to a lay audience even when he was writing on the most obscure subjects. Mr Lush, the deputy headmaster, hated florid writing; he taught his pupils to make their verbs do the work of description. A less able writer will always rely on adjectives and adverbs to do this job. Graves never did. This is what gives his prose such vitality and makes it so timeless.

The scandal of the headmaster, together with his failure to win the coveted scholarship, caused Robert's parents to move him once more in the autumn of 1908. His last preparatory school was Copthorne in Sussex and the year he spent here was pleasant, industrious and eventless.

★　　★　　★

School obliged Robert to deal with the troubling fact that he had a sexual identity. Amy had brought him up to think otherwise. Sex was not discussed in the Graves household, except to point a gruesome moral. Flesh was covered at all times. It was a disagreeable shock to Robert, then, when he saw other boys naked for the first time and observed that one of them was hirsute. His description of it – 'red hair, real bad, Irish red hair all over his body' – betrays the lingering, squeamish interest with which he later peered at putrefying bodies in the trenches.[19] Even as a small boy he was courting and exploring the sensation of horror. The feelings stimulated by the naked red-haired boy are closely related to those evoked by the notion of the living figure in the morgue or of imprisonment in the ruined castle of Harlech. By the age of nine, Robert was learning to thrive on images of fear and domination.

Girls frightened him if they showed themselves to have a sexual persona. He saw the red-haired boy in 1904, when he was spending a convalescent term away from Rokeby at Penrallt, a Welsh school where the air was expected to heal the effects of double pneumonia and measles. It was there, too, that the headmaster's small daughter and her friend trapped him in the garden and probed his underclothes to teach themselves about sexual anatomy. Graves told the story in *Goodbye to All That* as a repugnant memory, but it was an odd one. He was strongly built for his age. Could he really not fight off two small girls, or was he courting the experience of fear? It is not impossible that the story was a fabulous one: the reminiscence of little girls exploring sex in a garden has a suspiciously mythical slant.

Writing his autobiography at the age of thirty-six, Graves hunted for reasons to explain why he had been afraid of heterosexual relationships for so long. Searching back, he found a convenient memory of an occasion when he had been removed from Rokeby for an afternoon and sent to sit in the cloakroom of his sisters' school until they could join him for a family photograph. (The Graveses were addicted to these formal records of their happy home life.) Rosaleen and Clarissa were late; Robert was squirming with discomfort at all the giggles and stares directed at him by the time they arrived. His sisters seemed, he thought, to resent his presence and to look at him with anger. It was, he claimed, the memory of this humiliating episode and the little girls' probing fingers which had arrested his 'normal impulses' for years.

Life in a household run on the highest of Victorian principles and Amy's religious fervour had more to do with Robert's retarded sexual development than the glances of girls in a cloakroom, but he liked to explain his psychology by vivid cameos rather than venture into the soul-searching process of analysis. Better not to delve too deeply, for fear of what might be found. Better to gloss over the mysteries with a jaunty tale and a slick interpretation. If there were horrors there, let them find their way to the surface in the trance-state of his poem-writing.

This was Robert's firmly held view and he kept to it. We, observing, can see how Amy bound her eldest son to her with iron hoops of guilt and obligation; how her strict views about sex governed those of her son; how Robert's passion for his mother, that paragon of honour, caused him to place the women he loved on a shrine, however imperfect their behaviour. But Graves himself admitted to none of it, beyond the fact that his mother had encouraged her children to be strong moralists. She was a good woman, and that was all there was to it.

The older sisters also made a contribution to Graves's view of women. Rosaleen, in particular, was his collaborator and rival. Robert contributed rhymes to the house magazine begun by their mother; Rosaleen's rhymes were better and she could compose music to go with them. At school, Rosaleen shone where Robert sometimes lagged; in word games, she could always match or defeat him. When Graves wrote the novel *Antigua, Penny, Puce* in 1936 and presented his portrait of a chuckle-headed brother in the web of a scheming, brilliant sister, he was drawing in part on the memory of his own resentful admiration for Rosaleen. He never doubted that a woman could outwit a man and that it was in her nature to do so.

The heroes of his childhood were the three tall half-brothers, Philip, Richard and Perceval. Perceval, a charming idler, made the least impression with his stories of nights at the music-halls. Robert's hero-worship was reserved for Philip, who recovered from consumption to take a post in Cairo, and Richard, who went to Armenia in the Levant consular service. (These were very typical Graves career choices, of the kind which Robert fought hard not to make.) Both Philip and Dick were kind, lofty figures; they were, above all, free. Chained to the treadmill of academic expectation, Robert envied and admired them.

His first loves were formed after this pattern, innocent crushes on boys who seemed to defy convention. At Penrallt he singled out 'Ronny', a daredevil who climbed trees, killed pigeons with a catapult and broke all the school rules while never seeming to get caught.

Ronny appears in Graves's history of himself for a purpose. It is not clear from his account whether he ever exchanged more than a few words with his hero. Ronny, manly, active and carefree, exists in careful juxtaposition to Robert as he bends over a book of old ballads in the school library, the very picture of the burgeoning poet. Doubtless he did revere the boy, but Ronny's function in the story is to represent the other side of his nature. Perhaps as a result of his father's hard work in ensuring that compulsory games were put on the agenda of all the schools he visited, Graves formed at an early age the view that a real man had to push himself as hard on the physical as on the intellectual plane. Every aspect of life presented a test of character.

★　★　★

Relishing these tests, Graves had little enthusiasm for the quiet, conventional environment of Copthorne, his last preparatory school. Driven by the knowledge that he must succeed to win his parents' approval, he worked hard during his year there and was given extra Latin coaching by Alfred in the holidays. He was highly intelligent and he worked well, but the headmaster could not give Alfred and

Amy the firm guarantee of a Winchester scholarship which they wanted.

Alfred was a careful man – Philip, his oldest son, had been made to repay, with interest, the cost of his cure for consumption – and he wanted no risk of a heavy school bill on the eve of his retirement. Robert's weakest subject was Greek grammar. Charterhouse, of which Alfred knew little, had no Greek grammar paper.

The decision was made. After taking the top scholarship of the year, Robert Graves was sent to Gownboys House, Charterhouse, at the age of fourteen and three months.

CHAPTER TWO

1909–1913

UNHAPPY SCHOOLDAYS

CHARTERHOUSE STARTED LIFE IN 1611 AS A LONDON SCHOOL AND moved to Surrey in 1872. The Gothic style was in fashion for seats of learning and the newly venerable spires dominated the skyline above the River Wey and the little town of Godalming. The school had an illustrious past; the coats of arms on the library windows included those of Crashaw, Lovelace, Addison, Steele, Wesley and Thackeray. Vaughan Williams and Max Beerbohm were both sent there in the 1880s, but its function as a hotbed of creativity was less exalted than its architecture suggested. Charterhouse was not a happy school for individualists.

Its past was honourable but by 1909 its reputation had sunk to unprecedented depths. It is hard to understand how Alfred Graves, a school inspector, together with Copthorne's excellent headmaster, could have thought Charterhouse a suitable establishment for a studious and imaginative child. Any show of interest in work was despised throughout the eleven houses. Sport was the only admired activity and the boys who ruled the school were the 'bloods' who comprised the football and cricket teams. The other principal pastime was what the headmaster, Dr Gerald Rendall, dismissed as harmless 'amorousness'. This, Graves confirmed, was an adequate description for some of the romantic friendships between older and younger boys but not for the nightly assaults or the loveless sex by consent which took place between boys of similar ages.[1]

It was Robert's misfortune that he had been put down for the most notorious of the eleven houses. At Gownboys, according to Charles Graves who followed his brother there in 1913, conditions were so bad that each boy's cubicle was wired to sound an alarm if an intruder drew the curtain. The housemasters lived in quarters away from the boys and either noticed nothing or preferred to be oblivious. The headmaster was almost vacuous in his guilelessness: it was remarked later that he had the harmlessness of a dove without the wisdom of the serpent.[2] A dove was not what Charterhouse needed to lead it in 1909.

Robert's troubles began in his second term. Most were trivial; put together, they made for great unhappiness. There was, for a start, the problem of his own attitude. Taught by his mother to despise wealth, he was conscious now of looking either mean or poor in a school of businessmen's sons where there was none of the Graveses' scorn for trade. Amy's frugality meant that he was too short of pocket money to return tuck-shop treats and too cheaply dressed to escape derision. Used to holding his own in a contentious family, he seemed pushily talkative to his peers, and dully so, since he refused to discuss sex, the only topic of general interest.

It was not his fault that his parents had entered his full baptismal name on the school register and that this was the name which rang out at the daily roll-call. At a time when German goods were seen as a threat to sterling British industries, von Ranke was not a good name to have in a school packed with the sons of businessmen: 'I could,' Robert wrote, 'no doubt have passed off "Ranke" without the "von" as monosyllabic and English, but "von Ranke" was glaring.'[3]

Damned first as a German and then, for good measure, as a German Jew, Graves lacked the flippancy which might have protected him. He was desperate to defend himself. The hero of the school was Desmond O'Brien, a handsome Irish daredevil in the Ronny mould, who broke all the rules and did so with bravado. Seeing a chance to gain some credit, Graves declared his own Irish background. This did not improve his situation. Another Irish pupil in the same house as Graves was enraged that the contemptible German should claim to be his compatriot, and the bullying began in earnest. Ink was tipped over Graves's books, a water-jug over his bed; he was lunged at from dark corners; just before games, he would find that his sports clothes had been removed. Skilfully, the boy played on his prudishness, mocking his shocked reactions to sexual remarks and suggesting that his disgust concealed monstrous depravity. After several weeks of this treatment and with no friends to support him, Robert was near to having a nervous breakdown.

The Graves children were more aware of the change in their brother than were their parents. Clarissa, recording Robert's arrival for the summer holidays in 1910, noted that he addressed their mother by the name of the school matron: it seemed strange, too, when they all added parts to a family serial-story on the long train journey to Harlech, that Robert should contribute a vindictive account of beating up his little brother John for using words of three syllables.[4] None of them could know that he was revenging himself on the Irish bully, but they saw that he was unhappy.

Charles, resented by Robert ever since his new toys had been burned for fear of infecting his baby brother, was the chief victim of his despair. Bullied past endurance, he saved himself at last by pronouncing the terrible word 'Raca!' This, if the Bible was to be believed, threatened an instant end for both brothers in fire and brimstone; it had the desired effect of frightening the well-versed Robert into retreat. After this, he spent as much as possible of the summer weeks in Wales on his own, skulking in the rough, empty moorland above Erinfa.

By March 1911 Graves could bear it no longer. He wrote home begging his parents to take him away. Swearing them to secrecy, he told them about the way he was treated and the things he was expected to do at Gownboys; these details would, he hoped, convince them of the need to remove him.

Their response appalled him. Arriving at the school for his confirmation service a few days later, they reported the contents of their son's letter to his housemaster, Mr Parry, and asked for his advice. Parry, naturally, denied it all and the Graveses went cheerfully home after telling Robert to put his faith in prayer. The full extent of their treachery only became apparent that night, when Robert and his colleagues were told by Parry that he disliked informers, even though one of these despicable creatures had brought attention to the possibility that there was bullying in his house. To Robert, who had until now been the most dutiful of sons, this was an unforgivable betrayal. His trust in his parents had been severely shaken.

Exposed as a sneak, Robert's sufferings were bound to increase. His study was wrecked, he no longer dared to use the communal changing-room and he only escaped being beaten up on the football pitch after developing a psychosomatic heart problem. But the bullying continued until, in desperation, he decided to pretend that he had gone mad. This ruse was, for a time, effective; he was left to his own devices.[5]

⋆　⋆　⋆

'Since the age of fifteen poetry has been my ruling passion,' Graves wrote in the opening to *The White Goddess*. This tallies with the account he often gave to friends of having been converted to poetry while going through a particularly bad time at school. Ordeals, he later argued, were necessary and beneficial experiences. The more he suffered, and the more he courted suffering, the more convinced he became of this truth.

Alfred had already given him the grounding to become a poet by making him work at his Latin compositions in a way which challenged his son's skills.

> I had to be meticulous about quantity . . . And I had to make Virgil and Ovid my exemplars in metrical correctness . . . I learned exactly in what a *gradus ad parnassum* spirit eighteenth-century odes and pastorals were written; and how easy it was to compose mock-heroic satires on the Charterhouse Masters, from sheer boredom with the literary epic.[6]

It was not an experience which Graves had relished and it gave him a lasting distaste for virtuosity as opposed to inspiration. But Alfred's training helped to make a remarkable craftsman of him and Alfred's encouragement of the doggerel rhymes which he and Rosaleen wrote together gave Robert faith in his ability to become a poet.

His father's old-fashioned taste was all that he had to rely on when he began to ransack the shelves of the school library, and he was right never to publish the first rhymes which he wrote at school. But, by the summer of 1911, he had discovered Coleridge and identified his own nightmares in the vivid imagery of 'Christabel' and 'The Rime of the Ancient Mariner'. Drawing on his knowledge of the rugged, timeless landscape at Harlech, he set out to show fear as a seductive force. The result was 'The Mountainside at Evening'.

> Now even falls
> And fresh, cold breezes blow
> Adown the grey-green mountain side
> Strewn with rough boulders. Soft and low
> Night speaks, her tongue untied
> Darkness to Darkness calls.
>
> 'Tis now men say
> From rugged piles of stones
> Steal Shapes and Things that should be still;
> Green terror ripples through our bones,
> Our inmost heart-strings thrill
> And yearn for careless day.[7]

Echoes of the sinister nocturnal imaginings of the country child in Wordsworth's long autobiographical poem 'The Prelude' are too strong to be ignored. But there is a crucial difference. The young Wordsworth, hurrying home after laying traps and snares, is pursued by the spirit of his own guilt:

> and, when the deed was done
> I heard among the solitary hills
> Low breathings coming after me, and sounds
> Of indistinguishable motion, steps
> Almost as silent as the turf they trod.[8]

The difference is in the response. Wordsworth saw the product of a guilty conscience and made it into something unequivocally terrifying. Graves responded to the idea of a night-world haunted by phantoms with violent excitement: 'ripples' and 'thrill' are words which suggest ecstatic involvement. This sense of green terror was what he later described as the test of a true poem, when 'the hairs stand on end, the eyes water, the throat is constricted, the skin crawls and a shiver runs down the spine . . .'[9]

'The Mountainside at Evening' was the poem which changed Graves's life at Charterhouse. Its publication in the school magazine led to his being invited to join the Poetry Society run by Guy Kendall, a form-master in another house. Graves was the youngest of the seven boys who met each week at Kendall's home. Here, he made his first friend.

Raymond Rodakowski, half Scottish, half Polish, was a year older and in a different house. But for their membership of the Poetry Society, friendship would have been inconceivable. When they were walking back from Kendall's home one evening, Graves talked about the difficulties he was having. He was still jeered at for his name and he had just suffered the humiliation of finding one of his poems, raided from his study, pinned up in a room he was forbidden to enter, exhibited for general mirth and comment. Rodakowski sympathized and told him that he ought to take up boxing. It was, he said, the only way to impress the sporting 'bloods' who always feared a spoiling blow to their handsome faces. As a boxer, Robert would be able to hold his own in the school. And, since few boys did boxing, it would give the two of them an opportunity to meet. He also, and this meant much from a respected older boy, said that Robert was a good poet and a good person.

Graves took Rodakowski's advice and thrived on it. He did not become a happy schoolboy – he never forgave his parents for leaving him at a school he hated when he had begged for release – but he did learn to defend himself. His career as a boxer marked the switch from victim to aggressor; it also marked the stirring of his first sexual feelings. Boxing with Raymond in the annual display at the end of the 1911 autumn term, Graves responded to it as a form of lovemaking. In the first and more sensational version of his autobiography, he admitted to having experienced the match as a 'sex feeling'.[10] But he went no further. Amy's teachings had taken too strong a hold to permit anything more than an imagined transgression. What mattered was the sense of a bond with another boy, someone with whom he could share the thrill of physical action as well as the creative process of making poetry. His sisters had gone on to study music and art in London; Raymond more than filled the gap which they left in his life.

The Poetry Society had a short existence. Frank Fletcher, who succeeded Rendall as headmaster, was determined to lift the moral tone of the school. In the summer of 1912 he learned that two anonymous poems in the school magazine which hinted at romantic connections between pupils had been written by members of the society. The boy who disclosed the authors' names, and was called as witness against them by the headmaster, was Robert. Dr Fletcher acted decisively; the society was dissolved and the culprits were demoted from their monitors' posts.

It was no great loss – Kendall's teaching had been well-intended rather than inspired – but it is significant that the incriminating evidence came from Robert, for whom the society had provided an escape from isolation. The high moral standard which had been set by Amy made him capable of a most unlovable self-righteousness. In his own mind, he was clear; all that mattered was to tell the truth. This was the certainty which he would use as a weapon throughout his life. Knowing he was right, there was no room for doubt.

★　　★　　★

In the Christmas holidays of 1912, Alfred and Amy decided to take their children on a visit to Brussels. It was a holiday worthy of E. M. Forster's sharp pen. The family stayed in a pension where they all, children and parents, took daily French lessons from their landlady. In the afternoons they went ice-skating or looked at the shops. Alfred, a keen advocate of the cinema as a means of education, arranged visits to a suitably 'good clean show' with religious scenes and two unstirring love-stories. (We know that they cannot have been very stirring because Charles Graves remembered being told not to look when, a year later, a film showed a woman swaying after a glass of champagne. A screen embrace or kiss would have been unthinkable.)

Romance flourished, however, in the Graveses' pension. Two Irish sisters were staying there and one of them, Lola, fell in love with Robert. At seventeen, he was near to his full height of six feet two inches, strongly built, with high cheek-bones and thoughtful grey eyes. The irregularities of his face – a crooked smile because he minded about showing two broken teeth, and a badly set nose from a football injury – made him look less of a clean-cut schoolboy than his younger brothers. Used to performing in concerts at home, he had a good voice and an excellent memory for songs.

Perhaps Robert's eyes thoughtlessly rested on Lola as he sang a ballad in the pension's parlour. Miss Irwin was observed by the young Graveses to be captivated by their brother; he, however, was full of shame at being singled out and turned into an object for the mockery of his sharp-tongued sisters. There was no escaping her. It was a small pension and the evenings were spent in home entertainment, charades, recitals, everything which allowed Lola the chance to pair herself off with him. Already paralysed with embarrassment, Robert's nerve cracked when a religious painting crashed from the drawing-room wall one night, framing him and Lola before the company and increasing the merriment of his family. Looking back, he thought Lola's advances had been very charming. At the time, however, 'It frightened me so much, I could have killed her.'[11]

It was not just the fear of being laughed at which caused his feeling of revulsion. At home, Amy had trained her son to have a mind so pure that the very thought of a girl making advances suggested hellish degradation. At Charterhouse, mixing daily with boys to whom the sexual shape and behaviour of a woman seemed freakish and disgusting, Robert had been affected by that attitude. Lola's crime was to be a female behaving in a female way.

The Brussels holiday had not been a happy experience for Graves and his thoughts about sexual predators were still with him when he returned to school. It may have been a displaced sense of protectiveness which turned him towards 'Peter', the name by which George Harcourt Johnstone was known to his friends. Three years younger than Graves, he was a precociously clever aristocrat from a Yorkshire family, a nervous, good-looking boy with a narrow white face and dark hair. Widely read and with a remarkable gift for languages – he later became fluent in Russian, Arabic and Romanian – his literary heroes were the French poets Baudelaire, Mallarmé and Verlaine, to whom he introduced Graves.

An affinity was quickly established. It was ardent and undisguised enough for Graves to be called before the headmaster for questioning. Confronted by a pale, furious boy who compared his feelings for Johnstone to those of Shakespeare, Plato and the Greek poets, Dr Fletcher agreed not to pursue the matter.

Robert's feelings were more confused than he acknowledged. The most striking example of this came in his final term. A boy, knowing how he felt about Johnstone, told him that he had seen the choir-master kissing his friend. (It was the choir-master, incidentally, who had first rebuked Graves for his association with the younger boy.) Johnstone could not be blamed; the loved one was always sinned against in Graves's eyes. Instead, he went to the master and demanded his resignation. The man denied the charge, but collapsed when Johnstone chose to confirm it. He promised to resign at the end of the term; Graves, elated, rushed down to the swimming-pool and jumped in from the highest springboard, some twenty-four feet.

Moral outrage played a part in his behaviour, but Robert himself identified the underlying feeling as jealousy. It was hard for him later to be sure that his feelings were as pure as he would have wished. Had he been shocked or had he wanted to keep Johnstone for himself? Poems, in which Johnstone was the steady object of adoration, allowed him to fudge the issue with sentiment; in prose, he continued to evade it. In 1929 he was willing to say in *Goodbye to All That* that romance at public-school age was always homosexual and that he had only recovered from that tendency at the age of twenty-one. In 1957 he deleted the personal reference from his book; having turned against homosexuals, he could not accept that his own love for Johnstone had been in any way physical.

★   ★   ★

In love, Graves was forgiving; in friendship, he could be brutal. Johnstone could do no wrong; Rodakowski, Graves's first ally and supporter, was dropped shortly before he was due to visit Erinfa in the summer of 1913.

Fear was the cause of the break. Rodakowski had suddenly declared himself an atheist; he made it clear that he would not hide or compromise his belief in any circumstances. Graves, contemplating the likely reaction of his parents, decided to terminate the friendship. Rodakowski remained kind and affectionate, but Graves kept his distance.

Breaking the friendship meant that there could be no embarrassing scenes at Erinfa but that was only a part of the reason. Graves was afraid that Raymond could be right. He had already been shaken by the unremarkable nature of his confirmation, keenly anticipated as the climax of his religious experience. In the event, the only circumstance of interest had been that the boy who knelt at his side to be blessed fell off the stool. Alfred and Amy, standing proudly in the school pews, congratulated themselves on Robert's respectful attention to the Bishop of Zululand's address. Neither then nor for many years afterwards were they aware that their boy's confidence in God was wavering.

Graves did not dare to listen to Rodakowski. If he questioned the existence of God, the whole world of his childhood began to topple. Everything had been built on that belief. To be deprived of God was to be left in a void, and, worse, with the sense that he had been cheated by his parents. So he broke with his friend, but the doubts deepened into conviction and the feeling of savage, undirected resentment grew.

Looking back on his youth, Graves felt angry about all forms of parental pressure, but none more than the orthodox religion imposed by his fervent mother. He felt that he had given up one of his closest friends in order to avoid a row with his parents about belief, and that enraged him. He felt that he had been moulded to suit Amy and Alfred's expectations, not his own needs and interests. He felt that religion had been used as a threat, to tyrannize him into submission and guilt.

His bitterness was justifiable, and yet Amy's faith had given him a security which made its loss a poignant and resonant theme in his work. Indirectly she had provided him with one of his most powerful subjects, the search for God in human form. The two *Claudius* novels, published in 1934, portray a man who becomes a god. *King Jesus*, his novel of 1946, presents Christ as the most godlike of men. The White Goddess described in his famous study of 1948 is created by the imagination of poets. The yearning need for an omnipotent force continued to haunt him.

CHAPTER THREE

1913–1915

FIRST YEARS AS A POET

THE YEARS 1913–14 MARK A WATERSHED IN GRAVES'S LIFE AS HE turned away from his family and resolved to dedicate himself to becoming a poet. Contributions to *The Carthusian* show him trying his hand at every style from cockney songs to Tennysonian dirges. At home, he was provided with a cottage on the Erinfa estate by his mother – it was intended for all the children, but was monopolized by Robert and Rosaleen – in which to work on writing ballads and trying his hand at the complicated structure of the Welsh englyn. His skill increased; his subject matter remained as lively as cold tea. Apart from an occasional nervous nod towards the dark gods of the woods which was Robert's idea of a courageous stand against conventional religion, he wrote poetry that could just as well have been penned by his jaunty, competitive father.

Alfred Graves's interest in new work came to a stop shortly before the turn of the century. It was fortunate, then, for Robert's progress that George Mallory, a close friend of Rupert Brooke with a keen interest in the modern literary world, came to Charterhouse as an assistant master in 1912. Struck by Graves's confidence and brilliance in a school debate, he decided to make a protégé of him.

Mallory was in his mid-twenties and looked much less. A pictur-
esque, argumentative, untidy young man with a bright scarf always
knotted around his neck, he was frequently mistaken for one of
the boys he taught. Mountaineering and poetry were his twin
enthusiasms; in the spring of 1913 he asked Robert to join him
and some friends on a Snowdon climb. The experience strengthened
friendship into a feeling which was closer to a family relationship than
that of teacher and pupil. Long after Mallory's tragic disappearance
on Everest in 1924, Graves stayed in close contact with his wife
Ruth and their daughter. Mallory had been nearer to Robert in age
and character than his own admired older half-brothers, sharing his
love of poetry and his need to be constantly testing himself, pushing
himself to the limit.

As a teacher, Mallory imported from Cambridge an intellectual
love of debate. Among the subjects he set for essays were 'Honour',
'Candour' and 'Hypocrisy'. He made the Charterhouse boys act
instead of reading texts aloud and asked them to discuss and criticize
their own debating sessions. As a literary mentor he was invaluable.
His study, crammed with modern English and French literature and
poetry, was where Graves was soon spending all of his spare time.
Here he learned about the authors unmentioned, or disapproved of,
by his father. John Masefield's bawdy, violent, blasphemous poem
of 1911, 'The Everlasting Mercy', gave him a sense of excitement
which he never forgot, but he was also given his first introduction to
Shaw, Rupert Brooke, Wells and, most importantly, Samuel Butler.
Old-fashioned though they sound to us, these were the writers who
represented a new world for Graves.

One of Mallory's least successful ventures was a literary magazine
for the school, to be run by himself, Graves, Raymond Rodakowski
and another bookish boy, Cyril Hughes Hartmann. He called it
Green Chartreuse and persuaded his friend Duncan Grant to do a
cover featuring a liqueur-swigging monk. Graves's contribution to
the magazine – it only survived for one issue – was a story based on
memories of his first year at the school. By 1913 he could be almost
light-hearted about that miserable period.

His new ally introduced him to the London poetry circuit.
Through Rupert Brooke, Mallory had come to know Edward
Marsh, founder of the Georgian Poets. This nebulous group had
begun as a joke. During an evening which Marsh spent with Mallory
and Grant in the autumn of 1912, talk about the craze for little poetry

collections had led to the idea that they should publish a parody volume. Two days later Marsh decided it was worth doing something more serious as he entered his forties. He and Brooke would be the invisible editors. The poets they chose would represent a movement away from the flowery language and diction of the late-Victorian age and towards a realistic approach to everyday experiences. Their name, inspired by the country's new king, George V, would show that they stood for something modern. Harold Monro, who had just opened a haven for bright young poets, the Poetry Bookshop at 35 Devonshire Street in central London, where they were welcome to talk, eat and sleep, was invited to act as the publisher in exchange for a half-share of the royalties.

On 1 February 1913, Marsh visited Mallory at Charterhouse to read him a Masefield poem which he planned to include in the first anthology. Masefield, already well-known, was just the kind of modern but respectable figure needed to attract interest to the Georgians, but Marsh was also keen to publish new poets. When he made his next visit to the school, Mallory asked Graves to join them and to bring along some poems.

Graves was consistently singled out by homosexuals as an attractive boy during this period of his life. Mallory was not homosexual but Marsh was and part of his interest in Robert was due to the charm of a smouldering, soft-mouthed, strongly built boy who talked with stammering excitement of his literary hopes and looked as though his life depended on Marsh's verdict. He took the poems home and, while deploring their old-fashioned style and vocabulary, he recognized something original at work in them. He maintained contact. By the summer of 1914 he was prepared to say that Robert Graves had the makings of a Georgian.

For Graves, as for the older Siegfried Sassoon, whom Marsh was also monitoring at that time, he was willing to take endless trouble. Unlike John Squire, the editor who eventually took over the Georgian anthologies and gave the group its lasting reputation for babbling rustic mediocrity, he had an altruistic love of excellence. In 1913 Graves could not have fallen into better hands.

Alfred and Amy were not pleased by this new development in Robert's life. Poetry was a hobby. It could never be allowed to distract their son from his duty to get a university scholarship. Susan, Robert's half-sister, noticed that he was put under what she considered almost intolerable pressure by her father and stepmother as scholarship-time approached. The imposition of their wishes was apparent even in the choice of university. As Mallory's friend, Robert must have felt hungry for the literary company he heard of at Cambridge. But the Graves connections were with Oxford, where one of his cousins had just been awarded a history scholarship. The memory of how his parents had treated him when he begged to leave Charterhouse was strong as they urged him on to success with prayers and reproaches. Their anxious goading was never further than the daily letter away. It was hard not to hate them.

He sat for the exam at the end of 1913. His first selection of colleges rejected him; in the second choices, he was offered only a second-level award at St John's. Nervousness may have been responsible for a result which was less than Alfred and Amy had expected. Having missed no opportunity to urge him to succeed, they let their displeasure show.

Graves had been a model son at some cost to himself. He had been religious, dutiful, hard-working; the only signs of subversion had been in the outbursts of aggressiveness towards his younger brother and at his prep schools. Now, with the unconscious assistance of Mallory, he began the painful process of rebellion and withdrawal. The last straw had been the relentless pressure during the Oxford scholarship exam. The author who released his hitherto inexpressible frustration was Samuel Butler, one of Mallory's favourite novelists.

Butler, posthumously in fashion in the pre-war years, exerted a lifelong influence on Graves. His essay, 'The Humour of Homer', set the mood for Graves's rollicking translation of *The Iliad*, while his suggestion that *The Odyssey* could have been written by a woman provided the basis for one of Graves's most engaging novels, *Homer's Daughter*. But these were later works. The books by Butler which shaped his view of the family in 1913–14 were *The Way of All Flesh* and *Erewhon*. The expression of his own increasingly jaundiced view of family relationships came from the first, the formative ideas from the second.

The Way of All Flesh, a semi-autobiographical work, introduced him to Theobald Pontifex, the kindest and most reasonable man to the outside world, but a monster to his son Ernest. In everything that Graves read about Theobald and his wife Christina, he found himself discovering parallels with his own upbringing. Ernest, exhorted to put his faith in the power of prayer, is also betrayed by parents who carry his confidences to the schoolmasters and remind him of his filial duty on every possible occasion. The narrator, Graves noticed, felt it to be quite all right for Ernest to develop a strong dislike for both his parents and even to see them as his enemies. He was not prepared to do that himself, yet, but he was relieved to find such a stringent, worldly voice ready to speak up on his side.

But *Erewhon* was the book which excited him most and which he begged Rosaleen to read as well. 'There is no talisman in the word "parent" which can generate miracles of affection,'[1] Butler declared. To Graves, it was as if a weight had been lifted from his shoulders: Butler had said it; he was not alone in having such thoughts. His resentment was not, after all, a sin. The fault was not his, but the family's. Butler also showed that the happiest children are those whose parents let them take responsibility for themselves. In 1913 Graves was eighteen years old and he saw no hope of being given that generous freedom.

★　　★　　★

Graves made light of his failures and of family pressures in *Goodbye to All That*. There, he preferred to say that a classical exhibition had given him the liberty to enjoy his last year at school. In fact, he started to behave in a way that suggested considerable anger and resentment. On a skiing holiday with the family in December 1913 he opted for daredevilry, skiing down an ice-run for toboggans with a recklessness which would have killed him if he had not been able to rely on an extraordinary sense of balance. (He was later told by a celebrated climber, Geoffrey Young, that he had the best natural balance Young had ever seen.) A week or two later, staying alone with German relations at Zurich, he put himself at risk again, skiing through dense mountain woods and tobogganing down the main street of the city with Conrad, his favourite German cousin.

Returning to England, Robert was told by Alfred to work for a leaving exhibition from Charterhouse in order to help cover the cost of sending him to Oxford. He did not protest, but he bartered. He would work, but only if his father got him exempted from the school's official military drill. (He had spoken out in a debate during the previous term, with little support, against National Service and against war, saying that he would rather run away than fight.) Taking the bait, Mr Graves agreed.

Exemption gave Robert the time he needed, not for work, but for poetry, reading, and trying out his skills as a journalist. His anti-war speech had been made in support of Nevill Barbour, an ex-Copthorne boy who was now head of the school and editor of *The Carthusian*. When Graves returned at the beginning of 1914, Barbour recruited him as assistant editor. The collaborators set about their plans to reform Charterhouse, abolishing cricket in favour of tennis and banning all compulsory games, with an aggressiveness which had more to do with Graves than Barbour. He was on a crusade of private as well as public rebellion: the inclusion of organized games in the general school curriculum had been one of Alfred Graves's proudest achievements.

In a gesture which further suggests that Robert's principal target was his father, he printed a fictitious letter in the magazine. In it, the imaginary correspondent expressed displeasure that the young editor had, 'instead of giving your whole mind to the study of dead languages and ideas . . . been taking an intelligent interest in congenial work. It would be most regrettable if to gain some experience of life and a twopenny reputation for very indifferent verse and very inferior journalism, you were to neglect the study of the Classics on which your future bread and butter depends.'[2]

This was a direct parody of recent observations which the elder Graves had been offering to his mutinous son. But the interest of the letter is that it shows how much Robert had absorbed of Butler's savagely ironic style, and how well he was learning to use it. *The Carthusian* was not supposed to serve as a training ground for satirists and reformers; before the end of the term, Barbour and Graves were forced to resign.

Graves had espoused the cause of tennis as a substitute for cricket as part of *The Carthusian*'s crusade for reform. In fact, the only game he really enjoyed was football. Boxing had played little part in his life since the estrangement from Rodakowski in the summer of 1913. In March 1914, however, after agreeing to let his name be put down for the interhouse boxing competitions, he scored a remarkable success. Fortified with a concoction called cherry whisky – his first taste of alcohol since forswearing drink as a child – and with the knowledge that both Peter Johnstone and Charles Graves were in the audience, he won all five fights, using strong right and left swings which were not part of the ordinary school training. Charles, who had resented his older brother's lack of popularity as a hindrance to his own social progress at Gownboys, was delighted to see him being cheered at last. Richard Hughes, another new boy at Charterhouse and a Harlech neighbour, remembered it as having been 'one of the most exciting things I have ever seen'; Robert had been 'like the hero of a school story'.[3]

Having broken both thumbs in the contests, it was not surprising that Graves was beaten when he represented Charterhouse in the Public Schools Championship later in the term and arrived at Harlech with a black eye to show from the fight. When there was a fancy-dress evening at Erinfa, where a huge family party had gathered, he swaggered in dressed as a champion pugilist.

Graves kept his distance from the family nest during the Easter break, staying with friends and then spending ten days climbing in Snowdonia with Mallory and a group of experienced mountaineers. Describing the experience in an essay that year, he dwelt on the feeling of comradeship, of being one of 'a chosen band of people – people in whom one can trust completely'.[4] He felt closer to the climbers than to his family, bonded by the sense of a common cause.

The climbing holiday gave him his first taste of adult male comradeship, of a noble and honour-driven brotherhood which he rediscovered in the trenches in 1915. This, for the time being, was an emotion which moved him more powerfully than desire. His feelings towards Johnstone remained essentially protective and romantic; his attitude towards women had not altered since he had fled from Lola Irwin's attentions in the Brussels pension. Among men, engaged in active pursuits, he felt safe and certain.

The holiday also gave Robert a new perspective to apply in his work. Looking down from his perch on the rock-face, he gained the view of the buzzard who soars and hovers above the Welsh moors in 'Rocky Acres'. A startling shift in his perspective came when, watching a raven swoop and curve around their party on Lliwedd, the most dangerous of all the Snowdon precipices, he saw how the bird's flight disturbed the equilibrium of his fellow climbers, flattened against the rock. This was the vertiginous sensation which he learned to use in poems when he wanted to intimate danger and uncertainty. So, in 'Outlaws', written in 1919, he peers down through a sea of black undergrowth and then switches perspective to stare upwards, where 'Between the tree-tops, upside down / Goes the sky-track.'[5]

★   ★   ★

The last term at Charterhouse saw no softening in Graves's attitude to his family. For the mid-term exeat, instead of going home, he went to Abbotsholme, a progressive school in Derbyshire which had won the admiration of his friend Nevill Barbour and to which Robert wanted his youngest brother John to be sent. Robert had already been contemplating publishing an attack on Charterhouse in a newspaper; his indignation mounted after the incident already related in which, on Johnstone's testimony, he was persuaded that a master had tried to seduce his friend.

In the 1936 novel *Antigua, Penny, Puce*, Oliver Palfrey is constantly outwitted and betrayed by his sister Jane. Similarly Rosaleen, during this last term, passed on to her father everything that Robert wrote in confidence. After being informed about the seducing master, Alfred Graves learned that his son was bored with Classics and no longer wanted to go to Oxford. He may even have heard that Robert was thinking of running away to sea, a desperate thought indeed for a boy who hated sailing.

It was not the way a member of the Graves family was expected to behave. Alfred, anxious to bring Robert back into line, persuaded his brother Charles to write his nephew a letter of friendly warning from his editorial office at the *Spectator*. The letter was sent, along with a sovereign as a bribe, but the result was not of a kind to satisfy the brothers. The sovereign had been put to good use, Robert wrote back, to buy several of Samuel Butler's works. He said nothing about his plans.

Graves was in a black mood during his final term at Charterhouse, and ready to pick quarrels with anyone who made facetious allusions to his tender friendship with Johnstone. He had acquired a small circle of defenders but there was no shortage of mockers: the moment of general popularity which he had gained as boxing champion was gone. Once he found a fellow monitor of Gownboys scratching RG and GJ on a wall above twinned hearts and took revenge by pushing him into a bath before turning the taps on. The next day the monitors seized one of his poetry books and annotated it in blue pencil, to which Graves responded by knocking down the head monitor on the way to evening prep. The incident was seen and reported to the housemaster. Told that he had committed a brutal act, Graves announced his readiness to commit another if anybody else dared to touch his books.

Alarmed by his truculence, Parry called in the headmaster but this had little effect. Instead of apologizing, Graves delivered a stinging lecture on the lessons that Charterhouse could learn from Abbotsholme. Dr Fletcher decided to question his continuing friendship with Johnstone but here Graves's good faith was so evident that the headmaster decided against the expulsion which had been in his mind. Later, when Graves made visits to Johnstone at the school, Fletcher raised no obstacles; occasionally he even wrote him kind letters, passing on information about Johnstone's progress.

But it was Dr Fletcher's parting words which stuck in Graves's mind and which never failed to amuse him as an accurate prophecy of his habit of working through several drafts of everything he wrote. '"Well, goodbye, Graves, and remember this, that your best friend is the waste-paper basket,"' he said.[6]

He left Charterhouse on 28 July 1914 in a state of complete uncertainty about his future. Alfred was in Ireland with Clarissa and Rosaleen. His mother was at Harlech. Instead of joining her, he sent a letter to say that he was going to stay in London with a man whose life was devoted to reforming criminals. Two days later, however, as the news broke that Austria and Serbia were at war, he arrived home. Nothing more was said about his visit to London.

The mood at Erinfa over the next few days was fraught as accounts of German atrocities began to fill the papers. Amy took the view that her compatriots had gone mad; Alfred and his brothers swelled with jingoistic indignation. Nobody imagined that the situation would last beyond Christmas.

At Charterhouse, Graves had opposed war. Now, as war was declared, he saw a splendid opportunity to escape the family circle. The secretary at the Harlech golf club helped by informing the nearest regimental depot – the Royal Welch Fusiliers at Wrexham – that young Graves had been in the school's Officer Training Corps. He was told that he could come at once.

The family, hitherto despairing of moody, stubborn Robbie and his prospects, swelled with corporate pride to see such a transformation in the prodigal. Uncle Charles, who had been disgusted by the response to his letter, smiled on him again. On 12 August the Graves family rose at 6 a.m. to see the soldier-apparent on his way from Harlech station. For as long as they could see him, he stood waving to them from the carriage window.

CHAPTER FOUR

1914–1916

'SCHOOLBOY MILITANT'

GRAVES HAD JOINED A REMARKABLE REGIMENT, THE OLDEST IN Wales. The Royal Welch Fusiliers had first seen action at the Battle of the Boyne in 1690; since then, its two battalions had gained an almost unequalled twenty-nine battle honours, and all 'good bloody battle-honours', Graves noted with approval. Their part in the American War of Independence formed the background to the two *Sergeant Lamb* novels which he wrote during the Second World War; according to his own research, the regiment had with them then the original Tommy Atkins, assumed by most historians to have been a mythical figure. The Fusiliers prided themselves on their smartness (a misfortune for Graves, who was notoriously scruffy and remained so) and were unique in wearing five black flashes on the backs of their collars, a remnant from the days when pigtails were kept in a 'queue bag'. Their courage was legendary: George V, telling them of the difficulty he had in persuading Kitchener not to get rid of the Fusiliers' conspicuous black flashes, said he had carried the day by saying that there was no cause for concern since the enemy would never see the backs of the Royal Welch.[1]

The regiment also had some fiercely cherished traditions. They always went into battle accompanied by their own long-haired white goat. This precious mascot was also ritually led around the table at dinner on St David's Day, while the latest subaltern stood on a chair and put one foot on the table before consuming a raw leek and drinking a generous toast to the continuous roll of drums. On parades, the gilt-horned goat preceded the ranks of regimental pioneers, who marched in white buckskin aprons and gauntlets. Distinctive, too, was the fact that the 9th Battalion (not Graves's) went into the trenches with replica swords of those used at the Battle of Crécy, supplied by a colonel with a remarkable collection of medieval armour. (Officers, to put this in context, were still having their swords sharpened by armourers in the First World War.) The Royal Welch, then, was a regiment to stir the imagination. It was the only organized body – other than university – to which Graves ever voluntarily belonged and his love for it lasted until he died.

His loyalty did not spring up all at once; in October 1914 he told a schoolfriend that by joining the regiment he was violating all his anti-war principles and had no real knowledge of why he had done so, except, perhaps, to balance the family figures, which he put at ten on each side.[2] The truth of the matter was that he had jumped at a chance to escape from his programmed career and now, having made the commitment, he wanted to be involved. Nevertheless, he was not sent out to France until May 1915, ten months after enlisting.

One of Graves's most successful early poems, 'In the Wilderness', was written at Wrexham.[3] In it, 'The guileless old scapegoat' accompanies Christ on his journey into the desert to give comfort to 'poor blind broken things / Foul in their miseries'. Graves told friends that the animal was inspired by the regimental goat, and the Christ-figure strongly suggests an idealized soldier comforting the wounded and dying at the Front. For the time being, at least, Graves was prepared to transfer his worship from God to the regiment.

After three weeks of drilling at the depot, he was sent to help guard enemy aliens at Lancaster. The experience left bad memories. A faulty telephone gave him such a violent electric shock that he still dreaded handling the instrument ten years later. One of his first instructions was to supervise the escort of forty German waiters who had been fetched in handcuffs and chains from hotels in Manchester, the nearest industrial city. Another duty was to keep control of fifty Special Reservists, an endeavour which met with little success when they wanted to find drink or women in the town. To

Graves, obsessed with the memory of the fragile and aesthetic Peter Johnstone, whom he visited briefly at Charterhouse that autumn, the men's lewdness was disgusting. His feelings were reflected in a poem which makes it clear that, if not actually homosexual, he found it impossible to tolerate the fact of carnal intercourse between men and women without a shudder of disgust.

> Loutish he
> And sluttish she
> In loathsome love together press
> And unbelievable ugliness.
> These spiders spin a loathly woof![4]

Graves's unconcealed distaste for sexual talk or behaviour made him unpopular with the regiment. So did his intellectual arrogance. In *Memoirs of an Infantry Officer*, Sassoon gave a description of him at the time they first met late in 1915, when Graves was arguing against everything, as Samuel Butler had taught him to do. Theories about who wrote the Bible and whether Homer was a woman did not go down well with the officers, and Sassoon, while sympathetic, noted that

> he was a positive expert at putting people's backs up unintentionally . . . Also, as I have already hinted, he wasn't good at being 'seen but not heard.' 'Far too fond of butting in with his opinion before he's been asked for it,' was often his only reward for an intelligent suggestion.[5]

Graves was sent back to Wrexham, much to his relief, late in October. In January 1915 he spent a week's leave in London, staying with his parents in South Kensington at 18 Bina Gardens, a house which had been entrusted to Amy by her uncle, the German Consul, when he was forced to leave England in 1914. (Red Branch House had been rented out and Erinfa was full of Belgian refugees.) This was Robert's first experience of real London life – Wimbledon scarcely qualified as part of the city in those days – and he made the most of it. On the first night, he and Ralph Rooper, another Old Carthusian, went to *Henry V*, the first play Graves had seen in his sheltered life. (Neither Amy nor Alfred approved of drama, although Alfred put on pageants at Harlech after the war.) On the following night, having written from Wrexham to ask if they might meet, he went to dinner with Edward Marsh and gave him a sheaf of poems. He returned home late and his father, intrigued by this friendship with a prominent literary figure, asked for an account of the evening. Receiving a terse reply, he offered a prayer in his diary that his dear boy's character, still unresolved, would solidify 'in the right direction'.[6]

It is probable that Robert's sexuality was preying on Alfred's mind: Marsh was known for his attachments to young men. His father was not reassured the following day when Henry Devenish, a rather effete half-Portuguese schoolmate of Graves, appeared at Bina Gardens. Together the young men went off for an assignation with Johnstone in Sussex and missed the train back, arriving only an hour before Graves was due to leave for Wrexham. The family rose to the occasion. Alfred travelled to the station with him and Amy followed, bearing a parcel of sandwiches and underpants which she produced on the platform, oblivious to the fact that her son was no longer a schoolboy.

February 1915 brought a kind but harsh letter from Marsh. In it he criticized his new protégé for an obsolete technique and a priggish attitude. Writing back with resolute cheerfulness, Graves pointed out that it would be surprising if he had entirely escaped the influence of his father, 'a dear old fellow [who] . . . has been trying to mould me in the outworn tradition . . . I know I am a prig but three years' misery at Charterhouse drove me into it, and I am as keen as you for the regeneration of poetry.'[7]

His training as a soldier was showing results. In February 'Tibs' Crawshay, the adjutant, complimented him for successfully leading 1,100 men on a march, but his careless appearance, his vagueness and, absurdly, his failure to watch Crawshay's horse run in the Grand National, still counted against him. In March, when he asked his father to start looking for a publisher for his poems, he cut his leave down to two days, as anxious to show his dedication to the regiment as to escape from his parents' suffocating attentions.

Boxing, once again, turned out to be his salvation. Crawshay was delighted by reports that Graves had held his own for three rounds against the regiment's best boxer; it was, he said, a great incentive to the men. Graves was rewarded at last, although not with exactly what he had wanted. On 17 May 1915, he and four other officers were sent from unloading stores on the Le Havre docks to join, to their disappointment, not the Royal Welch but the scruffier Second Battalion of the Welsh Regiment. By 18 May Graves was asleep in a dugout at Cambrin, half a mile behind the front line. Writing home, he told his parents of a trench like a palace.

> Clay walls, bomb-proof ceilings, pictures on the walls, straw-filled berths, stoves, tables, chairs, complete with a piebald cat. I wasn't frightened by the guns which bang away all day and night. The noise is just like the Blaenau Festiniog slate-blasters, with the rocket-like whistle of the shells going over.[8]

The platoon of forty ragged soldiers put under Graves's command reflected the desperate need for recruits. The First Battalion had lost its quota of men five times over since August 1914 and there was no longer any concern with getting trained men for the Second Battalion. 'Enlist at the depot and get to France quick' was the way the Army advertised their need in Cardiff; the result, rectified some months later, was a motley assembly ranging from a fifteen-year-old who kept falling asleep on sentry duty, to a man of sixty-three, too old to understand the workings of a post-Victorian rifle.

Writing to Marsh to commiserate on the death of Rupert Brooke, a few days after his arrival in the trenches, Graves tried to describe the unreality of his new circumstances. On his first watch, he had paused to reprove a man for lying down barefoot; 'I shook the sleeper by the arm and noticed suddenly the hole in the back of his head. He had taken off the boot and sock to pull the trigger of his rifle with one toe; the muzzle was in his mouth.'[9] The sensation of being under fire was, he told Marsh, rather like spending a sleepy evening at the cinema and then suddenly finding yourself 'thrown on the screen in the middle of scalp-hunting Sioux and runaway motor cars . . .'[10] It was not, he added, a question of being frightened. He was not afraid.

At Wrexham, Graves had written a poem called 'It's A Queer Time' in which, taking Marsh's advice to heart, he used the simple words and images of childhood to express the horrors of war. The first three verses of this, together with 'The Poet in the Nursery,' were enclosed with the letter, and seem to have been approved. (Marsh's letters are unfortunately untraceable.) They marked the beginning of Graves's formula for war poetry. There was no spirit of protest in them: Graves clung to the idea that there was some hidden divine purpose in the destruction to which he was now a witness. This was his way of staying sane and keeping up the spirits of his men. What the poems set out to offer, often by means of an analogy with a shocking childhood experience, like the discovery of a dog's rotting body in a Welsh field, was an unblinking view of the reality of corpses, lice, mud and bursting shells in a limbo-land

> where the reek
> Of death offends the living . . . but poor dead
>   Can't sleep, must lie awake with the horrid sound
> That roars and whirs and rattles overhead
> All day, all night, and jars and tears the ground . . .[11]

The inspiration of the poems which Graves wrote in 1915 was drawn from the daily experience of living beside death. While the Georgian Poets achieved their poignancy by setting trench warfare against a lyrical view of rural England, Graves was unique in trying to see the war through the eyes of an imaginative child. The memory of his own childish terrors was strong enough for him to see a parallel. Occasionally, as in 'The Dead Fox Hunter', he sentimentalized war with the worst of them; this particular poem ended with 'the whole host of Seraphim' jogging in scarlet to the dead's man's heavenly meet. But the poems which carried the war back to the nursery, while not always successful, show that Graves was seeking an honest voice for his confused emotions.

In moments of privacy, he scribbled poems on whatever paper came to hand, envelopes, patrol diagrams, sentry records, and read his small store of books. These, conventionally, included Keats and Homer, predictably, Samuel Butler, and intriguingly, Nietzsche, whose views on the division between Apollo and Dionysus – skill and inspiration – would exert a powerful influence on Graves's later theories about poetry. He also wrote letters.

Horror and tranquillity appeared in constant juxtaposition in the family letters which his proud father sent Charles Graves for publication in a September 1915 issue of the *Spectator*. On the one hand, Robert provided cheerful accounts of teaching a French schoolgirl arithmetic in his billet and of an army cricket match played with a bundle of rags for a ball and a parrot cage, complete with dead parrot, for the wicket. On the other hand, references to the thunder of constant heavy bombardment make it clear that he was putting on a brave front in these light-hearted vignettes. None of the men could take more than three days in the trenches without a break. There were times when the whine of shells was like the din of gnats trapped in Graves's ears. It was not long before his nerves snapped. One night, the sergeant-major found him trembling on all fours in the trench, unable to stand for fear. On another, Graves found some soldiers tending a man who took three hours to die after losing the top of his head from a rifle-shot. That, he wrote home, was the sort of occasion on which jokes ceased to be a comfort.

All soldiers relied on reassuring letters to keep them sane at the Front. Graves's private solace was his correspondence with Peter Johnstone; a letter from him arrived every week. Other men made use of the army brothel at Béthune; Graves shunned it. In *Goodbye to All That*, he placed an account of the brothel between testaments of his attachment to Johnstone, or Dick, as Graves protectively renamed him in the book. The contrast between bought sex and pure love is emphatic. In 1915, however, Graves's faith in his friend's purity was badly shaken when his cousin Gerald wrote from the school to say that Peter was 'not at all the innocent fellow I took him for, but as bad as anyone could be'.[12] A few weeks later, a letter from Johnstone arrived to reassure him. It was true, he admitted, that he had been 'ragging about', a phrase which implied sexual attentions at that period, but he would now reform his ways. With this, because he was desperate to believe in the boy's virtue, Graves had to be content. Johnstone continued to be cherished as the anonymous love-object of his poetry. 'Dear, you've been everything that I most lack / In these soul-deadening trenches . . .' he wrote in '1915' and went on to recall the pleasure of 'Beautiful comrade-looks . . .'[13]

This sentimental poem, written in December and published in Graves's first collection, *Over the Brazier*, offers a clue to the riddle of his sexual feelings. Graves himself remained silent on the subject, only allowing, by 1929, that homosexuality was encouraged by life in single-sex English boarding-schools. He may never have been actively homosexual but he was strongly interested in it as a phenomenon, speculating eagerly on whether other poets were attracted to their own sex. Writing to Sassoon about the poet Charles Sorley in May 1916, Graves grew inquisitive: 'What did your Marlburian say about Sorley, and was he "so"? As his book contains no conventional love-lyrics and as he'd reached the age of 20, I conclude he was.'[14] On this assessment, Graves, aged twenty himself and with no conventional (in the sense of being addressed to a woman) love-lyrics to his name, must have thought of himself as 'so'. '1915', the only published war-poem which could be called a love-lyric, was written with Johnstone in mind.

Graves found it easier to get on with the men than the officers, both in the loquacious Welsh Regiment and in the stiffer Second Battalion of the Royal Welch, to which he was transferred in July when it was based at Laventie. But it was the officers with whom he identified. Mostly hunting men, the officers at Laventie were cool in their superiority. Dress on duty was immaculate; courage was the only way to win their respect. Off duty, they wore shorts and played polo as if the regiment had never left India.

It was a matter of honour with the Royal Welch to dominate no man's land until dawn. Graves was given his first taste of night patrol a few hours after his arrival at Laventie. His orders involved a two-hour stomach crawl into German territory under barbed wire and enemy flares; the prize was a glass container which appeared to contain only wine dregs and rainwater. The contents were not the point. He was praised for having carried out a dangerous mission.

The risks which Graves took on his night-patrol work were great and deliberate; he relished the admiration which he won by these feats of recklessness. One night, having offered to locate a reported group of Germans, he insisted on going across the wire even when a full moon shed a glaring light on the scarred territory of no man's land. The only hope of safety lay in scuttling forward from shell-hole to shell-hole, crouching among the dead until the German group had been identified and word sent back of where they could be bombarded. Shortly after this, leaving other Georgian Poets to apostrophize the moon's silent beauty and silvery calm, Graves wrote a poem about a child terrified of a moon that is 'cruel and round and bright' and 'drives people mad, / And that's the thing that always frightens me so.'[15] The moon, for him, would never again be a serene presence.

The sense of impending action was building to a climax by the end of August 1915 and Graves took his brief leave with reluctance. After a week, which he spent walking at Erinfa, he returned to find that his battalion had been moved back to Cambrin, where they were occupying the first trenches he had entered on arriving at the Front. This was the setting for his introduction to the harshest side of the war.

On 25 September the Royal Welch were decimated in a suicidal advance from Cambrin. It was, they learned afterwards, a decoy strategy to divert attention from the main attack at Loos. They had been sacrificed and there had been no victory to make it worth while. After two nights of bringing in dead men from where they hung on the German wires, Graves was confidentially informed that a planned second assault would also be a diversionary ploy. Of the five officers who had first come to Cambrin with him, he was the only survivor. In ten days, he had no more than eight hours' sleep. He was drinking, he estimated, a bottle of whisky a day, in order to stop himself from breaking down in front of the men. He never needed faith so much as now, after Loos, when he lost the last shreds of his belief that a divine power was guiding the war. More than forty years later, he was still noting the anniversary of Loos in letters to men born long after the war. It had, for him, been a terrible rite of passage.

On 3 October the Royal Welch were at last ordered to retreat. Graves, after a month of being shunted between doing night-work for the sappers and going back into the front line, was made a captain in the Third Battalion. He was marching with them towards the Hohenzollern Redoubt when they heard the distant racket of artillery. The message came to turn back.

> It had been another dud show, chiefly notorious for the death of Charles Sorley, a twenty-year-old captain in the Suffolks, one of three poets of importance killed during the war. (The other two were Isaac Rosenberg and Wilfred Owen.) So ended the operations for 1915.[16]

CHAPTER FIVE

1916

A NEAR ESCAPE

AT THE END OF NOVEMBER 1915, GRAVES WAS TRANSFERRED TO 'A' Company in the First Battalion of the Royal Welch, two miles north of Cambrin, where the men were attempting to dig new trenches. Graves found his new companions less old-fashioned and autocratic than in the Second Battalion but he still had difficulty in making friends among the young officers, who distrusted his intellectual brilliance. Provided with a batman to keep him neat and tidy, Graves felt that he at least looked the part. Among the rapid sketches he made of himself acting roles in *Goodbye to All That*, one for the late autumn of 1915 presents him 'in faultless khaki with highly polished buttons and belt, revolver at hip, whistle on cord, delicate moustache on upper lip, and stern endeavour a-glint in either eye, pretending to be a Regular Army captain'.[1]

Writing to Edward Marsh on 10 December, Graves told him that he had met Siegfried Sassoon from 'C' Company, 'a very nice chap but his verses, except occasionally, don't please me very much'. Sassoon, apart from a musician called Arthur Parry whom he had met in October, was the first officer to share Graves's literary interests. Sensitive, graceful and intrepid, Sassoon had the romantic qualities which had appealed to Graves in Peter Johnstone. But Sassoon was considerably his senior – he was almost thirty when they met – and in no need of protection. A hunting man, he achieved an instant and easy popularity in the regiment.

Sassoon, in Graves's opinion, was still too starry-eyed about war with his accounts of happy legions and blithe winds. Action, he thought, would sharpen his new friend's pen. Sassoon, in his turn, had reservations about Graves's work: he thought that Graves was overwrought and that his poems were still unfit for publication. 'Like his face, which had a twist to it, as though seen in a slightly distorting mirror), his mental war-pictures were a little uncouth and out of focus.'[2] So serious were his doubts that he wrote to his old friend and patron Edward Marsh to urge the folly of allowing Graves to publish his poems; Marsh disagreed.

Publication had become a reality. Alfred Graves, having persuaded Harold Monro to accept his own selection of Robert's poems, forwarded these, unrevised, to Marsh. Absence had softened Robert's feelings about his parents; touched, he urged Marsh to be kind to 'a most lovable old dear' when he came, self-invited, to lunch to discuss his son's work.[3] A few weeks later, Robert started planning titles for the book: 'Schoolboy Militant' was among the ones he liked best.

It took the death of another mutual friend, David Thomas, to jar Sassoon into the bitter vein which made him famous. Graves, only recently back from a respite as a training officer in Harfleur, felt none of Sassoon's anger against the Germans when Thomas died at Fricourt in March 1916. The death, nevertheless, meant more to him than any single loss. In 'Goliath and David' he saluted his friend as a hero in a hopeless situation.[4]

David Thomas's death bound Sassoon and Graves together as his closest friends. Whenever there was an opportunity they met to talk about poetry and books – Sassoon was astonished by the intensity of Graves's passion for discussing ideas – but appearances had to be kept up. Sassoon was the more self-conscious of the two, pretending that they were swapping a recipe for rum punch instead of their new poems. They were, Graves cheerfully noted, a disgrace to the battalion.

Sassoon was right to be anxious about Graves's nerves. To Marsh, Robert wrote that only the regiment now answered his desperate need for something to worship.[5] Struggling to emulate the courage of his fellow officers, his touching bravado reminds us how much of a schoolboy he still was.

> It's rather trying, having to go back into trenches after a three months' holiday, especially trenches like this where the two parties are so exceedingly embittered against each other . . . there are a lot of new terrors since last December . . . but I always enjoy trenches in a way, I must confess: I like feeling really frightened and if happiness consists in being miserable in a good cause, why then I'm doubly happy.[6]

In *Goodbye to All That*, when the time had passed for pretence, Graves admitted that he had been on the verge of a breakdown. He knew that it was imminent. 'It would be a general nervous collapse, with tears and twitchings and dirtied trousers. I had seen cases like that.'[7]

Boxing, in a roundabout way, came to his rescue again. Boxing with a broken nose had impaired his breathing, making it impossible for him to wear the new issue of gas helmet. He was told to get his nose fixed during his spring leave but the operation, carried out in London at Millbank Hospital on 6 April, was mishandled by the army surgeon. The pain was excruciating and he was kept in for a further ten days.

Eager though his family were to surround him, the experience of war had been an alienating one. He had reached the sardonic state of mind expressed in Richard Aldington's 1929 'jazz novel' about the war: 'The death of a hero! What mockery, what bloody cant!'[8] Sitting at meals with Alfred and Amy, he smelt not the thin fumes of vegetable soup but the odour of the trenches, stagnant mud, latrine buckets, chloride of lime, rotting sandbags, stale sweat, fumes of lyddite, decomposing flesh. Unable to bear acting the role of the gallant soldier for the family's benefit, he decided to break away. At the beginning of May he spent his army pay on buying one of his mother's little cottages on the Erinfa estate for £30. Whitewashed, with a beechwood writing table and periwinkles climbing over the window-sill, Gwithdy Bach gave him a life to dream about when the war was over. He thought about his future as a poet and of all the time to read which lay ahead of him. Oxford now seemed an inviting prospect, especially since Sassoon, who had left Cambridge without a degree, was willing to follow him there. Johnstone, too, had decided to try for Oxford after leaving Charterhouse, if the war permitted it.

Walking the moors failed to dispel the horror of his memories of the Front that spring, but Graves could still enjoy the beauty of 'bright sun and misty mountains and hazy seas and sloe blossoms and wild cherry and grey rocks and young green grass'. He wrote to Sassoon, too, about a 'wonderful' two days at Charterhouse with Johnstone, 'exquisite as usual', before begging his reckless friend to take care on his night patrols: 'for de Lawd's sake honey don't overdo it.'[9] Sassoon could hardly be blamed for reading more love into Graves's concern than was intended.

Staying nearby at Llys Bach in Harlech that year were the artist William Nicholson, his wife Mabel Pryde, and two of their children. Ben was a year older than Robert (his asthma was a principal reason for the family's removal from London). Nancy, aged sixteen, was the pretty, artistic, tomboy daughter in a family of three boys. Ben and Nancy were good company, funny, quick-witted and sharp-tongued, with the characterful charm of all their father's family. Graves liked them and envied them their tolerant parents.

His first volume of poems, retitled *Over the Brazier* by the publisher Harold Monro, and with a cover by Claud Lovat Fraser (another Old Carthusian) showing the Menin Arch, came out late in May. Charles Graves had pleased his nephew by giving it a friendly mention in the *Spectator*; other reviews were also encouraging. The *Observer* thought that Robert Graves would be 'most interesting to watch' while the *Times Literary Supplement* for 20–27 May 1916, having remarked on his 'repelling rawness', praised an ear for musical cadence which often 'lays a spell on the reader and achieves something like true beauty'. But this was to over-praise the book because it had been written by a young man in the face of death; Graves wisely dropped all the verses from it later, with the exception of 'In the Wilderness'.

At the end of May 1916 he was asked to rejoin the Third Battalion, in which he was now a captain, at Litherland, the depot on the outskirts of Liverpool which had replaced Wrexham as the Royal Welch's headquarters. Sassoon, his chief correspondent, heard of his new friendship with a charming subaltern of eighteen who was already addicted to cocktails, flirtation and swearing. 'It's a great grief to me,' Graves sighed piously, before admitting his greater source of despair. Peter Johnstone's mother, a strait-laced and strong-willed woman, had decided to investigate his letters to her son. She had been so shocked by the signs she found there of a dangerous influence on a pure young mind that she forbade Johnstone to write to, or see, Graves again. 'Complications too long to enumerate leave no loopholes of evasion for either of us, so I am now widowed, laid waste and desolate,' Graves concluded, adding that anything was better than the thought of Johnstone being killed.[10]

Litherland was a depressing place to be, situated next door to a giant munitions factory and with only a few old friends from the Wrexham days to keep him company. But July marked the beginning of the Somme offensive when all available men were needed to replenish the thinned forces at the Front. Graves was ordered to rejoin the Second Battalion in the trenches at Givenchy. Always superstitious, he had a sense of doom this time. Sitting beside the stoker on the train, he wrote to Edward Marsh, asking him to take care of his literary remains and to accept the last few poems which Rosaleen would be sending under separate cover.

A raid was already in progress when Graves arrived and Colonel Crawshay asked him to write it up for the regimental history. Watching as an academic, Graves noted that the men had, for the first time in two hundred years, reverted to the use of pikes, improvised by sticking butchers' knives to broomsticks with medical plaster. He was pleased to be with Crawshay again and with Dr Dunn, a remarkable man on whom the regiment's leaders depended for his shrewd judgements, both medical and military. But the officers gave Graves a hard time after rumour spread that he was the brother of a German spy who had taken the name of Carl Graves. If he had been a popular man the rumour would have been discredited, but Graves was still seen as an oddity, too loud, too assertive, too clever. Only Sassoon had discovered the loneliness behind his defensive exuberance.

On 10 July the battalion marched to Fricourt and then on to Mametz Wood, full of dead bodies and broken branches. Here Graves found a subject for one of his most determinedly realistic poems, a heavy-bodied German slumped dead against a tree. The sight was, he wrote, 'a certain cure for lust of blood'.[11] He offered the remedy to the civilians who never seemed to tire of bloody stories. If they could see as well as hear, Graves suggested, they, too, might lose their enthusiasm for war.

Survivors of 'A' Company, including Sassoon, were close by. Sassoon, now known as 'Mad Jack' for his exploits, performed another by taking, single-handed and in broad daylight, a Front stronghold, from which the German occupants fled at the sight of a man carrying bombs. Worried by these death-defying adventures, Graves sent a rhymed letter down the line, telling Sassoon how they would travel together to the East after a long rest at Harlech, where Graves would show him all his favourite settings for the Welsh myths. His own yearning to be there made itself felt in loving descriptions of the landscape and tales of wizards and unicorns among the desolate hills.

> You'll see where in old Roman days,
> Before Revival changed our ways,
> The Virgin 'scaped the Devil's grab,
> Printing her foot on a stone slab
> With five clear toe-marks . . .[12]

Sassoon was touched by this burst of affection. Sitting together in the dark evenings with guns booming along the valleys and the faint gleam of camp-fires showing in the mist, the two poets talked about a future together. 'And whenever I am with him, I want to do wild things, and get right away from the conventional silliness of life,' Sassoon wrote on 16 July in his diary, still under the spell of Graves's stories of the past.[13]

On 19 July Graves was told that his company would be in reserve for an attack on High Wood (Bois de Fourneaux). On the 20th, four days before his twenty-first birthday, he was caught by a fragment of a shell which burst eight paces behind him as they retreated from a barrage.

> I heard the explosion, and felt as though I had been punched rather hard between the shoulder-blades, but without any pain. I took the punch merely for the shock of the explosion; but blood trickled into my eye and, turning faint, I called to Moodie: 'I've been hit.' Then I fell.[14]

Dimly, he was aware of the stretcher-bearer saying that '"Old Gravy's got it all right"' before they carried him to the disused German dressing-station in Mametz Wood, where he was left to die. On the morning of 21 July Colonel Crawshay made out the official casualty list; on the 22nd, he wrote to commiserate with Amy Graves on the loss of a gallant son. The letter was prosaic, but Crawshay had many such letters to write that month. Sassoon, hearing the news on the 21st, was agonized by the loss. 'In him I thought I had found a lifelong friend to work with.'[15]

Colonel Crawshay's letter, which arrived for Amy on her son's twenty-first birthday, was premature; against all odds, Graves had survived the night and been taken, semi-conscious and screaming with pain, to a nearby field hospital. He fainted before arrival; a report reached Crawshay that he had died of wounds on the way. On 23 July he was put on a stretcher and taken to Rouen hospital by train. This journey, by his own accounts, was the worst part of his war experience; the horror of trains remained with him for many years, making a nightmare of even the shortest trip.

At Rouen, according to Graves's story 'Old Papa Johnson', he was both helped and hindered by a fellow invalid with a genius for impersonation; by the end of a week, a haemorrhage from laughing too much seemed a distinct possibility.[16] On 30 July his chest wound was drained. Four days later he was transferred home, to Queen Alexandra's Hospital in Highgate, with Alfred hard on his heels, begging for an account of the injury and its aftermath.

Most of the shell's effects had been superficial. Wounds on his hand, eyebrow, thigh and ribs had healed by the time he left hospital; an X-ray showed that the only severe damage was to the right lung. He was not, however, well enough to be released for a month. For the first two weeks he had difficulty in standing.

The relief of finding himself alive, if not in good health, was immense. By the end of the first week of August, Graves was almost unnaturally buoyant. His first response, as he told Marsh, was that he was out of the war, and 'with such jolly sick-leave prospects'.[17] He had high hopes that the news of his injury would soften the heart of Johnstone's mother. (It did not.) He was even ready to see the joke of having had his death announced in *The Times*, since the paper offered to insert a second (free) announcement of his recovery.

Shortly after Graves was wounded, Sassoon also returned to England with lung trouble (the official description was the all-embracing 'trench fever'). Harlech seemed the ideal place for them both to convalesce and work on their poems. Graves went ahead at the end of August and was driven up to Erinfa from the station in a car ceremoniously draped with flags. Two days later he was joined by Sassoon, whose gift for storytelling and love of golf made him instantly popular, as did his courteous attentiveness to Alfred's recollections of his encounters with Tennyson and Rossetti. Admiring him, Alfred and Amy must have hoped that some of his graceful manner would rub off on their surly son.

The Graveses did not understand how profoundly Robert had been affected by his experiences. They did not know that he had spent the whole journey to Harlech in tears after reading *The Times* and seeing almost every officer in the First Battalion on the casualty list. No other member of the direct family had been in the trenches and, like many other civilians, Robert's parents found it hard to imagine why young men should not be themselves again after a few cheerful weeks at home. But their son had changed. Portraits of him by Ben Nicholson and Eric Kennington before the end of the war show the remote, haunted eyes which still look out from studio photographs taken forty years later. He had been spared when his comrades had died. It was not an uncommon experience but it took an uncommon hold of Graves's mind. His death became for him a mythic event, the giving back to him of his life on (almost) his twenty-first birthday, as if he had been born again. In the poem 'Escape' he saw himself as Orpheus, descending into the Underworld to overwhelm Cerberus and make good his escape even as the guardian of death tried to block his way

> With monstrous hairy carcase, red and dun –
> Too late! for I've sped through.
>   O Life! O Sun![18]

Of all the people who surrounded Graves, only Sassoon was close enough in experience to understand his feelings. The time at Harlech was when their friendship came closest to being all that Sassoon had longed for, a perfect combination of intuitive sympathy and a shared passion for making poetry. For Graves, this was the first of many collaborative experiences with friends, and he loved it.

Literary decisions seem to have been evenly balanced, with Sassoon submitting to what he regarded as Graves's greater technical proficiency and Graves taking his friend's advice while revising, with what must have been a curious sensation, 'To His Dead Body', Sassoon's lament for his death. Graves did not, however, show Sassoon his other project at that time, a novel about his war experiences; this, he told Edward Marsh, was going to be the best war book ever written.[19] He had reached the sixth chapter by October, but Sassoon's diaries and letters show that he knew nothing about it.

One of the first people to hear about the novel (Graves abandoned it in 1917) was Robbie Ross, a gentle and cultured man in his early sixties, best remembered now for his kindness to Oscar Wilde. Graves was introduced to him by Sassoon that August. In September, when he was staying at Weirleigh, Sassoon's family home in Sussex, he wrote to announce that he was planning to finish the book in about three weeks. He was disappointed, however, that Ross did not approve of their plan to be the new Wordsworth and Coleridge, publishing their two sets of poems in a single volume like the *Lyrical Ballads*. 'I'm sorry,' Graves wrote, 'because old Sassoon's such a dear and we took some pains over co-ordinating the two sets of poems . . . However, I must remember that I'm a professional optimist . . .'[20]

Ross saw a good deal of Graves and Sassoon during the autumn of 1916 and evidently enjoyed the role of playing godfather to their talents. By October, he had replaced Marsh as their chief literary adviser. Ross had already urged Sassoon to follow up an invitation from Lady Ottoline Morrell, an enthusiastic literary patron who would be sure to help publicize his poems; Sassoon took Graves with him on his second visit to her celebrated country home near Oxford on 12 September.

Graves had heard of Garsington and Garsington had heard of him; Lady Ottoline read *Over the Brazier* and urged her guests to do the same, when it came out in May. Graves at this point was the better-known of the two young men, but Sassoon, in Lady Ottoline's eyes, was the rarer, more sensitive character. Her interest was all in him. Graves, by contrast, seemed 'an odd fellow with the face of a prizefighter' and an irritatingly possessive manner towards his friend.[21] Aldous Huxley, who very much wanted to make friends with the poets, thought they both had a rebuffing manner.[22] Lytton Strachey, eyeing Graves across the Garsington lawn a year later, confessed to his friend Dora Carrington that 'I found him (I need hardly say) attractive – tall and olive-brown complexioned, with a broken nose and teeth (the result of boxing) – with dark hair and eyes.'[23] But Graves, on the visit in 1916, was unapproachable. He was ill at ease among the pacifists who sheltered under Lady Ottoline's welcoming parasol; in their moral courage he saw only a shirking of duty.

In the middle of September, Graves returned to Harlech alone, to work on his novel and get his strength back by taking long daily walks. Slowly he began to pick up the threads of a normal life. Writing to Ross on 22 October, he spoke of 'being very jolly here' and of his new friendship with the Nicholsons. Ben had decided to rent Graves's cottage for the winter and the two of them were busy smashing holes in the walls to let in the light required for a studio.

In late November Sassoon and Graves returned to the army depot at Litherland, where they shared a hut and continued to edit each other's work. Sassoon, describing this period later in *Memoirs of an Infantry Officer*, used memory and hearsay to create an affectionate portrait of Graves, shaving with one hand and reading a book with the other, blowing smoke-rings, singing ballads and doing imitations of excitable Welshmen. They discovered a shared delight in the fantastic images and metaphors of the English Metaphysical Poets, sent to Sassoon by an admiring Lady Ottoline; together they laughed at her affectionate, breathless letters. For a Christmas present, Graves gave Sassoon a specially bound copy of *The Brook Kerith*, the novel in which George Moore, like Butler, argued for the survival of a very human Christ beyond the Cross and for seeing Paul's role as an ignoble one. (The book became immensely popular after the Battle of the Somme, when conventional faith wavered into doubt at the Front.) Sassoon was sceptical; Graves, while revolted by Moore's crude use of Irish dialect, found his ideas provocative and intriguing. The notion of a godlike man, rather than God made man, took root.

Goliath and David, Graves's second collection of poems, was too slight a volume to attract commercial interest; William Heinemann, who were planning to publish Sassoon's first book in May, wanted more poems from Graves, or none. Graves took Sassoon's advice and decided to publish the collection privately with the Chiswick Press in an edition of 200 copies. The day after making this decision he heard that he was being sent back to France on 22 January. He was not sorry. On the contrary, he told friends that he had deliberately deceived the medical board about his health in order to pass as fit for action. In December 1916 he had written to Eddie Marsh that he was incapable of writing poetry at Litherland.

My flow of poetry completely dried up the day I came here . . .
S. S. nags me about my professional ways but if I can't write

I feel it's most important of all to concentrate on being a good soldier and winning this war.[24]

Before returning to the Front as a 21-year-old veteran, Graves had two visits to make in London. One was to Robert Nichols, a young poet who had spent five months in hospital with shell-shock – and syphilis – after three weeks of non-active service at the Front. Nichols, whose first book of poetry was about to be published, wanted to dedicate part of it to Graves. He was not, Graves reported to Sassoon, of their temperament – a reference to Nichols's womanizing – but certainly worth encouraging. On the same day that he visited Nichols, he said goodbye to the Nicholson family at Apple Tree Yard, their studio house in St James's, off Piccadilly.

Graves was still uneasy about his feelings for women, but Nancy Nicholson, who seemed still almost a child, intrigued him. To Ben, who had been painting him and urging him to agree to their spending Christmas together in the Harlech cottage, he confided that he was impressed by her work. Her first published drawing, for the cover of *Vogue* magazine, appeared when she was fourteen and she was now producing delicate and original pen-and-wash illustrations very different from the strongly-lit and richly-coloured oils for which her father was praised as a portrait painter. Ben, still trying to break away from his father's fine but old-fashioned style, shared Graves's admiration for his seventeen-year-old sister who smoked, rode a motor bike and talked enthusiastically about women's rights. 'Yes. Nancy's drawings are damned good,' he wrote. 'And no harm in praising them if it comes to that, for she'll only laugh at you . . .'[25] It was Ben who had asked him to visit the family in London when the Welsh Christmas plan was abandoned, but the memory which Graves carried back to France was of Nancy, tall, slim and bright-eyed, in a black velvet dress. (Interestingly, an illustration for *Vogue* that year which Nancy publicly dedicated to Graves showed a slender girl in a full-skirted black dress.)

Graves's letters from Litherland show that he missed the tension of being at the Front, but Dr Dunn, who was still with the Second Battalion, bluntly told him that he was unfit for trench service and sent him to a billet with transport several miles behind the lines. The weather was colder than Graves had ever known. The River Somme was iced over; so were the plates from which they ate. The French had left the area. The houses were all wrecked by shells. Every night

Graves walked up to the trenches with the rations for the men; his own view was that only the daily tot of rum was keeping them from collapse. A brief meeting with Rodakowski, who was killed shortly afterwards, was his only pleasurable memory from this period.

Unfit though he was to fight, Graves needed to be back on the Somme, not just from a sense of duty but because it was where he could write, where he could find the key 'back to the dark corridor which I call other where' out of which his poems came.[26] In *Goodbye to All That* he admitted that he kept no records during this time; one of the reasons was that he was so deeply engaged in reading and thinking about poetry. Sassoon, charmed, sent Ross an account he had heard of their friend sitting up at night to work by the light of dozens of candles flickering around his bed. 'Isn't that a delightful – and unconscious – vignette of the authentic Robert?'[27]

Both Sassoon and Ross had come to feel a proprietary interest in Robert, especially since he had asked them to edit the 'Goliath' poems in his absence. Neither of them were pleased by one poem which he had submitted for inclusion: it was called 'To My Unborn Son'. The subject matter was undeniably sentimental but what irked them most was the fact that the poem showed Graves writing as a heterosexual, contemplating marriage and children as desirable goals. They took it out of the collection.

Graves may have been thinking of Nancy when he wrote that poem. Her influence is certainly apparent in 'Dead Cow Farm', written in France. Nancy believed firmly in the superior qualities of women and in the fact that they, not men, had once ruled society. This was the poem in which Graves first showed God as a woman. The tone was savage. Creation had emerged in mud; in the trenches, there was no chance of a poetic rebirth.

> Under her warm tongue flesh and blood
> Blossomed, a miracle to believe:
> And so was Adam born, and Eve.
> Here now in chaos once again,
> Primeval mud, cold stones and rain,
> Here flesh decays and blood drips red,
> And the Cow's dead, the old Cow's dead.[28]

In mid-February Graves won the admiration of his fellow officers when he was put in temporary command of the battalion. Called to

Brigade Headquarters to approve what seemed to him a foolhardy and pointless attempt to capture a German salient, he spoke his mind. The colonel of the Cameronians supported him and the attack was called off. A few days after this, a long and unsuccessful night hunting for two lost supply-horses put him in bed with bronchitis. Dunn ordered him back to Rouen hospital where the Royal Army Medical Corps major who had sent him home in July could hardly believe his eyes. '"If I find you and those lungs of yours in my hospital again, I'll have you court-martialled,"' he said, before asking where Graves wanted to be hospitalized. 'I said, at random: "Oxford."'29

Graves remained in Britain for the rest of the war. Increasingly he became aware that the conflict was being needlessly prolonged, but he clung to the idea that his own duty was to assume a cheerful manner. Insofar as he could, he suppressed his doubts, but his mind was haunted by what he had seen. Even the smell of flowers brought back the sickly odour of poison gas. He cried easily and often. Not only did telephones, trains, shrill noises, cause him extreme distress; so, unpredictably, did the presence of strangers. There was grief in the family for the seven German cousins who had died in the war; Graves was the only member who had to face the possibility that he could have killed one of them himself. In 1917 and 1918 he hovered on the brink of a nervous breakdown. Recovery took another ten years.

CHAPTER SIX

1917–1918

A CHANGE OF DIRECTION

GRAVES'S EXPERIENCES IN 1916 had affected him, physically and emotionally. There could be no question of returning to the Front after his collapse from bronchitis. Unwilling to accept that his nerves were no longer steady, he struggled hard to resume a normal life. In time, he hoped to be well enough for a foreign posting.

In February 1917 there was no question of his being posted anywhere. He was sent straight from Rouen to convalesce at Somerville College in Oxford. (Almost all the university colleges had undergone some such transformation during the war.) But the purpose of his cure was not simply to treat a bronchial condition; it had been recorded at Rouen that he was in a fragile mental state.

Released from Somerville after three weeks as physically fit, he was still nervous and prone to violent mood-swings. He spent his first week out of hospital in London, mixing with the people who were most likely to help him and Sassoon in their careers. Sassoon was back in France; Graves promised to keep an eye on the progress of his poetry collection, now titled *The Old Huntsman*. Publication had been postponed because of paper shortage, but Graves was optimistic. The collection was full of powerful writing, he told Edmund Gosse, a new literary acquaintance and one who wielded considerable influence; 'and, besides, the reviewers have all been squared . . .'[1]

Squaring reviewers was regarded by both Graves and Sassoon as good sense – neither of them, when writing to literary friends, ever missed an opportunity to mention the other's work as important – and they did all they could for each other in the way of promotion. So Robert now urged his father to write up Sassoon's book in *The Observer* and asked his uncle Charles to put a review in the *Spectator*. Eliot and Wyndham Lewis could already be distinguished as the new leaders of literary fashion by discriminating readers in 1917, but Graves and Sassoon, as war poets, were in a different camp. Death and comradeship in an open setting were the themes for which they were given respectful attention by civilian reviewers.

> Show me the two so closely bound
> As we, by the wet bond of blood,
> By friendship, blossoming from mud
> By Death . . .[2]

At the end of March 1917, Graves spent a few days at Erinfa, alone except for the old housekeeper, teaching himself the harp and firing off letters to his friends about 'a great poet, a chap called Skelton (1460–1525) of whom there's been no edition since 1843: a true Englishman and a man after my heart; wrote beautiful doggerel nonsense and thoroughly irresponsible and delightful jingles, though "the first scholar in the land" according to Erasmus.'[3] Graves had found a hero to place beside Samuel Butler; as with Butler, his liking was based on a strong sense of identification. Skelton, for him, became the first major English poet in a peculiarly English tradition, a man who had combined wit, honesty and scholarly brilliance while refusing to lavish praises on his patrons. This, increasingly, was how Graves viewed himself; in later years, when he was praised as 'the noblest defender of Skelton of our day',[4] he described himself as Skelton's heir.

In April, accepting that his weak lung made him unfit for further action in France, Graves took a teaching post at Wadham College, Oxford, turned into a training-school for officers. Having few local friends, he began making regular excursions to Garsington. Out of action himself, he was less inclined to despise the pacifists than he had been the previous year, and he found himself growing genuinely fond of kind, languid Ottoline, 'a ripper', and her chubby, flirtatious little daughter.

Garsington was an important place on the literary map for aspiring young poets. Besides meeting Aldous Huxley, Bertrand Russell, Clive Bell, Lytton Strachey and a smattering of politicians, Graves was befriended by L. A. G. Strong, a young Irish writer who promised to get his work published in *Blackwell's Poetry Magazine*, most prominent of the Oxford publications. Edmund Gosse, meanwhile, gave him a letter of introduction to John Masefield, who had just moved nearby to Boars Hill. Robert Bridges, the Poet Laureate, sent kind messages from there about his poems. Graves was invited to contribute to a new war anthology, *The Muse in Arms*, while Marsh accepted his submissions for the third collection of *Georgian Poetry*. He could be introduced to Garsington visitors as a young man with a future.

He was also a young man with a haunted past which clouded all his actions. His nerves were not up to the job of giving daily pep talks to cadets when his own memory of war was full of unspeakable horrors. He started to tranquillize himself with a strychnine tonic; one night he fainted and fell down the staircase from his college rooms, cutting his head. The wound was not serious but the signs of another breakdown were apparent. He was sent back to Somerville.

It was during this period of hospitalization that Graves described himself in *Goodbye to All That* as having fallen in love with a girl identified, in the revised edition only, as 'Marjorie', a probationer nurse with some talent as a pianist. If Marjorie did exist, and there is no external evidence in letters and diaries to suggest that she did, she was of very slight importance. Graves wrote that he ended their friendship when he discovered that she was engaged to a subaltern in France.

The romance with 'Marjorie' looks unlikely in the light of Graves's continuing and deep attachment to Peter Johnstone, a fact he disguised by falsifying the chronology in *Goodbye*. What, if anything, could he have felt for her at a time when he was using every endeavour to circumvent Johnstone's formidable mother and renew his friendship with her son? The story of Marjorie suited his later view of his sexual development; it looks very much as if she was a convenient fabrication.

'Convalescent home' had become a wartime pseudonym for a psychiatric hospital, of which many officers besides Graves were in dire need by 1917. In June, after a few weeks at Somerville, he was sent to Osborne House on the Isle of Wight. Once a favourite residence of Queen Victoria and the Prince Consort, Osborne had been turned into one of these informal asylums. Here, Graves told friends, his chief entertainment was a rag society which he had formed with a journalist inmate. The type of jokes they enjoyed suggests that he was going through a period of hysteria. One was to construct a model of a drowned sailor and prop it up on the beach to frighten fishermen; another was to dress up as Prince Albert and invent fantastic stories about their connection with him.

Graves needed to cheer himself up if he was not to break down completely; Osborne was primarily occupied by victims of shell-shock. Other inmates stuttered or walked aimlessly up and down; he himself had become a 'twitcher', unable to control his physical movements. His favourite refuge from the madness of his comrades was the local Benedictine monastery, which had a superb library. In the privacy of Quarr Abbey, he read his own little private store of books: Skelton, Keats, a ballad collection and his favourite Latin author, Apuleius, whose *The Golden Ass* led him into reveries about an ancient world ruled by witches and goddesses.

Putting together his third collection of poems was his main occupation while he stayed at Osborne. Heinemann had agreed to publish it as *Fairies and Fusiliers* and Graves was anxious to get preliminary reactions from his London mentors, Edward Marsh and Robbie Ross. Their enthusiasm confirmed his own belief that this was his best work yet. The child's acute though factual sense of tragic events remained a strong theme, but the most interesting of the poems were devoted to the idea that loyalty matters more than the cause. Occasional references show a glimpse of the fear and guilt with which Graves was wrestling privately. 'A Child's Nightmare' evokes the memory of a monstrous phantom who preyed on him when he lay wounded in High Wood, while 'A Boy in Church' looks beyond the serenity of the candlelit chancel to a dark hillside where 'The tortured copse bends to and fro / In silence like a shadow-show.' These are the lines which reveal how haunted Graves was by his experiences in France.

Sassoon had been wounded and sent home in April, in time to see his first book of poems well-reviewed. But Graves was the only critic for whose judgement he had respect; Sassoon was relieved to know that his friend approved of the savage tone of his most recent work. The satire reflected his growing disillusion with a war which he believed was being unnecessarily protracted. Slowly, he was coming round to the view that some action more startling than the writing of poems was needed to make an impact on events.

The letters which Sassoon wrote to Osborne from his mother's country home in June alerted Graves to the fact that his friend was also heading for a nervous breakdown, but not to the possibility that he might be planning a public protest: a letter dated 25 June admitted only that he had done something of which Graves might disapprove.

The explanation came on 10 July when Graves finally received a copy of a statement written by Sassoon with the help of that prominent pacifist and – in Graves's view – troublemaker, Bertrand Russell. In it, Sassoon called for an immediate end to war. For a civilian to make such a statement – Sassoon planned to circulate it to all leading journalists and politicians – was rash; for a serving officer to do so was unbelievably foolhardy.

Graves was anxious to help but Sassoon's protest could not have happened at a worse time. His fragile hold on normal life had been loosened after an anonymous friend had sent him a cutting from the issue of *John Bull* of 2 June, written by the popular magazine's owner and chief editor, Horatio Bottomley. 'A Revolting Charge: High Born Offender Goes Scot Free' was the attention-grabbing headline. Peter Johnstone had been arrested in his last term at Charterhouse for attempting to seduce a Canadian soldier, who subsequently reported him to the police. Bottomley's account was principally concerned with the fact that, as the grandson of an earl, Johnstone had not been sent to prison but put under the informal care of a psychologist, William Halse Rivers, whose colleague, Henry Head, had given evidence in court on Johnstone's behalf.

Graves did not break the connection with Johnstone (his account of events during this period in *Goodbye to All That* is again misleading) but the article gave him a profound shock. Despite the warning letter about Johnstone's behaviour from his cousin Gerald at Charterhouse in 1915, he had persuaded himself that the boy was guiltless. Now he had to face the evidence that, unless the soldier was lying, he had been wrong. And if Johnstone was homosexual, what was he? Graves had never attempted to analyse his feelings about men before. At a time when he was already in an overwrought state, the shock and stress were too much for him. He collapsed.

Graves was not, therefore, in a good state to rescue Sassoon from disgrace but he did not hesitate to try. A court martial seemed to him inevitable once the statement was published, and this was not an exaggerated supposition. After persuading the medical officers at Osborne that he was fit for leave, he took a train to Liverpool and went to the army depot at Litherland to plead with Sassoon's superiors for clemency. Sassoon, he suggested, was in no state to be held responsible for his actions. The colonel told him, to his relief, that they were ready to treat it as a medical case. All that was required was that Sassoon should attend a medical board at Litherland.

After holding discussions about Sassoon's situation with Marsh and Ross in London, Graves returned to Litherland, to learn that Sassoon, who was staying at a hotel in nearby Liverpool, had refused to attend the medical board. When they met, Sassoon seemed elated and to be eager for the court martial which he was convinced would bring maximum attention to his statement.

Graves's duty seemed clear. He deliberately set out to crush Sassoon's feverish excitement and make him see sense. With no knowledge of what the regiment had decided, he told Sassoon that the statement would not be given the publicity he anticipated. With his hand on an imaginary Bible, he swore that there would be no court martial and that Sassoon would achieve nothing but the contempt of his fellow officers. He was convincing. Sassoon, dismayed, agreed to appear with him before a medical board the following day.

The strain on Graves had been considerable and he broke down in tears three times while testifying to the board that Sassoon's mental state in the past month had been abnormal. It was what the sympathetic board wanted to hear; this was the way to let themselves and a young man they respected off the hook. Sassoon was instructed to report to Craiglockhart, a hospital for war invalids on the edge of Edinburgh, where he was, coincidentally, put under the supervision of William Rivers, the doctor who was treating Peter Johnstone for homosexuality. Graves, who followed Sassoon north after missing the train on which he was supposed to act as an official escort, stayed on for a few days at Craiglockhart, before returning to be fêted at Litherland for the dexterity with which he had resolved a nightmarish situation. Sassoon, unwittingly, had made a popular officer of Graves at last.

Graves's prediction that Sassoon's statement would gain little publicity proved to be wrong; it was widely discussed and published after being read out in the House of Commons by Lees Smith, a pacifist MP. Sassoon's name became firmly attached to the pacifist cause and it may have been for this reason that Graves decided to transfer the dedication of *Fairies and Fusiliers* from his friend to the regiment. He himself had never publicly opposed the war and he had no wish to be suspected of doing so, although he shared Sassoon's belief that it was being unjustifiably prolonged.

He was not usually so calculating. There may have been another reason. Writing to apologize for the altered dedication in the second week of September, Graves told 'Sassons' that he was anxious to avoid jealousy among '"friends and lovers"'.[5] He went on to mention only men's names: Marsh, Gosse, Ross and Masefield. It is possible that he was also thinking of Nancy Nicholson.

★　　★　　★

Graves had met Nancy again when he went to Erinfa for a few days at the end of August. Dressed as a bandit, she was just setting off for a fancy-dress dance when Graves arrived at Llys Bach, the Harlech house leased by her parents.[6] Impulsively, he decided to go with her and stayed until two in the morning. The next day he went to Llys Bach again and remained there until late in the evening. In early October, when he was hoping to be moved overseas from a new home posting – he was now attached to the Third Garrison Battalion at Kinmel near Rhyl on the north coast of Wales – he spent part of his autumn leave in London with the Nicholsons. Nancy, very upset that her favourite brother Tony was about to go out to France as a gunner, had just decided to become a land-girl, doing farm work. Her determination to do manual labour and exchange her velvet skirts for mannish breeches made an intriguing contrast to her delicate artwork. Seeing some of the illustrations which she was doing for a children's poetry book, Graves warmed to her still more. It was impossible that she could do such work and not share his own feelings about children. (Graves himself adored them. The colonel's children at Rhyl called him 'Georgy Giraffe' and honoured him with invitations to nursery teas and games of tiddlywinks.)

Johnstone's arrest had unsettled Graves's confidence in his judgement and caused him to wonder about his own preference for male company. He must have been aware by now that almost every man with whom he had a close friendship was a homosexual. He knew that this was not the way of life he wanted for himself, although his desire for women remained inhibited by Amy's emphasis on sex as a degrading activity, useful only for reproduction.[7]

Nancy's boyish directness and youth – she was just eighteen – together with the fact that she belonged to a more artistic and lively milieu than the Graveses, made her an appealing figure. Marriage and children would free him from his problematic male friendships and, perhaps, help to blot out the bloody images which haunted his nights and days. So he must have begun to think as he spent more time with the Nicholsons and saw their very different lifestyle.

Robert was still a product of his background, prim and shy in the company of strangers, easily shocked and startlingly uncultivated in all but his reading. Nancy's culture, by contrast, came from everything except books. In matters of art and music, she was far in advance of him.

Her father, known to his colleagues and family as The Kid, decided that the best way to start broadening young Graves's mind was to take him to a rather daring new revue; Robert was observed to enjoy it almost as much as Nancy. William Nicholson was a charming man and Graves and he were soon fast friends. Dandyishly elegant in a high-collared spotted shirt and green coat, worn with a yellow waistcoat and white duck trousers, Nicholson was more like an older brother to his children than a father, full of funny stories and terrible puns. His closest friends were Edwin Lutyens and Max Beerbohm, both of whom shared his sense of humour and love of practical jokes.

Nancy was fond of her father but she was more closely attached to her mother, a dreamy and rather melancholy Scot. Mabel Pryde (she was always called 'Prydie') was independent-minded enough to smoke, and to design all her own unusual, but modern, clothes. Nancy's affection for her had to do with a sense of fierce protectiveness. Mabel had sacrificed her considerable talent as an artist to look after her husband and children; she turned a blind eye to her husband's fairly regular flirtations. In her mother, Nancy saw resigned, down-trodden womanhood; this was the mainspring of her own fierce feminism. Robert Graves was one of the few men she had met who did not quarrel with her belief that women were the superior sex. He seemed, indeed, to accept her view on female supremacy as readily as the idea that if God was a man, God must be 'all rot'. They seemed destined to understand each other well.

★   ★   ★

On 12 October Graves left London to visit Sassoon at Craiglockhart. He was met at the station by a slight, handsome young man with a nervous stammer. On the way to the golf course where Sassoon was waiting to meet them, he introduced himself as Wilfred Owen, a poet and editor of the hospital magazine. His admiration for Sassoon was undisguised.

William Rivers, the doctor whom Graves had met on his first visit,★ was away at this time; instead of discussing their symptoms with him, as they had planned to do, Sassoon and Graves talked about the war, poetry, and Owen. Before he left, Graves was given a copy of 'Disabled', Wilfred Owen's most recent poem, and urged by Sassoon to offer friendly criticism.

Owen had become deeply attached to Sassoon as a friend and mentor after showing him some of his early work. In September, Sassoon praised and helped to revise 'Anthem for Doomed Youth' but he was perhaps too close to Owen to realize that the poems were not simply admiring imitations of his own style. It was Graves, not Sassoon, who recognized 'the real thing, a genuine new talent' as soon as he read 'Disabled'.[8]

Owen had not taken to Graves on first acquaintance; Sassoon was closer to his ideal of a poet than the sturdy, moody-faced visitor. Writing to his mother shortly after the visit, he told her that Captain Graves had been 'mightily impressed' by him as a 'Find' – but that he intended to find himself.[9]

His rancour died in the face of Graves's infectious enthusiasm for his work. The letters which he wrote to Owen that autumn not only show Graves's generosity to a man he rated above himself as a poet,

---

★ There is no direct evidence of this meeting between Rivers and Graves but the indications point towards it. Contrary to Paul O'Prey's assertion that 'Rivers was very interested in poetry' (*Collected Letters*, 1, p. 81), Rivers read it only for the purpose of analysing a poetry-writing patient's state of mind. By early August, shortly after Graves's initial visit to Craiglockhart, he was expressing an eager wish to see Graves's work. A letter from Graves on 9 August, promising to send him *Goliath and David* and asking Sassoon to 'salute for me that excellent man [Rivers]', suggests by the warmth of its tone that they must have met. Rivers would also have heard a good deal about Graves when he was treating Johnstone that summer. Rivers did not feel restricted to the confines of an official practice; the distinction between the people he treated (like Sassoon) and to whom he spoke as a friend (like Graves) was so fine as to be imperceptible. I am indebted to Pat Barker, who has written two novels about Sassoon and Rivers, for information and suggestions here.

but his intense awareness of craftsmanship. Taking 'Disabled' to pieces and pointing out where jingles, clichés and 'metrical outrages' had weakened the effect, Graves urged Owen to remember the basic rules. His letters show his warmth. They also show his own practical attitude to poetry.

> One can't put too many syllables into a line and say 'oh, it's all right. That's my way of writing poetry.' . . . Make new metres by all means, but one must observe the rules where they are laid down by custom of centuries. A painter or musician has no greater task in mastering his colours or his musical modes and harmonies, than a poet. It's the devil of a sweat for him to get to know the value of his rhymes rhythms and sentiments. But I have no doubt at all that if you turned seriously to writing, you could attain Parnassus in no time while I'm still struggling on the knees of that stubborn peak.[10]

As for Sassoon, at Craiglockhart he was writing some of the finest poetry to come out of the war but Graves was not altogether sure that he liked it. As he felt increasingly tender towards Nancy, his taste for savage satire correspondingly diminished. 'Don't send me any more corpse poems,' he pleaded in an undated letter, before urging Sassoon to fix his hopes on a new postwar world which would be, admittedly, emptier but 'wiser and happier than anything that has gone before'.[11] Their duty had not altered. They had entered a contract to fight; he disagreed with Sassoon that acknowledging that contract had become an act of cowardice. 'Sorry you think that of me,' he wrote on 17 October. 'I should hate to think I'm a coward. I believe though in keeping to agreements when everybody else keeps them . . .'[12]

By the end of October, when Owen was discharged as fit for general service, Sassoon had changed his mind. Rivers's gentle approach and the guilt which he felt about being separated from his battalion in France had undone his wish to be a solitary crusader against the war. He was impatient to return to the Front, but not because he felt fresh hope of victory. Graves's uncharacteristic display of optimism puzzled and irritated him.

It was, in part, an act, and one which imposed a considerable strain on Graves. Writing to Edmund Gosse on 24 October, he admitted to a difference in attitude between himself and Sassoon. 'He thinks he is best employed by writing poems which will make people find the war so hateful that they'll stop it at whatever cost. I don't. I think that I'll do more good by keeping up my brother soldiers' morale as far as I can . . . I suffer all that S. S. suffers, or nearly all, only I'm hiding it till after the war . . .'[13]

He had one cause for real happiness, his relationship with Nancy. In November he went to visit the farm at Hilton in Huntingdonshire where she was working as a land-girl with Smuts, her big black poodle, for company. Her short ruffled hairstyle and uniform of belted jacket, breeches and knee-length boots made her look like a handsome soldier; she had probably told Graves by now that her mother preferred boys. Robert helped her groom the horses and chop earth-clotted mangold roots while Nancy gave vent to her feelings about the way the local farmers talked about women. In softer moments she told him about Chaucers, the ancient house near Oxford where she had been born and where she dreamed of living one day when she was married. The following month Graves wrote to tell Robert Nichols about his new friendship. The letter makes it clear how anxious he was to distance himself from the homosexual circles in which he had been moving.

> I only tell you this so that you should get out of your head any misconceptions about my temperament. I should hate you to think I was a confirmed homosexual even if it were only in my thought and went no farther.[14]

Most of Graves's friends were aware of Nancy as a presence in his life by now. Sassoon was told that they were working on a children's book together and was asked to smooth down Ross, who had made his hostility clear by spreading stories of negro blood in Nancy's family. They did not know yet that he planned to marry her.

On 16 December Graves took Nancy to meet Edmund Gosse, proposed almost on the doorstep of his house overlooking Regent's Park, and wandered off for a two-mile stroll with her after completely forgetting their appointment.[15] At three in the morning, after walking through Putney in a driving blizzard, he appeared at Red Branch House and announced his news.

The engagement was welcomed by both sides of the family although the Graveses were unaware that Nancy had no intention of giving up her name or independence, or that she had only consented to a ceremony to please her father. The Nicholsons appeared to be prosperous, if a trifle bohemian, and they did not object to the idea of the young couple settling into Nancy's childhood home near Oxford, as Robert fancifully anticipated.* Nancy's mother's only stipulation was that Graves should let himself be investigated by Sir James Fowler, the doctor who had seen him at Rouen hospital in February. Graves was talking of a posting to Palestine and Mrs Nicholson did not like the thought of losing a son-in-law directly after the wedding.

The examination was made in December. After talking to Graves and noting that the right lung had shrunk to a third of its natural size, Sir James recorded a negative view. Any further active service would, in his view, bring back the nerve trouble. Graves could continue to serve, but only at home. The Nicholsons were much relieved by this verdict.

Writing to ask Sassoon to come to the wedding on 23 January, Graves could not resist the temptation to swagger a little about what was becoming – due to William Nicholson's circle of friends – a grand social occasion. There would be champagne at 11 Apple Tree Yard, he wrote, and all the best people would be there. But Sassoon saw the marriage as a betrayal of their own relationship. He declined to attend, offering the implausible excuse of a gas course in Cork.

Graves's 1929 account of his wedding was prefaced by the words: 'Another caricature scene . . .' His readers had been warned. He was writing at a time when his marriage had irretrievably broken down and when Nancy was in his bad books. His memories of a sullen, bad-tempered, champagne-swigging bride were neither kind nor accurate. Surprisingly, they have never been questioned.

In this retrospective account, Graves showed Nancy reading the wedding service for the first time that morning and becoming so angry that she could scarcely mutter the responses. But Graves was nowhere near Nancy on the morning of their wedding day. He was entertaining the Mallorys – George was his best man – at Red Branch House in Wimbledon, while Nancy slept on a sofa at Apple Tree Yard, the studio in St James's which her father had converted from a mews stable and loft on the advice of his friend Ned Lutyens, who lived next door. Shortly after she was woken by her father, Max

---

* 'When I am married and settled down as I hope to be one day at Chaucer's House at Woodstock I shall make it a sort of home for young poets – the Helicon Hostel,' Graves wrote to his friend Charles Scott-Moncrieff in December 1917, shortly before the wedding. (Scott-Moncrieff Papers, National Library of Scotland)

Beerbohm's sister Agnes arrived with the wedding dress which she had designed and made; it was a present to Nancy from her parents' rich and generous friend, Edie Stuart-Wortley. 'Wedding dress the most beautiful thing you can think of,' William reported to Ben, away in California, in a long and detailed letter the following day,[16] 'large pale romantic blue and white checked silk and the bouquet really good – as good as W.N. could make it anyway.' Nancy, too, looked 'simply and perfectly beautiful' and, as they set off in their friend Lady Sackville's loaned car for the short ride to St James's Church, Piccadilly, Nancy turned to her father and said, '"Father, this is fun."' It is impossible to equate this account with Graves's later description.

Goodbye to All That offers no details of the Graves family's presence that day, but William Nicholson wanted Ben to envisage it all. His letter started by describing Amy in a green velvet dress, showing off a most unnerving profile, and proceeded to Alfred, small and upright, perched beside his wife in a new grey suit and bowler hat and eyeing the bride's guests. Alfred, sighed William, is 'a dreadful bore of the 3rd water'. From the groom's parents, he proceeded to more general matters with a sense that it had been a day of triumph. Leopold Stokowski had agreed to play the organ, all their dearest friends had been present and Nancy and Robert spoke up in 'fine firm unashamed voices' before the vestry was swamped by 'a whole rash of the grave Graves family trying, without the least success, to make it seem an ordinary wedding'. William did not comment on his daughter's decision to keep her own name but he respected it. Signing the register after the service, she wrote the name she had always used and Robert, as a new convert to feminism, approved. To him, his wife would always be 'Miss Nicholson' or 'N.N.'

The Graveses were out of their depth at the reception which followed in the Apple Tree Yard studio, where the light and simple furnishings made Amy's taste for heavy mahogany look as dowdy as her dresses. William had ordered three dozen bottles of champagne and – a great treat in wartime – a cake from Gunter's, but the Graveses did not drink champagne and they did not know either the Nicholsons' smart friends or more than a couple of Robert's new literary ones. This second group was well-represented. Harold Monro, William Heinemann and his publishing partner, Sidney Pawling, Nancy's godfather, were there. Charles Scott-Moncrieff and Wilfred Owen had travelled from Shrewsbury, Owen bringing a set of silver spoons to show appreciation to one of his kindest mentors. Edward Marsh and Robbie Ross made up for the disappointing absence of Sassoon.

Amy had gone to unusual lengths with her appearance that day. Blissfully unaware of how William Nicholson had winced at the sight of her curious velvet costume, she shuddered when Nancy walked into the reception wearing breeches and smock, with a favourite red scarf from her father knotted round her neck. But William, having tied Marie Tempest's slipper to the back of Lady Sackville's car and waved the emancipated young couple off in it for their honeymoon night at a local hotel, saw only that his daughter looked lovely. He was sure that his 'Nance' had made a good choice, 'and a wise poet he was to choose the darling and this I will say'.

The Graves family returned to Red Branch House for a quiet evening. For William, the festivities ended with a call to Marlborough Street Police Station at one in the morning to collect his bedraggled poodle, Bingo, still wearing the satin wedding ribbons in which it had been arrested in Piccadilly after the service.[17]

After their night in London, Robert and Nancy spent the rest of their winter honeymoon at Llys Bach, becoming awkwardly familiar with each other – they were both virgins – and exploring the landmarks of the wild moorland which Robert had loved since childhood. It was, he told his friends, the happiest time he had known since the beginning of the war.

PART TWO

NANCY

CHAPTER SEVEN

1918–1919
YOUNG LOVE

TOWARDS THE END OF THEIR LIVES, IN THE LATE 1960S, NANCY and Robert finally agreed to share the responsibility for the failure of their marriage. The fault had been as much in the time and the situation as in a clash of personalities. At the age of twenty-three, Graves had plunged into marriage with a child bride in the hope of calming a storm of conflicting emotions. Sexually, he was still recovering from the trauma of confronting his own love for a boy he now believed to be a homosexual. He was also still in the early stages of prolonged shell-shock which made him – increasingly – neurotic and volatile. He was full of guilt about the men he had killed and about the members of his own regiment who had returned to the Front while he stayed securely at home in the later war years.

Financially, Graves was unready at this time to shoulder the responsibility of a wife and the four children they quickly produced. Apart from his war bonus and savings of some £150, he had nothing to live on but his disability pension, the tiny rent he could get for letting his two-roomed Harlech cottage and what he could beg or borrow from his parents. His mother had the money, and the authority to decide how much to release, and Amy was a reluctant giver. (She was also very possessive; no bride would have been considered good enough for her Robert. She had been against Nancy since seeing how she had signed the wedding register, as if she was ashamed, Amy thought, to call herself a Graves. This lack of cordiality did not increase Amy's inclination to hand over sums of money.)

Poetically, too, Graves showed signs of losing his way in the early years of his marriage; for this, he could hold Nancy partly responsible. Sassoon wanted him to continue writing poetry in the war vein. Nancy, who liked the idea of collaborations, backed his skill as a writer of ballads and songs. She could illustrate them and they might turn out to be money-spinners: Graves had told her the story of Alfred's 'Father O'Flynn'. Eric Pinker, Graves's literary agent, was enthusiastic and Ivor Novello, the immensely successful young Welsh composer of 'Keep the Home Fires Burning', was willing to set some of the songs to music. *Country Sentiment* (1920), Graves's fifth collection, of which he sent confident predictions to his friends, aimed to combine sweetness with satire; songs for Nancy, war-poems for Sassoon. It flopped.

Even *Country Sentiment* was riddled with darker thoughts than Graves was willing to acknowledge. His next book of poems, *The Pier-Glass* (1921), gives a clearer glimpse of the haunted mind with which Nancy was in daily contact. Most disturbing of all must have been her husband's growing belief that his torment was the source of his best work. In 'The Gnat', a poem which compares his mental state, horrifyingly, to the sensation of a metal-clawed insect boring into a man's brain, the cure is shown to kill the imagination. This was Graves's chief problem. He was tortured by his thoughts but he feared the consequences of being cured. What he wanted from Nancy was a calm and homely setting in which he would feel safe with his demons.

Nancy was a remarkable young woman, independent, confident and proud. Her misfortune was to be composed of opposites so that, for example, high professional ideals were often undermined by poor judgement of priorities. After promising to type Robert's poems for an impatient publisher, she might choose to work all night on designing the print for their kitchen curtains. Disapproving of servants and with advanced views on nutrition, she ended by letting her husband do most of the cooking. Rigid notions of how children should be brought up (bed at six o'clock and straight answers to all religious questions) proved hard to reconcile with a wish to treat the nurses as personal friends.

Everything to do with appearance was under Nancy's charge. She made furniture and even, after her separation from Graves, built a house. She decorated their homes, always using the same light sky-blue and deep green for contrast, with white muslin curtains at the windows and white floors to achieve an instantly identifiable Nicholson style. The children's best clothes were made by her, as were the crisply laundered blouses and heavy cotton skirts for which she abandoned her smocks and breeches in the early Twenties.

Nancy's intense response to appearances was utterly at odds with her husband's cheerful indifference. Graves lived by his ears not his eyes. He had to concentrate hard to take in anything visually; the Welsh landscape he used in his poetry offered a simple and barren world of mountains and moorland which required no detailed observation. His siblings noticed that Amy Graves was dowdy in her dress; Graves never did. He was the kind of man who could walk all day in different-coloured socks and never register it.

Nancy would have responded to the odd socks as sharply as to a slight on her sex. So extreme were her views that she once returned a picture by her brother, Ben, because it contained a displeasing colour; she would walk out of a room she had painted if a guest wore a colour that clashed with it. Later in life, she turned down a lucrative commission from a department store because mass production would have affected the colour of her hand-printed cloths. These inflexible aesthetics were brought to bear on her husband.

Graves was happy, at first, to laugh about Nancy smartening him up and getting him to wash his face. But he soon tired of it and Nancy grew weary of reminding him as he reverted to his old and careless ways, picking food off everyone else's plates – he cheerfully admitted to being a coarse feeder – and never noticing what clothes he put on. Their difference in attitude may never have been discussed: Graves was unaware of any fault on his side and Nancy had a horror of intimate exchanges. But she had an expressive face and no talent for hiding her hostility. The poems of the early years of Graves's marriage often appeal for a kind response which Nancy was evidently slow to give. 'The Patchwork Bonnet' starts in wistfulness, with the poet throwing a loving look at his wife's stern profile as she sits sewing. The baby cries out in fear. 'Then Mother turns, laughing like a young fairy' and Graves indulges in a poignant image of his wife and daughter as a Madonna and child, caught in silhouette upon the blind.[1] 'One Hard Look', a more direct appeal for tenderness, exposes his own vulnerable state of need, when '. . . one hard look / Can close the book / That lovers love to see.'[2]

They both wanted to start a family at once, but for different reasons. Graves saw children as an antidote to his memories of death. Nancy wanted to get the business of motherhood done and return to her artwork as soon as possible. This impatience made another contribution to their misfortunes. Completely uninformed about childbirth, she took two years to recover from the shock of her bad first experience. She went on to have three more children in quick succession. This, combined with perpetual worries about money, dragged down her health; by 1926, after eight years of marriage, the pretty, creamy-skinned girl was a shadow of her former self. A severe thyroid problem had produced a deadly fatigue, similar to the modern debilitating condition of myalgic encephalomyelitis, ME. Ringworm resulted in a loss of hair so complete that for a time she had to wear a wig. Exhaustion and stress had led to acute nervous strain. Most painfully for Nancy, life with four demanding children and a shell-shocked husband had left no time or creative spark for the vocation which mattered to her more than anything else.

There were also problems with the sexual side of the marriage. Graves, according to Nancy's later accounts, was an insistent but unsatisfactory lover. He had never slept with a woman before and sex, for him, was primarily a way of blotting out the horror of the nights in which his worst memories of the war returned. The act was necessary but the intensity of physical passion was a troubling experience for Amy Graves's puritanically-educated son. In 'Morning Phoenix' he gave a memorable account of his response to the sensation of desire as one from which he shrank with self-disgust.

> In my body lives a flame
>   Flame that burns me all the day,
> When a fierce sun does the same,
>   I am charred away.
>
> Who could keep a smiling wit,
>   Roasted so in heart and hide,

Turning on the sun's red spit,
Scorched by love inside?[3]

Another poem, 'The Kiss', ends with a description of the act of love as a hurried assault which ends in death-like isolation.

Is that Love? no, but Death,
    A passion, a shout,
The deep in-breath,
    The breath roaring out,
And once that is flown,
    You must lie alone,
Without hope, without life,
    Poor flesh, sad bone.[4]

For Graves, then, sex offered a momentary escape from the hell of his thoughts in much the same way as his daily game of rugger. By acts of violence he could eradicate, briefly, the memory of the greater violence which was always present in his mind. Nancy offered him no other opportunity to exorcize the past and neither, at first, did he want her to do so. But it grew hard when he realized how adamant she was. The war was never to be mentioned in their home. Nancy would not even allow a newspaper through the door, for this reason.

Had this been the whole story of their relationship, the marriage would not have survived as long as it did. But it was not the full story, not at the start. Graves sent a letter to Nancy every day they were apart in the first year of their marriage. (She later destroyed the correspondence, together with her diaries, leaving no private record before 1929.) Commiserating with Edmund Blunden over the death of the poet's first child in 1919, Robert described the guilt which he and Nancy felt about hearing of such sad events when they themselves were living in a 'heligoland of happiness'. Together they plotted a theatrical future, with Graves writing plays and Nancy designing sets. Together they laid plans for financial ventures such as the patenting of Nancy's 'golliwog' doll or a set of plates which she would execute to her husband's design. Their marriage was full of puns and jokes, until circumstances left no time or heart for laughter.

Knowing what followed, and deceived by Graves's own prejudiced account of a marriage he was determined to dismiss in *Goodbye to All*

That, biographers have looked too eagerly for signs of incompatibility. An early version of the poem 'Vain and Careless', usually cited as Graves's way of reproaching Nancy for these faults, reveals itself as a tender collaboration when first presented in magazine form. The 'Careless Lady' verse was written in Graves's hand on the corner of Nancy's full-page illustration of the giddy young woman.[5] What kind of reproach was this? 'The Troll's Nosegay', too, has been taken to refer to Nancy's capricious nature in demanding a winter nosegay for which she refused to express any pleasure.[6] But the poem was written at the beginning of 1919, when Nancy was still recovering from the difficult birth of their first child and from the potentially lethal Spanish influenza which she had caught from Robert. This was not the moment when he wanted to write a poem accusing her of whimsical ingratitude. Their marriage had never been closer. The lady of the poem who is so difficult to please carries more conviction as the poet's demanding muse, one who will not be satisfied until every flower – or image – is to her liking. This, after all, was the famous poem of which Graves claimed he wrote thirty-five drafts instead of his usual six or seven.

Nancy was not a muse. She was intelligent and literate – despite being an atrocious speller – and she enjoyed having poems read to her, but poetry never matched her feeling for art. She did not look for more from Robert than the creation of charming ballads to accompany her illustrations. Later in life, this might have mattered less. In his twenties, Graves was still hungry for literary mentors. His wife, loyally described to friends as one of his best critics, did not possess the voice of authority he was seeking.

★   ★   ★

After only a month of married life it was necessary for Nancy to return to her farm work at Hilton while Graves rejoined the regiment stationed at Rhyl. In the middle of February Charles Scott-Moncrieff helped him to transfer from the Third Battalion to the Sixteenth as a cadet trainer. By March Nancy had resigned from her job. She joined Graves, first in two tiny rented rooms in a Welsh farmer's bungalow and then as lodgers in Bryn-y-Pin, a small farmhouse above the army camp. Graves walked down the hill every day to his training duties; Nancy worked in a local market garden until the discomforting onset of her first pregnancy made her feel too ill to continue. Together they searched the local market stalls for the silver spoons and talismans Graves always loved collecting, while Nancy found funny, old-fashioned toys for their baby. Walking on the hills, they fantasized about the future. Their dream of a return to Chaucers, the ancient house near Oxford where Nancy had been born, had evaporated; instead they made fanciful plans for a farm to be run by poets and novelists. 'I do think a farm on the downs would be great fun,' Graves wrote to Charles Scott-Moncrieff (who was also a poet before he became the first English translator of Proust). 'You would manage the office,' Graves told him, 'S[iegfried] S[assoon] the horses, I and Nancy the ploughing, Alec Waugh perhaps the ducks and hens with help of his Barbara – a repertory theatre and printing press on the premises, and a bar parlour more famous than any Mermaid Tavern.'[7]

The opportunity to live in a more substantial home presented itself in the summer of 1918. The Nicholsons' friend Edie Stuart-Wortley had recently learned that her husband was missing, presumed dead. To comfort herself, she asked the Nicholsons, together with Robert, Nancy and Robert's sister Rosaleen, to spend the whole of June at Maesyneuadd, a house which she had been renting near Harlech while the Nicholsons rented Llys Bach. When the house party left, Nancy and Robert were told that they could stay on for as long as they liked during Robert's summer leave.

It must, at first, have seemed too good to be true. They had a beautiful fourteenth-century stone manor-house all to themselves. The hills rose behind it; to the front, there were tranquil views of moors and woods across a terraced lawn. But there was a drawback, an unfortunate one for anybody superstitious, and these were susceptible guests. Nancy, like Graves, studied astrology charts and saw ghosts in every passing shadow. 'It was,' Graves recalled in *Goodbye to All That*, 'the most haunted house that I have ever been in',

> though the ghosts were invisible except in the mirrors. They would open and shut doors, rap on the oak panels, knock the shades off lamps, and drink the wine from the glasses at our elbows where we were not looking . . . There was only one visible ghost, a little yellow dog that appeared on the lawn in the early morning to announce deaths. Nancy saw it one day.[8]

The dog's appearance gained in significance the following month when Nancy's mother died of influenza. Nancy was heartbroken; Graves later paid tribute to Mabel Nicholson as a woman who had sacrificed her vocation to bring up her children, and her independence by taking her husband's name. He went on to ridicule the idea of a Mrs Pericles of Athens.[9] It is an article which shows how strongly he had been influenced by his young wife's views on women's rights.

It was a year and a half since Graves had been in France. His correspondence with Sassoon, convalescing in a London hospital from a near-fatal shot in the head, was ostensibly about their different attitudes to their work, implicitly about their altered roles. Sassoon, still raging at the hypocrisy of war, could find little to praise in Graves's projected new collection, 'The Patchwork Flag', a combination of songs and war-poems.* Later Graves thanked Sassoon for stopping what he thought would have been a bad book; at the time he was hurt. Not even the munificent birthday present of £23 to match his years could soften the sense of Sassoon's hostility: he knew, as did all Sassoon's friends, that money was an easy gift from a prosperous young man. 'Old boy do you want me to stop writing altogether?' Graves wrote back. 'I can't write otherwise than I am now except with hypocrisy, for I am bloody happy and bloody young (with only very occasional lapses) and passionate anger is most ungrateful . . . Worrying about the War is no longer a sacred duty with me.'[10]

Graves tried to convince himself that this was how he felt by embarking on projects like 'The Penny Fiddle', a compilation of nursery rhymes to be illustrated by Nancy. The poetry tells another story. However hard he tried to concentrate on the soothing images and rhythmic chants of childhood, he could not get away from the hideous images which returned every few weeks in bouts of shell-shock. He could tell Sassoon that he was 'bloody happy'; the poems suggest that he was still guilty about having been allowed to escape death. 'Haunted' shows the past invading the daylit present with shocking clarity:

> . . . Strangers assume your phantom faces,
> You grin at me from daylight places,
> Dead, long dead, I'm ashamed to greet
> Dead men down the morning street.[11]

* This was the forerunner of the combination used in *Country Sentiment* two years later.

'Ghost Raddled' offers a still more disturbing glimpse of his hidden anguish. The poem purports to be about Maesyneuadd. In it, Graves wrote:

> Of demons in the dry well
> That cheep and mutter,
> Clanging of an unseen bell,
>   Blood choking the gutter.
>
> Of lust frightful, past belief,
> Lurking unforgotten,
> Unrestrainable endless grief
>   From breasts long rotten.
>
> A song? What laughter or what song
> Can this house remember?
> Do flowers and butterflies belong
>   To a blind December?[12]

The ghostly signals may belong to Maesyneuadd – but it is clear that the house stands for England and that Graves was questioning the validity of his own songs of flowers and butterflies in a time of devastation. The image of 'a blind December' had nothing to do with the house in which he had stayed in high summer, everything to do with the memory of death in the mud.

At the beginning of October 1918, Nancy and Graves were at last moving into a little Welsh cottage of their own when the news came that Nancy's brother, Tony, who had been on leave with them at Maesyneuadd, had been killed. He was just twenty-one. Graves, having already had the task of telling his wife of her mother's death, admitted to Sassoon that his main worry was that Nancy might miscarry when he reported this second tragedy. Never one to display her griefs – she had chosen not to go to her mother's funeral – Nancy appeared to take the news calmly, but she had lost her two favourite members of the family.

Robbie Ross, who had been giving advice to Graves on his new poems only that month, died on the same day as Tony Nicholson. Impressed by his wife's example of contained grief, Robert sent no notes or flowers. To Sassoon, however, he lamented the loss of a witty, generous and kind-hearted friend. It was Ross who had given him his first, specially bound, book of John Skelton's poems.

Graves had a new enterprise on his hands when he wrote this letter to Sassoon on 12 October. William Nicholson had decided that it might be fun to set up a small quarterly magazine, with his son-in-law looking after the literary contributions while he chose the illustrators. He would subsidize it and his darling daughter could contribute what and when she liked. This was *Owl*, which eventually ran to three numbers, two in 1919 and a special issue for Winter, 1923. The name developed from Nicholson's playful sketches of a fat and watchful bird; Graves added the quotation from Lewis Carroll that 'all owls are satisfactory'.

Financially, *Owl* was luckier for its contributors, who sometimes received £5 per page, than for its editors. Expensively priced at 12s 6d a copy, it failed for this reason and from lack of publicity. But for Graves, apart from the pleasure of working with his genial father-in-law, it offered a useful base from which to extend his circle of artists and writers by inviting them to contribute. On the illustration side, he made only one addition to William's list. Eric Kennington, a contemporary of Sassoon's, had exhibited a striking pastel head of Graves earlier in the year. The two men had liked each other at once and so had Celandine and Nancy, their wives. The Kenningtons were among the first close friends of their marriage.

Graves was conservative in his choice of *Owl* contributors: no Joyce, no Eliot, no Aldington, D. H. Lawrence, Wyndham Lewis or Aldous Huxley (but this was after Nancy, who hated Huxley's poems, lost his submission). Instead Graves and his fellow literary editor Walter Turner, the Australian music critic and poet, turned to Edmund Gosse, Walter de la Mare, Thomas Hardy, Arnold Bennett, Lytton Strachey, W. H. Davies, Hugh Walpole, Robert Nichols and, of course, Sassoon. Most of these writers belonged to an older generation; the only contemporary poet Graves was willing to consider at Sassoon's suggestion was Edmund Blunden, a newly-fledged Georgian. Compared to, say, the Sitwell-orientated magazine, *Wheels*, or *The Egoist*, in which the essays of Eliot and Pound were appearing, *Owl* was a traditional miscellany which took no risks. Graves could praise Strachey for 'the way the fish rose and gurgled at you when you baited them with Eminent Victorians', but he showed no similar wish to provoke *Owl* readers.[13] Eager though

Robert was to distinguish himself from his father, he was still almost equally old-fashioned in his literary tastes.

Lytton Strachey had nothing to offer to *Owl* – he claimed to have been intimidated by such an impressive list of contributors. But he remained intrigued by Graves and by the memory of conversations at Garsington, when he had become aware of 'strange concealed thoughts which only very occasionally poke up through his schoolboy jocularities'. The contrast between Graves's genial manner and his evident suffering had left a strong impression. 'Terribly tragic I thought.'[14]

*   *   *

The war ended, drearily for Graves, on 11 November. Nancy was still grieving for her brother. Jones Bateman, a young officer who had been with Graves through most of his service and acted as one of his most honest critics, had just died in France. So had Wilfred Owen who, Graves had hoped, was going to be transferred to Rhyl on his return. His last postcard to Graves arrived that day. With so few of his friends left, Graves had nothing to celebrate on Armistice Night. Instead, he left Nancy in the cottage while he walked alone in the dark, 'cursing and sobbing and thinking of the dead'.[15]

In December, anxious for his daughter's welfare in a small cottage with no help, William Nicholson took the advice of his closest woman-friend, Edie Stuart-Wortley, and rented a handsome new house for the whole family. It was bracingly situated on the South Coast at Hove with a strip of private beach running up to its doors. Here, on 6 January 1919, Graves's first child was born. She was named, but not, to Amy Graves's horror, baptized, Jenny Nicholson, it having been agreed that any daughters should take their mother's name. After overstaying his leave to be with Nancy for the birth, Graves rejoined the Third Battalion at Limerick in Ireland with the intention of getting demobilized as swiftly as possible and signing up as a student at Oxford, where he still had the right to take up his Classics exhibition at St John's. (Students had priority for demobilization and a grant of £200 a year.) Robert's plan was to read Agriculture for two years and become a farmer-poet, an idea which had the warm support of both Nancy and her father, who offered to sponsor the farm.

Brought up on Alfred's stories of his youth, Graves was quickly at home in Limerick. There were relations to visit, family anecdotes to be heard about his grandfather, the Bishop of Limerick, sad stories to be learned of the local Sinn Feiners who shook their fists at him as an English invader when he walked through the town. Limerick, despite this hostility, enchanted him and he crystallized his impressions in his account of a morning stroll along the main street.

> When the hour chimed, the door of a magnificent Georgian house flew open and out came, first a shower of slops, which just missed me, then a dog, which lifted up its leg against a lamp-post, then a nearly naked girl-child, who sat down in the gutter and rummaged in a heap of refuse for filthy pieces of bread; finally a donkey, which began to bray. I had pictured Ireland exactly so, and felt its charm as dangerous.[16]

Enticing to the imagination though this life was, Robert was impatient to get his papers signed and be done with soldiering. He had enough influential friends to secure a telegram ordering his release but it arrived, most unfortunately, the day before all demobilization in Ireland was being indefinitely postponed because of the Troubles. The adjutant, who had picked Graves out to help him arrange the St David's Day theatricals, refused to act on the telegram; Graves, shivering with what he recognized as the terrible Spanish influenza which killed thousands that year, decided to make a run for it. Armed with the essential signature of release from his colonel, he caught the last train out of Limerick before demobilization stopped.

A series of code-marks still had to be added to his papers, without which Graves feared that the demobilization centre in Wimbledon would send him straight back to Limerick. Luck was on his side. The man to whom he offered a lift from Paddington Station in his taxi – it was the only taxi available because of an impending rail strike – was the demobilization officer from Cork. He agreed to sign the vital papers for Graves's release in exchange for the lift.

His departure from Ireland had secured his freedom at the cost of his health: the influenza had gone from his head to his chest. When he arrived in Hove at the beginning of February, the Nicholsons' doctor diagnosed septic pneumonia from which there was little hope of recovery for a man with damaged lungs. Illness brought on a raging fever during which Graves was unaware that his wife and Mrs Stuart-Wortley had also collapsed with the influenza. Instead, half-conscious, he lay in bed composing 'The Troll's Nosegay' to a background of premature sobs from the housemaid as she tiptoed past the door. Graves had extraordinary powers of resistance; by 21 February he was well enough to ask his *Owl* colleague Walter Turner to come on a visit to 'Seasick Villa', so named by Nancy because it was full of vomiting invalids. They could, he added, offer oysters, a screaming baby – and a lot of bad jokes.[17]

★　　★　　★

On the day he was demobilized Graves had sworn that he would never belong to an organized body again. But he knew that he could not survive on his income from writing poetry. Oxford still offered a good temporary solution, if he could be assured of his grant, although he could not cope with the idea of living in rooms near the university, as Sassoon was now doing. City life was intolerable to him in his shell-shocked state; even a day-trip to London imposed a strain he found hard to bear. For the time being, then, he was thankful to accept Nancy's father's offer of Llys Bach, the Harlech house, until the lease expired in the autumn. They went there in March 1919 and stayed for seven months.

Llys Bach, or 'Slip Back' in its anglicized form, subsidized by William Nicholson, was a perfect place in which to forget their worries. They hired a pretty, well-educated maid, Barbara Morrison, and a doting Geordie nanny, Margaret Russell, who became a lifelong friend to Robert and his children. They lived, as Graves wryly observed later, as though they had an income of a thousand a year. The Army had given him no chance to learn about household economy; Nancy, with her confused ideas of justice, found it unbearable not to pay her new servants whatever they asked and then to give them more. But they were happy. Nancy worked on her delicate illustrations for Robert's poem 'Vain and Careless' and on their projected children's book, while Graves divided his time between finding suitable composers for his songs and writing reviews for Sassoon, who had been made the literary editor of the new and fiercely left-wing *Daily Herald*.

Socialism was the creed of the moment after the war. Suffering and death on such a massive scale could only begin to be justified by a new approach to education, culture and welfare; people who had fought together as a common body could not go back to a system which decreed that only one small class, of which there were few remaining heirs, should inherit the earth. Sassoon had temporarily become an extremist, looking to the Russian Revolution as a potential solution to Europe's decline. Graves, while never placing much faith in politicians to reform society, shared Nancy's conviction that the Labour Party offered the best future for Britain in 1919. Shocked by the cynicism of the Treaty of Versailles and reports of ex-servicemen being turned away by their former employers, he too felt like becoming a socialist. As always, however, he was more optimistic than Sassoon. 'As for your Lenin and Trotsky, I respect them for their thorough-going idealism,' he told him: '. . . But I think that despite Lloyd George, Clemenceau and the Capitalists, we can save Western Europe from so deep an operation and at any rate leave the bourgeoisie alive: being a bourgeois myself, I feel I want to remain alive.'[18]

Writing to Walter Turner on 29 May about his plans, Graves tentatively mentioned his hope of giving *Owl* a more political flavour. 'I have secret dreams of it as the organ of Labour (I mean of course "National") art and letters in the good days after the Revolution,' he wrote, but he cannot have been very committed to the idea since the rest of the letter was devoted to new projects.[19]

He was bursting with ideas in the summer of 1919. When Ivor Novello lost interest in his songs he turned to J. R. Heath, the local doctor, and started describing him as 'a first-class musician', a man who was esteemed in musical circles. (This, a gross exaggeration of Heath's pleasant talent, was typical of Robert's lifelong habit of championing mildly gifted friends because he liked their company. Heath was a very agreeable man.) Walter Turner heard, first, that Graves was going to make a big American lecture tour, and then that he was planning a career as a playwright. Nancy was going to collaborate, designing both sets and costumes. All they lacked now were the contacts.[20]

This new enthusiasm had been fuelled by a request from Sassoon to take over the job of writing a twenty-five-minute play for the annual theatricals in John Masefield's garden at Boars Hill. Graves responded with relish and dreamed of being a playwright until the Masefields' local vicar declared his disapproval of the subject, a religious spoof based on events in *The Way of All Flesh*; in 1919 Samuel Butler's hostility to Victorian family values still had the power to shock.

That summer at Harlech, Graves wrote a long and enthusiastic appreciation of Butler's anarchic novel about the evil influence of parents. Its tone may have been partly due to his irritation about the fact that his own parents, having sold Red Branch House, were settled at Erinfa, making it difficult to avoid daily contact. He had no quarrel with his sisters and brothers. Rosaleen stayed with them at Llys Bach for a few days and showed her own readiness to rebel against family tradition by adopting Nancy's boyish costume, while young Charles visited with stories of his first term up at Oxford, and of how Sassoon had asked him to play golf. But a happy visit from William Nicholson and his friend Edie Stuart-Wortley brought home to Graves all that infuriated him about his own parents. Edie, sophisticated, intelligent and broad-minded, was enormous fun (Nancy's brother Ben was hopelessly in love with her), and 'Sweet' William was endlessly amusing and good-humoured.

Robert had cause to be annoyed. Amy and Alfred were, while full of good intentions, interfering and manipulative. They had already urged Nancy's godfather, Sidney Pawling, to talk her into having Jenny baptized; Alfred had asked Eddie Marsh to stop Robert reviewing for a socialist paper. From Erinfa they criticized Nancy for being too friendly with the servants at Llys Bach, for the way she dressed and for using her maiden name. Much of this criticism was delivered indirectly through Robert. By July he had endured enough of it. Writing to Turner, he complained that his parents even told him off for letting Nancy carry her own coat. He felt like a siege prisoner at Llys Bach, 'family girt' in 'a stronghold to which no entrance can be won'.[21]

There was joy at Erinfa, however, over the news in late July that Nancy was pregnant again. It was not planned. Graves and she, under the emancipated influence of Edie, had started distributing leaflets on birth control to the Harlech housewives, but they had not been heeding the advice they dispensed. In his letters to Turner, Robert had been mentioning July as the month in which Nancy intended to start work on a regular basis.

A new child made the idea of going to Oxford in the autumn on a student grant seem less sensible. The problem of housing presented itself; Alfred's solution was that Robert should give up university plans and take a job as a schoolmaster. Reluctantly, Graves agreed that this was the prudent course to take.

Sassoon's visit to Llys Bach at the end of September, when Robert was still hesitating, was well-timed. He stayed for two weeks, enduring Nancy's abrasiveness for the pleasure of being with the man he still, in many ways, loved best. Almost every day he and Robert went for long walks on the moorland and Sassoon, as always, was astonished by the dazzling quickness and erudition of his friend. It seemed to him idiotic that Robert should throw himself away on being a schoolteacher and more idiotic still that he should go to Oxford only to study farming. He said so, and threw in the additional bait that Edmund Blunden was going to start reading Classics at Oxford that autumn: Blunden was the young poet Sassoon and Graves most admired, now that Wilfred Owen was dead.

He was speaking, as he probably guessed, to the converted. Early in October, Nancy, Graves, Margaret Russell and little Jenny left Llys Bach for a country home near Oxford, taking with them most of the oak furniture in the house as a present from Nancy's father. Before they left, however, Graves went to Portmadoc to be best man at William Nicholson's marriage to Edie Stuart-Wortley. Nancy was fond of Edie but she thought a year of mourning her mother had not been quite long enough. She refused to attend the service.

CHAPTER EIGHT

1920–1922

OXFORD: A TESTING TIME

THE FINAL INCENTIVE TO GO TO OXFORD HAD BEEN AN OFFER FROM John Masefield to let the young couple have the oversized cottage in his garden for £3 a month. Masefield, who had travelled to the Front and tried to report honestly on the horrors he found there, was a hero to all the young war poets. Graves felt grateful as well as honoured by the prospect of such a neighbour and friend; on the heights of Boars Hill, some five miles from Oxford, he could breathe fresh air and escape the claustrophobic panic which still overwhelmed him in crowded streets.

Oxford was hardly a swarming metropolis in 1920. Before the invasion of the *jeunesse dorée*, latterly known as 'the Brideshead generation', it was a sleepy hive of scholarship, its golden walls offering a well-maintained defence against the modern world.

Masefield and his family lived in a new house of bright red brick on top of the hill. Dingle Cottage stood next to it, looking across a segregated plot of wood-enclosed garden. At the front, the cottage, a pretty, rambling building, opened on to Ridgeway, a quiet road on which the appearance of a stranger was rare enough to cause comment. Every day Graves walked across Ridgeway and down the narrow twisting path which took him past the notorious house where Delilah Becker, 'the Jubilee Murderer', had killed her husband a few years earlier, to Mona Cottage where Edmund and Mary Blunden lodged for the autumn of 1919 with a charming old lady called Angel Heavens.[1] Mrs Heavens doted on Graves and he always had to pause and greet her before wandering on down the hill to his favourite spot, the famous view of Christchurch Hill from the field where Matthew Arnold had set 'The Scholar-Gipsy'.

Graves had become a privileged student by virtue of the company he now kept: locals called Boars Hill 'Parnassus' because of the elevated nature of its inhabitants. He had lost his early enthusiasm for Robert Nichols, a thin, intense young man who stalked the hill's shady paths with neurotic eyes gleaming under the brim of his enormous black hat. Like Edmund Blunden, Graves preferred the company of their older neighbours.

One of the oldest was Robert Bridges, the Poet Laureate, then in his late seventies and always kind and encouraging to young poets; Graves thought of him for a time almost as a second father. Another neighbour, Gilbert Murray, whose Greek translations he had read and admired as a schoolboy, was a comparative youngster – Murray was then in his early fifties – who talked as though Euripides lived just around the corner and shared his visitor's fascination with the subject of poetic inspiration. Murray's kind but formidable wife often dropped in at the cottage, occasioning a frenzy of wood and brass polishing, for Lady Mary was known to be a stickler for truth and cleanliness and Nancy was fiercely house-proud. But, much to Robert's disappointment, they saw less of their landlord, who spent all his day working in a remote garden hut, than of Masefield's brisk and frugal wife, Constance, who raised her eyebrows at Nancy's breeches and advised her to read more poetry if she wanted to keep her husband's interest. Nancy, who had not asked for advice, ignored it and laughed at her. In 1920 she still had no fears about her marriage.

Until now, Graves had only corresponded with Edmund Blunden; he proved to be as intelligent and agreeable as Sassoon had promised. (Blunden's tendency towards alcoholism was under control during this period.) Edmund was reading English after getting himself transferred from Classics; Graves, after dropping his farm-study plans, followed the same course. Away from their wives, the two men talked about the subject which still dominated every ex-soldier's thoughts: their wartime experiences. Nancy's prohibition of this topic had made Graves's craving to discuss the war the more desperate. Blunden, for a short time, answered that need.

Blunden only lasted for a term at Oxford before going to London to work as poetry editor for *The Athenaeum*. A return of shell-shock also prevented Graves from surviving the full course but he was there for almost three years and only just missed taking his final exams. Being at St John's College, where A. E. Housman had studied forty years earlier, had a special significance for him. Housman, whose *A Shropshire Lad* had been one of the most widely-read books of poetry during the war, was immensely admired by Robert for his combination of poetry and Classics. (Housman had, since 1911, been professor of Latin at Cambridge.) This was one point on which Robert's views were already fixed: mastery of Latin was for him an essential part of the poet's craft.

He was happy to follow in the steps of Housman but he was less impressed than he had anticipated by the education he received while he was at St John's. Later he exaggerated the faults of the course, claiming that he had been rebuked for preferring one poet to another. He was on safer ground in criticizing the university's old-fashioned emphasis on the eighteenth-century as England's golden age. It is hard to think of any young poet in the 1920s who admired the technical virtuosity of Pope and Dryden; the courses clearly needed adapting to a very different postwar mood. In Graves's case, two years of studying the eighteenth-century poets hardened dislike into loathing.

His tutors were both kind and understanding. Walter Raleigh, the head of the English School, who went out of his way to relax the rules for shell-shocked students, was referred to as 'that prince of dons' in a letter to Blunden.

Professor Raleigh's relationship with Robert was friendly but irregular. His personal tutor was Percy Simpson, an erudite, quick-witted man who once, memorably, tried to persuade him that there were forty-three degrees of humour; Graves remembered him as 'a darling'. Simpson's appreciation of the Jacobean and Restoration writers was infectious and Graves's first writings on poetry show how carefully he learned to read them. He still kept first place for Coleridge – 'I think Coleridge the best brain there ever was,' he wrote to Blunden on 6 August 1920[2] – but Simpson was behind his new enthusiasm for John Webster.

Graves did not regret coming to Oxford. He revelled in the chance to discuss poetry and to try his opinions out in debating societies, one of the skills in which he had excelled at Charterhouse. Dingle Cottage seemed ideal, too, but money worries continued to plague him. His hopes of selling the little cottage which he had bought from his mother collapsed when the buyer decided that he also wanted to acquire more than an acre of the woodland behind it. This belonged to Amy Graves and, to her son's disappointment, she refused to sell. She did, however, express great satisfaction about the birth of her first grandson, David, in March 1920. Amy had not changed her ways since she had idolized little Robert at the expense of his sisters; David meant far more to her than Jenny, or Catherine, born two years later. Amy talked of making David the heir to her family treasures; William Nicholson, in the meantime, paid Robert's outstanding debts.

Letters to his agent, Eric Pinker, at this time show how serious Robert's dreams were of earning enough by his poetry to survive without borrowing. *Country Sentiment* was to be published in the spring of 1920 and he was full of optimism about it. But his larger financial ambitions were pinned on 'The Penny Fiddle' with its songs set to music by H. R. Heath and illustrated by Nancy. If insistence could ensure success, the book would have outsold the Bible. Daily bulletins reminded Pinker that this was a potential best seller and to be sold as such: 'it's going to knock R. Caldecott, Stephen Crane [*sic*], Rackham and Dulac off the Christmas market so any publisher who wants it must pay.'[3] Finally, he wrote anxiously: '*Time*. It *must* come out by this Christmas, for urgent financial reasons.'[4] But Heinemann, the publisher who had expressed an interest, changed his mind and Graves was forced to appeal to Eddie Marsh for money instead. 'The Penny Fiddle' remained without a publisher until 1960.

One of Graves's most loyal supporters in the financial crises which dogged him during the 1920s was T. E. Lawrence. Lawrence had arrived at Oxford in the autumn of 1919 as a Fellow of All Souls and was working on the second draft of *The Seven Pillars of Wisdom*. Graves met him when Alfred visited Oxford in December and took his son to a dinner at All Souls. Lawrence, a slight, undistinguished figure with mesmerizing eyes, made a powerful impression at this first encounter, delighting Alfred with praises of his oldest son Philip's work in the Intelligence Department at Cairo and gratifying Robert by showing a familiarity with his poems. Lawrence was only his senior by seven years but he was a figure on the world's stage while Robert was still a young poet with a modest reputation. It was years before Graves lost the initial heady sense of instant rapport, and almost as long before he came to realize how often people had been affected in this way by Lawrence. He left the dinner hoping to meet him again.

The friendship that developed between them more than filled the gap left by Blunden's departure. By the spring of 1920 Graves was dropping in as a regular habit to sit in Lawrence's sombre, orientally furnished rooms after the first morning lecture. Sometimes Lawrence talked about some plan he had for livening up the university – driving the Magdalen deer into the All Souls quad was one proposal – or about his experiences in the desert. But most of their conversations were about poetry. It was as a poet that Lawrence had sought out Graves; he was looking for a new answer to his personal unease in the mastery of language and he believed that Graves could teach this to him.

For Lawrence, then, one of the most enjoyable aspects of the friendship was the chance to see Graves's poems in draft and to work through the revisions with him. His contributions were prominently acknowledged because of his fame rather than for their intrinsic value but Graves, understandably, never admitted that this was the case. He, for his part, was excited to have been singled out by Oxford's most celebrated resident and to be treated as a source of intellectual authority. He never fully penetrated the enigma of Lawrence's personality, despite writing a book about him in 1927, but he was fascinated by his air of cool and modest self-sufficiency. Lawrence was, for several years, his ideal, revered as an almost godlike being.

In June 1920 Nancy and Robert took the babies and their nurse on a visit to Erinfa. Nancy, maddened by Amy's criticisms of her clothes, her lack of religious faith and even the way she behaved with Jenny and little David, took refuge in long afternoon rests in her room; Amy, meanwhile, confided to her family that Robert did far too much baby-tending and Nancy far too little. Robert, resentful of her interference but bound by filial duty not to have a public quarrel, relieved his feelings in a wild night adventure.

The adventure consisted of taking a stranger on a midnight climb, on a moonless night, to the top of one of the ruined towers of Harlech Castle. Graves, an experienced climber, was confident of surviving, even when the stone edging on the walls broke away, leaving no way up but a leap in the dark. The man he took with him was not a mountaineer but a middle-aged married soldier, with whom he had started the evening by playing bridge. Why did Graves deliberately expose him to the risk of death?

The answer is so discreetly offered in Graves's autobiography that it has been overlooked. The man was a Canadian and 'at that time Canadian colonels interested me'. After bridge and a cold dip in the sea, Graves threw down his challenge not to the man but to his identity. '"I went bathing with you and it was cold. Now it's my treat. I'm going to take you climbing and make you warm. I want to see whether you Canucks are all B[ull].S[hit]. or not.'[5] It was a Canadian soldier who had accused Peter Johnstone of soliciting him and wrecked Graves's faith in the younger boy's sexual innocence. At the time, in 1917, he had not doubted the evidence. But later testimonies suggested that Johnstone might have been falsely accused by the man. Graves could have heard about this from William Rivers, the psychologist who treated Johnstone and with whom he himself was in regular communication, or from Henry Head, who gave the medical evidence at Johnstone's court appearance and who had also become a friend of Robert's. In the summer of 1920, when Johnstone was reading English at Merton College Graves had questioned him about the incident himself.★ If Johnstone or his doctors had suggested that the Canadian soldier had lied, Graves would have been angry enough to take revenge on the first Canadian officer he met. He paid a price for his recklessness; the shell-shock returned with unusual force after the climb.

The visit to Erinfa had been no holiday and they felt in need of one. In August, at Nancy's instigation, they left 'the nipcats' with their nurse, Margaret Russell, and went off on a long bicycling trip, carrying nothing but their knapsacks. Having forgotten to take any blankets, they were obliged to sleep in sunlight and ride by the light of the moon but this only added to the romance of the journey. Four days brought them to Dorchester and the Dorset home of Thomas Hardy. Happening to have a book of his own poems in his bag, Graves knocked on Hardy's door. It was the end of the day and they were invited, first, to stay and then to remain a second night. Reporting on his triumph to Blunden, Graves

---

★ The friendship, however, was over. In an undated 1923 letter to Marsh, Graves told him that he still could not think sanely about Johnstone, described to him by William Rivers as 'the most dangerous young man in England'. (RG, *Collected Letters*, 1, p. 150.)

admitted that Hardy had 'exceeded the most extreme expectations. Marvellous man!'[6]

Hardy, who had just turned eighty, was England's most cherished poet and, perhaps, the most influential. Bridges, while held in great affection, was out of tune with the times; Masefield was respected, not worshipped; Kipling was out of fashion. Eliot was not yet seen by everybody as an authority: 'The Waste Land' was still two years in the future. Graves had long admired and copied Hardy's style; many of his early poems show Hardy's effect on him in their tightly-rhymed form. It was one of these, 'The Cupboard', which Hardy singled out for praise in a kind letter to Graves, but his influence can also be detected in the bitter poem 'Apples and Water' in which a mother angrily forbids her daughter to offer anything to the soldiers marching past their door:

> Once in my youth I gave, poor fool,
>   A soldier apples and water;
> And may I die before you cool
>   Such drouth as his, my daughter.[7]

From Dorchester, the energetic cyclists pedalled on to Devon where they spent a week visiting Nancy's childhood nurse who now ran a village shop. Nancy threw herself into the task of rearranging the store with great success: by the time they returned to Boars Hill in mid-August she had decided that this was the way to make money and to have fun. She would start a shop on the hill, where none existed. Robert's brother, Charles, as editor of *Isis*, the university magazine, would act as their local publicist. Tourists and visitors would flood out from Oxford to see where the famous poets did their shopping and their worries about debts would be at an end. Nancy could see it all and Nancy, when gripped by an idea, was hard to resist.

Robert, still worried about money, was in no mood to object. Nancy's idea seemed to him a wonderful scheme. They went to work at once. A neighbour agreed to rent them a plot of land on which they erected a rigid wooden building to Nancy's design, with a suitably poetic sign outside showing a Celtic figure. Edie Nicholson lent them money to cover the timber and stock, while Alfred Graves sent words of kindly encouragement along with a new poem which he wanted Robert to show to Bridges and Masefield.

The shop opened with a flourish in the late autumn of 1920 after being publicized in the national press as 'the poets' store'. The Asquith family visited it; so did T. E. Lawrence. The smell of success went to Robert and Nancy's heads and they decided to expand it into a large general store. This was when things started to go wrong.

The next six months were a catalogue of misfortunes, culminating in financial disaster. Their partner, a Mrs Howard who Robert had naïvely supposed would attract business because she had an 'Honourable' attached to her name, showed no wish to soil her hands with the work of an assistant. Nancy, after unwisely sacking Margaret Russell in February for spoiling little Jenny, was too busy with the babies to run the shop alone. Robert was recruited to serve behind the counter while his wife bicycled around to collect orders and fetch supplies. The shop soon left no time for anything else. By May Mrs Howard's bookkeeping was discovered to have been inaccurate and Graves was seeking ways to recoup their losses. Putting in a manager merely diminished the novelty for their clients, who ceased to come, and added to their expenses; a national deflation lowered the value of the large amount of surplus stock for which they had already paid. In desperation, Graves wrote to the long-suffering Eric Pinker suggesting a series of articles about the shop in which he would provide intimate details of the shopping habits of their famous customers. He asked a fee of £50 an article and that the first of these should appear on the following Sunday; he also asked for an American sale. If necessary he would come to London to discuss it, although 'I am busy here and travelling upsets me'.[8] The papers showed no interest. And then Nancy discovered that she was pregnant again.

They were both near the end of their tethers. After three weeks of 'flu and a return of shell-shock, during which Nancy took charge, Graves went to see an unidentified professional neurologist – it could have been Henry Head or William Rivers – who recommended absolute rest. But rest was impossible. Far from making money, the shop had put them £500 in debt. Their hopes rose when an Oxford store expressed an interest in buying them out for a small profit but Constance Masefield did not want a commercial enterprise so close to her home. Graves had already been alarmed by rumours that a new experimental laboratory for developing a more lethal form of poison gas was going to be located on Boars Hill; Mrs Masefield's behaviour struck both Nancy and him as selfish. Impetuously, they announced that they would leave Dingle Cottage in June, at the end of the quarter.

They now faced the prospect of being both homeless and bankrupt. Even the building, on which they had spent £200, only fetched £20 for its timber value. Besides paying off their debt to his wife, William Nicholson did what he could for them by sending a £100-note – in a matchbox – and arranging to give Nancy an allowance of £120 a year to help with the children. T. E. Lawrence wrote sympathetically from Cairo and sent Graves four chapters of *The Seven Pillars of Wisdom* to sell for serial publication in America for whatever sum he could negotiate for himself, but he added the difficult provision that there should be absolutely no publicity in England. A deal was, however, achieved, producing another £200. This was enough, with the sale of their bankrupt assets, to meet the demands of their creditors, but they had nothing left to live on except the next instalment of Nancy's new allowance.

★   ★   ★

Outwardly Graves remained a loyal and devoted husband after this disastrous episode. Privately he blamed Nancy for their ruin. He was becoming unhappily familiar with the division in her nature between theory and practice. In theory, she had been wholly capable of running the shop and making a success of it – and of making life hard for him if he refused to support her. In practice, she had designed an impractical building, sacked the nanny when she could least afford the time to care for the children herself, left all the mundane work to him and blamed him when the newspapers failed to save them by buying their story.

In this mood, early in 1921, Graves wrote the poem which was finally called 'Love in Barrenness'. (It was published as 'The Ridge-Top' in *Whipperginny* in 1923.) Here he offered a striking image of a woman standing against the sky like a beautiful and triumphant statue of Victory. But Victory is always winged, and this woman has no arms; the landscape she has conquered is an empty and arid one. Her victory has cost her a heavy loss for an empty gain.

Like all Graves's finest poems, 'Love in Barrenness' is not what it first seems to be. It is presented as a homage. It turns out to be a piece of savagely ironic criticism:

O wingless Victory, loved of men,
Who could withstand your triumph then?

But there is pathos and sympathy here, too. Men do not love a wingless Victory statue, but they will not harm her because she is imperfect. He had promised to cherish Nancy. It was his soldierly duty to keep his vow. Equating love to an officer's commitment to his men made it easier to carry on, Graves found.

He could still enjoy Nancy's bold flights of fancy. How, he wondered to himself, did she imagine he was going to find a nice house for ten shillings a week in a local village when there were no houses being sold and when even ten shillings was beyond their means? Nancy was unshaken; her instructions were, as always, precise. What they wanted, Graves told the first house-agent he visited, was "'a cottage at Islip with a walled garden, six rooms, water in the house, just outside the village, with a beamed attic, and rent ten shillings a week." The house-agent said: "Oh, you mean the World's End Cottage?"'[9]

It seemed that he did. Standing at the end of a quiet cul-de-sac above the River Ray, where the pretty grey-stone village petered out into pastureland, the sublimely named World's End was exactly as prescribed, an early-seventeenth-century stone cottage with an apple tree in the garden, a loft big enough for two bedrooms, and its own water supply. It was for sale, not for rent, and the vendors wanted £500, but Nancy remained so confident that Graves decided to go along with whatever she suggested.

Amy Graves had already sent them the railway fares for a visit to Erinfa, having heard about their financial difficulties. At the end of April they went to Harlech with the children and, after some careful preliminary soothing of feelings, introduced the possibility of buying the Islip cottage on a mortgage. Any further loans were out of the question so far as Amy was concerned but she was prepared to accept a solution thought up by her husband. There would be no loan; there might even be a small profit. She herself would purchase the cottage and rent it to her son at £4 a month, thus keeping control of her capital and feeling that she had helped her family. An agreement was reached and, at the beginning of June, the Graves family visited Islip on an inspection tour. World's End was deemed adequate but cramped; Amy took reassurance from the fact that the vicar and his wife, with whom they had tea, seemed an agreeable couple, although she feared they would not approve of a wife who kept her maiden name and wore no ring. Amy did, however, make one stipulation: no trade was to be carried on from the cottage. She dreaded a repetition of the disaster of the shop.

On 15 June 1921, Nancy, Graves and the children left the black memory of their last winter at Boars Hill behind them and moved into World's End. Graves's favourite Tudor poet, John Skelton, had links with the village, a discovery which added to his sense of its perfection. Once again he had been allowed to escape catastrophe; being superstitious he was convinced that fate was at work on his behalf. He could hardly believe their luck. 'Islip is Heaven,' he told Blunden:

> Stone houses. Cricket. An old stone bridge where was a Civil War skirmish. Flowers. River. 4 Publics. A famous molecatcher. A square church . . . A retired serjeant major and a postman who was butler to My Lord the fifteenth Lord Valentia. A village schoolmaster with ambitions . . . Immmemmorial elmms as the bees say when they're not too hot . . . The people here are much the nicest-mannered lot I've ever struck in England; they think I'm dotty of course but have taken me for a village mascot already.[10]

They seemed at last to have found the perfect life. Nancy redesigned the inside of the cottage, painted it and made some of the furniture, while Graves played cricket as second batsman, revived the village football team and was eventually elected as a parish councillor. Having left St John's in March, he was now, at the age of twenty-six, free to concentrate on his writing, overshadowed only by Nancy's constant exhaustion and his own recurring shell-shock. This neurasthenic state was something which he now learned to use to his advantage.

★   ★   ★

Until 1918 Graves had shown no extraordinary zeal for work. In the postwar years he wrote as though his life depended on it. His brush with death was the spur. Eight thousand soldiers had died at High Wood; he had survived. For every famous dead war poet, there were fifty might-have-beens. Graves was terribly conscious of how little he himself had achieved before that fateful night. Who, if he had died in 1916, would have placed him above, say, a Grenfell or a Sorley? He had been spared – he knew it – for a purpose. That purpose was to become a poet.

At Islip, where he shouldered most of the burden of cooking, washing dishes and looking after the children, Graves did his thinking at the kitchen sink and kept a pad and pencil on the shelf for that purpose. Admirably, considering how poor they still were, he struggled not to prostitute his talent for easy money. Instead, between 1922 and 1926, he alternated between writing poems and books about poetry. The exceptions – a thoughtful anthology of ballads and nursery rhymes, a small edition of Skelton's poems and a novel, *My Head! My Head!*, dealing with a fairly obscure biblical mystery – could hardly be described as commercial gift.

Graves was determined not to squander his talent; it was incomprehensible to him that his clever younger brother Charles should have no greater ambition than to become a gossip journalist. Neither could he understand young John Graves's readiness to become a schoolmaster. When his kindly mentor Walter Raleigh, seeking to make life easier, offered to help him secure a minor professorial post (not at Oxford), he rejected it outright. His horror of becoming part of any organized body remained absolute; he knew that the poet was set apart to live by different rules.

The powerful, sinister poems of *The Pier-Glass*, published in March 1921, were the first conscious attempt he made to draw on his mental state for inspiration. While other poets used their emotional response to war to fuel their work, Graves, uniquely and courageously, used poems to explore his psychological trauma. He was not always sure what thoughts were at work until they reached a poetic form. Explaining the process to an intrigued Edmund Blunden, Graves told him that the mysterious and troubling imagery of his new poems was 'half an attempt to stand up to the damned disease [of shell-shock] . . . I wrote each [poem] not less than eight times before I understood what they were to be about . . .'[11]

*　　*　　*

In 1924 Graves published an enigmatic poem called 'From Our Ghostly Enemy'. In it, a man asks for his wife's advice about a presence which haunts him, spelling out his death wherever he looks. What shall he do? This is her answer.

> 'Speak to the ghost and tell him,
> "Whoever you be,
> Ghost, my anguish equals yours,
> Let our cruelties therefore end.
> Your friend let me be."'
>
> He spoke, and the ghost, who knew not
> How he plagued that man,
> Ceased, and the lamp was lit again,
> And the dumb clock ticked again,
> And the reign of peace began.[12]

Graves makes the speaker here into a woman who seems to represent his wife. But the ghost represents his own terror and Nancy's advice would have been the opposite to that given. Her counsel was always to suppress emotional feelings. The real adviser in the poem is the man who had more influence than any other on Graves in the early 1920s, William Rivers. It was Rivers who encouraged Graves to lay his ghostly tormentor by raising him again in his poetry.

Graves had been involved with Rivers ever since he visited Sassoon at Craiglockhart War Hospital in 1917 but he was still a little in awe of this quiet, authoritative man. By March 1921, when Graves told Blunden that he was 'the greatest living psychologist',[13] Rivers had already become his mentor on the psychological aspect of his literary work. In May Sassoon heard that Rivers had reacted favourably to his first short book about poetry – he had already written eight drafts of it – and that his faith in him was absolute. Rivers, Graves wrote, 'is really all that matters'.[14] With T. E. Lawrence no longer in England, Graves needed a new mentor-friend to stimulate and encourage him. By the end of the summer of 1921 he was visiting Rivers's rooms at St John's in Cambridge regularly, and Rivers also made several visits to Islip; Nancy, too, was devoted to him.

William Rivers was in his late fifties at this time. In his thirties and forties he had made pioneering studies of tribal life based on fieldwork in India and the Solomon Islands. His subsequent study of practical medicine was followed by three years of work with the war-damaged soldiers at Craiglockhart where he treated, as well as Sassoon, Wilfred Owen and another friend of Graves's, Frank Prewett, before returning to Cambridge as a lecturer in natural science. No formal teaching was required of him; Rivers's preferred method was to hold informal meetings for the discussion of a wide range of subjects. In the years after the war he was regarded by his colleagues as one of the most exceptional minds in England.

Even though, later in life, Graves pretended to have despised all forms of psychoanalysis, under Rivers's gentle influence he became fascinated by the connection between the unconscious and creativity. Many other poets had thought and written about this, but not from a therapeutic angle. Rivers encouraged his patient-friends – he made no distinction in his treatment – to recall everything that they had been taught to forget and to find a positive element in the memory.

Rivers taught Graves to see that shell-shock gave him special powers to draw on as a poet. In Rivers's view, the neurasthenic state which he had tried to suppress was his most potent creative source. Pain was the key. The cure was to write out of his unconscious and then use the poems to examine his state of mind.

Not all of Graves's attempts to do this were successful. Edward Marsh was not the only reader to be baffled by the abstract nature of the poems in *Whipperginny*, published in March 1923 and dedicated to Marsh. To him, the fact that Graves was still loyally ready to appear in the Georgian anthologies suggested that he belonged with this increasingly outdated band. What, he wondered politely, was the meaning of a verse like this, from 'The Red Ribbon Dream'?

> I stand by the stair-head in the upper hall;
>   The rooms to the left and right are locked as before.
>   Once I found entrance, but now never more,
> And Time leans forward with his glassy wall.

Graves did his best to explain. He was writing, he told Marsh, for ten years ahead, 'when knowledge of morbid psychology will be commoner than now'. (Morbid psychology was Rivers's speciality.) The poem showed Rivers's method in action; here he had written down a dream exactly as it came to him. He passionately disagreed with Marsh's tentative suggestion that he had lost his way. He sometimes had only a morning a week left over to write, after all his household duties. The best use of this time was '*surely* to write the necessary poems . . .'[15] The gentle, pleasing ballads which

Marsh longed for him to produce no longer seemed 'necessary' to him.

Sweetness was out; aggressiveness was in. The working title which he gave to *On English Poetry*, his first critical work, was 'Pebbles to Crack your Teeth On' and it was in this take-it-or-leave-it style that he chose to write. *On English Poetry* is an imperfect book but it is a fascinating one, old-fashioned romantic theory and shrewd new perceptions sitting alongside autobiographical snippets and thoughts about the poet's role in the light of Graves's newly-acquired ideas about ethnology and psychoanalysis. Rivers had introduced him to *The Golden Bough*, Sir George Frazer's famous interpretation of primitive culture, and the book shows that influence in its presentation of the poet as witch-doctor and leader, the oracular interpreter of dreams who chooses the nature of the god he will serve in his poetry. This is the first clear glimpse we have of Graves in his role as the prophet who works under the inspiration of his personal deity, the muse.

William Empson, who later acknowledged this early work to have inspired *Seven Types of Ambiguity*, his celebrated literary study of 1930, was intrigued by another aspect of Graves's book.[16] It was from here that he took the idea of equivocacy in language as a subject. 'In Poetry the implication is more important than the manifest statement,' Graves had written; 'the underlying associations of every word are marshalled carefully.'[17] The example which he used, and which impressed Empson, was the line from John Webster's *The Duchess of Malfi* when Ferdinand looks at the dead duchess and says, 'Mine eyes dazzle.' 'Dazzle', Graves showed, had a double meaning, conveying both the tears and the beauty which caused them to flow. It was in this hidden association, passing silently from the writer to the reader, that the power of the words lay. 'Poetry', he wrote here, 'contains nothing haphazard.'[18]

Following Rivers's advice to get his secret fears and traumas on to paper, Graves put some of his private thoughts into the book. He admitted to his horror of becoming a schoolmaster, the profession his father had wanted for him. He described the love he had felt for the soldiers who had served under him, and the fear of death, which had always to be hidden, as the fuel of his war-poems. Wistfully, he wrote of the adoration which Sassoon had inspired: 'the men would do anything for him.'[19]

He dedicated the book jointly to Lawrence and to Rivers, who was described as 'W. H. R. Rivers of the Solomon Islands and St John's College, Cambridge'. The reference to Rivers's earlier anthropological work was deliberate. Rivers's studies of primitive kinship had made him a leading authority on the subject of 'mother-right'. He believed that myths could be analysed to show that the earliest societies had worshipped a figure known as 'the Great Mother'. Nancy had convinced her husband that women once had – or should have – ruled society; Rivers produced the research to give this idea substance. It was he who introduced Graves to the idea of an early world governed by women. Other anthropologists acknowledged the existence of women as the chief heirs and heads of families in some early societies; Rivers encouraged Graves to look for a more general pattern and to assume that it would show widespread worship of a 'Great Mother' figure.

This was one of Rivers's most important gifts to Graves's fertile mind. It was his concept of a matriarchy which emerged in 1925 in *My Head! My Head!* as part of Graves's own mythology. It led directly forward to his rehabilitation of the Romantic poets' muse as a female deity. By the time of Rivers's untimely death in 1922, the idea which would take shape as the White Goddess was already in Graves's head.

CHAPTER NINE

1922–1923

PSYCHOLOGY AND POETRY

AMY GRAVES, VISITING THE COTTAGE IN ISLIP DURING NOVEM-
ber 1921, offered cheering words about the spiritual benefits to be
won through hardship. It was practical help rather than spiritual
consolation which was required. Nancy, whose third child was due
in early February, had been told to rest; Robert, while willing,
could not run the house, look after two children and his wife, and
write enough to keep and clothe them all. In December, after earnest
consultation, his parents agreed to release Clarissa Graves from her
duties as Alfred's secretary to help out at World's End for a few
weeks.

Clarissa, the most artistic of Robert's siblings, was the only one
of the family to understand the despair Nancy felt at not having
the energy or time for her painting. Clarissa liked and admired her.
While Amy and Alfred shook their heads over Robert's unfortunate
marriage, Clarissa saw World's End as 'a place of love and hard work
and a magic sense of home'.[1] It was here, not at Erinfa, that she chose
to spend the next two Christmas holidays.

Robert and Nancy, in turn, decided that the devout Clarissa's
prayers for their well-being must have remarkable power. Catherine

109

was born, with no difficulties, at the Nicholsons' new seaside house; when Graves arrived from Islip to see her and to take mother and baby home, he found Nancy in radiant spirits.

The pattern of events shows that Nancy was always in better health when she was with her own family; life with Robert and the children had become associated with anxiety. The recurring symptoms of an enlarged thyroid, followed by irritability and exhaustion, were in part a psychological response to a situation in which she felt helpless. She collapsed again in March, shortly after their return to Islip.

Graves, as his 1921 poem 'Sullen Moods' had already made clear, took responsibility for Nancy's depression. He blamed himself as an impossible companion, due to his traumatized state.

> Love, do not count your labour lost
>   Though I turn sullen or retired
> Even at your side; my thought is crossed
>   with fancies by no evil fired.
>
> And when I answer you, some days,
>   Vaguely and wildly, do not fear
> That my love walks forbidden ways,
>   Breaking the ties that hold it here.
>
> If I speak gruffly, this mood is
>   Mere indignation at my own
> Shortcomings, plagues, uncertainties:
>   I forget the gentler tone.[2]

Unwilling to acknowledge the fact of their incompatibility as a couple, Graves grew increasingly defiant. His parents were given no quarter if they dared to criticize his wife; when Sassoon appeared to be doing so, he was told to think of them as Shakespeare's phoenix and turtle, knit into a single creature. Graves underlined their togetherness by making Nancy read this letter and add whatever comments she felt appropriate. Her contribution was a sharp dig at Sassoon's friend, Lady Ottoline Morrell, an Oxford neighbour considered by Nancy to be foolish and over-social.[3]

The quarrel with Sassoon in the spring of 1922 was not of Nancy's making. It had been brewing for some time, due to Sassoon's strong sense that Nancy had separated him from his closest friend and that

Graves had gone along with this. Their correspondence the previous year, when Graves was still writing reviews for Sassoon at the *Daily Herald*, had been edgy and awkward. Graves needed the paid review work and he often wrote his pieces with careless speed. He hated it when Sassoon told him off for shoddy work; secretly, he despised the paper he was writing for.

Sassoon's own feelings came to a head on 19 April, when Graves unexpectedly called at his Piccadilly lodgings. Sassoon was in a nervous state; being with Robert always excited him. He was annoyed when Robert explained that he had just given a lecture for a society presided over by Edith Sitwell, a new acquaintance whose romantic style of verse he rather liked. Only a month earlier, Sassoon had loyally cut Edith's brother Osbert, an old friend, for daring to publish a parody of Graves. The least Robert could have done in return, he felt, was to stay away from the Sitwells for a little while. But Robert showed no remorse. Later in the day Sassoon bumped into him in the street, strolling with a small man in a long macintosh. T. E. Lawrence, now living in England again, was one of Sassoon's heroes. He longed to know him. To identify him as the stranger who appeared to be on almost brotherly terms with Graves on this particular day was the last straw. He made himself disagreeable to them both and went home in a state of fury at his own irrational behaviour.[4]

Pondering the relationship a month later, Sassoon showed absolute awareness of the chief problem which was that he still loved Graves in a way that Graves had never loved him. This, he wrote with some bitterness in his diary, had been the one male friendship which approached his ideal. 'But there was some vague sexual element lurking in the background of our war-harnessed relationship. There was always some restless passionate nerve-racked quality in my friendship with R. G. . . . .'[5] Was it there still? He was unsure. Writing to apologize for his peevish behaviour at their London encounter, Sassoon explained how depressing it felt to be passionately attached to somebody who responded to his affection with disapproval or indifference. The response came in Graves's best new psychoanalytic style, complete with such flourishes as 'epicritic' and 'protopathic'. But the tone was amiable. All he asked was that Sassoon should treat Nancy as an extension of himself and, which was harder for Sassoon to accept, that he should forget the Robert Graves he had known during the war.

. . . I am no more than his son and heir and so it is as an old
friend of my father that I want to meet you; my father had a
sort of hero-worship of you and I have heard him talk of you
with great awe even. That's exactly how I feel at present, that
I only know about you by legend.[6]

Sassoon was ten years older than Graves but it was hardly kind to
suggest that he belonged to the generation of Alfred Graves. Their
quarrel might have continued, had it not been for the tragic death,
a week later, of William Rivers, killed at the age of fifty-seven by a
severe intestinal obstruction. Walter Raleigh, who had just agreed to
supervise the book Graves wanted to submit for his doctoral thesis,
had died of typhoid fever the previous month, but this was an even
greater loss. Rivers had, in Graves's view, been 'the first scientist in
England'; it was as a friend that he mourned him.[7] Sassoon, who
had brought them together, shared his grief; recriminations were
forgotten for a time in a sense of mutual shock and regret. Mindful
of the fact that Rivers's last, unfinished book had been named *Conflict
and Dream*, Robert impulsively decided to write his own study of
dreams and to call it 'Conflict and Poetry'.

Sassoon was not the only friend he quarrelled with that year.
Edmund Blunden found it difficult to accept the jovial tone with
which Robert admitted that he had indeed been sharing his concern
about Edmund's drinking habits and the state of his marriage with
many of their friends. Always candid in his own views, Graves saw
no reason why he should not be so about the lives of those he
loved. He thought Edmund extraordinary to resent it, but expressed
delight at the news that the Blundens were, after all, happy in their
marriage.

The relationships with his fellow poets were the ones in which
he grew most excited: Eddie Marsh and Rivers's colleague Henry
Head were calmer characters who managed to ride out the storm
of Robert's turbulent moods with perfect success. Eric Kennington
and his wife remained devoted friends, as did the Mallorys. Islip
neighbours, especially those who belonged to the football team
run by Graves and the Labour Party which both he and Nancy
supported, found them a warm-hearted and spontaneous couple.
Their hospitality was far in excess of what they seemed able to
afford. The cottage was always full of visitors at Christmas; one
little boy, whose parents, the novelist John Buchan and his wife,

had sent him to join in the fun after contributing the Christmas tree, the turkey and the cake, found World's End bursting at the seams with at least twenty adults and even more children. Like Robert's sister, Clarissa, William Buchan thought World's End was full of vitality and warmth.*8

Three poets approached Graves in 1922. One, already mentioned, was Edith Sitwell, who was so charmed by Robert and Nancy that she started making plans to buy a cottage in Islip for herself and her dearest friend, Helen Rootham, so that they could meet every day. The second was a shy boy of sixteen. Peter Quennell, who was going to Oxford the following year, was brought to Islip by his father and invited to produce his work. Remembering how Mallory had helped him, Graves resolved to do all he could to support this gifted boy; he thought his work was just what Marsh would want for his Georgian anthologies and wrote to tell him so. This was the beginning of Quennell's literary career, and he did not forget it.

Graves never met the most important of the three. John Crowe Ransom, the American poet and professor at Vanderbilt University had just, with contributions from Vanderbilt students and colleagues, launched *Fugitive*, a small literary magazine which became the foundation of the 1930s school of New Criticism. Ransom had written an admiring review of Graves's *On English Poetry* when it appeared in America and hailed him as one of the most important English poets. They began to correspond in the spring of 1922, when Ransom sent a copy of *Fugitive* to Graves and asked him if he wanted to contribute to it. Instead Graves decided to spread Ransom's name in England. He began by turning the lengthy Preface to his latest poem, 'The Feather Bed', into an open letter of a most friendly kind to 'My Dear Ransome' [*sic*].9

The strain of writing his doctoral thesis on poetry, while looking after the children, doing all the shopping and attempting to keep Nancy's spirits up, was considerable. When Nancy suggested a holiday in August, Graves readily assented. The idea this time was that they and the three children would visit Rottingdean, a village on the Sussex coast where William Nicholson had leased for the summer a handsome house previously rented by Rudyard Kipling; they would round off the tour with a visit to Edie Nicholson's father, Lionel

* Joh Buchan's wife, Susie, was a relation of Edie Stuart-Wortley, who effected the introduction; a shared fondness for T. E. Lawrence bound the two men together. Graves dedicated his 1924 book, *The Meaning of Dreams*, to the Buchans.

Phillips, the Kimberley diamond magnate. Their transport was to be a horse-drawn van borrowed from the local baker.

The journey to Rottingdean was not a success. The shafts attaching the van to the horse were badly fitted; one of the children was jolted into falling on to the road. Frank Prewett, the farmer-poet neighbour on whose land they camped en route, was in a state of deep depression after quarrelling with Sassoon and Lady Ottoline Morrell; when they called on Lytton Strachey at his home near Pangbourne, he was out. Their plan to sleep in tents by the wayside was foiled by farmers who suspected them of being gypsies. Worse than any of this, it rained every day, making it impossible to wash and dry little Catherine's nappies. But they were given a warm welcome at Rottingdean, where Doris Ellitt, the young nanny who was looking after William and Edie's own new baby, took over the care of Jenny, David and Catherine. Recovering from a dreadful week on the roads, Robert relaxed into the affectionate relationship he always enjoyed with his father-in-law. 'My best friend' was how William referred to him, while signing his letters 'Father' or 'Kid'. No wonder, then, that Robert felt more at ease with him than with the old gentleman who signed himself, with great correctness, 'Your affectionate, Alfred P. Graves'. Even Lionel Phillips, their second host, was more fatherly than Alfred, entertaining Robert with stories of his first mining discoveries and arguing with him about socialist economics over the port.

Graves was fiercely loyal to Nancy and devoted to her family – her brothers were frequent visitors at the cottage – but the death of William Rivers left him even more conscious of how much he needed the mental spur which his wife was unable to provide. She was too exhausted to enjoy sex – and Graves was demanding in this respect;[10] neither did she enjoy the literary discussion on which he thrived.

This sense of a growing inability to find what he needed, and of weariness with his wife's refusal ever to seek peace in compromise, runs like a small cold current through the love-directed poems which Graves was collecting for his next book. No blame was attached to Nancy; 'Song of Contrariety' seems, indeed, to suggest that it is his own fault if passion wanes after he has sensed his wife's lack of desire. (It was written late in 1921.)

> At summons of your dream-despair
> She could not disobey,

But slid close down beside you there
And complaisant lay.

Yet now her flesh and blood consent
In waking hours of day,
Joy and passion both are spent,
Fading clean away.[11]

For stimulation, finding little at home, Graves turned to Oxford.

★   ★   ★

Oxford in 1922 barely extended beyond the university buildings. There were no more than thirty cars in the whole city. The first of the 'Brideshead generation' had arrived, but there were no cocktail parties and very few signs of wild behaviour. Even the famous Hypocrites Club was still dominated by tweedy beer-drinkers; the flamboyant influence of Harold Acton and Brian Howard had not yet penetrated the colleges. When Graves bicycled there to collect the groceries, he wandered around antiquarian bookshops, bought brass ornaments for the house or dropped into the rooms of a poetry-loving student for a talk. He was much admired by many of the students and dons; the talks which he occasionally gave in college rooms were well-attended. These were the occasions on which he forgot that he was a tired father of three and showed his mettle. Tom Matthews, a Princeton graduate who was in his second year at New College, Oxford, recorded one such evening in his memoirs.

The talk was based on the old nursery rhyme 'How Many Miles to Babylon?' Tall, loose-jointed and arresting-looking with his big broken nose, haunted eyes and hollow cheeks, Graves sauntered into the crowded room and swung into action. He started with his theory, taken from Rivers, that all poems emerged from a state of mental conflict. He used the old rhyme to illustrate his case. The author of the poem – it is anonymous – was conjured up by him with a mass of circumstantial detail which left his audience shouting and applauding. The description which Matthews gives could be of Graves on a platform at almost any stage of his life. His love of a dispute never lessened.

> [The] moment he stopped, they were on him. His first attacker
> was an older man, evidently one of a strong scatteration of dons
> among us. This academic, in a voice of mingled scorn and fury,
> wished Mr Graves to enlighten us, if he would be so kind, on the
> conflict in Tennyson's mind which produced 'The Charge of the
> Light Brigade'. Mr Graves did so – to general applause, if not
> to the satisfaction of his questioner. 'The Sinking of the Royal
> George?' [*sic*] 'Tyger! Tyger! Burning Bright'? Kipling? Eyes
> rolling with mischief, smiling almost apologetically, Graves
> fielded these hard-hit questions with deft ease, and no runs
> were scored by the other side. This was a game at which he
> excelled any of his present competitors, and it was a pleasure
> to watch him play.[12]

Such occasions left him hungry for intellectual battles. He found a
worthy opponent in Oxford that year in Basanta Kumar Mallik, a 41-
year-old Bengali who came to listen to one of his talks and stayed to
dispute his thesis. Mallik, by the autumn of 1922, had replaced
Rivers as the dominant influence in Graves's life.

Mallik was, on the face of it, an unlikely choice of friend. Sent
to Oxford in 1912 to study British political psychology by the
Maharajah of Nepal, he had taken his degree in philosophy at
Exeter College and remained on in a private capacity as an amateur
philosopher with a cult following, particularly at Balliol. Graves
hated philosophy. But then, he had thought that he hated psychology
until he began to talk to Rivers, and 'I had none of my usual feelings
with Basanta', he wrote in the 1929 version of *Goodbye to All That*,
the only edition in which a full account of this friendship was provided.
He also noted, as though this was a significant fact, that Mallik and
T. E. Lawrence had once lived in the same Oxford street. They were,
with Mallory Rivers, the most remarkable men he had yet known.

Charismatic, handsome and soft-voiced, Mallik charmed almost
everybody he met. Alfred Graves, on brief acquaintance, formed a
good impression; Nancy was almost as enthusiastic about him as was
her husband. Mallik, in turn, liked Graves and admired his intellectual
energy without understanding his poetry and without having his
ease of communication. He was not so well-read; Graves was
disappointed to find that he knew nothing about Herman Melville,
whose *Moby Dick* was a firm favourite of his own. Neither was Mallik
so literate; when he agreed to contribute a philosophical essay to *Owl*,

Graves had to rewrite it in intelligible form. It was still, for the lay reader, uncommonly obscure.

Graves had a genius for finding mentors whose ideas he could adapt to fit his own theories. Rivers's teachings on psychology and poetry were superimposed on all that Graves had read and, in particular, what he had read in Coleridge's *Biographia Literaria* about associative thought and the links between the psychological and poetic fields. Mallik offered him a doctrine of strict personal morality which suited Robert's puritanical nature admirably and which he assimilated without difficulty. He also introduced him to the belief, fashionable at that time, that all things are relative.

Relativity had its stimulating aspects. It was comforting to think that an unsuccessful marriage was no worse than a good one, that no one thing was more certain than another and, more significantly for Graves, that all things affect each other. By 1925, when he had absorbed Mallik's ideas and grafted them on to his own, they resulted in some remarkable poems. 'Alice', one of his best early works, is an exemplary piece of relative thinking, in which Alice discovers that the truth about the world beyond the looking-glass is just as true in its different way as the truth about her Victorian home. Alice, as the poet's alter ego, is free to go between the real world and the land where imagination makes its own truth. [13]

'Alice' was written in 1925. By this time, Graves had shaped Mallik's philosophy to suit his own vision of the poet as a being with superior knowledge. At first, however, he was completely dominated by his friend. Under his aegis, a book appeared in 1924. Its title was *Mock Beggar Hall* and the cold, pragmatic poems which it contains offer a startling contrast to the haunted – and haunting – images in *The Pier-Glass* collection of 1921. The critics who reviewed it were universal in their condemnation. Later Graves tried to suppress the book, just as he tried to conceal Mallik's brief hold over him.

No book by Graves can be dismissed out of hand. *Country Sentiment* is remarkable for two poems, 'Outlaws' and 'Rocky Acres', both of which survived to join the canon. *Mock Beggar Hall* also contains two notable poems, 'Knowledge of God' and 'Full Moon'. Both had been published previously, in 1923, as Graves's own contributions to *Owl*, which suggests that he rated them highly. Both are of strong biographical interest, since they anticipate the startling events which were soon to change the course of Graves's life.

'Knowledge of God' offers a weary image of time as a treadmill; it corresponds with Graves's account in *Goodbye to All That* of himself in the Islip years as 'getting through things somehow, anyhow, in the hope that they would mend'.[14] Graves would retain this idea of time's inexorability until Laura Riding arrived in 1926; what we can foresee in his poem is how strongly her idea of finite time would appeal to him.

> The caterpillar-years-to-come
>   March head to tail with years-that-were
> Round and around the cosmic drum,
> To time and space they add their sum
>   But how is Godhead there?

Mallik's insistence on self-watchfulness left little room for delusions. Graves's loyalty to Nancy had not lessened, but, in the last verse of 'Full Moon', a moon of icy sovereignty, he acknowledged the death of hope for his marriage.

> And now cold earth was Arctic sea,
>   Each breath came dagger-keen;
> Two bergs of glinting ice were we,
>   The broad moon sailed between;
> There swam the mermaids, tailed and finned,
> And Love went by upon the wind
>   As though it had not been.

'Full Moon' was written in the summer of 1923. At the beginning of that year, under Mallik's influence, Graves had been more hopeful. Alfred Graves, who was pressing him to look for a university post, was told, first, that Nancy did not want him to take one and then that Mallik, who planned a return to Nepal later in the year, wanted them to join him there. This hardly sounds as though the marriage was collapsing, but it is worth noting that the idea was dropped when they failed to persuade T. E. Lawrence to go with them (he claimed that a trip to India was much too desirable to be good for him). From now on, either Nancy or Robert, or both, were constantly looking for somebody who would share their married life.

In February they had had another disastrous holiday, living in tents with the children on the Oxfordshire farm belonging to Frank

Prewett and his gentle, deaf wife, Madeleine. The rain was relentless; after a week, they had crept home to Islip. Robert's mother had been urging them for some time to come to Erinfa and offering to pay for their rail tickets. In March, reluctantly, they accepted, hoping to recover their health and spirits.

Relations between Nancy and Amy were as fraught as ever. Each was determined that the other knew nothing about caring for children and neither was willing to give an inch. But Robert was relieved to find that his father was no longer nagging him to become a professor. Instead he had some suggestions to make about a new career as a playwright. Richard Hughes, their young Harlech neighbour, was making a small name for himself as a dramatist; if he could do it, surely so could a Graves? Alfred had, besides, rather a taste for play-writing himself; he relished the thought of collaborating with his son and giving him guidance. The result of these talks was a 'ballad opera' which William Nicholson did his best to sell to Charles Cochran, the London impresario, later in the year. Cochran, and others, rejected *John Kemp's Wager* as unplayable. But Robert had enjoyed writing it; he tried his hand again at writing plays in 1930 and in 1939, but without success. Having no grasp of the need for a different technique, he wrote his plays like dialogue novels; they could not, and did not, work on-stage.

While he was at Erinfa, it interested Robert to see that other members of the family were subjected to a similar level of pressure to succeed. He had never much cared for his youngest brother, John, but he felt for him now as, after getting poor results in his second-year exams at Oxford, he was exposed to the full glare of maternal disappointment. Amy could not bear failure in her children. She saw it as a sign of idleness. It is uncertain how much of Graves's own industry was a response to this ferocious discipline, but his feelings towards his young brother grew noticeably softer after this visit. John was asked to stay at the cottage, for as long as he liked.

Much though Graves hated travelling, he made several trips to London in the spring and early summer of 1923, staying at William Nicholson's studio in St James's and modelling for his friend Eric Kennington's figure of 'the intellectual soldier' on the war memorial, 'Soldiers Three', erected later in the year in Battersea Park. Sassoon lived close to Apple Tree Yard. Determined to recover his friendship with Graves, he called at the studio and paid Nancy compliments on her skill as an artist. This was well-received by Nancy, whose brusque manner had less to do with jealousy than with a girlish crush on Robert's elegant, delicate-featured friend. Sassoon found it hard to pity Graves as a bullied husband when he saw him in such good spirits, swapping jokes with Lutyens and Max Beerbohm. (Max, like Sassoon, was a godfather to little Jenny Nicholson.) Seeing Graves immediately after a meeting with Osbert Sitwell one day made it clear to Siegfried how much he loved him. 'He has all the humanity (and humility) which O[sbert] lacks', he noted in his diary that evening. 'There is nothing mean or malicious about R.G.' Full of affection, he promised himself that he would be nice to Nancy in future and treat her, as Robert asked, as 'a good chap'.[15] He was genuinely pleased when Graves suggested, a little later in the summer, that they might spend a few days together in a hut on Prewett's farm, as if they were back in the old days at the Litherland army depot. He refused, but he took it for a sign that their old friendship was almost restored.

CHAPTER TEN

1924–1926

LAST YEARS OF A COUNTRY POET

AFTER BASANTA MALLIK'S RETURN TO NEPAL IN OCTOBER 1923 regular correspondence was maintained and Mallik helped to get Graves's work published in India. Sam Harries, one of the Balliol students who had fallen under Mallik's spell, became Nancy and Robert's closest friend in 1925. Having graduated with a First in the summer of 1923 and become a tutor for the Workers' Educational Association, Sam spent most of his vacations at World's End. Nancy was noticeably happier when Sam was with them; it is possible that she and he had an affair with Graves's consent. Their fourth and last winter baby, born in February 1924, was named after him.

With four children under the age of six to be cared for, the strain on Graves increased. However hard he worked, there never seemed to be enough money even to pay their £4 rent to Amy every month. Once more he had to borrow from Marsh; Sassoon, too, continued to send occasional contributions. But Graves was a proud man. It irked him to be perpetually sponging off his friends.

Holidays were, of necessity, economical. In June, they camped again at Frank Prewett's farm. The place seemed to have a curse on it; this time Nancy and the children caught marsh fever while Robert was brought down by the bitter news that his friend George Mallory had been lost on Everest. The following week they heard that the young wife of a great friend at Balliol had died in childbirth. She had often attended philosophy discussions at the cottage, and both Graves and Nancy felt haunted by her loss. It was in memory of this unidentified woman that he wrote 'The Presence'.

> She fills the house and garden terribly
> With her bewilderment, accusingly
> Enforcing her too sharp identity,
> Till every stone and flower, bottle and book,
> Cries out her name, pierces us with her look . . .[1]

The poem can be read as an expression of general bereavement. Graves had lost so many friends.

Lawrence, having turned his back on his legendary fame in 1922, was in Dorset with the Royal Tank Corps, to whom he was known as T. E. Shaw. He had stayed in touch with Graves, but his letters no longer showed the relish for riddles, jokes and confessions which had marked their first correspondence. It was not so far from Wiltshire to Dorset, and Graves decided to arrange a meeting when he and Nancy and the children next went to stay with Edie and William Nicholson at Sutton Veny, a pretty manor-house on the borders of Wiltshire and Somerset which Edie had been given by her father in 1923. Lawrence gave no explanation of his sudden decision to seek anonymity, first as Ross and now as Shaw. To Graves, who continued to hero-worship him, it seemed a magnificent gesture. In his poem about Alexander the Great, 'The Clipped Stater', he wrote about a man who is made a god and rejects glory to join the ranks as an unknown warrior. Lawrence, he thought, had achieved that kind of nobility.

Everyone adored Sutton Veny, where life was always comfortable without being opulent, and where children who cried were the problem of their nurses, not their parents. Thankful for some peace at last, Robert spent his evenings chatting with Edie about psychology and poetry and his days working on *My Head! My Head!*, his biblical novel about Moses and Elisha's resurrection of the Shunammite's dead son. He had got the idea for it after reading Isaac Rosenberg's poem about Moses, and added his own thoughts about a golden age when 'woman was held to be of the gods and sacred'.[2]

The contrast between their two families had never seemed sharper. Having decided to rent out World's End for August in order to bring in some money, Robert and Nancy went with the children to Harlech for the month, expecting to stay at Erinfa. The house was full up and, despite appalling weather, they had to camp in the fields until Amy could be prevailed upon to find some extra bedding and take them in. Robert was eager to share his enthusiasm for the poems of John Crowe Ransom, which he had collected for publication by Leonard and Virginia Woolf's home-run Hogarth Press in the autumn. He had loved the poems enough to learn them by heart to recite as he walked across the fields around Islip, but Alfred saw only that they were blasphemous. His disapproval cast a blight, but Robert's high spirits had returned by the time Eddie Marsh, who was staying with Robert Bridges, dropped in for tea at World's End Cottage in October and found him presiding over a children's tea party with the village postmaster and his wife.

The Meaning of Dreams, which had begun life as 'Conflict and Poetry' and was written as an extension of dialogues with Rivers, was published in September 1924. It was an interesting but incoherent and carelessly planned book. The reviews were tepid. To students of Graves's work, it is a rich source book in which his essay on 'La Belle Dame Sans Merci' clearly shows that he was already attracted to the idea of a personal muse. Another useful insight can be gleaned from the final chapter, in which Graves wrote approvingly of a poet who lived in a *ménage à trois*. Coleridge was praised for sharing his home with a woman intellectually superior to his wife. Was this a piece of wishful thinking on Graves's part?

With no sign of financial relief, and knowing that he would need some form of qualification if he was to get an academic post, Graves delighted his parents by submitting his doctoral thesis in December. Amy and Alfred, visiting the cottage for a night, felt that their son was at last coming to his senses. They complimented Nancy on the neatness of the cottage and seemed pleased to meet some of their younger friends. When Clarissa came to stay for Christmas, she found Nancy and Robert happily arranging a fancy-dress party for the children with the help of their new maid, a thirteen-year-old called Daisy whom they had rescued from a rough life on the road with her father. Nancy, a skilled dressmaker, had sewn all the children's costumes.

The respite was brief. The little maid pined for her father and a free life and left. Amy and Nancy fell out again over how the children should be cared for and only a timely cheque from Eddie Marsh saved Robert from the creditors. In February 1925 his thesis, *Poetic Unreason*, was published. It was, like his previous critical works, a collection of gleefully iconoclastic essays, on everything from the pleasing tonality of the word 'manure' to the tragic quality in Edward Lear's luminous-nosed Dong. The critics were unimpressed. Sir Edmund Gosse, persuaded by Sassoon to make it his 'book of the week' for the *Sunday Times*, wrote a dismissive review which enraged Graves into thanking him for 'a lengthy, witty, and complete misrepresentation of my attitude in *Poetic Unreason*'.[3]

For all the originality of his ideas, Graves remained relentlessly marginalized. He was enjoying neither a critical nor a commercial success. The critics who had admired *The Pier-Glass* disliked *Mock Beggar Hall* and were puzzled by *Whipperginny*. I. A. Richards, hailing T. S. Eliot as the best poet of his generation in his influential book *Science and Poetry* (1922), appeared to see Graves as a younger Walter de la Mare, lost in a world of dreams and out of tune with the times.[*] For the wider public, he had passed into semi-obscurity with the ending of the *Georgian Poetry* series.

With his books selling in hundreds rather than thousands and four children to feed and clothe, Graves was in desperate straits. He had told Eddie Marsh in 1924 that it was only by working at a frenetic pace that he felt able to cure his neurasthenia but, by now, he was ready to do any kind of writing to pay the household bills. To Pinker, his agent, he admitted that he was willing to teach poetry to old ladies if they would give him money for it. He wrote rhymes to sell Huntley & Palmer's biscuits, and lyrics for a light opera; he translated German carols, wrote verses for children's annuals and edited a collection of nursery rhymes which, many years later, provided a foundation for the celebrated collection made by Iona and Peter Opie. Almost penniless, he was pathetically grateful when a neighbour bestowed an ancient car on them. Valued at £7.10, it started going wrong almost at once.

In this depressed state Graves was cheered to receive a sign that Sassoon was at last ready to treat him as a married man. He had resisted all invitations to come and stay at the cottage but, in March

---

[*] Richards, while not naming Graves, whose work he knew well, evidently had him in mind when describing de la Mare's nostalgic poems.

1925, he sent a copy of his new book of poems with a warm double inscription to Nancy and Robert. Graves responded joyfully: 'to have you as a friend again is the best thing that has happened here for years.'[4] In April, when Robert, Nancy and the children made a brief visit to London, the two poets dined together before Graves went back to Apple Tree Yard to see Paul Nash, who had already made his name as an officially appointed war artist, and who was illustrating Graves's forthcoming poetry collection, *Welchman's Hose*. The following day Sassoon joined them on a family trip to London Zoo. It was a happy occasion. 'R. G., as usual, was being gentle and patient with the children,' he wrote that evening. 'It always touches my heart when I see him with them. They are countrified little creatures, chubby and frolicsome.'[5] It was the beginning of a halcyon summer in their friendship, with lunches and dinners and even – an occasion which would have been unthinkable in previous years – a lunch between Nancy and Sassoon on their own.

The aquarium and the monkey-house were where Graves chose to linger on the visit to the zoo; the latter gave him the idea for a long satirical poem, *The Marmosite's Miscellany*. It was published under a pseudonym – although Graves's mild parodies of his contemporaries hardly rated such caution – by the Woolfs' Hogarth Press.

On his April visit to London, Graves decided that it was time to meet Leonard and Virginia in person since they were printing several of his works as well as his edition of Ransom's poems. Arriving unheralded at teatime, he poured out the story of life at Islip and of how splendid Nancy was. But Mrs Woolf, never having met Nancy, was unimpressed, and irritated by the length of his visit. Graves was 'a nice ingenuous rattle-headed young man', she concluded. She did not think much of his poetry, 'but what will you? The sensitive are needed too; the halfbaked stammering stuttering, who perhaps improve their own quarter of Oxfordshire.'[6]

Robert was, finally and humiliatingly, forced to accept that his father had been right: he could not support his family by his pen. In June 1925, shortly after being orally examined on his doctoral thesis, he began collecting recommendations for an American professorship at Cornell University. John Ransom had told him that he had a good chance of being appointed and he was full of hope. Armed with recommendations from Robert Bridges, John Buchan (Oxford's vice-chancellor) and another influential neighbour, Herbert Asquith, the Liberal leader, he applied for the post and was invited for an interview in London. But, perhaps because he was affected by nervousness after the train journey to London – his horror of travel had never left him since the nightmare journey to Rouen in 1916 – he did not make a good impression when he appeared before the panel of interviewers on 13 July. His application was rejected.

It was not a happy month. Sam Harries had gone to India in June to join Mallik. Late in July, news reached Islip that he had succumbed to typhus and, inconceivably, was dead. Harries had become one of their dearest friends. The shock was too much for Nancy; she collapsed with a nervous breakdown. In September, when she suffered a relapse, they were told that her best chance of recovery was to spend several relaxing months in a warm climate.

Luck, at last, seemed to be on Graves's side. Friends had been busy behind his back. E. M. Forster and Arnold Bennett were among those who had put his name forward for an appointment as Professor of English at the University of Cairo. Nancy, who hated the idea of living in a foreign country, nevertheless recognized her need to escape from a life of depressed poverty and, since Harries's death, grief; Graves, excited by the possibility of earning as much as £1,500 a year, posted off his earlier letters of recommendation, and was accepted.

An additional benefit of the post was that it would involve very little teaching, leaving time free for Graves to work at a study of modernist poetry on which he had persuaded T. S. Eliot to collaborate with him. William and Edie Nicholson had generously provided Doris Ellitt, their daughter's nurse, to take charge of the children at Islip and to go to Egypt with them. Dick Graves and Molly Preston, two of Alfred's older children, were both living in Cairo and Forster promised an introduction to the poet C. F. Cavafy in Alexandria. Only the problem of their domestic life remained. It seemed to them both that their marriage could only continue to work if they had somebody with them who could provide Nancy with company and Robert with intellectual stimulation. This had already become apparent in England; in Cairo, they feared that the problem would be exacerbated by their social isolation.

Their first thought was to invite Sassoon to join them and live on half of Robert's earnings; although touched by the suggestion, he declined. He liked Nancy better than he had in the past but he did not want to share a house with her and a man for whom his feelings remained nearer to love than friendship. Shortly after

Sassoon's refusal Robert heard that his salary was, after all, to be only £900 and that he was expected to stay in Cairo for three years. At first he panicked and thought of abandoning the project. But Nancy needed the sun and he saw little future for himself in England, where he had quarrelled with almost all of his literary contemporaries. At the end of November, struck by a new idea, he and Nancy wrote to someone who was already a friend even though they had never met, a female poet living in New York. This was Laura Riding.

★　　★　　★

It was Sam Harries who, leafing through magazines at the cottage one day in July 1924, had called their attention to a poem by Laura Gottschalk (her married name) in the February edition of *Fugitive*, the American magazine which published the work of Ransom's poetry colleagues at Vanderbilt University. (The best-known of these early *Fugitive* poets today is Allen Tate.)

Even after the relationship with Laura Riding had ended, Graves was still ready to cite 'The Quids' as a perfect example of intellectual irony. The poem, which won her an award from the *Fugitive* group, had been the first for which Laura had found a discriminating and appreciative literary audience. Technically, it was inferior to Graves's work, awkward in rhythm and clumsy in tonality. What shone through it was the intelligence of a writer whose airy mockery of the conventional world seemed entirely in tune with Graves's own way of thinking. He had written to Ransom, asking him to pass on a message of congratulation.

That summer, when Laura Riding's short marriage to Louis Gottschalk was already in disrepair, her thoughts were focused on the idea of connecting herself to the *Fugitive* poets and, in particular, to Allen Tate who was then unmarried. If Ransom conveyed the news of Graves's admiration, her response was not immediate.

Direct contact began the following year. In July 1925 Graves's extended essay, *Contemporary Techniques of Poetry*, was published. In it, Laura Riding was linked with Gertrude Stein. They were praised; so, in another category, were Thomas Hardy and Robert Frost. Almost every other contemporary of the author was dismissed as outdated or incompetent. 'The Quids' was singled out as one of Graves's favourite poems.

It is not clear when the correspondence between Riding and Graves began, but the nature of this book strongly suggests that he was already receptive to Laura's views by the early autumn of 1925.[7] He had been reading Stein's work for some time but he had not expressed such enthusiasm for it as he did now, and Riding greatly admired Miss Stein. He had previously expressed a fondness for Edith Sitwell's romantic lushness; Riding disliked Miss Sitwell's work, and Graves now lambasted Edith for her lazy rhymes. His mention of 'The Quids' sounds as if he was offering private homage to his invisible literary adviser. He had never before written in such an aggressive style, and Riding was uncommonly belligerent.

Their correspondence was devoted to literary topics; Graves became increasingly curious about her personal life. A letter to John Ransom in late August elicited some intriguing further details. Ransom, in his role as an old-fashioned Southern gentleman, had been unnerved by Laura's decision, shortly after receiving her *Fugitive* award, to join their strictly male group. Her efforts to promote the group had seemed to be a way of pushing herself forward; he had not liked it. She had, he told Graves, subsequently returned to her home city of New York where he understood that she was doing 'hack literary work'. After identifying her as a clever young woman of Polish-Jewish extraction, Ransom added the supercilious observation that she suffered greatly from the knowledge that she was English neither by speech nor tradition. Despite her difficulty with 'regular verse forms' and her wish 'to put more into poetry than it will bear', he was ready to concede that she was a remarkable young woman, 'very fine personally, but very intense for company'.[8]

Graves and Nancy had already read and admired enough of Riding's work to disregard the patronizing tone of Ransom's letter. It seemed to them both that Laura, if she could be persuaded, might provide the solution to their marital problems. From Nancy's point of view, a congenial female companion in a foreign country was a welcome idea; from Robert's, she would make an ideal partner with whom to work on his book of modernist poetry. He already had a clear view of her ideas about poets and was in agreement with them; Eliot, who had never sounded overenthusiastic about the collaboration proposal, was already mentioning other commitments. But, above either of these factors, the presence of a third person had already been shown by Sam Harries to ease the strain between a couple who did not want to separate but did not feel at ease when they were alone together.

For Laura, the invitation was well-timed. She was divorced from her kind but ineffectual husband. She had recently failed in an attempt to attach herself to Allen Tate and his young wife Caroline in just such a ménage as Robert and Nancy seemed to be offering. At the age of twenty-four, she was depressed about her inability to achieve significant recognition in her own country. Blessed with an invincible faith in her ability to influence events, she saw the invitation from England as a chance to bring her own vision of order and clarity to a confused Europe. She was willing to accompany Robert and Nancy to Cairo, and to work with Robert on his book, on the understanding that they would help to subsidize her journey and living costs.[9]

★　　★　　★

On 2 January 1926 William Nicholson and Robert walked along the platform at Waterloo Station to greet a slight young woman whose light-brown hair was pulled back from her pale face by a thin velvet ribbon, tied, like a child's, with a bow on the top. Her voice, clear and precise, carried only a hint of an American accent. Her large blue eyes glittered with intelligence; her nose and chin were, for a portrait painter like William, a touch too prominent. He also noticed, as Robert did not, that the young lady wore rouge, lipstick and eyeshadow; English girls still wore unvarnished faces when they were travelling alone. Looking at her, William Nicholson wondered if Nancy knew what she was doing.

The train to Oxford left from another London station, Paddington, to which Robert duly escorted their visitor. Writing to an American girlfriend a few days later, Laura described how she had felt. The attraction between them had been immediate, she wrote; sitting in the railway carriage together, Mr Graves and she had been dazzled by a sudden burst of light which filled the compartment. Lightning was the obvious explanation in a week of storms and floods; Laura felt they had been singled out by a supernatural power. They were, she said, struck speechless. At Islip, where the little River Ray was so swollen by floods that she took it to be the Thames, she had been led to a house in which everything had been designed and made by Nancy. To Laura, it was all wonderful. She had never before had a bath in a tub set beside a fire, and it was made all the more enjoyable by the knowledge that Robert had brought the water in pails from the garden well. She admired the clothes which Nancy had made for herself and the four children. Above all, as a young woman who had never before left America, she liked the kindness with which she was welcomed.[10] If, as seems probable, she had fantasized about a lost child of her own after cradling Allen Tate's newly-born daughter Nancy, the name itself may have added to her warm feelings towards Nancy Nicholson.

The feelings were mutual. When they left the cottage to spend their last few days in London at Apple Tree Yard, the strength of the trio was already apparent. Together they dined with Robert's parents, after which Rosaleen and Robert sang ballads. Together they went to a Harold Lloyd film, with Nancy and Robert each clasping one of Laura's hands as she sat between them in the dark. When they paid their round of farewell visits, they took their new friend with them. Everybody liked her. Nancy had been in a pitiful state for the past six months; it was impossible not to respond to the way she now clung admiringly to Laura's arm and looked to her for help in making the arrangements. A small scene which did not go unnoticed by Robert's visiting relations was of Laura quietly packing the steamer trunks while Nancy hurried out to the shops in search of the one commodity which would be superfluous in Egypt – cotton wool.[11]

Only Sassoon felt some instinctive uneasiness about the plan for which he was, indirectly, responsible. If he had accepted their invitation, they would never have thought of asking this Mrs Gottschalk to join them. The *ménage à trois* seemed to him a recipe for trouble. Nevertheless, he presented Robert and Nancy with a cheque to cover the cost of the Morris Oxford car they had set their hearts on taking with them. On 8 January 1926 he went to the docks to see them off. Nancy and Laura were wearing straw hats which made them look, at a casual glance, as if they were sisters. But only at first glance. Laura's hair was thick and waving, her cheeks unlined. Nancy was just two years older, but it was difficult to believe. Her face was gaunt and anxious; she wore a hat to hide the fact that her head, after a savage attack of ringworm, was almost bald. And Robert, who professed to love women, was to be alone with these two in a foreign country for the next three years.

CHAPTER ELEVEN

1926

DEMONS AND GHOSTS IN EGYPT

GRAVES HAD BEEN LOOKING FOR A WOMAN TO FIT HIS IDEA OF A goddess, an omnipotent being, since his conversations with William Rivers in 1921. He was ready, if he found such a woman, to elevate her to mythical status and to worship her. Laura Riding, who already believed herself to have uncommon powers, was the ideal candidate for the role. He wanted someone to revere; she knew she was destined to be a leader.[1]

'She is a great natural fact like fire or trees or snow and either one appreciates her or one doesn't,' Graves told a friend in 1933. The fact that Miss Riding was sometimes overbearing, he went on, had no relevance, 'except as a self-justification for resenting the fact of her'.[2] Laura, writing to the same young man the following year, told him that, if judged by the way she behaved and wrote, she expected to be described as self-willed, domineering and intractable'. She qualified the description by adding that only 'vulgarians' who failed to understand her would use such words.[3]

Reactions to Laura Riding's powerful character polarized into two camps. T. E. Lawrence, appalled by her apparent domination of a 'bewitched and bitched' Robert Graves, described a manipulative woman with Circe's taste for turning her adorers into slavish swine.[4] The novelist Antonia White was both attracted and repelled by her force of character and 'pronounced witchlike look'. Noting Riding's tendency to see herself as Christ with a mission to preach and enlighten, she added that she was 'very dangerous but powerful' in her personal relations.[5] Admirers testified to her kindness and patience in helping them to improve themselves. Some thought her mad. Few questioned her intelligence.

Born on 16 January 1901, Laura was six years younger than Graves. Her father, Nathan Reichenthal, from whom she inherited a diligent, enquiring mind and her deeply-set blue eyes, was a largely self-educated man. He was fifteen when his parents brought him to New York from Galicia, then a province of Austria, in 1884. He became, according to his daughter, a founding member of the American Socialist party. Laura, the only daughter of his second marriage, was named after his first wife. Her own mother, Sadie Edersheim, a German immigrant for whom Laura claimed a Dutch Sephardic background, had no intellectual ambitions.

Laura had left her past behind when she arrived in Europe, although Graves was shown some love-poems and told that she had written them for her fellow Fugitive, Allen Tate. Only after Nathan's death in 1938 did she reveal her feelings about her father. 'I know no one who has touched the like,' she wrote then. 'He was a *good* man.'[6]

She had no such regard for her mother and blamed her for the streak of instability she believed she had inherited. A few close friends were told about Bobby, her brilliant younger brother, whose death-wish had led to an early period of confinement in an asylum.[7] (Later, while harmless, he became an eccentric recluse.) Laura herself often behaved in a way which was disturbing to strangers. As a child, she had become hysterical when thwarted; the pattern did not alter as she grew older. Louis Gottschalk, her first husband, described her as 'high-strung to the point of fainting'.[8] Several London friends recorded incidents when Laura lay on the floor in hysterics, and they were not describing a girlish fit of giggles. When added to an obsession with death, a megalomaniacal belief in her magical powers, and an enduring paranoia about being robbed of her thoughts and words, derangement does not seem too extreme a word to use.

Nathan Reichenthal's strong political views and his respect for his daughter's mind made him eager to prepare her for a life committed to furthering his beliefs. He dreamed of making her into America's Rosa Luxemburg and supervised her reading and studies to this end. Compliant as an adolescent, Laura rebelled when she reached the age of fifteen, changing her name to 'Riding' as an act of independence and announcing that she was going to be a poet, not a politician. She had not, in her own view, broken faith with her father. She wanted to change society as much as he did but she believed that she could reform social behaviour through her writing and the charismatic force of her personality. They had loved one another, she told a friend in 1938, and they had not really been doing different things.[9]

Laura Riding did not, as she frequently explained, go hunting for truths. The truth was in her, for others to discover. Her business was to reveal it through the imposition of an exacting mental discipline on those who were willing to accept her guidance. The poet, she wrote shortly before meeting Graves, never allows himself to be shaped by past events. She compared him to the potter, who makes and sets the mould. The poet is a leader, she continued, a prophet and a warrior who never cares what damage he does because he knows that what he is doing is right. He would need to be harsh because he alone was making progress, and yet gentle in order to ensure that others followed him.'[10] She used the masculine pronoun but when Graves read this piece, he had no doubt that the poet-prophet she described was herself.

Graves saw Laura Riding's personality as a transforming influence in his life. Laura's error was to assume that she had also been the originator of his ideas, his poetic themes and even, in certain cases, of his mythical subjects. Graves, she convinced herself, had known nothing about the Greek hero Herakles and his attributes until she spoke of them. This assumption, of the son of a classical scholar who had himself taken prizes in Classics throughout his school career, was surprising, although not more so than the other allegations which she made against Graves in her old age.[11]

It is more helpful to look at their partnership from Graves's side and ask what it was that he needed to find in 1926. He wanted certainties. Laura provided them. He wanted to clear the confusion of shell-shock while retaining the raw contact with violent emotion, terror, shame, fear, on which he drew for his poetry. His relationship with Riding provided ample scope for these feelings. Weary of Mallik's relativity, he wanted to be in touch with sharp, clear-cut views again. Views did not come in a more aggressively black-and-white form than those originating in Riding's mind. He wanted to serve a poetic muse;

she knew she was destined to be followed and adored. But it was Graves's worship that exalted her.

Graves, although poor and struggling in 1926, was already a well-known poet on both sides of the Atlantic. (A miniature edition of his poems had been put in the doll's house at Windsor Castle, together with the verses of Hardy and Kipling.) Laura had come to Europe in the hope of making more of an impact than she had at home. After 1926 she made her name, to a modest degree, by letting her work be printed in books which also had Graves's name on the cover. No English publisher wanted to commit himself to Riding without Graves; when they did, they acted under pressure and Riding knew it.

Like all Graves's mentors, she was not the chooser but the chosen. Unlike her predecessors, Rivers and Mallik, she was also a poet and considered by Graves to be the finest of her generation. He never doubted it from the day he read 'The Quids'. 'By God, she was superior, indeed supreme,' he wrote four years after their estrangement.[12]

He was, and had cause to be, grateful to Riding for the rest of his life. In her, he found a companion with the energy, intelligence and confidence to challenge every assumption. The books which he wrote before working with her were, as he acknowledged, scrappy and often carelessly researched. Riding was meticulous; from now on, he got away with nothing less than his best. He never had a harsher poetry editor. Tirelessly, he quoted to friends Laura's lines on the need to destroy any poem which was not perfect. She was his trusted final judge.

If Riding was Graves's mentor, Graves was Riding's champion, setting her high above all mankind as a paradigm of personal and literary excellence. In 'Against Kind', he mocked the friends who expected her power to be displayed in some uncommon act or feat, as if she was no more than a tawdry miracle-worker.

> They waited for a sign, but none was given;
> She owed them nothing, they held nothing of hers.[13]

This was the vital truth about Laura which Graves intuitively grasped and drew on. There was no hidden message to await. She herself was it. By standing straight, a monument to her own singular vision in which time had ended and she was 'finality', she set him free to fly, defiantly, aslant, following the intuition he trusted above scholarship. At the end of the day, Laura had little influence on his poetry. He wrote, and thought, as he had before he met her; she was incorporated into his own idiosyncratic vision.

> The butterfly, the cabbage-white,
> (His honest idiocy of flight)
> Will never now, it is too late,
> Master the art of flying straight,
> Yet has – who knows so well as I? –
> A just sense of how not to fly:
> He lurches here and here by guess
> And God and hope and hopelessness.
> Even the aerobatic swift
> Has not his flying-crooked gift.[14]

*   *   *

The travellers arrived in Cairo in mid-January 1926 and, after four days in a hotel, established themselves in a dark second-floor flat in the city. Laura's unease – she thought the apartment was haunted – seemed prescient to the superstitious Graves when his youngest child, Sam, having only recently recovered from mumps, went down with measles. Much against his mother's wishes, Sam was taken to an isolation ward where a friendly English doctor arranged for him to be cared for by the nanny, Doris Ellitt. A week later, the other three children came out in spots and were also taken to the hospital. In Sam's case, measles led to an ear infection which caused severe – and lasting – deafness. It was not a good beginning to their stay in Egypt.

When Doris and her charges rejoined the adults a month later, she found them established in a more agreeable garden apartment in Heliopolis, just outside Cairo. There was, she noticed, a spirit of great affection between the three occupants; Nancy, disturbingly weak before their departure from England, had begun to blossom again. Laura had taken over the housekeeping and shopping. Nancy, who had bought a sewing-machine, was making Laura a whole wardrobe of clothes in her own plain and elegant style. She had also started giving Laura driving lessons in the Morris, a project which lasted until Laura grew too recklessly confident to be trusted at the wheel. (She did not drive again until long after her return to America in 1939.) When the children were well enough to be taken out, there were weekly expeditions, to explore the banks of the Nile and to gaze at the Pyramids and the newly-uncovered tail of the Sphinx. Nancy thought the Pyramids looked (her word) 'suburban'; Graves was fascinated by the contents of the Cairo museum and by the Egyptian myths. The ancient myth of Osiris's death at the hands of his brother and rival, Set, made a lasting impression on him; an evil contender in love became part of his personal mythology after the return from Egypt.

Graves did not visit the University of Cairo until early February, two weeks after their arrival. He was not impressed. Established in what had once been part of a harem, its rooms were swagged and gilded in the most flamboyant excesses of French rococo style. After the stimulating company of Laura, his academic colleagues seemed dull; his pupils, few of whom were able to understand his lectures, infuriated him by confusing Byron with Shakespeare and showing no interest in poetry.

It was not all bad. Only two lectures had to be given a week – and none at all when the students decided to show their respect for the four-week holy fast of Ramadan by staying at home. The curriculum was undemanding. The difficulty of making himself understood offered Graves the idea for a short and witty study of syntax which he called *Impenetrability*, while the lurid Egyptian curses he heard gave him some choice examples for a short work about obscenities, *Lars Porsena*.

Two of the pupils were agreeable enough to become their new tutor's friends. A rich Turk took him on a private tour of the Pyramids; a Greek student invited him home to tea with his three strong-minded sisters, Pallas, Aphrodite and Artemis, one of whom lectured Graves on Egypt's future as a country run by women. Outside university hours he haunted the bazaar, had his fortune told by moonlight beside Cheops's pyramid and visited a bat-infested temple dedicated to a headless monkey-god.

Dick Graves, a senior and respected member of the Egyptian civil service, was anxious that his half-brother's unconventional household should not attract too much attention. It was embarrassing for Dick that Nancy refused to be called Mrs Graves and that she and Robert insisted on going everywhere with their woman-friend. He could not make Robert understand how much it mattered to put on the tarboosh, the national red fez, when he went out, and why, at a royal soirée, he had disgraced himself by applauding the performers before the King had raised his hands. It was surely clear to him, when he took Laura Riding to official functions instead of his wife, that this would give rise to scandal?[15]

If Graves was aware of causing embarrassment, he showed no remorse. Conventions had never interested him. To Doris Ellitt, it seemed only that the three of them were happy and at ease together during the early part of their stay in Egypt. She saw nothing strange or inappropriate in her employers' relationship to each other and, since she was devoted to Nancy, her observations were most closely related to her.

The letters from this period confirm the nanny's impression. Nancy had found a lively and affectionate sister for herself, one who could give Robert the intellectual companionship he needed and whom she herself admired for her spirited independence. She loved Laura for taking an interest in her paintings and urging her to return to her career as an artist. Like Robert, she did not question their duty to subsidize their friend and guest. Both of them felt in Laura's debt for easing the tension between them by her presence. They began to describe themselves as 'a trinity'. Laura told American friends that there was nothing that she could not say to Robert and to Nancy. They shared everything. Robert was helping to revise her first collection of poems. She dedicated it to her half-sister Isabel – and to Nancy.

They began to collaborate soon after their arrival in Cairo. Robert had still not abandoned the idea of writing his survey of modern poetry in partnership with T. S. Eliot when he left England. By mid-February he was ready to tell Eliot that he felt happier about working with Laura, who 'is far more in touch with the American side than I am and is anxious to get ahead with it'.[16] Eliot was more than willing to resign his interest.

Difficult though it is to establish precisely who wrote what of the book which became *A Survey of Modernist Poetry*, Graves's letters make it clear that it was not the word-by-word collaboration described at the front of the book. In the summer of 1926 he wrote to tell Eliot that Laura had been working on two American poets while he was writing about Isaac Rosenberg. The final chapter, a homage to Gertrude Stein, was written by Laura and revised by Robert; elsewhere, a close reading shows a marked difference between the voice of Riding, girlish, combative and a little shrill, and Graves's own laconic clarity.

The guiding idea of discovering a hidden meaning in poetry belonged to him. Its first appearance was in the book he published in 1922, *On English Poetry*, where he had observed that 'the underlying associations of each word in a poem form a close combination of emotion unexpressed by the bare verbal pattern'.[17] Those underlying associations were what the two writers now examined as they worked in a quiet room in the Heliopolis flat. Here, Graves later claimed, he alone wrote the book's most influential section, an analysis of Shakespeare's Sonnet 129, 'Th'expence of spirit in a waste of shame', which showed that the original meaning had been falsified by eighteenth-century amendments to the spelling and punctuation.[18]

There is no reason to doubt Graves's claim. The analysis of the sonnet, clear, scrupulous, and showing Graves's own fascination with etymology, resembles nothing written by Riding at that time. One of the images used – a comparison of modernist poets to the brass buttons twinkling on a soldier's uniform – helps to confirm him as the author. Only Graves would have remembered how he, Robert Nichols and Siegfried Sassoon, three soldier-poets, had been described by John Masefield as 'the three morning stars', and have made the ironic link from star-shaped medals to the regulation brass buttons.[19] Such soldierly jests played no part in Laura Riding's prose.

★   ★   ★

Graves cannot have been wholly comfortable about a relationship which, while it made Nancy happier in the short term, threatened from the first to exclude her. His unease was apparent in a curious story, 'The Shout', of which he wrote the first draft in Heliopolis and which he liberally embellished with details about Celtic rites and superstitions, magic talismans and scholarly asides.

The story is of Rachel and Richard, a young couple who have promised each other total candour in their marriage. Rachel is often ill and depends on Richard to look after her and the house. Their trinity is completed when they meet Charles Crossley, a devilish figure with whom Rachel falls in love. Charles, who has magical powers, is capable of producing a sound which can kill, 'a shout of pure evil . . . pure terror'. The narrator shares Richard's luck in surviving the shout; Charles, demented with rage, kills himself in producing it.[20] Rachel and Richard here clearly represent Nancy and Robert, while an unconscious fear of Riding's supernatural powers – in which Graves sincerely believed – is behind the sinister figure of Crossley.

Doris Ellitt was convinced that there was nothing sexual between Graves and Riding while they were living in Cairo. She lived in the same apartment and saw nothing to suggest that theirs was more than an excellent working relationship.[21] Passion may not have been given a physical outlet but it showed itself in the poems which Graves wrote while he was living in Egypt. In one, he lingered with the hungry eye of a voyeur on the exposed and vulnerable area at the back of a woman's neck. (We know it is Laura's neck because he makes an explicit reference in the poem to a closely-bound chaplet. Riding was working on *The Close Chaplet*, her first poetry collection, while she was in Egypt.)

> The hair curtains this postern silkily,
> This secret stairway by which thought will come
> More personally, with a closer welcome . . .[22]

This whispered celebration of the sensual appeal of flesh struck a new note in Graves's poetry. Passion, in his previous love-poems, had always been associated with darkness, guilt and unhappiness. His mother's puritan views on sex had governed him too well in his marriage to an innocent and very young woman. But Laura, who was sexually far more emancipated than Nancy, banished his guilt and led him towards the light. For the first time Graves was able to think of sex without shame and to dream of an all-embracing love between equals. In late April, inspired by Laura, he wrote the tender and beautiful 'Pygmalion to Galatea'.

The poem is based on the classical story of Pygmalion's breathing life into a statue, and this throws an interesting light on Graves's view of his new relationship. He, as Pygmalion, watches himself in the act of formulating his ideal woman. It is a poem about creative power, in which we see how much the woman he loved was the product of his imagination. If he could see the strong-willed and ambitious Laura Riding as the merciful and generous Galatea, it is clear that he was not only in love but that he was able to blind himself to reality for the sake of his creative needs. This is how he wanted Riding to address him when, at last, they became lovers.

> 'Lovely I am, merciful I shall prove:
> Woman I am, constant as various,
> Not marble-hearted but your own true love.
> Give me an equal kiss, as I kiss you.'[23]

Laura, as she appears in the poems written in Egypt, was still to some extent the work of his secret dreaming. He knew her mind but not, as yet, her body. The poems tell us that he was joyfully anticipating the time when he would do so.

*　　*　　*

Graves left an account of the Egyptian interlude in his revised edition of *Goodbye to All That* only because, in 1957, anything to do with Suez was of interest to readers. He excluded a curious dedicatory epilogue to the 1929 edition in which he described Cairo as the birthplace for the Trinity,

> a unity to which you and I pledged our faith and she her pleasure. How we went together to the land where the dead parade the streets and there met with demons and returned with the demons still treading behind.[24]

He gave no clue as to what the demons were. The clearest answer seems to be that these demons had, by 1929, become anybody who opposed his relationship to Riding. We know that his Graves relations in Egypt disapproved of their unorthodox ménage in 1926; there may have been further protests from the university, which increased his impatience to leave.

The climate had been tolerable when they arrived in January 1926. By May, the heat had built to an almost unbearable level. The children got dysentery; Laura remained convinced that they were surrounded by unfriendly spirits; there was talk of a murder in a nearby house. Nancy openly expressed her unhappiness at the prospect of spending three years away from home. When Laura's sighting of a ghost was followed by a minor earthquake, Robert felt his old nervousness returning. No more than Nancy could he contemplate spending three years in this alien, haunted land, where jackals roamed the edges of the desert, while kites hung like predators over the flat city roofs, waiting for carrion. The inhabitants appealed to him as little as the country: 'Nobody has ever succeeded in liking the Egyptians,' he wrote to Dick Graves almost thirty years later. 'I certainly didn't.'[25]

In April 1926 Amy Graves heard that her son and his household were planning to return to England for the summer after selling the car to raise some money. Writing to Sassoon a month later, Graves admitted that he was hoping to find a way to go on an American lecture tour. (This abortive plan would have allowed him more time alone with Laura, since Nancy had made it clear that she wanted no more foreign trips.) By 10 June the Graves family, Doris Ellitt and Laura Riding were back at Islip. In July Robert told his distressed parents that he had posted his letter of resignation to the University of Cairo.

CHAPTER TWELVE

1926–1927

DISINTEGRATION

MONEY WAS THE FIRST PROBLEM WHICH CONFRONTED GRAVES
on his return to England. The sale of the car given to him by
Sassoon had raised enough money for the return journey from
Egypt. Beyond that, Graves had little to show for his brief tenure
as professor. The salary he had not forfeited by resigning had been
spent in Cairo and he was due for a sizeable income-tax bill. Alfred
and Amy, distressed by their son's decision to abandon lecturing and
by the continuing presence of Laura in his home, were disinclined to
help; T. E. Lawrence came to the rescue with a first edition of *The
Seven Pillars of Wisdom* which raised £330 and solved the immediate
worry.

If there were rough edges to the triangle of Robert, Laura and
Nancy, every effort was made to smooth them for public view.
Nancy was said to be hopeful of earning enough by her painting to
support them all. Writing to English friends, Graves painted a blissful
picture of life in the Islip cottage, where each of them took turns
caring for the children and where Laura and he continued working
on the *Survey* in an attic room while Nancy, who still intermittently
suffered from extreme lassitude, worked at her drawings in bed

below. If Nancy stayed at the cottage while he and Laura looked for a London workplace, that was her choice. Nancy, in her husband's version of events, was the loving contriver of their estrangement from her.

It is possible that Graves masked Nancy's real views in order to put the best possible interpretation on his own behaviour, but the evidence against this seems strong. How, to take the most obvious point, could he risk lying when Nancy, a truthful and outspoken woman, could speak for herself at any time? And her own actions seem to speak even louder: Nancy continued to design and sew clothes for Laura; she even gave Laura a locket containing her portrait.

Had Nancy continued to feel physical passion for Robert, the situation would have been unbearable to her. As it was, she may have been prepared to share or relinquish the not very satisfactory carnal side of the marriage. Graves himself later asserted in his correspondence with Nancy that she had only loved him as the father of their children, and that they had never understood each other's true feelings.[1] Catherine, their younger daughter, believes that Nancy saw her husband as a big, brilliant, boastful child to be humoured and indulged. If she did not take him seriously, she could, for a time, look kindly on his passion for Laura.

Suggestions have been made that Nancy and Laura became lovers and that this made a strengthening bond in the Trinity. The evidence on Nancy's side is non-existent; any passion she felt while Laura shared her home seems to have been displaced on to an unwitting Siegfried Sassoon. On her part, Laura Riding's 1927 essay, 'The Damned Thing', offers a contemptuous dismissal of active lesbian love.[2] It is unlikely to have been written by a woman engaged in a homosexual relationship.

Laura herself, while recognizing the need for Graves to present a harmonious trio for public view in England, quickly grew impatient with this convenient dishonesty. There was a different form of misrepresentation at work in the letters she sent to American friends. To them, she confided that Robert's wife suffered from nerves and that this made it difficult for her to live with other people. Laura asked Allen Tate's wife Caroline to look for a suitably quiet American house to which Nancy and the children could move.[3] (The idea can hardly have come from Nancy, who had made it clear that she never wanted to leave England again.)

A clue to Nancy's behaviour suggests itself from her own family. Her brother Ben was going through a similar period of difficulty in his first marriage to the artist Winifred Roberts. The emotional triangle here consisted of three artists, Ben, Winifred and their friend Christopher Wood. Winifred's dislike of London and the purchase of a house by Hadrian's Wall in Cumberland, enabled her marriage to survive for a few years through a judicious separation of lives. Nancy, who also moved to Cumberland in 1927, may have been following the apparently successful example of her sister-in-law, whose retreat there had been made earlier in the year. Nancy, like Winifred, was prepared to sacrifice a good deal to avoid a divorce.

Nancy was not yet ready to move in the summer of 1926, and Graves was not able to contemplate a sexual affair with Laura in the crowded surroundings of World's End. He had not lost his horror of cities. It says much for his obsession with Laura that he was willing, in July, the hottest month of the summer, to exchange the cool of the stone-walled cottage with the river running by for a stuffy basement flat in Ladbroke Square, west London. Rosaleen, who admired Laura and took vicarious pleasure in her brother's rebellion from the family orthodoxy, agreed to join them as their flatmate and chaperone. But Rosaleen had become a busy and successful doctor; they usually had the flat to themselves.

Here, at last, they made love. When, more than forty years later, an old friend asked for some details of the past, Graves told him that 'I once lived in sin in Ladbroke Grove [sic] with Laura and there wrote a poem called "Pure Death".'[4] At the time, however, such candour was out of the question. Friends were told that, while they worked together in one room, Laura lodged upstairs with the landlady. Even so, curiosity was aroused by the oddity of their situation. Awareness of Laura's vulnerability to gossip made Graves even more zealous on her behalf as he extolled her to his literary contacts.

'Pure Death' shows Graves moving towards Riding's idea of death as an almost voluptuous release. The lovers begin in feverish haste, bestowing everything they can find until, with a *frisson* of excitement, they realize that they have nothing left to offer each other. The last gift remains, 'the sinister, long, brass-bound coffin box' which 'unwraps Pure Death'.[5] Threatening though the poem is, it conveys the fever and wild elation of the first weeks of their physical relationship.

Louis Gottschalk could not have chosen a worse time to visit England and ask Riding to return home. In the summer of 1926 his ex-wife had everything she wanted in her grasp. Graves was besotted by her; Nancy showed no jealousy; the London publishers were, due to Robert's diligent attempts, showing a courteous interest in her work. Gottschalk's dreams were swiftly crushed; neither during the time he spent at the flat in Ladbroke Square nor on a weekend visit to the Islip cottage did Laura allow him to be alone with her for a moment. Unnerved by her distant manner, her new style of dress and a brand-new English accent, he slunk back to America where, by the end of the year, he had found a more obliging wife.[6]

On 14 September 1926 Sassoon received a note from Graves to announce that Laura and he would visit his Piccadilly rooms at 2.30 p.m. (Graves no longer waited for invitations; Laura had taught him to take the initiative.) Dreading the awkwardness of such an occasion, Sassoon invented an appointment with the dentist and left at 2.00. Returning a couple of hours later, he found a letter from Graves which he considered intriguing enough to copy into his diary. The tone was defiant and uncomfortable. The gist of the content was that, at Nancy's wish, Graves was going to spend a year in Austria with Laura. The first explanation given – tax avoidance was tagged on, as if of secondary importance – was that Nancy found it hard to do her artwork and keep the house clean if they were all there together, while they found it impossible to write if Nancy was doing housework. Separation was the only answer, for Nancy's sake. They would, Graves added with uneasy jauntiness, come back for a Christmas visit.

> And in the Summer, Nance and the children will come to us there. We are all very happy about it, though we'll miss each other very much of course, and especially we'll miss the children. Funny life, ain't it?[7]

Mulling it over, Sassoon decided that Nancy was desperate for a quiet life at any price. He did not approve and he refused an invitation to wave Robert and Laura off from Victoria Station three days later; instead he went to Curzon Street to get his hat stretched.[8]

The dismay of Graves's parents when they learned of the new development was only slightly assuaged by Nancy's brusque reassurances. Having already planned to take a holiday at the spa of Hof Gastein in Austria, they swallowed their indignation after receiving a furious letter from their son in Vienna, telling them to stop interrogating Nancy. Rosaleen assured them that the relationship with Laura was a purely professional one. Nancy said, however tersely, that all was well. Still the old couple remained uncertain. Robert and Laura were offered the rail fare to enable them to visit the Hof Gastein pension for a week or two.

Amy and Alfred had already received a second letter from their son, explaining the strength of his and Nancy's love for their American guest, when Robert and Laura arrived at the pension. A week of Miss Riding at her most charming was sufficient to persuade Amy that there was no cause for alarm. She noticed the portrait of Nancy hanging from Laura's neck and the affectionate way she spoke about her. She sympathized with Laura's sensitivity when she shrank with a blush at Robert's reference to her Jewish blood. As a mother, Amy was touched by Laura's evident concern for Robert. Both Alfred and she thought their boy looked tired and nervous, with the first threads of grey showing in his hair. Laura's influence was judged to be beneficial. When Graves and Laura returned to Vienna, they left such confidence behind them that it hardly seemed to matter that they had provided only a collection-box address through which to contact them.

Socially cut off by their weak grasp of the German language, Graves and Riding spent most of their time working in their rooms. Occasionally they went out to the cinema; once they went to hear Roland Hayes singing spirituals. The glory of Vienna exerted no apparent hold on their imaginations. They did not go to look at the great palaces, to walk in the Vienna woods or seek to catch the political and intellectual mood of the city in the cafés along the Karntnerstrasse.

It was during their time in Vienna that Graves began to discuss his interest in early matriarchal societies with Laura. The reason for doing so was a review which he was writing of Bronislaw Malinowski's most recent work, *Crime and Custom in Savage Society*, in which the anthropologist had disparaged the pioneering work of William Rivers. Graves, in leaping to the defence of the man he had so much admired, talked to Laura about the ideas which Rivers had given him. It was Rivers who had led him to read about the excavation of Knossos and to study the possibility of a female-based religion in Crete. In Egypt he had been intrigued by the cult of the goddess Isis; Laura and he now began to discuss the possibility of restoring the female to her position of rightful superiority. (Five years later,

Riding connived with Graves's presentation of her as Isis in his 'Dear Name, how shall I call you?'[9]

In Vienna they started work on a new collaboration, *A Pamphlet Against Anthologies*. As in the *Survey*, the writing of the collaborators is easily separated. Graves was the author of an erudite and entertaining analysis of the errors of geography and history in John Masefield's poem 'Cargoes'; Laura mocked Edna St Vincent Millay and joined Graves in reviling 'The Lake Isle of Innisfree'. (Graves's violent detestation of the poem and its author had much to do with his father's reverence for Yeats.)

Wedded though Graves was to Laura's belief that they stood alone and, in her case, above their contemporaries, he could not bring himself to be harsh about all the old friends he had left behind. While Laura despatched as 'inoffensive' the Fugitives who had helped to launch her career, he wrote affectionately of Edward Marsh as an anthology editor who 'kept in the background with a most unusual restraint, wrote no purple prefaces, paid his contributors generously, exercised no patronage . . .'[10]

★   ★   ★

The plan had been to remain in Vienna for a year, but in early January 1927 the travellers returned to Islip, having spent only three months abroad. Nancy was elated by the delicate prints for cotton furnishings which she had been designing while they were in Austria and the children were being looked after by Doris Ellitt. She seemed pleased to see them, but word had reached William and Edie Nicholson that Nancy was happier when Laura was not under her roof. Sassoon, too, was ready to query Nancy's supposed readiness to share her husband with another woman, having received a dejected letter from her just before her husband's return to Islip.[11] Shortly after the reunion of the Trinity, the usually easy-going William Nicholson announced that Nancy's allowance would be stopped until Laura left. It was the only means he had of forcing Graves to eject her. No response was made.

Doris Ellitt's account of this period is illuminating. Two rooms were rented in a nearby cottage to provide a working area for the collaborators and Doris offered to sleep there at night. She was glad to do so, since the situation at the cottage was becoming increasingly difficult to ignore.

> It was very clear that a break-up in the family was pending, and on one particular occasion Laura came to me crying because Nancy had asked her to return to America. The atmosphere now became very unpleasant.[12]

The problems intensified towards the end of February when the entire family went down with influenza, which was followed, in Nancy's case, by jaundice. Laura, presumably hoping to escape infection, went to stay with friends in Norfolk, leaving Doris in charge of six invalids. The young nanny's own health collapsed under the strain and she was ordered to take a rest-cure by the doctor.

Robert's impatience for Laura to return was unconcealed. On 11 March, Nancy, nervous and still unwell, decided to simplify matters. After hastily packing her bags, she took a train north to Ben and Winifred Nicholson's home in Cumberland. She asked Robert to send the children as soon as she had found somewhere for them to live. (Technically, since she left the children behind for a few days, this exposed Nancy to a legal charge of desertion. Later in her correspondence with Graves she expressed bitter regret for her impulsive flight. She was not allowed to forget it.)

If Nancy hoped to force an end to an intolerable situation, she was much mistaken. Left alone with the children, Graves instantly asked Laura to come to him at Islip. She did so. It was, the anxious Graves family heard, only a temporary measure dictated by necessity.

When Doris Ellitt returned to the cottage at the end of April, she found Robert and Laura living there alone. A few days later a letter from Nancy arrived, inviting Doris to join her and the children in Cumberland, a suggestion which was readily accepted. Graves and Laura, meanwhile, informed the two families and their friends that they were again going to rent a flat in London. There would, they explained, be regular visits between the three homes. Publicly, the Trinity remained in harmony. Privately, Doris Ellitt saw that Nancy was very depressed during the first six months at the new cottage, Walton Wood. 'Letters would come from Robert which caused her a good deal of unhappiness. It seemed pretty obvious that this was a final break.'[13]

★ ★ ★

Number 35A St Peter's Square, Hammersmith, consisted of the two upper floors of a four-storey house built in the 1830s. Like the rest of the square, it was built from London brick and rendered in stucco chiselled to look like handsome blocks of Ashlar stone. Above the flight of steps up to the front door, an eagle raised plaster wings, a mocking evocation for Graves of his family motto: An eagle does not hunt for flies. (Once, the square had offered a menagerie of plaster animals and birds; the eagles were all that remained from its more prosperous days.) Inside, a locked glass door separated the ground floor and upper maisonette from the basement.

The front windows of the house faced the east side of the square and, just beyond view, the small workers' houses of Black Lion Lane. The cross-route of the Great West Road was not yet built and only two little streets separated the southern end of St Peter's Square from the point at which the Thames curved and broadened to its widest stretch. When the tide was low, the pungent stench of the purple-black mud-banks reached the rooms where Graves and Laura lived. On a quiet day they could hear members of the Corinthian Rowing Club calling to each other as they brought the boats back to Lower Mall. A few streets off, a persistent barrel-organist disrupted the afternoons.

In the 1920s the area was rough and poor. Local families went scrabbling at daybreak for pieces of coal in the cinder yards by the river; the local newspapers told a daily story of drownings, assaults, and break-ins. It was, and continued to be, a part of London which attracted artists, who liked the expansive skies and changing lights of the river and found the prices cheap. By the early 1930s Hammersmith became a bohemian colony, inhabited by a few well-known writers, a smattering of architects and an ever-increasing number of painters. In 1927, Eric Kennington already had a canal boat and a studio at Durham Wharf, just to the west of the square where Hammersmith met the equally shabby fringe of Chiswick. But Graves had chosen this locality to be among strangers, not friends.

In 'Pygmalion to Galatea' Graves had laid emphasis on the importance of a free dependence for the woman he loved. His was the only name on the register of inhabitants at 35A and he was the sole payer of rent to Nelson Dawson, who lived four doors away and owned most of the houses on the west side of the square. But the flat was always said to be Laura's and friends were rebuked if they dared to suggest otherwise. Her ownership was one of the many fictions devised to contrive for her a position of independent power.

The lower floor of the maisonette, consisting of a small kitchen and two large rooms with long windows, was Laura's domain, although one of the rooms was officially set aside as Nancy's and occasionally sublet to a woman barrister when funds were low. This was all that most visitors were permitted to see of the flat. At the top of the last flight of stairs, Graves worked in a small room overlooking a concrete area and neglected garden at the rear of the house. Laura, a vigorous defender of Graves's privacy, kept daytime guard below and climbed the stairs at night to a bedroom they shared facing on to the square.

The maisonette was cheap and the landlord an obliging man, but money was short and Graves could hardly expect the Nicholsons, or even his parents, to subsidize his new way of life. T. E. Lawrence, away in India, was aware of his financial difficulties. He had long been fond of Graves and held him to be an honest and honourable man, even though he no longer always understood his poetry. When the publisher Jonathan Cape invited him in the early summer of 1927 to suggest a suitable candidate to write his biography, Lawrence mentioned Robert Graves as his first choice. Selfishly, he felt sure that Graves would write nothing offensive; generously, he wanted to help him to a lucrative commission. On 5 June, responding to Graves's innocent request for permission to write the book, Lawrence confessed his role in the arrangements. The terms were spelt out; Graves was welcome to look for holes in Lawrence's armour but his subject would not assist him in the search. Lawrence would have to be shown the finished typescript: there were certain things which he would not allow to be said.[14]

Given that Graves was only allowed ten weeks to research and write the book for autumn publication, he did a remarkable job. Lawrence's mother refused to help, but Lawrence, having indicated that he would not be involved, sent careful amendments and comments for each chapter he received. Eric Kennington, who had just moved to Chiswick Mall, lent his first, unrevised copy of *The Seven Pillars of Wisdom*; Lawrence's friends and military contacts helped to fill in the gaps. Graves himself was modest about his achievement, describing it as 'a journalistic job, done quickly and I hoped, inoffensively . . . the writing was as subdued and as matter-of-fact as I could make it.'[15] Apart from using a reference to

Lawrence's 'blind desire to be a literary artist' as a perch from which to scoff at anthologies and declare that 'the pursuit of "style" is a social practice of the vulgarest sort', he kept his personal views out of the book. This is the only point when the reader senses Laura's editing hand at work: 'vulgar' was her favoured term of literary derision.[16]

Nancy and the children came to the flat for three weeks in July 1927 when Graves was working at white heat on the book. When he had finished the typescript he went up to the cottage in Cumberland for a few days on his own.[17] (The Islip cottage had been sublet for a year from May.) Writing to his sister Clarissa in September, he told her that the location seemed to be ideal for the children and that he had liked Nancy's new home: 'Harlech country without motor cars or the Welsh.'[18] By the end of August he and Nancy had exchanged places again, she returning to Cumberland and he to St Peter's Square.

Living and working in close proximity to Laura strengthened Graves's sense of her genius. If he could now think more clearly, analyse himself more brutally and, on a more mundane level, answer a telephone without fear for the first time in ten years, he felt sure that it was due to her influence. Increasingly, he strove to make his poetry meet her conditions. Poetry, she wrote, 'should be harsh, bare and matter-of-fact.[19] Graves, accordingly, stripped his work of anything which might smell of sentimental weakness. He could respond to Laura's passion for an exact use of language. When, in 'The Cool Web', he wrote of the words with which children learn to 'spell away the fright' of the incomprehensible, he was also writing for himself. The only way to master his own neuroses was through the naming of his fears; words, in this respect, were his salvation. But, try as he would, he could not achieve the glacial intellectualism of the main body of Riding's poetry; the semi-mythical landscapes of his new poems gave imaginative depth to even the most sterile works. Allusions to the sand-hills of the Morfa plain and the ruined castle of Harlech, together with the use of identifiable scenes from everyday life, allowed the reader to respond on an imaginative level which Yeats had once described as too subtle for the intellect. Against his own endeavours, Graves remained more accessible and memorable than Riding in her musings on abstract concepts.

Present in the new poems, too, and not always agreeably, was Graves's pride in himself as a character scoured by Laura of traditional attitudes, conventional attachments. 'Dismissal' described his rejection of the hypocrisy of easy friendship and blind filial devotion. 'The Reader Over My Shoulder' set his newly-minted self in a position of triumph above the reader towards whom Laura had increased his hostility.

> For you in strutting, you in sycophancy,
> Have played too long this other self of me,
> Doubling the part of judge and patron
> With that of creaking grind-stone to my wit.
> Know me, have done: I am a clean spirit
> And you for ever flesh. Have done.[20]

Contempt on paper was all very well. In life, while the critics praised the originality of Graves's new collection, *Poems (1914–1926)*, they remained blind to Laura's worth. *The Close Chaplet*, published by the Hogarth Press, was damned with faint praise and sold only twenty-five copies.* Her long prose poem, *Voltaire*, fared little better. While an extract from their book on anthologies, when it was published in the summer issue of the *Calendar of Monthly Letters*, carried Laura's name on the contents page, only Graves was featured on the cover. (Graves and Riding instantly withdrew the poems which the *Calendar* was to have published in its next issue.) The contract with Jonathan Cape for the Lawrence biography had enabled Graves to ensure that Cape would also publish Riding's forthcoming critical works, but all of Eric Pinker's efforts on her behalf had failed to sell her sheaf of essays to the magazines which readily published Graves. In a bitter preface to *A Pamphlet Against Anthologies*, Riding rebuked the vulgarity of those English reviewers who had failed in the autumn of 1927 to mention that *A Survey of Modernist Poetry* had two authors.

Writing to Clarissa in late August Graves described the literary critics as 'rogues, fools and insanitary dustmen'.[21] The reason for his fury, although he did not explain this in the letter, was a recent review of Riding's poems in *The Criterion*, a quarterly magazine edited by T. S. Eliot. The reviewer, John Gould Fletcher, had praised Graves's poems on one page and dismissed Laura Riding's on another. Worse, he had described her work as derivative and pointed to Graves as an influence.

---

* It seems likely that the Woolfs, who had been publishing Graves's work since 1923, were encouraged by him to undertake Riding's book. She had found a US publisher, Adelphi, before leaving America.

Graves's indignation at this slight to the woman he revered was extreme. When Eliot mildly cautioned him about the furious letter which he wanted to be published in *The Criterion*, Graves responded by accusing him of using literary politicians instead of critics and of trying to evade the fact that Riding had been insulted. Eliot published the letter but he did not write to Graves again for almost twenty years. Laura contented herself with jeering references to him in her new book. It was easy to forget that Mr Eliot had once been a poet, she remarked there with self-comforting hauteur.[22]

Nerves, arrogance and a strong streak of truculence had put Graves at odds with most of the literary establishment since the early 1920s. Now, as his reputation began to grow, he exiled himself to a private world in which Laura Riding was the only authority. The more he despaired of others for failing to recognize her genius, the more passionately he devoted himself to her. But Laura needed more than the unquestioning faith of one man. She knew her worth. And what was worth without acknowledgement?

CHAPTER THIRTEEN

1927–1928

ST PETER'S SQUARE

GRAVES HAD SHOWN A DIVISION IN HIS PERSONALITY EVER SINCE the war. At home with his children he was kind, affectionate and playful. In the literary world he had become known as a quarrelsome, obstreperous, opinionated man whose belief that he was always right made it hard for even his oldest friends to maintain good relations with him.

Riding had equally rigid views and Graves knew nobody with a surer sense of their own worth. It seemed to him incredible that other poets failed to see her as a beacon of hope, an inspiration to them all. He never thought that love had blinded him. He refused to face the fact that his marriage was in shreds, his children separated from him, his name tarnished by scandal, all because of the fact that he could not live without Laura. She was a supreme being, not a home-breaker.

Graves did nothing by halves. In his later years he extolled his muses and exaggerated their beauty, their talent and their virtue out of all proportion to reality. And so, in 1927, he upheld and defended Riding. All the latent aggression which had built up in the years of hardship and disappointment since the war, was channelled into the crowning of his chosen muse. The personal justification he offered was that Riding alone had restored his faith in himself as a poet. She, and only she, had cleared the confusion from his mind. 'It is through the standards that she as a poet has clarified that I have been able to be more clearly the poet I unclearly was before,' he wrote eight years later.[1]

There was a natural sweetness and generosity in Graves's nature which had always made his truculence tolerable to his friends in the past. A few now tried to tease him back into good humour. E. M. Forster, told that he had a duty to visit Miss Riding at St Peter's Square, mildly enquired which of them was supposed to be Mohammed and which the mountain?[2] Tom Driberg, with whom Graves had made friends when Driberg was contributing to *Oxford Poetry*, was rash enough to ask if he could call Laura 'Mrs Graves', now that she shared his home. This was not well-received. It had, Graves wrote, made him

> so sick that I nearly asserted my Elemental, Virile and Sulky
> Personality and came to beat you up. There were two things
> bad about it, first that you had accepted L.R.'s hospitality and
> had been taken into our confidence about things, second that
> we knew you were homo, and therefore expected none of that
> conventional tin-arse filth which one finds in the hetero, about
> man and woman relationships.[3]

Bad temper was forgivable; but letters like this resulted in the hasty retreat from Hammersmith of almost all of Graves's friends. Undeterred, Graves explained it away by saying that they had all become so used to 'small talk' that they were at a loss in the company of serious-minded people.[4]

Sassoon did not like Laura Riding, but it was not she who was responsible for the rift which separated him from Graves at the beginning of 1928. The fault lay, in fact, less with either man than with the tension of their circumstances. Graves, while declaring himself at peace, had never been more nervy and emotional; Sassoon's difficult relationship with young Stephen Tennant, a capricious and neurotic homosexual, had sapped his energy and left him with no goodwill to spare for the rest of the world.

The first signs of trouble came in October 1927 when Sassoon sent Graves a stinging rebuke for daring to suggest to Sir Edmund Gosse that he might like to review the Lawrence biography in his weekly

Sunday Times column. Gosse, who resented such approaches, had consulted Sassoon, who offered to deal with the biographer himself. Given the fact that both Sassoon and Graves had unashamedly approached friends to review their poems a few years earlier, Sassoon's wrath on Gosse's behalf seems to strike a false note. But Graves was remorseful, writing to Sassoon that 'you and I have forgiven each other a lot in the last eleven years or so'; this was as near as a proud man could get to admitting that he had been in the wrong to approach Gosse.[5]

Graves's next misdemeanour was the result of pure tactlessness. Thomas Hardy died in January 1928. Sassoon had got to know him very well; Graves had met him only once, on his bicycling visit to Dorset. But Graves had just written the Lawrence biography, and it was he who was approached with an invitation to write a book about Hardy. Cape's advance of £500 for *Lawrence and the Arabs*, and the book's instant commercial success, had made Graves solvent; he did not need to accept this new proposal. Carelessly, generously, he passed the commission on to Sassoon, saying that he was sure Jonathan Cape would like to have his name on their list. Sassoon had already read, with displeasure, an article about Graves's alleged close friendship with the poet and novelist; the idea of discussing Hardy's biography within a week of his funeral seemed to him disgusting. He did not answer Graves's letter for two years.

Graves was not too distressed by the absence of his old friends; he had a mass of new ones to put in their place. Above all, he had Laura.

It is easy to exaggerate the grimmer side of Riding's personality. It should never be allowed to overshadow her charisma, or the fact that there was a girlish, playful aspect to her character which Graves loved quite as much as her exceptional intelligence. She was a far more brilliant conversationalist than her heavy prose suggests. She loved games, telling tall stories, dressing up in elegant clothes. She had the force of personality which can alter the mood of other people. When Laura was depressed, everybody felt sad. When Laura was happy, every day felt like a celebration. The fact that her depressions usually had to do with her having hoped for too much from somebody made it difficult not to sympathize with her. Her faith in herself extended to and embraced her friends, enabling them to do more than they had ever thought possible. It was for all these things that she was loved.

Knowing this, it becomes easier to accept the intimacy which made the first months in St Peter's Square so happy for them both. Together, they scanned Charles Graves's gossipy columns in the *Daily Mail*, walked along the muddy river-banks, hunted for bargains in cheap antique shops, dabbed themselves with red paint as they redecorated their kitchen. This was a bond so close that Graves could burst out laughing when he read Laura's mocking dissection of the 'phallus-proud' male in 'The Damned Thing' – and beg his friends to study it. In scorning men, Riding could be said to have scorned him but Graves was confident enough to separate the witty, contemptuous author from the passionate woman who shared his bed.

Their new friendships underline this lighter side of their relationship. They had first met Norman Cameron early in 1927 when his poems were being published in *Oxford Poetry* by W. H. Auden and C. Day-Lewis. A tall, frail, fair-haired young Scot of great charm and generosity, Cameron was dithering between a career as a poet or a painter. His inclination was towards poetry but his greatest university friend, John Aldridge, was an artist and about to set off on a landscape-painting tour of Europe. Cameron toyed with the idea of accompanying him, and decided instead to settle for writing and painting in a Hammersmith studio near St Peter's Square.

Cameron was probably responsible for introducing Graves and Riding to their most unusual friend. Len Lye was a New Zealander, whose first attraction for Graves was that he had spent two years studying tribal rituals in Samoa, where 'mother-right' formed part of the culture. In 1927 Lye came to work as a stoker and then as a batik printer in London. After living on Eric Kennington's canal boat and then in the equivalent of a chicken coop on the wharves, he moved to one of the Black Lion Lane cottages east of the square with Jane, his South African wife.

Thin, tall and bald with slanting eyes, Lye had an inquisitive, roving, salacious mind, an absolute disregard for convention and no money. (Kennington, Norman Cameron and Graves all helped to subsidize him.) His hobby was rumba-dancing; his passion was film-making. Long before Walt Disney's *Fantasia* Lye pioneered animation films, painting his images straight on to celluloid. Some of his best short works represented musical sound; on one occasion his neighbours were astonished to see him dancing out into the street with a paintbrush and a snaking coil of black film which was being coloured in time to the syncopated beat of a rumba record.

The atmosphere in the Hammersmith circle was cheerful and spontaneous. They met one another nearly every day. Mary Dawson, the daughter of Graves's landlord, has described a party at Norman Cameron's studio. Proceedings began with gin-and-bitters and the fashionable game of slapping a friend's face with a banana-skin by way of a greeting. Mary dutifully slapped Len Lye and joined in the fun.

> Then they stopped dancing and Robert Graves got up and shrieked and rolled on the floor, and Norman [Cameron] (who is really quite sane but tries not to be) made some toast. After this they sat round the stove and meditated, and became quite Russian; no one said anything for some time, until Lye remarked, 'Aw, I wish I was in bed,' and Laura said, 'Oh, I wish you were.' Then they all heaved sighs for some time, until a crash of glass without made everyone jump. Norman rushed out and came back and said, 'It's allright, it's only 2 burglars in British Grove.'

The highlight of the party was the news of a fire in a local factory which sent them all rushing out into the street to get a good view of the flames. It was, according to Miss Dawson's letter, a typical Hammersmith evening.[6]

★   ★   ★

Graves had not needed to apply to Gosse for a good review of his biography of Lawrence or to ask Edmund Blunden, just returned from three years in Japan, to be sure to write it up. *Lawrence and the Arabs* sold at a rate of over three hundred copies a day in the first weeks after publication. It made Graves well-known and, after eight years of penny-pinching, financially stable. He could afford to indulge a whim.

He had hankered after owning a printing press since the end of the war; Laura shared his enthusiasm for the idea of setting up their own small publishing company. Lawrence's friend Vyvyan Richards was their adviser; he chose an old Crown Albion press because it was – relatively – light and easy to use. (One of the best examples of

Albion press work remains the Kelmscott Press books produced by William Morris.) One day towards the end of November, the heavy machine was carried up the stairs of 35A and installed on the lower floor of their maisonette. A brass plate was hammered to the door, proclaiming this to be the headquarters of the Seizin Press. (They took Seizin from the old English term for ownership.)

Printing was less easy than Graves had supposed: laying the type was complicated and had to be done by a local Monotype firm, while Richards taught them how to dampen and pull the pages. The first book for Seizin was to be a dictionary for children.

Laura was not noticeably attached to children; the idea for such a dictionary suggests that Graves was missing his small tribe. Nancy, although she was prepared to make occasional trips to the flat on her own, objected to sending the children there since there were no spare beds or rooms in which they could sleep. At the end of 1927, still flush with the profits from *Lawrence*, Graves decided to buy an old barge, the *Avoca*, which was kept at the nearest of the wharves, and to do it up as a home for the children. When his brother John came on a visit, he heard that Graves intended to have the barge fit for habitation by January 1928 when the children and their nanny, Doris Ellitt, were coming on a visit.

It was a charming idea but an impractical one. January was the worst month in which to put three small children on to a dilapidated barge; the result was predictably disastrous. The children went down first with colds, and then with fevers. When Graves's sister, Rosaleen, visited the boat and discovered that Sam had severe bronchitis, Graves and Riding responded, somewhat hysterically, by sacking Doris Ellitt for incompetence. Nancy, who had not been eager to play a part in Graves's new scheme for extended family life, was forced to come down from Cumberland at the end of February and sort things out. Sam was despatched to his grandparents' in Wiltshire; after two weeks he was followed by his spluttering, wheezing sisters and brother.

It is an indication of Graves's devotion to Riding that he could worry about nothing except the effect that all this must have had on her. By way of compensation, he agreed to pay for a holiday in France.

Privately, he dreaded the idea; France was too full of painful memories for him to relish returning there. But Laura's American friend, Polly Antell, wanted to meet up with them in the south of France, while Gertrude Stein, a figure of considerable interest to Laura, held court in Paris. Usually dismissive of other female writers, Riding had praised Stein in the final chapter of *A Survey of Modernist Poetry* for using a language of divine ordinariness. It was Laura's idea that they should invite Miss Stein to publish something with the Seizin Press.

Graves's sentiments were less strong. He had been the joint recipient of Stein's elegant cards from 27 rue de Fleurus, embossed with her most famous line – 'A rose is a rose is a rose' – in a dainty silver ring of words. While he admired her insistence on the exact use of words, her style did not excite him. But this was a trip which he was undertaking for Laura's sake, and he liked Miss Stein for her enthusiasm about Laura's work. Anyone who recognized Riding's uniqueness was his friend. So he submitted to the holiday with a good grace, made friends with jovial Gertrude and her lank, intelligent companion, Miss Toklas, and sided with Riding in a furious literary spat with Eugene and Maria Jolas, the editors of *Transition*, a quarterly magazine of experimental writing, when they dared to dispute her scornful view of surrealism. Graves had no strong feelings on the subject but, during a trip devoted to making Laura happy, he would have defended her for saying that the sun was the moon.

In late June 1928 the travellers returned to London and enthusiastically applied themselves to their new vocation as publishers. Eric Pinker, thinking that they intended to be commercial, began suggesting authors and was rebuffed. Their plan was to produce what they called 'necessary books' in the promotion leaflet.

By giving Riding a press and encouraging her to print only the books which she thought 'necessary', Graves was giving her a firmer foothold in the literary world. He left the selection of authors to her; he wanted it to be her success. Her choices were capricious, and revealing. Len Lye was invited to contribute a book: although he was not a natural writer and had considerable difficulty in expressing himself, he supported Riding's beliefs. Cameron was recruited; so was Michael Roberts, a young poet in correspondence with Graves who had expressed admiration for their collaborative works. But, intriguingly, the brilliant generation of poets who were making their names in the late 1920s – Cecil Day–Lewis, W. H. Auden, Stephen Spender, Louis MacNeice – seem never to have been considered, although Auden was a keen follower of their publications. Success was not a helpful qualification for being published by Seizin.

Reports of life at St Peter's Square in the summer of 1928 convey an atmosphere of merriment. The children came for a second and more successful stay on the *Avoca* with a new nurse. Graves took them for long walks beside the Thames and set aside two hours in the late afternoon when they could visit him at the flat. Later in the autumn, when he was enjoying the critical success of his latest book, *Mrs Fisher; or The Future of Humour,* to which Laura had contributed many suggestions, Nancy made an impetuous visit to London and decided to stay.

Although we can never be sure what Nancy's thoughts were during this period, due to the fact that she later destroyed all her correspondence, she appears to have been feeling isolated in Cumberland. The children had brought back enthusiastic reports of their second holiday on the *Avoca* and of their father's high spirits. Listening to them, Nancy may have begun to think of the days in Egypt two years earlier when she, Robert and Laura had been so close to one another. It had been the spectacle of her husband's unhappiness which had driven her away; now that he had found the life he liked, she wanted to rejoin it and to share his relationship with Laura. The time had passed when she wished for Laura's return to America; now, she only wanted to find her way back into the warmth of the happy Trinity they had once been.

Graves and Riding were delighted by her decision, Laura because she was growing a little bored of being alone with Robert and his domestic problems, Robert because this was just the situation he had hoped to achieve. With Nancy on the boat, the children could stay there all the time. It was agreed that she would move down from Cumberland as soon as possible; she had installed herself on the *Avoca* by the middle of December 1928.

For her first Christmas on board, Nancy was asked to find room for Hart Crane, the wild, hard-drinking young homosexual poet with whom Laura had spent much of her time during her last weeks in America. Laura was devoted to Crane. Her eagerness for him to prolong his stay to almost a month suggests that she was beginning to tire of Robert's company. Certainly she was in low spirits when Crane left. He noticed that she became almost tearful when he prepared to move on to Paris.

Nancy rejoined the Trinity at the very moment when Laura was contemplating ways to expand it. Perhaps because she was sexually bored, perhaps because one man's love was not enough, she was ready to put Graves's devotion to a new test.

CHAPTER FOURTEEN

1929

THE HOLY CIRCLE

GRAVES, BY THE WINTER OF 1928, WAS SUCCESSFUL AND WELL-known. His biography of Lawrence had brought him a popular audience, his most recent collection of poems (*1914–27*) had been favourably received and, however unjustly, he was singled out as the writer chiefly responsible for *A Survey of Modernist Poetry*, a book which, while its sales were slight, had already begun to exercise an influence on ways of reading texts.

The year 1928 had also seen the publication of *A Pamphlet Against Anthologies* and of Riding's own *Anarchism is Not Enough* and *Contemporaries and Snobs*. These last two books were written with verve and scorn from a position of conscious superiority. Marianne Moore, Virginia Woolf, Wyndham Lewis, T. S. Eliot; the list of writers and poets condemned as vulgar or false by Laura Riding was a long one. Her readers, the critics whom she addressed as 'wisebottoms', 'children' and 'blinking intelligences', were informed in her 'Letter of Abdication' that she had become hollow with death and was, in a state of queenly tiredness, prepared to resign.

Laura's tragedy was apparent in that bold announcement. Having no perceived crown, she had no apparent position from which to abdicate. At Oxford, the poets clustered around Auden, Day-Lewis and Spender; at Cambridge, William Empson was the centre of a brilliant young literary group which included Jacob Bronowski, Julian Bell and John Davenport. None of these writers showed any interest in Riding's passionate statements in 1928–9 although her colleague was discussed, reviewed and read. In London, Graves's angry attacks on all those who failed to acknowledge her superiority did Riding's reputation more harm than good. She did not lack publishers, since Graves continued to insist that her books should be taken as part of his own publishing contracts. But she had not yet found the followers she felt destined to lead. Norman Cameron left the country to travel and then take a job as education officer in Nigeria at the beginning of 1929. John Aldridge was painting in France. Len Lye was busy making his first film, *Tusalava*. Even Graves, although always faithful, was committed to seeing as much as possible of the children on the *Avoca* while Nancy repaired and restored their new barge, the *Ringrose*, bought by Robert to give his family a more comfortable home. Laura's circle had shrunk to the American correspondents who were fed with regular details of her London life. The more perceptive sensed that she was impatient for change.[1]

★   ★   ★

It is not clear how Geoffrey Phibbs first came to hear of Laura Riding. His second wife, Mary Taylor, was told that he answered an advertisement in which Riding and Graves offered to sell a hand-printing press, possibly one which they had purchased and found unsatisfactory before they were helped by Vyvyan Richards to find their Albion machine.[2] But Phibbs was an eager reader of new poetry and his interest may just as well have been stimulated by reading *The Close Chaplet*. By October 1928 he was in a position to tell Graves that he had been reading Riding's work for six months and that she was the most important person in his life.

References, in this first extant letter, to a conversation the previous day show that Graves had been sufficiently intrigued to visit Geoffrey Phibbs in Ireland. In Dublin they had discussed 'Jocasta', the most striking chapter of *Anarchism is Not Enough*. Geoffrey had been left in awe not only of Riding but of her representative. Graves was a man who became physically more impressive as he grew older; at thirty-three, the craggy lines of his handsome middle age were beginning to emerge from the softer beauty of his youth. His mind, sharpened by daily argument and banter with Laura, was remorselessly clear. Geoffrey, used to being the dominant figure in Dublin literary arguments, found himself at a disadvantage.

> What you said yesterday about 'Jocasta' ought to have been and was valuable; but it made me so bluddy [sic] nervous that whenever I spoke afterwards I put things wrong which in the circumstances was a pity.[3]

During their discussion, Graves spoke of the need to discard all excess mental and emotional baggage if Geoffrey wished to reach Laura's 'active position'. This, as he had guessed, only served to increase Geoffrey's interest. To present her in the form of an intellectual and spiritual challenge was the best way he could ensure that Geoffrey would join the court. By the time Graves returned to England, Geoffrey was feeling eager to follow him. In his letter, he spoke of being tired of 'dissembling' and begged Graves to find him a job in London.

Geoffrey Phibbs is better known today as Geoffrey Taylor, the name which he assumed in 1929 and under which he collaborated with John Betjeman on two anthologies of landscape and love-poetry in the 1940s. (He was living near Dublin with his second wife and working as poetry editor of Ireland's leading literary magazine, *The Bell*, when he met Betjeman in 1941.)

Aged twenty-eight at the time of Graves's visit, Geoffrey was a year younger than Laura. He was the oldest son of a handsome Irish squire with conservative tastes and a flirtatious nature. His mother, who was only eighteen when he was born, was an Englishwoman, rich, strong-willed and artistic. Geoffrey grew up in Ireland, although he was sent to school in England. From the age of fourteen he lived at Lisheen, a large early Victorian house in Co. Sligo belonging to his father's family.

Pale-skinned and brilliant-eyed, with a lock of black hair falling over his face, Geoffrey in his twenties looked very like the young Yeats. Betjeman later wrote a tribute to him as a man of great integrity and almost electric intelligence. His charm, kindness and conversational brilliance are remembered by everyone who knew him. Idealistic and impulsive, he was also, as a young man, deeply shy. Despatched to France with an attractive girl by his mother when he was in his early twenties, he returned a virgin. Mrs Phibbs allowed her disappointment to show.

Too young to see action in the war, Geoffrey went from training with the Royal Irish Rifles to Trinity College, Dublin, and then to study entomology at the Royal College of Science. He became an assistant organizer of the new libraries being set up in Ireland by the millionaire philanthropist, Andrew Carnegie. In his spare time he wrote poetry. (Two small collections of his poems were published by the Hogarth Press 1928.) His passions were literature, naturalism and book-collecting; in conversation, he derided marriage and orthodox religion. He longed to escape from the old-fashioned way of life at Lisheen.

In 1924, to his father's displeasure, Geoffrey married a northerner, Norah McGuinness, who was eight years older than himself. A talented and ambitious artist, Norah readily accepted Geoffrey's theories about the way to conduct a modern marriage but frustrated him by her extreme modesty. Geoffrey was never permitted to see her naked.[4]

Their marriage was hardly more satisfactory than that of Graves and Nancy by 1928, when Norah told Geoffrey that, while on a visit to England to sell her book illustrations, she had allowed the libidinous novelist David Garnett to make love to her. Geoffrey's letter to Garnett has disappeared but the response to it indicates that, far from being distressed, he jumped at the chance to suggest a foursome household with David and his wife. Garnett, not sharing Geoffrey's enthusiasm for such modern compromises, put him off, saying that 'Four is too many: at the moment anyway'[5].

Shortly after this exchange, a telegram from Laura arrived, inviting Geoffrey, but not Norah, to come to Hammersmith and join Nancy, Robert and herself in a business relationship involving work for the Seizin Press. Geoffrey saw the possibility of a new foursome arrangement; Norah, sensing a more real threat to her marriage than David Garnett had been, decided to accompany him to London.[6]

If Geoffrey had any intention of staying with Norah in London – and it seems unlikely that he did – it withered under the spell of Laura's personality. Graves was out with Nancy and the children when the travellers arrived at 35A St Peter's Square. Laura registered the unpleasing fact that her admirer was accompanied by a good-looking woman, and took charge of the situation.

> Geoffrey was received with open arms – I was unimportant, an outsider, and must be got rid of. Laura, as cold as the cheap sparkling trinkets with which she was covered, accompanied Geoffrey and they brought me to the Regent Palace Hotel – thrust a bottle of brandy into my hand and said 'Drink this and forget your tears.' Then they left me in the desolate bedroom.[7]

Norah, after spending three days alone in the hotel, was rescued by a woman-friend with a home in Chelsea. After briefly returning to Ireland and asking her brother to send all of Geoffrey's books to St Peter's Square, she set off to do a course of painting in Paris by herself.

Geoffrey's initiation into the Holy Circle, as the Trinity had been renamed, could now begin. The religious flavour of the name was in keeping with the cabalistic ceremony of exorcizing Geoffrey's past. Under the supervision of Graves and Riding, he was asked to open the trunks of books – his precious library – sent by Norah's brother, so that they could be examined and censored. Any which were considered unworthy of his new existence were destroyed; he was invited to write 'Seizin Press' in the remainder to show that they were common property. This, for a young man who treasured his books, was hard. He did not really want his books to be part of a communal collection; after earnest discussion, it was agreed that he need not write the name of the press in all of them. He was then told to burn his clothes. Deprived of his property and clothing, he was judged to have been purified of the taint of Norah and his family. Astrological charts drawn up shortly after his arrival promised well for the future of the Circle. (Laura, like Nancy and Robert, was an ardent believer in horoscopes.)

The *Avoca* was loaned to Geoffrey to provide him with a little independence. He spent a certain amount of time on it, long enough for the children, living next door on the partly renovated *Ringrose*, to become attached to him and for an independent friendship with Nancy to be established. But the barge was intended only as a work area; his nights were spent at the flat. Graves and Nancy occasionally slept together on the *Ringrose*; on these nights, Geoffrey was expected to sleep with Laura. This presented a problem. Geoffrey's reverence for Laura was still as strong, but he was not physically attracted to her. To his extreme humiliation, he found himself quite unable to make love to her when he was called on to do so.[8]

Geoffrey did not discuss this misfortune and it is most unlikely that Laura said anything about it either. Sexual awkwardness did not lessen his awe. When she pointed to a clock one evening and announced that she could stop it by will-power, he did not doubt her. Like Graves, he believed that Laura Riding was capable of doing everything to which she applied her powers.[9] He was rewarded for his faith. Within three weeks of his arrival, a dictionary which Riding had planned to write with Graves was replaced by another, to be written with Geoffrey.

Superficially, the new scheme was working well. Rosaleen Graves told her shocked parents about the Circle holding barge parties and planning a summer walking tour in Germany. But Rosaleen had not had any private talk with Geoffrey. He had joined the Circle at the end of February 1929. A month later he was planning to return to his wife.

Laura Riding told a different story. In 'Opportunism Rampant', a subjective and as yet unpublished response to Martin Seymour-Smith's presentation of her in his 1982 biography of Graves, Riding stated that Geoffrey Phibbs invited her, on Easter Sunday, to run away with him to France and that she, for the good of the Holy Circle, declined.[10] This account does not tally with the other available evidence. On Easter Sunday, which fell on 31 March in 1929, Geoffrey wrote to an Irish friend, Tom MacGreevy, to confide that Robert Graves and his wife were 'victims of their own extraordinary set of values' and that Laura Riding had turned out to be 'a virago'.[11] The following day he went to lunch with his aunt, who lived in London, and failed to return to Hammersmith. He went, instead, to join Norah in Paris.

Geoffrey's letter of 31 March suggests that he was already plotting his escape. A private conversation with Graves on the morning of 1 April strengthened his decision. Graves, as Geoffrey explained in a letter posted to Laura from France, had seemed confused and unhappy: he had made it clear that the only life he could have with Laura was when Geoffrey was away. Geoffrey did not mention the fact that he had already decided to go when Graves spoke to him. It was less embarrassing to let Laura think that his sole motivation had been to alleviate Robert's unhappiness.

If Graves's initial feeling was one of relief, it soon gave way to concern and guilt when he saw how violently Laura responded to the news. She was hysterical with anxiety and, not unnaturally, furious with Graves for the part he had played. It was not possible that the horoscope charts and her own instincts had been wrong. She knew that Geoffrey had not really wanted to go. Graves was despatched on a fruitless journey to discover if he had returned to Ireland.

The letter from France was their first clue to his whereabouts; it had a Rouen postmark.[12] Len Lye was commissioned to wheedle the exact address out of Geoffrey's aunt by pretending he had a job to offer him. After taking the night ferry to Dieppe on 5 April, Nancy, Graves and Laura went straight to the hotel in Rouen and sent a message up to the room in which Norah and Geoffrey, at eight o'clock in the morning, were still in bed.[13] They were ordered to come down to the hall to discuss their plans.

Norah's immediate impression on entering the hotel hall was that the fierce-faced woman she had met in London, now festooned with sparkling paste ornaments and with *faux* diamond buckles on her shoes, was ready for a fight. Laura's manner, however, was gentle and conciliating. They had come, she explained, to invite Norah to join the Holy Circle. Norah and Geoffrey would be able to live in their own, separate London home. He would, while continuing to work on the dictionary, cease to be Laura's lover. All that was needed was their agreement.

The cabalistic aspect of the Circle had been apparent from the first ritual of burning Geoffrey's clothes. Norah now found herself witnessing a baffling exchange of signs and symbolic movements as Laura tried to exert her authority over Geoffrey. Norah left them to it and went for a walk until lunch, which was taken at a hotel just outside the town. This, although Norah did not know it, was Graves's choice. He was quite as superstitious as Laura, and the hotel stood on the site of the Rouen hospital in which he had been saved from death in 1916. It was, for him, a spot of talismanic power.

After lunch Norah was sent out on a short walk alone with Geoffrey.

> We walked. Geoff said that if I didn't go with them, he wouldn't
> – I sensed he was torn. However, I said I wanted to keep sane,
> and said nothing, not even losing Geoff, would induce me to go
> to what I thought was the madhouse of Hammersmith . . . So I
> just said 'No.'[14]

The effect of this declaration surprised them all. Graves, linking it to
his own near-death in the hospital, gracefully wrote in the 1929 version
of *Goodbye to All That* that Laura had 'seemed to die'. Norah, with
less diplomacy, wrote that '"God" in the Public Lounge threw herself
on the floor, had hysterics, threw her legs in the air and screamed.'[15]
Two waiters were summoned to remove her from the room.

The mission had failed. Later in the day Nancy, Graves and Laura
crept back to London while Geoffrey and Norah prepared to return
to Ireland.

★   ★   ★

Shortly after the expedition to France, an incident took place at
St Peter's Square which throws an interesting light on subsequent
events and indicates the strength of Riding's belief in her own
will-power.

Catherine Graves, then seven years old, was in the habit of visiting
her father in the late afternoon, as all the children were permitted
to do.[16] (This was, during the chaotic period of the Holy Circle,
the only opportunity they had to spend a little time with him.)
Arriving at about five o'clock one day, she was let in by Laura who
explained that Graves was out before inviting Catherine to come
and sit in her own room. After a time she persuaded Catherine to
sit beside her on the broad sill of the open window looking down
on the garden. Patting Catherine's hands, she told her a wonderful
story of a tree which grew just outside the window. Its leaves were
magical. Behind each leaf, just visible in the movement of light and
wind in the branches, was a delicious sweet. Laura was uncommonly
convincing. Catherine's only thought was to get hold of the tempting
sweets. Laura told her that if she stepped out of the window, a magic
staircase would rise from the ground to catch her feet.

Catherine was less ready to believe in a magic staircase than a
sweet-laden tree, but she did believe Laura's warning of a policeman
coming to punish her if she ever repeated the story. Terrified by the

thought of the fatal step she might have taken, she ran back to the barge without waiting to see her father.

The incident had a curious sequel. A book called *Four Unposted Letters to Catherine* arrived at the barge the following year.[17] The author was Laura Riding. Seeing the title, Nancy gave it to her daughter to read. The tone of the book was threatening. It began by reminding Catherine of what Laura had said about policemen. Now, Catherine learned, there were policemen all over the world and they were watching her. She was warned, too, about the danger of loving the 'wicked crooked person' who lived with Nancy. (This was Geoffrey Phibbs.) Her intention in writing this book, Laura explained at the end, had been not to cheer Catherine up or interest her, but 'not to do anything that I did not mean to do'.[18] Catherine understood this ambiguous message. Laura meant to warn her never to speak about what had happened at the flat that afternoon. She did as she was told and held her tongue until she was a middle-aged woman.[19]

★   ★   ★

Norah, who was given a warm welcome by Mrs Phibbs for bringing her son safely home to Lisheen, was allowed a few days of peace before the drive to recapture Geoffrey for the Circle was renewed. This time it took the form of objects sent by Laura, coins, pieces of coloured ribbon, even an old bus ticket. Each object was accompanied by what Norah identified only as 'symbolic signs'.

In mid-April, the pursuit accelerated. It was decided that Nancy should go to Lisheen and ask Geoffrey to come back to Hammersmith. Her reception was cool. After being kept shivering outside the house by Mrs Phibbs and Norah while they debated whether Geoffrey, who was in bed with asthma, should be informed of her presence, she was told that he was willing to talk to her. When he had dressed, Nancy and he went for a walk down the long avenue behind the house to discuss his plans. Geoffrey, who was very fond of Nancy and conscious of the trouble she had taken to find him, was infuriated when his father suddenly appeared on the driveway and ordered Nancy, whom he addressed as a 'scarlet woman' under the mistaken impression that she was his son's mistress, to leave his property. This was the moment at which Geoffrey took the dramatic step of dropping his father's name for his mother's. Geoffrey Phibbs became Geoffrey Taylor.[20]

Nancy left Lisheen with a promise from Geoffrey that he would rejoin them. The following week, Geoffrey and Norah returned to London. Norah, supposing that she had lost her husband to the 'madhouse', went on to Paris. But Geoffrey, instead of going to Hammersmith, took a train to Hertfordshire to seek the advice of a more experienced roué than himself. David Garnett counselled him to stay away. Geoffrey promptly sent a telegram to St Peter's Square, regretting his inability to rejoin the Circle.

Graves, as the only one of them who had a slight acquaintanceship with Garnett, was ordered by Laura to bring their runaway back. He set about his mission with zest, beginning with a telephone call to Garnett in which he threatened to kill Geoffrey if he did not return to Hammersmith. (This was subsequently reported by Garnett to Norah, whose account is by far the most extensive available.) An hour or two later Graves burst into Garnett's country home, swore at Garnett, and ordered Geoffrey to accompany him to London.[21]

Graves's behaviour by now was that of a man who had lost control of events. At the beginning of the month, his one objective had been to regain his relationship with Laura by forcing Geoffrey to leave the Circle. (Neither he nor his companions had been aware of Geoffrey's growing discontent; they all assumed, and continued to believe, that Geoffrey had only left because of what Graves had said to him.) Now he knew that Laura's forgiveness was contingent on his restoring Geoffrey to her. Graves did not ask himself why she wanted Geoffrey so much. That would have been painful, and Graves was good at blinding himself to what he did not want to see. What he saw was that Geoffrey was essential for the existence of the Circle and that Laura was acting, not for herself, but for the good of them all. She had, he later wrote to Edward Marsh, been 'desperately badly treated' by their guest.[22] Now it was Geoffrey's duty to admit that he had been in the wrong and submit to her.

Geoffrey was interrogated about his actions as soon as he arrived at the flat on the evening of 26 April. Laura was at her most persuasive but Geoffrey had become obdurate. He no longer believed that Laura knew best.

The dispute, which lasted for some hours, was resumed in the early morning. The four Circle members gathered to talk in the room on Laura's floor which overlooked the garden.[23] Emotions rose to boiling-point; the long sash-window was pushed up to its fullest extent. Geoffrey, exhausted by a discussion which allowed for no retreat, finally spoke in a way which made Laura realize that argument would not win her this battle. She left the room and returned to say that she had drunk some Lysol, a poisonous disinfectant. She showed no ill-effects. They may have thought that she was bluffing. But Graves, who had read all of her poetry and knew how often she had taken a leap from a window into her death-theme, must surely have felt uneasy when she sat down on the window-sill.

Believing, as she had with Catherine, that her will was strong enough to defeat death, or unhinged by the effect of the poison, Laura changed tactics. Swinging her legs up and over the sill she said, with some bravado, 'Goodbye, chaps,' and jumped.* They heard the slap of her body as it hit the concrete paving outside the basement door. Graves leapt out of the first window he came to, half a floor down on the staircase, in his haste to reach her. Nancy stayed upstairs long enough to telephone Rosaleen, a doctor, and to call for an ambulance before going down to the garden with Geoffrey. Graves's body was moving slightly; Laura appeared to be in her death-throes. For Geoffrey, who had never wanted to see Laura again, it was appalling to think that he was the probable cause of her death. Shocked and hardly conscious of what he was doing, he wandered around the local streets until his odd behaviour attracted the attention of the police.

Drugged with morphia by Rosaleen, Laura was taken to the Charing Cross Hospital, one in which Rosaleen had enough influence to ensure that she received the best possible treatment. She was diagnosed as having a bent spinal cord, four crushed lumbar vertebrae and a broken pelvis. Fears of a fractured skull proved groundless.

---

* Details vary as to which window and which storey were involved. Two things are clear. Laura fell into the 'area'. Graves jumped after her from a lower level. This precludes the front of the house, where the only 'area' was a narrow ditch and where protruding iron balconies on the raised ground floor would have prevented the body from falling into it.

There was, however, a large concrete area at the back of the house but the windows on the upper floor of the maisonette were much smaller than those on the third floor. Physically, it is not possible that Laura Riding could have jumped from one of these without first levering herself outside and clinging to the window-sill before releasing herself backwards. In a smallish room, with three observers, this is not a credible scenario. The third-floor sash-windows, however, were large enough for Laura to have sat on the sill without immediately causing alarm. The drop, from here, was sufficient to cause death or severe injury.

As for Graves, Laura (Riding) Jackson suggested many years later that he had used the fire-escape, but none of the houses on the west side of the square were fitted with fire-escapes in 1929. The fact that he had to spend a week in hospital being treated suggests a more violent form of descent.[24]

Dr Lake, the surgeon who examined her, was able to say that a complete recovery was not impossible.

Nancy had, meanwhile, tracked Geoffrey down to the foyer of their local cinema. They were both lost and unsure what to do. Geoffrey did not feel much inclination to patch up his marriage with Norah or to go back to his parents; Nancy dreaded the prospect of returning to a lonely life on the boat while Graves devoted himself to nursing Laura. Geoffrey was attached to the children and very fond of Nancy. They decided to set up home together and to see if they could not, cautiously, try to restore the Holy Circle on a new basis.

In ordinary circumstances, this might have been a reasonable hope of how life might resolve itself. But Geoffrey and Nancy were not dealing with ordinary people.

Laura's suicide-leap completed the reversal in her relationship with Graves. He, at first, had been the controller of events. It was he who had brought Laura over from America, taken her to Egypt, moved her to London and gone to Ireland to seek out Geoffrey Phibbs. Now, looking back to what seemed to him the fatal interview with Geoffrey on 1 April, he saw himself as the guilty party. He had driven Geoffrey away. If Geoffrey had not left the Circle – Graves still had no idea that he would have gone in any case – Laura would not have attempted to kill herself. Her full recovery was by no means certain. He saw himself as the man who had destroyed the life of the most remarkable woman he had ever known. No price could be too high for such a crime. There was, from now on, absolutely nothing that he would not do to show his devotion to Laura. His honour was at stake.

CHAPTER FIFTEEN

1929

GOODBYE TO ALL THAT

WHEN T. E. LAWRENCE WROTE TO HIS FRIEND CHARLOTTE SHAW, the wife of George Bernard Shaw, a month after Riding's dramatic leap, about the 'madhouse minds' at Hammersmith, he was full of pity for Graves and the struggle he would face to find the money to support four children and to pay Laura's hospital bills.[1] Commiserating with Graves, he described him to Mrs Shaw as 'a most excellent and truthful person, drowning in a quagmire'.[2]

Lawrence was a prejudiced judge, who saw his friend as the victim of a dangerously powerful woman. But Laura cannot be held wholly responsible for the volatility of Graves's behaviour in the weeks following the accident. Eleven years after the war he remained as nervous and hypersensitive as he had been in the early stages of shell-shock. Now, anguish and guilt deprived him of the ability to make balanced judgements. There was only one honourable figure in his version of the story, and she was the temporarily paralysed victim. Nancy, by allying herself with Geoffrey, had become tainted; their efforts to restore the Holy Circle to peace became, in Graves's mind, a vile conspiracy to bring more sorrow to Laura. She, in the first drugged days when she was lying in hospital, was not against the idea of reviving the Circle in a new form; it was Graves who was determined to force a break with the past. Laura was, perhaps, an unusually willing listener in her weak state. Graves, a persuasive and imaginative interpreter of events, was for some weeks her sole channel of information about Geoffrey and Nancy. Much of her own bitterness towards Geoffrey was based on how Graves chose to present him to her.

★   ★   ★

Initially, the main problem confronting both Graves and Nancy was how to deal with Geoffrey's revelations. The first conclusion the police drew was that Graves, as a jealous lover, had pushed Riding out of the window. When Nancy, as a witness, disproved this version, they moved on to the second possibility, a suicide attempt.

Suicide, in 1929, was a criminal offence for which Laura could be charged and deported. The papers exonerating Graves and charging Laura had already gone to the Home Office when Graves realized what the consequences of saving himself from a charge of attempted murder might be. Fortunately, Edward Marsh, one of the few friends with whom he had never quarrelled, was in a position to help. As secretary to Winston Churchill, then Chancellor of the Exchequer, Marsh was able to negotiate a case for extenuating circumstances which was informally put to the Director of Public Prosecutions in July, and was accepted.[3]

Graves was still unaware of Nancy and Geoffrey's plans to set up home together when he went into the Royal Homeopathic Hospital in Great Ormond Street for treatment on 2 May. Nancy visited him there the following day and explained the new situation, adding that Geoffrey and she both wanted to continue with the Holy Circle. This proposal did not suit Graves's plan to contrive a new future for himself and Laura, away from his wife and the cause of Laura's fatal obsession. On 4 May he sent Nancy two long and confused letters, rejecting their proposal and declaring his own enduring passion for Laura.[4] The handwriting in these letters was wild and they carried a note of desperate insistence.

> I love Laura beyond everything thinkable and that has always
> been so. Our love has always been strong, human, unques-
> tioned, in spite of my muddles. I do not fear her or worship

her or desire to possess her or anything that should not be.

After adding that he had learned enough never to press again on Laura in 'a wrong way', he turned to the subject of the children. By now, clearly, he had decided to make a new life without his family. His plans for them were expressed with a detachment of which his old hero, Samuel Butler, would have been proud. Butler sent the children of Ernest Pontifex in *The Way of All Flesh* to thrive on a fatherless river-life; this was exactly what Graves now proposed for his little brood.

> The children are yours; you are their mother. I am their father, but they are not my charges, I feel, only my friends. I hate being away from them but I do not feel anxious about them in a paternal way. I will always help you with them.

In the spate of letters which poured out following Laura's suicide attempt, many are undated, which makes it difficult to be certain about the exact order of events. Graves had already resumed contact with Laura by 6 May, when Geoffrey and Nancy visited her at the Charing Cross Hospital to try to make their peace. Graves, sending a report of this visit to Gertrude Stein as though he had himself been present, provided his first thoroughly vicious account of Geoffrey (Phibbs) Taylor.[5] Geoffrey, Miss Stein heard, had shown his 'mean goatish little independence' by threatening to throw Laura Riding out of the hospital window if she tried to destroy his relationship with Nancy. But, if this was so, why did Graves need to provide exactly the same details in an account to Laura of a conversation between himself, Nancy and Geoffrey on the *Ringrose* almost a week later?[6] It is likely that Geoffrey's uncharacteristic threat was the product of Graves's own imagination.

To Laura, for the rest of her life, Geoffrey was the devil. To Graves, he became the necessary scapegoat for his own guilt about Nancy and the children. His intention was to go abroad with Laura, to escape scandal and to provide her with a warm climate in which to complete her recovery, as soon as she was fit to travel. Some self-justification had to be made for the abandonment of his family. Geoffrey, a kind and honourable man, was mythologized as the villain whose evil influence had destroyed Graves's own happy relationship with his children and forced him to leave them behind. This bore no relation to the truth but it suited Graves's needs. Three years after Laura's accident, the easy-going William Nicholson was still having to tell his absent son-in-law that Geoffrey, to whom Nicholson was devoted, must not be referred to in correspondence as 'the devil'.

Graves's guilt-driven malice created an ugly situation. It worsened as the summer of 1929 went on. Geoffrey, having been forbidden to visit the World's End cottage with Nancy by an outraged Amy, found that Graves was blocking his efforts to find himself a job. His own naïvety was partly to blame for this. It was not wise of him to enlist Graves's support in seeking work at the *Times Literary Supplement*. Graves's prompt response was to warn the editor, Bruce Richmond, against having anything to do with an unsavoury character called Geoffrey Taylor.[7] Even a bookshop-owner in Oxford who asked Graves to provide a character reference for Geoffrey was warned not to employ him.

The main, and most ludicrous, dispute focused on Geoffrey's library, which was still at the flat. Geoffrey's view was that 175 of his books had not been inscribed as Seizin Press property and were, therefore, reclaimable. Graves refused to return them, saying that the books would cover the cost of having kept him at St Peter's Square for a month; Geoffrey pointed out that he had contributed £34, a fair sum for a month of board and lodging in 1929, and that he had done a good deal of unpaid printing work for the Seizin Press.[8] Changing tack, Graves and Riding pointed out that he had not yet returned the clothes they had allowed him to borrow.

Legal proceedings began on 25 July, when Geoffrey issued a writ for the restoration of all his books. Some had already been sold; a few more dribbled back to him in July and August. A further row in early September centred on the fact that Geoffrey had come in person to the flat to ask for his books, instead of sending a messenger as requested. The suit, which escalated to a summons for Laura to appear in court, was dropped when fifty books were returned to Geoffrey in September. The remainder were among the possessions which were shipped abroad for Graves and Laura Riding at the end of the year. A few remain to this day at the Graves home in Mallorca.

Graves marked his estrangement from Nancy as having begun on 6 May, the date of her visit to Laura in hospital. The letters exchanged in the acrimonious period which followed were the only ones from

Nancy which he chose to keep. All earlier correspondence from her was destroyed.

The letters show, in the circumstances, considerable forbearance. For Laura, Nancy expressed a steady and affectionate concern. If, by mid-August, she was ready to say that she was tired of hearing about 'poor, good Robert and lucky, bloody Nancy', when she was trying to keep herself and the children on eighteen shillings a week, it is hard not to sympathize.[9]

Her requests were reasonable. She wanted Graves to keep the *Avoca* for his own use or for sale and to give her £50 to convert the *Ringrose* into a permanent home for herself, Geoffrey and the children. She asked for help with £30 of outstanding payments on a car which she had bought, and enough money to send Jenny to a school at which she could concentrate on her chosen profession of dancing.

Graves was a willing giver, once he had been persuaded that Geoffrey was not going to stay on the barge. (There was a pathetic and short-lived attempt to deceive him; it was uncovered when Laura's half-sister, Isabel, who had arrived to help care for her, paid an unexpected visit to the *Ringrose*.) Believing Nancy to be living there on her own, Graves told his wife to raise what she could from the sale of the *Avoca*, agreed to pay the rent at Islip and offered £200 a year for the children. This was generous at a time when the demands on his pocket were heavy. Laura's operation and a seven-week stay at the Charing Cross Hospital had to be paid for, and she had insisted on a further four weeks of treatment in a private ward at the Royal Homeopathic Hospital.[10] Graves was thankful, at this point, for the arrival of £100 from Norman Cameron, presented in the tactful guise of a tuition fee for his instruction in mental discipline from Laura.

Even with Cameron's help, the future looked alarming. Until near the end of September, Graves was unaware that his mother was prepared to contribute to her two older grandchildren's school fees. Neither the Graveses nor the Nicholsons could be asked for help with finding a new home abroad for Laura and himself. It was in part financial necessity which made him decide to set aside the lonely business of working at the Seizin Press to write a book which would contain a most saleable commodity, a hard-hitting, firsthand report of life at the Front in the Great War

★   ★   ★

Goodbye To All That was not the first of the British war books to appear. This was C. E. Montague's *Disenchantment*, published in 1924, which was also perhaps the best of a stream of books setting out to expose the futility and folly of war. Herbert Read's *In Retreat*, a concise and objective account, was published in 1925. In 1928 Edmund Blunden's *Undertones of War* was widely praised for its lyrical, elegiac approach. Sassoon's *Memoirs of a Fox-Hunting Man*, also published in 1928, set the scene for the contrast between an idyllic, pre-war world and the savagery of war explored in his semi-autobiographical trilogy. The ferocious social comedy of Richard Aldington's *Death of a Hero*, published in 1929, came nearest to Graves in attitude but it made no claim to be an autobiographical work. Not even Aldington was driven by the angry recklessness of Graves as he set out to uncover and reject the whole of his past life, purging himself of falsehood for a new beginning with Laura Riding, the embodiment of truth.

Goodbye to All That was dictated to Jane Lye in Graves's eyrie study at St Peter's Square while Len, her husband, worked on a mural celebrating Laura's survival in the next-door bedroom. Although Graves never used this method of writing again, he believed that it contributed to the book's 'realistic sound.' Advising a young poet on how to write his memoirs forty years later, he urged him to borrow a tape-recorder. 'The vox humana is a great help,' he wrote to Keith Baines. 'Then correct the result.'[11]

The first draft was completed in two months, during which Graves spent three or four hours of each day at Laura's bedside. Her influence, even when unspoken, was considerable. The candour which gives the book its enduring vitality was fuelled by Graves's sense that she had liberated him from the shackles of duty and obligation. Now, at last, he felt free to say what he liked.

Graves must have known that he was stirring up a hornets' nest at home when he wrote the book. Alfred, busily writing his own memoirs, was dismayed to see his portrayal of the Graves family pre-empted by Robert's far less affectionate account. After failing to induce his son to postpone publication, he began to look into ways of getting the book prohibited. Jonathan Cape, Robert's publishers, had a better idea. They made an offer for Alfred's book, urged him to add a chapter about his disloyal son, and published it in 1930 with the significant title *To Return to All That*.

T. E. Lawrence, who had been shown the book in sections while it was being revised, took a different view. It was, he wrote to Robert on 13 September 1929, full of humour and exactly right in its presentation of 'wounds and nerves'. The characters were all full of life and he was especially pleased by the generous portrait of Sassoon. The construction, too, seemed to him excellent. 'A very good book.'[12]

Lawrence was privileged in being allowed to see the book at an early stage. Haste made Graves careless. When Edward Marsh received his advance copy, only a fortnight before publication, he was horrified to discover that his informal distribution of the quarter of Rupert Brooke's royalties to which, as his editor, he was entitled, had been described as The Rupert Brooke Fund. This, as Marsh ruefully pointed out, would bring droves of needy young poets to his door and, very possibly, the officials from the Inland Revenue. His letter was the gentlest of rebukes; Graves, abashed, promised to get an erratum slip printed, even if he missed the bonus of Christmas sales as a result. The main opponents to the book, however, were two of his oldest friends, Edmund Blunden and Sassoon.

Blunden's friendship with Graves was in disrepair long before he was commissioned to review *Goodbye*. It had already been scored with furious comments and subtitled 'The Welsh-Irish Bull in a China Shop' when he decided to seek Sassoon's views. The book was eventually annotated with some six thousand words of protest by Blunden, Sassoon, Ralph Hodgson and Dr Dunn, the RAMC doctor who had been attached to the Royal Welch.[13] The tone of most of the comments by Blunden and Sassoon is so malicious as to suggest that each was goading the other on for their private entertainment. (Each, we need to remember, was a competitor of Graves in the field of war memoirs; Graves had been an unenthusiastic reviewer of the first volume of Sassoon's trilogy.)

Many of their objections were trivial and irrelevant. Graves's headmaster was praised for having told him that the waste-paper basket was his best friend. Sassoon added several comments on Graves's extreme untidiness as an officer, and on the fact that he enjoyed discussing homosexual subjects. A comment on his having been too bourgeois to understand the difference between a note from Osbert Sitwell and his gamekeeper says more about Sassoon's snobbishness than about Graves's friendship with the Sitwells.

Sassoon was far angrier than Blunden, if we are to judge by the number of annotations that he contributed. He objected to what he saw as a misrepresentation of the events leading to his hospitalization at Craiglockhart, and to the inclusion of a private letter-poem addressed to Graves which contained some light-hearted comments on mutual friends, including Lady Ottoline Morrell. The comments in the poem were harmless – 'jolly Otterleen' was hardly an insult – but Sassoon felt that his confidence had been betrayed. The final straw was a reference to his mother. To the impartial reader, it is hard to see why he should have been so upset by Graves's account of an unidentified woman's attempts to have spiritual contact with her dead son. At the time, when they were both staying with Mrs Sassoon at Weirleigh, Sassoon had been equally bored and embarrassed. But now, in a year when his mother was seriously ill, Graves's mockery seemed blasphemous.

Six days before publication, on 18 November 1929, the publishers were compelled to substitute asterisks for the offending letter-poem and the passage alluding to Mrs Sassoon. But honour had not yet been satisfied. Two months later Sassoon wrote to castigate Graves for a journalistic book written with the help of a conveniently defective memory. After indicating that he was not alone in his objections, he gratuitously added that Graves was still going to be left £300 in his will, unless he made too much by his hack-work to need it.[14]

It was an insulting letter. Graves responded in kind, adding that one of Sassoon's cheques in the summer of 1929 might have spared him the necessity of writing the book. By the spring of 1930 their relationship was in tatters, reduced to insults and self-justifications. The friendship had weakened before the book was conceived. They no longer had anything but their memories of the war in common. Now, even those had become a battlefield.

★   ★   ★

Sassoon's rage, although ungracious, is understandable. *Goodbye to All That* is not a book which can be relied on for its factual accuracy, although Graves was pleased to be told by the military strategist Basil Liddell Hart in 1941 that some of the events which he felt he had imagined had really taken place and that the book was 'magnificently honest'.[15] He offered a defence of his method in 'The Whitaker Negroes', a story which was published in 1956. 'My imagination is not that of a natural liar,' he wrote here, 'because my Protestant conscience restrains me from inventing complete fictions;

but I am Irishman enough to coax stories into a better shape than I found them.'[16]

Laura Riding had little relish for Graves's literary successes when she had no share in them, and it may have been in deference to her feelings that Graves went out of his way in 1930 to dismiss *Goodbye* as a commercial project. In a series of articles for the popular press, he explained that he had taken care to put in everything which people wanted to read about: famous friends, hauntings, murders and royalty.[17] This was unnecessarily self-diminishing. The fascination of the book, even for readers who have no interest in the account of war, is the way in which, like a Victorian novel, it shows the development of a character and the effect on him of events beyond his control. As a child, he is seen in the rigid grip of an old-fashioned, conventional family, exposed to the crushing environment of boarding-school life before being jolted into maturity as a soldier at the Front. Just as the Victorian hero must experience illness or devastating loss in order to discover his true identity, so Graves is seen struggling with poverty and neurasthenia before Laura Riding can deliver him by helping to strip off the false coverings of the past. Only in the Epilogue, addressed to Laura, is the laconic, detached voice of the narrator replaced by that of the poet.

The 1957 edition ends rather flatly with a short summary of events subsequent to 1929. The Epilogue to the original book rang out like a triumphant Last Post, far more in keeping with the mood of defiant rejection.

> . . . no more politics, religion, conversations, literature, argu-
> ments, dances, drunks, time, crowds, games, fun, unhappiness.
> I no longer repeat to myself: 'He who shall endure to the end,
> shall be saved.' It is enough now to say that I have endured.[18]

★   ★   ★

In hospital, one of the presents which had pleased Laura most was a greenish-gold fillet of wire carrying her name in Greek letters which Graves found or had made at a Bloomsbury jeweller's shop. Often cited as an example of Laura's self-importance, it was only a pretty ornament, light-heartedly donned for special occasions. As with so much in their private relationship, the element of playfulness is easily overlooked. There was, however, nothing playful about Laura's behaviour at the hospital, where her demands and expectations drove Graves's sister, Rosaleen, to write of her as a borderline mental case. But her will to recover, however disagreeable an impression it made on doctors and fellow patients, was formidable. On 12 July, after a final month of homeopathic treatment and massage, she was well enough to be brought back in an ambulance to St Peter's Square. Graves, still hard at work on *Goodbye*, was waiting to carry her up to her bedroom. Helped by the Lyes and Laura's half-sister Isabel, he nursed her back to health. By the beginning of September 1929 Graves was able to tell T. E. Lawrence that she was strong enough to walk round a table with the aid of a stick. The time had come to start planning their new life abroad.

Laura had always been adamant that she did not want to return to America. Spain attracted Graves, for whom a Spanish phrase book which he had found and studied as a child had created an enduring interest. To a Latin scholar, Spanish presented the least difficulty of any foreign language; to a lover of etymological conundrums, it was a gold-mine. In the meantime, there was Gertrude Stein to consider.

Miss Stein had been kept informed of the tense situation leading up to Laura's accident. Graves had sent her a telegram on the day of the fall, begging her to come to London. One of the first letters which Laura wrote in hospital was to Gertrude; she was too exhausted to complete it without Graves's help.

Gertrude Stein was the only correspondent in the summer of 1929 who saw it as a benefit of the fall that Laura and Robert would be freed for each other. Her letters show that she liked Robert and admired Laura, 'so poignant and so upright' that she seemed doomed to suffer disillusionment.[19] In her view, their relationship deserved to survive. Her suggestion was that they should make their first step towards freedom by visiting her country home in Provence.

On 4 October Graves, Laura and a masseuse crossed the Channel to France. Rosaleen, who had been excluded from their friendship because of her refusal to stop seeing Nancy and Geoffrey, sent a last sad account to her parents of the abandoned children. (Geoffrey, too, had gone away, on a short academic posting to Cairo which would provide enough money for him to support his new family.)

> Poor little Sam went to Robert's flat up all the stairs to show him a lemonade powder he had and came back saying 'Father gone, Laura gone – all gone.'[20]

During the two weeks which Robert and Laura spent at a small pension near Gertrude's home in Belley, they were still hesitant about their final destination. Miss Stein urged them to stay, but Laura's enthusiasm for her had begun to wane, possibly because she disliked the sense of a rival who was loved for her wit and generosity. There was no room for a second star in this system.[21]

Spain continued to attract Graves; Miss Stein, who had spent some happy months with Alice Toklas on the Balearic island of Mallorca in 1914, aroused Laura's enthusiasm by describing it as 'paradise, if you can stand it'. Graves's researches informed him that the Baleares were identified by the ancients as the islands of pines and that the word derived from their skill with slings. The idea of 'an island of slingers' appealed; so did the prospect of living among people who were descended from the Moors and the Romans as well as the Carthaginians. Gertrude said that they were friendly and honest. The tourists had, so far as Graves and Riding could ascertain, overlooked Mallorca in their zeal for exploring the Spanish mainland.

The two travellers moved on from Provence to Freiburg, where a decision was finally reached to make their way to the island eulogized by Miss Stein. By the end of October they were on the night-ferry from Barcelona to Palma, Mallorca's capital. Graves's former friend, Walter Turner, spoke for the sceptical world on which they had turned their backs in a poem clipped by Graves from the *Sunday Times*:

> Untiring in knight-errantry
> The route from Yeats to Dante
> They rode not upon Pegasus
> But upon Rosinante.[22]

*　　*　　*

Turner's mockery of him as Don Quixote did not trouble Graves. He had already made up his mind to devote himself to serving the woman who, like he, had miraculously survived death. Her own interpretation of the fall as a demonstration of her powers had convinced him, if nobody else, that she was superhuman. Strength of character, rather than the doctors, had enabled her to defy fate and live. But he still blamed himself for the fact that she had been compelled to take such a dramatic step to express her despair about the Holy Circle. The guilty thought remained that, if he had not encouraged Geoffrey to leave them, none of this would have happened. Graves's duty now was to play the part of the guardian angel. Penniless and – with the exception of the Lyes, John Aldridge and Norman Cameron – friendless outside her own country, Laura was his responsibility. From now on, he dedicated himself to protecting her reputation, honouring her with gifts and showing an unquestioning deference to her wishes.

To others, this extraordinary resolve made Graves's behaviour in the 1930s look weak and almost pitiful. He seemed little more than a shadowy footman, a lackey on hand to serve Laura's will. He stopped writing letters, unless they concerned Laura. He delighted in adorning her with jewels and elaborate dresses. He bought property, only to transfer it to the name of his companion. He even agreed to become celibate because Laura no longer wished to sleep with him.

From the outside, the Riding-Graves ménage offered the sorry spectacle of a brilliant and captivating personality stamped out by the ferocious will of a termagant. But Graves had never cared how things looked to the rest of the world. Riding's inflexible certainty about what was right and what was wrong provided him with values in which he could trust. He honestly believed that her supervision was making him into a better – because a more honest – writer. It never seemed to him that there was anything unfair or unequal about their relationship. It was unimportant that he could earn more than she; Riding's contribution was beyond any commercial value.

This was the public case he made. There was also a private, psychological case. It was only by absolute subjection that Graves could absolve himself from a burden of guilt, one that he would never publicly acknowledge. He not only felt guilty about the circum-stances which had led to Riding's fall but about the delicate situation in which his love had placed her as the conspicuous mistress of a married man. He felt guilty, too, about the family he had abandoned. Brought up as a conscience-driven Protestant, he knew that a price had to be paid. The price was his devoted service to Laura Riding. She took the place in his mind of the regiment for which a serving officer had to be willing to sacrifice everything, even his life.

PART THREE

LAURA

CHAPTER SIXTEEN

1930

A LIFE ABROAD

THE FIRST VIEW OF PALMA FROM THE BARCELONA FERRY WAS OF the Gothic cathedral rising above the mirrored image of itself in a turquoise sea. In the light of a late October dawn it looked like a golden fortress, an encouraging symbol of the isolation Graves was seeking.

They spent their first nights in the overblown splendour of the Grand Hotel, their days exploring the town. Even after the benign climate of the south of France, it was a pleasant surprise to walk about in an atmosphere of perpetual summer. The air smelt of orange trees, the light was warm and brilliant. Leaning on a stick, Laura limped beside Graves as he made himself at home by hunting for bargains in the curio shops below the old city walls. The language, a loud, vigorous dialect loosely related to Catalan, was impossible to understand; initially they were relieved to learn of a scattering of English and American couples living on the island. Palma itself offered signs of a thriving German colony, but Laura pronounced her dislike of the German nation with such vigour that Graves had no option but to support her.

It was, ironically enough, a young German, a café artist whom they nicknamed 'the suffering Christ' for his anguished stare, who gave them the idea of looking for a home in Deyá. Palma was too noisy and too chaotic for Graves's taste – he still felt nervous in cities – and neither he nor Laura relished the thought of setting up home in the popular expatriate British suburb of El Terreno. Their appetites were whetted by the young artist's descriptions of Deyá as an unspoilt village in one of the most beautiful parts of the island. It was by the sea, and Graves liked to be within walking distance of a shore. Laura, having little experience of country life, was ready to follow his lead on this hunt for a home. The British Consul, Mr Short, had details of a cottage there which was secluded and available for rent.

The road to Deyá from Palma wound north across a broad plain, bringing the travellers to the rugged mountain setting of Valldemosa, where Chopin, George Sand and her children had stayed for three months in the Gothic monastery. From here, they took the vertiginous coast road which leads north-west to Deyá. They passed above Son Marroig, the palace-farmhouse once owned by the learned and eccentric Archduke Luis Salvador. Ahead, as they came in sight of a distant view of heaped crags above the Soller promontory and a bleak but well-tilled hillside falling away below them, lay the hidden village of Deyá.

Walking along the road past Casa Salerosa, their prospective home, with the sea lying some four hundred metres below them on their left, they caught their first glimpse of a long high ridge, tilled, terraced and crowned, like an Italian hill-town, with a spiralling cluster of rooftops rising to a church and graveyard. This was the upper part of the village. The valley in which the lower streets were concealed from view, showed from above only as a ravine quivering with the silver leaves of Deyá's ancient olive trees. Arriving towards the end of the afternoon, Graves and Riding could see the pale glimmer of charcoal-burners' fires in the dark woods which covered the hillsides encircling the valley. Rising above woods, hillsides and village, in the half-circle of a natural amphitheatre, was a gigantic wall of rock, cutting the village off from the outside world and lending it a sense of drama, of events awaited.

Watching the sun dye the soaring walls of the Teix mountain crimson before they blanched in the ashy glitter of the moon, Graves had a sense of being in the landscape to which he belonged. In its bleakness and simplicity, the combination of mountains, sea and grey rock, Deyá took him back to Harlech. There was no ruined castle here, but this, too, was a landscape made for legends. Deyá corresponds to the Greek word θεά, meaning, goddess. It seemed entirely credible that this place, where the moon shone brightly enough on the Teix's walls to make day of night, should have been chosen for a primitive place of worship. To superstitious souls like Graves and Riding, it was a setting of magnetic power.

There was nothing romantic about Casa Salerosa. The house was situated beyond the southern end of the village. It stood against an unirrigated hillside, which made it damp, and all its windows faced north, which made it cold. Like most Mallorcan cottages, it had a snug inglenook by a fireplace set well back into the building where, burning night and day, a wood-fire fought a losing battle against the clammy atmosphere. Laura, as an invalid in need of cosseting, worked close to the fire; Graves gallantly confined himself to a chillier room at the side of the house in which the Seizin press was installed when it arrived from England. Their talkative landlady, Mariana, was able to provide them with a maid for the equivalent of an English shilling a day. She, in turn, provided the Deyá villagers with an account of the new inhabitants.

It is revealing of the relationship between Laura and Graves that the common assumption was that Laura had come to the island with her butler. This was the unjust result of Graves's determination to secure respect for his companion. Marriage to Nancy had taught him that the woman, in a relationship, is always right and that her word should be law; in old-fashioned Mallorca, a man only took orders from a woman if he was being paid by her. Graves's deference was intended to act as a warning to anybody who dared to question the nature of their relationship. Instead, he led the villagers to suppose that he was in the employ of an eccentric spinster. (In Deyá, the post for newcomers was keenly studied: Riding's insistence on retaining her maiden name added to the confusion.)

The soft climate of their arrival was replaced by a vicious winter of raging winds and driving rain. Salerosa was isolated; Laura, staring out of the windows at the far end of the valley on which any gleam of sunlight seemed always to fall, talked longingly of a new home, and of company. They had few friends left to invite to Mallorca, but news of the extraordinary success of *Goodbye to All That* made it possible to dream of building a house of their own on the far side of Deyá.

Goodbye was published in November 1929, shortly after their arrival on the island. The first impression of 5,000 sold out at once and the book was in its fifth impression by Christmas, after selling 20,000 copies in the first week. In America, it was in its third printing by January 1930.

News spreads quickly in small societies. Within a month of their arrival, Laura and Graves had been befriended by Deyá's most enterprising inhabitant, Juan Marroig Mas, familiarly known as Juan Gelat. His kindness was disarming. He advised them on which village food shops they should patronize, did rough repairs in the house, and showed Graves the rough fisherman's path leading down to the sea-cove, the *cala*, at the foot of the valley. More importantly, he made them feel at home with stories of island gossip and provided the daily company and stimulation without which Laura pined in her semi-imprisoned state.

Gelat seemed to know everybody and to be able to arrange everything. Graves and Laura congratulated themselves on having found such a valuable friend in so short a time.

Dark and strongly built, with a round and smiling face shaded by the black fedora he wore on all occasions, Gelat was a shrewd profiteer with charming eyes, an easy, open manner, and a tolerant wife. He had already worked out the way to gain control in Deyá. His decrepit bus was the village's only form of daily contact with Palma. His diesel engines, set up in a ramshackle warehouse called the Fábrica, provided Deyá's electricity. When Gelat turned his engines off at ten every night, the villagers had to resort to the light of candles and oil-lamps.

Gelat had always been shorter on funds than on money-spinning ideas; Riding and Graves offered a splendid opportunity for him to build up his capital and provide work for his local friends. Most of the ruinous schemes on which they embarked in their six years at Deyá can be traced back to Gelat. Quick to see how their relationship worked, he always put his proposals to Laura, knowing that Graves would subsidize whatever she chose to do. Neither Riding nor Graves were good judges of character. In Laura's admiring eyes, their friend could do no wrong. To Graves, even after he had been bled dry by Gelat's projects, he remained 'an honest rogue'.[1]

They were, from the first, unhappy in Salerosa. Gelat was surely the man who, as they talked about Graves's golden flow of royalties from *Goodbye to All That*, pointed across the valley to a piece of land owned by Don Bernardo Colom, the father of his daughter's fiancé, and suggested that they buy it and build a house there. Foreigners, regrettably, were prohibited from owning land within five kilometres of the sea, but Gelat had the answer. They could register the property in his name. Officially it would belong to him, but what was officialdom between friends? By May, they had put down the first payment for a slab of land on which to build a house.

Their first visitors, Jane and Len Lye, came to stay early in 1930. Placed in a pretty nearby cottage, Ca'n Pa Bo, they were invited to take their meals at Salerosa. Here, although they were probably unaware of it, the Lyes ate their meals with Nancy Nicholson's silver cutlery while sitting on her mother's pretty ladder-back chairs. Graves, having 'borrowed' both canteen and chairs for St Peter's Square from the Islip cottage, had no compunction about carrying them off. He had a passion for silver and Laura deserved the best; Nancy's family owed her something for having been so disagreeable. So, it seems, his argument went. Nancy, who minded the loss of her possessions intensely, never saw them again.

The Lyes were expected to work during their visit. Len, who had designed the wrapper for *Goodbye*, drew book covers for their new Seizin poetry collections; Jane typed out letters, manuscripts and poems. A typist was always needed; when Jane left, Graves persuaded the British Consul's teenage son to take over the job.

* * *

The poetry and prose which Graves produced during his first year in exile reveals a divided mind. As a poet, he was ready unequivocally to declare himself the servant of his personal muse. The poems which appeared as *Ten Poems More* in June 1930 were written during the first winter months at Salerosa. In one of this collection, 'The Terraced Valley', Riding was presented as the mythical queen of Deyá. Here, Graves made a virtue out of his chosen state of servitude. To be deprived of his muse's authoritative and semi-magical presence became an experience of vertiginous terror; searching he,

> . . . found you nowhere in the whole land,
> And cried disconsolately, until you spoke

> Close in the sunshine by me, and your voice broke
> That antique spell with a doom-echoing shout
> To once more inside-in and outside-out.[2]

The poems collected in *Ten Poems More* were the first in which Graves clearly identified the vital qualities of the personal muse, or goddess-inhabited woman, as integrity, ruthlessness, and conviction. Conviction was, of the three, the quality he prized most highly. To others, Riding's confidence often seemed outrageous. When a friend suggested that even she was capable of error, she wrote back – in a letter which she subsequently published – to explain that she was infallible.[3] She could not be too didactic for Graves. The more grandiose her schemes and declarations became, the closer she seemed to come to the primitive goddesses who gripped his imagination. The more pain she caused him, the more he could rejoice in the sense of sacrifice. He did not say this at the time; he may not even have understood it. Thirty years later, he was able to see how he had been deliberately reliving his experiences as a traumatized and bewildered young officer.

> The pride of 'bearing it out even to the edge of doom' that sustains a soldier in the field, governs a poet's service to the Muse. It is not masochism, or even stupidity, but a determination that the story shall end gloriously: a willingness to risk all wounds and hardships, to die weapon in hand.[4]

Graves was romantic, quixotic and imaginative, but he also had a strong streak of common sense. One of Riding's most emphatic assertions was that time had stopped. Looking out of the windows of Casa Salerosa, Graves wished he could believe her. It was, for him, a comforting idea; but nothing could have been more visibly driven by the wheel of time than this little farming village with its inalienable cycle of olive harvests, saints' days and ploughing, the steady 'creak and groan of season',

> In which all moved,
> In which all move yet – I the same, yet praying
> That the twelve spokes of this round-felloe'd year
> Be a fixed compass, not a turning wheel.[5]

In his poetry, Graves was celebrating a new sense of certainty and liberation in the winter and spring of 1930. The pieces which he cobbled together during this period to make a sequel to *Goodbye to All That* show that he was still battling against his past. It is difficult to believe that the same man who was writing the ringing poems he published in June was responsible for the sour confusion of *But It Still Goes On*.

This book was written at the behest of Jonathan Cape who, having found one golden egg from Robert Graves, wanted his goose to keep laying. He had hoped for a cynical diatribe against modern mores, written in the same blackly ironic mood which had proved so successful in *Goodbye*. What he got, in the late summer of 1930, was a collection of short stories, some articles written about *Goodbye* for the *Daily Mail*, a botched play which gave the book its title, and a scrappy but intriguing journal kept by Graves in the months before he left England.

Cape, although he published *But It Still Goes On*, did not like the book. Neither did Graves's parents. There was plenty for them to object to. Graves had, in the first place, inserted a scornful account, omitted from *Goodbye to All That*, of himself as a young soldier on leave, being ordered by Amy and Alfred to push his father's Bath chair to church so that his parents might bask in the reflected glory of a hero from the Front. Criticized in his father's recently published memoirs, Graves took the chance to get his own back, and did so with a most unfilial truculence. When these betrayals were added to the fact that his uncompleted story, 'The Autobiography of Baal', showed God to be the Great Mother disguised as a phallic deity, and that Graves's eponymous play was a fairly frank presentation of lesbian and homosexual relationships, his parents' dismay and disgust were not to be wondered at. Amy could feel justified in having cut Robert out of her will when he left England the previous year.

The aggressive tone of the pieces in *But It Still Goes On* had less to do with Graves's views on society than with the anger he felt towards his parents and his unease about abandoning his children. In January 1930, the return of Geoffrey Taylor from Cairo to become their surrogate father had enraged Graves into deciding that he wanted nothing more to do with them. He wrote to Nancy, waiving his rights, and told her that all future communications would be made through a solicitor. By the summer, when he had completed work on his book, he was regretting his harshness and wondering whether

Geoffrey, 'the devil' as he had now become in the private mythology of Graves and Riding, had succeeded in turning his children against him. The principal reason for a two-month visit to England which Graves and Laura made in August–September 1930 was that he wanted to make peace with his small sons and daughters. (Jenny, the oldest, was then eleven years old.)

Everything was done to make things easy for him. William Nicholson tactfully invited Geoffrey to come away with him on a working trip; Edie asked Graves and Laura to stay with her at Sutton Veny, close to Nancy's new home at Tytherington in Wiltshire.

Against his expectations, Graves was impressed by the way Nancy had taken control of her life. She had rented two adjoining cottages, one for the children, the other for herself and Geoffrey. Here, looking stronger and happier than in the autumn of the previous year, when Graves left England, she was busy printing fabric and book designs on a hand-press, called The Poulk. Her refusal to meet Laura irritated him but he was relieved to find that the children seemed well, high-spirited and full of affection. Nancy raised no difficulties when he asked if he might take David to Mallorca for a year; it was his mother who put an end to this plan. Amy was paying the school bills. She made it clear to Nancy that she would stop doing so if any of the children went to Deyá. If Graves wanted to see his children, he would have to do so in England.

In September, Graves and Riding went to a meeting with Jonathan Cape. Money was needed to pay for the new house which they were building in Deyá; Graves agreed to Cape's suggestion that he should write a popular novel, to be called *No Decency Left*, which would carry on where *Goodbye* had left off. He started work on the novel soon after his return to Mallorca in October.

Jonathan Cape had expected a book by Graves, from which he hoped to make a fortune. What he got, in June 1931, was a book by Laura Riding, based on two drafts by Robert Graves. Laura herself, in a state of happy pride, informed Cape that all the best bits in the book were by her, while Graves admitted to John Aldridge, the artist he had chosen to design the jacket, that 'hardly anything' remained of his own work after Laura's revision.[6] Anxious though she was to forget it later, Laura was sufficiently pleased by her work at the time to ask for the authorship to be revealed and to attempt to get it republished with a sequel by her alone in 1934.[7]

The book did neither of its authors credit. Graves, presumably, was responsible for the basic idea, of an ambitious sales clerk, Barbara Rich, who, in the course of a single day, meets, marries and supersedes the princely ruler of a small democracy, Lyonesse. Barbara's passion for royalty and her love of control clearly stem from Laura, who chose a monarch among her list of 'likes' in 1935 and whose delusions of power had caused her to reject an editing job in the summer of 1930 with the explanation that she could not accept any position less than that of 'a centralizing force'.[8] What is surprising is that Laura Riding believed she had written, or rewritten, a potential best seller.

Cape did not share her enthusiasm. Having commissioned the book, he could not refuse to publish it. *No Decency Left* sold under a thousand copies and Cape published no more of Graves's books until 1949.

From England, the outlook for Graves's literary career seemed bleak. In February 1930, two months after leaving the country, he had been successful enough to be invited to write an article on the sensation of fame.[9] Two years later, his name was hardly ever to be seen in the papers or even in the literary journals to which he had always been a prolific contributor. A few – Auden was among them – were discerning enough to admire the wit and angular curiosity of poems like 'The Legs', which opened:

> There was this road,
> And it led up-hill,
> And it led down-hill,
> And round and in and out.
>
> And the traffic was legs,
> Legs from the knees down,
> Coming and going,
> Never pausing.[10]

The public found such poems baffling, while Graves's mystical poems of devotion to Riding were too abstract to reach beyond a narrow audience. To the general reader, and even to friends like Eddie Marsh, the romantic, haunted poet of the early 1920s and the witty, ironic narrator of *Goodbye to All That* appeared to have been replaced by a sour curmudgeon whose decision to abandon his children and turn his back on his country did not increase his popularity.

With such a reputation, Graves had, by early 1932, become almost as undesirable as his companion to mainstream publishers. It began to look as though, having become one of the most sought-after writers of his generation with the success of *Goodbye*, he might soon be reduced to distributing his works through the Seizin Press, hardly a good economic prospect for a man who was trying to finance the building of a large house. It did not help that, in 1931, rumours began to reach England that Robert Graves had set up a new *ménage à trois*.

CHAPTER SEVENTEEN

1931–1932

SUCCUBI OR SOLID FLESH?

THE STORIES ABOUT EVENTS WHICH TOOK PLACE IN 1931, SHORTLY after Graves and Riding returned from their visit to England, are bizarre. They include allegations of a sexual partnership set up by Riding for Graves's benefit, an illegal abortion for his mistress, the mistress being hounded out of Deyá with a whip, and of her return to become the mistress and, eventually, wife, of Riding and Graves's dear friend, Norman Cameron. The last statement is fact; the rest were a fantastic combination of fiction and circumstantial detail. They can be traced back to one source, Lucie Brown.[1]

In 1976 T. S. Matthews, an ex-editor of *Time* magazine, started to write his second book of memoirs, *Under the Influence*. Seeking material to flesh out the period before he and his young wife arrived on Mallorca in January 1932, and realizing that it would be fruitless to ask Graves himself at this late stage of his life, Matthews got in touch with John Aldridge's ex-wife, Lucie.

Lucie Brown, a slim, dark and, by all accounts, very beautiful woman in her early thirties, had arrived in Palma towards the end of 1931. She had told her relations that she was chaperoning a niece; her plan was to join her youthful admirer, John Aldridge, who was painting landscapes in Deyá at the invitation of Graves and Riding. Aldridge, a shy and charming 27-year-old, as blond as Lucie was dark, had not yet committed himself to her. Their relationship was affectionate, but platonic.

Writing about this episode in her life when she was in her sixties, in 1961, Lucie remembered the awe and excitement she had felt about being with such brilliant people as Riding and Graves. It was, she wrote reverently, 'like stepping into the centre of some Greek Myth and being accepted by the Gods. It was in this setting that John and my hitherto unresolved relationship became solid, blessed and, from then on, as serious as a marriage.'[2] (She married Aldridge in 1940.)

Fifteen years later, when Matthews approached her, she was semi-senile. The main source for her tales – Elfriede Faust – had been dead for forty years. This did not prevent Matthews from using Lucie's story as the basis for his own account of Deyá in the Thirties.

Lucie began the history of her first visit to the village by describing a conversation with a German girl who was staying in her Palma hotel. Elfriede Faust told her – or so Lucie recalled – that she had been living with Riding and Graves since early in 1931, and that Riding had encouraged her to have a sexual relationship with Robert since she 'was denying her own body sexually' to him. Still according to Lucie, Elfriede claimed that she had become pregnant by Graves and that Laura Riding arranged a home abortion: 'she [Elfriede] described how Laura had stood at the bottom of the bed to see that the illegal opp[sic] was carried out.'[3]

These events apparently occurred in the first months of 1931, before Norman Cameron arrived in Deyá and took a fancy to Elfriede. Lucie added a description of how Graves had talked to her about his own fondness for Elfriede and 'his torment of being deeply in love with Laura who wouldn't sleep with him'.[4] She placed this conversation a few days after her own arrival, and suggested it to have been a week or so later that Riding and Graves 'ordered' Elfriede to leave the island. Elfriede did so, but returned immediately and, against Laura's wishes, paid a furtive visit to the cottage in Deyá where Lucie and John Aldridge were staying. Later that night, in one of Lucie's finer descriptive flights, Laura Riding knocked on their door. She was

> dead white and [with] a whip in her hand which she kept cracking – there was no doubt that she could hardly wait to

use the whip. 'Where is Elfreda [*sic*]?' she demanded. I said I'd
no idea, she only came for a few minutes during the morning
– Laura said something scathing to me for treating Elfreda
with civility, Robert was giggling through this scene, and John
seemed unperturbed by it . . . I don't think Elfreda came to
Deyá again.[5]

Germs of fact lie buried in an exotic garden of fantasy and
half-forgotten gossip. How could Laura Riding, as a newcomer to
Deyá, have procured an abortionist, let alone overseen the operation,
in a Spanish, Roman Catholic village in the early Thirties? Not even
Gelat would have been able to help without risking the reputation
he guarded, as a would-be mayor of the village. Lucie appears to
have confused Elfriede's story with the fact that Laura did help to
deliver a child in Deyá two years later: the young mother, Mary
Ellidge, had a well-documented crush on Graves. The reference to
Laura's whip is evidently an embellishment of the cane on which
Riding still leaned for support in 1931. Elfriede's banishment, said to
have been to the Canary Islands, shows consideration for her fragile
health, not anger. Elfriede was tubercular, and Deyá was damp in
the winter months.

A few facts remain. Elfriede Faust was invited to come and live
at Casa Salerosa for a short time in 1931 when Graves and Riding
were feeling particularly friendless. Sexual relations between them
had been, of necessity, delicate since the injuries to Laura's back and
pelvis. By 1933 Riding was ready to make a virtue of necessity and
declare that 'bodies have had their day'.[6] But she had not, even by
then, entirely rejected sex; a letter which she wrote to John Aldridge
in 1933 has an addition in Graves's handwriting. It records the fact
that he and Laura have just enjoyed 'two fucks'. Graves inserted
the word 'lovely'.[7] Given the candour of this disclosure, and of all
Graves's correspondence about his love-life, it seems strange that,
when he wrote to John Aldridge in the summer of 1931, he only said
that Elfriede was living with them and that John would like her.[8] By
the summer, Elfriede was supposed to have borne him a child which
had been aborted in their home.

Looking back on the years when Laura decided that sex was for
those who lacked the power of thought, Graves recalled a period
of enforced celibacy which he had not enjoyed. 'Chastity in man is
obviously unhealthy but it gives one a sort of morbid magic . . .' he

wrote to his second wife in 1944, when she was nursing their third child in hospital. 'I know I was in a very bad state during those years with Laura . . . although I did learn to think.'[9] Confirmation of this can be found in Riding's own words. Late in 1933 she told a correspondent that Graves led a celibate life and that his 'brutal lapses', meaning his periods of sexual frustration, had never lasted long enough for him to find a sexual partner.[10] Why should Riding have said this, if Graves had already had a sexual partner living in their home?

Everything about Riding and Graves's relationship points away from Lucie Brown's account. He, at thirty-six, had only slept with two women before he came to Deyá, his wife and Laura. In his attitude to sex he remained a puritan, guilt-ridden and uneasy. The poems which he wrote while Elfriede was living at Salerosa suggest that he was tormented by his desires, not that he consummated them. In 'The Succubus', he warned himself against the danger of impure thoughts by conjuring up a hideous and predatory female 'with paunched and uddered carcase'. This 'hot-faced hag' seemed to be the unmasked face of his own longings.

Flesh, is she truly more gross than your lust is gross?[11]

Here, as in 'Down, Wanton, Down' a witty castigation by the poet of his penis for attempting to subvert his noble thoughts, Graves was struggling to extinguish his sensuality, not recording an affair with Elfriede Faust.

He was, and remained, unusually attractive to women, not least because he admired them so wholeheartedly. The most likely truth seems to be that Elfriede, a lively, naughty girl Graves drew on for his portrait of Erica, a young witch who appears in the novel *Seven Days in New Crete* (1949), was invited to Salerosa both for company and to give practical help, and that she fell in love with Graves. There are no real grounds for supposing that the relationship ever went beyond a light flirtation. In the spring of 1931 Elfriede happily transferred her devotion to their new visitor, the tall, witty and unattached young Scottish poet, Norman Cameron.

★   ★   ★

Cameron was at a loose end after two years of working in Nigeria. England seemed unadventurous, so he decided to accept his friends' invitation to Mallorca.

They looked more elegant than when he had known them in London. Laura had started wearing old-fashioned Mallorquin dresses in rich velvets, while Graves, somewhat against his inclination, had been coaxed into exchanging his flannel trousers for a suit or, at the least, a buttoned waistcoat and trousers which gave him the look of a handsome Irish bartender. (Socks were his sticking-point; he would do almost anything to please Laura but he would not, short of a dinner in Palma, put on a pair of socks.) To Cameron, it was hard to imagine more agreeable companions with whom to spend the rest of his life. Laura glowed with happiness when she was admired and applauded; Cameron had never doubted her brilliance. Her demure outrageousness was gracefully countered by the wilder humour and mischievous intelligence of Graves. In the spring of 1931, when *Poems 1926–1930* had just been published by Heinemann and Riding was still merrily improving *No Decency Left*, they had everything to look forward to. They were full of jokes and plans. They were even able to offer their guest a pretty girlfriend, although Riding had a few warning words to offer about the dangers of sex to the brain. (Cameron, like many of the guests who followed him, concluded that what Laura did not know about was unlikely to trouble her.)

Deciding to stay, Cameron made an offer for a house, Ca'n Pa Bo; Laura persuaded him, instead, to buy the plot of land next to their own and save them from the horror of having a stranger as a neighbour. Cameron, who was not a strong character, agreed. Ca'n Torrent, his bungalow, was built alongside Graves and Riding's half-completed home.

They called it Canelluñ, a slightly inaccurate translation of the Mallorquin for 'the far house', thinking, perhaps, of the distance it stood from Salerosa, on the opposite side of the Deyá valley. Set a stone's throw back from the road to Soller, it lay beyond the village outskirts and almost directly above the steep fisherman's track down which Graves strode, every day, for a short swim and, occasionally, the chance to stretch out naked on a concealed ledge. The garden, some two acres of English nostalgia, was laid out by Graves, who had a profound feeling for nature and its tranquil, soothing cycle of birth and death. They designed the house together, advised by Gelat. Clad, in the local style, with rough slabs of limestone and roofed with tiles, Canelluñ was never pretty. Its charm was in the ingenious features which its makers took pleasure in contriving for it. (Neither Riding nor Graves had ever owned a house before, if Graves's tiny Harlech cottage is discounted.) The kitchen cupboard hid a shaft and suspended bucket to haul up drinking water from a small well; the roof of a water-tank built at the side of the house provided a terrace on which to sit or dance on summer evenings. The floors were covered with gleaming, honey-coloured tiles; every room held a surprise: a cupboard with curved wooden doors, an unexpected niche.

On the lower floor, beyond the kitchen and hall, the Seizin press was set up in a small room which later became a library. Graves, looking for somewhere he would not be disturbed, made his study in the cool room behind this. Talismanic objects still crowd the room: the gold face of an ancient sundial, a batik by Len Lye of chaos and energy whirling out of an eight-branched tree. Graves wanted no view to disturb him; instead, his desk faced Lye's painting and a whitewashed wall. Laura, who often chose to work at odd hours of the night, preferred an upstairs study, next to her bedroom. They always, from the first year at Canelluñ, had separate bedrooms; nevertheless, a connecting cupboard provided the possibility of discreet exchanges.

House-designing was an enjoyable but expensive pastime; Graves spent the last of his royalties from *Goodbye to All That* with cheerful indifference. One week 4,000 pesetas (a sum equivalent to £2,600 today) went missing in the accounts for work being done by Gelat's men at Canelluñ. Full of embarrassment, Graves drew Gelat's attention to the fact, and was told that there had been a small error which would be adjusted. No further questions were asked.

A new threat to Graves's pocket developed in the summer of 1931. Gelat brought news that the previous owner of the Canelluñ site, Don Bernardo Colom, had been approached by some (probably mythical) Germans who wanted to build a hotel on the sea side of Canelluñ. The only way to defeat them was for Graves to buy the land himself. The area in question covered just under 36,000 square metres; the purchase, as always, would be registered in Gelat's name. To recoup their outlay, Gelat suggested that they ought to consider making a proper road down to the beach to replace the old Deyá track. The government would be sure to purchase it from them at a profit. (In the meantime, although he did not tell them this, it would be of great service to the smuggling operations which were carried on along that part of the coast.) How were they to fund the road? Gelat had the answer: by selling plots of the – still unpurchased – land of Don Bernardo Colom to their prosperous English friends.

Graves was full of enthusiasm for these schemes when he saw how happy they made Laura. Norman Cameron, who later felt that he himself had gone 'slightly mad' during that summer, agreed to invest 'an unspecified amount of money (in L. R.'s expectation, an amount limited only by my total then available capital)' in the new ventures.[12] Luna Land, as Laura's new domain was to be called, was envisaged as becoming an informal university devoted to teaching her apocalyptic view of life. They talked about a series of educational books to be written by Graves and Cameron under Riding's editorial supervision. The dictionary on which she had once planned to work with Geoffrey Phibbs reappeared as a Luna Land project.

Talk of educational projects turned Graves towards the idea of improving on Dickens's best-known novels. Dickens, in his view, had been a hack with a good story to tell; the best thing he could do was to prune away everything but the plot. Norman Cameron set to work on revising *The Pickwick Papers*, while Graves chose *David Copperfield*.

The venture was, in publishing terms, a disaster (it sold 306 copies in England and was never taken up in America) but Graves nevertheless enjoyed it. Norman Cameron had become one of his dearest friends and this semi-collaboration gave them the chance to indulge in daily discussions about poetry, life and Laura as they walked down to the shore or up through the live-oak forests to the Teix mountain's narrow paths. (Laura, even after her recovery, was no walker; she regarded it, like sex, as a waste of energy.)

Sadly, at a time when Graves was working on a book about a neglected and unhappy child, his behaviour towards his own eleven-year-old David became singularly cruel. Knowing that Nancy was upset at just having been cited in Geoffrey Taylor's divorce suit, David wrote to explain that he did not want to leave her to visit his father in the autumn, as Graves had proposed. Graves was furious. He wrote back to tell David that he was no longer his father's son, since he clearly cared so much more for his mother, and even for his grandmother. The effect of such a letter on a confused and withdrawn child must have been considerable.

Graves was still in a state of unreasoning fury with his family when Alfred Graves died in December 1931 and was buried at Harlech. He sent no condolences. He carried the war further in the following year, sending bitter and accusing letters to all of his siblings, chiefly on the theme of their failure to share his estimation of Laura Riding as the noblest of women. But, behind the bluster and aggression, there was a longing for reconciliation. He continued to beg for the children to be allowed to visit him; in a letter to his brother John, he admitted to a wish that Amy would drop her disapproving stance to 'come and see me and kiss me and be friends and go for long walks and enjoy the beautiful scenery'.[13]

★   ★   ★

By the spring of 1932, when Graves and Riding moved into Canelluñ, a Deyá group had begun to consolidate. Norman Cameron and John Aldridge were joined by Lucie Brown and a young American couple, Tom and Julie Matthews, together with their two small sons.

Matthews, having taken Riding for a woman in her forties, was amazed to discover from Graves that she was only thirty-one, born on the same day in 1901 as Matthews himself. Illness, work and two years in a damp cottage had taken their toll of Laura; Tom Matthews had, by comparison, led a charmed life. A handsome, sleek young man, he had skimmed through his time at Princeton and Oxford and married Julie Cuyler, his pretty childhood sweetheart. Before being hired by *Time* magazine, he was employed by Edmund Wilson to work on the *New Republic*. Wilson, who liked Tom and Julie enough to include them in his notional perfect dinner party with, among others, Scott and Zelda Fitzgerald, criticized them only for being a little too orderly, too well-regulated, and too rich.

Matthews was not quite so tranquil as he looked. Before coming to Mallorca, he and Julie had been enthusiastic followers of that consummate charlatan mystic, Geroge Ivanovich Gurdjieff. The novelist Katherine Mansfield had joined the Gurdjieff Institute in Fontainebleau shortly before her death in 1923; Matthews came to Deyá in search of a quiet house in which to write Mansfield's biography.

Chance brought Tom and Julie to Salerosa, where Matthews made the mistake of identifying Graves, while admitting that he had never heard of Laura Riding. This went down badly; Graves took his revenge by refusing to remember that Tom had once visited World's End Cottage with their mutual Oxford friend, Mary Somerville. Having learned to show a proper degree of awe at being allowed to know Laura, Matthews and his family were allowed to take over

Salerosa while Graves and Riding moved for a month to the far less accessible Ca'n Pa Bo – it stood high on the steep hillside of Deyá – until Canelluñ was completed.

The villagers watched these shifting patterns with interest. They had long since recognized their error in supposing Graves to be Miss Riding's butler: Gelat had made it clear that it was Señor Graves, not his friend, who had the money. Eyeing his elegant clothes, his fine new house and the two maids who now came to clean and wait at Salerosa, the local people grew attentive in their courtesies. The marked contrast in their greetings to him and to Laura infuriated Graves into taking action. He had long been convinced that women had a better right to be property owners than their menfolk. (Nancy and his mother both held this view, as did Edie Nicholson.) As the owner, a woman achieved independence and a measure of esteem; this was what he wanted for Riding. He had, besides, not yet made sufficient compensation for the pain and hardship he had caused her: her slight limp and difficulty in sitting without support were daily reminders of the fall, for which he still blamed himself. In 1932 restitution was made. Everything which Graves had purchased was transferred nominally to his companion. From now on, Riding could boast that she let Graves work in her home and that their friends stayed in her houses. This gift was no less than Graves was ready to offer any of the muses of his later years. It was one of the ways in which he chose to honour the women he venerated. In exchange, he expected their loyalty.

Sinister though even the most normal events came to seem in the later accounts of Lucie Brown and Tom Matthews, these early days of the Deyá group were in many respects easy and agreeable. Laura, surrounded by an admiring coterie and in charge of all their plans, was content. So, if he could escape to the privacy of his study, was Graves.

Laura worked late and often did not rise until midday; Graves's writing day usually began at seven in the morning, when the air was cool and there were no visitors to disturb him. He wrote fast, with fierce concentration, scratching across the paper with one of a fat jar of steel-tipped pens. He had no superstition about his writing materials, only about the objects which surrounded him. Many of his best poems started life on the back of old bus tickets, restaurant receipts and shopping lists. Rejected work went into the basket only when, always frugal with his own needs, he had used both sides of the paper, often for completely different work. The revised manuscripts were read again and corrected by Laura before being taken, on Gelat's bus, to a typist in Palma.

Life was not all work. They went to Palma every week. Tom and Julie Matthews went, furtively, more often, to play tennis, while Aldridge and Cameron researched the town bars with Lucie and Elfriede. Graves went to Palma principally for the fun of bargain-hunting. He was a happy man on the days he returned to Deyá loaded with household ornaments, gifts for friends and sparkling buttons for Laura's endless supply of new dresses.

In the evenings, before a dinner which Graves, always domestic, often prepared and cooked, the group met for drinks at the old café in Deyá opposite Gelat's business premises. The atmosphere here, sitting among the villagers who watched them with opaque interest, was light, with word quips, dear to both Graves and Laura, as the principal form of humour. Tom and Julie Matthews, for example, were temporarily renamed 'the Ben Beholdens' because they had rashly spoken of themselves as beholden for kindnesses received. Occasionally there were heated disputes: Aldridge was attacked by Laura for claiming that a squid, a decapod, differed in any way from the eight-tentacled octopus. (Laura's fits of contrariness were subsequently referred to by Graves as her 'octopus days'.) Cameron, on another occasion, was rebuked for failing to agree that a fluke was the same thing as a fake. Graves, whatever his private thoughts, invariably took Laura's side. Truth, as he had learned and their friends had not, was whatever Laura said.

The café visits often ended with a game of a local form of blackjack introduced by Gelat, in which Gelat always won and both Riding and Graves grew feverishly excited about their losses. Often, surely, they discussed the grand development plan for the road and Luna Land into which Tom Matthews, too, had now been drawn.

This halcyon period was short-lived. In March 1932, partly from a residual streak of prudence, partly from a sense that Elfriede Faust was not being kindly treated by Laura, Norman Cameron decided to leave Deyá and support his poetry-writing by getting a job in an advertising agency in London. Anxious to honour his investment promises, he presented Riding with the unfinished Ca'n Torrent house, adding a further 20,000 pesetas for completion and 10,000 for the laying of water-pipes. This was ill-received, as was his subsequent marriage to Elfriede. Five years later, when Elfriede was dead, his desertion was at last forgiven.

He was the first to go. Two months later, Lucie Brown, unhappy in a society in which, in the inimitable spelling of her memoir, 'Laura held the reigns in all things everyone cow towed to her', returned to England. The Matthewses followed in June. Their place was taken by a new couple.

Eirlys Roberts, a thin, quiet, good-looking girl with dark hair and amused eyes, was in her third year of reading Classics at Cambridge when her friend Jacob Bronowski begged her to accompany him to Deyá so that he would not have to be alone, as he supposed, with Laura Riding.

Cambridge entered a brilliant literary phase in the early Thirties and Bronowski was one of the brightest stars. Riding, delighted by his flattering review of her 1930 collection of poems, *A Joking Word*, had written to thank him; a correspondence led to an invitation to visit Deyá and work with her.

Riding had been looking for a secretary and acolyte; Bronowski, although she was displeased by his air of intellectual superiority, seemed a likely candidate. Shortly after his arrival, Bronowski was drawn into helping his hostess with work on an occasional journal, 'The Critical Vulgate', to which she wanted his Cambridge friends to contribute. The 'Vulgate's' aim was to pronounce on values. The problem, inherent from the start, was that only one person, the editor, would have authority over those pronouncements. Graves, as the associate editor, allowed Riding to speak for him. On values, he followed her lead unquestioningly.

Bronowski's extreme self-confidence grated on Graves, particularly when the young man offered to beat him in any competition of writing ballads or nursery rhymes. Graves was, on the whole, modest about his poetry in public, but this challenge stung his professionalism as badly as when somebody was foolish enough to query his knowledge of Latin. Eirlys seemed to him the more agreeable character; he liked her for sharing his interest in Roman history. Eirlys, in turn, was quicker than Bronowski to notice how, even when Graves was washing up plates or peeling vegetables, his mind was always busy. He never seemed to stop thinking about his work; his thoughts, it seemed to her, were more real to him than anything taking place in the room where he stood. Riding was far less detached. Eirlys was intrigued by the contrast.[14]

After a visit of a few weeks, Bronowski and Eirlys Roberts went home in August. They had enjoyed their stay enough to promise to return the following summer, when their time at Cambridge was finished.

★   ★   ★

Graves had good reason to be distracted during their visit. A month before they left, Don Bernardo Colom came to him with a demand for an instant cash part-payment on the land below Canelluñ. He wanted £1,500. If he did not get it he was ready to take money from the German property developers who, he said, still wanted to build a hotel near the beach. Graves had no money. He asked for a postponement of five months. At the end of the summer he made his decision. From the books on his study shelves, he pulled down his classical dictionaries and a companion to Latin studies, together with the works of the chroniclers of Imperial Rome. For the rest of August and most of September, he shut himself in his study and plotted out a novel about the intriguing and little-known life of the Emperor Claudius.

To outward appearances, the mood in January 1933 was festive when Graves agreed to a large 35,000 peseta mortgage on Canelluñ (approximately £24,000 today). His naïvety had, even by his standards, been breathtaking; the only explanation can be that he was desperate not to disappoint Laura's dreams about Luna Land. The mortgage funder, provided by Gelat, was Don Bernardo himself, lending out the money to buy his own land at a little above six per cent interest and demanding full repayment in six months' time.

But a celebration seemed in order. They had just received the good news that John Aldridge's mother was willing to invest £600 in the road-building scheme; they had also found a new publisher. Arthur Barker, an idealistic young man who had recently formed his own company, was ready to publish three new books by Laura, the abridgement of David Copperfield and Graves's most recent poems. All of these were due to appear in 1933 and Barker, fondly named Arthur by by Laura, also agreed to publish 'The Critical Vulgate'. (He had not been told quite how large this small journal had become.)

The only drawback was that Barker could not offer to pay well for publishing their projects. *Claudius* would have to salvage their fortunes. There was no visible alternative. This time, Graves decided to write his book alone.

CHAPTER EIGHTEEN

1933–1935

CLAUDIUS, AND A COURT

FRAUGHT AS THEY WERE BY ECONOMIC WORRIES, GRAVES AND Riding offered a warm welcome to visitors who were prepared to make themselves useful. The autumn of 1932 brought George Ellidge and his newly pregnant wife Mary to their door. A good-looking and bold-eyed girl, Mary cultivated a modest appearance for her first weeks on the island, hiding her statuesque curves under a flowing green cape and coiling her auburn hair around her ears in the manner of a Victorian governess. Her husband, a small, bright-eyed man with a charming smile and voice, made no objection when Riding explained that he must let his wife use her maiden name if they were to be friends. Nothing troubled George; he agreed at once, and Mary created a still better impression when she said that she was a trained typist. It was settled that, in exchange for free lodging at one of Gelat's village houses, George would work with Laura on *14A*, her *roman-à-clef* about events in St Peter's Square, while Mary would type Graves's novel.

The two Claudius books, *I, Claudius* and *Claudius the God*, are rightly the best-known of Graves's novels. They tell an extraordinary and engrossing story; the story of their making is of equal interest.

Graves wrote them in the year when Riding chose to end their sexual relationship, while still expecting him to act as her principal advocate and provider of subsidies. The reason she gave for this was that sex was a threat to the intellect and to industry. But, while he was demoted to the role of being her dearest friend, Graves can hardly have failed to observe that the men with whom Riding liked to work, closeting herself for hours of private discussion, were young and handsome. Matthews and Cameron were both good-looking. John Aldridge was beautiful enough to have been a film star if he had not been an artist; Ellidge was well-known for his attractive personality.

To some extent, then, Graves must have suffered a good deal in 1933 as he watched Riding flirting, first with Ellidge, and then with the man she often said that she loved best of them all, John Aldridge. We will never know whether Riding was deliberately hurting Graves by her behaviour, or whether she took his cheeerful, stoical manner at face value and assumed that he could cope with anything. She had heard him talking about his time in the trenches, his belief in the virtue of soldiering on; it must have been tempting for her to goad him, to see just how much this obedient worm of hers would take before it turned. The superficial answer was, seemingly, anything.

Graves had not altered his commitment to Laura Riding, and he still believed in her power, if she was helped, to influence events. He accepted her decisions, laughed at her somewhat studied jokes, and continued to defend her like a tiger against any sign of criticism. Publicly, he earned his friends' light scorn by his show of total adoration; privately, he knew exactly who controlled whom. *Claudius* is about a man who, surrounded by powerful women, achieves the position of ultimate authority without their realizing it. His manner towards them is almost craven, disguising a sharp intellect and an ability to manipulate events.

This interpretation is borne out by the violence of Laura Riding's response to the *Claudius* novels. It was not just a question of jealousy: *Goodbye to All That* had been enormously successful, and she had not punished Graves for it. But she detested the *Claudius* books from the moment that she first looked at the typescripts; they were said to be boring and unreadable.[1] They could not be mentioned in her presence; reviews had to be hidden from sight. What, one wonders, made these books so different from Graves's autobiography? Was it that they offered too harsh a reflection?

⋆   ⋆   ⋆

Claudius first took hold of Graves's imagination in September 1929 when he was arranging to leave England with Riding. He had just finished writing *Goodbye* and his mood was cynical. Claudius, in his early sketch for a possible book, was an ardent Republican, determined to expose the corruption of the Roman Empire and to give its leadership back to the proletariat. Where all previous historians agreed that Claudius was poisoned by his last wife, Agrippina, Graves planned to make him commit suicide and then to reveal him as the true author of 'The Pumpkinification of Claudius', a vicious satire about the readiness of ignorant people to make a god out of an idiot emperor. (The satire had in fact been written by Seneca, in revenge for his exile from Rome.)

Writing the idea up in his diary on 5 September 1929, Graves saw the book as an 'interpretative biography'.[2] As with all his subsequent novels, its first and strong appeal had been as a mystery, a puzzle to be solved. What was it that had turned Claudius, a mild and apparently simple-minded man, into a bloodthirsty autocrat, and caused him to marry a niece he hated? The answer Graves found in 1929 did not satisfy him; he abandoned the project.

Graves was by then already fairly well read in Roman history but he had not yet immersed himself in it. By the end of 1932, he was more at home in ancient Rome than in the dining-room at Canelluñ. Accused of having merely dipped into Suetonius and Tacitus for his accounts of Claudius, Graves asked his readers to note that he had also read Dio Cassius, Pliny,

> Varro, Valerius Maximus, Orosius, Frontinus, Strabo, Caesar, Columella, Plutarch, Josephus, Diodorus Siculus, Photius, Xiphilinus, Zonaras, Seneca, Petronius, Juvenal, Philo, Celsus, the authors of the *Acts of the Apostles* and of the pseudo-gospels of Nicodemus and St James, and Claudius himself in his surviving letters and speeches.[3]

It was not an empty boast. Eirlys Roberts, who read the typescript of *I, Claudius* for classical errors when she and Jacob Bronowski returned to Deyá late in 1933, was able only to query the coloured hem of a prostitute's robe. The authenticity of Graves's Rome astonished her. In conversation, he had given her no hint of the breadth of his knowledge.

Scholarly detail is not beyond the capacity of any hard-working writer. The strength of the *Claudius* books is in the personality of their imaginary author, the reticent, erudite Emperor in whom Graves recreated himself. He did so with superstitious care. In 'To Bring the Dead to Life', a poem written shortly after the publication of *Claudius the God*, he pretended to feel alarm at the hold which his hero had come to exert over him.

> Assemble tokens intimate of him –
> A ring, a purse, a chair:
> Around these elements then build
> A home familiar to
> The greedy revenant.
>
> So grant him life, but reckon
> That the grave which housed him
> May not be empty now:
> You in his spotted garments
> Shall yourself lie wrapped.[4]

This was the very opposite of the truth; writing about Claudius gave Graves the energy to continue with the punishing and masochistic course on which he set himself when he joined forces with Laura Riding. He was a man of uncommon, exuberant intelligence, who had trained himself never to let it compete with Riding's need to be the centre of attention and to be right about everything. Riding was not always right, and Graves knew it; nevertheless, he supported every assertion she made.

Claudius, for a whole year, offered him intellectual liberty and an escape from the exhausting role to which he had committed himself. He was still, on a few sweet occasions, allowed to share Riding's bed, just often enough to prevent him from straying; it was more usual for him to be called into her room to perform some small service, the finding of a lost piece of jewellery, the offer of a reassuring presence on a stormy night, a checking of her fire-escape rope. (Riding had a terror of storms and fires.) He knew that she was attracted to other men; she made no secret of it in her writings.

Still deeply in love with her, Graves knew Riding well enough to recognize the pointlessness of trying to influence or alter her. Instead he took refuge in his book. Their visitors noticed that he was like a man in a dream. He went through the motions of laying the table, laughing at jokes, accompanying them on trips to the village café; his eyes were remote. He seemed to be looking at another scene than the one before him.

As Graves became Claudius, so his subject inevitably came to share some of his author's habits and obsessions. The historical Claudius took no part in the campaigns of his brother Germanicus which Graves made his fictitious Emperor describe in detail. When Graves wrote that 'soldiers really are an extraordinary race of men, as tough as shield-leather, as superstitious as Egyptians and as sentimental as Sabine grandmothers',[5] he was thinking of the men who had served under him at the Front. For Claudius's defects, his stammer, his moments of memory loss, he drew on his own weaknesses. For the conversations of the young Romans in the book, he thought back to the squabbles at Erinfa in the long summer holidays of his adolescence. And when we find Claudius proudly quoting the Graves family motto, 'Aquila non captat muscas', in a public letter to the Romans, the figure bent over the desk in Canelluñ comes still more clearly into view.

These are some obvious points of identification. The more intriguing ones concern Claudius's account of his formidable grandmother, Livia, and Messalina, his promiscuous second wife. Graves cannot have been wholly aware of his betrayal of the woman to whom he proclaimed his unswerving devotion but it is impossible to read his descriptions of Livia, and even of Messalina's treatment of her credulous and adoring husband, without sensing that he was frequently exorcising either a personal experience or an unspoken suspicion.

Livia, referred to as 'the great Livia' in a later novel, *Count Belisarius*, is said to be 'an abominable woman' in the first pages of *I, Claudius*. As an empress who seeks deification to escape punishment by the gods for her crimes, Livia is hard to admire. In her daily life, she bears a striking resemblance to Riding at her most imperious. In her home, like Laura at Canelluñ, she imposes a regime of daily study and hard work. Like Laura, but without her unpredictable moods of gay indulgence, Livia has 'a faculty for making ordinary easy-going people feel acutely conscious in her presence of their intellectual and moral shortcomings'.[6] Describing Livia's aspirations, Graves again drew on his knowledge of Riding. 'Most women are inclined to set a modest limit to their ambitions; a few rare ones set a bold limit. But Livia was unique in setting no limit at all to hers, and yet remaining perfectly level-headed and cool in what would be judged in any other woman to be raving madness.'[7] This sounds startlingly like the woman who declared that she alone was 'infallible'. Even Livia's obsession with becoming a goddess became a reflection of Riding's demands for rich gifts and clothes, not only from Graves but from all their visitors. Riding, in the semi-deified state to which Graves had assisted her, regarded these offerings as tributes.

Graves had wanted others to see Riding as a more than human being, but he had never expected her, in her position of divine authority, to forbid him to sleep with her. Hoping for a change of mind, he resigned himself to celibacy. His bitterness surfaced in the fictionalized version of events. Messalina, too, persuades her husband that work should come before sex. She asks to be allowed to have a room to herself so that she can study Imperial papers at night. Claudius agrees.

> [Messalina] moved over to the New Palace that very evening. And for a long time I said nothing further, hoping that she would come back to me. But she said nothing, only indicating by her tender behaviour that a very fine understanding existed between us. As a great concession she did sometimes consent to sleep with me.[8]

On other nights Messalina sleeps with one of her lovers. Given the closeness to truth of the other events in the relationship between Claudius and his wife, it is quite possible that the young empress's promiscuity reflected Graves's worst fears about Laura Riding.

In fiction, he was free to show that he, not Riding, controlled their lives. Claudius uses his weakness and his vagueness as a cover, to help him to survive. In fact, the important decisions are taken by him. Livia cannot become a goddess without Claudius's assistance; she has to beg him to help her. When Messalina's treachery is discovered, her future depends on Claudius. Everything, finally, rests with him. It was this, even more than the portraits of herself, which Laura Riding must have found as unbearable as if he had jeered to her face.

★　★　★

Graves was always capable of concentrating on two or three projects at once. While most of 1933 was taken up by work on *I, Claudius*, he also found time to rewrite a book about the war by a Welsh miner's son, Frank Richards. There was nothing in the job for Graves but kindness and, eventually, a few pounds, but Richards had touched him in 1929 with his admiration for *Goodbye to All That* and pleased him now with his straightforward account of life in the ranks. It provided, Graves believed, a necessary balance to the officers' memoirs which had, until now, dominated the literary scene. He usually let Riding do all the rewriting of work by their friends; this was a private project. He spent two months on it and found both this book, *Old Soldiers Never Die*, and its successor, which he also rewrote, an enthusiastic publisher. He modestly waited until 1964 to write an Introduction in which he admitted his own contribution.

His other work was done for Riding. Whatever the relief that writing about himself as Claudius gave him, Graves could not begin to put a historical novel in the same category as his contributions to her 'Vulgate'. This, in his view, was a work of real importance, a communal manifesto which would spread Riding's clear values to every level of society. He felt nothing but pleasure whenever she asked him to take time off his novel-writing to contribute to it. In March 1933 he wrote a long and thoughtful essay on the Romantic poets; in May he contributed an erudite and charmingly whimsical article on his favourite people from the past. He chose John Skelton, Sir Thomas Wyatt, and, with what may have been an affectionate dig at Laura, a Protestant parson with a driving ambition to change the world.[9]

The high spot of the spring of 1933 was a drive down their newly completed road to the shore. The low spot was that Arthur Barker, the young publisher who seemed ready to devote himself to Graves and Riding, and who accompanied them on this ceremonial drive, had begun to express alarm about the vastness of the 'Vulgate' project. A book, and this was only to be the first 'Vulgate' volume, of more than a thousand pages of essays, almost all of them rewritten in Riding's slightly baffling prose, was not an appetizing project. Only Laura's promises that the *Claudius* books, too, would be his, kept poor Barker from flight. Even so, he disgraced himself shortly after his visit by making it sound as though he felt Robert Graves to be a more important person than Laura Riding. This was not an acceptable attitude. Both Riding and Graves were quick to chasten him.

John Aldridge and Lucie Brown came back to Deyá in the early summer. Laura was pleased by Aldridge's request to paint her portrait; Graves was delighted by the jacket illustration which Aldridge sketched out for *I, Claudius*, and happy to be reunited with the gentlest and most affectionate of all their friends. It often seemed to him now that John Aldridge was the only man beside himself who truly understood the importance of Laura's personality and thoughts.

Their visit offered a welcome few weeks of relief from the constant worry of debts. The road was built but Graves knew that he could not finish writing *I, Claudius* until August. In July he was due to pay back the £24,000 for which he had mortgaged Canelluñ to Don Bernardo Colom for a land purchase. The only income they were receiving at this time was a few shillings of rent a week from a cottage which Graves had carelessly agreed to buy as a convenient home for their visitors. Riding was worried enough to write to her half-sister in America, asking about the possibility of giving a lecture tour to raise funds. Graves, knowing that Sassoon had always been a willing lender in the past, sent a desperate appeal for a thousand pounds.

It sounded, at first, as though he might be given a favourable answer. Sassoon asked if his need was serious and then withdrew, explaining that Graves had given an insufficient account of his circumstances and adding, which may have been more to the point, that his funds were low. To Graves, this was outrageous.[10] Had Sassoon refused at once, he would have resigned himself; what he could not forgive was the fact that his hopes had been raised only to be dashed. Don Bernardo's gracious decision to let the July payment go by for another year, creaming off only his six per cent of interest, did not lessen his indignation towards Sassoon. An ugly correspondence which did neither man credit continued until October. It ended only when everything unpleasant and ungenerous had been said.

Partly out of a wish to make Sassoon feel guilty, Graves let him know that work on *Claudius* had damaged his eyes. (Since he worked by candlelight after Gelat's diesel-fuelled system was switched off, this was not surprising; from 1933 onward, he was compelled to use strong glasses for all close work.) He did not, out of a reluctance to reveal their extravagance, mention a more dramatic catastrophe. At the end of September 1933, a torrential storm swept away the new road. They still had not paid for it, and now it would have to be rebuilt. Moreover, they had not sold one of the plots of land by which they had hoped to subsidize it. John Aldridge's mother remained the only investor.

The hope of borrowing some money must have been in the minds of Riding and Graves that autumn when they wrote, separately, to his widowed mother, Amy, begging her to visit Mallorca and to make peace with her son. Loans were not mentioned but Amy, who had time on her hands after Alfred's death, was willing to agree to a spring visit the following year. Laura's careful representation of their relationship as a literary partnership, nothing more, made it easier for Amy to accept. She had never doubted that Graves was happier when he had somebody to work with. If this was all that bound him to Laura, she could almost regard them as a couple. She may even have begun to feel that it was a little hard on Robert that he should have received nothing from his father's will, as well as having been cut out of her own. Forgiveness was in the air.

The year 1933 was acknowledged by both Riding and Graves to have been disastrous, when worry had caused them to become irritable and quarrelsome. Graves had been almost malicious in his response to Laura's misfortune when she sat on a broken chamber-pot in July and scarred one of her buttocks with a crucifix-shaped wound. She had responded the following month by telling him that *I, Claudius* was a boring book.[11] As with Robert and Nancy, they both sensed that things were easier between them when they did not feel too isolated. Visits from an occasional couple were no answer. They needed the ease of a small society of like-minded friends to spare them from the intensity of each other.

The situation began to resolve itself in the early autumn. The frequent disappearances of Mary and George Ellidge to attend to their baby were made less annoying when Eirlys Roberts and Jacob Bronowski returned and expressed themselves willing to do as much work on the 'Vulgate' as Laura wanted, in exchange for rent-free lodgings at Ca'n Torrent. Eirlys agreed to work on a book about the role of women with Riding. (This, said later to be the forerunner of *The White Goddess*, was in part the result of Riding's many conversations with Graves about primitive culture and myth.[12]) Bronowski was, at first, happy to write for the 'Vulgate' and to let himself be edited by his collaborator. Graves, left free to work on the second novel about Claudius, relaxed into his private world.

At the New Year, the four of them conducted wild celebrations at Canelluñ. Bronowski sang a jolly, but incomprehensible, Russian song; Laura danced to the new jazz records which John Aldridge had brought out in the summer. Graves, with his mind on the scenes about Herod which he had just been writing, announced himself as Salome, come to perform a dance in seven veils made out of cotton sheets and a few yards of silk set aside for Laura's underwear.

The year continued in the spirit of festivity and games. When Honor Wyatt and her partner, Gordon Glover, both professional journalists, were invited to visit Canelluñ from the cottage they had rented, they were entranced by the spirit of good humour, industry and intellectual energy. It was clear to them both that they were being interviewed as potential friends on their visit. This did not offend them. Honor thought it was rather funny when she was told by Laura that Jacob Bronowski had noticed her dangling earrings and thought them common. She sensed no insult, only a way of testing her responses.[13]

Honor was right. Riding and Graves, observing the thin, stammering, good-looking young man and his cheerful, energetic little companion, thought they would make a good addition to the Deyá group. The fact that Honor and Gordon were hard-working and just able to support themselves by the articles they wrote, was an added advantage. They were welcomed in, to join the Ellidges, Bronowski and Eirlys Roberts as friends between whom there should be no secrets.

Even so, Honor noticed a few of these; when they played the Truth Game in the evenings, Laura was allowed to give any answer she liked while the rest of them were ordered to be absolutely honest. But, if this gave Laura an advantage, Robert evidently approved. They followed his lead without question and revealed all their secrets gladly. To Honor, everything about life in Deyá now seemed perfect, from the occasional meetings to eat buttered toast round the fire or to try to defeat Graves at shooting through a hollow-centred sugar bun with a bow and arrow, to the dinners cooked by Robert which Laura always sweetly thanked them for eating. Honor and Gordon agreed from the start that Robert was a genius and one of the most fascinating men they had ever met, but Laura, for Honor, was something more. In her old age, Honor was still willing to say that Laura took the place of Christ in her mind. And this, she was convinced, was Graves's own feeling about his extraordinary companion.[14]

Amy Graves did not take quite such a romantic view of life at Canelluñ when she arrived for an April visit with her youngest son, John. She saw that Robert looked tired and older than his years and that it was he who roasted the joints, peeled the potatoes, washed up, tended the garden, picked the fruit and filled the larder with home-made jams and chutneys. Laura's only practical contribution was to whip up an occasional froth of egg-whites and lemon for a birthday treat.

There was no doubt in Amy's mind that Laura ruled the roost with Robert's backing. She listened to her son when he explained that Laura's job was to act as a centralizing force; her editorial supervision was said to be of vital importance, not only to Robert's work, but to everything which was written by their friends and correspondents. Amy was not a great intellectual, and it is unlikely that she understood Laura's aims and principles. What she saw was that the shell-shock which had plagued her son during his years with Nancy had gone and that he had found what he had always wanted, an intelligent literary partner. Amy did not grow fond of Laura, but she was impressed.

For Graves himself, the visit marked the end of his war against his family. His father was dead. His mother was seventy-seven, old enough to enjoy being looked after and cosseted as she talked of Rosaleen's wedding and her grandchildren's summer visits to Erinfa. William Nicholson's affectionate, unreproachful letters told Graves that he was always welcome and sadly missed in their part of the family. Amy, too, now made it clear that she was willing to accept the choices Robert had made. Writing the *Claudius* books had led him into the lives of families for whom treachery and corruption had been a daily diet. Beside them, the disputes with his parents came into perspective. Seeing his mother again, he could love her and know that he was free. The squabbles continued; the years of rebellion were over.

*   *   *

I, Claudius was published in May 1934. It received eulogistic reviews. In July, Graves celebrated his birthday with champagne and a *Claudius* spoof play set in ancient Rome, with George Ellidge leading a cast of 'Canny Loons' as 'Emperor of the Month', while his wife Mary stripped down to her green silk camiknickers and, sitting astride a chair in a suggestive way, sang a Marlene Dietrich song. The mood among the group was euphoric.

By September 1934, *I, Claudius* had been reprinted four times by Arthur Barker and another four by Harrison Smith, the American publisher. The reviews were being matched by the sales figures. *Claudius the God* was published in November and was even more admired. Besides being awarded the James Tait Black Memorial Prize and, with a little help from Edward Marsh, the Hawthornden, Graves sold the film rights to Alexander Korda. As in 1927, when *Lawrence and the Arabs* had saved him from near ruin, Graves had proved his ability to write his way out of a financial crisis. After paying off his mortgage to Don Bernardo, his first concern was to rescue Laura's 'Vulgate' project. Arthur Barker had, as they feared, decided not to risk publishing it. Instead Graves approached Constable and offered them a generous sum to publish and distribute the 'Vulgate' – it was now renamed *Epilogue* – together with any other books written by himself and Riding, under a joint imprint with their own Seizin Press.

All of this should have delighted Laura, but it is not easy to be graceful about being supported, especially when the money derives from a book which appears to present the beneficiary in an unpleasant light. This was Riding's predicament. She resented the reviews which arrived for Graves by every post. She disliked the sense that she now owed the survival of the 'Vulgate' project to her companion. She could not wholly convince herself that her own tiny band of admirers were not looking with more respect at Graves than at her.

Riding's annoyance about Graves's unexpected success was ill-concealed. It may have helped to precipitate the departure of two members of the Deyá group at the end of the summer. After brusquely telling Laura that her editing of his poems was unhelpful and that she could not go on using spurious arguments to force everybody to agree with her, Jacob Bronowski returned to England. Eirlys Roberts, who left with him, retained the memory of Graves as a brilliant, attractive man who would always be able to survive in his relationship with Riding because of his ability to retreat into some private imagined world. He heard only what he wanted to hear, and so kept himself from being emotionally damaged.[15]

The explanation for the Ellidges' abrupt eviction in October is less clear. The official reason was that they had been spreading unkind gossip about Riding and Graves to Louise Addis, an American woman in Deyá whom Laura had been viewing as a potential friend.

The unofficial reason may have been that Mary's adoration of Graves was becoming an embarrassment. Honor Wyatt had been led to wonder if she was sleeping with him; in fact, they had exchanged nothing more than a kiss one day on a visit to the beach. It had, Mary remembered in her old age, been like a father's kiss.[16] (Mary's own father had died when she was young and this loss may have been partly responsible for her crush on Graves.) Laura had found this devotion irritating, sufficiently so to report to John Aldridge that Mary had caused scandal in the village by making 'a strong sex attack' on Robert.[17] If Graves had been tempted by this it is probable that he would, puritanically, have preferred the temptress to disappear. The revelation of their gossip provided an excuse for Riding to banish her friends, but it did not leave her feeling happy about having done so. To a new ally on the island, she admitted that both George and Mary had behaved very well about it, which suggests that she felt more guilty than injured.[18]

Graves's literary successes made him all the more determined to champion and defend Riding. It seemed unjust that he should be acknowledged as a figure of importance and offered awards, while she, who he knew was destined to change the world, remained in the humiliating position of his dependent. It was not what he wanted for her. She remained the most remarkable woman he had ever known, and he intended to make sure that others shared his view. Any attack on Laura now, however slight, met with a savage response. Mocking Laura in Deyá had become equivalent in his eyes to stamping on the national flag. It was an insult which he would not tolerate.

His victim, at the end of 1934, was Hans Rothe, a well-meaning but loquacious German who had been chosen to translate the Claudius novels. His crime was to query – behind her back – Laura's claim to be the owner of Canelluñ. Despite the fact that he had paid six months' rent in advance for Ca'n Torrent, he was ordered by Graves to leave at once. In his nervous haste to do so, Rothe forgot about some photographs which he had promised to give to a villager. This produced another furious tirade. Confiding his troubles to Louise Addis, Rothe gleefully wrote that Graves had actually declared national honour to be at stake if the photographs were not immediately despatched. Mrs Addis had refused to set foot in Canelluñ after Laura falsely accused her of stealing their (Nancy's) silver spoons. (Louise Addis was a silversmith.) Now, she was all ears.[19]

For Graves, the shrinking of the Deyá group signalled a welcome period of tranquillity. He did, however, need a new typist as he started work on a new novel, *Antigua, Penny, Puce*, which was intended to provide another healthy injection of cash into their coffers. Riding, too, needed assistance with the historical novel set in Troy which she had begun to write.* Their practical needs were satisfied in 1935 with the arrival at Ca'n Torrent of Karl Goldschmidt.

---

* Riding's surprising decision to write a historical novel, a genre on which she had heaped contempt in 1934, was carefully rationalized. *A Trojan Ending* was being written, not because she had any desire to compete with Graves as a historical novelist, but because the Trojan War was the only period in which she could see a vitality which made it relevant to her own age. Graves, who provided her with the necessary background details for a story which focused on the character of Cressida, was convinced that Alexander Korda, having seen a film in *I, Claudius*, would also see film potential in Laura's novel. Riding shared this conviction. Published in 1937, the novel was coolly received. No film offers were made.

CHAPTER NINETEEN

1935

UNDERLYING TENSIONS

'ABOUT KARL,' GRAVES WROTE TO A CLOSE FRIEND IN THE 1940S, when he was living in England:

> The first time I ever saw him in Spain, his face was distorted with anger against the stupidity of a bus-driver. I admire anger. It means real sensibility. That drew me to him. I have often since seen him in spasms of anger: once or twice directed against me for an imagined insult or a gross stupidity. I don't in the least hold it against him. He is a perfectionist in a manifestly cranky world and that he still has the power of anger is a tribute to an uncrushed spirit. (He has a lot of private distress which accounts for his not being able to control himself at times.) I love him dearly and know all his faults; and he knows all his own faults too.[1]

Karl Goldschmidt was twenty-one at the time of the encounter described here, which had taken place in the summer of 1933. His background helps to explain the willingness with which he allowed himself to be adopted and, although he would have disputed this, exploited by Graves and Riding. To him, they were a substitute for a lost family and an escape from years of hardship.

Karl's mother died when he was four. His father committed suicide when he was sixteen. Subsequently, living at his grandmother's house at Dortmund in Germany, he studied design. Expelled from his college for a minor misdemeanour, he was sent to work for strangers in Westphalia as a live-in shop assistant – his bed was under the counter – before he returned to his birthplace, Elberfeld (now Wuppertal), to draw signs for a big store. In 1933, after seeing a photograph of a Mallorcan village in a newspaper, he decided on impulse to make his way there.

In January 1934 Honor and Gordon Glover brought news to Canelluñ of a slight, nervous young German whom they had found living with a strikingly beautiful girl in the nearby village of Lluch Alcari. They had liked him very much. Graves and Riding had maintained their hostility towards the German colony on the island but, walking over to Lluch Alcari a few months later, Graves was amused to recognize the slight, dark-haired boy he had seen glaring at the bus-driver a year earlier. Karl was feeling in low spirits. His girlfriend had left him for an artist and he was having difficulty in making a living for himself. He was impressed when he identified Graves as the author of *Goodbye to All That*, which had sold well in Germany. He accepted a suggestion to visit Canelluñ and, if he liked, to earn a little money by typing.

Grateful to find himself among friendly and cultivated people, Karl soon agreed to start doing minor secretarial jobs, while Honor gave him English lessons. He had a prickly pride which they all came to respect, but small gestures – a little present, a flattering joke, invitations to the impromptu parties held at Canelluñ – easily won his affection. The test of his loyalty came when Jacob Bronowski, who had promised to find him a job in England, left the island. Karl hesitated, and decided to stay on in the little house in the village which he was now renting from Gelat. His reward came in November 1934 when Graves and Riding offered him 2,000 pesetas (£90) a year to become their typist. After proving himself willing to match the pace of his workaholic employers, Karl was asked in April 1935 if he would like to come and live rent-free at Ca'n Torrent. By now, Karl had become a much-loved fixture, to be scolded and humoured and supervised by Riding in a way which bound him ever closer to Graves, 'dear Rob' in Karl's new diary, as his fellow servitor.

Karl, better than anybody, understood Graves's devotion to Laura. He was not a poet, although his perfectionism and his rapid mastery of English were to make him a fearless sub-editor of Graves's prose work. (His skills as a designer were put to more immediate use for the Seizin Press.) He did not attempt to analyse their relationship, to explain to himself why Graves was supporting a woman with whom he had no sexual connection or to ask what it was that he received in return. It seemed unnecessary, when Laura was evidently such an exceptional woman.

In Karl's diary, more than in Honor's fond recollections, we catch a vivid glimpse of the woman Graves loved, both generous and cruel, delighting in presents, sulking when she did not receive a dress or piece of jewellery from a visitor, repairing a sudden burst of anger with an act of kindness, wanting affirmation of her singular strengths from everybody and reacting with violent emotion when her expectations were disappointed.

While merging with life at Canelluñ, Karl broke down the barrier between its inhabitants and at least two members of the island's German colony. This antipathy had no apparent rationale, but it was strong enough for Graves to have told the dismissed Hans Rothe that his behaviour was typical of a German, and for Riding to have persuaded Norman Cameron to take the plot of land adjacent to their own in order to prevent it from being bought by Georg Schwarz. All this now changed. Karl revealed that Schwarz and his housekeeper, Emmy Streng, had been kind to him when he was alone and miserable. Hostility evaporated at once, and Schwarz's arthritic renderings of Bach on his piano ceased to be a daily irritant on walks to the village shops. A sedate ritual of teas began, with conversation being conducted in halting Spanish since Riding had only a few words of German. Late in 1934, Graves began the generous task of turning Schwarz's memories of a German boyhood into readable form. (He had arranged for them to be translated by the wife of a local German novelist, Albert Thelen, since Karl's grasp of English was not yet good enough.) It was hard work, but he enjoyed it: Schwarz's descriptions of rural Germany reminded him of summer visits to his grandfather at Laufzorn.

★   ★   ★

When Riding and Graves had collaborated on *A Pamphlet Against Anthologies* in 1928, they had made it clear that they regarded the genre as despicable. Michael Roberts, a young poet and editor whom Graves had met and liked in the penultimate year at St Peter's Square, approached him in March 1935, hoping to persuade him to make an exception. This was for the 1936 *Faber Book of Modern Verse*, devised by T. S. Eliot.

Roberts was quickly made aware of the hideous mistake he had made in approaching Graves but not Riding; he rephrased his request, and was sucked into a voluminous correspondence. By the time the book was published, he had received twice as many letters from Graves and Riding as from the full total of his other contributors.[2]

The letters show the considerable tact needed in dealing with Riding and Graves as a unit. They took offence easily; their combined displeasure had the force of a royal slap. When Roberts, having been forced by Graves to include Riding, proposed to give her less space than her associate, there was an outburst. Roberts gave way: Graves's seventeen pages were reduced to ten, while Laura was given thirteen. (Riding's bullying manner was never more oppressive than in this exchange; Roberts was told to say 'honestly' that he required seventeen pages from her, unless he wanted Graves to withdraw his poems.[3]) Even the normal alphabetical rules of precedence were turned upside down. In one of his most charming letters, Graves explained that 'Graves and Riding' was like saying Pollux and Castor, or Sullivan and Gilbert, 'not to say bacon and liver or toast and tea . . .'[4] Roberts, amused, gave way, and printed Riding's name first.

It was unthinkable that the work of Riding should appear in a book without an explanation of her superiority to all other poets. Roberts did what he could in the Introduction; Graves, dissatisfied, rewrote this section, expressing his own heartfelt enthusiasm.

> [Her poetry] sails, it seems to me, as near as possible to being unevocative, and therefore like the most delicate, barely perceptible joke; it is intensely delightful. There is a kind of poetic art which is most perfect when it stands on the brink of non-existence.[5]

Two years later, Riding rebuked Roberts for such an inaccurate description of her work. The non-existence of which he wrote was in fact the true reality. Her poetry opened roads into this super-reality from 'temporarily journalistic existence'.[6] Her puzzling assertion that '"Poems is particularly to feel doom"' was meanwhile defended by Graves. This, Roberts learned, was no stranger than to say 'Mathematics is carefully to reckon numbers.'[7] It was in fact a good deal stranger, but Roberts had learned to let such claims pass unchallenged. He valued the friendship of Graves and Riding and he admired their devotion to their art. In all the mass of letters they had written to him, the one thing they had never bothered to discuss was money.

★   ★   ★

Publicly, Riding never had a stauncher defender than Graves; in fiction, he continued to take liberties with her character.

He had begun work on *Antigua, Penny, Puce* in the autumn of 1934 when he was still uncertain of how much money he stood to make from the *Claudius* books. Seeing it as a pot-boiler, he planned at first to publish the novel under a pseudonym. The story, his only modern one, full of wit and invention, was of a fight between a brother and sister over the ownership of a stamp album. The central theme, the distinction between ownership and possession, was prompted by his own curious situation as the non-owning possessor of a considerable amount of property in Deyá. The character of Oliver Palfrey, a novelist who admiringly reads the works of Graves's own pet hates, the Powys brothers and Mary Webb, was carefully distanced from himself: Oliver's sister, Jane, while occasionally evocative of Rosaleen, was a light-hearted portrait of Laura.

Who am I? was a favourite question of Riding's. In his novel, Graves provided some imaginative answers. Jane has the protean abilities which he saw in Riding, changing herself effortlessly from an art-gallery owner into an exotic dancer, from an astrologist into a cigarette manufacturer. She excels at whatever she does. Jane also displays Riding's manipulative skills; the other characters are effortlessly outwitted by her. As a matchmaker, a lover of elaborate clothes, player of games and teller of obscure jokes, Jane comes closer still to Laura. But Graves never criticizes her. It was more agreeable to see herself reflected in Jane than in Livia or Messalina; Riding willingly helped to revise the book and showed no hostility towards it.

Graves had only been working on his new novel for a month when the news came, in December 1934, that Alexander Korda, the most important man in the British film industry in the early 1930s, had bought the film rights of the *Claudius* novels. Graves was invited to condense his books for republication when the film came out. It was his first contact with the film world. He could hardly believe his good fortune when Korda followed this proposal up by telling him that T. E. Lawrence had recommended him to write the script for a film based on his life. Naturally, he and Laura wanted to share the news with their good friend, Gelat.

The year 1935 was a rosy one for Gelat. He began by persuading his newly prosperous friends to subsidize an electricity turbine at new premises, leaving the Fábrica free to be transformed into a café and dance-bar, which they were also to fund. Hearing that they were thinking of buying a car, he pointed out how much more convenient it would be if he had the car and could drive them in it. In return, he gave them the use of a pretty local orchard and meadow where the fruit which Graves loved to cook up for jams was particularly abundant. It was theirs, he said, but this was soon forgotten. The agreement had been a verbal one and the orchard remained the property of Gelat.

Graves and Riding, as always, saw only the thoughtful generosity of their friend. There was one benefit in his latest proposal. The orchard had been part of a large Deyá property, Es Moli, which Gelat had been commissioned to sell for an impoverished owner. Through Gelat, Graves was able to buy a house called La Posada from the Es Moli estate and to furnish it from another old house which Gelat was selling.

The Posada became his favourite home. A handsome but decrepit old house standing on the top of the Deyá hill next to the church, it was lovingly restored as a refuge for friends. Canelluñ and the cottage bought by Graves had been transferred to Riding's name, but no transfer was made of the Posada. Perhaps Graves considered living there at some point himself, remaining close but not united to Riding. The diary which he began to keep in 1935 at her suggestion is thick with references to the Posada, and to his affectionate feeling for it.

Graves was always generous when he had money. Laura's jewel-box, lined by him with velvet and silk and plush, glittered with his gifts in 1935. Nancy, who had been sent nothing for two years, was given £150 in arrears and promised £140 each quarter from now on. Graves's goodwill towards her increased in the summer of 1935 when he heard that Geoffrey Taylor had left her house to marry another woman who lived nearby. Told that Geoffrey and Mary Taylor remained on the best of terms with Nancy and the children, and that Geoffrey was even continuing to run the Poulk Press with Nancy, he chose not to listen. As far as he was concerned, 'the devil' had now shown his true colours and had lost his sinister influence over the children.

Here, Graves was making a typical distortion of the facts. The children had started to write him friendly letters only because he had, after a silence of three years, decided to communicate with them, inviting them to stay and grandly telling Jenny that he could arrange a film career for her through Korda. But Geoffrey's break with their mother did not alter their devotion to the man who had effectively been their stepfather for the past five years.

★ ★ ★

The untimely death of T. E. Lawrence in May 1935 opened Graves's eyes to the duplicity of the man he had once venerated. His first response to the shattering news had been to hammer out, overnight, a lengthy obituary which appeared, among many other places, in the *Evening Standard* under the startling headline 'Lawrence, by Myself'. The Lawrence executors, headed by T. E.'s brother, Arnie, were not pleased; Basil Liddell Hart, Lawrence's other biographer, sent Graves a friendly note to ask if his own name had been deleted from the Lawrence quotation which he had included about himself and another author of a Lawrence biography who 'seems to have no critical sense in my regard'. Cornered, Graves was forced to admit that this was so. He admitted, too, that he had included the quotation to make himself sound superior. Several letters later, he was mortified to learn that Lawrence had spoken of him to Liddell Hart in equally disparaging terms and that Liddell Hart had also been recommended by Lawrence to Korda as a potential screenplay writer. It is not surprising, then, that 'double-crossing' was a word which Graves repeatedly used of Lawrence in later letters to friends.

Liddell Hart, a superb military strategist, had Graves's measure from the start. He saw the pugnacity and liked it, just as he liked the quick, perceptive judgements and natural generosity of his correspondent. Neither man showed much concern when they learned that Arnie Lawrence wanted Korda to use Sassoon as the screenplay writer; the decision, Graves drily commented, was the

Lawrence estate's funeral, not theirs. When Graves suggested that they should combine their letters from Lawrence in two separate volumes to show the man in two different lights, Liddell Hart readily assented.

Their subsequent correspondence shows how Graves used letters as a way of thinking aloud. He was often almost unconscious of the person to whom he was writing. So Liddell Hart, bemused, learned that Auden was a 'parlour communist', Yeats a spiritualist and, therefore, a dubious poet, and D. H. Lawrence 'a bum poet' because he was 'a bum person. I can't understand people,' Graves went on, revealingly, '"admiring the work and not the man" in a poet. It's like saying that you like Gold Flake cigarettes apart from their suitability as smokes.'[8]

The conviction, held by both Graves and Riding, that the merit of a poem is directly related to the personal morality of the writer, helps to explain Graves's admiration for Laura's sometimes impenetrable poetry of the 1930s. If good poetry can only be produced by a good person, then, since Riding was a supreme being, her poetry must necessarily be the best. They both brought the same odd judgement to bear on their contemporaries. Yeats, who unsuccessfully approached them for contributions to his Oxford verse anthology when he visited Mallorca in 1935, was judged to have a vain and weak nature. This made it possible to argue that his poems had less merit than those produced by their young Cambridge friend, James Reeves. Reeves was a better poet because he was, in their view, a better man. The poetry was validated by the way of life.

It was to Riding that Graves looked for a definition of the right way of life from 1935 onwards as she searched for a way to confront the world-shaking events which threatened them from the shadows. Crisis predictions could be had by the sackful; only Riding was ready to offer personal solutions.

In the three *Epilogue* books, which were intended to spread Riding's gospel, she appears in the role of Socrates, knowing both the right question and the true answer. Graves took the role of the stooge, asking the questions she wanted to hear. The answers were not always reassuring.

In *Epilogue III*, he asked her to explain 'by what principle can one learn to think and live poetically, seeing all the varied fields of activity in a just proportion of importance . . .?'[9] Riding's response, that man must let death be part of his life-experience, was hard for Graves to accept, especially since, as he frankly acknowledged in this exchange: 'I have always feared death more than anything.'[10] Later, he allowed death into his life on a poetic level as part of the ritual death and rebirth of the poet-god in *The White Goddess*. In 1935 he knew only that Riding, like Chaucer and Homer, was the sole communicant of an age. He did not always understand her but he wanted others to see and share his faith in her. Whatever she said, was true. Whatever she asked, must be done.

Graves's diary offers a less persuasive account of his role as her pupil and follower than he was prepared to publish. In part, it confirms the picture of unity and ease which was later drawn by their most regular companions in 1935, Karl Goldschmidt and Honor Wyatt. There are reports of outings to Palma cinemas, evenings spent reading P. G. Wodehouse aloud, days of planning the garden and rearranging household furniture: all of this suggests a happy relationship in their last year-and-a-half at Canelluñ.

But the diary also conveys a period of almost continuous ill-health, for which strain as well as a poor diet were responsible. Graves indulged in binges of the kind which are usually related to using food as a substitute for affection. The endless reporting of gifts made to Riding, of additions to her wardrobe, of her flat jokes, is executed without warmth. Comments on Riding's inability to give up smoking for more than a few hours, on her having, on separate occasions, reduced the Canelluñ maids, a German friend and Honor Wyatt's mother to tears, are not affectionately made. An entry about a mental exercise in which Graves transposed his name into hers by a sequence of overlapping words, shows him choosing, among others, 'maneater', 'terrible' and 'arid'.[11] The sequence can be achieved with more agreeable words without difficulty, and Graves was a skilled player of word-games. None of these points in themselves have much significance; examined as a whole, they suggest that Graves was struggling to overcome feelings of resentment and despair. His need to believe in Riding as a force for good, of energy and intellectual integrity, remained strong. His problem was with reconciling his ideal with the demanding and neurotic personality of Riding in everyday life.

Epilogue I, published in the autumn of 1935, contained poems which celebrated Graves's continuing faith in Riding as the greatest poet and thinker of their time; but the context of these poems has to be considered. *Epilogue* was the vehicle, subsidized by Graves, through which Riding's gospel was to be spread. His panegyrics, while sincerely written, were intended to heighten the reader's awareness of her extraordinary qualities. 'The Challenge', couched in the form of a ballad about a boy prince coming to manhood, mythologized Riding's authoritative role, identifying her with the moon at which the young prince flies his hawk, only to lose both the bird and his kingdom.

> The Moon's the crown of no high-walled domain
> Conquerable by angry stretch of pride:
> Her icy lands welcome no soldiery.

Made wise by his loss, the prince decides to answer the moon's 'reasoned look' with submission, not rage.

> So peace fell sudden, and in proof of peace
> There sat my flown hawk, hooded on my fist,
> And with my knees I gripped my truant horse.

> Toward that most clear, unscorching light I spurred.
> Whiter and closer shone the increasing disc,
> Until it filled the sky, scattering my gaze.[12]

Here, as in all the poems published in *Epilogue I*, Graves urges the reader to accept Riding's intellectual supremacy, her superhuman status. But the images are chilling. In 'The Challenge' she is the moon; in 'To the Sovereign Muse' she is Fate, the spinner; in 'Like Snow' she is compared to the cold brilliance of crystals. Unable to love her physically, as he wished, he made an impenetrable icon of her.

To do so was a form of self-protection. Laura was living up to the nickname of 'Riding Roughshod' which Hart Crane had bestowed on her in New York, as she flaunted her sexual persona before the lover who was forbidden to touch her. In the 1935 *Focus* newsletters, she described her enthusiasm for 'it', the sex appeal represented by Elinor Glyn on her tiger-skin, and revealed the pleasure of showing off her naked, 'quite pretty' thighs at a Deyá tea party. She made taunting allusions to her love of violence and the sight of blood, and mocked Graves's understandable horror of such scenes after his war experience. She begged him to help her write 'Wishing More Dear', a poem which entreated her young protégé, James Reeves, to become more intimately affectionate with her. Graves remained fiercely stoical. This had been his chosen crusade: he was determined not to betray the commitment he had made to serve and honour Riding.

James Reeves had been a contemporary and friend of Bronowski's at Cambridge. He had been corresponding with Riding for two years before, after many pleas, he arrived in Mallorca for a month's visit in November 1935. He stayed with Karl at Ca'n Torrent. Riding was at first cast down by his looks and reserved manner. Small, moustached and pipe-smoking, Reeves projected an air of remoteness that was increased by the thick spectacles which hid his eyes. (He was almost blind.) Graves responded more quickly than she to the intelligence and fierce integrity of a man who became one of his dearest friends.

Reeves, like Graves, had a puritanical streak. His family, non-conformist teetotallers from the north of England, had struggled to give their children a good education; Reeves was now preparing to become a schoolmaster. Graves, remembering his own dread of the profession, was inclined to dissuade him.

The record of Reeves's stay is one of the liveliest episodes in the 1935 diary, although Graves himself was in continuously poor health and having to take daily runs with his newly acquired mastiff, Solomon, in order to reduce his weight. Reeves played his guitar for them and joined in dancing to records by Duke Ellington and Louis Armstrong. They went to the cinema and even, on one occasion, to a nightclub. James was enlisted to help work on the latest *Focus*, in which he wrote of his excitement that his poems were to be published by Seizin. But the reserve of which Laura complained is apparent: life in Deyá is said to be 'very nice', and so is the weather.

Epilogue I received a cool response when it was published in November; Reeves, as one of the contributors, was able to share in the mood of disappointment. However, optimism prevailed. On 7 December, the three contributors gathered to plan a grand itinerary for '*Epilogue* people'. The list of countries and states in which they expected to recruit followers was impressive: 'Holland Denmark Siberia Cochin China, Rimitara California New York Cyprus Turkey [*sic*].'[13]

A week later, Reeves returned to England. Initially, Riding had planned to accompany him to Barcelona with Gelat; in the end, she contented herself with 'sentimental farewells' on the boat at Palma.

The historian, Leopold von Ranke, Robert Graves's great-great uncle. *(Canelluñ)*

A Graves family portrait at Red Branch House, c.1907. *Back row, left to right*: Rosaleen, Perceval, Clarissa. *Second row, left to right*: Philip, Amy, Alfred, Robert, Susan. *Front, left to right*: Charles and John. *(Paul Cooper)*

ABOVE LEFT: Robert Graves in 1919. He gave this photograph to his friend, Walter Turner, in 1920. *(Francis Guilfoyle)*

ABOVE RIGHT: Nancy Nicholson and Smuts, her poodle, in 1917. Nancy presented RG with this photograph. *(Catherine Dalton)*

LEFT: Nancy and Smuts, 1917.
(Sam Graves)

BELOW: RG and Nancy on their honeymoon in Wales, 1918. *(Lucia Graves)*

ABOVE LEFT: Siegfried Sassoon in 1915, aged twenty-nine. *(Hulton Deutsch Collection)*

ABOVE RIGHT: Laura Riding, photographed by Ward Hutchinson, 1934. *(Canelluñ)*

BELOW: Geoffrey (Phibbs) Taylor, 1934. *(Mrs Mary Taylor)*

ABOVE: A group at the Deyá café. *Left to right*: Juan Gelat holding Solomon, RG's dog, Gordon Glover, Laura Riding, Honor Wyatt, Mary Phillips, Karl Goldschmidt, RG. *(Canelluñ)*

LEFT: Juan Gelat, c.1935. *(Canelluñ)*

LEFT: Some Deyá village women with Karl Goldschmidt and RG, 1935. *(Canelluñ)*

RG carrying wood from the field behind Vale House, 1941. *(Hulton Deutsch Collection)*

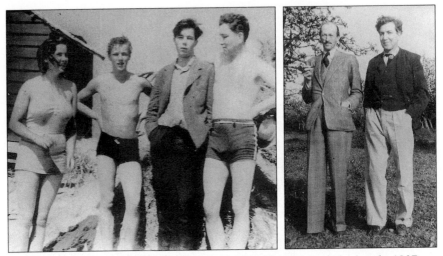

ABOVE LEFT: *Left to right*: Catherine, Sam, David and RG at the beach, 1937. *(Canelluñ)*

ABOVE RIGHT: Basil Liddell Hart and RG in Devon, 1940. *(Canelluñ)*

BELOW LEFT: RG, William, Beryl and their neighbour, Lord Falkland, Devon, 1941. *(Karl Gay)*

BELOW RIGHT: RG, Lucia and William at Brixham harbour, 1944. *(Douglas Glass)*

ABOVE: Beryl at Club Nautico, Palma, in 1950 on her wedding day. *(Canelluñ)*

ABOVE LEFT: Drawing of RG by Ronald Searle, 1950, done at RG's request. *(Ronald Searle)*

BELOW: RG, Beryl and Jenny (Nicholson) Clifford at Portofino, 1950. *(Wendy Toye)*

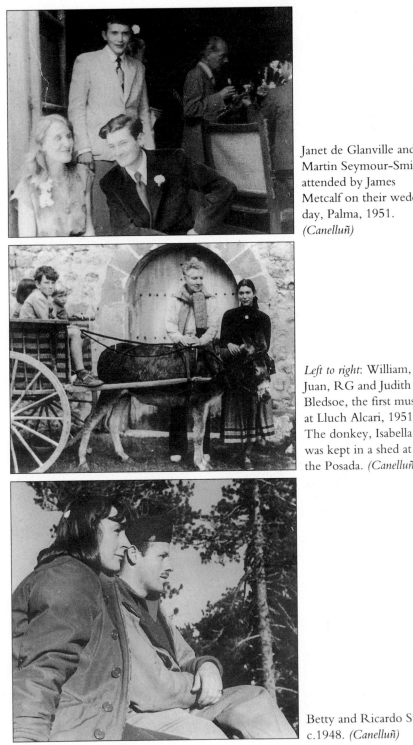

Janet de Glanville and Martin Seymour-Smith, attended by James Metcalf on their wedding day, Palma, 1951. *(Canelluñ)*

Left to right: William, Juan, RG and Judith Bledsoe, the first muse, at Lluch Alcari, 1951. The donkey, Isabella, was kept in a shed at the Posada. *(Canelluñ)*

Betty and Ricardo Sicre, c.1948. *(Canelluñ)*

ABOVE LEFT: Amy and Clarissa Graves at Erinfa, 1949. *(Canelluñ)*

ABOVE RIGHT: Jenny (Nicholson) Crosse at Torre Grillo, Rome, 1955. *(Canelluñ)*

BELOW: RG and Joshua Podro at the Posada, 1952. *(Canelluñ)*

Norman Cameron and his third wife, Gretl, at the Posada. *(Canelluñ)*

John Aldridge in the late Seventies. *(Lady Mancroft)*

Selwyn and Tania Jepson at Portofino. *(Canelluñ)*

RG and Karl (Goldschmidt) Gay in the Canelluñ study. *(Canelluñ)*

ABOVE LEFT: Len Lye and RG in Deyá, c.1960. *(Canelluñ)*

ABOVE RIGHT: RG with David Ben-Gurion and his secretary. *(Podro)*

BELOW: *Left to right:* Julie Gay, RG, Ava Gardner, Beryl, Lucia, 1958. *(Canelluñ)*

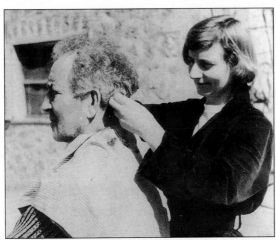

RG having his hair cut at
Canelluñ by Rene Gay.
(Canelluñ)

RG in his study at
Canelluñ. *(Tom Weedon)*

RG on his way down to the
cala at Deyá. *(Tom Weedon)*

Alastair Reid and RG on the 1958 American lecture tour. *(Canelluñ)*

Idries Shah and RG at
Deyá, 1962–3.
(Canelluñ)

RG and Lucia on her
wedding day in Deyá.
(Canelluñ)

THE THREE LAST MUSES

ABOVE: Margot Callas *(centre)* and RG, 1961–2. *(Canelluñ)*

RIGHT: Juli Simon, 1968. *(Canelluñ)*

BELOW: *Left to right*: Ralph Jacobs, RG, Cindy Lee, Beryl, Helen Morningstar, Lucia, at Café Indigo. *(Canelluñ)*

RG at Luggala, Co. Wicklow, 1975. *(Angus Forbes)*

She looked, Graves observed, 'worn out'. A few weeks later, they learned that their plot to introduce Reeves to another of their recent visitors, Mary Phillips, had been so successful that they were getting married. This proof of their matchmaking skills, after a less fruitful endeavour to pair Mary off with Gordon Glover, now estranged from Honor and their baby son, was an auspicious start to 1936.

★   ★   ★

Gelat was confident that Graves's 'investment' in his schemes would prove worth while; at the beginning of 1936, they appeared to be just one more way in which a generous and gullible man could be parted from his money. But Graves was no longer feeling quite so prosperous as he had a year earlier. The royalties and translation fees from the *Claudius* novels had enabled him to pay off the Canelluñ mortgage, but John Aldridge's mother was still waiting for her £600, Gelat needed more money to embellish his new café and Laura had set her heart on acquiring two more little houses to be rented out to friends. Nothing had come of their vague plans to make the Seizin Press a more businesslike venture; the *Epilogue* publications, while estimable, were a steady drain on Graves's shrinking funds.

With these financial worries in mind, Graves put his poetry aside to work on a revision of *Antigua, Penny, Puce*. Riding, anxious to soothe the publishers into an early payment, promised Constable that they would have it by May.

Mallorca remained cut off from political events. Their sense of growing international tension was gleaned from a weekly study of the newspapers and *Time*, the magazine which they read devotedly because Tom Matthews worked on it. The only local source of information, other than the village's one radio set, was Gelat.

There had already been a few sinister developments on Mallorca. Laura, the theoretical owner of their expensive new road to the shore, was summoned to Palma in the autumn of 1935 to explain its purpose and produce the appropriate authorizations. Graves appeared at the court in Laura's place and was allowed to return home unpenalized, but their dreams of selling the road to the Government for a profit were over. Gelat was convinced that they had been betrayed by his right-wing brother-in-law, Dr Vives. Political feelings in Deyá were running high.

In February 1936, events swung in their favour. The left-wing Popular Front won the Spanish election. Gelat, not hitherto known for his socialist feelings, saw a good chance of being made the new Mayor if he leaned a little more to the left. The Mayor's power in a small village was not to be dismissed; if he was appointed, Gelat's new business concerns were sure to prosper. So were his chief benefactors: Graves, bursting with excitement, wrote to his new friend Liddell Hart that he had never stood to gain so much.[14] Curiously, despite the strong views which both Graves and Laura had about personal integrity, they felt no concern about Gelat's cynical politicizing. His hold on their affections was so strong by now that they could see no fault in anything he did.

The mood of elation at Canelluñ was higher still in May, when, after a good deal of careful negotiating, Gelat was selected as the new Mayor of Deyá. Graves and Riding were invited to join the family celebration of his success, and to congratulate themselves on the shrewdness of investing in his schemes. Now, it seemed, they would all be rich.

Apart from the annoyance of learning that the formidable T. E. Lawrence Estate, headed by T. E.'s brother Arnie, intended to block the publication of his collaborative 'correspondence' project with Liddell Hart, Graves had seldom felt more cheerful. Amy no longer placed obstacles in the way of his children's visits to Deyá; after six years, he was eagerly anticipating seeing them in July. Reading their letters, he convinced himself that their feelings for him were just as fond as they had been before his departure.

This was only a partial truth. Both Jenny and David were old enough to find their father's desertion unforgivable; the fact that their letters were politely affectionate did not mean, as he thought, that he had escaped judgement. But Sam and Catherine were young enough to respond to their father's overtures with unalloyed happiness. Sam, in particular, endeared himself by making graceful references to Laura, a subject on which the other three children remained silent. Still struggling to overcome the profound deafness he had suffered since his hospitalization in Cairo, Sam was rewarded with a stream of loving letters, full of stories about Laura's cats and Robert's friendly dog and often ending in this fashion: 'We both send you much love and thanks and think you are a very kind boy to write so nicely to us. Your dear father, Robert.'[15] David, meanwhile, was invited to thrill to the news that their escort to Deyá would be a direct descendant of Sir Thomas Wyatt. This was Honor who planned to come with her baby, Julian.

At the beginning of July, Alan Hodge, a clever young Oxford graduate who had made a brief visit to Canellun at Christmas, returned to work on *Epilogue III* and Riding's planned series of school-books for children. While Riding struggled with her Trojan novel on a diet of cigarettes and black coffee, Graves helped Hodge on the school-book projects and completed his revision of *Antigua*. When, on 18 July, the news came that there were machine-guns in Palma and that all communication with the mainland was being suspended, he was too engrossed in his work to be bothered by outside events. Writing to Julie Matthews that evening, he told her about the impending visit by his children, about a novel, *The Heathen*, which they had helped Honor to write, about all the improvements they had made to the house and garden – about everything, in short, but a political crisis. There was, he casually added, some sort of martial law in Palma but he saw it as 'only a reflexion of Continental trouble, not trouble originating here'.[16]

The first serious indications of civil war came two days later. In the nearby village of Soller, a Fascist was shot while attempting to commandeer the post office; in Deyá, Gelat was ordered to hand over his mayoral duties to a non-political resident. Graves and Riding were shocked. On 21 July the first trucks of Franco's troops rolled through the village. On 23 July, the ardent right-winger Dr Vives escaped through the back of his village house in his drawers after Franco's men, believing him to be a socialist, fired on his front door. (Gelat was delighted; his friends wondered if he, perhaps, had given a false account of his brother-in-law's politics.)

The drama escalated rapidly in the next week; regretfully, Graves decided to cancel the children's visit. But he and Laura were determined to see things through. Their home had never seemed more beautiful to them than it did now in the late summer days. Every morning Graves, accompanied by Alan Hodge, marched down to the *cala*, as if in defiance of the hysteria which now prevailed in the village. He planned new additions to the garden. On 1 August, overcome by its loveliness and by the scent of the flowers, he wandered out to stand alone and stare at it by the light of the full moon.

It was his last opportunity to do so for ten years. The following afternoon, Riding and Graves were visited by a former British Consul from Palma. He told them that the last boat that would get them out of danger was sailing from Palma in a few hours' time. They could take one suitcase each.

They had been advised, not ordered, to leave: other foreign residents, both English and German, elected to stay and risk being ruled by Franco. Graves was eager to see his children again; Laura could not face the prospect of an isolated life with no visitors; Karl was ready to do whatever they wished. They decided to go.

They now had just two hours to reach the boat. Karl, wistfully, looked at the salads and jellies laid out in the larder for their dinner before packing his own bag. Graves fretted about their rudeness to Joän Junyer, a brilliant but deaf young artist friend, trained by Picasso, whom they had promised to visit that day. The suitcases grew increasingly unwieldy as they stuffed them with books, manuscripts, silver, and clothes. Gelat came, weeping, to receive the house-keys. Nothing, he promised, would be neglected. Their home would be safe.

There were more than a hundred and fifty refugees leaving Palma on HMS *Greville*. Laura secured a cabin; Hodge, Karl, and Graves shared a blanket on the deck. Laura, usually so decisive, was in a state of nervous collapse; the journey to England was one of the rare occasions on which Graves appeared as the controller of events. At Valencia, where they were transferred to a hospital ship for Marseilles, he persuaded the Captain that Karl, whose status as a German Jew put him at considerable risk, was a member of their party. When they reached Marseilles, it was Graves who made sure that Karl's passport was stamped before arranging the money transfers and tickets to get them to Paris. (The local bank had refused to lend them the necessary sum.) Laura had been reduced to tears in Marseilles by the American Embassy's refusal to grant her a visa; Graves saw that she was given one as soon as they reached Paris. She had become irresolute and helpless with fear; Graves had physically to carry her on to the train to Dieppe.

The last part of the journey was marred by the presence of the poet Roy Campbell, looking to them like an absurd caricature of a Spaniard in his cape and Cordoban hat as he eulogized Franco and drew their attention to some verses he had written at their expense. 'Apologized to L and me for libel on us in "Georgiad" or something,' Graves noted wearily, past caring what had been said.[17]

At Dieppe, Graves had found time to send a wire to their efficient friend Mary Somerville that they were now homeless refugees. When they reached London, Mary settled them temporarily into a handsome house on the edge of Regent's Park. The owner, Kitty West, had visited Mallorca once or twice and was sympathetic to their plight. She and her husband were away in Ireland and happy to lend their house for as long as it was required. Mary took Graves and Riding out to supper at the Café Royal on their first evening in London. Her guests were unable to make more than a polite pretence of enjoying themselves. They had been gone for less than a week and the sense of homesickness was already overwhelming.

CHAPTER TWENTY

1936–1937

A SENSE OF EXILE

ENGLAND WAS NO LONGER HIS HOME. WRITING ABOUT EXILE IN one of his semi-autobiographical short stories, Graves described it with feeling as 'the Devil's own fate'.[1]

Even though he had overcome the experience of shell-shock, peace was still essential for his own tranquillity. Deprived of his daily routine and his familiar landscape, Graves was restless and lost. Karl, who had enjoyed listening to the ballads he sang while he worked in the Canelluñ kitchen, noticed that he sang no more after their arrival in England. It is striking, too, that he suffered continuous poor health for the next two years.

They settled, after a week at Lucie Brown and John Aldridge's pretty old house in a sleepy Essex village, in a flat near the Marylebone Road belonging to Aldridge's mother. Graves had been happier in the country, but Laura was uneasy in a house run by Lucie and decorated to Lucie's taste.

Life achieved no regular pattern because it was lived in a state of uneasy suspense. Hoping each day to hear that they might be able to return to Deyá, they had no incentive to create a routine. Laura, often working until near dawn on her book about Troy, wrote with uncharacteristic pathos about Cressida's sense of being exiled from Tenedos, her island home; Graves, having finished correcting the *Antigua* proofs, had nothing but his increasingly difficult friendship with Riding to comfort him in the hot and dusty city. He made no attempt to communicate with friends who pre-dated his meeting with Laura. Only Eddie Marsh was greeted with all Graves's old affection. Neither he nor Laura had forgotten that Marsh's intervention had saved her from a suicide charge in 1929.

Graves was no longer in love with Laura. It seems that at times, he almost hated her. Antonia White, working in the same advertising firm as Norman Cameron, heard from Thea, a mutual friend, identified only by her first name in White's diary, that Graves had two quite different personalities. When he was with Laura, he would shun Thea and appear to defer in every way to his companion. When he was not with Laura, he was as friendly and cheerful as he had always been. Thea was not sure how to respond when he invited her to agree with him that Laura looked '"just like a witch"'.[2] This was hearsay, but it was revealing.

Laura, for Graves, had always been a cause. After the cause of defending and caring for her in the years following her fall, he had committed himself to the cause of her beliefs. Like an officer who does not particularly like the general under whom he serves, Graves put the cause first. He no longer showed any great desire to be alone with Riding. What mattered was the promotion of her role as a prophet and saviour at a time when the nightmarish prospect of a second world war was plainly visible to every thinking person. Fear was widespread enough for William Empson mockingly to accuse Spender, MacNeice, Day-Lewis and Auden of 'Waiting for the end, boys, waiting for the end' in his poem 'Just a Smack at Auden'. But, while other poets were negative about the future, Riding offered a positive solution – so long as she was allowed to be in charge.

The work Graves did with Laura now revolved around the recruitment of an 'inside' group who were willing to act on her wishes and allow her the role of a centralizing force. Here, as in earlier years, Graves was no weak appendage but a vigorous advocate and supporter. Whatever he might say behind Riding's back, he remained her most powerful ally.

The main 'inside' people were Mary Somerville, Honor Wyatt, Gordon Glover, Alan Hodge, John Aldridge, James and Mary Reeves and, after a chance reunion in a London square, Len Lye.

James Reeves swelled the numbers by adding his brother, David, and Harry Kemp, his friend from Stowe and Cambridge. Riding had been shown Kemp's poems when Reeves visited Deyá; a good-looking and industrious youth with pale blond hair and pink cheeks, he was flattered to be offered her help on *The Left Heresy*, a book against Communism. Kemp also brought in his girlfriend, Alix Eiermann. To Graves and Riding, the group showed itself as a university in miniature. With Mary Somerville as Head of Education at the BBC, John Aldridge designing and painting, David Reeves writing on furniture and Lye communicating through the film screen, they could see it as a real possibility that their influence would extend into every branch of the arts.

Norman Cameron was the only significant connection Graves and Riding retained with the London poetry world. To writers who had lived in Mallorca for six years, it was curiously irritating to hear earnest young English poets working themselves up into a fever about the Spanish cause when few of them had ever been there. Graves went, without enthusiasm, to a recital of poems by Stephen Spender and noted in his diary that it had been 'all about aeroplanes, politics and Spain . . . gloomy sissy voice . . . gloomy preface by Herbert Read'.[3]

Spender was not the only poet to invite his scorn. Writing an account of this period with Alan Hodge five years later, Graves did not hide his contempt for '"the canting lay" of the professional Communist'.[4] Louis MacNeice was said to have achieved the required level of realism in his work by writing 'on bourgeois subjects, such as lawn-mowing in Hampstead gardens'.[5] Dylan Thomas was dismissed as a windbag, amusing only for the stories which Norman Cameron had to tell of his quarrels and drinking evenings. Auden, in a period when he was brilliantly borrowing from every poet he admired, was dismissed as a shoddy imitator of Riding's work.

Graves's attitude was at odds with the mood of the mid-Thirties. Communism, or a gesture towards it, was almost obligatory; Graves missed no opportunity to denigrate it, although his contempt for a right-winger like Roy Campbell was equally vehement. Spain had given the young poets a much-needed cause for which to fight; Graves, who would have been admired for allowing himself to be marooned in Deyá, was hard to see as an heroic exile. His hostility to the young poets who now ruled the literary roost made him seem surly and a little dated. Even his age was against him. In the autumn of 1936 Graves was forty-one. Auden was not yet thirty.

Graves's diary makes it clear that he cared less about meeting poets than getting to know his children again. The younger three delighted him. Sam had become a handsome, open boy, while David's easy charm hid resentment so well that his father never suspected its existence. He made fourteen-year-old Catherine his favourite, taking her with him to publishers' meetings, to A. P. Watt, the new agent recommended by Basil Liddell Hart, or to shop for curios in the Caledonian Road. This was where Graves spent some of his happiest hours in London, fantasizing about his return to Deyá as he bought pretty knick-knacks for the house. Shopping, in his dislocated state, amounted almost to a mania. All he asked was that his acquisitions should be cheap; he loved to think that he had found a bargain.

Jenny, his oldest child, was less tractable than her siblings. While ready to make herself agreeable, she was determined to make Graves pay for the humiliations she had suffered. She had not enjoyed going to school in wooden clogs or having only one dress to wear for auditions; she had not, and never would, forgive her father for deserting them. She was more easily able to understand Geoffrey Taylor's need for a wife and children of his own than her father's willingness to let his children go hungry while Laura was presented with houses, clothes and jewels. She was not so spiteful as to seek a revenge; she simply refused to behave, as David, Catherine and Sam did, as though nothing had happened.[6]

The first – unintended – drama came within a month of Graves's return to England. Sarah Churchill, Jenny's best friend and fellow dancer in C. B. Cochran's revue *Follow the Sun*, eloped to America with their personable comic lead, Vic Oliver.

Jenny, thrilled to be in on the secret, talked about it in front of a journalist. At a time when the newspapers were short of frivolous subjects, the elopement of a politician's daughter made headlines. Graves was obliged to go, cap in hand, to Winston Churchill (then out of office under Baldwin's government) and beg forgiveness. Churchill liked his visitor and took the apology handsomely; he even listened to Graves's pleas for a speech on the need for political intervention in Spain. Some good had come of Jenny's folly, as Graves recorded in his diary.[7]

Jenny's life as a dancer took her into a precarious world which her father chose not to notice. Proudly attending her performances at the Dorchester Hotel, he saw the glamour, not the seediness, when Jenny appeared, turning cartwheels in a skimpy costume. Graves, in the two years since Mary Ellidge had done her best to seduce him, had succeeded in forcing his thoughts away from sex and into the realm of pure intellect. In this state of mind, he could convince himself that the pretty, almond-eyed girl dancing on the stage was part of the new sexless age of innocence proclaimed by Laura Riding. This naïve concept was rudely shattered for both of them when Robin Hale came to the flat to be interviewed as a potential member of the 'inside' group. (She had come on the recommendation of Norman Cameron, after a merry evening at his favourite haunt, the Café Royal.)

Robin Hale was the daughter of a celebrated suffragist, Beatrice Forbes Robertson. Sitting in the flat while her poems were examined by Laura, Robin talked cheerfully about her older sister, Sancha. Sancha, she said, told every man she slept with to add a threepenny bit to the jar by her bed; her sexual allure was great and the jar was almost full. Laura explained that sex was not to be admired or indulged in, unless for reproductive purposes. Robin Hale burst out laughing. Writing his diary that evening, Graves noted that she had defended sex as 'necessary and delightful. Had never come across L's point of view before . . . Knew every Pole in London.'[8]

Graves was already confused. His poems, as always, reveal more uncertainty and guilt than he showed in public. In 'Parent to Children', begun the previous month, he was ready to oppose, not just casual sex, but the act of procreation. After writing of 'bed-ignorance' as his excuse, he compared the products, his children, to war victims:

> I, who begot you, ask no pardon of you;
> Nor may the soldier ask
> Pardon of the strewn dead.[9]

Robin Hale's attitude undid this anguished puritanism. The month after her visit, he began writing 'A Jealous Man'. Nobody reading this poem can doubt the feeling which drives it. The puritan was struggling against the desires he knew he must not acknowledge. The struggle is painfully apparent.

This jealous man is smitten,
His fear-jerked forehead
Sweats a fine musk;

A score of bats bewitched
By the ruttish odour
Swoop singing at his head;

Nuns bricked up alive
Within the neighbouring wall
Wail in cat-like longing.

Crow, cocks, crow loud!
Reprieve the doomed devil,
Has he not died enough?[10]

It was during this period of tormented self-examination that Graves was forced to a new view of his daughter Jenny's lifestyle.

Tom and Julie Matthews had returned to London in the mid-autumn of 1936 and were taking part in the 'international' discussions which Riding had just begun holding for group members. On the last night of their visit, 5 November, Graves invited them and Mary Somerville to come and see Jenny open in her new revue. Graves noticed only that Jenny still disliked hearing him spoken of as her father; a note which he had written to her signed 'your dear father' met that night with a response curtly signed, 'Daughter'.[11] He thought nothing of it, but Tom Matthews was aware that Jenny was nervous and upset.

A month later, on 2 December, a cryptic entry appeared in Graves's diary: 'Jenny told me she was ill.' This was more serious than it sounds: the burning down of the Crystal Palace the night before went unremarked.

Jenny had, after a month of hesitation, plucked up the courage to tell her father that she had caught a venereal disease from Pat Moran, a young man with whom she was having a traumatic affair. Frequent references to 'an operation', quite unnecessary for venereal disease, suggest that she may also have been pregnant.[12] Graves instantly confided in Riding. Together, they sent for Nancy to come up from her home in Wiltshire and decide what was to be done. (Graves was, in fact, the last to know; Jenny had already talked to Nancy and to Geoffrey and Mary Taylor; they had insisted that her father must be told.[13])

Nancy's behaviour was, unsurprisingly, calm. She proposed to take Jenny back to Wiltshire and arrange for her treatment at a local hospital. When it transpired that the hospital was unwilling to deal with such a case, Graves arranged for her to go to the Belleville, a private nursing home in London. He agreed to cover all the costs himself.

The woman, in Graves's eyes, was always the victim when misfortune befell her. Jenny, while she stayed with her mother in the country, was showered with messages telling her how brave and good she was. Her father's predictable villain was Moran, transformed by his mythical imagination from a sharp young man capable of stealing Jenny's watch into a figure of diabolic cunning and wickedness. Jenny's continuing declarations of love became signs of Moran's sinister power over her. Nancy, who had heard enough from her husband about Geoffrey Taylor's demonic qualities to give a wry smile, was told that Moran had infected Jenny with the mark of a devil and that they must force her to burn his picture and break with him immediately. Exorcism seemed to Graves the obvious course. He could not understand why Nancy did not insist on it.[14] The violence subsided, but only after Graves felt that he had gained control of the situation.

Taking charge as he paid the Belleville bills and, despite increasing ill-health, made daily visits, did not enable Graves to control Jenny's emotions. In his diary, he puzzled over the reason why his daughter should always be 'ever so much nicer when I come alone'. It is possible that, knowing Laura was reading the diary, he wanted to convey a hint to her to stay away. Certainly, Jenny had shown no warmth when Laura visited her and lectured her on her duty to her parents. She looked coldly at the new nightdresses, underwear and sanitary towels which Laura thoughtfully presented. This was the woman who had broken up her parents' marriage. She had no intention of being grateful. Laura was reduced to writing letters of complaint to Nancy about Jenny's rudeness.

Worry and illness had not kept Graves from work during this hectic period. Korda, who had already agreed to let him rewrite the laughably anachronistic studio script of *I, Claudius*, commissioned a new screenplay based on his exile from Spain. Laura was not to be excluded from such an opportunity to promote her views; Korda extricated himself from a delicate situation by telling her that her own contribution was just 'too good' for him. This soothed Laura and placated Graves, for whom the film connection was full of promise. The Lawrence trustees had finally given their consent to the publication of the Liddell Hart and Graves letters; Korda now invited Graves to be an adviser on his film about Lawrence's years in Arabia. Full of excitement, Graves ignored the warning of Korda's friendly secretary, Elizabeth Wright, not to expect too much. Korda was never short of ideas; what he lacked in 1937 was the money to develop them.

A lucrative film deal would have been welcome to Graves, and this was the main reason why he was prepared to slog away grimly at the condensed version of his *Claudius* novels, to be sold when the film appeared. The £8,500 which he estimated he had earned from these books had already been spent and he and Laura were living beyond their means in a flat in Dorset Street in central London, surrounded by so many new possessions that they had required a van to move them. Things were not, however, so desperate that Graves felt he needed to accept a commission to write a book called 'In the Steps of Hannibal'. Why should he want to walk in anybody's steps but his own? he asked his diary before turning the offer down. There was little sign of financial despair in his decision to avoid tax by renting part of an Italian palace at Lugano for four months. (It was necessary that he should leave England at least two months before the tax-year ended on 5 April.) Laura and he left for Lugano in mid-February 1937, taking Karl Goldschmidt with them as their assistant and also as a necessary buffer for their increasingly tense relationship.

*　　*　　*

Their short-term tax haven was exquisitely beautiful, with a view of snow-tipped mountains, the lake nearby, and landscapes so lovely that Riding remarked that it was not the Swiss roads which were dangerous, but the prospects. It was also ineffably dull. There were, Graves glumly recorded, no antique shops and no pieces of china worth buying. Apart from a walk up Monte Salvatore or a visit to their former Deyá neighbours, Georg Schwarz and Emmy Streng, there was little to alleviate the monotony. The only excitement of a Lugano trip was to watch the lake-sweepers fishing out flotsam; Karl recalled an evening so dreary that he started taking light-bulbs out of the lakeside illuminations and planting them in the flower-beds.[15]

The atmosphere of mild depression at the Villa Guidi was not lifted by the news, which reached them at the beginning of March, that

Gelat had been imprisoned on unspecified charges. Schwarz, they noticed with indignation, appeared unmoved. Graves wept.

Karl, hammering away on his typewriter from morning to night, was perhaps the happiest of the three of them in Switzerland. In London, although he had always lived nearby, he had felt isolated; now, he was like one of the family. His devotion to Graves was increased by the fact that, when the German authorities suddenly threatened not to renew his passport, Graves came to his rescue. Swaggering a little in his best raw-silk suit and a panama hat, he looked the perfect English gentleman as he charmed the German officials into changing their minds. It is quite likely that this action saved Karl's life: Karl certainly thought so.[16]

While in Lugano, Graves had little to distract him from his work. He finished his laborious condensation of the two *Claudius* novels only to hear that Korda had abandoned the film a month after starting shooting. The given explanation was that Merle Oberon, selected to play Messalina, had been hurt in a car accident, but this was a convenient excuse. Charles Laughton's interpretation of Claudius was becoming increasingly discordant and bizarre. Some later film-buffs have judged it to be one of the most remarkable performances of Laughton's career. Korda lost his nerve, and Graves's book was left without a market.

Although his feelings for Laura had changed, Graves still delighted in her mind. One of the few pleasures of life at the Villa Guidi was that it gave him the chance to work on collaborative projects with her again. Together they revised novels by Honor Wyatt and Alan Hodge, both of which had been initiated by Riding, but their most serious collaborative task was on *The World and Ourselves*.

This work, intended to form the climax of the *Epilogue* series, had been born just after Christmas 1937 in the form of a circular, the 'international letter' which Riding sent to the four hundred people she saw as potential 'insiders'; she intended to study their responses and present them in a book which would offer hope to a doomed world. The list of people to whom this letter had been sent was a weird and wonderful one, ranging from Eddie Marsh and Christina Stead (who answered) to an antique-shop owner with whom Graves had made friends (who did not).

Answers were meant to arrive at the Villa Guidi by a specific date; Graves was ready to brandish his cudgels on Riding's behalf when Michael Roberts failed to reply, along with over three hundred others. In her Introduction to *The World and Ourselves*, of which the eventual responses – most of which were hesitant or scoffing – formed only a small part, Riding declared that no pressure had been put on correspondents; it is worth noting that, in Roberts's case, he was still resisting after five angry letters. Only the faithful shared Graves's belief that Riding's will-power could help to avert a world crisis.

Riding had, by now, almost abandoned poetry and her prose was becoming increasingly ornate and self-conscious. Graves, however responsive he was to her ideas, was not tempted to adopt her mannered style. The letter with which he answered her circular letter was a model of lucidity, and revealing of what he assumed their mutual aims to be. His argument was for individuality and privacy. 'Inside life', as he saw it, was the way life had always been in private households ruled by affection rather than law. The best thing which men could do to help 'inside' women was to refuse to conform to society's demands, and to resist the temptation to accept any form of fascist propaganda. His most vehement attack was reserved for the 'little Napoleons' who ruled the world.[17] In an exasperatingly confused and dissatisfying book, Graves's letter shone out for its honesty and its intelligence.

The success of Riding's 'international plan' became increasingly important to them both as the gap between his success and her failure, in commercial and critical terms, widened. *Antigua, Penny, Puce* had been well-received on both sides of the Atlantic. Riding's historical novel, *A Trojan Ending*, was published in March 1937 to muted or hostile reviews. Her plan for yet another dictionary, in which the meanings would be defined by herself, had not yet found a sponsor. There was, however, one piece of good news from America: Random House were ready to publish her collected poems. Graves, indignant about the lack of response to her call for a following, wrote a poem on a scrap of paper which he had picked out of a hedge on one of his walks. 'The Fallen Tower of Siloam' painted a picture of the wrecked world in which the poets chose not, as Riding had done, to give warnings, but to remain silent. The poets of Siloam escape harm and congratulate themselves on what the reader is intended to see as an empty victory.[18]

Homesick for Deyá when they were in England, Graves and Riding felt still more painfully exiled in Lugano. Graves noted in his diary that any day on which he felt well could be called a happy one; Riding, meanwhile, became convinced that the Villa Guidi was haunted by ghosts. (She could hardly be blamed: even the writing paper carried a logo of a skull and crossbones.) They were relieved when the four months were over and they could return to England, where Harry Kemp and his friend Alix Eiermann had found a suitable country house for them to rent as a foursome. But Graves's first stay was at St Mary's Hospital, where he was operated on for the removal of a painful boil which had developed into a fistula. The fact that, although this was only a small operation, it was judged necessary to keep him in hospital for three weeks is an indication of the poor state of his health.

CHAPTER TWENTY-ONE

1937–1938

THE COVENANT

PHYSICAL DISCOMFORT WAS NEVER ALLOWED TO GET IN THE WAY OF Graves's professionalism: before going into St Mary's Hospital, Paddington, on 20 June, he visited his new agent, A. P. Watt, to make a proposal. Since it remained, embarrassingly, the case that Riding's projects only attracted a publisher when a book by him was added as bait, he suggested that Watt should offer Laura's study of influential consorts of the past, *Lives of Wives*, together with *Count Belisarius*,[1] the novel he planned to write next. There was common ground here, which made it easier for Graves to suggest a twin sale: his book was about the Emperor Justinian's most famous general, while Riding was taking Justinian's wife, Theodora, as one of her subjects. Feeling, and looking, dreadful, he then went out to Denham Studios, to make sure that Riding was included in Alexander Korda's latest proposal for a screenplay – about life in the Thirties. (This, like most of Korda's proposed scripts, came to nothing.)

Even in hospital, Graves refused to rest. He spent much of his time thinking about *Belisarius*, and talking about the historical background with Sally Graves, the daughter of his oldest half-brother, Philip. Sally, a slim, dark-haired and rather beautiful young woman, had known Graves and Laura slightly since she was a girl of fourteen in the St Peter's Square days; now, as one of Laura's most intelligent admirers, she was a favourite among the 'inside' group. However, her uncle's thoughts were far from *Belisarius* and his niece when he wrote 'Leda' and 'The Florist Rose' in St Mary's.

Graves liked these poems enough to republish them in his final collection of 1975. In biographical terms, they are troubling. Graves, famously, loved women; what the poems suggest is that, by the summer of 1937, he could only control his desire by turning the image of a yielding woman into something abhorrent. 'Leda' shows the god's raped victim revelling in her degradation ('And there beneath your god awhile / You strained and gulped your beastliest.') 'The Florist Rose' goes to the opposite extreme and compares a neatly trimmed and presented flower to a cold coquette, foreign to the spirit of legend and romance, who 'Pouts, false-virginal, between bud and bloom';[2] The 'false-virginal' suggests that this simpering girl will behave like Leda as soon as she gets the chance. And so, sickened by the nightmarish images he conjured up, Graves kept himself in the required condition of unhappy celibacy.

Riding was always at her kindest when friends were ill. She made visits to Graves every day, and rejoiced with him over the news that Gelat had been released from prison. Talk of their friend brought back happy memories of life at Canellun. Much affected, Riding presented Graves with a letter. Written in the most courtly Spanish, it informed him, cheeringly, that she was his 'friend of the soul'.[3] To a man who was wrestling with images of the kind depicted in 'Leda', this was poor comfort.

Among the subjects of their talks at St Mary's was Beryl Pritchard, who had been brought into the group through a sexual partnership. Alan Hodge and she had become attached to each other in 1936, their final year at Oxford. The question was, whether or not she would make a suitable wife for Alan, to whom Riding and Graves were now devoted.

They seemed far younger than their twenty-two years. Alan, while articulate and intelligent, was shy and insecure; the novel which he was writing under Graves and Riding's supervision was, revealingly, altered as often as they asked. He was happy to be swayed by their judgement. His girlfriend, although quiet, was far less pliable.

Slight and dark-haired, Beryl had a creamy oval face and blue eyes which narrowed to slits when she was amused. The joke was, a little too often for comfort, a private one. Laura, who liked everybody to yield up their histories to her, was frustrated by Beryl's elusiveness and her slightly mocking smile. It sometimes looked suspiciously as though Beryl did not take her seriously.

There was not a great deal to be yielded up. One of a family of five, Beryl was the youngest daughter of an eminent solicitor and parliamentary agent and a quiet, conventional woman described by her non-believing daughter as a pillar of the Church. At Oxford, where she had been a student with Graves's niece, Sally, Beryl had read PPE (Politics, Philosophy and Economics) at St Anne's and joined the Oxford Union Labour Club. After an unhappy love-affair, Alan Hodge had seemed the perfect balm for her distress. He was kind, gentle, and weak. Beryl shared his enthusiasm for Graves and Riding and their dream of teaching people to cherish order and disciplined thought. But, exceptionally, she refused to be coaxed into writing novels, essays or poems. There was something in her manner which suggested that bullying would have no effect. Young though she was, Beryl knew exactly what she was prepared to do. She admired Riding's personality; she did not intend to be steamrollered by it.

Graves, from the start, was fascinated by Beryl; he refused to become worked up when Laura brought news that Beryl had, in some unspecified way, insulted her. A discussion about 'the Alan–Beryl position' was held, but no conclusion was reached. Their relationship continued to flourish gently under the mantle of the group, while Hodge started gathering anecdotal detail for Graves's new novel. (Cassells had agreed to the double offer of this and *Lives of Wives*, and were rewarded for their act of faith: they published Graves for the rest of his life.)

★   ★   ★

At Lugano, he had dutifully worked on 'The Swiss Ghost', a light-hearted thriller which he and Riding had conceived as a collaborative project. It had no future and Graves had realized this long before they decided to abandon the book. The relief of turning to the more intriguing subject of Belisarius was immense. T. E. Lawrence had given him the idea for a book six years earlier, but Claudius had overtaken it in his mind.

As with the mischievous satire on the deification of Claudius by

Seneca, so Belisarius's posthumous reputation had been blackened by the scurrilous pages of Procopius's *Secret History*. The most important questions about the great general remained unanswered. Why did Belisarius fail to command the loyalty of his troops? Why did he remain faithful to Antonina, a wife who betrayed him – according to Procopius – with their own adopted son? Why did Justinian show so little gratitude to the man who brought back all the spoils of Carthage to enrich his magnificent new church, Haghia Sofia? (Legend had it that the Emperor blinded the general and had him thrown on the streets to beg; more certainly, Belisarius was deprived of his property and only restored to favour when the Emperor saw that his own popularity was at risk.)

Graves did not begin writing the book until he was settled in the new home which Harry Kemp and Alix Eiermann – now Harry's wife – had found for the four of them to share in Ewhurst village, not far from Charterhouse School. They moved in on 7 July 1937. Laura disliked Highcroft, as it was named; Graves, less observant than she of the ugly brown and purple décor, was troubled only by the squalor and a faint, pervasive smell of damp, even in high summer. Prudently, he chose himself an airy, pleasant room on the first floor, overlooking the garden. After hanging up his map of Spain and a picture of his Deyá mastiff, Solomon, he set out the little talismanic objects which helped him to write, sent Sam and Catherine letters about the potential of the garden as a children's camp-site, and settled down to work.

Feeling his way back into the period of Belisarius occupied much of Graves's first weeks at Highcroft, although he was also working on a final polishing of his collected poems, to be published the following year. Alix, who had not seen the devoted way Graves attended on Riding in Deyá, was astonished to see him carrying Laura's breakfast to her room each morning. She did just the same for Harry, her husband, but it was not, surely, up to the man to do it? '"Lives of Wives,"' she remarked with an interrogative look; Graves, to her mild irritation, only laughed.[4] Perhaps, Alix decided, it had less to do with deference to Riding than with a passion for domestic work; on another day, she found him diligently shelling peas in his bedroom.[5]

At Canelluñ, writing the *Claudius* novels to save himself from ruin, Graves had shut himself in his study for most of the day. Life at Highcroft was more relaxed. The meals were taken care of by their housekeeper, Marie, a young girl who quickly became attached to Karl Goldschmidt. (They married in November.) A new entertainment offered itself in the form of Mary Lucy, a good-looking poetess whose admiration for Laura was soon replaced by a crush on Graves. His 'Leda' phase of seeing all women as vultures was cured by Mary's gentle overtures, but his pleasure at being flirted with waned when it became clear that Mary's interest in him had been reported back to her husband John, a man of jealous temperament. Graves began to avoid her.

There was, Graves's diary suggests, a concerted effort to turn Highcroft into a happy centre of activity, and to recapture the atmosphere of Canelluñ. While his younger children camped out in the garden, Harry, he and Laura played a new game which she had invented, of blowing strands of coloured wool along the floor. In the evenings, Harry and he held elaborate contests on the solitaire board. Archery, which he had enjoyed when he shot at sugared buns with a bow in Mallorca, became a passion again when Harry and Alix gave him a bow and arrows for a birthday present. He practised zealously and recorded his victories with pride. (It is no coincidence that archery plays a significant role in some of Belisarius's finest battles.) There were visits from members of the 'inside' group, songs around the piano, drinks in an idyllic local pub, a jolly visit to Bognor, evening sessions of reading comic novels aloud. Wodehouse remained their favourite.

Life should have been perfect. In his diary, Graves superstitiously blamed the house itself for the aura of depression which enveloped them as the summer faded. Everything seemed to go wrong. Alix heard that her father was dying and went to Germany to be with him. Harry, who was never happy unless he was living with a woman, became morose and contrary; there were long conversations about the problem of his disliking Honor Wyatt. (All members of the group were expected to love each other, while revering Riding; any expression of dislike was treated as a serious problem.) News of the sales of the Seizin Press books distributed in England by Constable was discouraging and Constable expressed a reluctance to continue with the partnership, even though they were heavily subsidized by Graves. Riding grew ill from overwork and too many cigarettes, while Graves became involved in a family row when his brother Charles, after talking to Jenny, told Amy Graves that her granddaughter was barely given enough money to live above the starvation line. (This was unjust; Graves had met all of Jenny's requests for money, and with very little protest.) He was more distressed, however, that Riding had ceased to treasure his gifts. Worse than the fact of her losing them, to him, was the undisguised evidence of her annoyance when he succeeded in finding and returning these lost trinkets. He could hardly have been offered a clearer sign of her growing indifference to his feelings. He remained too intent on pursuing his duty as her loyal lieutenant to see what was becoming apparent to his friends.[6]

Their hopes of returning to Deyá faded in the autumn of 1937 with the news that Italy had occupied Mallorca. Britain, Graves bitterly noted, appeared content to acquiesce. By mid-September, his dread of city life was outweighed by the gloominess of their country existence. A house with large, light rooms was found in pretty, agreeably shabby Alma Square, not far from Little Venice and some enticing antique shops. They all liked the area: Karl and his new wife found themselves a home nearby, as did the Kemps; Alan Hodge and Beryl Pritchard were already living within walking distance, in Adelaide Road.

Number 31 Alma Square was remembered by Graves as a happy period in his life, not least because it was here that he finally saw Riding in the position of authority which he had longed for her to achieve. The days passed in a pleasant routine, with work on *Belisarius* occupying his mornings and being resumed after a stroll to Paddington Street, where there was a shop full of the kind of curios which Graves loved buying. Here, in a single week, he bought a green stone fish, a little silver Persian horse, a glass bracelet, an engraving of a Spanish church and a Georgian tumbler. In the evenings, Laura often accompanied him on long strolls into the centre of London, to Hyde Park and Kensington Gardens.

Graves's younger children had enjoyed living in their garden tent at Highcroft. Taking his affectionate messages home to Nancy, they began to hope for a reconciliation between their parents. But when Graves wrote to Nancy in November 1937, it was to suggest a divorce. It had only been an idea; when David came to Alma Square with the news that Nancy had been unconscious for almost a week after a severe haemorrhage, Graves was horrified by the bad timing of his suggestion. The subject of divorce was hurriedly dropped.

Marriage was a frequent topic of conversation at Alma Square. Alan Hodge had discussed the possibility of his marrying Beryl on a visit to Highcroft; in December, Beryl told Graves she was not sure that it was a good idea. Graves offered nothing but the reassuring words which Beryl had not, perhaps, particularly wanted to hear. She married Alan at the end of January 1938. Graves, who usually enjoyed a party, was quite unable to get into the mood for the celebration of their wedding. His diary account was full of complaints; he left early with two new members of the 'inside' group, a sculptress called Dorothy Simmons, and her husband Montague, a part-time poet who worked at the Home Office.[7]

Belisarius was finished and ready for revision by the end of January 1938. Riding had been too busy with her plans to save the world from war to pay much attention to the book, but she did make one significant contribution before reading it. Graves had decided to tell the story through Antonina, Belisarius's lively, strong-willed wife, who sometimes went into battle with him and, on occasion, persuaded the Empress to take Belisarius's side against her mean-spirited husband, Justinian. Riding proposed that Graves should put the narration into the mouth of a fictitious slave, a eunuch in the employ of Antonina. It must have amused her to create a parallel to her own situation, with Graves appearing as the servile and sexually frustrated Eugenius. Graves, too, could get a morose pleasure out of such an analogy; there was always an element of masochism in the humiliations he chose to undergo. The change was made. The book suffered a consequent drop in the tension of the narrative.

Belisarius is, nevertheless, one of Graves's finest novels. The intrigue which takes centre-stage in the *Claudius* novels is here moved into the shadows, while the light falls with remarkable clarity on the scenes of war in North Africa and Italy. Liddell Hart thought it a superb book; Winston Churchill read and studied it for helpful ideas during the Second World War. Belisarius himself is made too one-dimensional by his unfailing decency, but Graves defended his right to paint a truthful picture of a good man in a dirty world. At a time when the subject of leadership was being discussed in every journal and newspaper, *Belisarius* seemed to him an inspiring example.

The revisions to *Belisarius* were made in February, during another period of anxiety about Jenny. Graves, endowed with a large intelligence, generously liked to suppose that all his children and dearest friends were equally remarkable in their gifts. Jenny was not just any dancer, but the finest young dancer of her age. So he told her, and Jenny, who was almost as much of a fantasist as her father, was willing to share his view. By February, however, her hopes had faded. A dancer who could not sing had no future in musicals, and Jenny had inherited none of her father's ease with a song. Like her mother, she was tone-deaf. Graves's promises of help brought nothing but disappointment. He had asked Korda to get her into films; Korda told her that he had nothing to offer at present. He had promised to get Noël Coward to make use of her talents; Coward replied that he could only help when Jenny learned to sing. In March 1938 she decided to embark on a new career as an actress with the Liverpool Rep. Her father was again convinced that this would be the start of an astonishing career.

From March onwards, Graves devoted himself to promoting Riding's work and pushing her role as a bringer of world peace; he pressed her dictionary on Cassell; he worked on a dramatization of her novel, *A Trojan Ending*, and wrote the jacket blurb for her forthcoming collected poems. He even planned to edit a book of tributes to Riding by members of the 'inside' group. When Nancy, rashly, wrote to tell him that she was tired of being told about the perfection of Laura, Graves, infuriated, raised the subject of divorce again.[8]

Nancy's rudeness was a small matter compared to the elation he felt at seeing Riding achieve all he had ever wanted for her. World events had begun to terrify thoughtful people by the beginning of 1938. Helpless in the face of what seemed to be an inevitable catastrophe, many found comfort in Riding's proposal to bring order out of mental discipline. At a time when almost the worst sensation was that of being unable to do anything, people responded to the idea of taking action into their own hands. 'Insider' recruits visited Alma Square steadily throughout March and April; at night, the 'inside' group met to hear how Riding proposed that they might prevent war. Basil Liddell Hart was among the new recruits; Mary Somerville was among those who left, disturbed by Riding's rejection of religious beliefs and any moral code she had not herself defined as acceptable.

On 28 April, Riding endowed the group with a new and hideous name, the Covenant of Literal Morality.* The sound of words no longer mattered to her; it was at approximately this time that she

---

* The Covenant was also, simultaneously, known as 'The First Protocol'.

rejected poetry as an unsuitable vehicle for the truth she wanted to convey. This was ominous; by 1938, Riding looked for acts of imitation among her friends. The 'inside' group, as the more astute of them soon realized, were not encouraged to have views of their own. Although it was never directly stated, Riding must have expected that Graves would follow her into this realm of a purer, if uglier, language. He did not; there is no trace in his writings of the late Thirties of Riding's ornate and somewhat portentous style. He never considered rejecting poetry for prose.

Graves attended all the Covenant's meetings and, by his presence, gave Riding a credibility which she still did not possess alone. This, presumably, was the reason why, when Graves was told he must go abroad again if he wanted to avoid paying British income tax, Riding chose to accompany him. But if she was wholly committed to the 'inside' group, why did she not stay and work with them in England? The reason was partly financial – she still depended on Graves to support her – and partly that he remained too useful to be dispensed with. She could not, yet, see an alternative to her partnership with Graves.

His own emotions were becoming increasingly unsettled by his feelings for Beryl. Graves's diary describes a curious evening when he and Riding went for a walk and gazed at the windows of Alan and Beryl's house near Primrose Hill before turning away. But Riding continued to hold him in thrall to her intelligence and clarity. At a time when the prospect of another war filled him with dread, he could not imagine life without the one woman he honestly believed might, through the influence of her uncommon personality, prevent that war from taking place.

★   ★   ★

At the end of June, accompanied by Beryl and Alan Hodge, while Karl stayed in London with his young wife, Graves and Riding travelled to the pretty old town of Rennes in Brittany. One reason for fastening on Rennes was that Alan had brought back good reports after a brief summer reconnaissance; another was that Gelat's sister and her family ran a fruit shop there. Anywhere that a member of Gelat's family lived was sure to be congenial; they were full of hope. The first few days, when they sat heavily smoking in the gloomy lobby of the Hôtel Central, did not bear out this sense of good fortune. No house that they saw, either in Rennes or in the nearby villages, suited their inclination; Graves was preparing to look elsewhere when they heard of a perfect home: the Château de la Chevrie. It was an eighteenth-century country house, ten miles from the town, with a pretty park, a lake and handsome rooms with oak-beamed ceilings. For £40 a year, it seemed a bargain.

Brittany itself enthralled Graves with its Celtic connections and legends. The château, too, appealed to the side of his nature which revelled in magic and superstition. The neighbouring woods had a reputation for being haunted by fairies and phantoms, while the dark, oak-panelled rooms of the house lent themselves to every kind of ghostly tale that an imaginative tenant could hope for. The owner had spent little of her time there, and the house was making a leisurely return to its natural state when they arrived. Mice, fleas, bees and bats had taken up residence; the first few days were spent in a fury of spring-cleaning. Furniture and pictures were put away, fires lit, rat dirt removed. A persistent and intrusive flock of bats were eventually tracked down to an attic, where Graves, Beryl and Alan dutifully beat them to death with wooden boards at Laura's behest. (Laura had a horror of bats.) A ghost, heard by Graves and seen in the act of spiriting away a poker by Beryl, added to their sense that this was a place filled with magical powers. Graves, mindful of his army days, divided and allocated special duties to each of them. He took charge of wood-chopping, kitchen-cleaning, flowers and bicycle maintenance, Beryl was asked to look after the purchase of groceries and household provisions, while Alan became the groundsman, lavatory cleaner and clock-winder. Laura's job was appropriate to her superiority; she was to make sure that the maids cleaned the rooms, and to supervise Modeste, the cook.

Riding, struggling to finish *Lives of Wives* and to keep up her correspondence with members of the Covenant, stayed in her room for much of the time; Graves, left alone with Beryl and Alan, became increasingly light-hearted. He took up bicycling for the first time in almost a decade, with the result that he was soon fit and thinner than he had been since leaving Deyá. Working with Alan on the grouping of words for Laura's dictionary was an absorbing pastime which neither man took too seriously; the quiet old rooms of the château were revived by the sound of their disputes and jokes. In the evenings, they played cards or went for walks to the lake in the park. The quartet had, almost without their noticing it, become a triangle.

The idea of renting a large house had been so that other friends should be able to join them at will. James Reeves's brother, David, came to live with them. So, when her husband started having an affair, did the young sculptress Dorothy Simmons. But this hardly affected the comfortable relationship between Graves and the Hodges; both Dorothy and David were working on projects under Riding's close supervision, which kept them fully occupied.

Life at La Chevrie was, although superficially tranquil, interrupted by moments of drama. After Elfriede's death, Norman Cameron had married Catherine, a woman Riding disliked; now, he announced that he was leaving The Covenant. David Graves infuriated his father by making it clear that he expected to be supported financially when he went to university. A bad review in the *Times Literary Supplement* of Riding's *Collected Poems* provoked Graves into sending the editor a savage letter of reproach. Alan Hodge, who had a weak head and a tendency to drink too much, became depressed about Riding's further revisions to his novel. He came back drunk from the village one night, announcing that he was the unerring voice of truth in all things. This sounded disturbingly like a parody of Laura's frequent declarations of her infallibility.

These were minor events. But, on a day when Graves found what he was sure was a magic hazel wand in a wood called Les Bois des Fées, and on All Souls' Night, when the château's tenants stood guard in what they thought was a magic grove, his superstitious instincts began to throb with a sense of excited apprehension. There was a sense of witchery in the air. Gradually, subtly, relationships at La Chevrie were beginning to shift and change.

The covert nature of Graves's remarks in his diary suggests that he allowed Riding to read it and took care not to arouse her suspicions; she would have needed to be very blind to miss the clues. 'We are getting very fond of Beryl,' he noted on 11 August, when they had been at the château for a little over a month. The following day, he noted that he and Beryl had talked about a ghost whose presence she had sensed in the kitchen. They went blackberry-picking together. In September Beryl invented a new solitaire game which Graves and she played almost every day. Karl heard from Alan of a strange occasion when Graves, hearing a crash of furniture, burst into their bedroom where Beryl, naked, was standing in front of the fireplace. Shaken, he beat a hasty retreat.[9] He made no reference to this occasion in the diary.

Animal references provided further clues. Laura had always been devoted to cats; at the château, where she kept none, Graves made space in his diary for doting comments – from a man who did not much like felines – on Beryl's absorbed interest in the two small cats and a hedgehog she had adopted. On his birthday, it was carefully recorded that one of Beryl's cats had given him a packet of Gauloise cigarettes.

The diary reveals, however indirectly, that Graves no longer thought Riding's jokes were interesting enough to be preserved; instead, he took admiring note of Beryl's sudden shafts of mordant wit. But the diary is most revealing in charting their progress from friendship to comfortable familiarity. Beryl and he cooked up jam together in vast saucepans, invented silly stories about the cats' secret lives, swapped jokes, and went on long walks. Some entries hint at a romantic development. Primroses are the flowers of dalliance; on several occasions Graves noted that he and Beryl had picked primroses together. When a girlfriend of Beryl's from her Oxford days visited the château, Graves told her about a dream in which he had seen Beryl walking towards him, smiling, and with her hands full of tiny flowers.[10] On one mysterious occasion, he noted that he had given Beryl a poem and then asked her to destroy it. It was significant, too, that he responded with intense anger when Mary Lucy attempted to revive his interest by writing that she was having clairvoyant feelings about him. Her intrusive flirtatiousness trivialized the sincerity of his own new feelings for Beryl.

The autumn of 1938 was the time when Graves began to think seriously about Beryl. The fact that she was twenty years younger than him, and that she was married to Alan, seems to have troubled him less than his own need to remain loyal to Riding. On 25 October, after a night walk with Beryl, he wrote 'The Suicide in the Copse', a black poem which argues that there is no escape, even in death; he took up the theme again in a poem which he presented to Riding on her birthday three months later. 'Dawn Bombardment' is an appeal for freedom by a group of captives who wait for rescue and bless each sign of the bombardment of their fortress.[11] He was, Riding told him a month later, quite wrong to see himself as a prisoner. The guns were his own to fire whenever he wanted. He was, implicitly, free to go.

Quite as powerful as the shift of Graves's love towards Beryl was the change which was taking place in Laura's mind in the late autumn of 1938. Karl was her confidant about the grief she felt when she heard that her father was dead. Riding had often thought of returning to America and seeing him again; now, she told Karl that only hatred of her mother was preventing her from doing so.[12]

She no longer felt hopeful about preventing war in Europe by the end of 1938, but America offered new opportunities for the Covenant. A return home, then, was already in her mind when news came from Tom Matthews of a glowing review of her *Collected Poems* in *Time* by his new poetry assistant on the magazine. In it, the reviewer had written that Riding and Rilke were the only two true poets of the twentieth century. The review arrived at La Chevrie in January 1939. Its author was the 38-year-old Schuyler Jackson.

Both Graves and Riding already knew about the Jacksons. On his first visit to Deyá, Tom had talked about his brilliant but volatile friend, a poet who had, for a time, shared his admiration for Gurdjieff's teaching. In Tom's mind, there was no doubt that Jackson was the most brilliant man he had ever known; he was a little in love with him. Both Jackson and his cheerful, sensible wife Katherine had been persuaded by Tom to become supporters of Riding's views; Kit Jackson had written one of the answers to her 'international letter'. When Riding heard herself described in such glowing terms by a man with a reputation for acute literary sensibility (this was according only to Tom Matthews), in a year when she was pining to return to America, her reaction was as powerful as it had once been to Robert Graves's admiration. She could hardly wait to make herself known to him in person.

Decisions were taken with impressive speed. By 6 February, Graves noted in his diary that they were thinking of going to America in the spring, 'to stay in Pennsylvania for a few months near the Jacksons and Tom and Julie'. Laura's letters to Karl, meanwhile, told him that they would certainly remain in the States 'until we see what next'.[13] By 5 March she was ready to tell him that she anticipated Schuyler with a sense of 'pure directness' which she had never yet known with anyone. She did not talk about this to Robert, she added; it was Karl's secret.[14]

The cheerfulness of Graves's mood was unshakeable. Even the news that Franco had taken Barcelona could not dismay him; a walk with Beryl to the moonlit lake on 10 February left him feeling 'thoroughly happy, somehow'. Riding, noting that he seemed to be on more intimate terms with Beryl than she could regard as prudent, began to offer advice and pointed hints. At first, she invented word-games in which the names carried a loaded meaning, conveying her approval or dislike; Schuyler Jackson was seen as a 'White' while Graves was a seemingly inferior 'Gallagher' or 'Fortaskew'. She proceeded from this covert approach to long private discussions and offers of moral guidance. Graves, knowing that Riding had completely forsworn all sexual relations, respected her integrity in such matters. He listened to what she said. 'Long talk about relations of L, A, B and me,' he also noted on 16 February. 'Talked most of night with Laura and *at last* got the thing right about joulting and swingering.' These were words devised by Lucie Aldridge to describe degrees of compatibility; a year later, he was still worrying because Laura had said Beryl and he did not have the right ratio of these ingredients to be a good influence on each other.

From a distance, the hubris of Riding's announcements seems breathtaking; but Beryl, too, accepted them and felt real anxiety if she acted in a way of which she thought Riding would disapprove. Riding's position had become almost that of an abbess, a pure figure whose own inviolability gave her the right to judge and regulate the behaviour of her novices. It never occurred to any of them to question her sudden wish to join the Jacksons. And yet Graves must have wondered what uncommon force was driving her when she shrugged off the news that, on 28 March, the Spanish Civil War was over and they were free to go home to Mallorca. Laura and he had always been united in their resolve to go back to Deyá at the first moment it became possible; now, Riding only wanted to return to America.

The plans were already well-advanced. Tom Matthews had good-naturedly agreed to provide, as a loan to Schuyler, the $25,000 needed to restore a ruined cottage on the Jacksons' farm in Pennsylvania. This was to be Graves and Riding's new home and, Graves hoped, a home for Beryl and Alan Hodge. He noted with touching pleasure that Laura's naming of the unseen house 'Nimrod' had created 'a bond of immediate intelligence between L[aura] and B[eryl]'.[15] That the two women should form a real friendship was now of great importance to him. He needed them both; he was overjoyed to learn that the Hodges were willing to follow him to Pennsylvania. His diary is not easy to interpret during this period, but his view appears to have been that Beryl and he would love each other, while Alan and Laura would occupy the roles of cherished friends.

The last April days at La Chevrie had a perfection which was almost unreal. The weather was serene and all the lanes and paths along which Graves and Beryl strolled were hidden by banks of wild flowers. On 3 April the news came that *Count Belisarius* had been awarded the Prix Femina; six days later, J. M. Dent fell into line behind a fairly reluctant Little, Brown and agreed to publish Riding's dictionary.

On 20 April, they heard the alarming news that their chosen liner, the *Paris*, on to which they feared their luggage had already been carried after being sent off in advance, had caught fire the previous night. The luggage was safe, and Graves and Riding set sail instead on the *Champlain*.

Beryl and Alan left France a few days later, promising to follow as soon as the new house was ready for visitors, while David Reeves joined the *Champlain* at Southampton.

For Graves, a poor sailor, the crossing was a grim one and not improved by the knowledge that he was travelling away from a familiar world and the woman he loved to live with people who were, however well-intentioned, complete strangers. Three weeks later, he was still describing 'a suffocating tiredness' brought on by the voyage.[16] He looked wan and depressed when Robin Hale, who had come with the Matthewses and Jacksons to meet the travellers, saw him on the New York docks. (Robin had moved from England to America in 1938.) She saw him hunting among the cases with a distraught look. A heavy box was dragged forward by a porter; Graves's face lit up again. It was, he explained, the crate which held his dictionaries. With his favourite books beside him, he felt safe again.[17]

CHAPTER TWENTY-TWO

1939–1940

MADNESS AND MAGICS

THE SITUATION TO WHICH RIDING FELT SO STRONGLY DRAWN WAS not dissimilar to the one she had encountered in 1926, when she joined the Graveses, routed Nancy and took up a position of supreme authority. As with Graves and Nancy, it was important that the Jacksons should both welcome her into their home before she could disrupt it.

They looked a perfect couple, smart and confident, with the ease which can be produced by a leisured, wealthy background. But the wealth had gone by the time Graves and Riding arrived, and so had whatever ingredient it was that had brought this unlikely couple together. Kit, a practical, cheerful sportswoman with a ringing voice and a jolly, almost puppyish manner, was still providing the money for a farming venture in which, year after year, her husband demonstrated his inability to grasp the basic principles of land economy. Schuyler, a short, arrestingly handsome man with burning eyes and the springing grace of an athlete, was now thirty-eight. He had first attracted Tom Matthews's fascinated interest in the early Twenties when he was writing poetry as a Princeton graduate. In his final year at university, Jackson was taken up by the last of the Georgian editors, J. C. Squire, with whose encouragement he moved to England, living – just after Graves's departure – at Boars Hill near Oxford. In 1922 he returned to America and founded a small press, The Open Road, through which he hoped to publish the work of young American poets. Since then, an unsatisfactory marriage and an unsuccessful career as a farmer had turned him into a sulky drinker who dreamed of escaping to a different life. His four children adored him, for Schuyler was possessed of almost as powerful a magnetism as Laura, and more charm; his wife endured the bad patches for the sake of the times when Schuyler seemed to become his dreamy, delightful self again. They both welcomed the idea of visitors who would give them a common interest: Laura's peace-bringing enterprise seemed to offer just that.

Laura Riding believed that everything she did in the summer of 1939 was undertaken out of pure selflessness, to save an unhappy family from destruction. It had never been possible for Riding to accept that she was capable of actions which were not inspired by the noblest of motives. But large justifications would be needed for her behaviour in America that year, both towards Kit Jackson and towards Graves.

The cottage on the Jackson farm at New Hope, Pennsylvania, was still uninhabitable on 28 April when the *Champlain* docked at New York. Arrangements were made for Graves and Riding to spend the first weeks with the Matthews family at Princeton, where Riding left a not altogether pleasant memory with Tom and Julie's sons of a powdered, perfumed little woman in heavy velvet clothes, who dismissed their nurse and took over their bedroom.[1]

The day after their arrival, Schuyler took them to see the farm at New Hope which Kit and he had bought in 1929, when he was twenty-eight and full of dreams of easy prosperity. After admiring the white, three-storey house in which the Jacksons lived, they walked out behind it to the half-restored cottage Laura had already named Nimrod's House. Poison ivy was thick on the ground and the clammy air buzzed with insects.[2] Nevertheless, writing to the sculptress Dorothy Simmons the following day, Graves reported that David Owle, the Cherokee who worked on the farm, was 'sweet' and that 'everyone is lovely to us'. Schuyler had seemed at first to resemble 'a stiff-necked army officer' and Kit an efficient woman doctor 'of the best sort', but they were 'not at all like that on second sight'.[3] Kit, presiding over their picnic lunch, had been loud and cheerful; Schuyler had said little but watched everything with a faint smile. This was also the day on which Graves wrote in his diary that 'L and S got things clear'.

It was not, as yet, apparent what this signified. Graves was, however, already less enthusiastic about their new life than Laura, and unable to admit it to her. A second letter to Dorothy Simmons was dictated by Riding. It said, again, that everything to do with the Jacksons and their farm was 'lovely', and that Kit was 'a mainstay for sensibleness, and calmness'.[4] Writing a third, and independent letter to Dorothy, Graves told her that the first week had been fraught with tension and that there was difficulty with Kit Jackson, although Laura was sure that she would be 'all right'.[5]

To Beryl and Alan, anxious that they should start for America as soon as possible, he wrote in a more positive vein. The four young Jackson children, ranging from four-year-old Ben to twelve-year-old Griselda, were described as wild but friendly. A car had been bought which David Reeves would drive for them. There were no bulls (Beryl had told Graves at La Chevrie that she was terrified of them) and 'Schuyler and Katherine are perfectly lovely people: this without any reservation. We are so happy here.'[6]

Laura wasted little time in deciding that Schuyler would join in the work on the dictionary: this was announced during the first week. Laura's altered manner had already begun to attract interest. Robin Hale, visiting the farm for a dinner a week after their arrival, noticed that Schuyler Jackson was now in excellent spirits and that Laura had become rather girlish and was wearing jewels, heavy make-up and an elaborate party dress. It was evident that there was something in the air between her and Schuyler. She was, Robin Hale thought, behaving like a coquette; Robert struck her as looking quietly frantic.[7]

On 13 May Graves told Dorothy Simmons that he had stopped keeping a diary. It had, he told her, been Laura's decision: 'Laura said it had a graveyard smell.'[8] This casual statement throws a sharp backward light on all the seemingly private comments Graves had made about Beryl at La Chevrie in his diary. He had never given more than a throwaway hint in it of his growing affection for Beryl, although both of them later agreed that their love had blossomed at the château. Laura had been suspicious of the way she saw Beryl looking at him, but the diary refused to provide the confirmation she sought. In the five years since Graves began keeping it at Riding's suggestion, the diary had served as a mirror into which she could peer for a pleasing reflection of her wit, her appearance and her industry. Now, with her eyes on a new future, Riding feared that it might present a less impressive figure at its centre.

No record was kept of that summer in America; the account on which biographers have tended to rely was given almost forty years later by Tom Matthews in *Under the Influence*. It is a fascinating book, but a prejudiced one, driven by Matthews's intense hostility towards Laura Riding. Reading his accounts of the daily discussions which she led, and of the way she exerted her formidable personality to impose her will, it is as well to be aware that Matthews was bending the evidence to fit a later view. Not all of his report is an exaggeration, however. The descriptions of Riding's manipulative use of her power over the new 'inside' group have been confirmed by another witness. Eleanor Fitzgerald and her husband Robert, the eminent classical translator, were urged by Matthews to join what was no longer called the Covenant of Literal Morality, as it had been known at Alma Square, but the Second Protocol.* Interviewed in 1989 by Riding's biographer, Deborah Baker, Eleanor Fitzgerald recalled her astonishment at being ordered by Laura to love her, and her dismay when Kit Jackson reported her to Laura for having used the word 'cult' to describe their group. Julie Matthews's explanation that Riding was 'Christ incarnate' and therefore entitled to expect their unqualified love, did not reassure Mrs Fitzgerald, who went home and cried for three days.[9]

Graves's deference to Riding's wishes was noticed by everybody. On one occasion, she told him to sit outside and read Dante's *Inferno* aloud to a lawn void of any audience but clouds of mosquitoes. Graves did it, knowing that he was being punished by Riding because of his wicked desire for another man's wife. The thought of Laura's own fierce purity made him feel all the worse about his sexual feelings for Beryl; to be stung by insects seemed a light penance for such a crime as his.

Alan and Beryl arrived in America in late May and took a hotel room in Princeton. To Beryl, whose love for Graves was already stronger than the sisterly affection she felt for her husband, the situation looked more promising than it had at La Chevrie. Riding's

---

* The First Protocol had marked the first stage of The Covenant.

interest was unmistakably focused on Schuyler Jackson, not Graves. 'The die,' in Beryl's view, 'was cast.'[10]

Time was now divided between the Matthewses' Princeton home and New Hope farm. Kit Jackson, who was becoming increasingly nervous and unhappy about her husband's assiduous attentions to Laura, retained two clear memories of this period. One was of Graves and Beryl sitting close together and whispering. Unaware of being observed, they looked like lovers. The other was of Graves meeting Kit in a passage at night with a worried look and whispering: 'Be careful. It's very dangerous.'[11]

Graves was no friend to Kit Jackson and there is a hint of melodramatic glee here. He had already hinted to Dorothy Simmons that Kit was being difficult; later, he told several friends that Kit had tried to seduce him by climbing into his bed. At no point did he show any wish to help or defend her; it is all too possible that it was he who first mischievously suggested to Laura that Kit was a practiser of the black arts.

When Nimrod's House was finally completed in early June, Graves moved in, together with Beryl and Alan. Riding elected to stay behind at the farmhouse and entertain her friends to dinner, almost as if she was their hostess. Tom and Julie Matthews noticed that she now took her place at the head of the table while Kit was relegated to a side-seat, a guest in her own home. One day Tom saw Kit lay her head on her arms. It was apparent that she was silently weeping. Kit herself remembered a battle of wills as she followed Laura round the house, undoing each small, proprietorial act which her visitor smilingly performed.[12]

One evening towards the end of June, Kit's control snapped. Watched by all the visitors, she stood up and pushed back her chair, telling the children to come for a walk. Griselda, the oldest daughter, remembers the brooding atmosphere which had culminated in this action; it seemed less alarming to go with their mother than to sit and face Riding's assertive glare of friendship.[13]

Riding ordered, successively, Graves, Beryl, and Alan to bring Kit back. Each attempt failed; Kit refused to listen to their supplications. Having distanced herself from her pursuers, she told the children to stop by a stream and look very hard for the fish. Her manner and tone frightened them. Griselda, crying, kept pulling at her mother's arm and asking what was wrong. It was, seemingly, the last straw. Kit could take no more emotional pressure. When

Schuyler Jackson finally reached his wife, he found her throttling Griselda.[14]

The following morning, Kit was taken to see their local doctor by Schuyler. Riding meanwhile informed Graves, Beryl and Alan that her decision to live on in the main house had been one of courageous altruism; she had sensed that there was evil in the house and had not spared herself to uncover it. Kit was not only mad; she was a witch. The ludicrous proof of her witchcraft, shown to Beryl, was a small triangular heap of new sanitary towels lying on the floor of Kit's bedroom.[15] When Tom Matthews arrived at the farm later in the day, he was called into Schuyler's study, where Riding explained what had happened.[16] She told him that Kit had confessed, after trying to kill her daughter, that she was a sorceress. Everything belonging to her was being burned or destroyed. The children were told that their mother was a damned woman. Neighbours were warned to beware of the return which Kit was sure to attempt from the asylum in which she had now been confined.

A similar ritual had taken place at St Peter's Square, when Riding ordered Geoffrey Phibbs to destroy everything associated with his wife Norah, thus protecting himself and his new friends from Norah's influence. Then, as later, the exorcism was a necessary part of Riding's ritual of invasion and replacement. The fact that she was able to convince others of an evil presence is a tribute to her charismatic powers of persuasion. Six years later, when the two Jackson daughters visited their father and Laura in Florida, they were offered evidence of Kit's satanic practices. Once, apparently, she had asked her husband if they could make love in a field of daisies; the only further tokens were some affectionate letters which she had written to Laura in the early summer of 1939. The affection was claimed by Schuyler and Laura to have been a perverted love.[17]

With Kit out of the way, there was no longer any need for pretence at New Hope about the relationship between Riding and Schuyler Jackson. Shortly after her departure, they went into his bedroom and remained there for two days. Riding then emerged with the cryptic news that, after all her harangues against sex, 'Schuyler and I do.'[18] There was no explanation, no apology; Graves was left to ponder the fact that he had endured six unhappy years of celibacy for what appeared to have been no more than Laura's whim. The only comfort for him lay in the thought that, if she found it acceptable to sleep with the married Schuyler, she must surely find it acceptable for him to sleep with the married Beryl. This was a naïve assumption.

From now on, Riding flaunted her sexuality. Her clothes became more elaborate, her make-up more emphatic. One afternoon she ordered Beryl to come over from Nimrod's House and sit by the marital bed while she and Schuyler rested.[19] When Kit, predictably, tried to return to the farm, Riding oversaw the arrangements to have her taken away in a strait-jacket.

It is unlikely that Riding ever saw the extraordinary private poem, 'The Moon Ends in Nightmare', written in June 1939, which became Graves's final diary entry, written at Nimrod's House. It has the rawness of a cry of pain as he realized – although he soon managed to talk himself out of this view – that he had worshipped at an empty shrine. Two years earlier he had written a poem, 'The Challenge', in which he identified Riding with the moon for her gift of a 'most clear, unscorching light'. Now, he watched the moon transform itself.

> In horror I cried aloud: for the same Moon
> Whom I had held a living power, though changeless,
> Split open in my sight, a bright egg shell,
> And a double-headed Nothing grinned
> All-wisely from the gap.[20]

Later references to a creek and the view of a tulip tree from the window show that the poem was written while Graves was living with Beryl and Alan at the restored cottage on the farm. The situation remained unbearable; the poem ends with the image of a lost spirit rapping at a window and being denied entry 'To a house not his own'. In mid-July, Graves left New Hope to stay in the soothingly conventional surroundings of Tom Matthews's summer home at Newport. Here he learned from Riding that Schuyler and she were now a couple. He was informed of their joint social arrangements. Graves was told, too, that their own relationship had been unbalanced by too much feeling, and then by too much 'thinking'. Schuyler had taught her to value emotion above intellect. She still, however, felt 'for' Graves, she told him, as opposed to having feelings 'about' him; she hoped that he would find a new ease with her.[21]

Riding, it appeared, had found instant serenity with her new love; Graves reverted into the old symptoms of shell-shock, a condition which was worsened by the fact that another war now seemed inevitable. To be in America at such a time, as an Englishman and an ex-officer, was against all his instincts, and these instincts were strengthened by the intolerable nature of the position in which he now found himself. Towards the end of July, he let Riding know that he planned to return to England to apply for war work. She responded coolly, suggesting only that he should take Griselda Jackson with him. Griselda would, she felt sure, be happier with friends in England than in America. (Griselda had been making no secret of her resentment of Laura.)

Graves's letters during this period show a state of utter confusion. To Dorothy Simmons, he wrote that he had never felt better and that he was leaving with reluctance.[22] Sassoon suddenly received a letter suggesting that they should try to revive their old friendship. (Sassoon, while amiable in his response, did not agree to a meeting: he had put his old male friendships behind him in 1934, when he married Hester Gatty.[23]) Nancy, having heard only talk of divorce in the past year, was asked if she was willing to heal their relationship. They owed it to each other, Graves told her.[24] It was as though he was making every endeavour to turn back the clock which Riding said had stopped. The most sensible response came from Lucie Brown and John Aldridge, who simply told him that their home in Essex was his for as long as he wanted to stay.

At the end of July, Graves returned to New Hope from Newport to make his farewells and, perhaps, to see if he had misunderstood Riding. He had not. The night before his departure for England, Graves was called into the couple's bedroom to be addressed by Riding on the subject of his relationship with Beryl. Schuyler, he was given to understand, had serious doubts about it, as did Riding. His recollection of the interview, seemingly the most painful of them all, was that Schuyler had worn a smirk of triumph as he watched Graves squirm. (This was later indignantly denied by Schuyler and Laura.)[25]

Beryl, excited by her first experience of this foreign country and unsure of whether she should leave her husband to live with Graves, a married man and one who seemed most uncertain about his own future, chose to stay on the farm. Graves still hoped to return; he left his dictionaries and trunk at New Hope. He travelled back to England with Alan Hodge, on his way to a journalistic assignment in Poland. During the voyage, they discussed Alan's marriage and Robert's feelings about Beryl. The Hodge marriage had not been a success and there was no animosity in these conversations. Hodge's own feelings were principally of hostility towards Riding, who seemed to have betrayed her principles.[26] Graves's were more confused. Emotionally and sexually, he felt drawn to Beryl; intellectually, he remained bonded to Riding and, honourably, obliged to uphold her actions. He wrote a play, *Horses*, during the crossing, in which two of the characters ceaselessly repeat a mantra of submission akin to the familiar statement of Riding's authority. 'You're right. You're right as usual. You're always dead right,' Hippo and Bill tell Anna.[27] Here, however, acknowledgement teeters on the edge of hysteria.

On 16 August, three days after his arrival in England, Graves held a meeting with Nancy in the presence of her father and David Graves, now down from his first year at Jesus College, Cambridge. Nancy had assumed from her husband's letter that he was ready to revive the marriage, an idea she was now willing to consider if Laura had resigned her claim. But Graves talked of nothing but Laura and never raised the possibility of a reunion with Nancy; after visiting Jenny to see how she was getting along in her new career as an actress, he retreated to the peace of Harlech for a few days. At the end of the month, he joined Lucie Brown and John Aldridge, renting from them the little chapel annexe to their house in Great Bardfield. From here, he applied to the War Office for whatever work they could give to a 44-year-old man.

On 25 September Graves wrote to tell Basil Liddell Hart, convalescing from a nervous breakdown in Devon, about his life. After explaining that the War Office's offer of non-combatant work in a dull corps had not seemed worth pursuing, he said that he was, in any case, intending to rejoin Laura in three weeks', time since his financial help was required.* He was, he added, reading up the background for a novel based on the experiences of Roger Lamb, a Royal Welch Fusiliers sergeant who had fought in the American War of Independence.[28] Reading the letter, Liddell Hart could not have guessed that Graves was in a state of acute nervous crisis, weeping before his friends, confiding in everybody.

Riding's mood had not been improved in Graves's absence by the hostility shown to her by Schuyler's children, or by Julie and Tom

---

* The fact that this provided Graves with his last hold over Riding may help to explain his astonishing lack of resentment.

Matthews's refusal to visit the farm. Beryl, who continued, wisely, to keep her head down and say as little as possible, had become an important figure at the farm. She was the only ally they now had, apart from Montague and Dorothy Simmons who had travelled out to join Schuyler and Laura. Against Kit Jackson's continuing assertions that she was 'right' and Laura 'wrong', it mattered more than usual to Laura to be surrounded by the few who were still able to see her as a model of rectitude.

By 19 August, Riding's attention was focused on the relationship between Beryl and Graves, all of whose letters were inspected by her with Beryl's amused consent. When Graves, rashly, tried to persuade Riding that it would be no more wicked for Beryl to sleep with him than it was for her to sleep with Schuyler, she responded as though she had been stung. It was, she wrote, either childish or vulgar of him to compare his relationship with Beryl to hers with Schuyler, especially on a sexual plane. Beryl, besides, belonged with Alan.[29] But even Riding could not force an estranged couple back into harness; Beryl's letters to Alan at this time urged him to join up with Alix Kemp, whose own marriage had fallen apart.[30]

By 26 September, Riding's feelings had hardened. Beryl was a threat to her power over Graves and, if only financially, she still had need of him. He was warned not to make 'a pseudo-Laura' of Beryl or to commiserate with Beryl for being dependent on Schuyler and Riding's goodwill. Reference was made to Beryl as having been in a mess ever since she had begun casting significant looks towards Graves at La Chevrie.[31] A present of a brooch sent from Graves via Riding to Beryl was not passed on to her.

Money was at the root of the relationship now, and Riding was desperately short of funds. When an erroneous over-payment to Graves was mistakenly paid into Riding's account by Random House, she refused to give it back: the money was deducted from the publishers' next payment to Graves. She also took the couple of hundred dollars which Graves had left in his American account, without his permission or knowledge. Regarding the property in Deyá, however, she was prepared to be generous. The Posada was in Graves's name; Riding offered to return everything else to him. She offered him the rights to their collaborative works as well, although she later changed her mind, furiously opposing any attempt by Graves to publish his part of any book in which she had participated. Regarding his personal possessions, she was grudging, refusing to return his precious dictionaries or the silver cutlery which had belonged to Nancy Nicholson's mother.

On 25 September Graves informed a shocked Dorothy Simmons that Beryl was on her way to join him in England. Beryl herself had finally reached the view that she would be wise to leave the farm, where Laura and Jackson had become vigorously committed to breaking her relationship with Graves. She wanted, above all, to be with him. 'I know that this is right,' Graves told Dorothy, 'and I know that if Beryl and I make a decent thing of our love, Laura and Schuyler will be only too glad to recognize it.'[32] Five days later, Laura sent him an urgent letter, asking him to return to America immediately. Graves, on this one occasion, ignored her orders. When Beryl arrived at Liverpool docks on 11 October, he was there to meet her.

Together, they returned to live temporarily with Lucie and John Aldridge at Great Bardfield. Graves had promised Beryl that Hodge would be his chosen collaborator and researcher for as long as Hodge needed work and a little income; he was as good as his word. Hodge, who had narrowly escaped being trapped in Poland at the time of Hitler's invasion, made his way back to England via Sweden in the autumn. He was promptly engaged to research the background for *Sergeant Lamb of the Ninth* and its sequel; he also worked with Graves on his next two non-fiction projects, *The Long Weekend* and *The Reader Over Your Shoulder*. Still attached to Beryl, while recognizing that their marriage was as good as over, Hodge found this a pleasing compromise.[33] His affection for Graves never diminished.

Graves continued, fantastically, to dream of acceptance by Laura and Schuyler in his new relationship, and to imagine that they could all live together on the farm. Laura appeared, for a time, to humour this dream. Hearing that Beryl was two months' pregnant in December 1939 she even wrote a letter of congratulation to the – prospective – three of them. This promised well; Graves began to consider a return to America in the spring as a real possibility. He had reckoned without Schuyler Jackson's pride.

Laura, it is clear, wanted Graves back as a financial provider since Schuyler had little aptitude for making money. Schuyler could hardly be expected to share this practical view; to him, Graves was a rival even though a handy provider of cash. In January 1940, seemingly under Schuyler's influence, Laura wrote a very different kind of letter. Graves was told to stay in England, and to understand that the Protocol, an 'infected' document, was going to be destroyed. Schuyler enclosed a letter of his own, saying that Graves, like Kit, had been unworthy of Riding's divine influence, that he was degenerate and that Beryl was the victim of his lust.[34] When Graves appealed against such a harsh condemnation, he was answered with a second and still more more hostile letter from Laura; this time he was addressed as 'Robert Graves!' She told him that all communication must cease, that their relationship had been a mistake and that he must burn all her papers when he went back to Spain.[35]

Riding was repeating her own history. She had, in the same way, asked one of her closest friends to burn all her papers in 1925 when she left her American life behind her. Now, having returned to it, she wished to destroy all traces of her life in Europe. The relationship with Graves, which had taken her there, was the most important part of that act of rejection. By jettisoning him, she completed her commitment to Schuyler Jackson, to whom she now devoted herself and with whom she continued to work on a new definition of language until his death in 1968.

Schuyler, according to a letter from Graves to Alan Hodge, was still communicating with Graves by telephone in 1941. 'He always wants the last word even if he has to wake one up in the early hours of the morning to bumble it alcoholically in one's ear,' Graves wrote.[36] But Schuyler's rantings no longer troubled him. Laura, in his view, had committed creative suicide by rejecting poetry, and emotional suicide by exchanging a noble partnership for marriage to a drunk and mediocre farmer-poet. Consciously, he put Laura Riding out of his life; unconsciously, she remained to operate on an ever more mythical plane in his mind.

PART FOUR

BERYL

CHAPTER TWENTY-THREE

1940–1943

A FAMILY LIFE

GRAVES AND BERYL SPENT THEIR FIRST SEVEN MONTHS TOGETHER in England living in the chapel annexe to John and Lucie Aldridge's home in Essex. (John and Lucie married during their stay.) Great Bardfield was a friendly, sleepy little village and The Place was a soothing home, a pretty old pink-walled house with a luxuriant wilderness of a garden presided over by John, and warm, oak-panelled rooms comfortably furnished by Lucie. The annexe itself was really too small for a couple, but with friends to whom they were so closely attached, this presented no problem; the house was theirs to share.

They made few new friends here, although Graves was delighted when he visited the local barber's shop to discover a slight, loquacious young Catalan, an ex-Republican captain called Ricardo Sicre who, after being rescued by friends from internment in a French camp, had ended up trimming hair in Essex. This was no job for a fighting man, in Graves's view; using his connection with Basil Liddell Hart, he found Ricardo a job teaching guerrilla tactics at a local army college before sending him to New York with a letter of introduction to Tom Matthews. Ricardo, a shrewd young man who made himself a fortune as a commercial entrepreneur during the next few years, did not forget Graves's kindness.

Graves spent much of his time at his desk. Riding's continuing raids on his pocket had left him short of money and it was impossible to predict when, if ever, he would recover the Mallorcan properties in which most of his funds were tied up. Now he had to think about supporting Beryl and the child who was on the way. The situation was a familiar one: in 1919 he had been worrying about how to provide enough money to keep Nancy and their baby daughter. The *Sergeant Lamb* books were to be published by Methuen, who had taken over the rights to the *Claudius* novels after the collapse of Arthur Barker's small firm. They were written at speed alongside *The Long Weekend*, a social history of Britain between the wars on which Graves was collaborating with Alan Hodge.

Graves began to write *Sergeant Lamb of the Ninth* and *Proceed, Sergeant Lamb* – they were divided into two books only to meet wartime library requirements – in the late autumn of 1939. Roger Lamb, a meticulous and orderly Dubliner with a keen interest in his appearance, was a very different character from Graves; that difference did not prevent Graves from identifying with him so closely that Beryl often saw him laying an extra place for the sergeant when they sat down to meals.[1]

An argument can be made for seeing these books, with their background setting of the American War of Independence, as Graves's way of mythologizing the war between himself and Schuyler Jackson on a national scale, but even references to the River Schuykill fail to yield anything more suggestive than a name. There is a villain, but he is not Jackson. John Martin, an agent of the Devil disguised as a priest, is 'a lean, lantern-jawed Irishman, with a black wet forelock and a cajoling tongue.'[2] The reference to a devil, Irish blood and the physical resemblance to Geoffrey (Phibbs) Taylor, who always had a lick of black hair falling over one eye, leave no room for doubt about who had inspired the character of John Martin.

The decision to write a picaresque novel, based on fact, about an eighteenth-century member of his own company, the Royal Welch Fusiliers, can rather be interpreted as an outlet for Graves's frustration at finding himself in a second war and ineligible for active service. George Orwell was alone among the critics in making a connection between Lamb's fierce loyalty and the passion Graves felt for his old regiment.[3] But it was the comparisons between the plain and lively style of the Lamb novels and that of the eighteenth-century essayist, William Cobbett, which pleased Graves most when he read the reviews; Cobbett's was the style which he thought showed English prose at its best.[4]

The novels deserved their warm reception. A stickler for detail, Graves had not left all the research to Alan Hodge. He had already read some eight thousand pages of historical background, together with a journal kept by Roger Lamb when, in November 1939, he appealed to his son David to hunt through the Cambridge libraries for a missing document, a memoir which Lamb had kept of the year 1812. Graves could not bear to think of what it might contain in the way of missing details. His anxiety was conveyed in typically dramatic terms. 'I *must* have it or I can't write the book and we will all starve,' he wrote.[5] David failed to find it, but Graves was more than ready to forgive his son's lack of concern when he heard that David was planning to apply for a commission to the Royal Welch as soon as he finished his English Finals. He could not, Graves told him, make a better choice: 'it is and always was a corps d'elite and . . . one always feels much *safer* in a really good regiment . . .'[6] Full of enthusiasm, he wrote off to every officer he still knew in the Royal Welch, urging them to look out for a letter from his son. To have David in the regiment would be almost as good as joining up again himself. This sense of identification was helped by the fact that his son bore a striking resemblance to himself and had just begun to write poetry.

The Long Weekend was a less personal book than the *Sergeant Lamb* novels and partly motivated by Graves's desire to offer Alan Hodge some discreet financial assistance. In return for his research work and for writing a first draft of several of the chapters, Hodge was told to claim as much of the advance as he wanted from Faber, their publisher.

The Long Weekend offered Graves a chance to review his thoughts about the first postwar decade which, in *Goodbye to All That*, had been seen from an intensely personal angle. The painful memory of his early married life and of his long commitment to Laura Riding's view of the world became less traumatic when set against a larger social context. But detachment was not Graves's forte, and Riding still occupied too large a part of his thoughts to be judged with indifference in 1940. A comparison between her and a spider, spinning its web out of itself, hints at the web of moral obligation in which Riding trapped her dutiful followers. An account of the drawing up of a code of values which had been the basis for the Covenant of Literal Morality (or the First Protocol) as a 'pleasant but arduous duty' makes too light of the happy weeks in Alma Square where Graves had joyfully and unstintingly worked to help Riding bring peace to Europe.[7] These personal and uneasy responses to Riding were out of place in a book which won admiration as an entertaining and well-informed social portrait of Britain between the wars. *The Long Weekend* also provided Graves with an opportunity to make amends for one past injury. After making a brief appraisal of books written in response to the Great War, he turned to his own. *Goodbye to All That* was, he wrote just over twenty years after it was first published, 'a reckless autobiography in which the war figured, but written with small consideration for anyone's feelings'. Since the preceding sentence referred to Sassoon, it was clear to whom this apology was being offered.[8]

★   ★   ★

John Aldridge's decision to enlist, and the need to provide a home where Graves could be visited by his older children as well as for the baby, were behind the resolution to start looking for a new place to live early in 1940. They found it on a visit to Basil Liddell Hart, who was living near Totnes in South Devon with a young Canadian, Kathleen Nelson. Graves was devoted to Liddell Hart, a dapper, quick-witted, charming man with a fondness for bright bow-ties and big cars. The fact that his sister Rosaleen Cooper and her family lived nearby added to the attraction of a home in the West Country. Graves caught sight of Vale House on a drive through the little village of Galmpton, close to Totnes, and decided, on the spur of the moment, to rent it. Kathleen Nelson agreed to supervise whitewashing and the installation of electric light; Rosaleen, together with two of Graves's children, David and Catherine, oversaw the unpacking of furniture and household goods. In May, Graves and Beryl moved in. They stayed at Vale House for six years. Their first three children were born here, William in the summer of 1940, followed by Lucia in 1943 and Juan in 1944.

The village of Galmpton itself was drab, and the chief attraction of the dilapidated eighteenth-century farmhouse was that it had enough space for all their visitors, and for the family of evacuees who, together with a local cleaning lady, provided their domestic help. The countryside surrounding Galmpton was richly verdant, however, with dense green woods and clay soil as red as the sails of the fishing-boats in nearby Brixham harbour.

Far more remote from London than the Aldridges' home in Essex, Galmpton was correspondingly more old-fashioned; it was not easy to gain acceptance at first as an unmarried couple with a baby son. But Graves's kindly and easy ways overcame an initial hostility. By the end of the second year, the villagers were calling him 'Captain' and stopping to admire the little boy whom Graves carried along on his shoulders when he went for a daily stroll.

Evidence of Graves and Beryl's own discomfort about their unconventional household can be discerned in the rapidity with which Beryl took the name of Graves by deed poll after Alan Hodge obligingly divorced her in 1943. She changed her name as soon as was decently possible; Nancy's obdurate attitude made marriage impossible until early in 1950.

Graves had asked Nancy for a divorce in September 1939, shortly before Beryl's return to England.[9] Nancy, still smarting from the hurt Graves had inflicted by suggesting a reconciliation and then failing to pursue it when he came back from New Hope, sent a cool response. On the first evening of Beryl's arrival in England, Graves tried again; this time, he made his first direct reference to a companion, describing Beryl as 'a lady' who had saved him from having a nervous breakdown in America, and adding that they hoped to have a child.[10] Nancy answered by saying she was so shocked that she would have to consult Graves's family about whether their children could be allowed to visit him.[11]

This was in the first rush of anger, when Nancy felt that Robert had let her down and made a fool of her; it did not help that she had shared her new hopes with the children. (Graves, early in 1940, was obliged to spell the facts out to his son David, telling him that he must stop hoping for a reunion between his parents: 'you must forgive me for this, but realize its impossibility.'[12])

Nancy had a strong streak of stubbornness in her nature. She accepted, reluctantly, that her children were free to visit Graves and Beryl if they wished. She was not prepared to change her name simply for the purpose of easing Graves's situation. At St James's, Piccadilly, in 1918, she had signed herself in the church register as Nancy Nicholson. Her solicitors showed discreet sympathy for her husband;

he, knowing the inflexibility Nancy could display when she felt she had cause, resigned himself to bringing up an illegitimate family.

The children did not endorse their mother's attitude. (It was Jenny, together with Graves's mother, who eventually persuaded Nancy to let herself be described as 'Nicholson alias Graves' and so allow a divorce to take place in 1949.) David became a regular visitor at Vale House when he was sent on a commando course in Devon in 1940–41. Jenny, too, made visits, first from the Liverpool Rep and then during her new provincial career as a journalist based in Bristol. Sam was often to be found staying with Beryl and Graves during the year he spent studying forestry at Dartington, a few miles from Galmpton, before going to Cambridge. Catherine, Graves's youngest daughter, was the most frequent visitor of the four. She married a scientist, Clifford Dalton, in 1941, providing Graves with the curious experience of becoming acquainted with his grandchildren and his own second brood of babies at the same time.

Basil Liddell Hart and Katherine Nelson moved north to Westmoreland in 1941, depriving Graves and Beryl of their closest friends in the neighbourhood and of the welcome luxury in wartime of a big car, in which they were taken on day-trips at least three times a month. The Liddell Harts' place was initially taken by their nearest neighbour in the village of Galmpton. Lord Falkland was a vain, roving-eyed old peer with the looks of an Elizabethan sea-captain and a family who had swashbuckled their way through history for several centuries. One forebear, a famous duellist, had been immortalized by Sheridan as Sir Lucius O'Trigger in *The Rivals*. Graves was no snob, but he loved a romantic background and a good yarn. Lord Falkland's recommendation of a relation who was prepared to do typing made him still more popular at Vale House.

Through this friendship, they met Irene Warman who lived nearby. The ethereal, sweet-voiced and bawdy-tongued grass widow of an intelligence officer – demoted to the rank of policeman in Graves's letters – Irene had naïvely been placed by her husband under the protection of the philandering peer. Her daughter, Sweet Pea, became little William's playmate; Irene was often to be found in the untidy Vale House kitchen, trimming Lord Falkland's magnificent beard while he regaled the household with stories of his ancestors. Karl, interned until October 1940 when he changed his name to Gay and volunteered for service, found Irene's wit and pretty face irresistible when he came to live at Galmpton in the summer of 1944, after being discharged from the Navy with a nervous breakdown. His marriage to Marie had failed and he was in a vulnerable state. Graves, deep in his books, was startled to learn that Karl and Irene had fallen in love. He had not even noticed a friendship.

Agatha Christie was their most famous neighbour, although Graves had difficulty in recognizing her as the detective novelist when she appeared at the house one day, introducing herself as Mrs Mallowan. Agatha was pleasant, but stately; Graves visited her handsome house for uncomfortably formal teas and resigned himself with good humour to being teased about his dishevelled appearance. She was, he told James Reeves, 'a very sweet person'.[13] But he preferred her husband, Max, the eminent archaeologist, who was able to broaden Graves's knowledge of the ancient societies in which women had been worshipped. Mallowan's name is one of the few mentioned in gratitude at the beginning of *The White Goddess*.

Galmpton marked the beginning of two enduring friendships. One was with George and Joanna Simon, whose second daughter Julia became Graves's last muse in the 1970s. He first met her parents at Brixham harbour in 1944; the rapport was immediate. George, short and sturdily built with a strong Manchester accent and a permanent expression of mild anxiety, was a leading radiologist at St Bartholomew's Hospital; his wife, Joanna, a tall, fair, graceful young woman with family connections in the London art world, introduced Graves and Beryl to her art-student friends, pretty Irish twins called Peggy and Duffy Fitzgerald who became regular and welcome invaders of Vale House. They lost touch with the twins, but the Simons remained among their closest and most loyal friends.

Graves's friendship with Joshua Podro had a more professional element. Joshua was, Graves wrote to a friend in 1954, 'the gentlest sweetest man in existence'.[14] Born Podrushnik, he was a Polish Jew whose press-cuttings agency had been transferred to Paignton in Devon shortly after the beginning of the war. Graves met him through a distant von Ranke relation who was also living in Paignton.

Podro was an intellectual who had devoted all of his spare time to study of the rabbinical aspects of Jesus's teaching. His library of Hebraica was known to academics as one of the best in the country, and with his knowledge went an open mind. Graves was fortunate to meet him in 1943, when he was working on *King Jesus*, a novel which had led him into an absorbing study of many of the pre-Christian sources;[15] Podro's first contribution to the book was to shake Graves's conviction that the Pharisees were a corrupt equivalent of the modern Church Commissioners. Podro persuaded him to take a more respectful view of these remarkable men.

In Devon, this was the only friendship which provided Graves with the mental stimulus on which he thrived: Fanny Podro, a homely, kind, cake-making lady, was a less likely friend for Beryl, and most of Graves's visits to Paignton were made alone. Here, sitting in Joshua's workroom, the two men talked for hours about myth, ritual and pre-Christian history. A good deal of what was discussed with Joshua Podro found its way, although in a rather different form, into *The White Goddess*, which Graves wrote, and rewrote, alongside *King Jesus* in 1943–4.

★   ★   ★

Graves's children were quick to make friends with Beryl, warming to her evident love of their father and her readiness to take them on their own terms, as Laura Riding had never done. Beryl's own family, although initially concerned by the fact that she had chosen such an unconventional lifestyle, accepted that the problem was not of Graves's making. Her mother, Lady Pritchard, like Amy Graves, wrung her hands at the thought of three grandchildren born out of wedlock; Sir Harry, a kind and cheerful man, took a more pragmatic view of the situation. He liked and admired Graves and was pleased to see his daughter settled with a man she evidently adored. Beryl's twin brother, Hardinge, was a frequent visitor to Vale House before he was sent overseas in 1943; her sister and brother-in-law, Evelyn and Jack Neep, a generous, wealthy couple, were equally well-disposed.

Several of Graves's close friends found it impossible not to draw comparisons, to Beryl's disadvantage, between her and Riding. Tom Matthews, visiting Galmpton in 1942, was convinced that Graves, having settled for an inferior woman, was doing everything he could to recreate the earlier and more powerful relationship. Beryl was ill in bed during much of his visit: Matthews contrasted her voice, 'querulous, weakly strident, upbraiding, complaining, impatient', to that of Robert, 'anxiously conciliatory, humble, apologetic. Exactly the tone he had used to Laura.'[16] Beryl was blamed for trying 'to do something that was not natural to her – to rule the roost – ' with

Graves's encouragement.[17] The blame was laid on Graves, but the criticism was of Beryl, contemptuously described as 'a child-wife'.[18] Anxious to justify himself, Matthews added that 'other friends' had shared his impression.[19]

There was some truth in this. Dorothy Simmons, who was living at New Hope farm in 1940 and thus very much under Riding's influence, wrote to express her strong disapproval of the relationship.[20] Honor Wyatt, while accepting that Graves and Beryl were in love, shared Matthews's belief that Beryl's 'bossiness', as she termed it, was the result of her wish to be seen as another Laura, and that Graves encouraged this.[21] Karl Gay was more subtle in his criticism. Staying at Vale House for six months in 1944, he took his meals into the dining-room and ate there in solitude, rather than share the 'filthy' table at which the others ate. A fastidious man, he was revolted by what seemed to him an atmosphere of squalor. At Canelluñ, he had been enchanted by the high standards of cleanliness and order on which Laura insisted. His angry response to conditions at Vale House indirectly expressed his resentment of slight, untidily dressed Beryl for being so unlike Laura Riding.[22] Other visitors to Galmpton had nothing worse to say than that the house was 'a little chaotic',[23] and 'rather bohemian'.[24]

The criticism was, perhaps, inevitable. Graves had defended Riding's principles and supported her ventures for over ten years with a passion which suggested love. His feelings for Beryl had been well hidden until they were thrown together at the Jacksons' farm. It was impossible for those friends who had not understood how cerebral his relationship with Riding had become by the late Thirties to understand what it meant to him to be offered, for the first time in his life, a loving, uncomplicated partnership in which there were no tests, no ordeals, no quixotic ambitions. The fact that Graves continued to search for a muse-figure should not be allowed to overshadow the importance of all that Beryl had to give him.

Writing to Beryl on 25 September 1939, shortly before her arrival in England, Graves described his relief at the way in which they kept a check on each other's more extreme moods 'by gentleness not violence. This gives us the lovely calmness we both find in each other's company.' Returning to the theme of peace at the end of another letter written on the same day, he told her that he was never free from 'that tightness in the solar plexus which means that I am away from home and can't really relax until we are together again'.[25]

Calmness was something which he had never known with Laura Riding; it was at the heart of the first ten years of his relationship with Beryl. The letters written by them both in December 1944, during the period when Beryl was in hospital for the birth of their third child, Juan, testify to a love based on trust, tenderness and intense affection. 'Darling darling,' Graves began one letter on Christmas Eve, before agreeing with Beryl that Juan's birth seemed mystically linked to the birth of their love at La Chevrie; a week later, he told her that little William seemed to love the Evening Star, 'and it *is* a beautiful thing and very special for people in love like you and me'. 'Ever always very truly (meaning it) yours and yours only – Robert', he ended another letter. His apology for having rushed a new poem, 'To Juan at the Winter Solstice', into print without consulting her – 'I never feel right about a poem unless you pass it' – suggests that Beryl's frankness was as welcome as Laura's corrective supervision had been. Homely details, of visitors, new cooking inventions, books that he was reading to the children, books that he himself had read or was working on, confirm the reader's sense of a relationship that was mature and harmonious. Beryl's letters are, of the two, the more overt. 'Most of the time I'm just lying here and thinking about you,' she wrote from the hospital in an undated note. 'Goodness how I do love you and it's so wonderful to think that it has all really happened.'

Their love was not without obstacles. Ill-health, caused by persistent gynaecological problems, often made Beryl sharp and anxious. In a letter of 1944 about the way he had been looking after William and Lucia while she was in hospital, Graves gently hinted that she worried about them too much and that, 'as soon as you stop worrying, all seems perfect'. Beryl's answer was contrite. He was right: 'My only fear is of the tiredness and crossness, which I know is the only thing that comes between us. Actually I'm sure that being so much in love takes up a lot of energy.'[26] Three years later, nothing had changed. 'How I miss you but please don't be cross . . . You worry too much!' Graves told her in September 1947 while Beryl, having promised to be less anxious, wrote back in yearning tones: 'Never loved you so much as I did last night.'[27]

Graves was used to living with women in poor health. A thyroid deficiency and exhaustion had almost prostrated Nancy Nicholson in the mid-Twenties; his 1935–9 diary records the frequency of Laura's collapses from nervous exhaustion; his letters to Beryl show him running the household while working on three different books in 1944. To Graves, child care, washing-up and jam-making were all pleasant, routine activities which produced the necessary blankness of mind for creative thought. Kathleen Nelson, while admiring his insouciance, was horrified when he showed her how he propped young William's milk bottle in his mouth with a pile of books while he did the washing-up at Vale House.[28]

The influence of Beryl on Graves's work was swift and profound. The year 1939 marks the beginning of a new phase in his poetry which set him on the road to fame as one of Britain's greatest love-poets.

Graves's critics were ready for a change. Reviewers of his 1938 *Collected Poems* had regretfully noticed the absence of 'a delightful and glancing wit' and any use of romantic imagery.[29] Reviewing *No More Ghosts: Selected Poems* (1940), the last book which falls into Graves's 'Laura period', Stephen Spender praised his 'always remarkable, often beautiful, often arid, cantankerous, difficult and forbidding poems'. After comparing his finest work with the best of Auden and Eliot, Spender voiced the largest problem with Graves. An insurmountable intellectual barrier had been erected between the poet and his reader, 'something in Mr Graves's powerful will and intellect which obstructs him from writing always with such a naturalness and freedom'.[30]

Spender made an exception of the last poem in the collection, 'To Sleep', a poem in which Graves bridged the emotional leap from Riding to Beryl. The poem begins with his memory of La Chevrie, and of the despair he had felt, tortured by jealous dreams and frustration. The last five lines move into the present with an image which displays Beryl, as she appears in many of the poems, as his passive and beloved bed-companion:

> Now that I love you, as not before,
> Now you can be and say, as not before:
> The mind clears and the heart true-mirrors you
> Where at my side an early watch you keep
> And all self-bruising heads loll into sleep.

'To Sleep', 'Despite and Still', 'Mid-Winter Waking', 'The Door', 'Through Nightmare' and 'She Tells Her Love While Half Asleep', all published in Graves's 1945 collection, show that Beryl's gentle and transforming presence was at work. Intimacy has replaced reverence. These poems read as if murmured across the pillows; they are full of a spirit of tender protectiveness towards a cherished and vulnerable equal, where the poems to Riding had been written to a superior being.

'Despite and Still', a poem which could as easily belong to the seventeenth century as to the twentieth, binds the lovers together by their weaknesses and pleads for harmony: Beryl, here, is addressed, not represented:

> Have you not read
> The words in my head,
> And I made heart
> Of your own heart?
> We have been such as draw
> The losing straw –
> You of your gentleness,
> I of my rashness,
> Both of despair –
> Yet still might share
> This happy will:
> To love despite and still.

'The Door' celebrates the trivial incident of her visit to his study and makes of it a miracle, a moment in which all fears are held in abeyance. In 'Mid-Winter Waking', 'Through Nightmare' and 'She Tells Her Love While Half Asleep', he returns to the bedroom, to show his companion lying peacefully at his side and, in what is one of his most perfect poems, murmuring her love.

> She tells her love while half asleep,
>   In the dark hours,
>   With half-words whispered low:
> As Earth stirs in her winter sleep
>   And puts out grass and flowers
>   Despite the snow,
>   Despite the falling snow.

★   ★   ★

To the reader, the gap between these love-poems and those in which Graves began, in 1944, to celebrate the Goddess, is disconcerting. The superhuman being described in 'The White Goddess' has Beryl's blue eyes, but there is nothing of Beryl in her high brow, 'white as any leper's' or 'hair curled honey-coloured to white hips'.[31] In 'To Juan at the Winter Solstice', composed when Graves was writing some of his most tender letters to Beryl in hospital having their third child, he showed the Goddess again, crooking her finger to summon her victim to his ritual destiny.

> Water to water, ark again to ark,
> From woman back to woman:
> So, each new victim treads unfalteringly
> The never altered circuit of his fate,
> Bringing twelve peers as witness
> Both to his starry rise and starry fall.[32]

Nothing could seem further from the spirit of the love-poems to Beryl. Yet Graves told her that it contained the same feeling 'as in the poem about sleep which was about you'.[33] 'To Sleep' had celebrated his new life after a period of nightmarish uncertainty. Now, in a myth which soothed him with the sense of time as a circle, held in place by the poets whose songs preserved the past, he saw Beryl as a part of the unending story of life and death. The very act of her giving birth to Juan brought her into the realm of myth as he wrote of the rebirth of the naked king in the grove of the Goddess. His union with her, and her bearing of the new solstice child for whom he felt a superstitious reverence, were locked into the poem's assurance of an unending ritual: 'There is one story and one story only.'

Was it a commitment or a warning? In the same month that Graves wrote this poem, he gave Beryl a typescript to read in hospital and asked her to check it for inaccuracies. 'Please note any historical breach of the historical fact that all families in Crete were descended from the mother until the fall of Cnossus (at the end of this book) and even afterwards (except in the Greek colonies) and that girls had free sexual relations before marriage in honour of the Mother Goddess.'[34] Described here as 'The Cretan Novel', this is evidently an early version of *Seven Days in New Crete*, which it has always been assumed that Graves began writing in 1947 after his return to Mallorca. In fact, he was then working on a second draft; the book was first written in 1944 as a blueprint for life under the rule of the Goddess. Playful references in the dialogue to the poems of Edward Lear, which Graves was reading to William for the first time at Christmas 1944, provide additional confirmation of this earlier date.

The typescript cannot have made pleasant hospital reading, although Beryl's reaction to it has not been preserved. A Butlerian fantasy of a mysterious kingdom in which the traditional worship of the Mother Goddess Mari has been maintained, it is in part a spoof on the notion of a society governed by poets. Graves was not yet sure how seriously he wanted to pursue his new religion. Edward Venn-Thomas, a simple but good-hearted man, is summoned to New Crete, ostensibly to tell the inhabitants about the late Christian epoch, unofficially, to help the Goddess to spark some life back into the island by causing trouble on her behalf. Edward's attendance at a bloodthirsty local ritual in which the wild women devour the flesh of their last king corresponds with one of the most startling passages in *The White Goddess*, of which Graves had recently completed a second draft. (The first was written at Easter 1944.)

The figure of principal interest to Beryl in the book was Antonia, Venn-Thomas's wife. Since there is a good deal of Graves in the husband, even to his hatred of being in London for any length of time, she could reasonably suppose that the character of Antonia was based to some extent on her. The portrait was affectionate, but detached. She is, we learn, sharp-tongued.

> What I liked about her [Antonia] was that she had no special talents . . . she neither wrote, painted, acted, sang, nor played a musical instrument, and cards bored her. She drank an occasional Dubonnet or dry sherry – for her sake I stopped mixing my drinks and reverted to my English conventions – and had neither illusions nor ambitions. Her prejudices . . . were all half-humorous. But though she had no special talents I recognized that she had genius: the subtle and peculiar genius of being herself, knowing herself and always rising superior to the situation. If she said something witty, as she did quite often, her words came out so simply and casually that one didn't realize until too late that they deserved applause. Antonia was, in fact, a lady . . . I was consistently happy with her.[35]

To be consistently happy is not to be in love; the account is full of admiration, but it lacks passion. It is even more strikingly detached when read in context; Graves prefaced it by an account of Venn-Thomas's relationship with the violent, brilliant and capricious Erica, a character in whom he combined elements of Elfriede Faust and Laura Riding.

★   ★   ★

The love which Graves found with Beryl in the 1940s was of a comfortable, tender sort, well-spiced with humour. What it lacked was the tension, the element of despair and hope which he needed to inspire him. That is why his letters, and his poems to Beryl, returned so persistently to the time at La Chevrie when their love had seemed impossible. It was as if he needed to recover the sense of anguish. This, indirectly, was being communicated to Beryl through his books by the mid-Forties. She had been advised. The messenger from the Goddess would always come from outside the family circle.

> *The White Goddess* is anti-domestic; she is the perpetual 'other woman', and her part is difficult indeed for a woman of sensibility to play for more than a few years, because the desire to commit suicide in simple domesticity lurks in every maenad and muse's heart.[36]

Beryl's role as a wife and mother was not to be threatened. Graves loved and respected her, but not, after the first year, as a muse. The love he needed was of the unobtainable woman. With Beryl at his side, however, he would be able, as he later put it, to go out and fly his kite in every thunderstorm that promised to excite his imagination.

CHAPTER TWENTY-FOUR

1940–1943

A WRITING LIFE

GRAVES'S OUTPUT IN THE 1940S WAS PRODIGIOUS.[1] THE EXCUSE he made to friends, as if anxious to explain an energy which put his contemporaries to shame, was that each book was being written to pay off the tax due after the last advance. He had, it was true, a British income-tax bill of some £1,500 to meet on his return from America in 1939, but his choice of subjects over the next ten years hardly bears out this allegation of commercialism: one project, a collaboration with Alan Hodge on the writing of good English, was fondly known to its authors as 'A Short Guide to Unpopularity'. A book about Milton's first wife in which Graves gave the poet short shrift was rejected by his American publisher, Random House, as far too provocative to be sold as a historical novel. *The White Goddess*, aimed at the handful of people who cared about poetry, not at the general public, almost ended its days being published by *Wales*, the small literary magazine in which its first chapters had appeared. *King Jesus*, while written in a period of widespread speculation about the mythical element in Christianity, was a shot in the dark by Graves as far as its audience was concerned: his interest was in the unfashionable subject of showing Jesus as an enemy of ancient female power. A goddess-oriented account of Jason's voyage with the Argonauts was not a likely subject to capture readers looking for light relief from the subject of war. A futuristic satire about a matriarchal society governed by poets was an equally strange choice for a man desperate to pay his tax bills.

There are, in fact, only three books from the Forties which can be said to have shown a touch of financial acumen in their subject matter. The *Sergeant Lamb* books allowed Graves to pursue his own interest in the history of the Royal Welch Fusiliers, but he was also well aware of their marketability in wartime. A rollicking account of the scheming Doña Ysabel Mendana's expedition to the Solomon Islands, *The Isles of Unwisdom*, only lifts itself above the run of costume romances by a wealth, almost a superfluity, of historical detail. Here, for once, we can agree with Graves that the book was a pot-boiler.

Graves had finished writing *The Long Weekend* by June 1940; two months later, he was hard at work on *The Reader Over Your Shoulder* or, to borrow Graves's useful abbreviation, T.R.O.Y.S. It was published in 1943, by Cape in England and Macmillan in America. As a handbook to style, it has never been bettered. But it was more than a grammar book in Graves's mind. In the opening chapters, he suggested that lack of clarity in communication was a threat to the security of the country. This was the view which had, however unclearly, been put forward by Riding in her attempts to bring peace to the world. Having been banished from both the dictionary project and the First and Second Protocols, Graves used T.R.O.Y.S. as his own way of dealing with Britain's ills. Good English, he was not afraid to say, was a 'moral matter, as the Romans held that the writing of good Latin was'.[2] Riding had tried to establish a new set of moral principles; Graves offered his guidelines for good prose in just the same spirit of schoolmasterly authority.

The pattern for the book is close to that of Riding's *The World and Ourselves*, published in 1938. There, she had printed her own views and then taken the letters of sixty-five correspondents to pieces, showing their faults and virtues in long appendices. In T.R.O.Y.S. Graves began by offering his view on the importance of recovering a mastery of the English language, laying a heavy emphasis on the wisdom of a good Latin education, and praising his old hero Samuel Butler as a master of clear writing. He then proceeded to analyse and rewrite the texts which were provided by, among others, T. S. Eliot, the scientist Sir James Jeans, the mathematician A. N. Whitehead, and

I. A. Richards who was recognized as the leading authority on the English language. The method, and the belief in an unambiguous language as the basis of a healthy society which Graves expressed here, showed his affinity with Riding. He felt that he was taking on the job which she, in rejecting the Protocol and separating herself from her friends, had abandoned.

It was not written in a dutiful spirit. A good deal of the life and fun of the book lies in knowing the background to some of the pieces. 'I should dearly like to test I. A. Richards and the Basic Englishers,' Graves told Hodge when he was first collecting material for the book;[3] he was remembering that Richards's hostile report on Riding's dictionary project had lost her a potential American publisher. Richards, having submitted a passage from his *Principles of Literary Criticism* for examination in T.R.O.Y.S., was consequently punished with a savage analysis.[4] It was, Graves commented, impossible to make a coherent statement out of such a muddled passage as that written by Richards on the arts as a storehouse of recorded values. 'Also, the argument is incomplete, repetitive and disordered, and the language an uneasy mixture of Victorian literary incantation and bald modern laboratory exposition.'[5] Louis Gottschalk, Riding's former husband, received a relatively light cuff on the head for failing to take lessons from journalists in the art of plain writing.

Only one of Graves's victims protested that he had been unjust: Helen Waddell good-humouredly denied that she had written her introduction to *The Wandering Scholars* in a hurry, or that the writing showed any signs of carelessness. Her critic backed off, praising her for being 'entirely admirable . . . as busy and as patient as myself'.[6]

*   *   *

The Story of Marie Powell: Wife to Mr Milton was the next book which Graves undertook. Writing to a friend in 1941, he admitted to having disliked Milton ever since discovering that he had tried to suppress Skelton's poems; nothing had happened to lessen his hostility. (Graves seldom changed his views; a lifelong dislike of Virgil seems to have been founded on his belief that the poet was a sycophant; Yeats never escaped from the trough of Graves's disdain.) Taking as his thesis the curious notion that Milton was a trichomaniac so distracted by the beauty of a young girl's hair that he decided to make her his first wife, Graves concocted a lively story written from the point of view of the unfortunate first Mrs Milton.

Random House, the American publisher to whom the book was offered in the autumn of 1942, were alarmed by Graves's approach; Milton seemed to them too great a poet for such cavalier treatment. The reviewers, when the book was published early the following year, shared this view; but the readers were enthusiastic. The Cassell edition of 10,000 copies sold out immediately; in America, the more courageous Creative Age Press, a small New York publishing house, was delighted by a sale of 20,000 copies in the first two months of publication in 1944.

Graves, as so often, won his audience with a strong narrative, clearly told, and with a wealth of absorbing historical detail, which here created a convincing background to the story of a seventeenth-century Royalist household. His unconcealed disapproval of Milton was softened by the liveliness of his account of Marie Powell as a pretty young girl who married to save her parents from financial ruin. Marie's mystical ability to communicate with Mun, her absent soldier-lover, shows the superstitious side of Graves's nature; detailed accounts of English folklore reflect his abiding fascination with the pagan rituals in which many of the old English sports and festivals had their origin. *Wife to Mr Milton* shows the two sides of Graves's nature in perfect balance: the iconoclastic schoolmaster hammering away at a poet for whom he has no sympathy, and the passionate, other-worldly seer-poet firmly believing in Marie's ability to receive telepathic messages through the power of love.

★   ★   ★

Living at Galmpton, Graves had little contact with the literary world. He was not an admirer of Cyril Connolly's *Horizon*, looked on by many of his contemporaries as the main literary focus in the war years.[7] He was, however, concerned by the lack of young poets to respond to this war in the way that he and his friends had done in 1914–18. In October 1941 he wrote an article for *The Listener*, deploring this situation and suggesting that a shortage of paper had led to a situation in which the big publishing houses were only ready to commit themselves to work by established figures. The only poet-soldier he could single out was Alun Lewis, a young Welshman who had won wide admiration for

'All Day It Has Rained' and 'The Soldier', the second of which Graves quoted in his article.

A radio talk with Stephen Spender in November 1941 gave Graves another chance to praise Alun Lewis. This time, Lewis plucked up the courage to write to him, initiating a long and friendly correspondence. Alun Lewis had not yet been posted abroad but, despite Graves's cordial invitations, they never met. (Lewis died in Burma in 1944.) The roles of master and pupil were quickly established; for Graves, it was a poignant reminder of the poetic education which he and Siegfried Sassoon had given to Wilfred Owen in another war. His enthusiasm for Lewis's work was strong and generous; it was typical of many associations in which he acted as mentor and adviser. His suggestions were sweeping. Lewis, an ardent admirer of Yeats, was told to reconsider him as a manipulator of glamour rather than as a true poet; his enthusiasm for David Jones, the author of *In Parenthesis*, met with an equally cutting response. Jones, in Graves's view, was a plagiarist, a crime from which even his connection with the Royal Welch Fusiliers could not exonerate him. 'I do not like synthetic work, from Virgil on through the centuries . . . and, in the case of D[avid] J[ones], I knew too many of the sources.'[8] Lewis did not allow such subjective pronouncements to influence him, but it was from Graves that he learned the importance of finding his own values and judging himself, instead of trying to assess his merits by comparing himself to other poets.

Alun Lewis's poetry was less close to that of Graves than Edward Thomas, another poet for whom Graves had scant respect. But Lewis's admiration for Graves's work and his judgement was immense; writing to him in March 1942, just before being sent to India, he said that Graves's opinion 'was of more value to him than any other man's'.[9] From India he wrote to ask Graves if he would help Gweno, his wife, to draw up a list of suitable poems for his second volume. (*Raider's Dawn* had already been published, with Graves's approval, in 1942.) Graves chose a selection and wrote a Foreword to Lewis's second book, *Ha! Ha! Among the Trumpets*. It was published, posthumously, in 1945.

*　　*　　*

A reference by Lewis in November 1941 to plans to start a journal of Welsh literature which would extend from the tenth-century poet

Taliesin to Dylan Thomas met with mild enthusiasm from Graves.[10] He was, however, prepared to say that he preferred Taliesin, whom he had read in translation, to Dylan Thomas. Three years later, the most casual reference to Celtic poetry could be guaranteed to produce a stream of ideas. The Graves of 1944 would have corrected Lewis's dating and told him that Taliesin was a sixth-century court bard, and a far less interesting character than the Taliesin he had recently identified in an ancient riddling poem as the son of Cerridwen, the White Goddess in her Welsh form. In 1941, Lewis's remark prompted only courteous interest. What happened to Graves between 1941 and 1944 to send him in search of an all-powerful goddess, demanding human sacrifice?

There have been many illuminating studies of *The White Goddess* but little movement away from the notion that the principal biographical events behind the book were a formidable mother, a traumatic experience in the First World War and the thirteen-year relationship with Laura Riding. References to Jung's theory of archetypes have proved hard to avoid. Graves denied ever having read a word of Jung, but Jung's description of the female anima (the male image of the female) as a woman who is both unobtainably erotic and possessed of an ancient and superior wisdom, leads us directly towards Graves's concept of the Goddess.

The theory that Graves's Goddess was based solidly on personal experience was first expounded by Randall Jarrell, the American poet and critic, in 1956.[11] Jarrell suggested that Graves was divided between the 'logic-chopping regimental explainer' who descended from the von Rankes, and the poet who is 'Baby, Lover, Victim howling in dreadful longing for the Mother who bears, possesses, and destroys'.[12] This, one might assume, makes a case for seeing Amy Graves, still in good health and back on good terms with her son in the 1940s, as the Goddess. In the second part of his argument, however, Jarrell points his finger in another direction. Laura Riding is described here as the Goddess's original, a personality of 'seductive and over-mastering force':

> Judging from what Graves has written about her . . . I believe that it is simplest to think of her as, so to speak, the White Goddess incarnate, the Mother Muse in contemporary flesh . . . it was only after Graves was no longer in a position to

be dominated by her in specific practice that he worked out his general theory of the necessary dominancy of the White Goddess, the Mother–Muse, over all men, all poets.[13]

So, we must assume, Laura Riding returned to Graves's mind with irresistible force in 1943 when he began work on the book. The device of the Goddess, Jarrell went on to suggest, allowed Graves to take Riding's place. If he alone could interpret the Goddess's wishes, he took all of the Goddess's power into his own hands.

> He has become, so to speak, his own Laura Riding. There is only one Goddess, and Graves is her prophet – and isn't the prophet of the White Goddess the nearest thing to the White Goddess?[14]

There are some problems with this view. One is that Graves had been separated for four years from Riding before he began the research which led to the creation of the White Goddess. Why, if he was driven by the need to recreate her in this form, did he show no interest in the subject between 1940 and 1943? Why did he take care in *The White Goddess* to make the distinction between the Goddess and Laura Riding, who is described as an ideal muse and a model for women poets?[15]

Jarrell's suggestion, that Riding is the original of the Goddess, is unsound. Riding, as Graves clearly stated in his book, was in the difficult position of being both a woman poet and a muse. A woman, in his view, could not have a male muse; the muse was always female. The muse is not the Goddess but a woman who, for a period of time, is filled with her divine strength and thus able to act as an inspiration to the poet who loves and serves her. Riding did come to believe that she had powers which gave her an almost godly status, but it was Graves who had encouraged her in this belief. His interest in an ancient civilization ruled by women and goddesses preceded his friendship with her and directed the way he behaved towards her. It would be more accurate to say that Riding had been fitted, in 1926, into the niche where Graves needed to place a female deity, and that her departure in 1939 left a vacuum waiting to be filled.

The proposal then, that Laura Riding inspired Graves to write *The*

White Goddess carries little conviction. In fact, the book was initiated by a traumatic personal event in Graves's life.

Early in April 1943, Graves received a telegram to say that his son David had been reported missing. By June, the newspapers were carrying accounts of his death. He had been killed while attacking, single-handed, a Japanese stronghold on the Arakan peninsula in Burma. His recommendation for a VC was rejected only because the attack had failed.

Graves talked very little to his friends about David's death; to Sam, who followed his older brother to Jesus College, Cambridge, in 1945, he was able to show a little of the grief he felt. 'Dear David,' he wrote to Sam, 'all my memories of him are good ones; he never gave me the least unkindness or trouble or anxiety; and I still have continual pangs about him.'[16] The following year, he chose the poem written by his son which he had liked best and lovingly revised it for publication in *The Cambridge Review*. Its first line must have haunted him: 'It will be small loss, never to return.'

Graves's own sense of loss, and of lost opportunities, was intense. This was uppermost in his mind when he wrote to Basil Liddell Hart in the spring of 1944 about 'a deeply rooted religious habit of sacrificing one's son'.[17] Indirectly he was acknowledging a responsibility. It was he who had encouraged David to go to war, who had helped him to get into his own regiment and allowed himself the fantasy that he, through his son, was participating in the action. His new young family surrounded him, an unconscious and daily reminder of all that he had not done for the son he had lost. David's death acted as a catalyst for his backward leap, into a world where the death of a heroic young man could be seen as a poetic sacrifice demanded by the Goddess. Rational thought was of no use to him; what he needed and sought was some grand poetic scheme into which David's death and the nightmarish memories of war which now returned so vividly could be absorbed. The Goddess was already in his mind; in the summer of 1943 he began to revise his view of her and to extend her powers.

CHAPTER TWENTY-FIVE

1943–1946

THE WHITE GODDESS

WHEN GRAVES ADDED A POSTSCRIPT TO *THE WHITE GODDESS* IN 1961, he was ready to believe that the idea had been produced by a mysterious conjunction of talismanic objects on his writing-table.[1] Randall Jarrell was right in this respect; having invented the Goddess, Graves became increasingly eager to demonstrate her control over his life. As her personal bard and rescuer, he felt it his duty to speak for her on every possible occasion.

During the first period of Graves's curatorship, the Goddess was clearly defined as white, because of her association with the moon and because the colour white suggested the double image of purity and terror Graves wanted. The haunted pallor of the moonlit cliffs that rise above Deyá may have placed the colour in his mind; having read Herman Melville's novels as a young man, he was fascinated by the author's exploration, in *Moby Dick*, of the feelings evoked by whiteness. Melville's observation that visitors to London were far more chilled by being shown a White Tower than a bloody one stayed in his mind and was quoted in his book.[2]

The Goddess was defined as a being of triple form, representing the three female life-stages of bride, mother and, in her most sinister aspect, the Crone, or Layer-Out. She was not a goddess in her own right, but the mould from which all goddesses were created. Although Graves often seemed to have his tongue in his cheek when he talked of her powers, his belief in her was sincere. In earlier days he had described poetry as his religion. If the word 'poetry' is replaced by 'the Goddess', his attitude becomes clear.

From where, originally, had she come? Frazer's *The Golden Bough* is usually cited; Graves had been familiar with most of Frazer's work since his conversations with William Rivers in 1920–21. Frazer provided him with the idea of a sacrificial king whose death and renewal could be identified as an actual or theatrical ritual performed in many different societies. But the idea of a goddess who is both the murderess and the muse probably came from Jane Harrison, the remarkable Cambridge Classics don who, at the turn of the century, argued for the existence of an original matriarchy. She was not the first to do so; her own sources include the sturdy German historians who took matriarchy for their subject in the nineteenth century. (Graves insisted that he had not read the German authors, but his study of Harrison makes it hard to accept that he followed up none of the German sources which are discussed and named in the main body of the text. Graves's reading habits show that he was, almost to a fault, a follower-up of footnotes and references.) What singles Harrison out and makes her likely to have been the most powerful influence on him is not only the richness of her prose and the vividness of her imagination, but the aptness of her chosen illustrations. The wasp-waisted, bare-breasted priestesses in Harrison's books bear an uncanny resemblance to Graves's accounts of the appearance of the Goddess's followers. The beautiful, raging maenads, 'the wild white women' of Gilbert Murray's translation of Euripides's *The Bacchae*, are described by Harrison as possessed, magical and dangerous. These are the qualities which Graves's Goddess bestowed on the muses.

The book in which Harrison discussed the cults and rituals surrounding the maenads in detail was *Prologomena: A Study of Greek Religion*.[3] Here Harrison connected Greek and Celtic traditions in a way that Graves would do later. More strikingly, in her account of the Orphic mysteries Harrison made a clear connection between the maenad and the muse. Orpheus dies at the hands of the maenads, the women who represent a wild, irrational force. He is rescued by the muses, who bury his magical singing head in a sacred grove. 'Who are the Muses?' Harrison asks. 'Who but the Maenads repentant, clothed and in their right minds . . . The shift of Maenad to Muse is like the change of Bacchic rites to Orphic; it is the informing of savage rites with the spirit of music, order and peace.'⁴ This is the spirit in which Graves presents the rites of the White Goddess, progressing from terror and violence to order and calm; it is also the source of the thrilling tension of his mature love-poetry, in which emotion is invisibly restrained by classical discipline. Orpheus, first used in 'Escape' in 1916, is the poet-hero of several of his finest late poems.

The Goddess had already made her first appearance by Easter 1943, when Graves was still at work on *The Golden Fleece*. 'I am carrying the whole weight of Classical History and myth about in my mind from sink to coke-house . . .' he wrote to Karl Gay, who was then just getting himself transferred from the Army to the Navy. 'It is a frightfully interesting story to write.'⁵ In the Introduction he explained that it was an example of how a myth could be reinterpreted to suit the politics of a new generation. The original theft of the Fleece had taken place, in his view, in the last years of goddess-rule; later poets had chosen to embellish and revise the tale in order to diminish the Goddess's role. But, having rebuked the mythographers, Graves showed that he was not above borrowing from them to improve his plot. Orpheus, a notoriously late addition to the story, appeared among his own Argo crew.

In the introduction to *The Golden Fleece*, the White Goddess is presented, first, as Isis and then in her modern counterpart as Mary; 'for as Queen of Heaven the Goddess still claims the moon, the snake, the fetich cross, the blue garment, the stars, the lilies, and the Divine Child as her attribute.'⁶ (Here, Graves was already moving towards his next book, *King Jesus*, in which Christ would die trying to defy the ancient rule of the Goddess.) Affectionately and with a touch of homesickness, he opens *The Golden Fleece* in Deyá where, we learn, the Goddess lives when she is not on the island of Samos. The nymph we meet in the orange grove at Deyá is severe, but charming; she lacks the quality of sublime terror which the Goddess later gains. True, she orders the death of her visitor, but even this is done in a spirit of gaiety, as if in a fairy story. 'Besides, he was a bent, bald, ugly old fellow, an exile, and a Dolphin man, who would bring no luck to the grove.'⁷

Graves was writing the last chapters of *The Golden Fleece* when the news of David reached him. This was the point at which Harrison's synthesis of the maenad and the muse acquired a new and personal relevance. David's death was assuredly in his mind as he wrote the elegiac last words of the book.

> Orpheus also died a violent death. The Ciconian women one night tore him to pieces during their autumnal orgies in honour of the Triple Goddess. Nor is this to be wondered at: the Goddess has always rewarded with dismemberment those who love her best, scattering their bloody pieces over the earth to fructify it, but gently taking their astonished souls into her own keeping.[8]

Graves had already planned his next two books when he finished writing this novel. One was to be an examination, as Claudius had been, of how a man could become a god; in *King Jesus*, he expected to prove that Jesus had been a Jewish prophet and Messiah whose misguided faith in a paternalistic religion had led him to the Cross. The second book he wanted to write, together with Alan Hodge, was a history of English poetry.

Reading the letters which Graves wrote to Hodge in the late summer of 1943, it is clear that the agenda for *The White Goddess* was already set. Throughout his life, he would confound his more hesitant contemporaries by taking what seemed to be a leap in the dark to arrive at the same conclusion that they, by a careful process of elimination and comparison, would duly reach. By July, he was convinced that the Celtic bards had been the guardians of the old, original stories, which had reached them from Greece, of an ancient goddess-worshipping society. Where William Blake and the eighteenth-century Druidists held that Albion had been the cradle of civilization, Graves identified Albion as the shrine to which all secrets had been brought for safe keeping. By the end of the summer he was searching for a link between Ireland's three Brigids and a threefold female figure in early Welsh literature.

Graves was not alone in turning back to the bards. His extreme hostility to both David Jones and Dylan Thomas may have stemmed from the fact that they were working in a similar field, when Graves wanted it all to himself. The poetry of the 1940s, which has been called the New Romanticism, and which was a reaction against the contemporary flavour of much of Auden's verse, was united by the sense of a loss of vision and a belief in the poet's ability to create a private mythology from ancient knowledge. The exponents who set out to recover this power included Jones, Thomas, Vernon Watkins, Kathleen Raine, John Heath-Stubbs and George Barker. Graves, in writing *The White Goddess*, became their spokesman.

In the autumn of 1943, a young Welsh correspondent, Lynette Roberts, sent him a curious work by a nineteenth-century Welsh academic, Edward Davies. Davies's mind, as was evident to both Roberts and Graves, was unbalanced. It was Davies's investigation of Celtic myth, nevertheless, which provided the clue Graves had been looking for.[9] He had already made a division in his mind between romantic, muse-inspired poetry and the conscious appliance of technique, which he described as Apollonian. Davies, by providing the key to a druid alphabet based on tree worship, opened the way not only to a pre-Christian calendar but to a possible interpretation of the secrets guarded by the riddle-loving bardic schools. The astonishing effect can be seen in a letter Graves wrote to Alan Hodge a few weeks after reading Davies's book.

> The Moon was the Muse in Greece and worshipped on Helicon either with left-hand or right-hand practices, as the Goddess Kali is in India. In Britain she was Danu, Brigit, Any and Merion; and she dwindles and ends as Maid Marion, of the Robin Hood play . . . She appears and reappears in English poetry as Mab, Fairy Queen, Titania, Lamia, [La] Belle Dame Sans Merci, Christabel, The Phantom of Life in Death etc.
>
> The technique of Moon poetry is altogether different from that of Sun poetry, which derives from the Druidic schools of Ireland, Wales, Brittany, and pre-England, written in honour of the god Belen, who corresponded with Apollo of the Orphic mysteries.[10]

If Davies's book had not come Graves's way, he would have found another to serve his purpose. It was, he strongly believed, a family gift of the Graveses to make an intuitive leap to the answer before finding the proof. When Sam, in the summer of 1946, wrote from Cambridge to say that he was thinking of taking up history instead of architecture, his father was delighted. 'The particular gift that runs in the Graves family is historical,' he told his son, 'the intuitive assessment of historical evidence – an ear for what rings false . . .'[11] It seemed to him an eerie proof that he was on the right track when he found that one of his forebears had shared his fascination for druid alphabets and that another, William Rowan Hamilton, had made a seemingly random connection in mathematics which, years later, was discovered to be accurate. In *The White Goddess*, Graves boasted that the answers to the long riddling poem with which he began the book had been clear to him long before he looked for confirmation. Intuition was inspired – and always verifiable.

In 1943 he had been consciously directing his researches towards *King Jesus*. But, by Easter 1944, when the house was full of guests, Graves found it irresistible to begin setting down his new ideas about poetry. He wrote his first draft in a few weeks and called it 'The Roebuck in the Thicket', intending to reveal the roebuck as the unicorn. (Sears, Roebuck put in an objection, which necessitated a new title.) The imposition of a curfew (this was because of naval manoeuvres) in the Galmpton–Brixham area created, he told Karl, a 'film' between himself and reality as he found himself a prisoner in his own home; this was the trancelike state in which he wrote his first version of *The White Goddess*.

He had two cases to make. One was for the supremacy of Celtic poetry. The other was for the importance to poets of preserving a romantic tradition of service to the Goddess in the form of her human incarnation, the muse. Graves had been pleading on her behalf since the 1920s, when he wrote in 'Outlaws', one of his finest early poems, of 'Incense and fire, salt, blood and wine / And a drumming muse'. She had been an ambiguous creature, manipulated by the 'aged gods of power and lust' in those confused days of his early puritanism; now, he was ready to celebrate the power of an adamant, intuitive, sexual deity, through and for whom he could inflict humiliation and torment on himself as, being a puritan at heart, he needed to do. Laura Riding, finally, had escaped his controlling vision, leaving him to solace himself with domestic tranquillity. The Goddess was his compensatory invention. The muses he later sought out and moulded in her image would be, on a poetic level, his possessions in a way that Riding had never allowed herself to become.

Graves gave his book a subtitle: 'A historical grammar of poetic myth', juxtaposing the dusty sound of a school book with the image of bard and harp that 'poetic myth' suggests. But it was not written for schoolrooms, and the scholars who went to wearisome lengths to demonstrate the non-existence of a triple goddess, an original matriarchy or a tree alphabet were not performing a useful service. Graves's decision to omit footnotes did not make him, as George

Steiner suggested in one of many adverse comments from academic reviewers, a charlatan. The decision was deliberate. His intention was not to inform but to stimulate, and to show the advantages of thinking poetically, that is, on several levels at once. 'The whole point is the method of thought, not the results,' he wrote to Karl Gay, 'and as many examples as I can give, the better. It warms up towards the end, and I don't think there's a dull chapter.'[12] Karl, who arrived at Galmpton to start typing a clean copy in August 1944, worked on it without comment; he might have shared the view Graves nervously expressed to another friend, Alan Hodge, that it was 'the damn queerest book of the century – heaven help us all!'[13]

Large books were not welcome in wartime when there was a serious shortage of paper. Jonathan Cape rejected it and added, condescendingly, that he would give the author a dinner if he could find a publisher willing to take it on. An unnamed American publisher, having refused it, gave Graves satisfaction on another level by 'almost immediately' hanging himself in a garden, dressed in women's clothes. This, to Graves's myth-loving mind, was a clear sign that the Goddess was on his side.[14] Happily, she did not need to show any such violence to T. S. Eliot who, finding the book baffling but impressive, agreed to press for its publication with his fellow editors at Faber and Faber, who had done well with *The Long Weekend*. With that achieved, Eliot also agreed to the enormous list of expansions and revisions that were made before publication in 1948, increasing the book's size when paper remained in short supply; he refused to consider Graves's offer to waive his payment in order to see it in a single volume. In the publisher's catalogue, to Graves's satisfaction, Eliot himself described *The White Goddess* as a 'prodigious, monstrous, stupefying, indescribable book'.

The White Goddess pleads for a return to the romantic and mythological approach to poetry, but the Victorian schoolmaster in Graves is in evidence as he condemns the illiteracy of 'a cockney civilization'. How, he asks, are poets to understand the myths when these can only be impressed on a child's mind by 'a severe Classical education'? Why is there no official canon of 'two or three hundred books which every educated person may be assumed to have read with care'? What has happened to the time when adults as well as children feared ghosts, when poets could identify a fallow deer from a roebuck, when it was not remarkable to be able to identify a quotation from a mid-Victorian sermon?[15]

If this sounds as though Alfred Graves had risen to tap his son on the shoulder, Graves's notion of the ideal civilization is all his own. In describing it, he makes an eloquent argument for returning poets to a position of honour in society.

> To know only one thing well is to have a barbaric mind: civilization implies the graceful relation of all varieties of experience to a central humane system of thought . . . But that so many scholars are barbarians does not much matter so long as a few of them are ready to help with their specialized knowledge the few independent thinkers, that is to say the poets, who try to keep civilization alive . . . [The poet's] function is truth, whereas the scholar's is fact . . . Fact is not truth, but a poet who wilfully denies fact cannot achieve truth.[16]

In Graves's concept of a society guided by poets who follow the Goddess, a single system of thought does become imaginable, but only on a poetic level. When Laura Riding rejected poetry, she did so on the grounds that the language of poetry was not capable of conveying absolute truth; Graves has turned the argument around to say that the truth which the poets have to offer is based on knowledge, intuition and a recognition of the source of their inspiration, the Goddess or muse. This is truth, not in terms of fact, but of revelation.

Not all poets are fit to wear the crown Graves offers. He makes it plain that there have been very few poets who were widely read enough to become leaders. Only Ben Jonson and John Skelton are singled out: Graves evidently sees himself as their proper heir.

The most notorious page in *The White Goddess* forms part of the climax in which Graves released his most powerful and – to him – frightening emotions. In life, he was still disturbed by the sight of blood, by the act of sex, by any divergence from good manners in polite society. On the surface, he was a conventional, old-fashioned, slightly prudish man. *The White Goddess* unleashed the violent feelings which Amy Graves had taught him to suppress and deny, but only into the world of his imagination. Assisted by the Goddess, he was able to sabotage the lurid images of war which David's death had revived, by pushing them back into the ancient world of ritual human sacrifice. No poet could hope to understand the nature of poetry, he wrote,

> unless he has had a vision of the Naked King crucified to the lopped oak, and watched the dancers, red-eyed from the acrid smoke of the sacrificial fires, stamping out the measure of the dance, their bodies bent uncouthly forward, with a monotonous chant of: 'Kill!kill!kill!' and 'Blood!blood!blood!'[17]

Graves's attitude to the Goddess who presides over this scene is ambivalent. 'The poet is in love with the White Goddess, with Truth: his heart breaks with longing and love for her,' he wrote in this same section. A few lines further on, with no further explanation than that the author Solomon is 'a sour philosopher', he offers a lengthy quotation showing women as sexually insatiable vampires. The clue to his own attitude is given here as a Latin pun. '*Odi atque amo*': 'to be in love with is also to hate'.[18] On one side, he longed for women to resume their role as raging Bassarids or maenads; on the other, he could write with fastidious distaste of having seen an American woman (Kit Jackson is not identified by name) reproducing the Dionysiac ritual 'in faithful and disgusting detail' during a mental breakdown.[19] As a champion of women's superior powers, he was redoubtable; as a lover, he remained torn between lust and purity. In the White Goddess myth, the division could be made real; the notion of a continuing war over Isis between the Egyptian Osiris and his priapic rival, Set, allowed him to see his own conflicting needs as part of the unending story passed down from poet to poet. Retrospectively, he could see Geoffrey Taylor and Schuyler Jackson playing Set's role to his Osiris; as time went on, the pattern would repeat itself. The men who fell in love with Graves's muses were shocked by the fury of his opposition. They did not, could not, understand that they entered a story which offered them no escape from the role of the evil rival.

★   ★   ★

Writing to T. S. Eliot in January 1945, Graves told him that he had been like a man on two kettledrums the previous year, with his left hand on 'The Roebuck in the Thicket', as *The White Goddess* was still known, and his right hand on *King Jesus*.[20]

He started writing the story of *King Jesus* in the summer of 1944. It was based, in part, on the discussions which he had been holding since the previous summer with Joshua Podro, who lived nearby and who was the only Hebrew scholar he knew. Podro, Graves later told Tom Matthews, who strongly disapproved of the book, had been 'an angel of revelation . . . a sort of Uriel'.[21] Podro's contribution had been to an aspect of the book which presents Jesus as a Hebrew Messiah, an uncompromising and difficult man who had almost nothing in common with the Christian figure presented in the Gospels. Graves took care of the rest. When Podro expressed mild uneasiness about Graves's decision to connect Jesus to Dionysus, Graves shrugged it off. He had, he said, discussed it all with the vicar at Brixham; there were no problems with the idea.[22] Nevertheless, Graves was prudent enough to let his story be told by a Greek living in the Roman Empire in the 1st century AD; such a man could be assumed to have confused rumour with facts.

The sources for Graves's thesis were, as he acknowledged in his Appendix, remote; he was clearly determined to bludgeon his critics into silence when he informed them that his studies of secret Essene lore preserved in miscellanies of Irish poetic doctrine 'yield their full light only in the light of Babylonian astrology, Talmudic speculation, the liturgy of the Ethiopian Church, the homilies of Clement of Alexandria, the religious essays of Plutarch, and recent studies of Bronze Age archaeology.'[23]

It is in this Appendix that we hear, for the first time, about the 'analeptic' method, Graves's grand name for the ability of a poet or novelist to imagine a way into the past, and about 'iconotropy'. This was a word devised by Graves for what he saw as the wilful misinterpretation of matriarchal myths to show men as the superior beings. Among the examples he cited here was the sexual union of Pasiphaë and the Cretan bull, from which emerged the Minotaur. The myth relates that Pasiphaë, a nymph of Crete, fell in love with a white bull which King Minos had decided was too beautiful for the annual sacrifice. Hidden in the wooden body of a cow, she made love to the bull, and produced the Minotaur. In Graves's interpretation, presented in the Appendix to *King Jesus*, the myth hid a ritual event in which King Minos put on a bull's mask to be wedded to one of the priestesses of the moon goddess. A live bull would have been killed as part of the ceremony.

The myth of Pasiphaë was one which had particular resonance for

Graves. Either as a chaste priestess of the moon goddess or as the nymph of the later myth, she had disgraced herself. She had already made an appearance in 'Lament for Pasiphaë', a poem which he wove into the text of *The Golden Fleece*. This was the poem in which he reconciled himself to the loss of Laura Riding. She, like Pasiphaë, had 'shone for all', and shown supreme impartiality, in Graves's view, until 'Spring's cuckoo', encountered in the spring of 1939, pushed Graves out of the nest and caused Riding to betray her integrity. This is barely a poem about Pasiphaë at all, but about Graves's mourning for a woman he continued to honour.

> Faithless she was not: she was very woman,
> Smiling with dire impartiality,
> Sovereign, with heart unmatched, adored of men,
> Until Spring's cuckoo with bedraggled plumes
> Tempted her pity and her truth betrayed.
> Then she who shone for all resigned her being,
> And this must be a night without a moon.
> Dying sun, shine warm a little longer![24]

King Jesus, published in 1946, was one of Graves's most successful books, selling out of its first edition of 12,000 copies in England in the first week of publication and reaping the benefits of what Graves told Eliot was 'a storm of controversy' on both sides of the Atlantic.[25] Tom Matthews, despite his prejudice against what seemed to him a blasphemous interpretation, agreed to provide the Preface to a long article which Graves wrote about the book for the *New York Herald Tribune* of 4 February 1947; by then, it had been sold in five countries, easing Graves's financial worries.

Reviewers had preferred *The Golden Fleece*. *The Times Literary Supplement* dismissed *King Jesus* as 'an ingenious farrago . . . a copious narrative stiff with learning';[26] in *The Nation*, Robert Fitzgerald, an old friend of Tom Matthews, was distressed by inaccuracies and 'a certain anti-Christian pettishness and uneasiness that all Mr Graves's powers cannot dispel'.[27] The reviewer for *The Listener* was among several who had been sufficiently intrigued by Graves's reference to anachronisms in the Gospels to hope that he would soon provide a more detailed commentary. Graves was ready to oblige; by the time he came to read the reviews, he was already deep in correspondence with Joshua Podro about a study of the Gospels and the influence on them of Simon Magus, perceived by Graves as a villainous rewriter of the true story of the Jewish, non-Christian, Christ. They would, Graves told Podro, be doing Jesus a favour.

> [The sense of] Jesus in our midst is like that of a ghost who has a confession to make or a message to deliver: he is pathetic, outraged, distressed that nobody will listen, he protests that he did *not* mean what he is said to have meant, that he is *not* God, that he is loyal to God, that he is a Jew not a Gentile . . . Well, we shall see.[28]

★   ★   ★

Six years in England and without Riding had not softened Graves's view of his fellow poets. He was ready to profess admiration for Louis MacNeice and George Barker, but he remained cool about Spender and dour about Auden. Invited to appear in a new anthology by Ronald Bottrall, he was only prepared to do so if he was given as much space as Eliot and Yeats, holding himself superior to both. When Eliot asked him to sign a plea on behalf of Ezra Pound, interned in an Italian camp, Graves refused on the grounds that it would seem to be an endorsement of Pound's poetry. His unfavourable view of David Jones has already been recorded. Dylan Thomas, who had sent his poems to Graves in the early Thirties, was now dismissed as a writer of beautiful but incomprehensible verses. (Every word of a poem, in Graves's view, had to make sense in the whole; Thomas seemed to him more in love with melody than with meaning.) His loyalty was to old friends, like Norman Cameron, happily settled by 1945 with a comforting Austrian woman, and James Reeves. Neither had made the wholehearted commitment to poetry which Graves believed was crucial, but he was always willing to break his rules where friends were concerned. These two, and Alan Hodge, were the poets with whom he had chosen to appear in a small Hogarth Press collection, *Work in Hand*, published in 1942.

His legendary kindness to younger poets had been put into practice shortly after his arrival in Devon. Martin Seymour-Smith, then a schoolboy who wrote poems in all his spare hours, Derek Savage, Terence Hards, Ronald Bottrall; all were poets who drew on Graves for encouragement and assistance in the Forties. As always with Graves, it is difficult to overlook the contrast between his harshness to the successful and his kindness to those less gifted than himself.

These were friendships which were chiefly maintained by correspondence. By the end of 1945, Devon was full of British tourists and empty of friends. Only Irene Warman and Lord Falkland remained. Joshua Podro had taken his press-cuttings business back to London, where he was able to offer employment to Karl Gay. The Liddell Harts had already gone; Agatha Christie and her husband, who remained, had never been more than friendly acquaintances. Sam was reading history at Cambridge, Catherine was a busy mother, and Jenny, who had become a highly professional war correspondent, had married Alex Clifford, a fellow reporter at the Front, in 1945. There was nothing to keep Graves in England. He had enjoyed making a visit to Erinfa to look at his father's old books on bardic literature, and he had enjoyed, too, getting to know his sister Rosaleen's children during the Galmpton years but the family was not, to him, home. Unpleasant though it was to contemplate living under Franco's rule in Mallorca, Deyá was where he longed to be.

CHAPTER TWENTY-SIX

1946–1949
RETURN TO DEYÁ

IN JANUARY 1946, HEARING FROM JENNY THAT SHE WAS PLAN-
ning a trip to Portugal and Spain, Graves asked his daughter to
visit Deyá and look up the Gelats. The news she brought back
was encouraging. The constrictions of life under Franco sounded
no more repressive than those in wartime Britain, and Canelluñ
had been maintained as if they had left it only the other day; she
had even found a half-finished letter to herself lying on her father's
desk. Graves was overjoyed. Later that year, enthusing to Joshua
Podro about the Mallorcans, he told him that 'their sense of moral
obligation and personal honour is the highest in Europe'.[1] With his
second family, Graves imagined that he could regain the years when
the price of living abroad with Laura had been the loss of his small
sons and daughters.

Preparations to leave England began in April. Travel was still
problematic in 1946 and Graves had to use all his skills at pulling
strings to find a way to fly himself and the family to Spain. They
packed up the house at Galmpton at the end of the month, donating
the furniture to Catherine as a compensation for the university
education which Graves had been too poor to subsidize in 1941.

He was richer now; before they left, he decided to give Beryl, Irene Warman and the children a taste of luxury at Brown's Hotel in London while he made the final arrangements about visas. On 15 May, the family went to Croydon airport, where a specially chartered air-taxi was waiting for them.

The journey, for all but an elated Robert, was exhausting. The plane was only just large enough to hold the family, the pilot, the navigator, and the luggage. Buffeted by winds, the younger children were sick and in no state to enjoy meeting Gelat's sister Anita when they made a stop at Rennes, or to share their father's amusement when the plane almost hit a flock of sheep when it landed at Barcelona, or to match his patience at the twenty-four-hour wait there before the British Embassy in Madrid could arrange permission for them to proceed to Mallorca, which was still a military zone. At Palma airport, the children looked on with embarrassment as their father was embraced and wept over by two strangers; Gelat, little changed by ten years, had brought his son, also called Juan, to help welcome them home.

The village, although almost empty of foreigners, seemed unchanged and the children were rapidly at home. To Beryl, however, suffering acutely from bleeding haemorrhoids and with no knowledge of Spanish, the new life offered a considerable challenge. 'It was very strange at first,' she told her ex-husband, Alan Hodge, 'not least because of the evidences of Laura in the house, the strange designs she drew on the walls, the clutter of furniture in her rooms, empty and half empty bottles of medicines, and all the other things.'[2] Graves seemed as anxious as she to make the house theirs. Laura's workroom became a bedroom for Lucia and Juan, while William was moved into Graves's monastic single room. The study downstairs was kept as it had been, but the press room next to it was converted into a library. The Seizin days were over and Graves was anxious to sell the handsome old Albion machine, seen now as 'a nice toy' which took up too much room.[3] Twenty years later, it was still being occasionally used.

In 1939 Laura had asked Graves to burn all her manuscripts and letters when he returned to Deyá; all those that could be found in 1946 without much trouble were sold in two sacks of scrap paper to a Palma merchant; what later turned up was burned in the garden the following year. 'She left a lot of unhappiness behind but we are clearing it off gradually', Graves wrote to Hodge, concluding, 'unhappiness breeds clutter.'[4] Many years later, Beryl found one more manuscript in the attic and sent it to Riding, who remained convinced that this had been the source for ideas of female superiority expressed in *The White Goddess*. The fact that Graves had almost completed the book by the time he returned to Deyá did not alter her view of him as a vandal, but Riding had an unusually protective belief in her rights of creative ownership.

The oddity is not how much evidence of Laura was removed from Canelluñ, but how much was left, and remains. Pictures and ornamental plates hang where Laura placed them; a batik by Len Lye celebrating her miraculous survival from the fall in 1929 still hangs at the foot of the staircase. A chair which Gelat had made to fit and support her slight frame became the one in which little Juan sat at family meals.

Alan Hodge was the only person to whom Beryl was ready to admit the problems of their new life; others heard how delightful it was to have warm weather and to be away from the traffic and the Devon tourists. Dutifully, Beryl attended the feasts held in her honour, experimented with Spanish cooking, squirrelled away the last of their sugar, powdered chocolate and instant coffee from England and tried not to miss the company of English friends. Laura, too, had been frantic with loneliness in the first months, but Deyá had been her chosen home. To Beryl, although she came to love it, even the glorious mountains which enclose Deyá offered a threat in the first years. Canelluñ's atmosphere was gloomy and its position remote from the village. The most she could achieve was not to communicate her sense of despondency as winter approached and with it a cloying dampness to which Graves himself seemed oblivious. There were no entertainments; Franco's Spain had put an end to dancing and card games. At Galmpton, Beryl had thought nothing of wearing a skirt as short as a child's; in Franco's Deyá, such freedom was unthinkable. When the children were sent to school in the village, the only available option was for William to go to the strict Falangist schoolmaster while Lucia and Juan were turned over to the nuns and taught to kiss the Cross. This, for a woman as hostile to orthodox religion as Beryl, was hard to take. She was not even able to laugh when Graves joked that he would have been a Catholic if he had needed to choose a faith.[5]

Nothing could crush Graves's pleasure at being back in the village where he felt he belonged. If there is a consistent note to his letters about the return to Deyá, it lies in a robust determination to make the best of everything. Busy on amendments to *The White Goddess*, he made light of the impossibility of getting help in the house (all the local women had taken work as glove-makers and no regular maids could be found for the first two years), of the difficulties with currency conversion (partially solved by the opening of accounts in Tangiers and America) and a 600 per cent rise in living costs since he had left the island. He joked about the use of ground olive stones to make petrol and prided himself on the way they managed to support themselves by turning most of the Canelluñ garden over to vegetables and compost heaps. Their friends from England could not visit them, but Graves, engaged on his books, felt little need for company. When he wanted to communicate with his old friends, he wrote them letters.

A secretary was the only luxury with which he could not dispense. Beryl was fully occupied with looking after the house and children when she was not confined by ill-health to her bed; knowing that the job with Podro's London press-cuttings agency had proved unsatisfactory, Graves wrote to suggest that Karl should come back to live, as he had before, at Ca'n Torrent. The news that Irene Warman would accompany him was well-received; Irene, besides being pretty and amusing, would be able to help look after the children. Karl and Irene arrived in 1947 and the crisp rustle of Karl's morning entrance with a sheaf of typescript and a neat list of editorial queries became as familiar a part of the Canelluñ routine as his conscientious reproaches when Graves had been careless in his haste to finish an article or review. 'Actually, we all lived in fear and trembling of him,'[6] Beryl wrote to a friend in the 1960s; but the children had never taken Karl's wrath or his indignant 'For Chrissake!' too seriously. Graves, who knew him even better than they, was always aware of the kindness and loyalty which underlay Karl's fierce manner.

Travel remained problematic but, in June 1947, Graves decided to accept a suggestion from his young friend Ricardo Sicre, who was still based in New York, that he and the family should take a holiday at his parents' home in the Spanish Pyrenees. Any holiday seemed better than none; Graves accepted. But the Sicre home was dank and remote, and the visit was not a great success. When Graves went for a walk in the local valley, he was bitten by a viper.

The pain was extreme – his leg was still swollen a month later – but the experience gave him a new idea for *The White Goddess*.

After the snake-bite his sight had been temporarily 'silvered over', or so Graves was eager to imagine. Silver Island had been identified as a name for the final resting-place of the sacred kings. A study of the myths showed that many of the heroes had died from a poisoned heel, their one vulnerable point. The pain, for such discoveries, was well worth enduring. The vision of a Silver Island increased his conviction that hallucinogenic experiences were behind many of the ancient mysteries and oracular sayings.

They returned to Deyá in July and were almost immediately plunged into a family crisis. Gelat had given young William a red bicycle for his seventh birthday: it had become his favourite new toy. Riding it home one day, William was knocked down by a car filled with tourists. His right foot was badly injured; a month after he had been unsuccessfully treated at the Palma hospital, amputation was recommended. Instead, while Beryl returned to Deyá, Graves took William to a Barcelona clinic where he was operated on by a surgeon skilled at grafting skin.

For William, the month in Barcelona, during which he had his father's sole attention, made up for some of the pain he had experienced during his initial period of treatment in Palma. Graves was an affectionate father, but his mind was seldom engaged by the children's games and chatter. His thoughts were always on his latest work commitment and everything he did and talked about was related to that central, unswerving interest. Even in the hospital, all of the time not spent telling stories or singing ballads to William was given up to revising and expanding the futuristic novel set in New Crete which he had started writing at Galmpton in 1944.[7] It was, he wrote to Ricardo Sicre in Madrid, meant to show 'how to stabilize society without boredom or tyranny' and it was based on his belief that friendship was the only thing worth having in their own 'horrible' epoch.[8] Friendship, for Graves, still carried the weight of significance with which Riding had endowed it. Like her, he continued to believe that a circle of right-thinking friends could affect the mental attitude of a generation.

Graves had always liked Barcelona; his stay was long enough to make him consider the possibility of moving there. It might, he felt, suit Beryl better; he was aware that she had been putting a brave face on her discomfort in an isolated Mallorcan village. But he also wanted to bring her to the city for a more practical reason: the hospital was an excellent one and the doctors were confident that they could perform a successful operation on her haemorrhoids. His letters persuaded her: in September, she arrived for an operation and to take over the role of William's companion, while Graves returned to his work and the other children.

This was the order of his priorities. Graves's letters to Beryl in hospital show a near-obsessive fascination with time-keeping where the children were concerned. Rather than describing their games or sayings, he reported on ways in which he had contrived to do things for them at the maximum speed. Everything, always, was geared towards providing more time for his work.

He had never been busier. The Cretan novel had provided a light-hearted interlude at a time when he was already engaged on four other projects. Penguin had invited him to translate Apuleius's *The Golden Ass*, a task which appealed to him not only because it contained a vivid account of a goddess and her powers, but because it would require him to search for the exact contemporary vocabulary to catch the earthy, lively voice of the original Latin. He had also agreed to collaborate with a 'studious, stranded, sentimental but reliable German historian' called Otto Kubler, on a novel about the discovery of the Solomon Islands.[9] (As Graves's description here suggests, there was little rapport between the two men; the following year, Kubler allowed Graves to take over the project.) A long list of additions to *The White Goddess* was being drawn up for Eliot's agreement; at the same time, Graves was deep in research for the book in which he and Joshua Podro hoped to show Jesus as he had appeared before Christian scholars tampered with the Gospels.

In September 1947 all of these projects were laid aside while Graves began to review his essays for publication. Several were taken from the books which he had written with Riding; since she had resigned her claims on them in 1939, making an exception of the American rights, he apprehended no difficulties so long as she was given proper acknowledgement. Unwisely, he assumed that Riding's renunciation of poetry meant that she had no interest in reprinting her views on it.

The essays, pruned and revised to show a coherent line of thought, were published after some savage exchanges between Laura Riding, Graves and Eileen Garratt, the American editor at Creative Age Press who had published *The White Goddess*. An early essay on *The Tempest* was expanded to include its author's new belief that the story of the witch Sycorax and her hideous son was a variant of the history of the folk-hero Taliesin, told, Graves charmingly supposed, by Shakespeare's Welsh schoolmaster. The essays, which appeared under the title *The Common Asphodel*, remind us also of the schoolmaster in Graves, delighting in the analysis of original manuscripts, in discussions of technique and, in one of his most dazzling pieces, 'Lucretius and Jeans', in the sheer fun of discovering analogies where none had seemed to exist. Few collections of literary essays have revealed so much of their author's nature; here, more than in Graves's letters, we see a disciplined, imaginative, original mind at its mental peak. Here, too, there is ample demonstration of the love of craftsmanship and technique which Graves called the 'Apollonian' side of his work.

Laura Riding was in his mind for other reasons than the essay revisions in 1947. A year after his return to Mallorca, he was anxious to assert his property rights. Norman Cameron was willing to resign any legal claim he might still have to Ca'n Torrent, which he had made over to Riding, but a letter from the Jacksons' lawyers in October 1947 suggested that Graves's troubles were not over. 'The fact is,' he told the Aldridges, 'I am allergic to lawyers' letters calling me a swindler and saying that since I now have taken possession of the property (which I haven't) I must damn well pay $500 into their bank, or else.'[10] An exchange of letters between Riding and Gelat produced a more satisfactory result, but one which left Gelat with power of attorney to act on Riding's behalf. The house deeds were transferred; but the act was meaningless, since foreigners were still forbidden to hold land or to build houses within five kilometres of the sea. Graves, however, was content to accept an arrangement whereby Gelat would provide him with olives and wood in exchange for farming the land for himself. It was, in Graves's view, a comfortable understanding between friends.[11] It never occurred to him that he did not, and never had, owned the property for which he had paid.

Beryl, writing to a friend in England at the beginning of 1948, lamented the fact that conversation in Deyá seemed to revolve around olive crops and the black market, with occasional discussions about 'art'.[12] She was feeling a little flat after the departure for America of their closest English friends, Archie and Cicely Gittes, a couple who had stayed on in the village throughout the war and who were always ready for a pleasant evening of gossip and singing, with Archie improvising descants against Graves's pleasant tenor as they rambled through the old ballads Graves loved.[13] The Gitteses' departure left only two or three couples with whom they could spend an agreeable evening; nevertheless, Graves was able to tell his sister Clarissa that fourteen people had sat down to a real Christmas dinner at Canelluñ in December 1947. There had been a Christmas tree, stockings on the children's beds, turkey, champagne, plum pudding, tangerines and brandy. Christmas in England, he added with pardonable pride after doing most of the cooking himself, had never been so complete.[14] New Year's Eve was livelier still, with a lot of 'dancing and nonsense' at the bullfighters' club in Palma, where Graves boasted to his sister of having downed fourteen glasses of brandy before consuming the traditional twelve grapes at midnight.[15]

A piece of news which transfixed the Graveses shortly after this came from Montague and Dorothy Simmons. Never having abandoned their faith in Laura, they had gone out to work with the Jacksons in the citrus fruit enterprise which they had started at Wabasso, Florida. Laura, her face partly paralysed by a small stroke, had been welcoming, but goodwill had rapidly evaporated when the Simmonses realized that Schuyler intended them to act as the domestic helps. After refusing to do the household laundry, they had returned, penniless, disillusioned and unemployed, to England. Graves could not resist writing to express regret that they had not listened to his warnings. The Simmonses laid the blame on Schuyler, seen by them as a bullying husband who had crushed Laura's brilliance and reduced her to drudgery. Their old friendship with Robert and Beryl was now resumed.[16]

Business and pleasure dictated that the Graveses should spend at least a month each summer in London. In July 1948 the family stayed in Maida Vale at the large, comfortable house belonging to Graves's niece Sally and her husband Richard Chilver; the following year, they rented an even more central house from friends of Sally's. For the children, these were the times of their first meetings with Beryl's parents and with their grandmother, Amy, a tall, forbidding old lady dressed in black. Graves pottered around antique shops, went to see his niece Diana's husband, Michael Gough, in a Sartre play and taught William to row on the lake in Regent's Park. William enjoyed this visit; he was even taken along to visit T. S. Eliot at Fabers' office and allowed, by Eliot's kindly dexterity, to win a game of rigged cards while his father put forward proposals for his new book about the Gospels. The first edition of *The White Goddess* had sold out; Eliot was willing to listen.[17]

The months when Ricardo Sicre had struggled to make money in New York by giving Spanish classes to Tom Matthews and his friends were long past. By 1948 Ricardo Sicre and his Canadian wife Betty were Graves's most financially successful friends, due to Ricardo's entrepreneurial skill as an American citizen selling goods to a commodity-hungry Spanish market. Ricardo had acquired a circle of glamorous and influential friends. His debt to Graves had not been forgotten but, as he and Betty returned in the late Forties to live in Barcelona and then Madrid, he had another favour to ask. He had written a novel, based on his upbringing in a village in northern Spain. He wanted Graves to work on it and to recommend it to a publisher. Graves did as requested and *The Tap on the Left Shoulder* was duly published, with his help; in return, Graves had the support of a formidable financier with a wide range of connections that were to prove enormously useful.

Sicre's first and main act of assistance concerned the land and houses which Graves still believed he owned in Mallorca. In 1949, when old Gelat died, he had left all the 'Graves' property to his own son Juan Gelat, a fact of which Graves remained unaware for ten years. When young Gelat finally admitted that he was indeed the new owner, Graves could not believe that his old friend had been so unscrupulous. Ricardo Sicre was the mastermind in the complicated negotiations to recover, by further payments to the Gelats, what was rightfully his. It was Ricardo who pulled strings to have Canelluñ placed within the boundaries of the village so that it could be owned by a foreigner; it was Ricardo, too, who acted as the necessary Spanish middleman to whom young Gelat was persuaded in 1960 to sell the property and land. Graves discreetly made the payments to Ricardo who, in turn, had all the property transferred into Beryl's name.* Without Ricardo Sicre's help, it is likely that Graves would eventually have lost all of his Mallorcan assets to the Gelat family.[18]

Ricardo was also the man to whom Graves turned for advice on currency and banking arrangements, a major concern for a busy writer whose money was earned abroad. When Graves felt that he needed commercial advice – he seldom took it – Ricardo was there to offer it and to provide the contacts. Graves, offered access to a

---

* This made sense as Beryl was twenty years younger than Graves. To put the property in her name at this stage reduced the eventual likelihood of death duties.

world of bankers, film stars and producers, was as fascinated as a child at a fair.

His own celebrity was growing. His 1938–45 collection of poems, widely read, had won admiration for the section in which he celebrated both his new love for Beryl and his sense of a universal, unending myth known only to poets. In the summer of 1948, *The White Goddess* was published. Reviewers on both sides of the Atlantic greeted it, after a six-month pause for reflection, with a mixture of bewilderment and admiration. Graves himself had described it to his friend James Reeves as 'a very capacious and fantastic mare's nest for poets to lay their heads in for years to come'[19] and it was from the poets that he received the tributes he valued most. Lawrence Durrell was one of the first to send a letter of unqualified praise. Even poets who had found fault with the detail, like John Heath-Stubbs, the first to point out that Graves's red-legged cranes must have come from observation of a badly-coloured print (as they had), found much to admire. 'I believe in the tradition of poetry for which you stand, and have tried to follow it, however ineffectually, in my own work,' Heath-Stubbs wrote in 1948.[20]

Ten years later, Roy Fuller told Graves that it had been a revelation to discover that what his own poetry lacked was a sense of the White Goddess. 'I realized I had been starving it of something it vitally needed that was there in my life but not finding a perspective in my verse.'[21] Ted Hughes and Sylvia Plath were among the younger poets who acknowledged the book as a formative influence; Hughes won *The White Goddess* as a school poetry prize and read it when he was at Cambridge in the early Fifties. When he met Sylvia Plath, this was one of the first books he wanted her to read. In 1967, when inviting Graves to take part in a London poetry festival, Hughes told him that it remained 'the chief holy book of my poetic conscience'.[22]

Poetry, in the late Forties, took a back seat to prose in Graves's life. A collection was published in 1948 but he had written fewer than six poems a year since starting work on *The White Goddess*. Such a reduced output did not prevent an increasingly respectful attitude developing towards his work. 'I must be getting old or something – shortage of grand old men, so they are grooming me for the position,' he wrote to his sister Clarissa in 1950, after hearing of Kathleen Raine's two-page appraisal in the *Times Literary Supplement*.[23] But, at fifty-five, he was bursting with energy and ideas. He looked magnificent; Cicely Gittes, his Deyá neighbour, remembered feeling uncommonly glad that she was already on her knees by the fire when Graves first walked into her home in 1946. If she had been standing, she was convinced that his presence would have turned her limbs to jelly.[24]

The haemorrhoid cure had not ended Beryl's discomfort. In July 1949 she had a further operation, gynaecological this time and 'very aesthetic', Graves told Alan Hodge. The following month they went to visit Jenny and her husband, Alex Clifford, in the beautiful little castle above Portofino which they had bought two years earlier. Tom and Julie Matthews were also staying with Jenny and there was additional pleasure for Graves in meeting Jenny's godfather, Max Beerbohm, for the first time in thirty years. His last recollection of Max had been of seeing him and William Nicholson annotating a London magazine with saucy caricatures. Max, in his old age, had lost none of his charming insouciance, but Graves eyed his house's proximity to the noisy coast road at Rapallo with horror. In 1949 tourism had yet to leave scars on Deyá.

From Portofino, they travelled on with the children to England where, since Beryl was still weak, William was put in the care of a young chaperone, Martin Seymour-Smith. Martin escorted William to suitable London sights, while Graves visited Amy in Harlech before returning to go over the details of the projected Gospel collaboration with Joshua Podro at his home in north London.

Graves liked events to conspire in his favour. He had been delighted by the appearance of a new star in the 'Ship' or 'Argo' constellation when he was writing *The Golden Fleece*. Now, with the recent discovery of the Dead Sea scrolls and the establishment of Israel's new status in 1948, the timing seemed right for a book which would give Jesus back to the Jews. But it was frustrating to have so little time for work in sociable London; Podro was persuaded to make two visits to Deyá, one in the autumn and the other during the spring of the following year.

The Nazarene Gospel Restored, although one of Graves's least studied books, is one of his most erudite and fascinating. His enthusiasm for the project was immense. As a lover of riddles and puzzles, he saw the decoding of the Gospels not only as a valuable task but also an entertaining one. There were occasional bitter disputes between the collaborators. Even when Graves cited the respected Hebrew scholar Raphael Patai as his source, Podro found it hard to endorse the idea of Jesus undergoing a coronation ceremony and a ritual breaking of his leg in full-blown matriarchal style. But the joy for Podro of working with Graves was too great to be forfeited for a difference of opinion.[25] Against his own judgement, Podro allowed the coronation scene to be included and agreed to stop trying to give Graves lessons in Hebrew.

Graves's enthusiasm was infectious. As always, he spilt it over his correspondents with reckless indifference to their likely degree of knowledge or interest. Cicely Gittes was puzzled to receive an account of the latest Gospel confusion to have been sorted out in response to a letter she had written about Christmas presents.

> Today's little problem was why did Matthew X.29 say only two sparrows were sold for one farthing, and Luke XII.6 that five were sold for two farthings? Once one has solved this problem the sense appears. Answer: Luke put 'five for a farthing'; by mistake, an editor wrote 'no, two' having consulted Matthew; subsequent stupid editors thought he meant farthings, not sparrows, and amended accordingly . . . I can't make out how biblical critics have failed to solve potty little problems like this, but I suppose to have DD to one's name is a hindrance not a help.[26]

★   ★   ★

Education in Deyá was beginning to be a problem by 1949. Lucia liked nothing but ballet-dancing; Juan had not progressed beyond drawing lines of tidy 'O's in his books; William's teacher was unsatisfactory. Originally, a plan was made for Martin Seymour-Smith to come as a tutor; this idea was postponed and they decided instead on William Merwin, described to Cicely Gittes at the time of his arrival in September 1949 as an intelligent Princeton graduate who had been teaching the royal children in Portugal, and who would be bringing his wife Dido. A little over a year later, Merwin was being referred to in less equable terms as 'eloquent, industrious, cruel and sly', although he was acknowledged to be 'a good tutor when he knows our eyes are on him'.[27] Merwin's later letters to Graves suggest that he never knew what he had done to incur his wrath. He had, in fact, done the unforgivable, which was, so Graves believed, to attempt to seduce Judith Bledsoe, the poet's first muse. (There was, according to both the muse and Merwin, no seduction, although Bledsoe agrees that she may have allowed Merwin to flirt with her.[28])

Graves had been a devoted husband to Beryl in everything but legal name during the first years they spent living in Devon. It was only after he had written *The White Goddess* and declared to the world that he was her man, bound to her service, that he began to feel the need for a muse to torment and inspire him. The first signs of the search had been given before they left England. Irene Warman's pretty face and lively ways caught his interest for a time. He told her that she was appearing to him in his dreams and suggested that it was a sign of her significance in his life.[29] Irene did not take the suggestion seriously. In Deyá, shortly after meeting the Gitteses, Graves went to visit Cicely alone one day. She, like Irene, was unusually pretty and strong-willed. Graves revealed that she was beginning to influence some of his poems, and suggested that they should go away for a week together. Cicely, by her own account, hesitated only for a moment before deciding that her duty lay with her husband. Graves took the rejection with perfect good humour, and never again proposed anything in the nature of an escapade.[30] His behaviour, in both these cases, was romantic rather than aggressive, but it came as no surprise to Cicely Gittes to learn, in 1950, that Graves had found himself a muse. She did not imagine that it would trouble Beryl; to their friends, it was clear that Graves would always need and depend on his wife.

For her husband's sake, Beryl put up a remarkably convincing front. The hints of the humiliation she felt are so minute that they can easily be missed. Beryl's loyalty was of the old-fashioned kind that stiffened the backs of army wives in the days of the British Empire. She accepted the muses, treated them as her friends, and scolded them if they seemed to be treating Graves unkindly. By behaving honourably herself, she created a sense of obligation in them. They were never called muses either by Graves or by Beryl; they were the young women who, possessed for a time by the power of the Goddess, came to inspire his poetry. Beryl, as much as Graves, accepted that this was the work of fate.

The muses were, as the creatures of the Goddess, free of all blame. If they had affairs with other men, as all of them did, the men were blamed for it. The only sin a muse could commit, in the eyes of Graves and Beryl, was to abandon her poet. If she did so, the Goddess instantly left her body. She had beauty, strength and power only so long as she played her chosen part.

CHAPTER TWENTY-SEVEN

1950–1956
JUDITH

GRAVES OBTAINED HIS DIVORCE FROM NANCY LATE IN 1949; in May 1950 he married Beryl. It was, he told Cicely Gittes, 'a particularly nice wedding at the Consulate' with flowers and champagne. They had left the children at home, but Karl and Irene, Joshua, Norman and Gretl Cameron, were all present; the day was rounded off with a visit to a friend's yacht, and ices in Palma.[1] Three months earlier, Norman had spent a less happy time trying to console Nancy on the day of the divorce.

In December 1950 the slightly prudish James Reeves was astonished to receive a letter from Graves announcing that the Goddess 'appeared in person in Deyá during the last full moon, swinging a Cretan axe . . .'[2] Cicely Gittes had received a less exotic account of the Goddess in November. She had revealed herself as 'a tall American footloose beauty who goes about in long black trousers, and paints'.[3] A month later, she heard that the girl was twenty-two – Judith was, in fact, seventeen but Graves was unaware of this – and that Beryl and he had

loved her exceedingly, but our neighbours and (let's face it) employees Karl and Rene [*sic*] and William's tutor [William Merwin] and wife started a witch hunt against her. Beryl and I said: 'Oh if only Cicely were here!' Girl in question knew all the rare old songs that you and I make a test of taste and virtue, and sang them as they deserve; wasn't that queer?[4]

Graves was not in love with Judith in the way that the term is usually understood. He needed a muse on whom to focus the devotion, the ritual of sacrifice and pain which he had described in *The White Goddess*. Marriage had forced home on him the fact that contentment was hostile to the spirit of his poetry. Judith came to the right place at the right time.

Writing about her in his short story 'The Whitaker Negroes', in which her name is changed to Julia Fiennes, Graves described Judith Bledsoe as a mixture of Irish-Italian on her father's side and New Orleans-French on her mother's. She was 'young, tall, good-looking, reckless and romantic. She had come "to take a look at Europe before it blows up."' In conversation, he claimed that they spoke in 'a joking verbal shorthand [which] for us expressed a range of experience so complex that we could never have translated it into everyday language'.[5] This sense of a semi-mystic rapport was also established with Judith's successors. In each case, Graves encouraged them to discover and share his own sense of a magical bond between the poet and the wild, free, elusive young woman he had chosen to adore.

Judith Bledsoe's own account begins with a handsome father she never knew, leaving her with a need for glamorous and mature substitutes. She found her first older man when she left her mother's Hollywood home to live in Paris with an artist called Marvin. She visited Mallorca on an impulse holiday with another woman and, when they quarrelled, went to Deyá in the hope of meeting the author of *I, Claudius*. She was a talented artist, but her fantasies circled around the film world; her vague dream was that Graves might help her towards a film career. After a week during which Graves noticed an unusually good-looking girl wandering around the village on her own, an invitation to dinner was transmitted through Karl. Dressed in her best clothes, Judith walked out along the quiet road to Canellun, where she was greeted by a brown-haired, pale-skinned woman with dark-lashed eyes of deep, transparent blue. (Judith was, and remained, struck by Beryl's beauty.) Beryl's friendly manner put her at ease, but Graves was 'jumpy and disconcerting'

> He came into the room like a storm and laughed a lot, too much. The next day, he came to see me on his own. I did have a dangerous quality then, *enfant sauvage*, which was quite seductive to older men. I told him that I would like to have a child with nut-brown hair and that it would have blue eyes and that I would call it Darien. Robert said: 'Bite me and I will engender it.' And so I did.[6]

This is the odd incident on which Graves based the poem 'Darien', one of four which were directly addressed to Judith. In the poem, however, Judith was translated from a flirtatious wild young girl into the all-powerful muse, swinging her axe as she strides from peak to peak of the island. The use of the axe to decapitate the poet shows one side of Graves's mind influencing the other. He had been reading the Apocrypha as background for *The Nazarene Gospel Restored*. One of the most startling stories in the Apocrypha is of Judith, a spinner of wonderful stories who uses them to seduce Holofernes before she swings her axe to cut off his head. Graves fused Holofernes with the poetic singing heads of Orpheus and the Welsh god Bran in the poem 'Darien'. Magic and myth were perfectly married in his mind.

> 'See who has come,' said I.
>
> She answered: 'If I lift my eyes to yours
> And our eyes marry, man, what then?
> Will they engender my son Darien?
> Swifter than wind, with straight and nut-brown hair,
> Tall, slender-shanked, grey-eyed, untameable;
> Never was born, nor ever will be born
> A child to equal my son Darien,
> Guardian of the hid treasures of your world.'
>
> I knew then by the trembling of her hands
> For whom that flawless blade would sweep:
> My own oracular head, swung by its hair.[7]

It was clear to Judith from the beginning what her role was to be.

Apart from one naked dip in the sea, suggested on the spur of the moment by Graves, the relationship was not overtly sexual. Graves was still sleeping with Beryl, although not frequently. Just as he and Laura had discussed their intimate lives with all their close friends, so Judith was informed on rare occasions that 'Beryl was very nice to me last night' until she asked him to stop talking about it. His affection for his wife was never in doubt. He told Judith that 'Beryl is the funniest woman I have ever met'. Within the house, Beryl remained in control. Outside it, she trusted Graves to draw the line between myth and reality. *[8]

Judith's influence on Graves lasted for a little more than a year; during that time, she was often absent. Fond though she became of both Graves and Beryl, she was absorbed in her own affairs. In January 1951 she returned to Paris, where her artist lover, Marvin, was challenged by Irwin, a younger suitor. Judith became unhappy and confused by their insistence that she must make a choice between them; instead, she fled back to Deyá and was taken into Canelluñ, to be treated as a sick and indulged child. Given a bedroom renamed The Seed Room, dressed in Laura's old silk dressing-gown and offered such suitably symbolic gifts for a muse as plates of nuts and fig bread, she grew happy again, until Marvin's arrival on the island caused a new sense of confusion. Understandably, he did not like her close friendship with Graves. Marvin grew sullen; Judith grew miserable. She returned to Paris; Marvin, armed with neither money nor an address, set off in pursuit. Graves was not displeased by this display of passion; a true muse was expected to make men mad with desire.

Judith rejoined the Graveses on their annual summer visit to London. This was a social summer; she was introduced to Peter Ustinov, the cartoonist Ronald Searle, who was greatly taken by her, and to a handsome Irish boy whom Graves appeared to be offering as a possible match.[9] Hearing talk of his friendship with other young female poets, she assumed that her role as a muse was on the wane. This was a mistake.

In the summer of 1952 Judith returned to the island with Irwin, to whom she had become engaged. They lived with her mother at

---

* It was during this period that Graves later believed William Merwin to have assaulted Judith. His memory was clearly at fault: in November 1950, he was telling Cicely Gittes that Merwin and his wife were conducting a witch-hunt against Judith (Karl and Irene Gay to the author, October 1993; see also n. 4).

a house in the village of Soller, not far from Deyá; inevitably, word of her return reached Graves.

'I could never believe that Robert would do what he did then,' Beryl Graves has written.[10] What he did, according to Judith Bledsoe, was to take a taxi to Soller, burst into the cinema where the couple were watching a film, seize Irwin by the shoulders and tell him he had no right to be with such a noble woman. When the police came, summoned by Irwin, they blamed the man they identified as a tourist, and apologized to the celebrated local writer. Graves went home to dinner; Irwin spent the evening under arrest. Shortly afterwards, in a state of fury with Graves, the couple returned to Paris. In Deyá, the story was refined in a mill of second- and third-hand chatter. Before long, it was being said that Graves had gone on a donkey to Soller to challenge his muse's boyfriend to a duel.

Graves did not let go easily. Shortly after meeting Judith, he had invited her to illustrate *Adam's Rib*, a short interpretation of the Book of Genesis in which he argued that the story of God creating Eve from Adam's rib was a Hebraic substitute for a far more ancient story of a hero being murdered by his rival for Eve's favour. Using Judith's supposed artistic obligation as his excuse, he besieged her with letters, many of them with additional messages from Beryl, begging her to return. By 1953 Judith's mother, Escha, was forced to ask him to desist. In 1954, newly married to Irwin and staying in Soller with her mother, Judith had a private visit from Beryl, asking her to come and see them. She refused, although both she and Escha Bledsoe made visits to Canelluñ in later years. At Irwin's request, the letters from Graves were burned.[11]

As muse-relationships stand in Graves's life, this was a relatively benign experience. He, although disturbed, could see a comic side to his behaviour: writing to James Reeves in 1951, he complained that he was being punished with rheumatism and a ricked back for pursuing young ladies.[12] Beryl evidently understood the relationship's mythical significance and decided to support it; Judith was, for a time, flattered and excited. In 1951–2 Graves, willing himself into the desired sensations of ecstasy and anguish, produced half a dozen poems about muse-love. They are good poems, but their mythical trappings make them less immediate and universal than the earlier ones to Beryl. They raise the question of whether Graves had a growing hunger for beautiful young women which he chose to disguise as poetic inspiration, or whether Judith and her successors were providing him with the crucial emotional tension which he could no longer find in his marriage and which he needed to fuel his love-poetry. Did he believe, as his poems suggest, that Judith, as the Goddess's agent, had sought him out? Even at this early stage of the muse years, no tidy lines can be drawn between lust, art and superstition.

Graves himself was anxious only that his new love-poetry should not be considered artificial. He had always argued that the poet's work and his life are inseparable; it appalled him that people might think he had fabricated his emotional tension for the sake of his poetry. Writing 'A Plea to Boys and Girls' in January, 1956, a few years after his relationship with Judith, he asked that his readers should

> . . . call the man a liar who says I wrote
> All that I wrote in love, for love of art.[13]

Judith was right to suspect that she had competition for her role. In the spring of 1952, a gifted young Canadian poet called Jay Macpherson, visiting her father in London, received a kind and encouraging letter from Graves. A friend had shown him her poems and he had been struck by their mythological content. (Graves had recently started work on *The Greek Myths*.) After being vetted by George and Joanna Simon in London, Jay was invited to Deyá and was offered the chance of having the old Seizin Press revived to publish her first collection, *Nineteen Poems*. She accepted both proposals; she spent four summer months living at the Posada with William's new tutor, Martin Seymour-Smith, and his fiancée, Janet de Glanville.

Jay, a slim, striking girl with dark hair reaching to her waist, was welcomed into the Graves circle. Beryl was now expecting a fourth child and, when the family went to London in the autumn, Jay often took her place at the parties to which Graves wanted to go. At one of these, given by Lynette Roberts, she watched him improvising an African dance before he settled down to grumble about the rotten nature of English literary society in which the critics only praised each other's books. The outsiders, he told her, were always the best. 'Robert,' Martin Seymour-Smith warned her, 'only likes unsuccessful poets.'[14]

Jay Macpherson was offered the job of acting as nanny and governess to Graves's younger children while Seymour-Smith tutored William. She refused. Much though she liked and respected Graves, she did not feel comfortable about his behaviour as a father. There were no story-reading sessions or songs at Canelluñ although Graves always seemed ready to sing folk-songs and ballads with strangers. She disapproved of his claims that each of his children was destined to be a genius and, pleasant though they were, saw little evidence of their supposedly remarkable qualities. William tried hard to please, but seemed doomed to disappoint a father who liked wild and exciting behaviour. Lucia, who was the brightest, was spoilt; Juan was uncontrollable and moody.[15]

This was Macpherson's personal view; against it should be set the fact that Graves was sufficiently anxious that his children should have a good education to rent, from September 1951, two flats in Palma, where the best schools on the island were to be found and where Lucia could go to dancing classes. Here, during the term-times, he and Beryl lived, with Martin Seymour-Smith tutoring William in the upper flat during the afternoons after school closed, while Janet de Glanville worked as Graves's translator and researcher on one of his most important books, *The Greek Myths*. Despite occasional visits to the cinema and to the bullring, Graves did not enjoy living in Palma; the block of modern flats was ugly and depressing; he had never liked city life. It was a sacrifice which he made for the sake of the children and to give Beryl a little freedom from the village. He welcomed the long summer holidays when they returned to live in Deyá.

Macpherson's view of Graves as a friend, adviser and scholar was less harsh. She had seen how hard he worked on *The Greek Myths* while she was in Deyá. When she met up with the family again on their annual visit to London, he was no less busy, but time was always made for the intruders who came to show Graves their poems, to ask him to do Latin translations or for his views on mythology. He was, she noticed, an attentive listener. All ideas interested him; none was mocked or dismissed. Everything was of value to a mind which excelled at making dazzling connections.[16]

Jay Macpherson's recollection accords with that of Derek Savage, who, clasping presents of a pineapple and a book of poems, visited Graves's rented flat in Church Row, Hampstead, to pay his respects in 1952.

Savage, a poet and critic, had been a rival to Martin Seymour-Smith for the post of William's part-time tutor, a plan which had been overturned by the fact that he had four young children of his own. Graves could not see a way to house them all and, reluctantly, took back his offer. Savage's first impression at their London meeting was of a man whose melodious, dated voice contrasted oddly with the appearance of 'an old sailor, wearing dungarees and with carpet-slippers over bare feet'.

Their meeting was interrupted by three other visitors who had come to pay their respects to Graves, but Graves himself removed any sense of awkwardness.

> As we sat and talked – about Burma, and about Herr Professors, and Shakespeare and psychoanalysis – and as Robert's bare toes fiddled in and out of his carpet slippers, while he sat with hands clasping his blue-trousered knees, I corrected my first impression and compared him mentally to those wood-engraved, laurel-crowned portraits of Ben Jonson. Then again I thought he himself would make an excellent Roman Emperor, given the appropriate costume. This historical novelist seemed very much a man of the ancient world.

Integrity was the word which Savage used to sum Graves up, 'a really admirable human quality of being all in one piece, cut out of the same solid material throughout'.[17] It was a quality which Graves had seen and admired from childhood in his mother.

★　★　★

Amy Graves died at the beginning of 1951. She had been in regular contact with Graves since his return to Deyá, and he, mature enough to be untroubled by her lectures on the moral dangers of living in sin, humoured her with a steady flow of little presents, cards, and loving notes. He saw her for the last time in the summer of 1949; she was delighted to learn, the following year, that he had married Beryl.

It is one of the many contradictions in Graves's nature that, while he was ready to lament the caprices of his muses in the full glare of the public eye, he was incapable of expressing any more profound form of emotional loss. Only in his letter to Sam, his son, had he allowed a glimpse to show of the misery he felt about David's death in 1943. He appeared more upset when Norman Cameron's flat caught fire in 1951 than when Cameron died two years later, aged only forty-eight. Yet Cameron had been one of his dearest friends. It was not that Graves did not grieve, but that he had never found a way of dealing with death since his first war experience of it. Instead he threw himself into the task of getting Cameron's poems published and wrote an affectionate Introduction for a man he considered to be one of the best poets of his generation.

Graves chose not to go to his mother's funeral in Wales but he devoured the minute account sent to him by his daughter Jenny: of his brother Charles expecting to be waited upon by the family, of his sister Clarissa singing the hymns in a trembling soprano, and of the unfeigned grief of the local people of Harlech who shared the view of Jenny and her father that Amy Graves had been 'such a very good woman . . . the parson and the curate were really sad and read every word as if they meant it'.[18]

His lack of demonstration of grief did not mean that Amy's loss went unmourned by her oldest son. To Sam, who had adored his grandmother, Graves wrote that Amy 'had been far more talented than she realized, especially as a writer'.[19] These are the words of a devoted son; Amy's writing in the memoir which Graves had read is humourless, saccharine and awkward. To Dick, his brother, who had now reached the height of his diplomatic career as Mayor of Jerusalem, he wrote a more revealing letter. It wounded him that Dick had been the only member of the family to commiserate with him; too late, Graves realized that his quarrels with his parents in the early Deyá years had coloured the family's view. It had not occurred to them that he would miss a mother who had cut him out of her will in favour of his children; only Dick heard that he felt bereft.

Robert could see no point in keeping on the house in Wales for the family; Erinfa without Amy, he sadly told Dick, would be like Vienna without emperor or court.[20] (Clarissa, who never married, did, nevertheless, retain the house for many years.) Bequeathed his mother's gold brooch, Graves was amused to discover from the Mallorcan assayers, to whom he took everything gold he received, including medals, that it was mere gilt. It was his only tangible legacy from Amy. Less tangibly, she had given him his sense of honour, his relish for hard work and an enduring respect for strong-minded women.

Another bereavement followed. Writing to comfort Tom Matthews in 1950 for the fact that his wife, Julie, had died of cancer, Graves told him that Jenny's husband, Alex Clifford, had Hodgkin's disease. Clifford died in the spring of 1952; Graves, again unable, to express his regret directly for a man he had liked and admired, wrote both his obituary, for *The Times*, and his epitaph, praising Clifford's compassion and honesty. Jenny, sad enough to sign a letter written in April 'Jenny Lose Heart (almost)', startled Graves and shocked Nancy by marrying Patrick Crosse, a Reuters journalist based in Rome, less than six months after Clifford's death. [21]

Jenny was shrewd enough to make use of her father's connections – and, in particular, his friendship with Ricardo Sicre, the man who knew everybody and had a reputation for being able to fix almost anything – to promote her own career as a journalist and would-be scriptwriter. She returned the favour by introducing Graves to a new circle of friends on his visits to her homes in Portofino and – after her marriage to Crosse – in Rome. It was through Jenny that he met Selwyn Jepson, a thriller writer who was to become an invaluable adviser and arranger of his English affairs, setting up accounts to pay for the children's education, acting as a deputy parent, negotiating the sale of manuscripts letters. Kaye Webb, who set up Puffin children's books, her husband Ronald Searle, and the choreographer Wendy Toye were among other friends of Jenny's who visited Deyá and entertained the Graveses on their annual visits to London. The Jepsons, knowing Robert's passion for 'The Game', a new form of charades which caught on in the Forties, used to summon Wendy Toye to join them for a session of play-acting whenever Graves dined with them in their Mayfair flat; in Portofino, Wendy coaxed him into posing with their celebrity neighbour, Rex Harrison. [22]

Wendy Toye, a shrewd observer and one who had known Jenny since she was in her early teens, was aware that the relationship between father and daughter was not without stress. Jenny had never forgiven her father for his first desertion of the family; in 1954 she wrote to tell him, indignantly, that she thought his treatment of Sam and herself had been 'painfully unfatherly'. Sam had recently spent his honeymoon at Deyá; not only had he received no wedding present, but he had been invited to admire a new gift from his father to Beryl. It was not, Jenny added, that she felt anything but delight that Lucia should have managed to dance on her points for the first time, but could he remember having known or cared when she, his first child, had done the same? [23]

The accusation went home; it is possible to see Graves's long, unfortunate flirtation with films in the Fifties as an extended apology to Jenny. This was the world which she, far more than he, wanted to join. He did everything he could after 1954 to ensure that Jenny had a part in his own film projects.

★   ★   ★

However much money Graves earned, he never had enough. It was not that he was personally a spendthrift; it would be hard to find a man who spent less on himself. (The bargains he found on antique stalls were almost always given away to friends.) His weakness was the generous and proud one of wanting to play the role of general provider. The friends who visited Deyá were told to put all their local purchases on his account and were offered daily hospitality; young writers who came to him to ask for help never went away empty-handed. If he went out for a meal in Palma with friends, it was always he who paid the bill. The result of this lavishness was a permanent shortage of money. Lucrative film deals offered him a way to keep up the open-handed way of life he liked to lead.

Graves was hard at work on *The Greek Myths* at the beginning of 1952 when the first siren call came to make himself some easy money as a scriptwriter. The man who approached him was Will Price, an American Southerner of great charm and some learning. Price had already done a few low-budget films; his colleague and producer, Forest Judd, believed that he could raise money for a film based on *The Arabian Nights*. They wanted Graves to write a script, to be called 'The World's Delight'.

An offer of $5,000 made Price's suggestion hard to refuse. By the summer of 1952, however, Graves was beginning to wish he had listened to Ricardo Sicre, who advised him to concentrate on writing popular novels if he needed money. Price had spent a pleasant month in Deyá, during which it became apparent that he had a fatal fondness for drink and women: the visit ended with Graves having to order Price's disruptive girlfriend home and lend him close to £300 to pay his hotel bill. By the time the script of 'The World's Delight' was ready to be shown, it was clear that Forest Judd was, after all, unable to make a credible presentation. Still, Graves had been paid $2,000, and Will Price, when sober, had been delightful company. The idea of a 'golden dream', as Graves called it, had been planted; it grew into a large but barren tree. He was still dreaming of a second career in films or Broadway musicals in the mid-Sixties, but success eluded him, just as it had in his early attempts at play-writing. The only film which ended by being made was the television adaptation of *I, Claudius* twenty years later.

★   ★   ★

Deyá revolved around Graves in the early 1950s. To Alan Hodge's new wife, the daughter of the poet Conrad Aiken, he seemed the swaggering king of a miniature world in which he shone as the only achiever.[24] The implication – that Graves preferred lording it among mediocrities to striving among equals and that it was this which kept him in Deyá – is not wholly fair. Graves's fame grew steadily throughout the Fifties; had he returned to England, there is no doubt that he would also have been lionized and honoured. This was the period in which young men like Kingsley Amis were writing reverent letters to tell Graves that he was the best English poet of their time. 'All my friends agree,' Amis told him.[25] Magazines and newspapers sent out their best journalists to interview him; on his visits to England, he was besieged with literary invitations.

There was nothing self-serving about Graves's wish to remain in Deyá; his circle of friends there was founded on affection and kindness rather than out of a need for adulation. The ferocity of the period when Laura Riding had refused to speak to those who failed to accept her rules had been replaced by Beryl's gentle hospitality. Old-fashioned courtesy made it difficult for either of the Graveses to turn away any stranger who came to the door; the price was a perpetual stream of visitors. They were made welcome, but they were not necessary fodder for Graves's self-esteem.

The village had changed. Old Gelat had been replaced by his hard-faced son, always on the lookout for a deal and a way to squeeze a few more pesetas out of the foreigners.[26] Their old friends had left, to be replaced by a principally American colony of artists and writers. A few of these played a small but crucial part in Graves's life. Bill Waldren, a painter and photographer, was helped by Graves to start a museum and arts centre in the village after he made some archaeological finds in the Deyá area; Mati Klarwein, an Israeli painter, used his camera, quite innocently, to open Graves's eyes to the beauty of Margot Callas, Judith's handsome successor in the muse role. But the two who became particularly attached to Graves were Alston Anderson, a young Jamaican writer educated in America and France for whose one book, *Loverman*, Graves wrote the introduction, and James Metcalf. A sculptor with a passionate interest in primitive styles, Metcalf described Graves as having given him a complete education in anthropology.[27] He, in turn, agreed to provide the woodcuts for *Adam's Rib*, the commission originally offered to Judith Bledsoe.

Metcalf's lessons in smith-work gave him an interesting insight into the way that Graves's mind was working at this time. Accompanying Graves on his daily stride down to the sea, Metcalf explained the way he had been taught to control the symmetry of a work in hammered metal 'by guiding the hammer blows with concentric circles inscribed with a compass from a point in the centre of the piece of metal'. Graves was intrigued. 'As if discovering a truth that had always existed, he said, "why, certainly the word Cyclops means 'ring-eyed'." When Metcalf looked up Cyclops in *The Greek Myths* two years later, he read that the Cyclopes were early bronze-smiths, inspired by concentric circles, and that 'the smith would guide himself with such circles, described by compass around the centre of the flat disc on which he was working'. With amusement and surprise, Metcalf recognized the description of his own method of working in metal. He had not, until then, thought of himself as the heir of Cyclops.[28]

By 1953, Graves was too busy on the task of decodifying the myths of Greece to spend much time worrying about what reviewers would say about *The Nazarene Gospel Restored* when it was published late that year. He was willing to predict that it would cause chaos in the religious world – and return to thinking about the myths. For Joshua Podro, a less experienced writer, it was dismaying to have to wait almost six months for the first response to their book.

The reviews of *The Nazarene Gospel Restored*, when they appeared in 1954, were ferocious. The presentation of Jesus as an apocalyptic extremist and the collaborators' hostility to Paul were enough to provoke wrath in some of the most traditional quarters. A few scholars and readers were willing to risk disapproval to honour an original and courageous book; the American scholar Moses Hadas and the Canadian novelist Robertson Davies were among these admirers. But the small heap of praise was too light to tip the scales. Graves, playing his cards close to his chest, carefully mentioned only enthusiastic responses to friends like Tom Matthews; he was unwilling to disclose how many had been vitriolic. The *Manchester Guardian's* reviewer was compelled by furious letters from Graves to apologize for calling Podro 'a renegade Jew'; it was not so easy to force a retraction out of the reviewer in the *Times Literary Supplement* who questioned one of their sources for a Galatians text. Podro, unused to skirmishes, was distressed by the experience of public contempt; Graves, as always, leapt into the ring and went for his opponents with both arms flailing.

Given that he was also working on at least three other projects, the energy he put into defeating this one sceptical critic was remarkable. Alan Pryce-Jones, the outgoing editor of the *Times Literary Supplement*, was made to regret that the review had ever appeared when it became clear that Graves was ready to go to court if a retraction was not printed. The reviewer held his ground; in May 1954 Graves told the *Times Literary Supplement's* solicitor, Charles Russell, that he intended to bring a case of libel against the paper. To the consternation of the editor, he carried out his threat. With Podro's friendly solicitor, Mark Haymon, freely representing the collaborators in exchange for a signed copy of Graves's poems, and supporters like C. H. Dodd, editor of *The New English Bible*, willing to back their textual source, Graves was bursting with confidence. It was not misplaced. The source was upheld, the case was settled out of court, a retraction was printed, and Graves was awarded the costs of bringing the case. His record of it, never published but sent to Podro and Mark Haymon, exists in a poem titled 'To the Times Reviewer':

> When you open your Bible, beware
> That you read it with absolute care:
> Oh, beware that the Bible
> Don't lead you to libel
> And scandal in Printing House Square.[29]

Graves was ebullient; Podro never recovered from the strain.

In 1953 and 1954 Graves, who had been lending money to anyone who seemed in need and rarely getting repaid, was working at full stretch. Malcolm Muggeridge, who had taken over editing the book pages at *Punch* from Anthony Powell, offered him 35 guineas for any stories he cared to send. Graves welcomed an easy new source of income. Writing far too rapidly to please Karl, he churned out lightweight articles and stories of Mallorcan life for *Punch*. At the same time he began working as a regular reviewer for the *New Statesman*, where Janet Adam Smith, the widow of his old friend Michael Roberts, was the literary editor. In one article for *Punch*, he related with pride that he had never written less than five hundred words a day in the past twenty-five years;[30] in 1953–4, this was a gross under-estimate of his daily output.

As an essayist and reviewer, Graves became hasty and careless in the mid-Fifties. In poetry, he continued to prune, rewrite and reject, priding himself on the number of drafts he wrote and on the number of poems which he destroyed. His BBC broadcast, 'A Poet and his Public', delivered in the autumn of 1954,[31] simplifies the way in which a poet can tell good poetry from bad by comparing it, as he did in a poem written that year, to a housewife smelling fish to test it for freshness, or to a shopkeeper letting a coin ring on the counter. The public, he was ready to tell them, had nothing to do with his choices; he did not write his poems for them, but for other poets, and himself.

With his prose, however, Graves was sliding in the opposite direction. *Homer's Daughter*, a novel published in 1955, was written with the hope of a big serial sale in America; in his letters to Selwyn Jepson, who was to have negotiated the sale, he used a businesslike language which comes strangely from a poet still ready to break his heart with love for the White Goddess. Nausicaa, the Sicilian princess who is the supposed author of Homer's *Odyssey* – Graves took this idea from a whimsical lecture by Samuel Butler entitled 'The Humour of Homer' – is described as 'a tight little body [who] would have made a very good shore-officer in the WRNS'.[32]

The American publishing firm of Doubleday had, bravely for a house with a strong religious list, published *The Nazarene Gospel Restored*, but they entered Graves's bad books when they subsequently rejected *The Greek Myths*. By making an offer for *Homer's Daughter*, one of the Doubleday editors, Ken McCormick, realized he had a chance to recapture a valuable author for the firm. The price to be paid was the fact that they would have to publish a novel which neither he nor his fellow editors much liked; the reward was that it opened the door for Doubleday to become the chief US publisher of Graves's poetry.

Homer's Daughter is, as the reviewers were quick to say, well below the standard set by *I, Claudius*. Stuffed with gratuitous detail and heavy with anachronisms, it was praised solely for having characters who speak as if they are alive: that, after the laurels heaped on Graves's early works, was tepid homage. Several of the reviewers, a little weary of the White Goddess, noted that Mr Graves had seized the chance to ride his hobby-horse again and turn Ulysses into a divine king whose voyage symbolized seven years of escape from ritual death. For the biographer, the book offers two points of interest. In its sole account of a marriage, it shows a shrewish and demanding wife prone to menstrual problems and with an extremely hostile attitude to lovemaking; this, regrettably, seems to have been Graves's jaundiced view of his own marriage by the mid-1950s. He was kinder to himself than to Beryl. Nausicaa's lover, one we are intended to see as a most attractive man, is described as having legs which are muscular but a little out of proportion with his long back – this was Graves's own physique – as well as soldierly virtues. He is also a skilled boxer. Graves's dry view of marriage and his willingness to present himself as a handsome hero suggests that his desire for a muse had not subsided.

CHAPTER TWENTY-EIGHT

1953–1956

A FOX WITHOUT A BRUSH

WRITING TO LYNETTE ROBERTS, THE YOUNG WOMAN WHO HAD been one of his chief researchers for *The White Goddess*, Graves described the relief he felt when he turned from writing prose to poetry. Only then, he told her, could he release his 'madder and essential self'.[1] But it was a study of mushrooms, rather than poetry, that released the wild side of his mind in the autumn of 1953, when Gordon Wasson, an American banker friend of Ricardo Sicre's, came to visit him for the first time.

Wasson's acquaintance with Graves began in January 1949 when his Russian wife Valentina sought Graves's views on the type of mushroom eaten by Claudius before his death.[2] The Wassons shared his belief that the poison had been administered by mixing the deadly *Amanita phalloides* with a harmless dish of wild mushrooms; they were intrigued by Graves's suggestion that Seneca's satire, *The Apocolocyntosis of Claudius*, had given a secret away in its title. The colocynth is a poisonous wild gourd; Graves deduced that two doses of poison had been given to the Emperor: the mushrooms and then the gourd.

The discussion marked the beginning of an absorbing correspondence. Graves had already made the discovery that mushrooms had once been a forbidden form of food; from this he drew the conclusion, with which the Wassons agreed, that mushrooms had been used for their hallucinogenic effects in primitive rituals and were therefore regarded as sacred. Here, perhaps, was the solution to early descriptions of ambrosia and its effects. Graves himself believed – an idea which was later appropriated and examined in greater depth by Wasson – that *Amanita muscaria*, or the fly agaric mushroom, had been one of the first hallucinogenics to be used. As an inquisitive child, Graves had licked one and been terrified by the sensation of burning heat and the immediate swelling of his tongue.[3]

Beryl, ever since the birth of their fourth child, Tomas, in January 1953, had been feeling too ill and depressed to be congenial company; Graves was delighted to spend his October evenings at Canelluñ with Wasson, 'the most civilized American I have ever met', talking about the mushrooms which he had managed to bring back from Mexico and hearing about the effect which he had found them to have. For Graves, who had been forced to rely on his imagination to describe the ritual orgies of the Goddess, this had a particular fascination. Bubbling with excitement, he told Selwyn Jepson that Wasson had taken part in an ancient mushrooming ceremony with a primitive tribe of Indians which had resulted in 'a very excellent divinatory message', and that he had managed to bring back some of the mushrooms in a preserving solution, to be examined by 'Paris savants'. Graves's envy of Wasson's firsthand experience of the mushroom drug was unconcealed.[4]

His mood of intoxicated speculation about ancient oracular rituals was interrupted by a sober invitation from Trinity College, Cambridge, to deliver the prestigious course of Clark Lectures the following autumn. Mindful of his passion for bardic literature, the college warned him that the mention of anything before Chaucer was forbidden. Graves was not discouraged. The chance to speak his mind at the university which he still loyally disdained as 'the other place', and the fact that William had just been offered a place at Oundle, a public school not far from Cambridge, for the autumn of 1954, combined to persuade him to take up the offer. And, although Graves never admitted it, his vanity was flattered. It was the most significant form of academic recognition he had yet achieved and, although he liked the role he had described in *The White Goddess* as that of the fox who has lost his brush, it was pleasant to be sought out. Having beaten the Trinity term of six weeks down to three, in order to get back to Deyá as soon as possible, he agreed to give the lectures.

In January 1954, Graves was alerted by Basil Liddell Hart to a new book about T. E. Lawrence; the artist Eric Kennington, who had seen the proofs, described it as poisonous. The author was Richard Aldington and, by April, Graves was also ready to agree that he deserved harsh treatment in return for a ruthless attack on Lawrence's integrity. (Aldington, with disagreeable unctuousness, excused Graves for having written a too favourable life on grounds of credulity and hero-worship.) Graves's first review, for the *News Chronicle*, was partly based on the facts fed to him by Liddell Hart; when the *New Republic* commissioned him to expand on it, Graves decided to present Lawrence as 'a pure-hearted romantic truth-teller' whose 'vivid, waking fantasies (diabolical even)' had been stimulated by the experience of being physically assaulted and humiliated.[5] Was Graves describing Lawrence or himself? He was not in the habit of analysing the characters or motives of his friends, preferring to paint them in whatever colours he fancied. It seems more likely that he imposed on Lawrence his own duality, the pure, hard-working family man and the fabulist poet, waiting for another muse to come striding over the Deyá hills to torment his imagination with lustful fantasies.

Beryl, never cast in this role, delighted him by her return to health in the spring of 1954. He had anticipated it in 'Rhea', a poem written almost two years earlier. 'Rhea' is about a woman who can cope, through oblivion, with every storm that comes. Beryl is seen here in an idealized form, closer to the Goddess than the muses in her regal indifference to the chaos which rages around her. This was how Graves wanted Beryl to be, how he believed she really was. 'Thanks for liking Rhea. That is how I saw Beryl, to whom I am married', he wrote to a young poet, Keith Baines, who had been seeking his advice.[6]

> Discrete she lies,
>
> Not dead but entranced, dreamlessly
> With slow breathing, her lips curved
> In a half-smile archaic, her breast bare,
> Hair astream.

The house rocks, a flood suddenly rising
Bears away bridges: oak and ash
Are shivered to the roots – royal green timber.
She nothing cares.[7]

It was with poems like 'Rhea' and the icy, mesmerizing, 'Counting the Beats' – 'Counting the beats, / Counting the slow heart beats, / The bleeding to death of time in slow heart beats, / Wakeful they lie' – that Graves earned the respect of a new generation of poets in the 1950s.[8] A few, like Keith Baines, responded to his rallying-cry for the poet to re-establish himself as diviner, truth-teller and worshipper. Among the dry, sardonic minds of the Movement poets – Philip Larkin, D. J. Enright, Kingsley Amis, Donald Davie, Thom Gunn – where there were reservations about Graves's romantic theme of a universal myth of sacrifice, he was admired for the elegance of his forms and for the controlled emotion of his more dispassionate poems.

When young poets came to Graves for advice, and they did so in their scores after *The White Goddess*, they found an honest critic with a nose for nonsense. Gentle on minor defects of rhyme or metre, he was blunt about the need for absolute clarity. So, writing to a young Midlands poet who came to live in Mallorca in 1954, Graves pointed out that his last offering had gone 'a stage beyond common sense' with its allusions to green music and pillows raped beyond repair. Music could be many things, but not green; a raped pillow was not poetic; it was merely confusing.[9]

The poet was Alan Sillitoe and Graves became a lifelong friend and adviser both to him and to his wife, Ruth Fainlight. She remained a poet and became a fine one; Sillitoe, gifted with a less certain voice, took a hint from Graves to write an honest book about Nottingham, his home town. The idea had been planted for one of the most influential novels of the Fifties, *Saturday Night and Sunday Morning*, published in 1958.

Finding time to talk about poetry with Alan Sillitoe was particularly generous in the spring of 1954, when Graves had committed himself to going over Beryl's translation of a Spanish classic, *The Cross and the Sword*, to be published under his name in America, and to undertaking two translations for Penguin Books: *Pharsalia* by Lucan, whom he detested, and *The Twelve Caesars* by Suetonius, whom he admired. He was also revising and checking *The Greek Myths* and dealing with some further aggressive attacks on *The Nazarene Gospel*. But the most problematic task before him was the writing of the Clark Lectures.

A friend of Jay Macpherson's, Stephen Pike, had been keeping Graves abreast of literary life at Cambridge. From Pike, he knew that he was becoming a respectable figure. F. R. Leavis had praised the critical methods he had used in *The Common Asphodel*; Empson had started describing him as a founding figure of modern criticism.

There was a contrary streak in Graves's nature which opposed such easy acceptance; he wrote the Clark Lectures in a spirit of mischief, relishing the task of being provocative. 'How university professors hate me!' he exclaimed to Selwyn Jepson with undisguised joy.[10] He did not, he told James Reeves, mean to be amiable in his discussions; to Janet Adam Smith, he made fun of his delight in being an independent critic.

> Wouldn't it be nice if I could genuinely admire Yeats, Pound and Dylan Thomas, not to mention Auden, and the later Eliot, and the later (Dr) [Edith] Sitwell; and play fool with the boys; and win my C.B.E. and take tea with C. S. Lewis and Dorothy Sayers and like it! Or even pretend to? What's wrong with me?[11]

This was the mocking spirit in which Graves wrote his series of brilliant but destructive talks for Trinity College, shocking even such modish members of the Movement as John Wain, a fervent admirer of Graves's poetry, into accusations of philistinism.[12] But Wain was protesting after the event; nobody had warned Graves to be cautious about what he said. Karl Gay had never criticized his employer's poetry or literary criticism; Martin Seymour-Smith, who might have felt able to restrain him, had left Mallorca when William no longer needed private tuition. Beryl enjoyed and encouraged her husband's outrageous side. 'I don't remember a single discussion of ideas in which they didn't completely corroborate each other's views,' observes James Metcalf, who believes Beryl to have had a 'very close philosophic relationship' with her husband in the Fifties.[13]

Graves's letters to his friends that summer suggest a certain nervousness as he begged for news of contemporary poets and their literary tastes; in his study, however, he was full of fire. Just as, in *The White Goddess*, it had suited him to describe himself as a fox without a brush, now he was a scholar without a Chair, a poet who was prepared to offer his personal principles at Cambridge, nothing more: 'nobody is obliged to agree with me.'[14]

Ted Hughes, who had left Cambridge in the summer of 1954, returned to hear the Clark Lectures. Many students travelled from Oxford and London to hear them, and to see Graves. Hughes enjoyed the vigour of Graves's attacks on received opinions;[15] others, John Wain among them, were shocked.

Graves's lively savaging of Pope, Milton and Dryden might have been allowed to pass muster; his insistence that Irish poets represented the best work of every age could have been called familial patriotism. It was the third and last lecture, 'These Be Your Gods, O Israel!', which provoked the most outrage. He began with a comparison to a small boy throwing a brick through a window behind which a row of young poets kneel in awe. His targets were Yeats, Pound, Eliot, Auden and Dylan Thomas; along the way, he paused to mock Stephen Spender's habit of predicting literary fashions as skilfully as an editor of *Vogue* and went on to attack two reputations in a single throwaway pronouncement. This was the sentence which came back to haunt Graves, as his critics and reviewers wondered at what point mischief becomes malice.

> Need I also dwell on the lesser idols now slowly mouldering: on sick, muddle-headed, sex-mad D. H. Lawrence who wrote sketches for poems, but nothing more; on poor, tortured Gerard Manley Hopkins?[16]

The critics of the Clark Lectures were numerous. 'Even Martin [Seymour-Smith] has had his little yap,' Graves told James Reeves in November 1955 when the lectures were published in book form.[17] Donald Davie and the writer Herbert Read were among the most vigorous opponents. In 1961 Read joined forces with Edward Dahlberg, who lived in Mallorca and resented his exclusion from Graves's intimate circle, to write *Truth is More Sacred*, a book in which Graves was presented as salacious, boastful and weak in his scholarship.

Graves was always more aggressive on a platform than in life, and he was not nearly so much of a lone fox as he liked to claim. His professed aversion to the British literary establishment needs to be taken with a pinch of salt. He often saw Cecil Day–Lewis on his visits to England; one of his first dates before embarking on the Cambridge lectures was a dinner with Stephen and Natasha Spender. Despite Graves's frequent disrespectful comments in private about the work of 'Stainless Stainforth', he had grown fond of the tall, gently-spoken poet and his Russian wife. Although Graves was considerably older, Spender's jaundiced view of the younger generation of poets and novelists made him seem almost a middle-aged contemporary.

*　　*　　*

Among the modern poets commended by Graves in his lectures – they included Laura Riding, Frost, Cummings and Alun Lewis – was Siegfried Sassoon. Graves met Sassoon twice, purely by chance, during the three weeks that he spent at Cambridge, once at Oundle, where Sassoon's son was was also a pupil, and once in King's College Chapel. Sassoon, who was on the verge of converting to Roman Catholicism, had long regretted his vilification of Graves's war memoirs. He had, he now felt, overreacted in a state of personal crisis. It was a relief to both men to make their peace, but the friendship was never restored. They neither corresponded nor sought each other out again.

Shortly after delivering the Clark Lectures, Graves paid a visit to Montague and Dorothy Simmons who were running a privileged establishment for delinquent boys in Hertfordshire. Here they introduced Graves to their star pupil, a handsome, dark-haired youth of twenty. His name was Robin Blyth and he was both persuasive and literate; Pound's prison cantos acquired a new poignancy when Blyth quoted them in his reform-school surroundings. The Simmonses said that Robin was due to inherit £48,000 when he came of age but that he had no guardian to sign the papers releasing the money or to keep an eye on him. Impulsively, Graves offered to take on the role; Robin was invited to Deyá, where he was permitted to stay in the Posada under the local supervision of Karl and Irene Gay, while Beryl and Graves returned to Palma for the spring term of Lucia and Juan's schools. Having signed the papers by which he assumed responsibility for him, Graves had set Robin Blyth free to run through his fortune as fast as he pleased.

If Graves liked somebody, he could not rest without the assurance that his view was shared. With this in mind, he would exaggerate the person's merits and swell their sense of self-importance. A girl who could paint or dance reasonably well, and who seemed to have muse potential, would be described as a great artist; Robin, arriving on the scene in the year that James Dean died, was cast as the romantic outlaw without a cause. Sharing this view of himself, Robin began signing his letters 'Robin the rebel'. This was ominous enough but, when he began to cause mayhem in the village, Graves refused to intervene. Karl's daily letters to the Palma flat became increasingly frantic. Robin had sworn at Irene, punched Bill Waldren, driven Graves's old car into the ground and told the inhabitants of Deyá that the owner of Canelluñ was a currency fiddler. Graves answered by saying that Robin was no wilder than Ricardo Sicre had been at his age, when he was a dashing young captain in the Republican army. The analogy was significant; Graves had been entranced in 1940 by Sicre's stories of his escapades and womanizing. Outrageousness, when romantically presented, could always enthrall him. Robin's crass behaviour seemed, in his affectionate eyes, poetic. 'Dearest Karl, we are all miserable sinners and I am always ready to make mistakes,' he wrote in response to one of Gay's angry letters, 'but [I] will hang no dog until I have given him a bad name myself.'[18]

In March 1955, still full of confidence, Graves wrote to tell Dorothy Simmons that Robin was a great success and that he had spent some of his inheritance on buying a pretty house in the nearby village of Lluch Alcari. 'He has a brilliant mind,' she heard, '[and] always keeps his promises.'[19]

By the summer of 1956, having lent a considerable sum against the new house which Blyth was now unable to repay – he had already spent the entire £48,000 – Graves was forced to ask Ricardo Sicre for help. Sicre, after scolding him for his gullibility, agreed to buy the house, Sa Guarda, for a sum which would free Graves and allow Blyth to clear his debts. (Sicre allowed Graves to continue borrowing the house for the use of guests.) Three months later Graves heard that Blyth had been arrested for breaking into a yacht and being found in possession of a loaded gun. Still forgiving, he hurried off to see what he could do to help: he was able to arrange a release if he would guarantee Blyth's departure from Mallorca. In October 1956 Blyth made a last call at Deyá before leaving the island, 'with a girl called Judith', Graves noted with a wistful flicker of identification as he remembered Judith Bledsoe.[20]

Blyth left behind, by way of mementoes of his comet-like career, a silver Land-Rover which he had bought the Graveses in 1955, a dog and a gramophone. On the deficit side, his affair with James Metcalf's wife had hastened the end of their marriage. Graves, who was more interested in tricky or doomed relationships than happy ones, made this the subject of a poem, 'Call It a Good Marriage'.[21] As with his own relationship to Beryl, he was able to say of the Metcalfs that it was good, because

> They never fought in public,
> They acted circumspectly
> And faced the world with pride;
> Thus the hazards of their love-bed
> Were none of our damned business –
> Till as jurymen we sat upon
> Two deaths by suicide.[22]

Robin Blyth's compulsive need to borrow large sums of money had been ill-timed for Graves. The years 1955 and 1956 were made financially difficult by Spanish tax demands and by the heavy cost of entertaining friends and supporting his family. Unhappily, it was during this period that Will Price began to revive his hopes of the film world. Early in 1955 Price arrived in Mallorca with promises of a television 'spectacular' version of 'The World's Delight', Graves's *Arabian Nights* script. He was told to expect a windfall of some $13,000. In July he was still waiting for it. Writing to James Reeves, just after he had celebrated his sixtieth birthday with fireworks, the annual play, dancing and sixty guests,* he described Price as a reformed character and boasted of Ingrid Bergman's eagerness to play Nausicaa in a film of *Homer's Daughter*. Will Price had suggested that she would, if she was keen enough, pay handsomely for the option to retain that right. Nothing solid had yet materialized; he admitted that he was 'in great need of large cash'.[23] A year later, Bergman lost interest and described herself as too old for the part. The $13,000 windfall still had not appeared.

It was in the hope of restoring his finances that Graves agreed to take on the job of rewriting and adding a chapter on brainwashing to a popular book by a neurologist at St Thomas's Hospital. George Simon, who also worked there, counselled him to have nothing to do

---

* The annual birthday celebration was shared, from c.1955, by Graves with William and Lucia, both of whom were born in the summer. It was often held on a fiesta day between June and September. The guests included villagers and friends of the children. Rockets, games and a play always formed part of the fun. (Beryl and Elena Graves to the author, February 1995)

with William Sargant, a charming man known for his eccentric views on lobotomy and hallucinogenic drugs; Graves, as always, refused to hear ill of a man he admired and who was, in the words of one of his young colleagues, 'one of the doyens of psychiatry in his day'.[24] *Battle for the Mind* would, Graves confidently told Karl, be 'an epoch-making book'; his reward was to be a third of the royalties after its publication.[25] (This was not until 1957.)

He was living on pipedreams; by August 1955 both Sicre and Wasson, two of his richest friends, were seriously worried about his position. His poetry, it was true, had never been more highly praised and there were rumours that his name had been put forward for the Oxford Professorship of Poetry. (He was rejected, on this first occasion, on the official grounds that he lacked the appropriate academic qualifications; unofficially, there was still strong feeling among members of his old college about his desertion of Nancy and his children.) To successful businessmen like Sicre and Wasson, it was shocking that an eminent poet should be relying on hack-work to survive; to Graves, it was the price for living outside the system.

Sicre's first solution was to tell Graves to take a year off to write a best seller on a subject to be chosen by his friend, Harold Matson, a commercial and highly successful American agent. When Graves refused, Sicre and Wasson tried to arrange a lucrative posting to Princeton for a term. Here, too, there was a problem. Graves hated being away from Deyá. He had only agreed to take the Cambridge post when the time had been halved. Offered $5,000 for a visit of four months, he refused.

The sense of financial desperation which haunted Graves's letters at this time was barely hinted at in the diary which he had started to keep again in the Fifties. Glamour appeared to cloak him and all his ventures. A visit from Tom Matthews and his new girlfriend, Martha Gellhorn, was followed by the arrival of Ava Gardner, sent by the Sicres to consult Graves about her role in a film with a Roman setting. Graves, having quaked with alarm at the thought of entertaining such an exotic creature, was charmed by Ava's friendly, downright manner. His hopes of writing a film, set in Spain, in which she would appear, came to nothing, but the friendship lasted. Her mixture of vulnerability and toughness, her readiness to drink herself senseless and to fall in love with unsuitable men, all endeared Ava to Beryl and Robert. This, among all their experiences of the film world, was the one relationship which survived as a loving friendship. At Graves's memorial service in 1985, the photographers turned from the family to focus on the face of a woman who had become as much of a hermit as Greta Garbo. For the sake of a man in whom her trust, unusually, had proved well-placed, Gardner was willing to face them.

Alec Guinness, while never so intimate, became an affectionate acquaintance. In the spring of 1956, Graves approached him about playing the lead in the *Arabian Nights* film; Guinness, whose enthusiasm for this project cooled rapidly, was more interested in the idea of playing Claudius. After taking William back to Oundle for the summer term, Graves stopped in Paris where he now had a wide circle of English and American friends, including James Metcalf, Harry Mathews, a young American poet, and his wife, Niki de Saint Phalle. Graves's mission on this Parisian stopover was to discuss a *Claudius* remake with Vincent Korda, who had taken over London Films after the death of his brother, Alex. Korda was interested, if a scriptwriter and a female star could be found; discussions continued in London against a background of lunches at the Savile Club with Selwyn Jepson, and dinners at the Ritz with Beryl's rich and generous sister and brother-in-law, Evelyn and Jack Neep. The omens were all of prosperity, but Graves was not reassured by the talk of negotiations. Sicre's warnings not to put his trust in films had begun to take root. Despite Jenny's optimism about the film projects, he preferred for the moment to trust his prose to make enough money to give his children a good education. Recruiting Joshua Podro and a friendly London bookseller to act as his researchers, he began to read up the background for a new book which he intended to be a popular best seller.

They Hanged My Saintly Billy was Graves's fifteenth and last novel. Set in the eighteenth century, it was, in its author's words:

> full of sex, drink, incest, suicides, dope, horse-racing, murder, scandalous legal procedure, cross-examinations, inquests and ends with a good public hanging – attended by 30,000.[26]

This was just the kind of swaggering description with which Graves had tried to sell himself to an uncertain public in the early 1920s; now, however, he had an audience and a more polished product to offer them. His hero was William Palmer, known as the Staffordshire poisoner. Graves gave himself the task of proving that Palmer had been wrongly accused. Relying on newspaper reports and on a voluminous number of Victorian retellings of Palmer's life, fleshed out with borrowings from Thackeray and Dickens, Graves produced a book which excels in its racy, vivid detail of low-life in a provincial eighteenth-century town. He had, he said, modelled his technique on Defoe. He wrote the novel, with a relish he never showed for his film-writing, in three months, and threw himself into devising publicity campaigns. Both Cassell, the most loyal of his London publishers, and Doubleday in the United States, were urged to set up a public demonstration outside Madame Tussaud's on the day the book was published, protesting against the injustice of keeping Palmer's effigy in the Chamber of Horrors.

The campaign was carried out and contributed to the immense success of the novel when it was published in the summer of 1957. Reviewers were sceptical of Graves's thesis. 'As always,' the *Times Literary Supplement* sighed, 'reasonable surmise is tangled with remote possibility.'[27] Ralph Partridge, writing in the *New Statesman*, thought that 'for all this fine writing, Mr Graves has been wasting his time and ours'.[28] Partridge had missed the point. The book is not a legal document. Whatever the flaws in Graves's argument, the merits of his last fictional work outweigh them. Few of his novels are more revealing of his skill at assimilating detail and his delight in sniffing out and unravelling a mystery.

The next job to which Graves applied himself was the revision of his first great success, for republication in paperback by Penguin. Reading the book (*Goodbye to All That*) again for the first time in twenty-five years, Graves was impressed by its energy and dismayed by the carelessness of his writing; judging by the rude comments about his own work which he scribbled on the daily batches of revised typescript which he handed over to Karl, he had forgotten the appalling pressure under which the book had been written. His main concern now was to tighten up the grammar and to lay a stronger emphasis on his Celtic heritage than he had cared to do in the days when the very word Celtic conjured up old Alfred Graves quivering in the grip of bardic enthusiasm. But he was also anxious to get rid of the earlier version's ending, with its homage to Laura Riding. The visit to Cairo at the beginning of their relationship was, after careful thought, allowed to stand; Britain's involvement with Suez made Egypt too topical a subject to be deleted.

December brought more enticing hints from the film world. Alec Guinness, who had been talking business with Jenny in Rome, shared her belief that a film of the *Claudius* novels might still be made if they could persuade the Italian actress Anna Magnani to play Messalina. But Graves had already taken the decision to look elsewhere for money. While Jenny, groaning about the blinding migraines from which she had begun to suffer, went off to Paris to help Lady Diana Cooper with the writing of her memoirs, Graves finally decided to go on 'a smash-and-grab raid'[29] of the American universities who were willing to pay richly for his time.

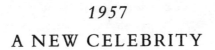

CHAPTER TWENTY-NINE

1957

A NEW CELEBRITY

GRAVES HAD BECOME DESPERATE FOR MONEY BY THE MID-autumn of 1956. To Tom Matthews, he wrote mournfully that all his golden dreams had turned to dust, 'but I don't care; I go slogging on.'[1] Five days later he told Karl that, with three years of Spanish income tax in arrears, he felt that he might as well be dead.[2] This was over-dramatic: his sister Rosaleen and his daughter Catherine had noticed nothing amiss when they visited Deyá two months earlier. It was true, nevertheless, that Graves was finding it impossible to see how he could survive financially without writing a steady stream of novels and articles and sacrificing the time he needed for his poetry.

His Spanish tax demands were only a part of the difficulties which confronted him. In 1950 he had disturbingly described a writer as a man with a golden brain who picked it off in layers 'for his greedy dependants until he died a hollow-skulled imbecile, gold dust and blood under his fingernails'.[3] His dependants were not particularly greedy but, by the end of 1956, the prediction that he would destroy himself to keep them satisfied seemed more accurate than ever. His bank accounts were almost empty. William's last

361

two years at Oundle had to be paid for and Juan and Lucia were in urgent need of a better form of education than was locally available. Juan, in particular, needed stimulus. He had made no progress at school; a letter in which Graves described him to Tom Matthews as 'beastly-sweet and crazy as ever' shows that he had accepted that there was a problem with his handsome but volatile and sometimes violent child.[4] Having Juan at home was proving too much of an ordeal for either his parents or the Gays to cope with on a permanent basis.[5] Hearing good reports from the Sicres of the École Internationale at Geneva, Graves decided to send Lucia and Juan there together. Swiss schools were among the most expensive in the world. Graves was also determined that Tomas, his youngest child and the apple of his eye, should receive a full English education.

What was offered to the children of Beryl could not be withheld from his grandchildren, particularly when Graves remained full of guilt about his failure to pay for the education of Sam and Catherine. Karl's wages had just been increased; the annual visits to England with the children had to be covered; they were employing a gardener and two maids to help Beryl, while Juan Gelat the younger was a regular producer of bills for agricultural work on the land. In short, Graves was trying to maintain the life of an English gentleman abroad. To do so with no capital and a wholly unpredictable income was no easy matter. This was the problem which Graves was pondering when an invitation to lecture at Mount Holyoke in western Massachusetts arrived at Canelluñ.

It was not the first time Graves had been approached by American colleges. In Britain, the publication of the Clark Lectures in 1955 had aroused pompous indignation; even the usually supportive William Empson confined himself to rejoicing that Graves remained 'so wonderfully active, as the lady in Dickens said about Vesuvius'.[6] In America, however, reports of his provocative talks only heightened curiosity about a man whose liberating and imaginative views on myth and religion had already gained him the status of a cult figure. The Ivy League colleges were prepared to pay him, and to pay him well, for the privilege of being shocked.

Graves had been less desperate in 1955. Even now, he was daunted by the difficulty of making the arrangements for such a trip, by the prospect of being away from Mallorca for any length of time and, above all, by the thought of being alone in a country of which he had such unhappy memories.

The person who persuaded him to face up to the experience was a young poet called Alastair Reid. When Reid, with the assistance of Ken McCormick at Doubleday, offered to devise the schedule and act as his travelling secretary, Graves began to think that an American trip, if brief, might be a more agreeable experience than he had imagined.

Reid had, since their meeting in 1954, become one of Graves's closest friends. He had published a slim book of poetry and was teaching English at Sarah Lawrence College, when he first began spending his vacations in Deyá and writing occasional articles on Spain for the *New Yorker*. Like Graves, he fell under the spell of a dour, unchanging landscape in which nothing appeared to have altered for centuries.

> The overall feeling is one of suspension; the great wall of the mountains hangs over the village, and time moves as imperceptibly as the shifting shadows on the rock face . . . Everything felt irregular, odd, the houses on one another's shoulders, the fields in the landscape that formed acoustical traps, transmitting odd conversations or the sound of an axe across the deep valley. Mallorca still lived then by the agrarian round . . .[7]

As James Metcalf was spending an increasing amount of time in Paris, Reid succeeded him as Graves's favourite companion. As a Scot and a poet, he may have seemed to take Norman Cameron's place. Like Metcalf, Reid would come to Canelluñ early in the morning when Graves was watering the garden or tending the compost heaps he named after visitors and friends; together they would walk down to the *cala*, talking about anything that had taken Graves's interest. In 1955, when Graves was under heavy pressure with too many projects, he invited Reid to do the initial translation of Suetonius's *The Twelve Caesars* in exchange for a share of the royalty payment. Reid was confident enough about his own skill as a translator to suppose that the first draft would be the final one; every day Graves was able to improve on his work and bring it to life. When Graves talked about ancient

Rome, he seemed to the dazzled young Reid to be standing in the Forum.[8]

Reid became almost a member of the family in 1955–6. To the Gays, resentful, perhaps, of his intimacy with Graves, he seemed too conscious of his own inventiveness and charm;[9] to the children, to Beryl and to Graves himself, he was a life-enhancing companion. When Peggy Glanville-Hicks, an enthusiastic American composer who had fallen in love with Greece, wrote in 1955 to ask if she could turn *Homer's Daughter* into an opera, Graves instantly put Reid's name forward as the librettist.*

It was Graves who had the idea that the long, conversational letters which they exchanged when Reid was away in America or on long sailing expeditions, should be collected under the title 'Quoz' and offered to Doubleday. He, as much as Reid himself, saw the advantage there would be in allowing the young man to work alongside Ken McCormick on the arrangements for an American lecture tour; this, surely, would facilitate the progress of 'Quoz'. (It did not; McCormick, who had already rejected *Jesus in Rome*, second Graves–Podro collaboration, declined to publish it. It remains an intriguing source document.[10]

In January 1957, free of work for the first time in many years, Graves tidied all his files and started writing his talks for the tour, which now encompassed Mount Holyoke, New York University, and Boston's Massachusetts Institute of Technology. Working on a lecture about the Goddess, he found himself turning back to one of his earliest sources of inspiration, William Rivers. Beryl, eyeing his unruly white hair, shabby sandals and a jacket which looked far too tight, suggested that some personal attention might be a good idea. Dutifully, Graves went to Palma to order a new suit and, for the first time in many years, a smart pair of leather shoes.

Against all his expectations, Graves not only survived but enjoyed his fortnight in America. Surrounded by old friends like Cicely Gittes, Len Lye, and the ubiquitous Will Price, with Alastair Reid willing to do everything from pressing his suit to arranging his transport, Graves was courted, fêted, commissioned and praised until a less modest man's head would have spun. Writing to

---

* Reid completed the libretto in 1959 but asked, after hearing Glanville-Hicks proclaim Graves as her sole librettist on a radio programme, that his own name should be removed. Graves, like Glanville-Hicks, remained mystified by what was, to them, an inexplicable decision.

Beryl at the end of the first week, he was able to tell her that his talk on the Goddess at MIT in Boston had been sold out, that he had been interviewed on television with the fashionable striptease queen, Gypsy Rose Lee, that he expected to bring back $3,500 and that 'my table manners have been perfect'. Mount Holyoke, comprising twenty-eight 'palaces' (Graves's word) full of charming girls, had given him an ecstatic reception. 'Won't pretend that it's not great fun,' he added, honourably, after confessing that he was just off to spend an evening discussing mushrooms with the Wassons in New York, 'but I'll be glad to be back to you.'[11]

E. E. Cummings and Robert Frost were, with John Crowe Ransom, the American poets for whom Graves had shown an unswerving admiration since the early 1920s. Frost shared his love of pure language and a spirit of mischief which could turn malicious when either man was crossed. But Graves, in his later, muse-ridden phase, was closer to Cummings in the tightly-crafted poems which celebrate witty, sorrowful, inescapable love. In life, too, the two men were quickly in sympathy with each other; one of the happiest evenings recorded in Graves's diary for the American visit was spent with Cummings and his wife Marion at their home in New York, 'laughing much and chattering'.[12]

Graves felt like a conqueror. He had never been treated like a celebrity before; the experience intoxicated him but he did not, on this trip, feel any threat to his values. To talk on television with Gypsy Rose Lee required only a sense of humour; when Ken McCormick told him that he had been asked to appear on the famous $64,000 quiz show, his confidence wavered. It was no use, he told McCormick in his letter of refusal; 'I am the ignorantest man alive and couldn't win $64,000 even on a Babe Ruth quiz.'[13]

Alastair Reid, while disappointed by McCormick's lack of interest in 'Quoz', was delighted by Graves's success and surprised by the ease, cheerfulness and wit which he showed in dealing with his vast audiences. Not having seen Graves's performances at Trinity College, he had not expected such assurance, or even such stamina. Only Cicely Gittes was blunt enough to tell Beryl that her husband owed it to his American audiences to get a new set of false teeth. Having sat among a group of women at the MIT lecture, she had picked up a touch of dissatisfaction. A poet who talked with passion about his devotion to the Goddess needed to have a romantic image; there was nothing romantic about the old-fashioned plates which glinted and whistled behind Graves's full and ruddy lips.[14]

Usually superstitious – he was still a nervous follower of horoscopes, card-readings and omens – Graves was in such a jubilant mood about the trip that even the presence on the plane home of Toscanini's coffin, disguised by a white cloth as a buffet-table, was a subject for jokes.

Composting, making marmalade and picking wild asparagus with Beryl, sighing over his ever-growing pile of correspondence, he barely paused for a day before resuming his work schedule in Deyá. His main new project was a children's version of *The Greek Myths*. But film projects were again uppermost in his mind.

Will Price, affable as ever but a little more desperate, had talked to Graves about a new idea when they met in New York. This was for a film of Graves's novel, *Wife to Mr Milton*. While talking this through, Price had made it clear that he meant to be included in the ongoing plans for a film of *Claudius*, to be made the following year. Graves, who could never resist Price's charm and humour, agreed. But Jenny, who was still hoping for a 1958 *Claudius* starring Alec Guinness and Anna Magnani, was furious. On 7 March 1957 she wrote her father a sharp letter from Rome, telling him to forget the whole project rather than humiliate her by associating with such pitiful figures as Will Price and Vincent Korda.

Ricardo Sicre had been observing Jenny's attempts to take on the role of her father's unofficial film agent with a cynical eye. Sicre had a large number of influential friends in the film world of Rome to which Jenny wanted, passionately, to belong. He had allowed her to use his name as an introduction to many of these people because he knew that this would please her father. But he, better than Graves, knew that Jenny's claims to experience in films had no foundation.[15] With his usual brutal frankness, Sicre advised Graves in 1957 to drop his daughter from the film plans; she was being more of a hindrance than a help. Graves listened – and did nothing. He did not have any great faith in Jenny's negotiating skills but he was determined to offer support at a time when she was suffering a personal humiliation.

This had its roots in a report she wrote for the *Spectator* from the Labour Congress in Venice. In it, Jenny had named three British politicians while putting their drinking habits in a most unflattering light and indicating that the Italians had been outraged and amazed by their behaviour. By March 1957, a month after the report was published, Graves already knew that his daughter was in deep trouble and that her only fault had been one of indiscretion: a libel suit had been filed against the paper by the three politicians, who maintained that Jenny's article was a gross misrepresentation of their behaviour at the Congress. (Ten years later, they admitted that her report had been entirely accurate.[16])* This was not a time at which Graves wanted to inflict any additional distress on his daughter, so he ignored Sicre's advice and followed that of Jenny, however wrong-headed. Since she was no shrewder than her father in dealing with film producers, Graves's film career remained nebulous.

Visiting London in April and May 1957, Graves again stayed with his niece Sally and her husband, Richard Chilver, in their house near Little Venice in Maida Vale. Still enjoying his sense of prosperity after the American tour, he did little work and spent most of his time seeing members of the family and catching up with old friends: the Liddell Harts, the Podros, the Reeveses. Invited to appear on television with Malcolm Muggeridge, he felt full of confidence. Muggeridge, in company with almost every television interviewer who worked with Graves, was forced to let his guest dictate the pace and style. Humour, Graves had decided, was the secret ingredient needed for broadcasting; he used it to mask discomfort. His voice, both clipped and melodious, sounded as though it had been preserved from an earlier era; his eyes, baffled by the camera lights, darted about uneasily, giving him a cunning look. The only television programmes on which he ever appeared at ease were those shot at his own home, in his own landscape: sitting in a studio in London or New York, he looked, and sounded, trapped.

He enjoyed having lunch with the Spenders and hearing that Stephen wanted to come and interview him in Deyá in the course of a summer visit. It was satisfying to decline Harold Macmillan's offer of a CBE with the explanation that poets had no need of being

* The *Spectator* prostrated itself in abject apology on 20 September, blaming all on the reporter. It still failed to escape damages. On 22 November, the politicians were awarded £2,500 each and Jenny's career as a journalist was over. In the newspapers, it was reported that she had broken down in tears when the verdict was announced.

honoured for public services, since their work was essentially private. But the occasion from which Graves derived the most pleasure was a two-hour discussion with Robert Frost at his London hotel. The admiration was mutual: Graves had been the first person the American poet had asked to see. Frost was the older by twenty years but they talked the same language, spoke from a shared understanding of their craft.

Graves celebrated his sixty-third birthday in the summer of 1957; superstitious as always, he told friends that he had reached 'my fateful year of the grand climacteric'.[17] This belief in the number sixty-three as having a peculiar significance dates back to the early eighteenth century, according to the *Oxford English Dictionary*; Graves is not the only man to have assumed that 'the grand climacteric' heralded a period of change in his life. His age was beginning to prey on him; in one of his talks that summer, he wondered at what age it became indecent to write love-poetry in the spirit of a young man.

An essay about the sacred origin of the mushroom was what absorbed him most as he pursued the idea that mushrooms, perhaps, had been the initial form of stimulant used in the Dionysiac rituals. Strangely, for a man who believed that the best poems are written in a suspended state of 'glamour-trance', Graves never allowed himself to imagine that the frenzies of the ancients could have been produced in any other way than by stimulants. He wanted mushrooms to fit his thesis; by the mid-Sixties, many others were willing to regard the mushroom as sacred.

The Spenders' visit to Deyá was followed by one from Brendan Gill, who had come to interview Graves for the *New Yorker*; borrowing back Sa Guarda, the house which Ricardo Sicre had bought to rescue him after he had funded Robin Blyth's extravagant purchase the previous year, Graves used it to entertain Alec Guinness and his family while they continued their talks about a film of *Claudius*. Bridget Boland, a neighbour of Jenny's in Rome, had written the screenplay for one of Guinness's first successes; it was agreed that Graves should start working on *Claudius* with her in September.

Mallorca was becoming fashionable; Graves's diary for that summer drips with the names of famous visitors. Happy to be an invisible Prospero, he was beginning to tire of being pointed out as the local monument. Unable to visit the *cala* without being approached with invitations to a drink or to write an autograph or to read a poem, he took to swimming at Ca'n Floquer, a strip below Sa Guarda which

Karl Gay had secured for the family. Here, the Graves family had their own little boat-house – and peace.

Graves was full of confidence again. Writing to one correspondent about his reasons for turning down an offer to abridge Frazer's twelve volumes of *The Golden Bough*, he explained that he had no time. 'Too much big business with films and TV series – embarrassing, but I set myself to make money last year, and down it comes like water from a breached reservoir.'[18] After the financial worries of the previous year, it gave him huge pleasure to distribute some of his new funds on enjoyment. The annual birthday party was held in August that year; when Alec Guinness and his family had settled into Sa Guarda, they were invited to a grand celebration at Canelluñ, with fireworks, dancing, a Punch and Judy show, a skit on Samuel Beckett written by Graves's Jamaican neighbour, Alston Anderson, and a ballet performed by Lucia and the Gays' daughter, Diana. Four days later, on 5 August, Graves heard that Poland was ready to pay £800 to publish *Claudius*. Money, suddenly, had become easy to make.

The Guinnesses, while friendly, had little in common with Graves's more private side; he was happier when they were followed by the Reeves family, who spent a month staying at the Posada. It was a chaotic visit, but Graves was among old friends again and travelling back into his first years in Deyá as he and James settled down to sing folk-songs and ballads after dinner, just as they had done in 1935.

In September, while Beryl went ahead with Juan and Lucia, Graves travelled to Geneva where his children were about to start their first term at the École Internationale. Lucia, they were confident, would be happy; Juan was watched with a more anxious eye. Bridget Boland arrived to work with Graves on the *Claudius* script during his stay in Switzerland, but for once he found it hard to put himself back into imperial Rome.

Cicely Gittes, without being aware of the significance, had been amused by Graves's insistence on the old-fashioned habit of taking a chamber-pot to his room when he and Reid stayed with her in New England.[19] It was no joke to Graves. Increasing discomfort and a horror of incontinence finally drove him to ask a doctor in Geneva about the possibility of prostate cancer. This, as he later admitted to friends, was the terror which had haunted him since, when he was only twelve, Amy had informed him that it had been the cause of her father's lingering death. The Swiss doctor did not give a clear response; for two more years Graves lived in pain and with the secret fear of a painful and humiliating death.[20]

Haunted by mortality, and glumly preparing to have two of his last teeth pulled, Graves wrote a poem, 'Around the Mountain', in which he asked and answered a question which was preying on his mind. Was it, at his age, worth the pain and risk to discover passion again? He compared the experience to that of a man who left his warm home to spend all night circling a mountain in search of desire, a forgotten sensation. If he took that dangerous route, how far would it be safe to go?

> Whoever makes the desired turning-point,
>   Which means another fifteen miles to go,
> Learns more from dawn than love, so far, has taught him:
>   Especially the false dawn, when cocks first crow.
>
> Those last few miles are easy: being assured
>   Of the truth, why should he fabricate fresh lies?
> His house looms up; the eaves drip drowsily;
>   The windows blaze to a resolute sunrise.[21]

The poem indicates that Graves was not yet ready to take one of his walks to the edge, but he was thinking about it. A few months earlier, he had studied himself in the shaving glass and come to a different conclusion.

> I pause with razor poised, scowling derision
> At the mirrored man whose beard needs my attention,
> And once more ask him why
> He still stands ready, with a boy's presumption,
> To court the queen in her high silk pavilion.[22]

Graves was under no illusions about the folly of such an attitude. 'The Face in the Mirror' is his equivalent to one of Rembrandt's late self-portraits, a brutal itemization of a body in decay, of furrowed cheeks, wrinkled forehead, grey hair and missing teeth. Even the last lines, which seem at first glance to ring out a triumphant assertion of his right, yield up a weight of pathos in their placing of a troubadour boy behind the ageing features. There is a kind of heroism here. What is immediately striking, however, is the fact that Graves was publicly setting up the circumstances for the next muse to appear. His readiness to find her and put himself to the test was a secret he shared with his readers.

★　★　★

Graves's second successful trip to America at the beginning of 1958 followed Christmas with Jenny in Rome and a visit to Yugoslavia with Beryl, culminating in a skiing holiday for the family at Lech in Austria. Juan, a natural sportsman, was in his element; Graves, who had not skied for fifty years, was more cautious but delighted with the success of his holiday plan. Jenny, too, seemed to be getting over the disappointment of the *Spectator* case; their visit to her in Rome had been almost imperial in the level of its grandeur, with meetings with Ingrid Bergman and Roberto Rossellini following parties in palaces and dinners at embassies. Enjoying the reverence with which he was received wherever he went abroad, Graves allowed himself the moment of irritation which comes to all those who feel themselves to be prophets outside their own countries. Italy, he told Karl Gay, 'is treating me rather as America did, and as England never has and never will'.[23] Forgetting that the reasons were mostly of his own making, he grew resentful.

While staying with Jenny, Graves worked on the last of his four talks for the American trip in February 1958 during which Alastair Reid had again agreed to act as his assistant.

It lasted for three weeks and took Graves on a whistle-stop tour of seven major cities. The pace was chaotic; he was not only booked to give talks and readings and do signings, but was to appear on chat shows and in debates, where his opinion was solicited on such subjects as step-parenting and nudity. In New York, Reid took him to have tea with Auden and noted with glee that their host was far more nervous than Graves and that, after the guest had gone, Auden had declared Graves to be '"by instinct"' a homosexual.[24] Graves's diary was less revealing, stating only that he had taken tea with Auden on 10 February.[25]

The low spot of the trip came three days later in Ann Arbor, when Graves found himself walking seven blocks in the icy Michigan winds in the hope of finding a can of beer; the static in the university buildings here was so extreme that he thought he was experiencing an electric storm. In Chicago, a more congenial city, he stayed at a party until dawn and found himself succumbing to a cough on his way to Bloomington the following day. At Dallas, where he stayed with friends of Gordon Wasson's, he had a fever of 101 and was only able to deliver his talk after being given a double shot of penicillin. Arriving at Austin the following day, he gave his favourite lecture, on the connection between mushrooms and religious ecstasy, and was delighted to find that the audience included a man knowledgeable enough to discuss the significance of mistletoe in folklore with him afterwards. 'Now, (thank God) finished my engagement tour,' he wrote in his diary on 17 February.

The grind was over, and the fun was still to come. On 18 February, dressed as a clown, Graves went to a Texan masquerade ball, 'drank champagne and mixed with four hundred fantastic guests until 2 a.m.' Two days later, staying with Len Lye and Anne, his second wife, in New York, he was becoming blasé enough to record that 'everyone . . . including the Press' was at another party where he drank and talked into the early hours. The following evening he was out again, at Auden's birthday party, with 'scores' of guests, until midnight. The last day came and Graves, in a panic, realized that he had bought none of the list of purchases requested by his family. His final hours in New York were spent shopping. Laden down with vegetable seeds, spark plugs, nightdresses for Beryl, suits for William, plasticine for Tomas and Tom Lehrer records for them all, Graves was taken to the airport by Reid and met, at the other end, by Beryl, Tomas and the entire Gay family. 'Warm winds,' he wrote, contentedly. 'All well.'

*　　*　　*

Graves had decided, rather whimsically, to use Ronald Searle as the illustrator of the translation of *The Iliad* on which he worked steadily for Doubleday after his return. His approach was not a conventional one. Unlike the Latin translations he undertook, in which his success stemmed partly from the ease with which he entered the mind of the original writer, he imposed his own view of Homer in his version of *The Iliad*. Homer, he decided, was a bit of a joker, a man who liked to share a laugh at the gods and heroes with his audience. Friends were told that it was an easy job and that he was lacing the prose with lyrics in the old Irish style. The result is curious and uneasy, as if the tale of Troy had been confused with the humorous adventures of Don Juan. Searle's caricature drawings should not be criticized; he produced them to Graves's specifications, winks and all.

The other main work of the summer, before setting off on a brief autumn expedition to Minorca in search of 'goddess stones', was on the *Claudius* script, since Alec Guinness now wanted Graves as the principal scriptwriter with Bridget Boland as his consultant. (Boland's first screenplay had not appealed to the producers whom Guinness had approached.)

By now, the modern world was beginning to enter Deyá. William had started to bring parties of young friends to stay when he returned from Oundle. Lucia and Juan played pop music on the portable gramophone as they sat out on the Canelluñ steps. The village was crowded with young Americans. Surrounded by youth, Graves refused to play the grandfather he was; his diary shows him dancing while Alston Anderson and Mati Klarwein played the drums, holding a fiesta for a hundred and twenty guests and going to restaurants in Palma with groups of amiable, but fairly ordinary, young people to whom he was a meal-ticket and something of a curiosity. Few of them had read his work; most knew that it sounded smart to admire *The White Goddess*. Gradually, Graves was becoming that popular freak of our times, somebody who is known more for their name than their work. The reverence of the young American students had given him quite a taste for being a popular idol. He was not, perhaps, so old as all that. Having survived his year of the 'grand climacteric' without mishap, he bought himself a leather jacket a month after transforming Beryl's life with the installation of an Aga cooker.

Living in this circle of adulation, Graves sometimes lost all sense of how he might sound to the outside world or of how he was perceived. Would he, in earlier years, have thoughtlessly confided his financial successes to James Reeves, who was always short of funds, with the announcement, 'I love money, don't you?'[26] Would he have added to Reeves's humiliation by telling him, with a modicum of tact, that his only chance of getting his selected poems published was with a Foreword written by Graves himself, 'not that I wouldn't like the job'?[27] Keith Baines, the obscure author of one slim volume of poems, was advised on the need to have a sense of humour when writing big musicals and appearing on television.[28] Cicely Gittes, asking for news of William's A-level results, was answered with accounts of Alec Guinness's plans for *Claudius* and of a new scheme for a Broadway musical.[29]

Graves was no less kind than he had always been: Alan Sillitoe's first novel was urged on Doubleday, James Reeves's poems were highly praised in an autumn radio broadcast, and Daryl Hine, a young Canadian poet whose play for the summer fiesta party had been a dismal failure, was solaced with the offer of one of the Palma flats for his free use. (Hine was less pleased when Graves, in a sudden fit of financial caution, sent him a bill for the rent.[30])

Spending an increasing amount of his time among people who were not his intellectual equals inevitably had its effect. In 1958 Graves was beginning to lose some of that fierce, clear sense of poetic values which Laura Riding had held before him like a banner. Riding now seemed a pathetic figure, obsessed by a dictionary which she and Schuyler Jackson had still failed to complete; Graves did not see the shabbiness of his own new aspirations. Writing to James Reeves to wonder aloud if he might be in danger of becoming a hack if he took on too much work, he was spared an honest answer.

A few of his friends and critics were ready to express disapoint-ment with the way his career was developing. Tom Matthews, in 1958, wrote a harsh review in *Time* magazine of *5 Pens in Hand*, a collection of essays, poems and short stories which Graves had cobbled together shortly before his first American trip. It was threadbare and Matthews said so. Graves, when Matthews wrote to apologize for his bluntness, professed absolute indifference to anything Tom might want to say and then admitted that he had been hurt. Why, if he did not like the book, had he bothered to review it? To Graves, it was an act of dishonour to give a friend a bad review; a good one, or none at all, was his own policy.

In England, too, there was a murmur of dissatisfaction with *Steps*, a similar miscellany published in 1958. Philip Larkin, while ready to describe Graves as being 'as good a poetic mentor as the young are likely to get' and falling under the spell of Graves the reviewer and Graves the conversationalist, 'so charming the reader that the original book is forgotten', noted the ephemeral nature of *Steps* and raised the interesting question of Graves's division between inspiration and control. If, Larkin asked, his poetry was written in a state of sacred trance, why was he so proud of the number of times he revised each work? Where did the magic trance come in, if the poem had to go through at least five drafts before it could be regarded as satisfactory?[31] The *Times Literary Supplement* expressed pleasure that Graves had become 'a happy man' before allowing itself a demure giggle at his abrasive comments on other twentieth-century poets, remarking that it was surprising 'just how catty a gentleman of the old school can get'.[32] John Wain was not so mild. Graves, he felt, had been corrupted by his American success and had started to opt for easy ways to make money. *Steps* seemed to him to be a 'volume of barrel-scrapings' in which the poems had been tacked on as makeweight.[33]

There was reason for concern, summed up in Wain's scornful use of the phrase 'package deal' to describe *Steps*. Graves's dedication as a poet remained absolute, however, and the poetry which he was writing in the 1950s stands with his best. Here, he was still holding in balance the romantic, moon-haunted love-poetry and the ironic, witty, metaphysical work which Wain, among many others, considered the more remarkable. The poetry, the work he most cared about, was beyond reproach, but Graves had begun to compromise the way in which he offered it to his readers, just as he had begun to sacrifice his much-vaunted integrity to the pursuit of easy money. The argument, that he had to provide funds for an expanding family, never altered; the difference was that Graves no longer seemed to care about the form in which his work went out, so long as it produced quick cash in return.

CHAPTER THIRTY

1958–1960

ILLNESS

AT THE BEGINNING OF 1958, GRAVES HAD BEEN ASKED BY his half-brother Dick to visit Israel during the year of its tenth anniversary. The invitation was issued in Dick's role as Mayor of Jerusalem, on behalf of the Israeli government. It was, Graves told his brother, 'the greatest public honour I have ever been paid.'[1] The trip, eventually scheduled for January 1959, rapidly developed into something approximating a presidential visit; Graves's fearless presentation of Jesus in *The Nazarene Gospel Restored* as a revolutionary Jew whose life had been hijacked by Saint Paul, had won him a large audience of admirers in Israel. Guessing that Dick would be nervous that his mischievous side would get the better of his sense of ceremony, Graves reassured him. 'I will tread circumspectly . . .' he promised. 'On my best behaviour – which can be magnificent.'[2]

Graves's genito-urinary problems were still causing him considerable pain when he set off on his tour. But, after a miserable crossing from Naples – he hated boats and was confined to his bunk for most of the journey – he surrendered himself to a taxing month of meetings, discussions and expeditions around a country he had only imaginatively explored in his researches.

Israel fascinated him. For the first time in years, he made no effort to write anything except a daily diary; the nature of this, normally a flat record of routines, visitors, purchases and schedules, changed into a heroic attempt to keep track of all the information he was receiving. As an honoured visitor, he lunched with Golda Meir and went for a morning stroll with Ben-Gurion, attended by the press. But it was the contact with Israel's past rather than its struggling present which absorbed him. Occasionally, the combination of the two provided a fruitful image. Gethsemane, he noted, could only be seen through the thorns of a barbed-wire fence. At Solomon's mines, or at the place where he supposed them to have been on the Red Sea, he found that the talk was all of German and American investment in copper-mines. Solomon's massive excavations had exhausted less than 40 per cent of the dark-green copper ore buried in sandstone.

Graves had a good reason to be interested in Solomon. A year earlier, he had been contacted by Alexander Cohen, a Broadway producer who was a great admirer of his poetry. Cohen's idea, which captured Graves's interest at a time when his hopes of a *Claudius* film had faded, was that he should write the words and lyrics for a musical about Solomon and Sheba. They might, Cohen thought, be able to secure Lena Horne, then the most successful black female singer in New York. As a director, he suggested Tyrone Guthrie, for whom Graves had considerable respect.

Invited by Graves to co-write the script, Guthrie had refused. He would, he wrote, prefer to be treated as 'an experienced elderly lady who might have ideas about what will, or what won't, work in the theatre'.[3] In compensation, he let Graves know that he too would be visiting Israel early in 1959, and suggested that they might start discussions there.

Graves had already drafted notes for a first act during the boat journey from Naples. After his second long conversation with Guthrie in Tel Aviv, he grew elated. 'Have lost scarf, knife, lighter, etc. (Sign of confidence),' he noted, pleased by his indifference to the loss of three treasured objects. Normally, such an occurrence would have filled him with superstitious alarm; with his thoughts fixed on a Broadway success, he felt untouchable. Here, at last, was the sure-fire success which he and Jenny had been waiting for.

Israel was an experience Graves never forgot and to which he often referred, but he was in poor health and he had given himself no pause for rest during his stay. He was offered no chance to do so when he left, as Jenny swept him off to Rome, to start work with her on the script each day while socializing at night in the way that she adored. The pace proved too strenuous; home again in Deyá on 5 February, Graves managed to write a long commissioned article on Israel for *Holiday* magazine before he collapsed. Even in bed, he kept working; propped against the pillows, he revised the proofs of his new *Collected Poems*.

There was no time to be ill; Cohen wanted the script of *Solomon and Sheba* to be on his desk by April. By 19 February, Jenny, on a ticket paid for by her father, had arrived to act as his collaborator. They worked nine- to ten-hour days for a fortnight, Graves composing the required twenty lyrics and providing the broad outline, culminating in the love-scene between Solomon and Sheba, for Jenny to develop. They gave no thought to dialogue; instead, Graves provided well-researched scenes which were more attentive to historical detail than achieving a dramatic plot. The script was sent off on 4 March; the following day, Graves went to his local doctor to see what could be done about the urinary problems which were becoming increasingly painful. A course of treatment provided him with a few weeks of improved health.

The first response to the script was encouraging; Cohen made enthusiastic noises and, when the Guthries arrived to stay at the Posada, Graves was told by Tyrone that he was a true professional. Shortly afterwards, the *New York Times* announced, prematurely, that Lena Horne would be appearing later in the year in a musical written by Robert Graves; a dramatic hit seemed to be within his grasp at last.

In April, Graves prepared himself for the first serious television documentary to be made about his life. It was to be presented in celebration of his new poems. Huw Wheldon's film for the BBC *Monitor* programme, shot over several days, showed Graves in his everyday routine, talking about his work. Wheldon was one of the few interviewers who managed to persuade his subject to drop the air of puckish naughtiness which he cultivated for television, and to be himself. Unusually, most of Wheldon's questions elicited clear and unevasive answers. England was still, Graves said, the source of his poetry; a poem was for him a way of enshrining a piece of experience. But, confronted with a leading question about the 'troubled' nature of his love-poetry, Graves shied away. While prepared to admit that 'poetry to me rather means trouble',[4] he pretended to see the question as an enquiry about pessimism. He was not, any more than Thomas Hardy, a pessimist, he told Wheldon, but that, as they both knew, was not the answer that Wheldon had wanted. The delicate subject of the influence of a living muse on some of his poetry was dropped.

The fact that Graves was ready to spend evenings watching West End musicals when he went to London with the family in May 1959 shows that he was taking his new enterprise seriously. Cohen, however, felt that he had not taken it seriously enough. The problems, which began with Miss Horne's disconcerting refusal to play Sheba, escalated. Guthrie was taken off the project and Graves's suggestion that his friend Peggy Glanville-Hicks should compose the music was rejected; they were not, as Cohen and his colleagues reminded Graves, putting on an opera. They wanted the script rewritten. Graves was outraged to learn that this did not mean he would get a second payment.

All summer long, the letters and cables flew to and fro among Cohen, Graves and Jenny. Guthrie, gently, told Graves that a plot outline and twenty lyrics were not enough; Alex Cohen was right to insist on a rewrite. He also backed Cohen's insistence on the use of a well-known composer. But not even Graves's name could persuade William Walton, Bernstein or Britten to commit themselves to what seemed to them an ill-conceived venture. Graves, too, when told that he must contrive a spirited copper-bargaining scene between Solomon and Sheba, began to feel serious doubts about the project for the first time.

One of the great merits of living in Deyá was that it enabled Graves to detach himself. Viewed from Canelluñ, the musical quickly fell into perspective as an interesting but unimportant experiment. To Jenny, however, it had become a mountain which must be climbed. Goaded on by her unconcealed longing for a Broadway success, Graves continued to participate in the discussions with Cohen. But his hopes for the musical waned. When the time came for the annual birthday play, Solomon and Sheba seemed to have found their proper level, with Mati Klarwein starring as Solomon, while the young Sicres, Gays and Tomas Graves flounced across the stage as a gaggle of concubines, wives and irate husbands. In 'The Lost Chinese', a short story which he wrote that summer, Graves amused himself by sending up Alex Cohen as 'Sammy Samstag, the Broadway impresario', who enthusiastically applauds a new script before demanding a complete rewrite.[5]

Graves could afford to be cynical. He had found another and easier way to make some money. Ever since June, he and Karl had been scrambling around the attics of Canelluñ, hunting out manuscripts and old drafts of poems for which the University at Buffalo, then the biggest literary collector in the US, was willing to pay $30,000. In his interview with Wheldon, Graves had spoken of his affection for the Charterhouse headmaster who advised him to make good use of his waste-paper basket; now, as somebody who had for years been keeping the contents of his baskets to use as second and third drafts, Graves was thankful for his frugal habits.

Physically he remained in poor shape, complaining in his diary of recurrent pain and exhaustion. A little socializing gave him pleasure, a dinner with friends in Palma, a moonlight beach-picnic hosted by Alastair Reid and Mary, his young second wife. But there were too many visitors that summer for a sick man to enjoy. His sister Rosaleen's family filled the Posada and were instantly succeeded by the Reeveses; Canelluñ itself was the focus of what he wearily described as 'a teenage summer with the record player going on the whole time and Wm, Lucia and Tomas, each with a dozen friends, using the house as a hotel'.[6]

Graves's poems that summer focused on his marriage. In 'The Quiet Glades of Eden', first titled 'Proclivity to Vice', he hinted at a longing for violence which seems to have been lacking in the gentle marital relations he compared to a cool drink of water, pleasant and wholesome. The poem makes it plain that he needed something wilder and darker, a pain against which to test himself.

> If it should please you, for your own best reasons,
> To take and flog me with a rawhide whip,
> I might (who knows?) surprisedly accept
> This earnest of affection.[7]

In 'Joan and Darby', a still more directly autobiographical poem, he wrote of a love which had lasted for twenty years without ever achieving that mystical sense of twinned spirits he sought from his muses. The warning signs of restlessness were clear.

> Other seasons, other thoughts and reasons,
> Other fears or phases of the moon:
> In loving-kindness we grow grey together –

> Like Joan and Darby in their weather-lodge
> Who never venture out in the same weather.[8]

He could brood on his emotional needs, but he was not feeling strong enough for the self-imposed ordeal of muse-love. After a further visit to his Mallorcan doctor revealed that he had a growth on his prostate gland, he found it impossible to put his grandfather's death from prostate cancer out of his mind. Stoically, he made arrangements through his medical friend William Sargant, to undergo the modified operation which was only available in England. Sargant was able to put him in touch with Mr Mimpriss, the top genito-urinary surgeon at London's St Thomas's Hospital and to promise that, even on the National Health Service, he would have a private room in which he could work in peace. Mimpriss saw him at the beginning of September 1959 and decided that the operation should not be delayed. Graves went into hospital the following week.

Even in normal circumstances, a prostate operation is an uncomfortable and distressing affair. In Graves's case, three operations were needed due to the fact that he was found to have a rare and initially undiagnosed blood disease. The first operations, on 7 and 19 September, were undertaken by Mimpriss; after an unusually heavy loss of blood, it was decided that Graves should be kept in St Thomas's until 27 September. By the 16th, when Jenny was his regular daily visitor, he was working on the *Iliad* proofs and accepting visits from several friends, including Alec Guinness and Jerome Robbins, chosen by Jenny as a likely director for *Solomon and Sheba*. Beryl arrived in London on 18 September. Four days later, Graves suffered a severe haemorrhage and had to be operated on in the absence of Mr Mimpriss after 'some memorable pain', as he tersely noted in his diary. This was the period recorded in 'Surgical Ward: Men' where Graves described his refusal to submit to morphine, addressing 'Lady Morphia' as a dangerous and testing mistress.

> Her scorpion kiss and dark gyrating dreams –
> She in mistrust of whom I dared out-dare,
> Two minutes longer than seemed possible,
> Pain, that unpurposed, matchless elemental
> Stronger than fear or grief, stranger than love.[9]

He was given a massive blood transfusion of forty-five pints, well over three times his original liquid content, as he weakly boasted to his friends. Despite being too ill to face seeing even his family, he managed to complete two more articles for *Holiday* magazine. By 29 September, although still in hospital, he was elated by visits from Sam Spiegel and David Lean to discuss the possibility of working on their film about T. E. Lawrence.

'Glad it's over,' he wrote on the last day of the month. But the following week brought further haemorrhages; the blood specialist, who had been away on holiday, now diagnosed a rare condition of fibronolysis; Graves's blood was failing to clot because of a minor form of haemophilia, transmitted to men through the female line. It was this which had turned what should have been a fairly routine operation into a life-threatening experience. His family and friends had been terrified; Graves's own immediate concern was for his virility. The Gays, welcoming him back to Deyá in early November, were instantly informed that he was just as potent as he had been before the operation.[10] The fear of impotence continued, nevertheless, to worry him and to create a need for him to prove himself sexually in the next few years. Apologizing to his wife in 1962 for his frantic pursuit of a beautiful young woman over the past two years, Graves told her that he had not been himself since the 1959 operation.[11]

★　★　★

Installed for his convalescence in a ground-floor bedroom at 108 Clifton Hill, the London home of his niece Sally Chilver, Graves was inundated by visitors in October 1959. Margaret Russell, the children's old nurse, came; so did the vicar of Great Tew in Oxfordshire, last seen in 1925. John Aldridge came to sit by the bed and sketch him; Ricardo Sicre, always businesslike, brought news that Sam Spiegel was prepared to pay $10,000 for a film option on Graves's *Lawrence and the Arabs*. Lawrence's brother, Arnie, also arrived in a businesslike spirit; in exchange for recommending him to Spiegel as a consultant on the film, he wanted Graves to back his attempts to persuade the Lord Chamberlain to veto a new play about Lawrence.

The play was Terence Rattigan's *Ross*, in which Alec Guinness had been chosen to play Lawrence's role. Fond though Graves was of

Guinness, he disliked the play almost as much as Lawrence's brother. 'I'm sorry about Alec, but to play a sadistic, vain, unbalanced queer would have done him no good,' he wrote to Karl Gay on 13 October,[12] after hearing that the request for an embargo had won the Lord Chamberlain's support. Guinness continued to defend a play which he thought honest and powerful.[13] Rattigan, uneasily aware that Graves and the Lawrence Estate made a powerful combination, offered to consider any alterations or cuts which Graves might suggest. No suggestions were made.

Graves's hostility to Rattigan's interpretation of Lawrence as a brave but confused masochist with strong homosexual tendencies was not contrived. His friendship with T. E. Lawrence had developed when he was still conscious of having been deeply in love with Peter Johnstone. Rattigan's play suggested to him that he could have been committing himself to another such attachment with Lawrence. Since those early years, Graves had repressed any latent sympathies he might have felt for homosexuals, addressing the subject of perversion with a zeal that was beyond eccentricity. (One of his most imaginative claims, made in 1970, was that men who drank milk were more likely to become homosexual than those who did not. Thus, homosexuality was on the increase in America because all the boys drank milk shakes.[14])

Given Graves's desire to see Lawrence as a heterosexual, his response to Rattigan's uncompromising portrait was not surprising. Neither was the fact that he wanted to control the way in which Lawrence was presented on film. If there was an element of venality in his interest – he still liked the idea of making easy money – there was also an element of loyalty. Lawrence had been good to him, and Graves had shared Basil Liddell Hart's anger at the misrepresentations made in Richard Aldington's scurrilous biography. Above all, he was anxious to protect the reputation of a man who had always been generous to him and whom, for a time, he had worshipped as a hero. Graves was not always a good judge of character, but his powers of intuition meant much to him. He wanted Lawrence to be known as the kind of man he had believed him to be.

Weak and still dizzy from illness and antibiotics, he returned to Deyá at the beginning of November. On the first day, he was only strong enough to stroke their two poodles, who were gratifingly pleased to see him, and talk to a few neighbours who came to welcome him home. After two more days, he was able to stay out of bed for the whole of Tomas's first day at school although not as yet in a state to consider adding a new compost heap to the 1958 hillocks he had named for Ralph Vaughan Williams and Sir Arthur Bliss. By December, however, he was ready to join forces with Ricardo Sicre in making the final arrangements to recover his property from the hands of Juan Gelat. Heartened by the knowledge that he was, at long last, the owner of all that he had (twice) paid for, he was ready to go to a party given by Nancy Cunard, a friend from the past who had published some of his and Riding's poems. Nancy was almost unrecognizable as the pale and elegant 'Ivory' he and Laura had admired, but the evening stayed in his mind. 'Watched boatlike moon sink into the sea. Beryl wearing her new green suit,' he noted in his diary.

Beryl, as he knew, had been greatly alarmed by his decline in hospital; his diary references to her in the next few months were unusually tender. He worried about her when she became ill for a week and felt happier when he could note that she was 'well enough to start worrying'; when they went to London together in January 1960 he wrote in his diary that only Beryl could understand why he had refused an honorary doctorate from the University at Buffalo, just as he had rejected Harold Macmillan's offer of a CBE. He disliked awards.

Graves had never been consistent in his declarations. Shortly after making this observation in his diary, he began packing his bags to go to America in order to be awarded the Gold Medal of the National Poetry Society. One good reason for accepting this honour was that Robert Frost, his favourite American poet, had promised to attend the ceremonial dinner. On 15 January, three months after a hospital experience which had nearly killed him, he left London for a third American lecture tour, sponsored by Doubleday. Family commitments prevented Alastair Reid from accompanying him; instead, Graves took his daughter, Jenny.

PART FIVE

THE MUSES

CHAPTER THIRTY-ONE

1960–1962

MARGOT

EARLY IN 1960 GRAVES WROTE AN ESSAY, 'THE CASE FOR XAN-thippe', in which he offered a defence of Socrates's reputedly shrewish wife.[1] Women were never at fault, in Graves's view. Xanthippe had clearly irritated her husband by asserting the superiority of intuition to reason, a view which Graves enthusiastically supported. Further to this, he suggested that Xanthippe had upset Socrates by taking a poet for a lover; Socrates had revenged himself by spreading the word around that his wife was a nagging harridan.

There are no grounds for these spirited assertions; Graves's suggestion that Xanthippe's flirtation with a poet might explain the absence of all but a handful of poets from Plato's Republic tells us only how little philosophy he had read. (This aspect of *The Republic* was based not on the teachings of Socrates, but on Plato's own ideas.) What is of interest is that the fictitious poet-lover, evidently far more alluring than Socrates, is assumed to have an absolute right to seduce Xanthippe. She is his chosen muse and nothing can therefore be allowed to prevent the poet from possessing her.

Graves's view of the poet's entitlement to a muse, on a sexual or platonic basis, became inflexible in the 1960s. The muse, standing for the intuitive feelings Graves held to be vital to the poetic spirit, was his defence against an increasingly mechanized and technological age which threatened the sacred gift of imagination. From 1960 until he was no longer able to hold a pen, Graves always had muses. His need of them was far greater than theirs of him. He had persuaded himself that he was incapable of writing poetry unless he had a living source of inspiration, a woman who, while she loved him, held the power of the Goddess in her hands. When she ceased to love him, she ceased to have power. The muses were, in fact, good-looking women reinvented by Graves to suit his own vision of the Goddess.

Graves's relationship with three successive muses dominated the decade and the work he produced during it. Increasingly, he deleted his earlier poems from collections to make more room for muse-poetry. By 1965 half of his *Collected Poems* comprised muse-poetry; by 1975, when the final edition of his collected poems was published, muse-poetry took up more than two-thirds of the book.

Did Graves know what he was doing? Not entirely. The 1960s mark the beginning of his slow and sad decline into senility. Mental deterioration at this early stage took the form of a personality change, as he became increasingly convinced that he was chosen to act, with the help of the muses, as the Goddess's human spokesman. By 1965 he was behaving in a way which would have seemed incredible, from the point of view of his dismayed family, at the beginning of the decade.

The principal reason for this alteration can be traced back to the traumatic experience of his prostate operations. A transfusion, due to his clotting deficiency, of more than three times his circulating volume of blood would have killed a less resilient man; such a transfusion robbed him of all his ability to fight infection. But the hospital records have more to reveal than this. They show that Graves was a heavier drinker than he publicly admitted and that, as a result, he required unusually large amounts of anaesthetic for his three operations. The fact that he was also a heavy smoker led to furring of the arteries and the starvation of oxygen to the brain during his operations, which, in turn, would have induced an imperceptible series of mini-strokes, or multi-infarcts.[2]

Evidence of mental deterioration is hard to produce because of the oddity of Graves's normal characteristics, and the eccentricity of many of his beliefs, long before 1960. He had described the peculiarity of the Graves family's manner at the beginning of *Goodbye to All That*;

he did so again, with easy mockery, in one of his talks given at Mount Holyoke, when he looked back on a lifetime of absentmindedness, stuttering, and forgetting what was going on around him, or even where he was.[3]

All of these idiosyncrasies became more noticeable as time passed, but there was little to suggest a decline in the first few years of the decade. In the words of one old friend who had known him for thirty years: 'Robert simply became more Robert'.[4] Even in the mid-Sixties when admirers started to squirm at his references to the rape of the moon, secret plots by the CIA and the dangers of feeding milk to homosexuals, eccentricity and old age, rather than madness, seemed the appropriate diagnosis. And these strange assertions could be made to seem reasonable when they were put in the general context of Graves's beliefs. The first moonshot was indeed a horrifying invasion to a poet who believed in the moon as an inviolate source of inspiration and strength. His daughter Catherine had convinced him that the death of her husband, Clifford Dalton, in 1961, was closely related to the CIA's interest in his work as a scientist for the Australian Atomic Energy Commission.[5] His theories about milk-drinking homosexuals evidently derived from the Spanish saying that 'A man does not drink milk'. Graves was not yet judged to have lost his wits. He had always been known for his unconventional views.

If Graves's bizarre behaviour in the 1960s was due to the onset of senility, it must be added that he was more than ready for the dangers and excitements of an increasingly eccentric lifestyle. Encountering student youth in the late Fifties and early Sixties opened his eyes to a freedom which he had never known. As a young man, he had gone straight from the Army into marriage and family life before entering a relationship with Riding in which he relived the harsh discipline of a puritan upbringing. William had been born the year after Graves's relationship with Riding ended; his life since then had been, as he saw it, a perpetual struggle to produce money for his demanding tribe. He had never had time for enjoyment. There were plenty of young men and women around in the Sixties to tell him that from now on he owed it to himself to follow every new chance of adventure which came his way.

And so, under the influence of a deteriorating mental condition and his own impulses, Graves began to change his appearance and his ways. He became notorious, not only for his muses, but for his overt interest in every pretty young woman who came near him. He became an enthusiastic supporter of Sufism and experimented with drugs. Having urged, in *The White Goddess*, that every student should be made familiar with a canon of some two or three hundred works, he now urged them to avoid 'the dragon of Compulsory Literary Orthodoxy – "CLO" for short – ' and invited them instead to read Sufi texts and to worship at the shrine of the Black Goddess of ultimate wisdom.[6]

None of this did any harm to his reputation among the young. The academic establishment winced, but the student audiences revelled in Graves's genial iconoclasm and laughed at the jokes with which he illustrated his arguments. His straightforward manner, upright bearing and air of conviction gave authority to even his wildest assertions. He was a legend, but a very approachable one.

The only woman who might have influenced his behaviour, Beryl, made no attempt to do so. She had seen what had happened to Graves when Laura left him, and had respected his commitment to a woman of fierce intellectual power. Having known Graves's relationship with Laura at close quarters, it was impossible for Beryl to look on the muses as serious rivals.

Beryl was a loyal woman with a deep love for her husband and an unquestioning faith in his genius. Whatever Graves did, was done with her knowledge. Stoicism was her chosen course; the photographs in her albums bear witness to it.

* * *

On 4 February 1960, Graves had the first dinner alone with his wife since leaving for the US lecture tour in mid-January. He had, however, kept her informed by letter, reporting that Jenny, although sweet, was unstoppably loquacious, and that he had enjoyed the formal presentation of his medal far less than a private dinner with Robert Frost on the previous day. He had been leading a hectic social life, staying up unusually late at a party given by Jerome Robbins, now thought by Jenny to be the ideal director for a film of *The White Goddess*. But they had not yet found a producer; Robbins was, perhaps, relieved to have the excuse of work on the choreography for the film of *West Side Story*.

Both Robbins and Jenny were present on the evening which was, for Graves, the highlight of the visit. On 31 January, together with

Jess MacNab, a young American art historian who often visited Deyá, they assembled at Wasson's luxurious Manhattan apartment on East End Avenue to taste the Mexican mushrooms containing the hallucinogenic psilocybin and, after a suitable period, to listen to the religious invocations which Wasson had recorded while watching a tribal mushroom ceremony.

Graves was a receptive subject. The following year, an Oxford student audience heard about his experience of the ancient world's vision of Paradise. (Graves believed that images of Paradise from all over the world coincided because they were all based on mushroom visions; he also noted that the word for 'mysteries' can be made to derive from the Greek word for 'mushroom-springing', while one root Arabic word for a toadstool is identical with that used for 'divine rapture'. Here was evidence of 'a pre-Islamic hallucinogenic practice of immense age'.[7])

The drug-taking and the vision it produced was, Graves told his listeners, a wholly beneficial experience. He had seen Paradise, in the form of a mountain-top Eden full of bright streams and flowers; he had known, briefly, the intoxicating sensation of an absolute mastery of knowledge. The images had remained clear in his mind for over a month, although he was ready to admit that the drug-trance was a passive and uncreative state compared to the poetic trance in which he produced his work.

Graves was, as so often in his life, ahead of the times. Aldous Huxley had already described the effects of taking mescaline. At the beginning of the Sixties, the medical profession was just starting to investigate the possibility of using psychedelic drugs to treat mentally disturbed patients. But the acid age had not begun; for many of Graves's young Oxford audience, this was their first authoritative account of 'tripping'. Graves himself disapproved strongly of drug-taking as a habit or outside a controlled environment. His own two or three experiments in Wasson's home were made out of scientific curiosity; in Deyá, where he was surrounded by drug-takers, he turned a blind eye to a practice he refused to indulge.

The main purpose of Graves's visit to America had been to accept a Gold Medal. To the Poetry Society, the honour was in the conferring of the award, not its value; Graves took a different view. In his speech, he expressed pleasure that his work was thought to have reached an assayable value; home in Mallorca, he was outraged to learn that this value was no more than that of a lick of gold on a coin of bronze. The committee were informed, after a brisk and cool exchange of letters, that Graves was going to spend the accompanying cheque for $100 on purchasing the sort of medal they should have given him. Authenticity mattered to him more than the committee understood; he was extravagantly pleased, on being awarded the Queen's Medal a few years later, to discover that this was the real thing. His work had finally been valued at its true worth.

Accolades were beginning to be showered on Graves. Shortly after his return to Mallorca at the beginning of February 1960 he was invited to London to accept Christina Foyle's Poetry Award. Flying over for the day, he surrounded himself with old friends and members of the family; home again, he resumed his voluminous correspondence with the eminent Jewish scholar and anthropologist, Raphael Patai, on a collaboration which Patai had suggested during his recent American visit. This, Graves's last prose work, was *Hebrew Myths*.

For young poets like Ted Hughes, admirers of *The White Goddess* and *The Greek Myths*, it seemed logical that Graves would follow these with 'The Celtic Myths'.[8] Nobody could have been better suited to the task, but Graves, after all his work on *The Nazarene Gospel Restored*, was more interested in the idea of examining the stories of the Old Testament and exploring the history behind them. It was more intriguing to look for a Jewish source to an old Welsh song, which told how Adam lay at Hebron for five hundred years without a soul, than to continue exploring the origins of Taliesin.[9] Patai, a diligent and meticulous man, was prepared to do much of the spadework for the book, leaving Graves free to theorize and, on occasion, to dazzle his collaborator by the accuracy of his intuitions.

Graves was still working on the revised version of *The White Goddess* in 1960, and she was much in his mind when he went with Beryl to America in May for the official reception of his manuscripts by the University at Buffalo. In New York he held discussions with a new friend, William Morris, who had started his own literary and dramatic agency, about a film of *The White Goddess* on which he planned to collaborate with Alastair Reid. They stayed with Gordon Wasson and here Beryl was persuaded to join them on a second mushroom trip. Cicely Gittes, visiting Wasson's home on East End Avenue the following day, found Beryl ironing Robert's shirts in the middle of a gloomy red bedroom of immense size. Both

Beryl and Graves were quiet and pale; the synthetic substitute used on this occasion had produced no celestial visions and left them feeling queasy for several days.[10] Even a party of all their young American friends who had become regular summer visitors to Deyá seemed more of a trial than a pleasure in these circumstances.

The summer days in Deyá passed uneventfully on, with nothing more exciting for Graves to report in his diary than the building of a new water-tank and dining-room extension at Canelluñ. Patai was working on the first draft of *Hebrew Myths* in New York; Graves was free to continue revising *The White Goddess*. He had begun to wonder who should play the Goddess in the film, for which the omens seemed good, when he was introduced to Margot Callas.

Their first meeting was at a dinner given by Mati Klarwein, their Israeli friend in Deyá. Klarwein had befriended Margot when she came over from Ibiza to work as a waitress at Ca'n Quet, the small hotel that faced Canelluñ across the valley of Deyá. In the summer of 1960 Margot returned at the suggestion of Mati, who liked her spontaneity and wit, while admiring her classical beauty. A Greek-Canadian with a touch of Irish blood, she had a sumptuous figure, dark, curling hair and a strong, lovely face. Her first marriage was over; while unambitious, she was shrewd enough to know that her looks had a value worth exploiting.

Graves was instantly smitten. A few days after the dinner party, Margot came to Canelluñ with Mati Klarwein who was in the process of making a film about the village. Margot's scene required her to appear naked to the waist; there must have been a touch of naughtiness in Klarwein's decision to set this scene in the Canelluñ garden, with Graves and his family looking on.

A friendship developed almost at once. Less than a week after the scene in the garden, Margot and Graves were going off for long walks and swims together. In 'Lyceia', a poem written that June, he described her as a slender Artemis, walking alone and proud in a circle of wolfish admirers.[11]

Graves did not keep his excitement about Margot all to himself. Alastair Reid, whose brief second marriage had come to an end, was invited to agree that she had the perfect face for *The White Goddess* film, for which Reid had just begun writing the screenplay. But Graves did not tell Reid that he had already begun to take possession of Margot in his poetry. He had found his muse.

It had become usual for Graves to write the play for his birthday celebrations; this year, he admitted in his diary that he had been obliged to burn the first plot for it. It seems likely that he had made too candid a disclosure of his feelings. The week after the revised play had been performed, Margot was invited to join in the discussions with Graves and Reid about *The White Goddess* filmscript. Together, the three of them watched her half-naked appearance in Klarwein's strange little film. Later that day, Graves gave Margot a sheaf of poems and told her that she had been their inspiration.

The decision had been made, and yet Graves continued to pretend to himself in his diary that the debate continued. 'In bed with cold, brooding; reassured by Beryl. Poem "To Myrto"' he wrote on 30 July. 'Day of decision; and no troubles found', began the entry for the following day.

Beryl probably guessed what was going to happen as soon as she saw Margot stripping off her shirt in the Canelluñ garden. She had already made her own decision, which was to support Graves in whatever he felt he needed to do for the sake of his poetry. He had told her that Judith Bledsoe had been important for his work; it was apparent that Margot was to perform the same useful service. She seemed a very agreeable and polite young woman. Tactfully and kindly, Beryl made expeditions to Palma in order to leave Graves and his muse alone; she may have preferred not to be a witness to the extravagance of her husband's devotion to Margot.

James Reeves was more judgemental when he arrived with his family to stay at the Posada in August. He had been puzzled by what Graves meant when he wrote a letter in June to say that he was too happy even to write poems. Observing that Margot Callas was being involved in every plan that was made after his arrival, Reeves finally understood what this state of elation meant. He was not impressed by talk of muses; to him and to his young daughter Stella, it seemed that they had been invited to Deyá for a purpose: to keep Beryl occupied while Graves dallied with his girlfriend. They felt both embarrassed and scornful.[12]

Their reaction was understandable. Handsome though Graves was in later life, he looked an inappropriate companion for a girl who was only a few years older than his son William. And, ready though Beryl was to show that she approved of Margot, whom she liked, she could not control the fact that she appeared to be a neglected wife, devoting herself to the cats and dogs with the same humorous tenderness that Graves showed for his young protégée. To the Gays, who shared

James Reeves's feelings of distaste, it was apparent from the start that Alastair Reid, an attractive, clever and amusing young man, was likely to capture Margot's interest when the excitement of being a muse had worn off.

Initially, Margot was moved and flattered by Graves's adulation. The relationship was, occasionally, a sexual one;[13] passionately in love, Graves needed very little response to make him happy. By September, when Beryl and he were touring the French battlefields on their way to England for a three-month visit, he had cast Margot in the same mould that he had chosen for Judith Bledsoe, his first muse. Judith had been 'wild and innocent, pledged to love / Through all disaster' in his poem 'The Portrait';[14] 'Under the Olives' described her successor in the same terms as 'Innocent, gentle, bold, enduring, proud.'[15]

The muses triggered Graves's emotional responses; the single woman he celebrated in all of them was an ideal. Readers of his poems can easily distinguish between those devoted to Laura and those to Beryl, but the love-songs and poems poured out for the last four women in his life are all stitched from the same piece of cloth. All are one, because all are seen as incarnations of Graves's own Goddess. He said as much himself when he wrote the poem 'In Her Praise'.

> This they know well: the Goddess yet abides.
> Though each new lovely woman whom she rides,
> Straddling her neck a year or two or three,
> Should sink beneath such weight of majesty
> And, groping back to humankind, gainsay
> The headlong power that whitened all her way
> With a broad track of trefoil – leaving you,
> Her chosen lover, ever again thrust through
> With daggers, your purse rifled, your rings gone
> Nevertheless they call you to live on
> To parley with the pure, oracular dead,
> To hear the wild pack whimpering overhead,
> To watch the moon tugging at her cold tides.
> Woman is mortal woman. She abides.[16]

Soon afterwards Margot left for a trip to North America. Graves did not see her again for an interminable six months during which, occasionally, she sent an answer to his letters. Her elusiveness increased her suitability as a muse. By causing pain, she was, as far as Graves was concerned, fulfilling her destiny as a vessel of the cruel Goddess.

★   ★   ★

The Graves family spent the autumn of 1960 at a large London house in Kensington Park Road, conveniently near to the Portobello Market where Graves made weekly raids on the silver and glass stalls. Still hoping for more than an advisory role on Spiegel's film about Lawrence, he dismayed Alec Guinness by asking for tickets to see him in Rattigan's *Ross* (the Lord Chamberlain had withdrawn his embargo on the play). This was embarrassing enough, given what Graves had said in 1959 about the play's depiction of Lawrence, but Guinness was more worried by Graves's announcement that he intended to sue Rattigan for having made use of his Lawrence biography without permission. By doing this, Graves hoped to ensure that Rattigan would not be asked to replace him as a consultant on the film. He did not fulfil his threat. As it happened, Spiegel, the producer, wanted neither of them to be involved; Graves had to be satisfied with meeting the director, David Lean, and giving Peter O'Toole some tips about the characterization of Lawrence.

Graves had been saddened in August by the news that his favourite half-brother, Dick, had died of cancer; in London, Beryl spent much of her time visiting her father to comfort him after the death of his brother, Clifford. Graves had plenty to occupy him in her absence. He went on the *Brains' Trust* programme with A. J. Ayer and gave a poetry reading at the New Festival Hall. On television with John Betjeman, he talked about his latest publication, *The Penny Fiddle*. This was the book which, when he was young and poor, he had tried and failed to sell as a children's book of nursery rhymes to keep the creditors at bay. Then, he had offered it with line drawings by Nancy; now, illustrated by Edward Ardizzone, it was picked as a children's book of the month and placed in the front of every bookshop window. Some 20,000 copies were sold.

But Graves was, as always, happier being informal. The occasions he enjoyed most on this visit were his trips to the Portobello Road, his long walks with Alastair Reid, who was now rewriting the *White Goddess* screenplay with his help, and meetings with old friends.

Loyalty was one of Graves's strongest qualities, and living away from England increased his determination to stay in touch, whenever he could, with the people who were like part of an extended family to him. Year after year, he made the same round of visits, to the Reeveses, to Tom Matthews and his second wife, Martha Gellhorn, and to John Aldridge who had left his wife Lucie to live with Norman Cameron's widow. Two new friends acquired this autumn were the novelist, Laurie Lee, whose love of Spain created an instant bond of affection, and a young folk-singer, Isla Cameron.

Graves's enthusiasm for helping friends and for exaggerating their talents was sometimes destructive. Alastair Reid had already warned him that he had no right to behave like a magician, casting a trance of glamour over everybody he liked by insisting that they possessed phenomenal talents.[17] Laurie Lee was worldly enough to shrug off Graves's failure to persuade Ava Gardner that Lee was the only man capable of writing a screenplay for television worthy of her talent; it was harder for Isla Cameron to resist his declarations that she was going to become the greatest folk-singer in the world. Charming though this side of Graves was, he carried it too far. Minor poets like James Reeves had been led to hope for more, perhaps, than they could reasonably have expected by Graves's assurances of their prodigious talent. Hopes were blighted, not by intention, for Graves was always a kind and generous-hearted man, but by his inability to draw the line between myth and reality.

In January 1961, Alastair Reid, after delivering the *White Goddess* screenplay to William Morris in New York, found himself travelling back to England on the same liner, the *Leonardo da Vinci*, as Margot Callas, who had gone to America after making an autumn visit to her mother in Canada.

In Reid's recollection, it seemed entirely appropriate to the myth of the Goddess that they should have an affair; Graves had, after all, decribed the battles between the gods of the waxing and waning year, Osiris and Set, as though rivalry was predestined. But this may have been Reid's way of justifying to himself behaviour which he knew would cause distress; certainly, he had no strong desire to tell Graves what had happened. Margot found it easy to persuade him that discretion was the wisest course. She told him that she herself would explain their relationship to Graves when she felt that the time was right. She gave no indication when that would be.[18]

Graves suffered a moment of anxiety himself when he discovered that Reid and Margot were returning from New York on the same ship. He had no idea whether it was a coincidence or whether they had planned to do so, but it disturbed him. In his diary, he noted that he had started to write a poem called 'Ugly Thoughts' before reproaching himself for being too fanciful. He destroyed it. There were other things on his mind in January: Idries Shah had arrived on Mallorca, together with Dr Gerald Gardner, one of England's leading experts on witchcraft.

CHAPTER THIRTY-TWO

1961–1963

BETWEEN MOON AND MOON

IDRIES SHAH, TOGETHER WITH HIS BROTHER OMAR, WAS CLAIMED by Graves to be in the senior male line of descent from Mohammed and to possess the secret mysteries of the Sufis.[1] This was the account which the Shah brothers had given him of themselves.

Idries impressed Graves from their first meeting in mid-January 1961. A slight, dark, conventionally dressed man of thirty-seven, Idries had the same easy, self-contained manner that had struck Graves when he met the philosopher Basanta Mallik in the 1920s. Idries, like Mallik, was a man who seemed to hold the key to a new way of looking at the world. Like Mallik, he was under the illusion that he was teaching Graves; in fact, he had little of value to reveal to him.

The Shah brothers met Graves at a time when he was already looking for an endorsement of his new, muse-ridden way of life. Graves welcomed a philosophy which fitted in with his own ideas about intuition and the value of talismanic objects, while adding a spiritual dimension. When he agreed to write a Foreword to *The Sufis*, a book written by Idries and published by Doubleday in 1964, Graves took the opportunity to stress what Sufism signified for him.

He ignored the Sufi belief in number as a principle of human being and the root of science; this had no relevance to his life. Instead he emphasized the fact that the Sufis acknowledged a force of mental power which could be created by telepathic communication. To Graves this was a sign that the Sufis shared his view of the poet and his muse as able to become a powerful force for good when harnessed together.[2]

This was a case of Graves reading into Sufism what he wanted to find. In the 1930s he and Laura Riding had been convinced that like-thinking people could alter world patterns of behaviour by a combined force of thought-waves. Even with Judith Bledsoe, Graves had been more excited by the idea of what their combined mental powers would produce than by anything so uncomplicated as physical lust. He filled his diary with references to the 'cosmic coincidence' of his relationship with Margot. If he wrote her a letter and put it away in a drawer, he believed that she would know its contents. Sufism lent authority to a view he already held, but wanted to substantiate.

It was not long before Graves's friends were being urged to take advice from Idries Shah on every aspect of their lives; as usual, Graves was cheerfully imperious in expecting everyone to share his enthusiasm. A few refused to do so. Ricardo Sicre would have nothing to do with the Shah brothers and began to fear that Graves was losing his last shreds of judgement; Gordon Wasson, sceptical of Idries's claims to know all about secret mushroom rituals in the East, begged Graves to stop passing his own discoveries on to Shah. Jenny Nicholson wrote a bitter letter to ask her father why Idries was supposed to know more about their family and its needs than they did themselves.[3] Neighbours in Deyá, while ready to agree that Idries was charming and courteous, found it hard to accept him as the great healer and mystic described to them.[4] Graves, as usual, had thrown his glamour-cloak around the shoulder of somebody he liked.

Idries seemed to have brought good fortune to Graves by the mere act of his presence. His arrival on Mallorca in January 1961 heralded the return of Margot. Graves and she went to Madrid together, where they met up with Alastair. Nothing was said about Margot and Alastair's new relationship; Graves was eager to suppose that everything was just as it had been six months ago. Margot was introduced to Ava Gardner, who liked her, and to Ricardo Sicre, who took a dim view of all Graves's muses. Margot gave Graves a black Cordoban hat; he did not forgive her for offering Ava the one he presented to her in return. His gifts were magic talismans, and to be cherished. He had meant the hat to symbolize a bond between them.[5]

Graves returned alone to Deyá after a week to write up a new talk about 'baraka', a word given to him by Idries, which he compared to the old-fashioned sense of the word 'virtue'. A stone or amulet could contain baraka for him, but so could a relationship. In February he was still ready to believe that the love between him and Margot had baraka; lovingly, he revised the poems which he had written to her, which were to dominate his new collection that summer.

He had no knowledge yet of having been betrayed, but the poems are haunted by a sense of unease. In one, 'Ruby and Amethyst', he drew a wistful contrast between two women; one, based on Beryl, is faithful, honest, self-reliant; the other, an elusive woman who refuses to commit herself, is more highly prized. In 'Troughs of Sea', he allowed himself to consider the prudent choice: to end his irrational passion, drown it in the sea. But the image of that act was made so terrifying, a replay of his vertiginous early poems of plunges to nightmare depths, that refusal seemed the wiser choice.

> Waves tasselled with dark weed come rearing up
> Like castle walls, disclosing
> Deep in their troughs a ribbed sea-floor
> To break his bones upon.
>
> – Clasp both your hands under my naked foot
> And press hard, as I taught you:
> A trick to mitigate the pangs
> Either of birth or love.[6]

These poems were a very public declaration of his love for Margot; James Reeves was shocked when he saw them published in *The Observer* as a collection early in 1961. His reproaches were unluckily timed; they arrived in April, the month in which Graves learned that Alastair and Margot had gone to live together in a mill-house in France for an indefinite period. Graves told Reeves on 29 May that Beryl had shared his horror at behaviour which involved 'Satanism and devious lying'. The accusation of Satanism is uncomfortably reminiscent of the talk of Geoffrey Phibbs's devilry and the allegations of witchcraft laid against Kit Jackson, with Graves's connivance, in 1939.

Reid himself was still unaware of the level of hostility his behaviour had aroused. Graves often talked about the White Goddess and muse-love in a deceptively lighthearted way; only Beryl understood how intense his obsession was. When, therefore, Alastair wrote a cheerful letter at the end of the summer to explain that Margot, while loved by them both, belonged to neither of them, he was aghast at the fury of Graves's response.[7]

Margot, as the muse, was exonerated from whatever pain she might cause. Causing pain was part of her function as the tool of the Goddess. But Alastair Reid had forfeited any chance of future friendship. He was cast, as the letter to Reeves had hinted, as an agent of the devil, and even as the devil himself.

Pain, from the point of view of muse-poetry, was a beneficial experience; within a few weeks of hearing about Margot's flight, Graves was writing 'Lion Lover'. Here, he acknowledged that he had courted disaster, undertaking

> Cruel ordeals long foreseen and known,
> Springing a trap baited with flesh: my own.[8]

This suggests resignation, but Graves had not given up the battle yet. Writing to James Reeves in May, he told him that 'Beware, Madam' was going to 'make the hair rise on some lovely necks'.[9] 'Beware, Madam!' warned Margot to put her trust in the true poets, a soldierly band of 'single-hearted lovers / Who adore and trust beyond all reason, / Who die honourably at the gates of hell.' Alastair is the serpent of whom she must beware.

> Beware, madam, of the witty devil,
> The arch intriguer who walks disguised
> In a poet's cloak, his gay tongue oozing evil.[10]

Forgiveness for Reid was out of the question. Although Graves hotly denied that he showed any malice towards his rival, the evidence is against him: Betty Sicre remembers having threatened to end all communication with Graves until he called off what she regarded as a vendetta.[11] Graves's behaviour was a near-exact repetition of the way in which he had tried to ensure that Geoffrey Phibbs became unemployable in 1929. He told friends that Reid owed him money; when Reid wrote to ask for specific details, he was met by silence.[12] Reid's most regular source of income was from his work for the *New Yorker*; Graves wrote to its editor, William Shawn, threatening to make no further contributions until they took Reid off their payroll. Shawn did nothing; both men continued to publish their work in his magazine.[13]

Margot did not make life easier for Graves by her own reluctance to let go of her role as the cherished muse. In July, after spending four months with Alastair in France, she returned, against Reid's wishes, to Deyá, for the annual birthday celebrations.[14] Graves was overcome. 'Happiest day of year,' he wrote in his diary, imagining that this signalled the end of her relationship with Reid. A week later, Margot was back in France and Graves's hatred of Alastair had doubled its strength.

Throughout his emotional traumas, Graves remained professional. In May, he performed well on his annual lecturing visit in the United States; during the summer, he worked on the addresses he was to deliver at Oxford in the autumn.

He had heard the news about Oxford at the beginning of the year. Auden, from whom he was to take over the five-year post as Visiting Professor of Poetry, had supported his election. He sent Graves a friendly letter, offering to let him have the name of his own writer for the traditional Latin oration.[15] (It must have delighted Graves to answer, coolly, that he would be writing his own Latin speech.) But the main worker behind the scenes had been Graves's old friend Enid Starkie, who visited Deyá with her husband in the early Fifties. She was the rallier and persuader who urged her colleagues to give Graves the MA without which he could not, technically, be permitted to hold the post.[16]

Graves's second brood were beginning to leave home. William finished his three years of reading geology at London University in the summer of 1961. After refusing an invitation to go mushroom-hunting in Mexico with Gordon Wasson, he decided to go to Texas where some friends of Wasson's had offered him an introduction to the oil world. The choice was deliberate; William had suffered from being the son of a famous man and had not, as yet, shown any sign of having inherited his father's literary gifts. He was intelligent, but he was not an intellectual. Wisely, he struck out for a world in which his father's name meant little or nothing.

Lucia, who looked like becoming the most academic of the family after applying herself to books instead of ballet-dancing, was at a loose end in her pre-university year. In August she accompanied her father on a brief trip to Greece, where he was appearing in a television film, before going to share a flat with Stella Reeves in Madrid until she went to read Modern Languages, specializing in Catalan, at St Anne's, Oxford. Juan, lacking in academic skills, was written up in his father's letters as a skier of near-Olympic prowess. Once, he had dreamed that Juan would become a poet; now, he placed all his hopes in eight-year-old Tomas, a bright, cheerful little boy. He was put down for Bedales, an English public school which encouraged individual artistic talent to flourish.

Raphael Patai had been doing most of the work on the *Hebrew Myths* during 1961; in September, he and his wife Ann came to Mallorca to go over some of the finer points of the argument. They stayed, at Graves's insistence, at the Posada and survived the shock of discovering that they shared an outside privy, where a plank with a hole cut in it bridged a small, dank pit, with the Graveses' donkey, Isabella. The Patais, who had wanted to stay at a local hotel, were puzzled that Graves thought such a primitive house would provide them with a more agreeable experience.[17]

Patai was an observant guest. He has given an excellent account of Graves as he appeared in the early Sixties, and of his way of life.[18] They worked together in the mornings and swam or walked in the afternoons, Graves going out in shorts, ankle socks and a short-sleeved white shirt with a wide straw-brimmed hat. His body, thinner by a stone after the traumatic loss of Margot, was lean and muscular. His face, in Patai's view, 'was a perfect human counterpart in miniature of the rocky Majorcan coastline'.[19]

To a man who was used to working in a scholar's environment, it was baffling to understand how Graves could tolerate the constant disturbance of visitors wandering in and out of the house. Equally distracting was Graves's own habit, which Patai remembered from their conversations in New York, of wandering off in all directions from the subject in hand. There was one route towards which his thoughts seemed always now to tend; Karl caustically explained that his employer was having problems with the latest incarnation of the White Goddess. When Patai left, he was given a letter to post from Barcelona to Margot's French address.

It was the poetic side of Graves which impressed his guest most during his visit. He spoke, in a matter-of-fact voice, about his belief in ghosts, and about the ancient matriarchies which he believed had once governed most parts of the world. He talked, too, about his enduring conviction that he had been saved for a purpose from death in the First World War. Patai, a rational man, was startled to find himself falling under the spell of what he described as the 'magic aura that emanated from the personality of Graves'. Against his own judgement, he was persuaded that there was another route to knowledge than scholarship,

> that beyond the world of mental exertion, rational judgement, events that could be observed and categorized, results that could be reached by deductive processes, there was another world that revealed itself only to a chosen few, a world in which logic was not king, and certainties were reached by an intuitive grasp akin to revelation.[20]

In October 1961, pausing for a brief sentimental visit to the Château de la Chevrie, Beryl and Graves travelled to England in the silver Land-Rover which dated from Robin Blyth's disastrous visit. Fired by his talks with Patai, Graves was in the right mood to deliver an address which he had written earlier that summer for the Hillel Foundation on the difference between Hebrew and Greek myths. It was given to an audience of 1,300 and was, so Graves told Patai, 'a resounding popular success'.[21] The size of the audience and the fact that Graves had presented the Hebrew myths as the source of Western democracy should have guaranteed this; in fact, the lecture triggered an outburst of fury from the more conservative rabbis who thought that a charge of falsehood had been levelled at their sacred texts. Graves, as usual, rode out the storm with good cheer and without retracting a word.

For the rest of the autumn, Graves and Beryl moved between Sally Chilver's Maida Vale home, a gloomy Edwardian flat on Boars Hill, and a set of rooms in the centre of Oxford, provided by his old college, St John's, for teaching purposes. By 1965, the fifth and final year of his Oxford tenure as Visiting Professor of Poetry, Graves was able to attract audiences of well over a thousand, many of them travelling from Cambridge and London; even in 1961, his first year, the audiences who came to hear him at the Oxford Playhouse were twice the size which had been anticipated. In his opening term, Graves told the students about his dislike of Virgil, whose work as an 'anti-poet' he contrasted to the tradition of dedicated 'muse-poets', reaching back from himself, via Coleridge and Keats, to his beloved John Skelton. This took up the first two lectures; the third was a more intimate discussion of the meaning of the term 'personal muse'. Graves was ready, as he had not been in the Thirties, to acknowledge Laura Riding as one of a sequence of muse-women briefly invested with the Goddess's powers. 'I know a good deal about the Muse now,' he wrote to Tom Matthews, 'and am able to separate the mythic from the personal better; I feel now that I failed Laura no less than she failed me . . . We were premature.'[22]

The return to Oxford had been an unnerving prospect; he was relieved to find himself welcomed back by old university friends like the medieval scholar Nevill Coghill, who now looked as startlingly like one of the emperors whose heads circle the Sheldonian as did Graves himself. Boars Hill was peopled by strangers, but the colleges were unaltered. Much though Graves cherished his role as the warrior at the gate, he was content, for a short time, to be given the sense that he did also have a place inside the city. It had been, he wrote to Patai in December, 'a wonderful time'.[23]

★　　★　　★

Raphael Patai was one of the few men to escape being taken into Graves's confidence about his feelings for Margot over the next two years. In her absence, Graves continued to pour out his love and his frustration in a stream of poems which, remembering James Reeves's comments, he hesitated to publish. They were personal and they could be seen as a betrayal of his wife, but so, arguably, could the Oxford lectures and tutorials at which, until his retirement in 1965, he had continued to dilate on the role of the muse and a black goddess of wisdom whose domain lay beyond the torments devised by her crueller, paler sister.

Margot, even to Graves's adoring eyes, did not appear to have the miraculous healing qualities of the Black Goddess, but she was, until the summer of 1963, the source of his inspiration. Her departure with Alastair Reid in April 1961 had prompted poems of grief and bewilderment. When he returned to Deyá after delivering the Latin oration at Oxford in June 1962, he found a letter telling him that Margot was alone again and that she contemplated making a visit to Mallorca at the end of the summer.

Graves was overjoyed. When William returned from his first oilfield experiences in July, he found his mother grieving for her father, Sir Harry Pritchard, who had recently died, and his father in the process of buying a pretty ruined house for Margot to use as her private home. He was always with Beryl, but he talked, incessantly, of Margot.

Not all of Graves's friends were able to understand that the more passionately he swore to devote himself to Margot, the more he felt obliged to defend and honour his loyal, astonishingly discreet, wife. So, when their Jamaican neighbour, Alston Anderson, wrote Beryl a letter in which he used explicit sexual language, he was sternly rebuked. 'She is NOT a person to write obscenities to. Do you realize what you wrote to her?' A sentence or two on, Graves chided Anderson for indulgence. 'I'm afraid you've got to the point of no return in your drinking and doping. It's bad for work, too.'[24] The warning was a kind one – Anderson, a heavy drinker, was dead within two years – and yet the whole letter seemed inappropriate from a man who extolled hallucinogenic experiences and talked only of his love for the 'other woman'.

To Graves, the division was clear. If Margot inspired him, his debt to Beryl was all the larger. Her loyalty was a crucial ingredient of the lethal emotional cocktail he had mixed for himself. He knew exactly what he owed to her. And so, as his passion for Margot grew increasingly extravagant and public, and as the interviewers relentlessly bent their questions in the direction of muse-love, he felt impelled to defend the woman he seemed to reject.

Laura Riding knew nothing of Robert Graves's relationship with Margot, but she had read *The White Goddess* and she had probably heard about his references to her as a personal muse in the 1961 Oxford lectures. Since the literary magazine *Shenandoah* was well known to her, she had probably also heard about its plan to devote a whole issue to Graves, including an essay by Auden entitled 'Poet of Honour'. In July 1962 she began a long public campaign to expose what she felt to be the truth about her former partner.

Riding was not inclined to be courteous. Writing to the *Times Literary Supplement* on 16 July 1962, she referred to three decades of 'thieveries from my thought' by Graves, a 'fundamentally vulgar' man. Graves, as a regular reader of the *TLS*, must have seen the letter, but he made no comment.* For him, Laura Riding belonged in the past. He had no more interest in her; writing to Tom Matthews in 1960, he referred to her as having 'knowingly' thrown herself into a bottomless gulf when she renounced her vocation as a poet in 1939.[25] He continued to admire and praise her poetry, but her influence over him had been broken when he erected the White Goddess as his personal deity in her place. For Riding, however, Graves now replaced Geoffrey Phibbs as a daemonic figure in her personal mythology. Graves, of the two men, was the more despicable, in that he had made himself famous through his use of her own ideas. This was the belief which fuelled Riding's hatred of Graves for the last three decades of her life.

Graves spent a sociable and cheerful summer in Deyá, waiting for Margot's promised arrival. Dick Graves's grandson Simon Gough had made, with the help of young Tomas Graves, a new theatre for the annual birthday play, laying concrete steps into the side of a hill to create a miniature amphitheatre under the vast natural one created by the Teix mountain. The theatre opened, in front of an audience which included Ricardo Sicre, Cicely Gittes, Isla Cameron, James Metcalf and his new Mexican wife, Pilar, with *The Oracle*. This was more successful than many of the birthday plays had been in the past; Ursula Vaughan Williams, writing to Graves in the autumn, requested a second performance for which she and Ralph were prepared to bring appropriate robes and wreaths.[26]

Graves had met Kingsley Amis when he gave his Latin oration in June. He liked him. In August, Amis, together with his wife Hilly and their three children, was a guest at the Posada while he gathered material for an article about Graves. Like all those who came to interview Graves in the Fifties and early Sixties, Amis was struck by the breadth of Graves's knowledge and by the playful manner in which he discussed what were evidently serious beliefs. Amis was charmed, but he was also exhausted by the time he returned to England; Hilly had watched with sympathy as her rotund husband toiled up and down the hillside behind his military-marching companion. Graves, at sixty-seven, could still outwalk everybody he knew.[27]

Frank though Graves was in his discussion of muse-poetry and

---

* It may have been only coincidence but the main theme of Graves's 1962 Oxford addresses was poetic vulgarity. He had only rarely used the word before; it had always been a firm favourite with Laura.

of the real woman who was needed to inspire it, interviewers learned little about his family life or his longing for privacy in the summers when visitors swarmed through the house at all hours. So Amis was not shown the rough steps up to the little shepherd's hut above Canelluñ which Graves planned to use when writing his poems and letters. Neither was he told about Graves's concern about his daughter, Catherine Dalton, whose husband's premature death the previous year had left her with very little money and five children. Graves sent cheques, but it was Jenny who flew out to Australia and listened, sceptically, to Catherine's theory that her husband had been deliberately eliminated.

Beryl made no public objection to Margot. She allowed her husband to assure their friends that she, as much as he, had been shocked by Margot's affair with Reid. It was easier and less embarrassing to treat a muse as a family friend;[28] nevertheless, she found a reason to go to England just as Margot returned to Mallorca. At the end of August, Graves wrote to reassure her that their marriage remained intact. Margot was staying at the Posada – her house was not yet ready – and getting along beautifully with everybody. Rosaleen, his sister, had just left, he had finished writing his third lecture and everything was calm and happy. 'You know I love you, you, you,' he went on, 'with all the natural warmth of my heart and with all the gratitude and admiration and devotion you could ever demand, and still more so because you do not grudge me this other strange thing with M.'[29]

During the autumn, Beryl, Graves and Margot lived a shared life. Margot, together with Beryl, attended the first of the 1962 Oxford lectures; when the Graveses returned to London, to rent an over-heated house in Montagu Square, Margot was an almost daily visitor. To the reader of Graves's diary, she sounds like a cosy member of the family, but Selwyn Jepson, who had been requested to have her to stay for a weekend, was not so sure. Always blunt, he told Graves that his wife Tania saw Margot as a home-breaker, while he saw a good-looking troublemaker who would always be able to take care of herself. Like James Reeves, he was baffled by Graves's desire to publicize what seemed to them a most improper relationship.[30] Graves's own view, that discretion was a form of dishonesty, was not acceptable to these more conventional husbands.

★   ★   ★

'I am very up and down these days,' Graves wrote to Isla Cameron at the beginning of 1963. He spoke of feeling confused by his movements between America, Oxford, London and Spain, 'but this is my home and this is where I work, under Karl my peppery task-master'. Isla had asked how Margot was, to which he responded, tartly, 'I guess she's all right from a couple of cables she sent her lawyer about a Palma flat. She always is.'[31]

Intuition or carelessness made Margot behave in exactly the way Graves required to produce the tension between hope and despair in his poems to her. Having shown nothing but affection for him throughout the autumn, she left England for New York, where, wistfully, Graves asked some of his younger friends to keep an eye on her.[32]

Margot asked for money; then she asked for help in legal arrangements about her Palma flat; then she asked for contact addresses in New York. Graves did as she requested and was rewarded, as he sadly noted in his diary, with silence.[33] To the Amis family, who returned to rent a house while Kingsley did a formal interview with Graves, no trauma was apparent;[34] internally, Graves was raging with grief and jealousy of imagined rivals. He poured his feelings out in some of his best late poems, the agonizing 'A Last Poem' ('A last poem, and a very last, and yet another – / O, when can I give over? / Must I drive the pen until blood bursts from my nails . . .') and 'The Three-Faced', printed here complete.

> Who calls her two-faced? Faces, she has three:
> The first inscrutable, for the outer world;
> The second, shrouded in self-contemplation;
> The third, her face of love,
> Once for an endless moment turned on me.[35]

On 28 April, Graves went to New York on a lecture tour. Having hoped that Margot would be at the airport, he noted, with disappointment, that nobody had come to meet him. But a few days later, James Reeves received a letter written from Gordon Wasson's home in New York, telling him that 'all the unhappiness of three years has peeled away. I wrote a poem two days ago beginning: "Not to sleep all night long, for pure joy . . ." which is one of the few poems of utter happiness ever written.'[36] Since the only events recorded in Graves's diary for that day are a lunch with Margot and a meeting with his American agent, Willis Wing, the source of the joy is clear.

His happiness was short-lived. Margot had been unwilling at first to reveal that she was living with a man. He was, Graves told Idries Shah on 6 May, rich and sweet and young; this had not prevented Graves from speaking his mind. Margot had been understandably furious, before showing signs that she might be ready to relent.[37] On the same day that he wrote to Shah, Graves sent Margot a painful and self-humiliating letter, filled with phrases from his poems. After praising the 'goodness and directness and simplicity' of her new companion, he urged her to realize that she still needed a poet just as badly as he needed a muse. The argument he made was a curious one. He did not suggest that Margot should give up her friend, but that she should follow his own example and try to live two private lives which would be 'wholly clear and reconcilable'.[38]

A week later, Graves flew to Boston to give a lecture at MIT to an audience he assumed would be composed entirely of scientists. He called it 'Nine Hundred Iron Chariots'. Cicely Gittes, who was present, was astonished by the hostility of his tone.[39] A composer herself, she was conscious that many of the listeners were musicians as well as scientists; it embarrassed her to hear them being addressed as though they were incapable of understanding anything outside a test-tube, and being ordered to follow the Goddess's irrational commands. But this had always been Graves's attitude. Science, to him, was the enemy of everything he revered, and scientists were foreigners to the state of creative trance. Their only chance, in his view, was to listen to the voice of the Goddess; his words suggested that they would never be privileged to hear her.[40]

Graves was still tightly in control of his personal unhappiness when he returned to New York, to go to a drinks party given for him by the Patais – they could not know that this was the kind of social occasion Graves most hated – and to give a public talk at the 92nd Street YMCA on the *Hebrew Myths* with Patai. He managed it with élan. Patai was unaware that any personal crisis existed.[41]

Graves had, as he was bitterly aware, a certain remaining usefulness for Margot because of his contacts. Before he returned to Deyá, he went to see Richard Avedon about some photographs of her, to which he proposed to offer accompanying poems. Margot, full of gratitude, came to the airport to see him off.

He should have been devastated. His spirits were low during the next month. But, when Kenneth and Kathleen Tynan visited Deyá in mid-July, they found Graves in high spirits, 'charming and skittish . . . he impressed us by diving into the sea from the highest rock.'[42] Even before Margot disclosed that she had a lover, he had begun to look for an alternative source of inspiration.

★   ★   ★

By the time that Amelia Maria-Theresa Laraçuen arrived to spend the summer of 1957 in Deyá, she had become Cindy Lee, the wife of a professional diver, Owen Lee. Owen occasionally accompanied Alastair Reid on his long sailing expeditions to South America; Cindy and he, together with their friends Margie Alston, Ralph Jacobs and Helen Morningstar, formed a small American group who spent their summers together in Deyá and who, occasionally, joined Graves for dinners in Palma.

Cindy was in her late twenties in 1957. A small, striking-looking woman with curling dark hair and a lively, attractive face, she had a partly Mexican background and a ferocious temper. In 1961 she asked Graves for protection from the police after stabbing her husband with a knife in a quarrel and leaving him for dead.[43] Lee survived; the marriage did not.

Cindy's name appears in Graves's diary entries for his visits to New York in 1960 to 1962. He never saw her alone. Usually she was with Ralph Jacobs, a gentle homosexual schoolteacher. In 1962 she came to Deyá with a new boyfriend, a young American poet called Howard Hart. A heavy drinker, Hart had not appeared to advantage, but Graves was inclined to take a charitable view of his behaviour. Hart was, he wrote to Jacobs, 'a bit out of his depth here, that's all'.[44]

This letter was written in January 1963, when Graves was in despair about Margot's absence in New York and begging Jacobs to find out what she was doing. But he was also becoming increasingly attached to Cindy. Jacobs had warned him earlier in the month that Cindy had a difficult nature; Graves responded sharply. Cindy was not to be referred to as if she was 'a neurotic casualty . . . Cindy's fine.'[45] In his diary, he noted that Cindy had given him an idea for a new poem.

The fact that Cindy could be seen as a source of inspiration shows that Graves's thoughts were straying from Margot three months before his visit to New York. On 10 May, four days after Graves's quarrel with Margot's boyfriend, he noted in his diary that 'Cindy shopped for me'. Before the end of the month, Cindy knew enough for him to inform his diary that she felt Margot had treated him badly. When the Tynans visited Graves in July and found him so charming and skittish, he had the best of reasons to be in high spirits. Cindy was in Deyá and seeing Graves almost every day. By the early autumn, the question only remained of whether Margot was prepared formally to relinquish her role as the poet's muse. Margot, who was making arrangements for her wedding to the film producer and director, Mike Nichols, was now happy to do so.

CHAPTER THIRTY-THREE

THE POET AND HIS MUSE

Who here can blame me if I alone am poet,
If none other has dared to accept the fate
Of death and again death in the Muse's house?
From 'Ibycus in Samos', 1962

The moment has come to ask exactly what Graves's relation to his muses was, and how much, with the female inspirations of his later work, he was – consciously or unconsciously – repeating his earlier life with Riding. Who controlled whom? Conventionally, Graves is seen as a man who loved women and who bound himself to them. That is a simplistic interpretation. The muses, among whom Laura Riding must be included, were shaped to his imaginative needs, not he to theirs. The muse-relationships of his later life show striking parallels with the earlier, formative one.

But you, my love, where had you then your station?
Seeing that on this common earth together
We go not distant from each other
I knew you near me in that strange region,

So searched for you, in hope to see you stand
On some near olive-terrace, in the heat,
The left-hand glove drawn on your right hand,
The empty snake's egg perfect at your feet –
                    From 'The Terraced Valley', 1930

We stood together, side by side, rooted
At the iron heart of circumambient hills,
Parents to a new age, weeping in awe
That the lot had fallen, of all mankind, on us
Now sealed as love's exemplars.
                    From 'Iron Palace', 1965

The first of these two poems was written for Laura Riding, the second for Cindy Lee. The setting is identical, the mountain-bound valley of Deyá, linked to Delphi in Graves's mind as a place filled with ancient magic. Thirty-five years apart, the two poems celebrate the idea of a muse whose magical powers to heal and enlighten link her to the poet, her creator. Riding comes to the valley at the summons of the poet. Cindy is chained to it by the poet's will:

Woman, wild and hard as the truth may be,
Nothing can circumvent it. We stand coupled
With chains, who otherwise might live apart
Conveniently paired, each with another,
And slide securely graveward.
                    From 'Iron Palace'

Graves's poems of homage and acts of servitude suggest that Riding was the dominant member of their partnership. The facts point in the opposite direction. He fitted her into the fantasy of powerful, unattainable womanhood which can be traced all the way back to his childish awe of Amy Graves.

In 1920, Graves wrote the poem 'Outlaws' in which his youthful sense of the muse-woman as a forgotten source of poetic power was reflected in a vision of a drumming muse 'Banished to woods and a sickly moon / Shrunk to mere bogey things / Who spoke with thunder once at noon / To prostrate kings.'[1] His conversations with Dr William Rivers in 1920 and 1921 opened his eyes to the possibility of a primitive world in which women had ruled their tribes and been placed by men above the gods. By the summer of 1924, when Graves wrote the short novel *My Head! My Head!*, he had established to his own satisfaction and, doubtless, with the approval of his feminist wife, the existence of such an epoch. He used the book to describe, in Elisha's words, a period when it was thought that women were – when they walked alone – possessed by ghosts who, in time, were born as their children:

> and woman was held to be of the gods and sacred because she was possessed of those ghosts whom she bore as children: the mother ruled and all the possessions of the family were the mother's right.[2]

Men, in Elisha's account, established themselves as rulers and erected male gods only after the connection had been made between intercourse and childbirth. 'Thus the mother lost her rule in the family and the father assumed it easily, for he was of greater bodily strength. This was the beginning of our present misery when woman was despised and put into subjection to men . . .'[3]

My Head! My Head! was the book in which Graves set out the ideas which eventually led to *The White Goddess*. By 1924 he already saw it as his duty to redress the injustice done to women and resolved, when he found the appropriate woman, to acknowledge her powers, for 'a god is nothing, a shadow, a ghost, unless he be obeyed; then listen to the sequel.'[4]

The sequel was Graves's discovery of Laura Riding, a brilliant and little-known young poet who had begun publicly to describe herself as a prophet in 1925. Her clear vision of herself and her belief in her supernatural powers made her an ideal candidate for Graves's requirements of a living goddess. (The distinction between the Goddess and the woman she inhabited was not yet clearly drawn in his mind.) He trumpeted Riding's miraculous qualities to everybody he knew, demanding that they honour her. He encouraged Geoffrey Phibbs to join them, adding the necessary rival to the myth which was central to his idea of the Goddess who stands, like Isis, between rival brother deities. He satisfied his belief that Riding, like the women chiefs of ancient societies, should have first right over all family possessions by putting the Deyá properties in her name. He lambasted anybody who questioned her authority. He continued to venerate her until, by renouncing poetry and her mission to bring peace to the world, she forfeited her position as his muse.

Graves is often presented as a champion of women. This did not mean that he recognized them as the intellectual equals of men. The qualities he praised were those which made them suitable muses. When he spoke of Laura Riding and – in his Oxford lecture on the personal muse – of Margot, as being natural facts, unassailable as forest fire, he was honouring what he saw as the womanly gifts of instinct and intuitive knowledge. He was ready to use women as his assistants; publicly, he overlooked the contributions they made to his work. Thus, while privately admitting that Eva Meyerowitz's book of 1952, *Akan Traditions of Origin*, had been an immensely helpful source when he was writing *The Greek Myths*, a debt which Graves generously repaid by working over one of her typescripts in detail, no public acknowledgement was made. His failure to acknowledge Riding's contribution to his view of the Goddess was the chief cause of her bitterness in later years.

His was the controlling hand. Generous though Graves was to his muses, he, finally, reserved the right to divest them of authority and ownership if they betrayed him. The Goddess, in Graves's increasingly complex interpretations of her authority, could leave a woman as abruptly as she entered her. When he turned to a new muse, the Goddess turned with him and endowed her with miraculous powers. But those powers were clearly said by Graves, in his poem 'In Her Praise' and elsewhere, to have a limited time-span of three or four years. When the White Goddess proved insufficiently binding, he discovered a black one who stood above her.

This imaginative control did not mean that Graves escaped pain in his muse-relationships. Neither did he wish to do so, regarding love as a soldierly virtue in which pain was part of the discipline. Laura and Cindy caused him more emotional damage than any other women, but Margot was not far behind. Having knowingly courted the distress for the sake of his poetry, Graves bore no grudges towards its givers. 'I need no pity from my friends,' he wrote in 1964. 'These things are occupational hazards for poets . . .'[5] As a giver, he was as munificent as Timon of Athens. Laura had been offered everything he could afford to bestow; Cindy was given enough to build herself a house in Mexico, together with a home in Deyá, jewels, and the copyright of all the letters and poems Graves wrote, as he believed, under her inspiration. The best present which she could offer in return, he told her, was simply to go on receiving.[6] His muse was most obliging in this respect.

In life, he was generous to his muses; in his poetry, he made them pay heavily for their betrayals. Here, they were ceremoniously stripped of their powers when they began to lose interest or to find other men. All his old puritanical horror of sex rose up again in the 1963 sequence of poems which presented Margot as a treacherous and lustful Eurydice, beyond the rescue of Graves's heroic Prince Orpheus.

'Food of the Dead' and 'Eurydice' are among the most disturbing poems Graves wrote about women since his disgusted vision in 'The Succubus', in the 1930s, of a slobbering, paunchy, lust-driven phantom. In 'Food of the Dead', Margot, having betrayed him once with Reid, has again 'warmed the serpent at her thighs / For a new progress through new wards of hell'.[7] In 'Eurydice' the progress begins. 'Speak, fly in her amber ring; speak, horse of gold!' Graves writes, referring to gifts which he had made to Margot and which are described in his diary:

What gift did I ever grudge her, or help withhold?
In a mirror I watch blood trickling down the wall –
Is it mine? Yet still I stand here, proud and tall.

Look where she shines, with a borrowed blaze of light
Among the cowardly, faceless, lost, unright,
Clasping a naked imp to either breast –
Am I not oppressed, oppressed, three times oppressed?

She has gnawn at corpse-flesh till her breath stank,
Paired with a jackal, grown distraught and lank,
Crept home, accepted solace, but then again
Flown off to chain truth back with an iron chain.[8]

This is the ugly side of Graves's love, ugly because it shows him cannibalizing the life of an agreeable and graceful young woman to suit his own mythical ends, ugly because it is not a finished poem – the earlier, more careful Graves would not have allowed that double use of 'chain' – and ugly because it is so at odds with his creed of honour and integrity to publish this hideous caricature of a chosen muse. A Rochester or a Pope might have done the same, but those poets had not spent their lives proclaiming a passionate wish to honour women.

'To Beguile and Betray' is the poem which predicted the end of Margot's musedom. Here Graves declared it to be an inevitable consequence of her loss of 'the divine need-fire / By true love kindled in [the muse-women]'.

> Have you not watched
> The immanent Goddess fade from their brows
> When they make private to her mysteries
> Some whip-scarred rogue from the hulks, some painted clown
> From the pantomime – and afterwards accuse you
> Of jealous hankering for the mandalot
> Rather than horror and sick foreboding
> That she will never return to the same house?[9]

The reference to the hulks or ships links the rogue to Alastair Reid, who went on long and adventurous sailing expeditions every year, while Mike Nichols, who was more engaged by the theatre than by films in 1963, is the pantomime clown. Denying jealousy, Graves reveals it by the way his rivals are turned into caricatures while he remains the noble and generous Orpheus.

By careful arrangement of his muse-poems into sequences, Graves reconstructed life as a myth under his own control; he terminated Margot's musedom with the sour 'I Will Write', although it was not his final poem to her. Divested of power and romance, she was presented as a fickle girlfriend with a light regard for her promises to write letters. And who cares? is the mood of this poem, which ends, 'There are no mails in a city of the dead.'[10] The next poem, 'Bird of Paradise', marked the beginning of sequence XVI, a celebration of Cindy Lee.

★ ★ ★

William Graves had been away working in oilfields and, thus, absent from Deyá for most of Margot's reign as muse. In September 1963, after spending a few days with his father at Delphi, where Graves was being filmed as he introduced plays acted by the Greek National Theatre, William received a letter from him. It said nothing about the archaeology course at Oxford which Graves had encouraged him to take. Instead, it carried an enthusiastic account of Cindy Lee. Cindy, Graves reported, was really called Emelia [*sic*] Maria-Theresa Laraçuen, and her father's family had been heroic fighters in Mexico. Idries Shah and Graves had both been astonished by her disclosures. 'It's staggering what lies behind that fun and games façade,' Graves told his sceptical son.[11] At about the same time, Graves told Ralph Jacobs, confusingly, that he and Cindy had just been out to dinner in Palma, leaving Beryl at home, but that he would prefer Ralph not to gossip about their relationship because 'trouble has been made with Beryl'. Beryl, it seems, had for once expressed hostility to a muse-relationship, and was distressed by the fact that Graves was being so public about his new love. In the same letter to Jacobs, Graves tried to justify his behaviour. The term 'muse' was rejected. Cindy was something finer.

> 'Muse' connotes cruelty and suffering, and the Muse always goes back to cohabitation with serpents and eating corpse flesh. Cindy is not that sort . . . only good comes of our new bond of understanding.[12]

To someone unacquainted with the poems in which Margot was being transformed into a necrophiliac Eurydice in the autumn of 1963, the distinction was a baffling one. Knowing Cindy as a neurotic and wild young woman, it was hard for Jacobs to guess what the nature of this new understanding might be.

By the time of the third autumn series of Oxford lectures in 1963, Graves had formulated a poetic explanation for his need to move on from Margot to Cindy. The Black Goddess, a figure loosely based on Sufic concepts and on the various well-known cults of black madonnas and virgins, was introduced to his student audience as a higher figure than the White Goddess and the muse she inhabits. The Black Goddess will only accept the poet when he has passed, uncomplaining, through all the trials set by her white sister. With that achieved, she is able to offer him a certain and enduring love.[13] This was to be Cindy's role.

To his friends, it was easier to see Cindy as an unsuitable mistress than as a Black Goddess. She had sexual magnetism, and it was that which they felt had drawn Graves to her. Patai, who only encountered her briefly in New York in 1964, noticed the look she gave him and disliked her for it. 'I was seized with pity for the ageing poet caught in the web of a fickle muse.'[14] To two open-minded neighbours in Deyá, Cindy appeared to answer a need Graves felt for strong, unconventional women. They observed her outrageous behaviour, and that Graves humoured and enjoyed it. On one occasion, in a restaurant, they saw Cindy upturn a bowl of Indonesian food on Graves's head by way of showing that she disagreed with him. Graves laughed.[15]

Graves's insistence on Cindy's goodness and her power to help him enabled him to gloss over the less presentable side of their relationship. He was sexually enthralled by her and the letters which, in 1964, told American friends that they had achieved a new non-sexual union suggest that this had not been the case in 1963.[16]

What was apparent to Graves's friends must also have been apparent to Beryl. Publicly, she continued to support her husband; the trouble referred to in his letter to Ralph Jacobs is likely to have been of the kind caused when well-meaning friends urge a loyal wife to defend her rights. A loyal wife, in these circumstances, often feels more humiliated by the intrusive friends than by the relationship which she has decided to accept. Beryl continued to take the view that acquiescence was the wisest course. Saying nothing, she looked on with rueful sympathy as her husband, increasingly, exposed himself to ridicule, both in the village and among their English friends, by his extravagant devotion. She did not believe in the miraculous powers which Graves claimed for Cindy, but she knew, better than most, that it was an essential part of Graves's mythology that Cindy should have these attributes.[17]

The few letters from Cindy Lee which are available show a warm, confused, immature mind.[18] She was, evidently, torn between being proud of her role as a muse and alarmed by the prospect of a lifelong commitment. In a letter of 1964 to Ava Gardner, whom she greatly admired, she confides that she has no intention of becoming an old man's nurse-companion, being unable to offer 'the good and excellent care' that Beryl can give. She thinks it a pity that Graves is so determined not to grow old in the way Beryl wishes. She complains bitterly about the food in Mallorca, the coldness of the winter months and the boredom she feels when Graves is not around, for 'he's the sun, verdad'. She devotes the rest of the letter to descriptions of gold sandals and her newly found sense of kinship with Ava and her friends. 'You're REAL people.'[19]

In America, both Cindy and Graves confided in their mutual friends, Ralph Jacobs and John Benson-Brooks, a composer who had come into Graves's life through a meeting at one of Len Lye's parties in New York. The letters between Benson-Brooks, Jacobs and Graves show that both men were devoted to Graves, and seriously worried about the effect on his health and mental stability of an affair with a volatile and drug-dependent young woman. Their advice went unheeded; however badly Cindy betrayed him, Graves always had an explanation, and a hope that things would improve.[20]

Cindy Lee has proved impossible to track down. Even the affectionate letters of her friends, Benson-Brooks and Jacobs, make it hard to conceive of her as the inspiration of some of Graves's loveliest late poems and songs. The answer, of course, is that the muses themselves were no more than flints to the iron. Cindy Lee's character is as irrelevant to Graves's poetry as Laura Riding's. The poems show what he sought from these women, not who they were. All were recast in Graves's own mould, as incarnations of a goddess who made them a gift to his inspiration.

★   ★   ★

'My trouble is that I know too much of the craft of poetry, so that even non-poems read beautifully,' Graves wrote to Ruth Fainlight in 1969. 'But O how bored I can be, reading them a month later.'[21] Six years later, he had lost the power to make such judgements and all these 'non-poems' were thrown into the embarrassing, unwieldy *Collected Poems 1975* which was his last.

Purists will always prefer the early work. There are, undeniably, aspects of the Sixties poems which jar: the recurring emphasis on a male code of honour and on a permissible female code of deception; the talk of unbreakable bonds and mystic understandings; the decorative symbols which appear as Graves, a self-conscious Leo, identifies himself with rampant lions and blazing suns while Cindy becomes the palm tree which represented her in the I Ching (Graves learned from her to study this with avid interest). Among these ornate formulations, however, there are delicate songs and ballads to show how complete Graves's mastery of the traditional genre remained, and sour poems like 'Wigs and Beards' to demonstrate his enduring gift for satire. There are also a handful of lovely, mocking love-poems which deserve a place in every twentieth-century anthology. As his letter to Ruth Fainlight suggests, his craftsmanship remained, giving him masterly control of form, technique, vocabulary. But Graves had convinced himself that his craft was of no value unless he had an object of love, and pain, on which to deploy it. Deprived of that emotional torment and ecstasy, he foresaw and feared the death of his inspiration.

Writing to his sympathetic but anxious friends in the years 1963–7, he constantly used the song-refrain, 'But I'm sticking to the Union' to emphasize his determination not to give up. It was a time of unbearable tension, when Graves seemed to everyone who knew him to be sad and humiliated. But the poems often tell another story, of a grandfather whose refusal to grow old soberly meant that he could write with the gaiety and tenderness of a man half his age. The muses did not bring him joy, but they gave him the will to write and, at the best of times, a feeling of triumph.

> The King of Hearts a broadsword bears,
>   The Queen of Hearts, a rose –
> Though why, not every gambler cares
>   Or cartomancer knows.
>
> Be beauty yours, be honour mine,
>   Yet sword and rose are one:
> Great emblems that in love combine
>   Until the dealing's done;
>
> For no card, whether small or face,
>   Shall overtrump our two
> Except that Heart of Hearts, the Ace,
>   To which their title's due.[22]

CHAPTER THIRTY-FOUR

1963–1967

THE BLACK GODDESS

CINDY LEE CONTINUED TO DIVIDE HER TIME BETWEEN MALLORCA and America in 1963–4. She was in New York early in 1964, having been put in charge by Graves of the arrangements for his annual lecture tour. At the beginning of February, Graves heard that his daughter Jenny had died in England of a brain haemorrhage after being hospitalized for a week. Her collapse, after lunch with friends, was sudden, but there had been signs that she was far from well when she came to Deyá in the autumn to talk about film and musical projects. 'Poor Jenny . . . Her visit here was most peculiar and sad,' Graves wrote to Selwyn Jepson.[1] Jenny had become the closest to him of all his children. In many ways, he had seen his own character reflected in hers. Jenny, like her father, was generous, romantic and determined. She had fought all her battles bravely; she had refused to be discouraged by her defeats. She had a life-enhancing quality of her own which had won her many friends; she had earned her father's respect by her readiness to speak up on behalf of her siblings when she felt that Graves – always 'Robert' to his daughter – was not doing all that he should for them. Even their ill-fated film ventures had seemed enjoyable when Jenny was there to share them with. He would miss her.

As always, Graves offered little public indication of grief. The fact that his passport was in Barcelona while the visa was being renewed gave him a good reason not to attend the funeral; William went in his place. Graves's own contribution was his resolve to finish writing the story of Solomon and Sheba as a tribute to Jenny; his enthusiasm for the project was fired by the sense that Cindy was now playing Sheba to his own Solomon. (The project was never completed, although Graves did, in 1973, publish a version of Solomon's *The Song of Songs*, with an additional commentary.)

The writer Richard Hughes came with his family to the Posada as Graves's guests at the end of January 1964, while Douglas and Jane Glass, friends from the Galmpton years, stayed in another of the family homes. Hughes enjoyed himself, but he got no work done during his month-long visit and was impressed by Graves's self-discipline. He heard about the plans Graves had to restore two houses opposite Deyá's new museum as an arts centre; there was talk, too, of turning them into homes for William and for Lucia, who had announced that she wanted to marry her drummer boyfriend Ramón Farrán as soon as she had finished her degree at Oxford.

Graves joined Cindy at the end of February in New York for a hectic schedule. Promoting the *Hebrew Myths* on radio with Raphael Patai, he was, Patai noticed, 'his usual self: witty, rambling, somewhat disconcerting.'[2] Privately, he complimented Graves on the meticulous stylistic changes which he had been making to the final proofs of their book. Both men were delighted with it.

Duty did not prevent Graves from attending to his muse. Determined to please, he allowed Cindy to drag him out to late-night parties, the last of which ended in an all-night 'jam session'. He rearranged the dates in his diary to conceal the fact that the trip ended by his taking Cindy to Madrid for four days before returning to Palma. In Madrid, Cindy was introduced to Ava Gardner and to Ricardo Sicre. Ricardo was unimpressed. 'She's plain awful and does not have a brain on her shoulders . . .' he wrote to Karl Gay. 'At least Margot had a bit of spark.'[3]

The relationship had become close enough for Graves to write to Ava from Deyá that he and 'Aemile', as he now called her, were sharing a bed while he wrote one of his lectures for Oxford.[4] He was ecstatic; Cindy grew bored and restless after a few cold weeks in Mallorca.[5] After her departure, life at Canelluñ reverted to normal for a short time as Graves busied himself with supervising the restoration of the new houses and with a revival of the old Seizin Press to produce the poems of Terence Hards, who had been unable to find a British publisher. Graves's kind action paid off; *As It Was* was well reviewed and Hards, an old friend of Graves's, was overjoyed to be in print after years of obscurity.

Cindy continued to dominate Graves's thoughts in the summer of 1964. He was distressed when he discovered that she had resumed her affair with Howard Hart, a man who continued to obsess her in just the way that she obsessed Graves. There had always been a rival in Graves's poetic myth of his relationship with the muse, but he was never able to regard Howard Hart as more than a token competitor for whom Cindy, in her goodness, felt some lingering concern. Writing to Idries Shah, he declared the new 'compactness and certitude' of his poetry to derive from his love for Cindy. 'Although on the everyday level she's unpredictable and even scatty, on the durable level she's as firm as a rock: I don't worry about how and what and when.'[6] By the end of August, he had even begun, astonishingly, to consider leaving Beryl for Cindy; justifying his behaviour in advance, he told Ralph Jacobs that 'my life with Beryl is neighbourly, nothing else'.[7]

For the penultimate autumn term of Oxford lectures, Graves insisted that Cindy should accompany Beryl and himself. In London, he divided his time between them. Beryl was taken to a lunch with Ken and Kathleen Tynan, during which she offered to adopt their unhouse-trained pet, a slow loris. (Renamed for Ralph Jacobs, Ralphie subsequently shredded the Canelluñ curtains and terrified the maids. Relegated to a caged area of the garden grotto, the loris was declared by Beryl, who was not above making fun of her husband's superstitious beliefs, to have oracular powers.) Graves took Cindy shopping for dresses in the Portobello Road and had long discussions about their combined power to make extraordinary things happen. On Hallowe'en Night, Cindy told John Benson-Brooks, they had spoken to each other 'from the very core of one's world . . . Robert felt so good that he painted his face black, filled a small box with bones, got a wand and cast spells.'[8]

Graves's own poetic mythology was slowly being overtaken by the effects of the damage to his brain during his prostate operations.

By the end of 1964, while still believing that he was acting as a poet should and following his muse, he had begun to behave in a wild and unpredictable way more easily explained by his mental deterioration than by any poetic thesis. Beryl had been the quiet central figure in his life for nearly twenty-five years. She had defended his muse-relationships and provided the affection and care he needed. Now, she was repudiated as Graves planned to give up his marriage, his family and even his poetry in order to live with Cindy Lee.

To him, the future seemed clear and simple. Cindy had given him back his youth. Canelluñ had become the place in which he was expected to behave like the grandfather he was, but when he was with Cindy, he felt free to do as he liked; Beryl seemed to him to have a comfortable life, surrounded by friends and with her tribe of cats to dote upon: 'Beryl would rather have her cats on the bed than me,' he told one friend in 1964.[9] To himself, he argued that Beryl, always understanding, would respect his need for a new life. By December 1964 he had decided to make the break. John Benson-Brooks was told that he and Cindy were going away together in the spring of the following year, 'to live secretly and understand and think out the problems of love and poetic reality together: and record our findings.'[10]

Beryl was also informed of her husband's plans in December. Controlled as always, she wrote to tell Douglas and Jane Glass that Robert was going to leave her, 'perhaps for ever'. The house would not feel the same, she went on, after they had spent so many years in it together.[11] 'Beryl has been marvellously good and true and patient,' Graves wrote when Glass tried to remonstrate with him, 'but I continue obsessed . . .'[12]

It was not only because of a wish to be with his muse that Graves dreamed of escape. He had begun to fall out of love with the village. Deyá had changed from a quiet, industrious community into a haven for drug addicts and pushers, poets who wrote no poetry, artists who painted no pictures. He mocked them in 1967 in one of his best satirical poems, 'Wigs and Beards', using them as a modern parallel to England's bad old squirearchy, who

> . . . remain true to the same hell-fire code
> In all available particulars
> And scorn to pay their debts even at cards.
> Moreunder (which is to subtract, not add),

Their ancestors called themselves gentlemen
As they, in the same sense, call themselves artists.[13]

Money had, for many years, been Graves's substitute for the love
which more demanding children might have expected from their
father. Now, as he began to recognize that his creative powers were
waning, he argued himself into thinking that he had done enough
for his family. With his seventieth birthday in sight, he decided that
he had earned the right to be free.

A decision had already been taken that Juan should go to Australia
and become a forester or logger, since he had expressed a liking
for an outdoor life. (His father's dream of seeing him, first, as an
Olympic skier and then as a professional photographer, had come
to nothing.) Lucia was engaged and William, who had abandoned
his archaeological course at Oxford after finding that his thesis on
Mallorcan artefacts had already been covered by another student, was
in love with a Spanish girl and planning a future in Deyá. There were
houses enough for all of them and Graves was confident that he had
taken the necessary steps to guarantee Beryl's security. Arrangements
could be made through Selwyn Jepson, his English financial adviser,
to pay for the schooling of Tomas and even for the education of his
grandchildren, through royalties and the sale of manuscripts. The
one obvious casualty in his plans was Karl.

Karl had always been invaluable as a researcher, typist and second
editor (Graves made all final changes himself) and he had been as busy
as ever on the *Hebrew Myths*, smoothing the edges of what he called
Patai's 'rabbinical prose'[14] for the book's publication in 1964. Patai
wanted to produce a sequel; Graves refused. He was tired of writing
prose books, he said; in fact, he was now incapable of writing them,
a fact which Karl himself realized.[15] His services were no longer
required; there was no place for an efficient typist and copy editor
in Graves's plans for a new life. Karl had, moreover, been rash
enough to express his hostility to Cindy.[16] Graves was always ready
to attack anybody who failed to share his own view of his current
muse, so Karl was not altogether surprised to receive a letter from
his employer in March 1965 telling him that he must prepare himself
to leave Ca'n Torrent and find himself a new job.[17] Financially,
Graves promised that he should have whatever he needed; later in
the year, he fixed on a sum of £6,000. Karl left Deyá at the end of the
summer for America, and took charge the following year of the

poetry collection at the University at Buffalo. The correspondence between the two men continued, their relationship astonishingly unbroken in its affection and mutual regard.

In the last week of February 1965, Graves set off on a lecture tour that would take him to New York, Syracuse, and New Haven. Three weeks later, he flew south to Mexico, leaving Ralph Jacobs to tell Beryl that no mail was to be forwarded to him. One cable did get through; William, after expressing a hope that his father would one day come back to Deyá for a visit, asked to be given the Posada as a home for himself and his wife. Graves, envisaging a life abroad, agreed.

The dream was short-lived. Cindy's descriptions had not led Graves to imagine that Puerta Vallarta would be a depressing shanty town situated, like Deyá, between the mountains and the sea, and filled, like Deyá, with American dreamers and drug-takers. Ten years later, Puerta Vallarta became a fashionable colony; in the mid–Sixties, when it was used as the location for filming Tennessee Williams's *Night of the Iguana*, it was squalid. Cindy had her own friends there, including Howard Hart, and Graves did his best to join in and pretend to be one of them. After two weeks, he was involved in a car crash and injured his head; when he decided to go to Mexico City to have himself examined, Cindy elected to stay behind. Her lack of interest or concern was, even to Graves, apparent and a poor return for the effort he had made to rescue her from a new affair with a boy young enough, he speculated, to be her son. Having spent £2,000 on his muse and her friends, Graves was forced to appeal to Gordon Wasson for help to get himself home. Mexico had, he admitted to John Benson-Brooks, been an ordeal, but 'only good can come of ordeals' and Cindy, too, had suffered, he was sure.[18]

On Easter Sunday, 16 April, he arrived back in Deyá. Beryl, according to the memory of Karl Gay, observed only, with some coolness: 'So you're back.'[19] Her detachment did not last; Graves's letters in the following weeks were full of grateful references to the way Beryl had nursed and comforted him.

Graves's capacity for inflicting pain on himself and triumphing over it remained impressive. At the beginning of May, still suffering from the injury to his head, he collapsed from shock and exhaustion; in early June, Cindy was forgiven, songs were being sung with a jolly girl from North Carolina and he was showing off his vigour by walking twenty-two miles, many of them uphill.

The object of this walk was, in part, to punish William by showing up his inferior physical strength. Now that he had returned, Graves bitterly resented having given away the Posada to his son. It was the house which he had always enjoyed lending to people he liked – the comedian Spike Milligan, a new friend, was now told he could not stay there because William had 'grabbed' it.[20] More seriously, Graves had decided that the Posada was the one house which might tempt Cindy to remain in Deyá. She came back to the village in the early autumn and was told, first, that the house was hers and then, when William and his wife protested, that she could instead have its old Spanish furniture. William's resistance was taken to mean that he was actively opposed to Cindy.[21] Gradually, just as with Laura, a wedge was being driven between Graves and his family, and, again, the wedge was of his own making. His children had been ordered to be affectionate to Riding in just the way that William and Elena, his young wife, were now commanded to be friendly with Cindy. To resist was a sure way to incur parental displeasure.

Cindy was in Deyá in September to witness Graves's satisfaction at being awarded the Italia Award for *The Anger of Achilles*, his 1959 translation of *The Iliad*. She came to the house every day, while Beryl sat upstairs with the cats, and perched in his study, working on a chalk portrait which was, at Graves's insistence, reproduced in his 1966 collection for Doubleday, *Love Respelt*. (The English limited edition published by Cassell in 1965 also carried illustrations by Cindy, whose talent as an artist was modest.) But, when Graves returned to Oxford for his final series of lectures, he had to comfort himself with the thought that his muse was mystically rather than physically present; she had gone back to New York, where Howard Hart was waiting for her. Beryl, who had been studying Russian for three years, took the opportunity to make a three-week visit with Ruth Fainlight to Moscow and Leningrad, where Graves's newly translated work and Alan Sillitoe's recent visit guaranteed them an enthusiastic welcome. (Fainlight described the journey in her 1994 poem, 'Sugar Paper Blue'.)

His last lecture at Oxford, Graves wrote to a new friend in Scotland, William Stewart-Henry, was a triumph. Twelve hundred people attended it; none were aware that the lecturer had two spiritual allies on the platform. Omar Shah, Idries's brother, had promised that he would communicate as he stood in the Hindu Kush, dressed in turban and pantaloons and holding up his Afghan sword; Cindy, her eye on the clock, was supposed to be standing by in New York, Graves's emerald engraved with Athena's owl blazing from her forehead. At the party which followed the lecture, Graves saw a glass break of its own accord, and knew it was a message from Cindy. 'If it hadn't happened, I'd have lost faith in love,' Graves told Stewart-Henry, 'but in poetry, there are no "ifs", as you know.'[22]

Quoted, Graves can sound absurd. In life, he remained disconcerting, warm-hearted and inspiring, as much at home with English dons and with Greek professors as he was with the Oxford students who saw him sunning himself on the quad grass and, on one memorable occasion, shinning up a tree to demonstrate his skill at fruit-picking.[23] Common to all their recollections is a sense of Graves's enthusiasm and kindness. Min Wild, who sent him her first poems in the mid-Sixties when she was just thirteen, remembered how he encouraged her by analysing her work, telling her that 'words are a poet's only riches' and signing his careful letters as 'your devoted colleague'.[24] Spike Milligan, who had first met him in December 1963, thought of his new friend as 'a Colossus, so massive, so wise, so learned, so witty, and so simple with it all – so unpretentious'. He was overjoyed at finding a man who treated him not as a buffoon, but as an equal.[25]

Hugh Lloyd Jones, Regius Professor of Greek, had been at pains not to meet Graves during his 1961–5 tenure at Oxford. Admiring his poetry, he dreaded the quarrel he felt sure would break out over *The Greek Myths*, a literary but fanciful work, in his own view. They met in Graves's last term and Lloyd Jones fell under his spell.

> I have seldom felt a more instant rapport with any human being. Long after dinner, Robert accompanied me to my rooms in Christ Church, and we talked until the small hours. After that he signalled me whenever he was coming to England, and we met either in Oxford or, more frequently, in London. We talked a good deal about poetry . . .[26]

Lloyd Jones was especially struck by Graves's gift for Greek translation, despite the fact that his knowledge of the language had never been profound. Lloyd Jones had recently come across some fragments of an early Greek poem; when he recited the lines about a beautiful young girl, Graves 'was instantly attentive. "Write

that down for me," he said, "with a translation between the lines."'
Lloyd Jones did as requested. The next morning, Graves presented
him with a translation which caught the spirit of the original more
closely than he had imagined possible.[27]

> 'Astymelusa!'
> Knees at your approach
> Suddenly give, more than in sleep or death –
> As well they may; such love compels them.
> 'Astymelusa!'
> But no answer comes.
> Crowned with a leafy crown, the girl passes
> Like a star afloat through glittering sky,
> Or a golden flower, or drifted thistledown.[28]

One of the most striking features of the conversations and correspondence between Graves and Hugh Lloyd Jones over the next
few years was the regularity with which Graves referred to his
experiences in the Great War. The pain he suffered for his muses
was never, perhaps, painful enough to exorcize the guilt he felt for
the lives he had taken. As he grew older and more confused by the
modern world, he returned to what had been the most traumatic
experience of his long life.

Since the mid-1920s Graves had been attentive to the dates of the
battles in which he had fought, noting their anniversaries at the top
of his letters and often including some anecdote about them in the
text. Now, in his seventies, he began to seek out some of his old
colleagues, to talk with them about a time which everyone in his
circle of family and younger friends seemed to have forgotten. In his
poems, he placed increasing emphasis on the need for men to display
the soldierly qualities of honour, truth and chivalry. In life, he took
an increasingly protective attitude towards women, guarding them
as he felt a soldier should. On one occasion, seeing a young girl he
knew being treated in what seemed to him a discourteous way in a
London restaurant, he offered to fight a duel on the spot. His manner
made it clear to his amused but impressed audience that, although
well over seventy, he was entirely serious in his challenge.[29]

★　　★　　★

Graves had never been a greedy man, but he had been persuaded by friends who were financially shrewd that he would be wise to avoid being taxed twice. The scheme he entered in 1962, also used by Graham Greene, was organized by Thomas Roe, whose company, Roturman, bought copyrights and then acted as middlemen, receiving the payments in Switzerland and transferring them to the authors' accounts. This, in itself, was not illegal, but Roe was discovered in the summer of 1965, three months after Graves's inglorious return from Mexico, to have been handling forged money. Roe was put in gaol and the company was suspended. Until the case was settled, Graves was unable to touch any of his writing income. None of his debts, including money owed to Karl, could be paid.

Selling the newly converted Deyá Arts Centre was an act of panic which produced little financial relief and caused bad feelings; it meant that Bill and Jackie Waldren, who had been friends of the Graves's since the Fifties, had to be evicted from their rent-free flat in the building which they had worked to make habitable. (They remained in the village and continued to run the archaeological museum for a time.) Larry Wallrich, a book dealer living in Deyá, produced a more practical solution. He had already helped Graves to sell some of his old books. In the autumn of 1965 he agreed to look for a buyer for the Graves family papers; in February 1966 the University of Southern Illinois offered $37,000.[30] The money was not, however, received until the end of the summer.

Lack of money concerned Graves less than the thought of his elusive muse. Searching for ways to bind her to him in the early summer of 1966, he found an old village house and started to redesign it as a home for her. Shortly after receiving the payment for his family manuscripts and letters, he also trustingly sent Cindy the money to purchase land and build a house for them both at Puerta Vallarta. This was the first step towards a dream he had not yet given up – of making a new life for himself in Mexico. The money sent constituted almost all of the $37,000 archive payment; £6,000 was kept back for Karl Gay. Beryl was not told about her husband's gift to Cindy, a fact which had unfortunate consequences when Graves lost his memory in later years.

To his family he seemed to be in low spirits, but in London that summer Graves demonstrated that he was still capable of putting on a remarkable show. When, after agreeing to help raise funds for the Mermaid Theatre, he appeared there for an evening performance in

June with Spike Milligan, the audience were so entranced that they refused to leave. Graves, dapper and merry, delighted them by dancing, singing and improvizing along with Milligan and thirteen-year-old Tomas, who was brought on stage to play his guitar.

Semi-amateur occasions like this, at a small, friendly theatre, in company he enjoyed, allowed Graves to excel. He was less happy the following month at the Albert Hall, where young Jonathan Boulting had persuaded him to participate in an evening devoted to muse-poetry. The idea was badly-timed; by 1966, the energies of the younger poets had begun to focus on the war in Vietnam. Love-poetry was not in fashion. The audience, according to one hostile reviewer of the evening, Christopher Logue, thought that Graves was a pompous old bore and let him know it by heckling him.[31] Logue did not add that, before reading his poems, Graves had rolled up his sleeves and offered to take on the protesters.

Despite his gallant public performances, Graves was a sick man, troubled by nausea and bouts of crippling stomach pain. The cause was diagnosed as gallstones. In October, it was arranged that he should have his gall-bladder removed at St Thomas's Hospital. Graves refused to take the operation seriously, although it is not a minor one. His thoughts were fixed on a plan to join Cindy in Mexico as soon as he was well enough to travel. Once again, he set out to justify his bizarre behaviour to Cindy's friend, Ralph Jacobs.

> Beryl has been suffering terribly from the waiting and sorrow and tension, as we all have. This will clear up everything. Beryl is really waiting to start up being something on her own, not a mere housekeeper unpaid. She and I have great feeling for each other, which made things difficult. I didn't want to abandon her and she couldn't trust Aemilia . . .[32]

The letter does not explain the cause of Beryl's mistrust, but, as a shrewd and sensible woman, she may have been better able than Graves himself to see the hopelessness of his fantasy. Cindy had, for most of 1966, been living in America and Mexico with her lover, Howard Hart. While grateful to Graves for enabling her to build a house in the place she loved, she had no wish to share it with him. She had, so Graves told Jacobs, described the house as 'eternally' his, but that did not mean that she expected him to come and claim it. When Graves wrote to announce his plans, Cindy found reasons to postpone them. She did not quite dare tell him never to come to Puerta Vallarta, but she made it clear that he would not, in the near future, be welcome.

Weakened by his operation, Graves was shattered by this denial of his hopes. The sense of betrayal was strong; even so, he could not bring himself to end the relationship. He wrote that it was over, and then, that it was going through a difficult patch. To his friends, he offered hopeful rationalizations. Cindy was suffering from hypoglycaemia, he decided, after reading up the symptoms, and so was not responsible for the things she said. There was always in his mind the possibility that she would change her mind. His dream of rescuing her from his rival remained strong.

Guided by Selwyn Jepson, he decided to take back the house he had created for her in Deyá, for which he had not yet paid, and to use it instead as a guest-house for friends. As the Torre Susana, it was unofficially bestowed on the next muse and then on Graves's youngest child, Tomas. (Margot had meanwhile chosen to pass the ruined house which had been given to her on to Juan Graves, who eventually restored it.) The house in Mexico remained the property of Cindy. Warned by Jepson to be careful about the fact that she still had the copyright in all of his letters and could, if she wished, sell or publish them, Graves could not believe that Cindy would do anything to harm him. 'I've given Aemilia the copyright and she'll use it honourably,' he had told Jepson in 1964.[33]

All her deceptions had not weakened his faith in her. The rule held; a muse could do no wrong. To Ava Gardner, looked on by now as a younger sister to whom he could confide all his secrets, Graves sent a wistful defence of his beloved, and quoted a saying of Laura Riding's which had come to have a strangely consoling ring as he endured the rejections of his muses:

> She's very brilliant; but one can't ride a chariot with a lion *and* a mangy buffalo in the shafts. 'To each is given what defeat she will.' Sad, sort of. At her best, she's supreme.[34]

A month after the operation, although still distressed, weak and on a strict diet, Graves set off on one of his arduous American tours. Professional pride saw him through. On 24 November, wearing a yellow rose in the lapel of his new dinner-jacket, he addressed six thousand teachers in Texas. Primed with champagne, the only drink which he was permitted by the doctors, he survived a five-city tour and demonstrated his ability to drink a Doubleday editor, Sam Vaughan, under the table while remaining, to all appearances, in perfect control.[35]

CHAPTER THIRTY-FIVE

1967–1969

THE LAST MUSE

GRAVES HAD ASKED CINDY LEE TO COUNT ON HIM WHEN SHE needed help; the calls began in January 1965 when she told him, first, that she needed money to visit her mother in Texas and then that her mother was also short of funds. Still in love with her, although he tried to persuade himself that he was not, Graves remained generous: Doubleday were told to send Cindy a cheque for $500, deducted from Graves's American royalties. Writing to Hugh Lloyd Jones, one of his most sympathetic correspondents on the subject of muse-love, Graves exonerated Cindy of cupidity by claiming that, as a woman, she was incapable of honour; later, he admitted that she had two sides to her nature.[1] Still under her influence, he passed from bitterness into resignation.

> Though once true lovers,
> > We are less than friends.
> What woman ever
> > So ill-used her man?
> That I played false
> > Not even she pretends:

> May God forgive her,
> For, alas, I can.[2]

This is one of the few late Cindy-period poems which deserve to survive; most were written on automatic pilot, insisting, long after the final curtain had come down, that she and Graves were bound together, loving as none had ever loved before.

By the summer of 1967, however, a new mood had entered Graves's work. In 'Fact of the Act', first published in July, he invoked a young girl on the brink of her first love-affair. The theme from now on would be of a love that defies convention and time by spanning two generations. The hollow, tired tone of the later poems to Cindy is replaced by a sweeter voice of loving experience. The embarrassing insistence on intellectual and creative equality between poet and muse becomes a tender solicitude, a pretence of delegated power.

> It is for you, now, to say 'come';
> It is for you, now, to prepare the bed;
> It is for you as the sole hostess
> Of your white dreams –
>
> It is for you to open the locked gate,
> It is for you to shake red apples down,
> It is for you to halve them with your hands
> That both may eat.[3]

The reason for this change of mood was that a new – and final – muse had made herself known. Julia – always Juli to Graves in life, and Julia in his poetry – was the younger daughter of his old friends George and Joanna Simon. Her older sister Helena was his god-daughter; he had known both girls and their brother, Christopher, for all of their lives. All three of them hero-worshipped him. (Christopher's interests, Classics and archaeology, were influenced and assisted by Graves; when he went to Balliol, Oxford, Graves asked Lloyd Jones to keep an eye on his career.)

Juli had made her first visit to Deyá in the summer of 1966, when she was just seventeen; in the unremarkable poem 'How It Started', Graves later recalled the evening when she summoned him to join a group of teenagers dancing in the garden.

Since girls like you must set the stage always,
With lonely men for choreographers,
I chose the step, I even called the tune;
And we both danced entranced.[4]

Juli visited Graves again when he was in St Thomas's for his gall-bladder operation. When her parents had left the hospital, she told him that she was in love with him. Confused and unhappy about Cindy's capricious behaviour, Graves accepted her declaration as a sign. It was part of his belief that the woman who was to be the muse should always be the first to identify herself.

Her role as a muse was not immediately established: Graves was still emotionally tied to Cindy, although he did his best to pretend that the feelings he had were purely of concern for her welfare. For Juli, however, the sense of commitment was immediate and absolute. She had a budding career as a ballet-dancer, which meant that she was seldom in Deyá for longer than a summer, but the relationship with Graves became the most important thing in her life. For him, it was a return to innocence which allowed him to see himself as the romantic, mythical unicorn laying his head in the lap of a pure virgin; for her, it was a 'magical twinning' of two forces, poetry and dance, which allowed them to span a gap of fifty-four years.[5]

Partly for the sake of her parents, Juli was anxious to keep her function secret. She borrowed Helena's role of god-daughter as a shield; Graves did his best to respect her wish for discretion, but he had never been a keeper of secrets. Priding himself on his candour, he was used to discussing his love-life with his friends, while broadcasting it to the world in his poetry. Nobody was deceived about his sudden interest in his 'god-daughter', but neither was anybody who loved him able to disapprove: Juli was alone among the muses in radiating a gentleness and goodwill that could never be regarded as a threat to the poet's happiness. Beryl, who had been much tried by the period when Graves was under Cindy's influence, shared his affection for Juli and was able to ease the embarrassment which George and Joanna Simon felt about seeing their daughter adopted as a muse. With Beryl's assurance, they knew that no harm would come to her;[6] the sexual side of the relationship emerged only when Graves sensed a threat to Juli's purity.

In the poems Graves wrote for his last muse, he achieved a new serenity; all that was missing from them was the audacity of the best love-poems he had written for Laura Riding, Judith Bledsoe, Margot Callas and Cindy. Lovely though many of the final poems are in their cadences and images, they do not compare with the poems he had written for Beryl in the 1940s. Craftsmanship disguised the fact that his creative powers had dimmed.

★　　★　　★

Two forms of solace had been offered to Graves when he was hospitalized in the autumn of 1966. One was Juli's gift of herself. The other was Omar Shah's gift of a twelfth-century version of *The Rubáiyyát of Omar Khayyám*. Known as the Jan Fishan Khan manuscript, it was said by Shah to have been in the possession of his family for many generations. He did not offer to let Graves see the original. That, it was explained, would not be easily possible because of its sacred nature as a family heirloom: what Shah offered, instead, was a crib of the verses from which Graves could make a new translation. To a less trusting man than Graves, it might have seemed a shaky basis from which to attack Edward Fitzgerald's famous version of the *Rubáiyyát*, but Graves never thought of questioning Omar's word of honour. His only disappointment was 'that the divine love he [Khayyám] felt for his friend from Shiraz was a comrade love, without the least hint of bodily love . . . I had hoped it was love for a woman and would give a precedent for my impossible love for Aemilia [Cindy] and hers for me . . .'[7]

Graves had always admired the Shah brothers and he believed the story of their illustrious family background. He accepted Omar's explanation of the *Rubáiyyát* as a profoundly religious collection of poems which enshrined Sufi beliefs (not a view which was generally held);[8] Edward Fitzgerald had, in Omar's view, poisoned the spirit of the original by presenting Khayyám as a non-believer and aesthete.

Attacking accepted views was meat and drink to Graves; by November, he was eulogizing Khayyám to Tom Matthews – 'What a hell of a poet HE was!' and describing Fitzgerald as an 'arch-murderer'.[9] Having started by working until midnight in hospital by the light of a green-shaded lamp, he had almost completed his translation by February 1967.

Graves never doubted the authenticity of Omar Shah's crib. When his translation was published in November 1967, it appeared, to the outrage of most of the eminent Persicologists, as 'the original rubáiyyát of Omar Khayyám'.[10] Encouraged by Omar Shah, Graves asserted that Fitzgerald had bowdlerized a masterpiece, while he (Graves) had faithfully translated the words of Khayyám's original poem. (Shah had failed to grasp that the rubáiyyáts, or quatrains, were not written as a single poem and that they had never been intended to have an ordered sequence.) Backed by his collaborator, Graves continued to make declarations in his most bullish style. 'I understand that it will not be long before the Royal owner of the A.D. 1153 document satisfies the world's appetite for the truth,' he wrote to *Life* magazine; 'whereupon any English Persicologist who cannot face the facts will have either to resign his lectureship or consult a psychiatrist.'[11]

Faced with increasingly hostile criticism and with aspersions being thrown on the credibility of his source, Graves appealed to Omar to produce evidence of the manuscript and clear him of charges of literary fraud. He was answered by evasions and talk of the importance of trust and honour between friends. The manuscript was not produced, neither was any further evidence of its existence forthcoming.

Graves, admirably, continued to maintain his faith in the Shah claims. Scholars were less generous. In the spring of 1969, J. C. E. Bowen, who had made his own translation in 1961, travelled to Afghanistan and introduced himself to the head of the Shah family, who had supposedly looked after the Jan Fishan Khan manuscript until it passed to the father of Omar and Idries. With understandable satisfaction, Bowen recorded in 1972 that 'the bright-eyed courteous old man told me that he had no ancient manuscript in his possession and had never heard of Omar Khayyám'. A convincing case was made to show that Omar Shah's crib had been based instead on a late-Victorian translation made by Edward Heron-Allen. The sequence and even the errors in Heron-Allen's version were identical to those in the alleged Jan Fishan Khan manuscript.[12] The 1972 letter in which Bowen put all these discoveries forward in *The Listener* was never answered by Graves or the Shah brothers.

Graves's translation of the *Rubáiyyát* and the claims he stubbornly continued to make regarding the Jan Fishan Khan manuscript did considerable harm to his reputation, but this was not yet apparent in 1967. When John Masefield, who had been Poet Laureate for over thirty years, died at the beginning of the year, Graves was invited to deliver the June memorial address at Westminster Abbey.

This amounted to a public placing of the mantle on his shoulders. No direct approach had been made, but Graves was confident that it would come, and he was ready to accept. Writing to John Benson-Brooks in April 1967, Graves told him that he intended to do the job of being the Laureate cleanly and with a good conscience.[13]

The news had come at an auspicious time; Graves was in high spirits after a successful BBC interview at Canelluñ, followed by his first role as an extra in a summer film being shot in Palma. The star was Michael Caine; Graves appeared in *Deadfall* as an eccentric participant in a ballroom scene, dancing with exuberant glee.

His physical problems appeared to have been cured by the operation on his gall-bladder; in the summer of 1967, Graves was more concerned by the deep depression into which his son Juan had sunk after his return from Australia. Ignoring the advice of his old friend George Simon, Graves decided to consult Dr William Sargant at St Thomas's. Sargant suggested a course of pills, which he provided in a large bottle labelled with instructions. His diagnosis was, it seems, at fault. Certainly the result was disastrous. Told that he must at all costs continue the treatment, Juan became increasingly hyperactive and suffered an identity crisis, hyperventilation and, finally, a breakdown.[14] At the end of July he was flown out from Palma and taken as an emergency case into St Thomas's where his anxious father visited him every day. Juan's life was saved and he was able to return to Deyá in August. The depressions continued for another three years and form a sad leitmotif in Graves's letters during that period. Anxiety about Juan was the reason for Graves's failure to take part in the first London South Bank Poetry Festival in the summer of 1967, at which Ted Hughes had asked him to join Neruda, Lowell, Auden and Anne Sexton.[15]

The other key event of 1967 for Graves was his trip to Australia in October to see his daughter Catherine and her five children. Jenny, visiting her sister in 1962, had been alarmed by Catherine's conviction that her late husband was the victim of a sinister plot. Nancy had shared Jenny's concern. In 1962 Graves had been equally sceptical, but a conversation with a colleague of Catherine's late husband in April 1965 had changed his mind. This was the year in which Graves had been ready to elope with Cindy to Mexico; as he became noticeably more unstable, he found it easier to believe conspiracy theories. Writing to Catherine early in 1966, he compared Dalton's death to the assassination of Kennedy by 'a hired and well-protected marksman . . . Ordinary people can't believe it; it's too much like *I, Claudius* . . .'[16]

The Australian holiday was a great success. In a letter to Spike Milligan, Graves related how he had been taken opaling and had bought back some 'beauts' and how, at the end of a formal cocktail party in Canberra, he had made all the guests sit on the floor to sing songs and tell stories. On another occasion, after giving a lecture, he and a genial professor had ended up 'singing alternate songs by Dowland and by American folksong hillbillies on the damned virginals, no less. It just shows.'[17]

Graves, as he was the first to acknowledge, had lost touch with his daughter before he went to Australia. When he returned, he wrote, for the first time in many years, to Nancy. (Nancy had kept in regular contact with Catherine.) He had, he admitted, been uncertain what to expect:

> but by very careful check-ups with the grandchildren, Sir Mark Oliphant and other central characters I came to the conclusion that she had been completely accurate in her statements, and has one of the most extraordinary minds as well as the most enormous courage of anyone I have met for years.[18]

Catherine's belief in a conspiracy had taken an alarmingly strong hold on her father's mind. He ended his letter to Nancy by explaining that he had brought his teenage granddaughter Caroline back to Deyá, to save her from being kidnapped. Three years later he encouraged and helped Catherine to publish an account of the circumstances surrounding Dalton's death in 1961. Some of her revelations, including the illegal dumping of plutonium at Maralinga, were later substantiated; others remain in the category of puzzling, but unprovable, events. To Graves, however, there was no doubt after 1967 that his daughter was right.

Graves's readiness to believe in a Khayyám manuscript he had never been allowed to see was merely foolish; his plans to elope with Cindy Lee can, perhaps, be put down to an old man's romantic folly. But his readiness to embrace the idea that his son-in-law had been murdered was a more serious sign of his increasing mental deterioration. It was not the only one. He was becoming obsessed by thoughts of injustice. In June 1967 he wrote to Alan Hodge, as one of the two founder editors of *History Today*, to ask if the periodical was in the pay of the CIA. 'Everyone seems to be in that position now, except myself,' he added.[19] In January 1968 he informed an incredulous Selwyn Jepson that Catherine was being persecuted by the CIA;[20] in 1970, one of his friends was told that Catherine 'is avenging her murdered sister Jenny and her own husband', while John Benson-Brooks heard in 1971 that she had written 'the daringest book of the century'.[21] The critics and readers did not, at the time, share his view.

The case of Stephanie Sweet shows Graves defending a less dramatic miscarriage of justice which appealed to him because the victim was pretty and young, while her attacker, Sergeant Parsley, was a sturdy representative of everything Graves most disliked about England. Stephanie, a friend of his daughter Lucia, had been charged as the absent and unwitting tenant of an Oxfordshire cottage in which her subtenants were shown to have been using drugs. Miss Sweet was found guilty of managing the premises and fined. In July 1967 she wrote to beg Graves for help and advice; in April 1968 *The Times* published an article in which he argued that the judgement should be revoked. Graves himself was delighted by the successful outcome; in a footnote to an essay titled 'An Absolute Criminal', he noted that the case had made legal history.[22]

Letters and essays were the only form of writing other than poetry to which Graves was now prepared to commit himself. He toyed with the idea of a book about his views on love, began making notes for a further revision of *The White Goddess* and wrote part of a three-act play about Saint Paul, but none of these projects was completed. Essays were less arduous, but even these required more revision than they had done in the past, when he had the help of Karl Gay. At the beginning of 1967, he was delighted with the prospect of being paid a dollar a word by *Playboy* to write about reincarnation; by the autumn, after rewriting the piece several times, his enthusiasm had waned. Far easier, since it required little independent thought, was the turning of his mother's memoirs, which he first read early in 1967, into one of his best short pieces – it is almost inventive enough to be called a short story – as 'Miss Briton's Lady-Companion'.[23]

At the other end of the spectrum was 'Genius', published in *Playboy* in August [1968]. All the old elements of Graves were on show here, but as if in an artful parody. Lucidity was replaced by contention, perception by clusters of baffling assertions. A genius was defined as someone who uses intuition to reach their discoveries.

Napoleon, Hitler and Alexander the Great were presented as geniuses who 'were really psychopaths conning themselves with their own boastful legends until they ruined their countries and died shamefully with no sons to succeed them'. In other parts of this strange essay, Graves argued that city doctors are incapable of diagnosis because they have lost their sense of smell, and that creativity can only be sustained by the continuous process of falling in love. From a man of seventy-three, this sounded like hollow bravado.[24]

Graves was losing his ability to make a convincing case for his opinions, but his intellectual curiosity was as strong as ever. In January 1968, rallying from the disappointing discovery that Cecil Day-Lewis was, after all, to be the new Poet Laureate, he retreated into academic speculation. Writing to his Scottish friend Stewart-Henry, he told him that he was newly fascinated by what appeared to be strong connections between Arab, Persian and Irish beliefs in the eighth and ninth centuries, and ended by complimenting Stewart-Henry on his erudition. 'It is too late at seventy-two for me to become a scholar, but I recognize the real ones when I meet them.'[25]

Graves was surprisingly calm about the news, which came to him from Selwyn Jepson in February 1968, that Cindy was preparing to sell his letters to whichever publisher would make the highest offer. Jepson was disgusted by her commercial attitude and worried by the hurt that publication would cause to Beryl; Graves, while accepting that there was need for concern, said he would always love her. He was still confident that Omar Shah would vindicate his *Rubáiyyát* by producing the original manuscript, and he was looking forward to a March discussion of the book between himself and Shah at the Festival Hall. 'Our academic enemies are libelling us with venom, but we hold the ace, so it's rather fun,' he wrote to Isla Cameron.[26]

In London, he stayed with the Simon family and went to see Juli dancing in *Aïda*. In April he went with Beryl on the first of two visits to Hungary.

'I am . . . very fond of Hungary,' Graves told an interviewer two years later, 'I suppose because they have always brought me good luck and have more poets to the square mile than any other nation in Europe.'[27] Invited there by PEN in 1968, he was given a rapturous reception. Photographs from the visit show that there were queues a street long in Budapest for his autograph; Graves delighted his audiences by telling them of the songs by Kodály which his father had translated, and then singing them in their own tongue. He also told them that Hungarians had the same understanding of poetry as the Irish and Welsh, a declaration which was intended, and received, as the highest of compliments.

The 1968 visit to Hungary marked the beginning of an eventful summer. After the brief trip to Moscow which followed, Graves and Beryl returned to three months of an exhausting invasion of Canelluñ by their friends and relations: 'Beryl and I are the only people not on holiday,' he wrote to Spike Milligan.[28] Juli, Margot and Cindy were briefly all on Mallorca at the same time. Margot, now divorced, had come to stay at Lluch Alcari with her baby daughter and a nanny; Juli was charmed by her and the Graves family welcomed Margot back as though she had never been away. To Juli, enjoying her first summer as principal muse, it was a happy time, marred only by the sense that trouble was being made behind her back by a rival.

Graves's feelings for Cindy were wholly unaffected by the knowledge that she was doing her best to exploit their relationship for as large a sum of money as she could get. Writing to Milligan, he told him that Cindy was living in a cottage for the summer with a new and very young boyfriend, Peter Weissmuller (the family were old friends of the Graveses). 'Cindy', he announced, was 'absolutely at her best'.[29]

Cindy was not so willing as Margot had been to relinquish her role as muse. At the end of July, Graves told Selwyn Jepson that he had been obliged to send her away because of the lies she had told him about Juli Simon and that she tried to lay all the blame for her own behaviour on Howard Hart.[30] There may have been another reason for Graves's wish to have his former muse out of the way for a brief period. Cindy left for England in July, shortly after Graves was invited to become the first Son of Deyá. It was a ceremony for which he was required to appear as a dignified family man; he was perhaps unwilling to risk having a young woman regarded as one of the disliked 'hippie' colony present as one of his guests. But it would have been unlike Graves to put public opinion before loyalty to his muses.

Graves had not always pleased the villagers. There had been anger in 1962 when he used his friendship with the Spanish Minister of Information and Tourism to prevent a scheme to erect a hotel, chalets and a concrete solarium above the beach. Thanks to his intervention, a preservation order was passed on Deyá and, subsequently, on the whole of the north coast. This move was not welcomed by the

commercially-minded Deyáns, but it was Graves's influence with
the minister which resulted in the village, after years of Gelat's shaky
electric turbine, being converted to a modern system which provided
light at all hours.

In the Mayor's speech, mention was made of the tourists Graves
had brought to the village. The irony of this observation cannot have
escaped all of the audience. The year 1968 marked the beginning of
Deyá's worst period as a colony for drug-takers. Graves took pride
in his new title, but his affection for the village had reached its lowest
point. Writing to Isla Cameron in London, he told her horrifying tales
of police raids on the cafés, of

> a naked girl found drugged, raped, tied to a tree and infected
> with syphilis; three insane people (including one with a knife
> who said he would kill anyone who did not believe he was
> Jesus Christ); a spot of bad magic . . . The village is slowly
> separating into the Goodies and the Baddies.[31]

Isla's response was not as sympathetic as it might have been;
Graves had persuaded her to let Cindy and Peter Weissmuller use
her London flat while they were away from Deyá. Returning to find
her neat home looking as though it had been hit by a tornado, Isla
was almost ready to let the friendship go. A cheque, and a disarming
admission of culpability from Graves himself, healed the breach.

The end of the summer restored peace at Canelluñ. A visit by
the Simons was followed by one from John and Gretl Aldridge; at
Graves's request, John painted the first portrait he had undertaken
since the jacket of *I, Claudius*. It was Graves's own idea to have
himself painted as though he had been hewn out of the landscape;
he asked to be shown as if he was made out of chalk, loam and
gravel; this, in the startling, rock-coloured painting which appeared
at the Royal Academy Summer Show the following year, was what
Aldridge achieved. It is, Graves noted, 'the only good portrait of me
ever'.[32]

At the end of October, Graves heard from the new Poet Laureate
that he had been invited to receive the Queen's Medal for Poetry;
Day Lewis proposed that they should go together, he to receive
his insignia, Graves his award. Graves accepted at once, despite his
declared aversion to public honours, and regaled his friends with
accounts of the occasion. 'I love the Queen. She is one of us. Need

I say more?' he wrote to two new friends.[33] Spike Milligan was told that the Queen had instantly recognized his regimental tie. Clarissa, his sister, was given a fuller account.

> I told the Queen, when she gave me the gold medal, that I am a loyal subject and my family has been since the 12th century (the first occurrence of our crest and name and motto [was] in 1188) and that I was most deeply grateful to her for the gift – but that I accept nothing from Prime Ministers.[34]

In his correspondence with Cecil Day-Lewis, Graves had raised the question of who was to become the new Oxford Professor of Poetry in 1968. Edmund Blunden, his own successor, had retired early. Candidates for the empty Chair included Yevgeny Yevtushenko, whom Graves despised, Kathleen Raine, Al Alvarez and Roy Fuller. Writing to Day-Lewis, Graves urged him to cast his vote for Enid Starkie. She was not a poet, but she had supported Graves's own election. Starkie's husband was dead and she was still recovering from a severe car crash; Graves took the view that she should have the Chair because she needed encouragement. Day-Lewis, however, felt that a poet was the best candidate for the post and voted for Fuller, who was duly elected.

The perversity of Graves's choice was typical of his wish to put friends before literary politics, and of his indifference to public opinion. The same quality stood him in good stead when the reviewers, who had been breathless with praises for the past ten years, suddenly turned against him. It is not clear why *Poems 1965–1968* should have caused so much displeasure, since it contained some of Graves's best late love-poetry. It may have been that there was discomfort about the readiness with which he publicized his muse-loves to the world. It may have been simply that love-poetry was out of fashion. Graves himself laughed it off, saying that his success went in fifteen-year cycles and that this response had been predictable. It 'makes me laff', he wrote to Isla Cameron, and cheerily quoted the *Listener* reviewer who compared his poetry to '"shabby, peeling, Georgian stucco"'. For himself, he had no doubt of his superiority to the poets of the younger generation. 'The trouble is that they have nobody worth a damn to offer [in my place] instead; I do wish they had.'[35] His letter to Isla suggests that he was more worried by the fact that Peter Ustinov, whom he liked, had not bothered to come and visit him while he was staying on the island. 'Probably shy,' he decided; 'last time I gave him an 18th c. Russian silver snuffbox.'[36] He was reassured a few weeks later, when Ustinov invited him to come with Beryl for a dinner in Palma.

CHAPTER THIRTY-SIX

1969–1985

THE EMPTY ROOM

BAD HEALTH PLAYED A PART IN GRAVES'S DECISION TO STAY behind when Beryl, Margot Callas and Tomas Graves made a visit to the Soviet Union at the beginning of 1969. Beryl loved going there; Graves, who described Russia as uninspiring, was glad of the excuse of illness to remain at home.

His respite of good health after the gall-bladder operation had been brief. The acute digestive problems returned late in 1968, but the specialists he visited could find nothing wrong. Neither, yet, was anybody fully alert to the fact that Graves's mind was becoming confused. When Spike Milligan received an almost exact replay of one letter in another a week later, he was puzzled, but not alarmed. Only the increasingly conscientious way in which Selwyn Jepson handled Graves's financial affairs suggests that someone was beginning to sense a special need for care.

Throughout 1969 Graves continued to pour out a stream of poems to Juli in which Sufi beliefs and the conceits of the seventeenth-century Metaphysical Poets were entwined, often to dazzling effect. When they were published the following year, he made a reference to the danger to a 75-year-old of plagiarizing himself. Repetitions are, in fact, very few; many of the late lyric poems and songs show Graves writing of the same subjects that he had treated as a young man with a freshness which astonishes in a great-grandfather.

Call down a blessing,
On that green sapling,
A sudden blessing
For true love's sake
On that green sapling
Framed by our window
With her leaves twinkling
As we lie awake.[1]

James Reeves was among those who felt that Graves had reached an age when he should stop falling in love; a curious correspondence in 1968–9 about Reeves's sudden interest in the poet Trumbull Stickney becomes explicable when we know that Stickney was famous for his hopeless and idealized love-affairs. Graves was not prepared to take the hint. Stickney, he told his friend, was a poet with whom he felt little sympathy.[2]

Corresponding with his American publisher in 1969, Graves showed that intermittently he remained alert and in control. When informed that Doubleday intended to subtitle his new poems 'An ardent suitor lovingly chides the proud muse', he responded tartly: 'I don't. It just looks silly.'[3]

The year 1969 was best remembered by Juli Simon for 'a most calamitous summer'.[4] The reason for this was that Graves had responded badly to the discovery that his young muse was capable of having a sexual relationship. And yet, as with Margot Callas and Alastair Reid, it is almost possible to see Graves as having created the situation for a betrayal.

It was Graves's idea that Juli, as the theoretical owner of the Torre Susana, originally bestowed on Cindy Lee, should live there when she visited Deyá, and act as hostess to friends judged by Graves to be suitable. The friends he chose were Sonja Guy, a gentle, good-looking girl whom he had previously persuaded to befriend Cindy, and her fiancé. Juli, dark-eyed and dark-haired, with a dancer's slender limbs and graceful movements, had the additional appeal of being known – for the secret was not well kept – as Graves's muse. As might have been predicted, Sonja's fiancé was attracted to her. His engagement to Sonja survived his brief escapade with Juli, but Graves's sense of his muse's purity was temporarily unsettled. He responded, as he had done with Margot, by blaming the fiancé; a muse could never be allowed to be at fault. In the shepherd's hut above the house which he had converted into a private study, he wrote poems with titles which were indicative of his mood: 'Iago', 'Man of Evil' and 'Against Witchcraft'. In the same dark mood, he wrote one of his most bitter poems about old age. The last verse of 'Troublesome Fame' was a grim reflection on his own condition:

> But Fame attendant on extreme old age
>   Falls best. What envious youth cares to compete
> With a lean sage hauled painfully upstage,
>   Bowing, gasping, shuffling his frozen feet –
> A ribboned hearse parked plainly down the street?[5]

Cindy had left Mallorca to travel around India in February 1969. By August, Selwyn Jepson had discovered where to reach her and had offered her a deal to drop her plan to publish the letters; Graves's casual response to the news suggests that he himself would not have cared much if she had gone ahead. He had never been embarrassed by his muse-relationships or anxious to conceal them from the world. He went along with Jepson's arrangements for Beryl's sake, not his own. For the sum of $12,000, Cindy agreed to release Graves's side of the correspondence, together with her letters to him, to the University of Victoria, to remain unseen until ten years after the death of Graves, or his wife, whichever should fall the sooner. The glimpses of this correspondence found in the few stray letters held in other collections do not suggest that it will add much to our knowledge of Graves, although it may deepen our sense of his passionate commitment to Cindy and his longing to see her as the wise and loving Black Goddess he had proclaimed her to be.

He still loved her. Even now, when he had found a replacement, he could not put her out of his mind. In 1970 a student returning to America was asked to deliver a necklace to Miss Cindy Lee, of Walnut Creek, California. A year later, hearing that she was stranded in Turkey without funds, Graves came once more to the rescue. There was no further contact between them.

★ ★ ★

Interviewers had become used to the fact that Robert Graves's opinions were often eccentric. Those who came to Deyá in 1969 and 1970 found it hard to tell if they were being teased, sidetracked, or offered some special insight. Sometimes Graves pulled down from his shelves the weighty 1857 publication *Transactions of the Ossianic Society* and told his visitors to make themselves comfortable and enjoy his favourite book. (It could be relied on to give him peace for at least an hour.) Asked when he planned to visit America again, he shook his leonine head and spoke in horror of the CIA. Many heard about the Stephanie Sweet case and about Catherine Dalton's book; others were lectured about the connection between a failure in creativity and short hair. Remembering that Juli was still anxious to remain unmentioned, he kept quiet about a visit he made to Venice in March 1970; Juli was dancing there, and he wanted to help celebrate her twenty-first birthday. Pointed questions about ballet-dancers were diverted with observations on the ugliness of modern nightclub dancing, 'a mindless perversion' from the romantic perspective of a poet.[6]

The subject which preyed most on Graves's mind in 1970 was what he regarded as a betrayal by his old friend, Gordon Wasson. In 1969 Wasson had published *Soma: Divine Mushroom of Immortality*. Graves responded to it with a review for *Atlantic Monthly* which he included in his 1972 collection, *Difficult Questions, Easy Answers*.

His distress stemmed from the fact that Wasson had made no acknowledgement of his own contribution to the study. The use of the mushroom in ancient religious rituals was no longer in doubt: in his book, Wasson argued that Soma, the plant deity worshipped by the ancient Hindus in 2000 BC, had been the fly agaric or *Amanita muscaria* mushroom. Graves had endorsed Wasson's view and had contributed many useful suggestions and ideas, more especially in the early years of his research. He was particularly disappointed that Wasson had failed to make any reference to the use of Soma in the Greek mystery rites. Twelve years earlier, as Graves wrote in *Atlantic Monthly*, he himself had written an article in which he argued that Soma was the 'nectar' of the Greek gods. He had also suggested that Dionysus's first birth, from a lightning bolt, linked him to mushrooms, which were once believed to spring up where lightning struck the ground.[7] Wasson had read the essay and been intrigued by it; he now chose not to acknowledge it as an influence.

Wasson's private response to Graves's review shows that he was conscious of the omission. Many of Graves's contributions to the study of psychoactive mushrooms had been inspirational, but Wasson's reluctance to mention his debt to his old friend was understandable. As Graves himself wryly admitted in his review, 'Any mention of my work in academic books is so suspect as to detract from their sales value and general acceptance'.[8]

★ ★ ★

The years 1971–2 marked a swift deterioration in Graves. The operation on his nose during the First World War had been badly done and the specialists shared Graves's own view that his digestive problems might stem from leaking sinuses. An operation was carried out in the spring of 1971 and Graves again required an unusually heavy administration of anaesthetic. The result this time was swift and alarming; he lost his short-term memory. Even the old songs which he had been able to sing without hesitation since he was a boy now eluded him. After a second operation on his sinuses in 1972, Graves told Karl, in May, that his grasp of names had gone,[9] and John Benson-Brooks, in August, that he had been having 'what one may call a nervous breakdown'.[10] To Selwyn Jepson, in September, he admitted that he could only think very slowly. He was, nevertheless, collecting notes for a play about one of his favourite villains, Saint Paul.[11]

One reason for wanting to write a play was to keep his mind working. Another was that *Claudius*, having failed as a film project, had at last achieved a degree of success as a stage play. Graves had long ago signed away all his dramatic rights, but he could still hope to profit from a popular film or stage success in terms of book sales and he continued to show a keen interest in *Claudius*'s progress. In 1965, partly as a result of the enthusiasm of Dirk Bogarde, the BBC had shown a documentary containing all the footage preserved from the original unfinished Korda production. In 1968 Tony Richardson, who was filming *Laughter in the Dark* on Mallorca, brought the actor Nicol Williamson to Deyá to discuss the making of a film, with Williamson playing Claudius; in 1970 Alec Guinness again expressed an interest in the part. In July 1972 John Mortimer's adaptation of the two

Claudius books, commissioned by Tony Richardson, had a short run
at the Queen's Theatre in London, with the lank, lugubrious-faced
David Warner playing the leading role. Graves took Juli to see it,
joined the first-night party and told his friends that he was delighted
by the way Mortimer had preserved the spirit of the original.

A further development occurred in 1973, with talk of a full-scale
television adaptation of his most famous books. Summoned to
London for discussions, Graves began to feel in better shape than
he had for the past two years. 'Now that my health is coming back
perhaps my memory will also,' he wrote to Jepson in February.[12]
He agreed to be filmed for a surprise tribute to Spike Milligan and
joined forces with John Betjeman to save one of London's best-loved
landmarks, the Albert Bridge, from being pulled down. He went to
a Burns Night celebration with Juli Simon and to Oxford, where
he had been made a Fellow of St John's, to stay a night with John
Carey, a Merton don. Carey was impressed by his kindness to the
students who sought him out; he was struck, too, by the range of
his knowledge and by the elegance with which Graves could play
on words. (Asked to think of a word which added a syllable by the
loss of a letter, he was given the answer by Graves himself; 'beautify'
becomes 'beatify'.) He was puzzled, however, by Graves's angry
references to a man who had 'robbed' him of his manuscripts.[13]

This, sadly, was a further indication of the confused state of
Graves's mind at a time when he was feeling short of money. Having
forgotten the arrangement which had been made with the University
of Southern Illinois through Larry Wallrich, he decided that the book
dealer must have cheated him and stolen his manuscripts for a private
sale. Furious, he spread the story to everybody he met. Not until
Wallrich wrote him a stern note to say that he was ready to go
to court, did Graves back down. 'I have suffered from a bad
loss of memory these past six months,' he wrote to Wallrich in
September 1972, 'so if I have wronged you by misrepresentation,
please forgive me. I hope it will come back.'[14] Wallrich, who had
already suspected that something was badly wrong with Graves's
mind, sent back an affectionate note and a recommendation to visit
an acupuncturist.

Graves was still writing poems. He told his friends that Juli,
too, had become a poet. His hopes of recovery were now pinned,
fantastically, upon her. Towards the end of the year he wrote a
forlorn poem, unpublished, called 'Unless'.

How can I hope to retrieve lost memory,
Lost pride and lost motion,
Unless, defying the curse long laid upon me,
You prove the unmatchable courage of your kind.[15]

In his heart, he probably knew the truth. Introducing his tenth collection of essays and reviews, *Difficult Questions, Easy Answers*, in 1972, he noted that 'it is likely enough that this will be the last'.

★　　★　　★

Laura Riding was unaware of Graves's condition; had she known about it, she might perhaps have been less ferocious in the onslaughts she made on his reputation at this time.

The source of Riding's anger was the question of who had written what in their 1927 collaboration, *A Survey of Modernist Poetry*. Her anger was, at first, indirectly expressed. Writing to William Empson in 1970, she asked for an explanation of Empson's failure to mention the *Survey* in a 1947 edition of his own book, *Seven Types of Ambiguity*. He had, she noted with asperity, acknowledged a debt to Graves's work but none to the *Survey* or to herself. It is not at all clear why Riding waited twenty-three years to make this protest, but she was not satisfied by Empson's explanation that he owed more to Graves's own early critical writings than to the *Survey*. Rubbing salt into the wound, Empson added that he found it impossible to believe that the analysis of Shakespeare's Sonnet 129 in the *Survey*, generally considered the most significant chapter in the book, had not been written by Graves. He drew her attention to a letter in *Modern Language Quarterly*, published in September 1966, in which Graves had confirmed this. Having stated that he was quite unaware of having been, at any time, influenced by her work, Empson added that he had no intention of making the public acknowledgement which Riding demanded. 'I really will not tell a lie to encourage that [belief],' he wrote in April 1971 in answer to one of her longest and most elaborate letters. 'I have already been punished enough.'[16]

This letter ended the Riding–Empson exchange. It marked only the beginning of Riding's war against her former collaborator. While Graves continued to insist, when asked, that he had learned from her 'a general attitude to things, rather than verse-craft',[17] Riding made her case for having been victimized, plagiarized and misrepresented by Graves. The energy she put into pursuing her former collaborator was considerable. 'Laura is active again and seems to hate me more than ever,' Graves had written to Harry Kemp in 1970.[18] He was no longer capable of defending himself when Riding published, in 1974, her most damning, and inaccurate, attack on him in the *Denver Quarterly*.[19] Copies of the article were sent by Riding to all the leading literary magazines with a request that they should take careful note of the contents.[20] Her final attack, written in 1975, was posthumously published. The subject here was not the *Survey*, but *The White Goddess*, written, Riding claimed, as an act of revenge in which Graves had murdered her ideas and distorted her personal character into that of the revered and detested goddess muse.[21] Riding remained, until her death in 1993, unable to accept that Graves's ideas of matriarchies and of an all-powerful muse goddess had predated his partnership with her, and that her own goddess-like reign in Deyá had been contrived and supported by him.[22]

★　★　★

Thoughts of the Great War had never been far from Graves's mind. His concept of the military virtues had governed him for fifty years and his passion for his regiment, the Royal Welch Fusiliers, was undiminished. It was, then, a great delight for him to be invited to the regimental dinner in London at the beginning of 1974. There, the officers were shocked by his meandering conversation and heavy silences; his family were dismayed to find afterwards that he had wandered off and sat waiting to go home in a stranger's car. In fact, the dinner was one of the last official events which he was able to enjoy. 'It was', he told Selwyn Jepson, 'a splendid occasion with a speech in honour of David [Graves] – and of me – which moved me very much.'[23]

Constant anxiety about money to help the family and a renewed burst of affection for his old comrades turned his mind to the idea of writing, at last, a proper sequel to *Goodbye to All That*. He had, for years, insisted that there would be no successor and that all he wished to say was contained in his poetry. Now, with an ominous insistence that he was only going to write it for cash, he attempted to outline the story to Selwyn Jepson. The letter, a long and rambling one, shows that he could no longer keep to a coherent line of thought.

James Reeves visited Deyá in July 1974 together with his daughter

Stella and her husband. Canelluñ, as always, was lively and crowded with friends and relations; Graves, their host, drifted among them like a ghost. To the friends who had known him in other times, the change was poignant.[24]

His memory had gone, but he could read his poems aloud, write one or two – and talk. To those who had not known him before, he seemed the embodiment of poetry. Tall and strongly-built, with the eyes of a seer and a shock of white curls crushed under the black Cordoban hat, a type which no visiting tourist could wear without incurring the old man's wrath, he still looked magnificent. An audience of boys from Westminster School listened with respect when he came to tell them, not about poetry, but of how, with magic, he could make a bonfire's smoke change direction.[25] James Reeves's son-in-law relished the deadpan humour with which Graves nodded at a tree and informed him that it was an edible oak. 'Just as well to know. You need never starve now if there is an invasion.'[26]

Graves was still able to attend an occasional dinner at his old college, St John's, and, in February 1975, to urge the President, Sir Richard Southern, to acquire a bronze bust called 'Don Roberto' by Carmen Feldman.[27] (This was done.) When, in May that year, he went with Beryl to Ireland – his first visit since 1918 – to give readings at University College, Cork, and the Peacock Theatre, Dublin, the poet John Montague was bewitched by him, although saddened by his confused addresses. Graves, who stayed first with Mary Lucy's son, Sean, visited the Guinness family with Montague after they had read their work together on-stage. Montague was also his companion on a sentimental visit to his grandfather's grave. Recalling the occasion for a radio programme some years later, Montague described how Graves had pointed to a star as they stood by a lake in the Wicklow Mountains and how, the moment they reached the house, 'the star just disappeared . . . he had become the kind of poet that he wanted to be. He had got magic powers.'[28]

When Derek Jacobi and the cast of the television production of *I, Claudius* were visited by the author on set in London in 1975, they were dismayed. Jacobi, who had met Graves in Mallorca several years earlier, noticed that he spoke just once as he walked among them. He stopped beside the actor who was playing Tiberius, George Barker, and said that he was the right height for the part. At lunch, he told the actors that he was a hundred and forty years old. Beryl, to the cast's relief, laughed it off by saying he had been a hundred and twenty at breakfast.[29]

In July 1975, for his eightieth birthday, Beryl arranged a massive celebration at Canelluñ. Twenty-eight members of the family came. Honor Wyatt's son, the actor Julian Glover, who had been asked to give a recital of Graves's poems in the little open-air theatre, was checked when Graves himself appeared, standing on the ground above the theatre, looking down at him in horror. Crying out, 'Plagiarist!', he was led back to his chair in the house.[30]

A decision to visit China in 1975 was abandoned. The following year, along with seven members of the family, Graves visited Poland to spend some of the royalties which could not be taken out of the country. He was found wandering through the streets at night, lost and afraid. In Mallorca, too, he began to grow uncertain about the roads and paths he had walked for fifty years. When the *Claudius* series was shown on television to huge acclaim, he could not comprehend that it was connected to a book he had written. In London, the cast hoped, but did not believe, that a telegram from Mallorca saying Claudius would look after them – the book was thought to have a jinx on it – came from Graves. Most guessed that Beryl had sent it.[31]

★   ★   ★

'It is a family habit of ours to live far too long,' Graves had written to Alastair Reid in 1956.[32] Until 1978 he remained stronger, physically, than many younger men. He could still keep up a rapid marching pace, swing himself up into a tree to pick olives, and tend his compost heaps. Until 1980 he was able to find his way to a neighbour's house for tea and a disconnected form of conversation every afternoon; sometimes he got lost and was brought home by one of the villagers. He wrote his last poems in 1975; after that, Beryl took over all correspondence, often choosing to say no more than that her husband's eyes were bad or that he was tired.

For friends of long standing, it was not always easy to accept Beryl's courageous determination to share Graves with the world in his last years. Canelluñ was a hospitable house and Graves had always lived his private life in public; she saw no reason to change that way of life because he was infirm. Some, like Honor Wyatt, were distressed to see him dressed like a child in a baby-blue caftan and being given children's presents in brightly coloured paper for his eighty-fourth birthday. Many were grieved by the fact that Graves's mind had evidently turned back to the war, engendering terrible guilt. 'I am in hell,' he said to Honor Wyatt, when she visited him in 1979.[33] To his nephew, Paul Cooper, he spoke of having killed more than a hundred Germans.[34] Some old friends, like Ricardo Sicre, found it unbearable to visit him; others, like Spike Milligan, appreciated being asked to help Beryl put Graves to bed, or to change his clothes. Judith Bledsoe was among those who came to see Graves in his final years.

The success of *I, Claudius* on television meant that Graves's two books about the Roman Emperor became best sellers around the world. He had always said that Claudius would look after him; oddly, and appropriately, it was the royalties from the *Claudius* sales which paid for his nursing care and enabled him to remain at home until his death.

He showed no signs of recognition at all from 1980 on. Beryl, who did not accept that his understanding had gone, continued to read Shakespeare to him in the afternoons. His bed was moved into the little library which had once housed the Seizin Press. On 7 December 1985, he died. He was buried in the churchyard which crowns the hill of Deyá, under a plain slab marked with his name. A memorial service later in the month was held in London at St James's, Piccadilly, where he had married Nancy Nicholson in 1918. The Last Post was played by a Royal Welch Fusilier.

*　　*　　*

Nancy Nicholson had died in 1977. Peace had been made between her and Graves after he wrote her an affectionate letter on their fortieth wedding anniversary in 1968. Beryl, Graves's widow, and the three sons of his second marriage, continue to live on Mallorca, as does Irene Gay who returned with Karl from America to live in Palma. Tomas Graves has retrieved and revived the Seizin Press, which is now devoted to limited editions of Graves's published, and unpublished, work. William is in charge of the literary estate; Lucia, who owns Ca'n Torrent, continues to translate Graves's work into Spanish. Sam and his family visit Deyá from the Spanish mainland, Catherine and hers from New Zealand; Margot Callas and her daughter Daisy make occasional trips to the island. Juli, whose feeling for Graves has never diminished, bought a house for herself in the village and visits it every year.

Deyá, out of season, is still recognizable as the village Graves and

Laura Riding saw when they first came to the island in 1929. At Canelluñ, or Ca N'Alluny, as it is now more properly named, Graves's study is kept as it was with all his talismans in place. In the passage leading to the room in which he died, his black Cordoban hat hangs on the wall.

NOTES

FOR FULL DETAILS OF ROBERT GRAVES'S WORKS, SEE THE bibliography that follows this section. The Graves Archive at St John's College, Oxford, was being expanded while I was in the course of preparing this book; where possible, I have tried to supply that as the place where the letters cited can be found. Many of them were read by me while they were still in private hands, and it may be that not all of these have yet been catalogued as part of the St John's archive.

Graves usually revised his poems for later publications. I have quoted from the original versions except where indicated.

Abbreviations used in the Notes are as follows:

Berg	Berg Collection, New York Public Library
BL	The Manuscript Collections, British Library, London
Brotherton	Brotherton Collection, University of Leeds
Buffalo	University at Buffalo, State University of New York
Canelluñ	Collection of Mrs Beryl Graves
Deyá	Collection of William and Elena Graves

Donohue   Donohue Rare Book Room, Gleeson Library,
          University of San Francisco
HRC   Harry Ransom Humanities Research Center,
          Austin, Texas
Lilly   Lilly Library, University of Indiana
Morris   Morris Library, Southern Illinois University at
          Carbondale
RG   Robert Graves
St John's The Robert Graves Trust at St John's College,
          Oxford
UCLA   University of California at Los Angeles
Victoria University of Victoria, Victoria, BC

CHAPTER 1: *1895–1909* YOUTH

1 Robert Graves, 'Miss Briton's Lady-Companion', *The Crane Bag* [1969], pp. 192–202.
2 Amy Graves, 'Memoir' (copy held by William Graves).
3 Amy Graves, 'Memoir'.
4 RG to Ava Gardner, 9 October 1966 (St John's).
5 'Not at Home', 1962, *New Poems 1962* [1962].
6 RG, 'My Best Christmas', *The Crane Bag*, pp. 183–6.
7 As n. 6.
8 RG, *Goodbye to All That* [1957], p. 31.
9 RG, *Goodbye to All That*. The quotation here is taken from the 1957 revised edition and does not appear in the earlier one. Hereafter, all quotes will be from the 1957 edition (cited *GTAT*) unless indicated [1929].
10 RG first met this story in Lady Charlotte Guest's translation of *The Mabinogion*. He drew on it for *The White Goddess* [1948].
11 Jenny Nicholson to RG, 20 February 1951 (Canelluñ).
12 RG, *The Crane Bag*, p. 198.
13 RG, 'Down', in *The Pier-Glass* [1921].
14 RG, *GTAT*, p. 35.
15 RG, 'Rocky Acres', *Country Sentiment* [1920].
16 Evidence of this trait is particularly apparent in Alfred Graves's diligent pursuit of Edmund Gosse and John Squire, editor of the *London Mercury* (UCLA).
17 A. P. Graves, *To Return to All That* (Jonathan Cape, London, 1930), pp. 275–6.
18 RG, 'The Abominable Mr Gunn', *Collected Short Stories* [1964], p. 94.

19 RG, *GTAT*, p. 22.

CHAPTER 2: *1909–1913* UNHAPPY SCHOOLDAYS

1 The account of Charterhouse given by Graves is confirmed by G. D. Martineau in *The Charterhouse We Knew* (British Technical and General Press, London, 1950).
2 Rev. E. M. Jameson, at the memorial service for Dr Rendall, 21 January 1948.
3 RG, *GTAT*, p. 38.
4 Richard Perceval Graves, from his collection of family papers (Berg) quotes this collaboration on pp. 66–7 of *Robert Graves: The Assault Heroic 1895–1926* (Papermac, London, 1987).
5 The account given of these events in *GTAT* [1929] and 1957 appears to be accurate and I have followed it here.
6 RG in the second of the Clark Lectures, published as *The Crowning Privilege* [1955] (Penguin, Harmondsworth, 1959 edn), p. 45.
7 Dated 1908 and identified in 1938 by RG as his first published poem (*The Carthusian*, 1911).
8 From Wordsworth's 'The Prelude', 1805, Book I.
9 RG, *The White Goddess* [1948] (Faber, 1961, rev. edn), p. 24.
10 RG, *GTAT* [1929], p. 75.
11 RG, *GTAT*, p. 23.

CHAPTER 3: *1913–1915* FIRST YEARS AS A POET

1 Samuel Butler, *Erewhon*, 1872 (Penguin, Harmondsworth, 1970), p. 176.
2 RG, *The Carthusian*, April 1914, p. 284.
3 Richard Hughes, Introduction to *An Omnibus* (London, 1931).
4 RG, *GTAT*, p. 58.
5 RG, 'Outlaws', *Country Sentiment* [1920].
6 RG, *GTAT*, p. 53.

CHAPTER 4: *1914–1916* 'SCHOOLBOY MILITANT'

1 Major E. L. Kirby, *History of the Royal Welch Fusiliers* (Pitkin, London, 1974).
2 RG to Cyril Hughes Hartmann, 25 October 1914 (Imperial War Museum, Special Misc. M4).

3 RG, 'In the Wilderness', *Over the Brazier* [1916].

4 RG, 'Oh, and Oh!', *Over the Brazier*.

5 Siegfried Sassoon, *Memoirs of an Infantry Officer*, 1930 (Faber p/b, London, 1985), p. 78.

6 Alfred Graves's diary, quoted by Richard Perceval Graves in *Robert Graves: The Assault Heroic 1895–1926* (Papermac, London, 1987), p. 78.

7 RG to Edward Marsh, 3 February 1915 (Berg).

8 A. P. Graves, *To Return to All That* (Jonathan Cape, London, 1930), p. 323.

9 RG, *GTAT*, p. 89.

10 RG to Edward Marsh, 22 May 1915 (Berg).

11 RG, 'Limbo', *Over the Brazier*.

12 RG, *GTAT*, p. 103.

13 RG, '1915', *Over the Brazier*.

14 RG to Siegfried Sassoon, 2 May 1916, *Collected Letters*, 1, (Moyer Bell, New York and London, 1988), p. 48.

15 RG, 'I Hate the Moon', *Over the Brazier*.

16 RG, *GTAT*, p. 141.

CHAPTER 5: *1916* A NEAR ESCAPE

1 RG, *GTAT*, p. 150. He added this sardonic sketch of himself to the 1957 edition. In 1929 RG was less inclined to mock his soldierly aspirations.

2 Siegfried Sassoon, *Memoirs of an Infantry Officer* (Faber p/b, London, 1985), p. 108.

3 RG to Edward Marsh, 10 December 1915, *Collected Letters*, 1, pp. 37–8.

4 RG, title poem in *Goliath and David* [1916].

5 RG to Edward Marsh, 9 February 1916 (Berg).

6 RG to Edward Marsh, 15 March 1916, *Collected Letters*, 1, pp. 42–4.

7 RG, *GTAT* [1929], p. 252.

8 Richard Aldington, *Death of a Hero* (Chatto & Windus, London, 1929), p. 31.

9 RG to Siegfried Sassoon, 2 May 1916, *Collected Letters*, 1, pp. 45–6.

10 RG to Siegfried Sassoon, 27 May 1916, *Collected Letters*, 1, pp. 50–1.

11 RG, 'A Dead Boche', *Goliath and David*.

12 RG, 'Letter to S. S. from Mametz Wood', *Fairies and Fusiliers* [1917].

13 Siegfried Sassoon, 16 July 1916, *Diaries 1915–1918*, ed. Rupert Hart-Davis (Faber, London, 1983).

14 RG, *GTAT*, p. 181.

15 Siegfried Sassoon, *Diaries 1915–1918*, 21 July 1916.

16 RG, 'Old Papa Johnson', *But It Still Goes On: A Miscellany* [1930].

17 RG to Edward Marsh, August 1917 (Berg).

18 RG, 'Escape', 1916, *Goliath and David*.

19 RG to Edward Marsh, September 1917 (Berg).

20 RG to Robert Ross, 16 September 1916, *Robert Ross: Friend of Friends*, ed. Margery Ross (Jonathan Cape, London, 1952).

21 *Ottoline at Garsington: Memoirs of Lady Ottoline Morrell, 1915–1918*, ed. Robert Gathorne-Hardy (Faber, London 1974), p. 162.

22 *Ottoline at Garsington*, ed. Gathorne-Hardy, p. 200.

23 Quoted by Michael Holroyd in *Lytton Strachey*, II (Holt, Rinehart, New York, 1968), p. 231.

24 RG to Edward Marsh, 17 December 1916 (Archives of the Royal Welch Fusiliers, Caernarfon).

25 Ben Nicholson to RG, 12 November 1916 (Canelluñ).

26 RG to Keith Baines, 12 October 1958 (private collection: Janet Boulton). The original sentence reads: 'It is wrong to refuse to play games with ordinary people, so long as one doesn't lose the key back to the dark corridor which I call other where, or stay out too long.'

27 Siegfried Sassoon to Robert Ross, 18 March 1917, *Robert Ross*, ed. M. Ross.

28 RG, 'Dead Cow Farm', *Fairies and Fusiliers*.

29 RG, *GTAT*, p. 201.

CHAPTER 6: *1917–1918* A CHANGE OF DIRECTION

1 RG to Edmund Gosse, 23 March 1917 (Brotherton).

2 RG, 'Two Fusiliers', *Fairies and Fusiliers* [1917].

3 RG to Siegfried Sassoon, 26 March 1917, *Collected Letters*, 1, pp. 66–7.

4 Harold Edwards to RG, 9 June 1956 (Deyá).

5 RG to Siegfried Sassoon, 13 September 1917, *Collected Letters*, 1, pp. 82–4.

6 Richard Perceval Graves, *Robert Graves: The Assault Heroic 1895–1926* (Papermac, London, 1987), p. 182 (no source given).

7 This view is implicit in all Amy's writings and helps to explain the extreme prudishness of her son before his marriage.

8 Quoted in Dominic Hibberd, *Owen the Poet* (Macmillan, Basingstoke, 1986), p. 120.

9 Dominic Hibberd, *Wilfred Owen: The Last Year* (Constable, London, 1992), p. 52.

10 RG to Wilfred Owen, n.d. (October/November 1917) (English Faculty Library, Oxford).

11 RG to Siegfried Sassoon, n.d. (October 1917) (Berg).

12 RG to Siegfried Sassoon, 17 October 1917 (Berg).

13 RG to Edmund Gosse, 24 October 1917 (Brotherton).

14 RG to Robert Nichols, November 1917, *Collected Letters*, 1, pp. 88–9.

15 RG to Edmund Gosse, 4 March 1919 (Brotherton).

16 William Nicholson to his son Ben, 24 January 1918 (Ben Nicholson Archive, Tate Gallery).

17 As n. 16.

CHAPTER 7: *1918–1919* YOUNG LOVE

1 RG, 'The Patchwork Bonnet', *Country Sentiment* [1920].

2 RG, 'One Hard Look', *The Pier-Glass* [1921].

3 RG, 'Morning Phoenix', *Treasure Box* [1920].

4 RG, 'The Kiss', *Treasure Box*.

5 RG, 'Vain and Careless', *Owl*, 1919.

6 RG, 'The Troll's Nosegay', *The Pier-Glass*.

7 RG to Charles Scott-Moncrieff, 24 March 1918 (National Library of Scotland, Coll. 7423).

8 RG, *GTAT* [1929], p. 227.

9 RG, 'Books at Random' by 'Fuze' in *Woman's Leader*, 14 May 1920.

10 RG to Siegfried Sassoon, 26 August 1918, *Collected Letters*, 1, p. 101.

11 RG, 'Drink Your Red Wine', as in the unpublished 'The Patchwork Flag' (Berg). It was subsequently published, revised, as 'Haunted' in *Country Sentiment*.

12 'Ghost Raddled' was first published in *Owl*, 1919, and subsequently published as 'The Haunted House' in *Country Sentiment*.

13 RG to Lytton Strachey, 3 January 1919 (BL, MSS. 60669).

14 See ch. 5, n. 23.

15 RG, *GTAT* [1929], p. 28.

16 RG, *GTAT*, p. 229.

17 RG to Walter Turner, 23 February 1919 (Donohue).

18 RG to Siegfried Sassoon, 13 January 1918, *Collected Letters*, 1, p. 106.

19 RG to Walter Turner, 29 May 1919 (Donohue).
20 RG to Walter Turner, 26 July 1919 (Donohue).
21 As n. 20.

CHAPTER 8: *1920–1922* OXFORD: A TESTING TIME

1 In the 1929 edition of *GTAT*, RG enlivened the Boars Hill period by stating that the Blundens had lodged with Mrs Becker, the murderess, not Mrs Heavens; p. 361.
2 RG to Edmund Blunden, 6 August 1920 (HRC).
3 RG to Eric Pinker, 30 March 1920 (British Library, Pinker, 2072)
4 RG to Eric Pinker, 18 May 1920 (BL, Pinker), 2072
5 RG, *GTAT* [1929], p. 365.
6 RG to Edmund Blunden, 20 August 1920 (HRC).
7 RG, 'Apples and Water', 1920, *Country Sentiment* [1920].
8 RG to Eric Pinker, 17 May 1921 (BL, Pinker 2072).
9 RG, *GTAT* [1929], p. 384.
10 RG to Edmund Blunden, 12 July 1921 (HRC).
11 RG to Edmund Blunden, 10 March 1921 (HRC).
12 RG, 'From Our Ghostly Enemy', first published in *London Mercury II*, December 1924.
13 RG to Edmund Blunden, March 1921 (HRC).
14 RG to Siegfried Sassoon, 29 May 1921, *Collected Letters*, 1, p. 126.
15 RG to Edward Marsh, 17 December 1921, *Collected Letters*, 1, p. 130–1. RG identified the poem as influenced by Rivers's suggested method in an undated note in the Canelluñ Collection, but he also wrote to Marsh about Rivers, describing him as 'my mentor' in the study of Freudian self-analysis. The most important difference between Rivers and Freud from Graves's point of view was that Rivers found Freud's idea of dreams as wish-fulfilment impossible to equate with the dreams of shell-shocked soldiers. Rivers did, however, give Graves a respect for Freud which he later either forgot or rejected, claiming to know nothing about his methods.
16 For William Empson's acknowledgement of this book as his chief influence, see Ch. 11, n. 18.
17 RG, *On English Poetry* [1922], p. 14. This book was published three months earlier by Alfred A. Knopf, Graves's US publishers since 1917.
18 Ibid., p. 32.
19 Ibid., p. 68.

CHAPTER 9: *1922–1923* PSYCHOLOGY AND POETRY

1 Clarissa Graves's diary, quoted in Richard Perceval Graves, *Robert Graves: The Assault Heroic, 1895–1926* (Papermac, London, 1987), pp. 263–5.
2 RG, 'Sullen Moods', *Whipperginny* [1923].
3 RG to Siegfried Sassoon, 31 May 1922, *Collected Letters*, 1, p. 134.
4 Siegfried Sassoon, *Diaries 1920–1922* (Faber, London, 1981), 29 April 1922, pp. 150–1.
5 Sassoon, *Diaries 1920–1922*, 2 June 1922, p. 162.
6 RG to Siegfried Sassoon, 31 May 1922, *Collected Letters*, 1, pp. 134–5.
7 RG to Siegfried Sassoon, n.d. June 1922, *Collected Letters*, 1, p. 143, where it is wrongly dated July.
8 William Buchan to the author, 12 May 1994.
9 RG, *The Feather Bed* [1923]. The misspelling of Ransom's name can be blamed on the publisher rather than the author.
10 Mary Taylor to the author, June 1994, describing her own conversations with Nancy Nicholson in the 1930s.
11 RG, 'Song of Contrariety', *Whipperginny*.
12 T. S. Matthews, *Under the Influence* (Cassell, London, 1977), p. 118.
13 RG, 'Alice', *Welchman's Hose* [1925].
14 RG, *GTAT*, p. 263.
15 Siegfried Sassoon, *Diaries 1923–1925* (Faber, London, 1985), 6 June 1923, p. 34.

CHAPTER 10: *1924–1926* LAST YEARS OF A COUNTRY POET

1 RG, 'The Presence', 1924, *Welchman's Hose* [1925].
2 RG, *My Head! My Head!* [1925], p. 6.
3 RG to Edmund Gosse, n.d. 1925 (Brotherton).
4 RG to Siegfried Sassoon, 2 April 1925, *Collected Letters*, 1, pp. 157–8.
5 Siegfried Sassoon, *Diaries 1923–1925* (Faber, London, 1985), 24 April 1925, p. 237.
6 Virginia Woolf, *Diary 1925–1930*, ed. Anne Olivier Bell (Hogarth Press, London, 1980), 27 April 1925, pp. 12–14.
7 The date at which the correspondence between Graves and Riding began cannot be clearly fixed but it seems to have started early in 1925.

8 Graves's biographers and the editor of his letters suggest that Ransom's letter was written in September 1924; however, its contents indicate September 1925.

9 The details of Riding's finances at this stage are unclear. Elizabeth Friedmann, her official biographer, believes that she paid for her own passage to Europe, possibly with the help of her half-sister, Isabel. Mrs Friedmann has no evidence of the amount of money Riding brought with her; Deborah Baker in *In Extremis: A Life of Laura Riding* (Grove Press, New York, 1993), p. 123, suggests $150. Both biographers concede that Riding's estranged husband might have continued to subsidize her to some degree, but his apparent reluctance to lose her cannot have made him a willing giver. It seems clear that Riding would have been dependent for most of her support on Robert and Nancy, and that this was rationalized as an exchange for the work she would undertake. (Elizabeth Friedmann to the author, 20 October 1993 and 14 May 1994)

10 For the details of Riding's reactions to World's End Cottage, I am indebted to her most recent biographer, Deborah Baker, *In Extremis*, p. 122.

11 Sally Chilver to the author, March 1993.

CHAPTER 11: *1926* DEMONS AND GHOSTS IN EGYPT

1 Laura Riding Gottschalk, 'A Prophecy or a Plea', *The Reviewer*, April 1925.

2 RG to James Reeves, undated but datable from content to 1933 (Berg).

3 Laura Riding to James Reeves, n.d. May 1934 (Berg).

4 T. E. Lawrence to David Garnett, 4 May 1929 (Bodleian Library, Oxford).

5 I am indebted to Susan Chitty, Antonia White's daughter, for letting me see these observations, made on 1 September 1937, in an unpublished passage from her mother's diary; Antonia White, *Diaries 1926–57*, ed. Susan Chitty (Constable, London, 1991).

6 Laura Riding to Karl Goldschmidt (subsequently Karl Gay), 24 December 1938 (Lilly).

7 Karl Gay in interviews with Deborah Baker, 1989, and the author, October 1993.

8 Joyce Piell Wexler, *Laura Riding's Pursuit of Truth* (Ohio State University Press, Columbus, 1979), p. 7.

9 See n. 6.

10 See n. 1.

11 Laura (Riding) Jackson, 'Some Autobiographical Corrections of Literary History', *Denver Quarterly*, Winter 1974, pp. 1–33.

12 RG to Nancy Cunard, November 1943 (HRC).

13 RG, 'Against Kind', *Poems, 1929* [1929].

14 RG, *Poems, 1926–1930* [1931].

15 Catherine Dalton (RG's daughter) in an interview with the author, August 1993.

16 RG to T. S. Eliot, 16 February 1926, *Collected Letters*, 1, pp. 163–4.

17 RG, *On English Poetry* [1922], p. 25.

18 See also Ch. 8, p. 107 and n. 16. In *Modern Language Quarterly*, September 1966, there are contributions from Graves and Empson concerning the writing of the *Survey* and the influence of Graves on Empson.

19 The letter from Marsh giving this information to Nichols was passed on to Graves, who in turn conveyed it to Sassoon on 3 July 1917, *Collected Letters*, 1, p. 74.

20 RG, 'The Shout', 1929, *Collected Short Stories* [1964].

21 Doris Ellitt to the author, 5 April 1993.

22 RG, 'The Nape of the Neck', *Poems (1914–1926)* [1927].

23 RG, 'Pygmalion to Galatea', was first published in the *London Mercury*, May 1926, and then in *Poems (1914–1926)*.

24 RG, *GTAT* [1929], p. 444.

25 RG to Dick Graves, 21 January 1952 (Victoria).

CHAPTER 12: *1926–1927* DISINTEGRATION

1 RG's bitter correspondence with Nancy is in the Nicholson Papers at the Lilly Library, University of Indiana, Bloomington.

2 Laura Riding, 'The Damned Thing', *Anarchism is Not Enough* (Jonathan Cape, London 1928).

3 Deborah Baker, *In Extremis: A Life of Laura Riding* (Grove Press, New York, 1993), p. 57.

4 RG to Harry Kemp, 21 July 1969 (Berg).

5 RG, 'Pure Death', first published in *The Nation*, November 1926, and subsequently in *Poems (1914–1926)* [1927].

6 Joyce Piell Wexler, *Laura Riding's Pursuit of Truth* (Ohio State University Press, Columbus, 1979), p. 8, and Baker, *In Extremis*, p. 136.

7 RG to Siegfried Sassoon, 18 September 1926, *Collected Letters*, 1, p. 169. The date given in Sassoon's diary is 14 September 1926.

8 I am indebted to Sir Rupert Hart-Davis for these details from Sassoon's unpublished diary of 1926.

9 RG, 'Dear Name, how shall I call you?', *To Whom Else?* [1931].

10 RG and Laura Riding, *A Pamphlet against Anthologies* (Jonathan Cape, London, 1928), p. 192.

11 This letter from Nancy to Sassoon can only be identified by a letter which RG wrote to contradict its contents on 18 January 1927. Here he declared that they were all 'very happy' and that Nancy now admitted that her complaint had been meant as a joke (Morris).

12 Doris Ellitt to the author, 7 April 1993.

13 As n. 12.

14 RG, *T. E. Lawrence to his Biographer*, [1938], pp. 45–6.

15 Ibid., p. 47.

16 RG, *Lawrence and the Arabs* [1927], p. 160.

17 Graves seems to have made an earlier trip to Cumberland. In a letter to Clarissa Graves he mentions a visit to Nancy in June 1927 (Donohue).

18 RG to Clarissa Graves, n.d. but contents suggest October 1927.

19 Riding, *Anarchism*, p. 11.

20 RG, *Poems (1926–1930)* [1931].

21 RG to Clarissa Graves, n.d. but contents suggest August 1927 (Donohue).

22 Riding, *Anarchism*, p. 94.

CHAPTER 13: *1927–1928* ST PETER'S SQUARE

1 RG to Michael Roberts, 4 April 1935 (Berg).

2 E. M. Forster to RG, n.d. 1927 (Canellun).

3 RG to Tom Driberg, n.d. but contents suggest late 1927 (Christ Church, Oxford).

4 RG to L. A. G. Strong, n.d. but contents suggest 1928 (HRC).

5 RG to Siegfried Sassoon, 4 November 1927, *Collected Letters*, 1, p. 181. When the quarrel was resumed in 1931, Sassoon based his attack on the fact that Graves had insulted Gosse, to which Graves responded that Gosse had gossiped about his private life (*Collected Letters*, 1, pp. 198, 201).

6 Mary Dawson to Rhoda Dawson, 4 November 1928 (private collection: Mrs Bickerdike).

CHAPTER 14: *1929* THE HOLY CIRCLE

1 Deborah Baker's 1993 biography of Riding, *In Extremis*, demonstrates that she was open to the point of indiscretion with her American contacts about her English relationships.

2 Author's interview with Mary Taylor, September 1993, based on the full accounts given to her by Geoffrey (Phibbs) Taylor in the early years of their marriage. I am also indebted to Mary Taylor for her descriptions of Geoffrey's family and character and of her conversations with Nancy Nicholson.

3 Geoffrey Phibbs to RG, 28 October 1928 (Canelluñ).

4 As n. 2.

5 David Garnett to Geoffrey Phibbs, n.d. (Berg).

6 Norah McGuinness to T.S. Matthews, 6 March 1978 (private collection: Mrs Pamela Matthews). This unsolicited account was written to a stranger whose book about Graves and Riding, *Under the Influence*, she had read and to which she wished to add circumstantial details. Mary Taylor confirms the details to have matched the account given to her by her husband in the mid-Thirties.

7 As n. 6.

8 As n. 6.

9 Author's interview with Bernard and Pamela Myers, 16 August 1993. (Based on Geoffrey Taylor's many conversations with Bernard Myers, a close friend, and with Pamela, an associate since the period when John Betjeman, the outgoing literary editor of *Time & Tide* in 1953, appointed Taylor as the unofficial poetry editor, a post he kept until 1956. Both Bernard and Pamela Myers were given accounts of the events in 1929 which confirm, and sometimes amplify, the detailed record provided by his widow, Mary Taylor.)

10 Laura Riding, 'Opportunism Rampant (Berg). I am indebted to Deborah Baker for comments on this manuscript, written *c*.1983. Riding's other account of the events of 1929 was a novel, *14A*, written with George Ellidge in 1934. It was withdrawn when Norah McGuinness threatened to sue for libel. In it, Riding appears as Catherine, who is regarded as 'sacred' by her friends.

11 Geoffrey Phibbs to Tom MacGreevy, 31 March 1929 (MacGreevy Papers, Trinity College, Dublin).

12 Undated note by Geoffrey Phibbs (Canelluñ).

13 As n. 6.

14 As n. 6.

15 As n. 6.

16 Author's interview with RG's daughter, Catherine Dalton, August 1993.

17 Laura Riding, *Four Unposted Letters to Catherine* (Hours Press, Paris, 1930).

18 Riding, *Four Unposted Letters to Catherine*, p. 51.

19 As n. 16.

20 As n. 6.

21 RG describes this episode in the Epilogue to *GTAT* [1929].

22 RG to Edward Marsh, 16 June 1928, *Collected Letters*, 1, p. 188.

23 The details of the defenestration are based on the accounts of Norah McGuinness, Mary Taylor, RG in *GTAT* [1929], and on personal observation of the premises.

24 This information is based on interviews with Hammersmith Planning Department, English Heritage, three long-term residents on the west side of St Peter's Square and a personal examination of the property, both inside and outside.

CHAPTER 15: *1929* GOODBYE TO ALL THAT

1 Although it may yet emerge that Laura Riding's half-sister, Isabel Mayers, helped to meet the bills, the evidence currently available suggests that Graves took total financial responsibility for her medical treatment.

2 T. E. Lawrence to Charlotte Shaw, 22 May 1929, *The Letters of T. E. Lawrence*, ed. M. Brown (Oxford University Press, 1991), p. 421.

3 RG's first appeal to Marsh was on 13 May 1929 (Berg).

4 RG Nancy Nicholson, 4 May 1929 (Lilly).

5 RG to Gertrude Stein, n.d. (Beinecke Library, Yale University).

6 RG, 'Report' to Laura Riding, 12 May 1929 (Canelluñ).

7 Bruce Richmond to RG, 10 June 1929 (Canelluñ).

8 Messrs. Wainwright & Pollock to RG, 1 August 1929 (Canelluñ).

9 Nancy Nicholson to RG, n.d. but evidently written in August 1929 (Canelluñ).

10 See n. 1.

11 RG to Keith Baines, 26 February 1953 (private collection: Janet Boulton).

12 T. E. Lawrence to RG, 13 September 1929, *Letters*, ed. M. Brown, p. 429.

13 The annotated copy of *Goodbye to All That* is at the Berg Collection, New York Public Library.

14 Siegfried Sassoon to RG, 7 February 1930, RG, *Collected Letters*, 1, pp. 197–201.

15 Basil Liddell Hart to RG, 14 July 1941, RG, *Collected Letters*, 1, pp. 300–1.

16 RG, 'The Whitaker Negroes', ¡Catacrok! [1956]; *Collected Short Stories* [1964], p. 319.

17 RG's articles for the *Daily Mail* appear in *But It Still Goes On* [1930].

18 RG, *GTAT* [1929], p. 446.

19 Gertrude Stein to RG, n.d. (Beinecke Library, Yale University).

20 Richard Perceval Graves, *Robert Graves: The Years with Laura 1926–40* (Weidenfeld & Nicolson, London 1990), p. 120. There seems to be a discrepancy in dating as Rosaleen Graves's letter to her mother, dated 21 October 1929, is said to have been sent by Amy to John Graves on 5 October 1929.

21 Laura later said that she had been bored by Miss Stein's interminable conversations about the weather and her poodle, but this is out of keeping with Gertrude Stein's fame as a conversationalist who charmed all her guests. It seems more likely that Laura felt herself outshone and wanted to move on.

22 W. J. Turner in the *Sunday Times*, 25 February 1929.

CHAPTER 16: *1930* A LIFE ABROAD

1 RG to Ricardo Sicre, 17 October 1956 (Canelluñ).

2 RG, 'The Terraced Valley', *Ten Poems More* [1930].

3 Laura Riding, quoting a letter from herself in *Everybody's Letters* (Arthur Barker, London, 1933), p. 174.

4 RG, 'The Duende', *Poetic Craft and Principle* [1967], p. 109.

5 RG, 'The Felloe'd Year', *To Whom Else?* [1931].

6 RG to John Aldridge, n.d. 1931 (Berg).

7 In *Denver Quarterly* (Winter 1974) Laura (Riding) Jackson denied that she had written any part of *No Decency Left*. The fact that the book was published under the pseudonym of Barbara Rich has made it difficult for the true details of its authorship to be established. In the same article, Riding claimed to have been the sole author of all work published under the name of Madeline Vara. On 30 November 1935 she had written of the pseudonym to John Aldridge, that it was everybody and nobody. The recent piece on Nietzsche, she went on to tell him, had been written

by Robert (Berg). The essay on Nietzsche had appeared in *Epilogue I*, Autumn 1935. The author was Madeline Vara.

8 Laura Riding to Michael Roberts, from Salerosa, n.d. (private collection: Janet Adam Smith).

9 RG, 'What It Feels Like to Be Famous', *Daily Herald*, 7 February 1930.

10 RG, 'The Legs', first published in *To Whom Else?* [1931]

CHAPTER 17: 1931–1932 SUCCUBI OR SOLID FLESH?

1 My scepticism about Lucie Brown's memoir is not shared by Richard Perceval Graves in *Robert Graves: The Years with Laura 1926–40* (Weidenfeld & Nicolson, London, 1990), pp. 154–65.

2 Lucie Aldridge to Beryl Graves, 14 November 1961 (Canelluñ).

3 Lucie (Brown) Aldridge, an unpublished memoir (private collection: Mrs Pamela Matthews).

4 As n. 3.

5 As n. 3.

6 Laura Riding, in *Authors Today and Yesterday* ed. Stanley Kunitz (H. W. Wilson, New York, 1933), p. 565.

7 Laura Riding to John Aldridge, 14 March 1933. The addition is written by RG in purple crayon (Berg).

8 RG to John Aldridge, n.d. but contents indicate the summer of 1931, *Collected Letters*, 1, p. 215.

9 RG to Beryl Graves, Christmas 1944 (Canelluñ).

10 Laura Riding to Kenneth Allott, 21 September 1933 (Buffalo).

11 RG, 'The Succubus', *Poems 1930–1933* [1933].

12 Norman Cameron to RG, 13 January 1943 (Canelluñ).

13 RG to John Graves, quoted by R. P. Graves, *The Years with Laura*, p. 181.

14 Eirlys Roberts in an interview with the author, April 1993.

CHAPTER 18: *1933–1935* CLAUDIUS, AND A COURT

1 Mary Ellidge, in a letter to Richard Perceval Graves, quoted in *Robert Graves: The Years with Laura 1926–40*, p. 219.

2 Graves published this as part of his 'Journal of Curiosities' in *But It Still Goes On* [1930].

3 Quotations from the *Claudius* novels in this chapter are taken from the

Vintage edition of *I, Claudius* (Penguin, Harmondsworth, 1978) and the Penguin 1968 edition of *Claudius the God*. The passage quoted here is from p. 7 of *Claudius the God*.

4 'To Bring the Dead to Life' was written in the spring of 1935 and first published in Michael Roberts's anthology, *The Faber Book of Modern Verse*, in 1936.

5 RG, *I, Claudius*, p. 231.

6 Ibid., p. 31.

7 Ibid., p. 28.

8 RG, *Claudius the God*, p. 177.

9 A collection of 'Likes' by various hands was originally planned as a book. These ended as a small collection in *Focus*, 4, 1935, a newsletter printed by Riding and Graves on the Seizin Press and distributed privately to their friends.

10 Sassoon's response has been lost; we only have RG's summary of its contents on 26 June 1933 on which to rely (*Collected Letters*, 1, pp. 222–4).

11 See n. 1.

12 Laura Riding, *The Word 'Woman' and Other Related Writings*, ed. Elizabeth Friedmann and Alan Clark (Persea Books, New York, 1993). This was its first publication.

13 Author's interview with Honor (Wyatt) Ellidge, 18 February 1993.

14 As n. 13.

15 Author's interview with Eirlys Roberts, August 1993.

16 See n. 1.

17 Laura Riding to John Aldridge, n.d. (Berg).

18 Laura Riding to Karl Goldschmidt, n.d. 1934 (Lilly).

19 Hans Rothe to Louise Addis, 23 December 1934 (Victoria).

CHAPTER 19: *1935* UNDERLYING TENSIONS

1 RG to Joshua Podro, n.d. 1944 (private collection: Michael Podro).

2 Janet Adam Smith, Introduction to *The Faber Book of Modern Verse* (London, 1936, reissue, 1982), p. xxvi.

3 Laura Riding to Michael Roberts, 12 April 1935 (Berg).

4 RG to Michael Roberts, Introduction, *Faber Book of Modern Verse*, (reissue, 1982), p. xxxiii.

5 RG to Michael Roberts, n.d. (private collection: Janet Adam Smith).

6 Laura Riding to Michael Roberts, 4 March 1937 (Berg).

7 RG to Michael Roberts, 13 February 1937 (Berg).

8 RG to Basil Liddell Hart, 21 December 1935, *Collected Letters*, 1, pp. 262–3.

9 RG and Laura Riding, 'A Private Correspondence on Reality', *Epilogue III* (Seizin/Constable, London, 1937), p. 124.

10 RG and Riding, 'Private Correspondence', *Epilogue III*, p. 109.

11 RG, Diary, 8 March 1935 (Victoria).

12 RG, 'The Challenge', *Epilogue I* [1935], republished in *Collected Poems* [1938].

13 RG, Diary, 7 December 1935 (Victoria).

14 RG to Basil Liddell Hart, 20 February 1936, *Collected Letters*, 1, p. 265.

15 RG to Sam Graves, n.d. 1936 (St John's).

16 RG to Julie Matthews, 18 July 1936, *Collected Letters*, 1, pp. 271–2.

17 RG, Diary, 31 December 1936 (Victoria).

CHAPTER 20: *1936–1937* A SENSE OF EXILE

1 RG, 'God Grant Your Honour Many Years', in *Collected Short Stories* [1964], p. 222.

2 This is an unpublished passage in Antonia White's diary for 1 September 1937.

3 RG, Diary, 14 November 1936 (Victoria).

4 RG and Alan Hodge, *The Long Weekend* [1940], p. 334.

5 Ibid., p. 339.

6 Author's interview with Catherine Dalton, August 1993.

7 RG, Diary, 24 November 1936 (Victoria).

8 RG, Diary, 7 October 1936 (Victoria).

9 RG, 'Parent to Children', *Collected Poems* [1938].

10 RG, 'A Jealous Man', *Collected Poems* [1938].

11 RG, Diary, 5 November 1936 (Victoria).

12 Mary Somerville was also asked for advice about where a discreet operation could be performed, and suggested 'a woman-surgeon to go in the worst comes to the worst case'. RG to Nancy Nicholson, n.d. (Lilly).

13 Mary Taylor to the author, 12 January 1993.

14 RG to Nancy Nicholson, n.d. (Lilly). RG's behaviour should be considered in the light of the later 'exorcism' of Schuyler Jackson's wife, Katherine, in 1939.

15 Karl Gay to the author, 16 August 1993.

16 Karl Gay to the author, 30 August 1993.

17 RG in *The World and Ourselves* by Laura Riding and 65 Others (Chatto & Windus, London, 1939), pp. 120–5.

18 RG, 'The Fallen Tower of Siloam', *Collected Poems* [1938].

CHAPTER 21: *1937–1938* THE COVENANT

1 The final title of *Count Belisarius* came later from the publishers. In the text, I have used the book's working title of 'Belisarius'.

2 RG, 'Leda' and 'The Florist Rose', 1937, *Collected Poems* [1938].

3 RG noted this in his diary, 1 July 1937 (Victoria).

4 Harry Kemp in an interview with the author, April 1993.

5 As n. 4.

6 Based on interviews with Harry Kemp, Beryl Graves and Jane Aiken Hodge, widow of Alan Hodge.

7 RG, diary, 29 January 1938 (Victoria).

8 Nancy Nicholson to RG, summer 1938 (Lilly).

9 Karl Gay to the author, October 1993. Karl heard about this incident from Alan Hodge.

10 Isabel Hawking, a friend of Beryl's from their years as Oxford students, to the author, April 1993.

11 RG, 'Dawn Bombardment', *Poems 1938–1945* [1945].

12 Laura Riding to Karl Gay, 24 December 1938 (Lilly).

13 Laura Riding to Karl Gay, 3 February 1939 (Lilly).

14 Laura Riding to Karl Gay, 5 March 1939 (Lilly).

15 RG, diary, 16 March 1939 (Victoria).

16 RG to Dorothy Simmons, 3 May 1939 (Berg).

17 Robin Hale to the author, July 1993.

CHAPTER 22: *1939–1940* MADNESS AND MAGICS

1 Deborah Baker, *In Extremis: A Life of Laura Riding* (Grove Press, New York, 1993), p. 387.

2 RG, 'Cambridge Upstairs', *¡Catacrok!* [1956] pp. 39–40.

3 RG to Dorothy Simmons from Hibben Road, Princeton, 30 April 1939 (Berg).

4 RG to Dorothy Simmons, written with Laura Riding and partly at her dictation, 3 May 1939 (Berg).

5 RG to Dorothy Simmons, n.d. but the contents indicate mid-May 1939 (Berg).

6 RG to Beryl and Alan Hodge, May 1939 (Buffalo).

7 Robin Hale to the author, July 1993.

8 RG to Dorothy Simmons, 13 May 1939 (Berg).

9 Baker, *In Extremis*, pp. 389–90.

10 Beryl Graves to the author, 19 August 1993. In the same letter, she states that there was no sign of madness in Kit Jackson's behaviour when they first arrived in May.

11 Letter from Katherine Jackson to the author, 23 August 1993, in which she refers to Riding's 'witcheries'. RG's increasing intimacy with Beryl is said by Mrs Jackson to have been apparent to everybody there.

12 Griselda Ohaniesson and her mother, Katherine Jackson, in separate letters to the author of 6 April and 23 August 1993.

13 Griselda Ohaniesson to the author, 6 April 1993.

14 As n. 13.

15 Beryl Graves to the author, 19 August 1993.

16 T. S. Matthews, *Under the Influence* (Cassell, London, 1979), p. 208.

17 Baker, *In Extremis*, p. 396.

18 Alan Hodge gave this account to Martin Seymour-Smith, *Robert Graves: His Life and Works* (Paragon, New York, 1988), p. 336. There are no other accounts of the incident.

19 Beryl Graves to the author, 27 August 1993.

20 RG, 'The Moon Ends in Nightmare', inserted in the last page of his diary following the entry for 6 May 1939.

21 Laura Riding to RG, 22 July 1939 (Buffalo).

22 RG to Dorothy Simmons, n.d. but contents indicate late July 1939 (Berg).

23 Siegfried Sassoon to RG, 16 August 1939 (Morris).

24 RG to Nancy Nicholson, n.d. (Lilly).

25 Laura Riding to RG, 15 September 1939 (Buffalo). This letter recites the contents of RG's previous letter to her in detail. RG's original letter has not been found.

26 Alan Hodge talked about this period to his second wife, Jane Aiken Hodge, to whom I am most grateful for providing details during an interview in June 1993.

27 RG, 'Horses: A Play Chiefly for Children', in *London Calling* ed. Storm Jameson (Harper, New York, 1942).

28 RG to Basil Liddell Hart, 25 September, 1949, *Collected Letters*, 1 [1984], pp. 286–7.

29 Laura Riding to RG, 17 August 1939 (Buffalo).

30 Beryl Hodge to Alan Hodge, 21 August 1939 (Buffalo).

31 Laura Riding to RG, 26 September 1939 (Buffalo).

32 RG to Dorothy Simmons, 25 September 1939 (Berg).

33 Jane Aiken Hodge to the author, June 1993.

34 RG's letter to Karl Gay of 26 January 1940 (*Collected Letters*, 1, pp. 290–1) gives a full account of the contents of Laura and Schuyler's letters to him.

35 As n. 34.

36 RG reported this in a letter to Alan Hodge, 20 March 1941, *Collected, Letters*, 1, pp. 299–300.

CHAPTER 23: *1940–1943* A FAMILY LIFE

1 Beryl Graves to the author, June 1993.

2 RG, *Proceed, Sergeant Lamb* (Methuen, London, 1941), p. 94.

3 George Orwell, *New Statesman & Nation*, 21 September 1940.

4 RG to Alan Hodge, 3 March 1941, *Collected Letters*, 1, p. 298.

5 RG to David Graves, 13 November 1939 (Lilly).

6 RG to David Graves, 22 January 1940 (St John's).

7 RG, *The Long Weekend* [1940], pp. 200–1.

8 Ibid., p. 216.

9 RG to Nancy Nicholson, 2 September 1939 (Lilly).

10 RG to Nancy Nicholson, 11 October 1939 (Lilly).

11 Nancy Nicholson to RG, 14 October 1939 (Lilly).

12 RG to David Graves, n.d. 1940 (St John's).

13 RG to James Reeves, 1 September 1944 (private collection: Stella Irwin).

14 RG to Dorothy Simmons, 30 January 1944 (Berg).

15 RG later believed the meeting to have taken place with Joshua Podro in 1941; the Podro records clearly indicate 1943.

16 T. S. Matthews, *Under the Influence* (Cassell, London, 1979), pp. 229–30.

17 Ibid., p. 230.

18 Ibid,. p. 229.

19 Ibid., p. 230.

20 Dorothy Simmons to Beryl Graves, 12 January 1940 (Canelluñ).

21 Honor Wyatt, in an interview with the author, 18 February 1993.

22 Karl Gay, in an interview with the author, 18 February 1993.

23 Kathleen Liddell Hart in an interview with the author, February 1994.

24 Joanna Simon in an interview with the author, 15 May 1993.

25 RG to Beryl Hodge, 25 September 1939 (Canelluñ).

26 RG to Beryl Graves; Beryl Graves to RG, December 1944 (Canelluñ).

27 RG to Beryl Graves; Beryl Graves to RG, September 1947 (Canelluñ).
28 Author's interview with Kathleen Liddell Hart.
29 *The Times Literary Supplement*, 19 November 1938.
30 'Graves Superieur' by Stephen Spender in *New Statesman & Nation*, 21 September 1940.
31 RG, 'The White Goddess', *Poems and Satires [1951]*.
32 RG, 'Juan at the Winter Solstice', first published as a Christmas-card poem for friends, December 1944.
33 RG to Beryl Graves, Christmas Eve, 1944 (Canelluñ).
34 RG to Beryl Graves, 31 December 1944.
35 RG, *Seven Days in New Crete* (US title: *Watch the North Wind Rise*) [1949], p. 209.
36 RG, *The White Goddess* [1948]. The revised 1961 edition is referred to throughout, unless an alteration, as here, has been made to the 1948 text; p. 449.

CHAPTER 24: *1940–1943:* A WRITING LIFE

1 The full list of RG's prose works in 1940–50 is; *Sergeant Lamb of the Ninth* (US: *Sergeant Lamb's America*) [1940]; *The Long Week-end* [1940]; *Proceed, Sergeant Lamb* [1941]; *The Story of Marie Powell: Wife to Mr Milton* (US: *Wife to Mr Milton*) [1943]; *The Reader Over Your Shoulder* [1943]; *The Golden Fleece* [1944] (US: *Hercules, My Shipmate*) [1945]; *King Jesus* [1946]; *The White Goddess* [1948]; *Seven Days in New Crete* (US: *Watch the North Wind Rise*) [1949]; *The Common Asphodel: Collected Essays on Poetry 1922–1949* [1949]; *The Isles of Unwisdom* [US: 1949; UK: 1950]; *Occupation: Writer* [US: 1950; UK: 1951]; *The Transformations of Lucius, Otherwise Known as the Golden Ass* (a translation) [1950].
2 RG and Alan Hodge, *The Reader Over Your Shoulder* (T.R.O.Y.S.) [1943], p. 39.
3 RG to Alan Hodge, 23 October 1940, *Collected Letters*, 1, pp. 195–6.
4 RG and Alan Hodge, T.R.O.Y.S., pp. 254–63, on I. A. Richards, *Principles of Literary Criticism* (Kegan, Paul & Co., London, 2nd edn, 1926).
5 RG and Alan Hodge, T.R.O.Y.S., p. 263.
6 RG to Helen Waddell, 3 August 1942 (Canelluñ).
7 Beryl Graves to the author, June 1993.
8 RG to Alun Lewis, 15 November 1941, *Collected Letters*, 1 [1984], pp. 307–9.
9 Alun Lewis to RG, 1 March 1942, *Collected Letters*, 1, pp. 311–12.

10 RG to Alun Lewis, 15 November 1941, *Collected Letters*, 1, pp. 307–9.

11 'Randall Jarrell, Graves and the White Goddess', *Yale Review*, XLV, 1956, pp. 302–14 and 467–80 (proofs, Berg).

12 *Yale Review* proofs, pp. 302 and 304.

13 Ibid., pp. 473–4.

14 Ibid., p. 476.

15 Camille Paglia, in *Sexual Personae* (Penguin, 1991), p. 672, claims that Graves disapproved of women poets and that lesbian poems were particularly abhorrent to him. The references are to pp. 446–7 of *The White Goddess*. Here, far from showing disapproval, Graves suggested that Laura Riding was the ideal female poet; he went on to describe the qualities of the ideal female as poet those of being 'impartial, loving, severe, wise'. Sappho was cited by him in the same section as another ideal female poet. Graves followed this by defending Sappho against the notion of her as an 'insatiable' lesbian. This hardly suggests disapproval.

16 RG to Sam Graves, 31 October 1945 (St John's).

17 RG to Basil Liddell Hart, 1 May 1944, *Collected Letters, 1*, p. 321.

CHAPTER 25: *1943–1946* THE WHITE GODDESS

1 RG, *The White Goddess* [1948], pp. 488–9. See also ch. 23, n. 36.

2 *White Goddess*, p. 67.

3 Jane E. Harrison, *Prolegomena to the Study of Greek Religion* (Cambridge University Press, 1903).

4 Harrison, *Prolegomena*, p. 465.

5 RG to Karl Gay, n.d. 1943 (Lilly).

6 RG, *The Golden Fleece* [1944], pp. 24, 27.

7 Ibid., p. 37.

8 Ibid., p. 371.

9 Edward Davies, Chancellor of Christ's College in Brecon, wrote two books, either of which could have given Graves the clue he needed. One was *Celtic Researches, on the Origin, Traditions and Language, of the Ancient Britons* (London, 1804). The other was *The Mythology and Rites of the British Druids* (J. Booth, London, 1809).

10 RG to Alan Hodge, November 1943 (St John's).

11 RG to Sam Graves, 3 November 1946 (St John's).

12 RG to Karl Gay, 1 January 1946 (Lilly).

13 RG to Alan Hodge, 8 August 1944 (St John's).

14 RG, 'The White Goddess', a lecture published in *5 Pens in Hand*

(Doubleday, New York, 1958), p. 72. The story has proved impossible for the author to verify.

15 RG, *White Goddess*, pp. 458–9.

16 Ibid., p. 224.

17 Ibid., p. 448.

18 Ibid., p. 448.

19 Ibid., p. 458.

20 RG to T. S. Eliot, 22 January 1945, *Collected Letters*, 1, pp. 327–8.

21 RG to Tom Matthews, 29 August 1946 (private collection: Pamela Matthews).

22 RG to Joshua Podro, 7 June [1945] (private collection: Michael Podro).

23 RG, *King Jesus* [1946], pp. 420–1.

24 RG, 'Lament for Pasiphaë', *Poems 1938–45* [1945].

25 RG to T. S. Eliot, 10 December 1946, *Collected Letters*, [1988], pp. 36–7.

26 *King Jesus*, reviewed in the *Times Literary Supplement*, 7 December 1946.

27 *King Jesus*, reviewed by Robert Fitzgerald in *The Nation*, 26 October 1946.

28 RG to Joshua Podro, April? 1946 (private collection: Michael Podro). The letter carries the Galmpton address and mentions their travel plans.

CHAPTER 26: *1946–1949*: RETURN TO DEYÁ

1 RG to Joshua Podro, 3 December 1946 (private collection: Michael Podro).

2 Beryl Graves to Alan Hodge, June 1946 (Berg).

3 RG to Karl Gay, 24 June 1946 (Lilly).

4 RG to Alan Hodge, 29 June [1946], *Collected Letters, 2* [1988], pp 29–31.

5 Beryl Graves to the author, October 1993.

6 Beryl Graves to Pamela Matthews, 30 January 1978 (private collection: Pamela Matthews).

7 William Graves, interview with the author, October 1993.

8 RG to Ricardo Sicre, 8 December 1947 (St John's).

9 As n. 8.

10 RG to John and Lucie Aldridge, 17 October 1947 (Berg).

11 RG to John Aldridge, 21 February 1948 (Berg).

12 Beryl Graves to Douglas Glass, January 1948 (private collection: Christopher Glass). Douglas and Jane Glass were friends from the

Galmpton days. Douglas Glass, a photographer, took many of the most frequently-used photographs of Graves, at Galmpton in the Forties and at Deyá in the early Fifties.

13 Cicely Gittes to the author, July 1994.

14 RG to Clarissa Graves, 3 January 1948 (Donohue).

15 As n. 14.

16 The letters between RG and the Simmonses are in the Berg Collection, New York Public Library.

17 William Graves to the author, March 1993.

18 The letters in which RG and Ricardo Sicre discussed the property arrangements are at St John's, Oxford.

19 RG to James Reeves, 30 March 1946 (private collection: Stella Irwin).

20 John Heath-Stubbs to RG, 14 August 1948 (Canelluñ).

21 Roy Fuller to RG, 25 April 1948 (Canelluñ).

22 Ted Hughes to the author, October 1994; Ted Hughes to RG, July 1967 (Canelluñ).

23 RG to Clarissa Graves, 23 December 1950 (Donohue).

24 Cicely Gittes to the author, June 1994.

25 Michael Podro, in an interview with the author, June 1993.

26 RG to Cicely Gittes, 31 December 1949 (St John's).

27 RG to Cicely Gittes, early 1951? n.d. (St John's).

28 William Merwin to the author, August 1993; Judith Bledsoe in an interview with the author, March 1993.

29 Irene Gay to the author, April 1994.

30 Cicely Gittes in an interview with the author, June 1994.

CHAPTER 27: *1950–1956* JUDITH

1 RG to Cicely Gittes, 18 May 1950 (private collection: Cecily Gittes).

2 RG to James Reeves, 14 December 1950 (private collection: Stella Irwin).

3 RG to Cicely Gittes, 20 November 1950 (Gittes).

4 RG to Cicely Gittes, 25 January 1951 (Gittes).

5 RG, *Collected Short Stories* [1965], p. 304.

6 Judith Bledsoe in an interview with the author, March 1993.

7 RG, 'Darien', *Poems and Satires* [1951].

8 Bledsoe interview, March 1993.

9 The identity of the Irishman has not been established, but it may have been Robert Kee, who went with Daniel Farson to interview Graves in Deyá later in the year.

10 Beryl Graves to the author, 21 April 1993.

11 Bledsoe interview, March 1993.

12 RG to James Reeves 1951 (Irwin).

13 RG, 'Plea to Boys and Girls', *5 Pens in Hand* [1958].

14 Jay Macpherson, in an interview with the author, August 1993.

15 As n. 14.

16 As n. 14.

17 Derek Savage, *Focus* on *Robert Graves and his Contemporaries*, Spring 1994, p. 13.

18 Jenny Nicholson to RG, 20 February 1951 (Canelluñ).

19 RG to Sam Graves, 14 December 1951 (St John's).

20 RG to Dick Graves, 3 February 1951 (Victoria).

21 Jenny Nicholson to RG, April 1952 (Canelluñ).

22 Wendy Toye, in an interview with the author, May 1993.

23 Jenny Nicholson to RG, 18 August 1954 (Canelluñ).

24 Jane Aiken Hodge, in an interview with the author, June 1993.

25 Kingsley Amis to RG, 25 October 1954 (Canelluñ).

26 Karl Gay to the author, October 1993.

27 James Metcalf to the author, December 1993.

28 As n. 27. The reference is to *The Greek Myths*, vol. I, pp. 32–3 in the US Moyer Bell edition of 1988. The book was originally published by Penguin in the UK and US in 1955; George Braziller published an original US edition in 1957.

29 RG's poem, 16 June 1954, is printed in *Collected Letters*, 2, p. 139. The letters from RG about the *TLS* court case are in the Podro Collection.

30 RG, 'Varro's Four Hundred and Ninety Books', *Punch*, 8 September 1954.

31 RG to Selwyn Jepson, 10 March 1954 (Victoria).

32 RG, 'A Poet and His Public', *The Listener*, 28 October 1954.

CHAPTER 28: *1953–1956* A FOX WITHOUT A BRUSH

1 RG to Lynette Roberts, 1951?, *Collected Letters*, 2 [1988], p. 87.

2 RG to Gordon Wasson, 26 January 1949, *Collected Letters* 2, p. 53.

3 RG to Gordon and Valentina Wasson, 6 March 1949, *Collected Letters*, 2, p. 54.

4 RG to Selwyn Jepson, 4 November 1953 (Victoria).

5 RG described his intentions to Selwyn Jepson on 6 February 1955 (Victoria).

6 RG to Keith Baines, n.d. 1954? (private collection: Janet Boulton).

7 RG, 'Rhea', 1952, *Collected Poems* 1955.

8 RG, 'Counting the Beats', *Collected Poems 1955*.

9 RG to Alan Sillitoe, 26 July 1954, *Collected Letters*, 2, pp. 137–8.

10 RG to Selwyn Jepson, 23 March 1954 (Victoria).

11 RG to Janet Adam Smith, 16 June 1954 (private collection: Janet Adam Smith).

12 John Wain to RG, 2 August 1961 (Canelluñ).

13 James Metcalf to the author, December 1993.

14 RG, *The Crowning Privilege: The Clark Lectures 1954–55* [1955], p. 5.

15 Ted Hughes to the author, October 1994.

16 RG, *The Crowning Privilege*, p. 157. Put on the defensive, Graves later claimed to have been one of Hopkins's first supporters in *A Survey of Modernist Poetry* [1927].

17 RG to James Reeves, 8 November 1955 (private collection: Stella Irwin).

18 RG to Karl Gay, 19 April 1955 (Lilly).

19 RG to Dorothy Simmons, 14 March 1955 (Berg).

20 RG, diary, 20 October 1956 (Beryl Graves).

21 James Metcalf confirms that this poem was written in response to the end of his first marriage (Metcalf to the author, December 1993).

22 RG, 'Call It a Good Marriage', *Steps* (London: Cassell, 1958).

23 RG to James Reeves, 27 July 1955 (Irwin).

24 R. W. Lloyd-Davies to the author, 31 October 1994.

25 RG to Karl Gay, 19 April 1955 (Lilly).

26 From RG's own blurb for the jacket of *They Hanged My Saintly Billy* [1957].

27 *The Times Literary Supplement*, 31 May 1957.

28 *New Statesman & Nation*, 25 March 1957.

29 Beryl Graves to the author, October 1993. This was how Graves light-heartedly described the tour to his family and friends.

CHAPTER 29: *1957*: A NEW CELEBRITY

1 RG to Tom Matthews, 1 October 1956 (private collection: Pamela Matthews).

2 RG to Karl Gay, 5 October 1956 (Lilly).

3 RG, *Occupation: Writer* [1951], p. 275. (This was first published in the US, by Creative Age Press, in 1950.)

4 RG to Tom Matthews, 1 October 1956 (Matthews).

5 Juan Graves to the author, November 1993; Karl and Irene Gay to the author, October 1993.

6 William Empson 'In Eruption', *New Statesman & Nation*, 1 October 1955.

7 Alastair Reid in an address delivered at the University at Buffalo, in State University of New York, 1985.

8 Alastair Reid in an interview with the author, June 1993.

9 Karl and Irene Gay to the author, October 1993.

10 The author is grateful for the use of a copy of 'Quoz' held by William Graves.

11 RG to Beryl Graves, 5, 12 and n.d. February 1957 (Canelluñ).

12 RG, diary, 13 February 1957 (Beryl Graves).

13 RG to Ken McCormick, n.d. February? 1957 (Berg).

14 Cicely Gittes to Beryl Graves, 10 February 1957 (Canelluñ).

15 Ricardo Sicre to the author, April 1993.

16 Jenny's article was titled 'Death in Venice'. Details of the trial are in the Canelluñ files. Auberon Waugh, in *Will This Do?* (Century, London, 1991, p. 251), described 'the famous *Private Eye* lunch at which Richard Crossman announced that he, Aneurin Bevan and Morgan Phillipps, General Secretary of the Labour Party, had all perjured themselves in the famous libel against the *Spectator* which had jocularly suggested that they had all got drunk at a socialist conference in Venice.' Waugh adds that the lunch-time revelation was later reported in *Isis* by one of the guests, Tina Brown. I am indebted to Mr Waugh for his help here.

17 RG to Joshua Podro, 24 July 1957 (private collection: Michael Podro).

18 RG to John Brown, 28 August 1957 (Berg).

19 Cicely Gittes to the author, June 1993.

20 Ricardo Sicre to the author, April 1993.

21 RG, 'Around the Mountain', *Steps* [1958].

22 RG, 'The Face in the Mirror,' *5 Pens in Hand* [1958].

23 RG to Karl Gay, 23 December 1957 (Lilly).

24 Alastair Reid in an interview with the author, June 1994.

25 These quotes are from RG's diary (Beryl Graves).

26 RG to James Reeves, 26 November 1958 (private collection: Stella Irwin).

27 RG to James Reeves, 9 March 1958 (Irwin).

28 RG to Keith Baines, 12 October 1958 (private collection: Janet Boulton).

29 RG to Cicely Gittes, 26 August 1958 (private collection: Cicely Gittes).

30 Jay Macpherson in an interview with the author, June 1993.

31 Philip Larkin, *Manchester Guardian*, 2 December 1958.

32 *The Times Literary Supplement*, 9 January 1959.

33 John Wain, *The Observer*, 11 January 1959.

CHAPTER 30: *1958–1960* ILLNESS

1 RG to Dick Graves, February 1958 (Victoria).

2 As n. 1.

3 Tyrone Guthrie to RG, 20 December 1958 (Canelluñ).

4 Huw Wheldon, '*Monitor*' BBC interview with RG, 1959. Reprinted from *Monitor: An Anthology* (Macdonald, London, 1962) in *Conversations with Robert Graves* ed. Frank L. Kersnowski (University Press of Mississippi, Jackson, 1989), pp. 49–57.

5 RG, 'The Lost Chinese', *Collected Short Stories* [1964], pp. 272, 280.

6 RG to Alan Sillitoe and Ruth Fainlight, 21 September 1959, *Collected Letters*, 2 [1988], p. 183.

7 RG, 'The Quiet Glades of Eden', *Food for Centaurs* [1960].

8 RG, 'Joan and Darby', *Food for Centaurs*.

9 RG, 'Surgical Ward: Men', 1960, *More Poems 1961*.

10 Karl Gay in an interview with the author, November 1993.

11 RG to Beryl Graves, 26 September 1962 (Canelluñ).

12 RG to Karl Gay, 13 October 1959 (Lilly).

13 Alec Guinness to RG, 31 September 1959 (Canelluñ).

14 RG to Edwin Newman, in interview of 1970 reprinted in *Difficult Questions, Easy Answers* [1972].

CHAPTER 31: *1960–1962* MARGOT

1 RG, 'The Case for Xanthippe', *The Crane Bag* [1969], pp. 60–8.

2 I am grateful to Dr Eve Hammer and to Dr Eleanor Moskovic for information about the likely causes of Graves's deterioration after 1959 (February 1995) and to William Graves for allowing me to study the hospital records supplied by St Thomas's.

3 RG, 'Tyger, Tyger', *The Crane Bag*, p. 133.

4 Honor (Wyatt) Ellidge, in an interview with the author, April 1993.

5 The circumstances of Dr Dalton's death in 1961 are discussed in *Without Hardware: Cases of Treason in Australia*, the book which Catherine Dalton wrote in 1970 and which was republished by Ochre Press, Towamba, in 1980.

6 'A Significant Lecture at Mount Holyoke', *The Crane Bag*, p. 132.

7 RG, *Oxford Addresses on Poetry* [1961], p. 121.

8 Ted Hughes to the author, October 1994.

9 RG and Raphael Patai, *Hebrew Myths* [1964], p. 47.

10 Cicely Gittes in an interview with the author, June 1993.

11 RG, 'Lyceia', *More Poems 1961*.

12 Stella Irwin in an interview with the author, May 1993.

13 Alastair Reid in an interview with the author, June 1994.

14 RG, 'The Portrait', *Collected Poems 1955*.

15 RG, 'Under the Olives', *More Poems 1961*.

16 RG, 'In Her Praise', *New Poems 1962*.

17 Alastair Reid to the author, June 1994.

18 Alastair Reid to the author, November 1994.

CHAPTER 32: *1961–1963* BETWEEN MOON AND MOON

1 RG, Introduction to *The Sufis* by Idries Shah (Doubleday, New York, 1964).

2 As n. 1 above; 'Nine Hundred Iron Chariots' in *Mammon and the Black Goddess* [1965].

3 Ricardo Sicre to the author, April 1993; Gordon Wasson to RG, June 1962 (*Collected Letters*, 2 [1988], p. 218); Jenny Nicholson to RG, 10 August 1962 (Canelluñ).

4 Janet Boulton to the author, October 1993. Janet Boulton and her husband Keith Baines were living in Deyá during the early period of Graves's friendship with Idries Shah.

5 RG, diary, 17 February 1961 (Beryl Graves).

6 RG, 'Troughs of Sea', *More Poems 1961*.

7 Alastair Reid to RG, n.d. but contents indicate August/September 1961 (Buffalo).

8 RG, 'Lion Lover', *New Poems 1962*.

9 RG to James Reeves, 29 May 1961 (private collection: Stella Irwin).

10 RG, 'Beware, Madam', *New Poems 1962*.

11 Betty Lussier in an interview with the author, June 1993.

12 Alastair Reid to RG, 4 February 1962 (Buffalo).

13 Betty Lussier to the author, June 1993; Alastair Reid to the author, November 1994.

14 Alastair Reid, as n. 13.

15 W. H. Auden to RG, n.d. but Spring 1961; unsourced quote in Martin Seymour-Smith, *Robert Graves: His Life and Works* (Paragon, New York, 1988), p. 507.

16 Dr Michael Dunnill to the author, 21 January 1995.

17 Raphael Patai, *Robert Graves and the Hebrew Myths* (Wayne State University Press, Detroit, 1992), p. 254.

18 Ibid., pp. 257–61.

19 Ibid., p. 259.

20 Ibid., p. 261.

21 RG to Raphael Patai, 18 December 1961, *Robert Graves*, p. 264.

22 RG to Tom Matthews, 5 August 1961 (private collection: Pamela Matthews).

23 As n. 21 above.

24 RG to Alston Anderson, 4 July 1962 (Canelluñ).

25 RG to Tom Matthews, 22 April 1960, *Collected Letters*, 2, pp. 195–6.

26 Ursula Vaughan Williams to RG, 7 October 1962 (Canelluñ).

27 Lady Kilmarnock (Hilly Amis) to the author, November 1993.

28 Based on the author's conversations with Beryl Graves, October 1993.

29 RG to Beryl Graves, 23 September 1962 (Canelluñ).

30 Selwyn Jepson to RG, December 1962 (Victoria).

31 RG to Isla Cameron, 9 January 1963 (Victoria).

32 RG to Ralph Jacobs, 24 January 1963 (Canelluñ).

33 RG, diary, entries for January and February 1963 (Beryl Graves).

34 Lady Kilmarnock to the author, November 1993.

35 RG, 'A Last Poem' and 'The Three-Faced', *Man Does, Woman Is* [1964].

36 RG to James Reeves, 2 May 1963, *Collected Letters*, 2, p. 225.

37 RG to Idries Shah, 6 May 1963, *Collected Letters*, 2, pp. 225–6.

38 RG to Margot Callas, unposted, 6 May 1963 (Canelluñ).

39 Cicely Gittes in an interview with the author, June 1994.

40 RG, 'Nine Hundred Iron Chariots', *Mammon and the Black Goddess*.

41 Patai, *Robert Graves*, p. 345.

42 Kathleen Tynan, *Kenneth Tynan* (Weidenfeld & Nicolson, London 1987), p. 213.

43 Jakov Lind and Annie Truxell to the author, January 1995.

44 RG to Ralph Jacobs, 24 January [1963] (Canelluñ).

45 As n. 44. (It is worth noticing that RG, while fiercely opposed to homosexuality in his public interviews, was a devoted friend to several homosexuals, including Ralph Jacobs.)

CHAPTER 33: THE POET AND HIS MUSE

1 RG, 'Outlaws', *Country Sentiment* [1920]. The version quoted here is from *Collected Poems 1975*.

2 RG, *My Head! My Head!* [1925], p. 51.

3 Ibid., p. 52.

4 Ibid., p. 91.

5 RG to Ava Gardner, 8 October 1964 (St John's).

6 RG to Cindy Lee (also known as Aemelia Laraçuen, 17 May 1965 (HRC).

7 RG, 'Food of the Dead', *Man Does, Woman Is* [1964]. The sequences described are the division, by Roman numerals, of his work into sections; thus, this book comprises XV–XVII.

8 RG, 'Eurydice', *Man Does, Woman Is*.

9 RG, 'To Beguile and Betray', *Man Does, Woman Is*.

10 RG, 'I Will Write', *Man Does, Woman Is*.

11 RG to William Graves, October 1963 (St John's).

12 RG to Ralph Jacobs, 10 October 1963 (Canelluñ). For Jacob's comments on Cindy, see ch. 32, p. 412.

13 RG, 'Intimations of the Black Goddess', *Mammon and the Black Goddess* [1965].

14 Raphael Patai, *Robert Graves and the Hebrew Myths* (Wayne State University Press, Detroit, 1992), p. 374.

15 Jakov Lind and Annie Truxell to the author, January 1995.

16 RG to John Benson-Brooks, 9 April 1965 (Canelluñ).

17 Based on the author's conversations with Beryl Graves, October 1993.

18 The two undated letters used here are in the possession of William and Elena Graves (Deyá).

19 Cindy Lee (as Aemilia Laraçuen) to Ava Gardner, 19 March 1964 (Deyá).

20 The letters from John Benson-Brooks and Ralph Jacobs to RG are in the Canelluñ Collection.

21 RG to Ruth Fainlight, 12 February, 1969, *Collected Letters*, 2 [1988], pp. 277–8.

22 RG, 'Sword and Rose', *Man Does, Woman Is*.

CHAPTER 34: *1963–1967* THE BLACK GODDESS

1 RG to Selwyn Jepson, 12 February 1964 (Victoria).

2 Raphael Patai, *Robert Graves and the Hebrew Myths* (Wayne State University Press, Detroit, 1992), p. 359.

3 Ricardo Sicre to Karl Gay, 20 April 1965 (St John's).

4 RG to Ava Gardner, 19 March 1964 (St John's).

5 Cindy Lee to Ava Gardner, 19 March 1964 (Deyá).

6 RG to Idries Shah, 21 May 1964, *Collected Letters*, 2 [1988], pp. 240–1.

7 RG to Ralph Jacobs, 30 September 1964 (Canelluñ).

8 Cindy Lee to John Benson-Brooks, November 1964 (St John's).

9 Honor (Wyatt) Ellidge to the author, 18 February 1993.

10 RG to John Benson-Brooks, 10–14 December 1964 (St John's).

11 RG to Douglas Glass, 17 December 1964 (St John's).

12 RG to Douglas Glass, 15 January 1965 (St John's).

13 'Wigs and Beards', *Poems 1965–1968* [1968].

14 Karl Gay in an interview with the author, November 1993.

15 As n. 14.

16 As n. 14.

17 RG to Karl Gay, n.d., *Collected Letters*, 2, pp. 246–7.

18 RG to John Benson-Brooks, 22 April 1965 (St John's).

19 As n. 14.

20 RG to Spike Milligan n.d. (quoted in *Dear Robert, Dear Spike: The Graves–Milligan Correspondence*, ed. Pauline Scudamore (Alan Sutton, Stroud, Glos, 1991), p. 20.

21 Based on the author's conversations with William and Elena Graves, December 1992.

22 RG to Henry Stuart, 3 December 1965 (National Library of Scotland).

23 Paul Driver to the author, July 1994; Andrew Fraser to the author, October 1994.

24 Min Wild (formerly Lynne Smith) to the author, February 1993.

25 P. Scudamore (ed.), *Dear Robert, Dear Spike*, p. 134.

26 Sir Hugh Lloyd Jones to the author, 29 November 1994.

27 As n. 26.

28 RG, 'Astymelusa', written in October 1966, first published in *Oxford Magazine*, 1968, and republished in *Poems 1965–1968*.

29 Christopher Hudson to the author, November 1993, recalling an occasion on which he observed Graves's old-fashioned chivalry.

30 The sum is approximate, based on family recollections of what was received after the broker, Wallrich, took his commission. (William and Beryl Graves to the author, February 1995).

31 Christopher Logue, *Daily Telegraph*, 22 June 1966.

32 RG to Ralph Jacobs, 29 September 1966 (Canelluñ).

33 RG to Selwyn Jepson, 20 April 1964 (Victoria).

34 RG to Ava Gardner, 10 November 1966 (St John's).

35 Sam Vaughan to the author, January 1994.

CHAPTER 35: *1967–1969* THE LAST MUSE

1 Hugh Lloyd Jones quotes Graves back to himself in a letter to RG, February 1967 (Canelluñ).

2 RG, 'Song: Though Once True Lovers', *Poems 1965–1968* [1968].

3 RG, 'Fact of the Act', *Poems 1965–1968*.

4 RG, 'How It Started', *Poems 1968–1970* [1970].

5 Julia Simon in an interview with the author, Spring 1994.

6 Joanna Simon in an interview with the author, May 1993.

7 RG to Idries Shah, n.d. October 1966, *Collected Letters, 2* [1988], p. 254.

8 This is based on the account given by J. C. E. Bowen in *Translation or Travesty: An Enquiry into Robert Graves's Version of Some Rubáiyyát of Omar Khayyám* (Abbey Press, Abingdon, Berks, 1973).

9 RG to Tom Matthews, 15 November 1966 (private collection: Pamela Matthews).

10 This was incorporated into the title of the US edition of RG's *The Rubáiyyát of Omar Khayyám* [1968].

11 Quoted in Bowen, *Translation or Travesty*, p. 4.

12 J. C. E. Bowen, *The Listener*, 3 August 1972.

13 RG to John Benson-Brooks, 1 April 1967 (St John's).

14 Based on interviews by author with Juan, Elena, Beryl and William Graves, Winter 1993; RG to Karl Gay, 28 July 1967 (Lilly).

15 Ted Hughes to RG, July 1967 (Canelluñ).

16 RG to Catherine Dalton, 2 January 1966. Quoted in Catherine Dalton, *Without Hardware* (1970, new edn, Ochre Press, Towamba, 1980), p. 213.

17 RG to Spike Milligan, November 1967. Quoted in *Dear Robert, Dear Spike – The Graves–Milligan Correspondence*, ed. Pauline Scudamore (Alan Sutton, Stroud, Glos, 1991), p. 73.

18 RG to Nancy Nicholson, Dalton, *Without Hardware*, p. 213.

19 RG to Alan Hodge, 26 June 1967 (private collection: Jane Aiken Hodge).

20 RG to Selwyn Jepson, January 1968 (Victoria).

21 RG to John Benson-Brooks, 5 January 1971 (St John's).

22 RG, 'An Absolute Criminal', *The Crane Bag* [1969].

23 RG, 'Miss Briton's Lady-Companion', *The Crane Bag*.

24 RG, 'Genius', 1968, *Difficult Questions, Easy Answers* [1972], pp. 12–13, 14, 15.

25 RG to Henry Stuart, 16 January 1968 (National Library of Scotland).

26 RG to Isla Cameron, n.d. February? 1968 (Victoria).

27 *Conversations with Robert Graves,* ed. Frank L. Kersnowski (University Press of Mississippi, Jackson, 1989), p. 111.

28 RG to Spike Milligan, 18 June 1968, P. Scudamore (ed.), *Dear Robert, Dear Spike.*

29 As n. 28.

30 RG to Selwyn Jepson, 22 July 1968 (Victoria).

31 RG to Isla Cameron, 2 August 1968 (Victoria).

32 RG to Isla Cameron, 28 September 1968 (Victoria). John Aldridge's portrait of RG is in the National Portrait Gallery, London.

33 RG to Colin and Heather Thompson, 17 December 1968 (St John's).

34 RG to Clarissa Graves, 14 January 1971 (Donohue).

35 RG to Isla Cameron, 28 September 1968 (Victoria).

36 As n. 35.

CHAPTER 36: *1969–1985* THE EMPTY ROOM

1 RG, 'Olive Tree', *Poems 1968–1970* [1970].

2 RG to James Reeves, 4 January 1968 but misdated by RG as 1967, *Collected Letters,* 2 [1988], pp. 265–6.

3 RG to Ken McCormick, 12 April 1969 (Berg).

4 Julia Simon to the author, December 1994.

5 RG, 'Troublesome Fame', *Beyond Giving: Poems* [1969].

6 Frank L. Kersnowski (ed.), *Conversations with Robert Graves* (University Press of Mississippi, Jackson, 1989), pp. 144–67.

7 RG, *Difficult Questions, Easy Answers* [1972], p. 96.

8 Ibid., p. 109. Wasson was less honourable in publishing a 1972 paper on the murder of Claudius in which Graves was only glancingly acknowledged to have made a contribution to his thesis. Graves had provided Wasson with the classical background by which Seneca's satire could be seen to hold a clue, and had also confirmed the most likely form of mushroom used to poison the Emperor. In Wasson's paper, this information appears to have been discovered by Wasson himself. (Botanical Museum Leaflets, Harvard University, vol. 23, 3, 1972).

9 RG to Karl Gay, May 1972 (Lilly).

10 RG to John Benson-Brooks, 26 August 1972 (St John's).

11 RG to Selwyn Jepson, 4 September 1972 (Victoria).

12 RG to Selwyn Jepson, 13 February 1973 (Victoria).

13 John Carey in an interview with the author, spring 1994.

14 RG to Larry Wallrich, 7 September 1973 (Morris).

15 RG, from 'Unless', 1974 (unpublished poem in the Berg Collection).
16 William Empson to Laura (Riding) Jackson, 25 August 1970 and 29 April 1971. The correspondence between Chatto & Windus, William Empson and Laura Riding is held at Yale University, New Haven, Conn. See also *Modern Language Quarterly*, September 1966.
17 Kersnowski (ed.), *Conversations with Robert Graves*, p. 106.
18 RG to Harry Kemp, 16 June 1970 (Berg).
19 Laura (Riding) Jackson, 'Some Autobiographical Corrections of Literary History', *Denver Quarterly*, Winter 1974, pp. 1–33.
20 Arthur Crook (then the editor of the *Times Literary Supplement*) to the author, 24 January 1995.
21 Laura (Riding) Jackson, *The Word 'Woman' and Other Related Writings*, ed. Elizabeth Friedmann and Alan Clark (Persea Books, New York, 1993), pp. 205–11.
22 Elizabeth Friedmann in an interview with the author, 21 April 1993.
23 RG to Selwyn Jepson, 7 February 1974 (Victoria).
24 James Reeves, 'The Graves I Know', *The Malahat Review*, 33 (1975), p. 148.
25 David Eksurdjian to the author, November 1994.
26 Michael Irwin, in an interview with the author, April 1993.
27 RG to Sir Richard Southern, 10 February 1975 (St John's College Archive, Oxford).
28 John Montague in *A Story Worth the Telling*, Radio 3, 2 August 1982.
29 Derek Jacobi in an interview with the author, 28 April 1993.
30 Julian Glover in an interview with the author, June 1993.
31 Jacobi interview, April 1993.
32 RG to Alastair Reid, 1 June 1956 (Buffalo).
33 Honor (Wyatt) Ellidge, in an interview with the author, 18 February 1993.
34 Paul Cooper, in an interview with the author, March 1994.

ACKNOWLEDGEMENTS

MY LARGEST DEBT OF GRATITUDE IS DUE TO THE GRAVES FAMILY AND, in particular, to Beryl, Elena and William, who helped me with their encouragement, support and unstinting hospitality. They have allowed me to talk to their friends, study their personal letters, borrow their books in vast numbers and interrogate them about their past. Their greatest gift was to leave me free to draw my own conclusions. They could not have been kinder, or more helpfully candid. I am also grateful to Elena for reading the final manuscript, and to Beryl for reading part of it, in order to correct inaccuracies.

The late Karl Gay's editorial eye was as sharp as it had been when he was working for Robert Graves; without his reading of the central section of the book, there would have many more slips and errors. His assistance has been tireless and it has provided me with a file of letters which I shall treasure.

Supposedly, you can tell a man by his friends. In Graves's case, it has been difficult not to be moved by the loyalty, the affection and the humour he inspired. My thanks are due to all these friends for allowing me to interview them, and persecute them by post, fax, and telephone. My questions were often intrusive and far from good-mannered; I thank them, too, for honest answers. I wish some of them could have had a larger part in the story to which they contributed. I felt ready to write a whole book about the families of Robin Hale and Honor Wyatt; I would have liked to spend weeks talking with Lady Mancroft about John Aldridge, her half-brother, with Mary Taylor about Geoffrey (Phibbs) Taylor and staying with Pam Matthews, the most hospitable of them all.

Numerous patient acquaintances and poetry critics have allowed me to solicit their views of various parts and stages of the typescript; they have saved me from such mortifying slips as keeping Edward Thomas – a poet Graves inexplicably despised – alive until the 1920s. (He died at Arras in 1917.) I hope they will think that their efforts were worth the candle.

I am also indebted to Jane Birkett, Anthony Goff, Joanna Goldsworthy, Ellen Levine, Douglas Matthews and Marion Wood for the great contribution they have made to the book.

Thanks are due, for permissions and for the use of materials held in public collections, to the under-mentioned: Vincent Giroud at the Beinecke Library, Yale University; Francis Mattson at the Berg Collection, New York Public Library; the Bodleian Library, Oxford; the BBC Sound Archives; Erina Laffey at the British Film Institute; the British Library; Christopher Sheppard at the Brotherton Collection, Leeds University; Michael Basinski and Robert Bertholf at the University at Buffalo; Mrs Ann Wheeler at the Charterhouse Archives; Dorchester County Museum; Mrs Valerie Eliot; Thomas Fisher at the Rare Book Library, University of Toronto; Benjamin Watson at the Gleeson Library, University of San Francisco; Cathy Henderson at the Harry Ranson Humanities Research Center, Austin; Nigel Steel and Martin Taylor at the Imperial War Museum; the Board of Management for the estate of Laura (Riding) Jackson; Miss J. Cox at King's College Library, Cambridge; Heather Munro and Saundra Taylor at the Lilly Library, University of Indiana; University of California at Los Angeles; Karen D. Drickamer at the Morris Library, Southern Illinois University at Carbondale; Robin Smith at the National Library of Scotland; Andrew and Tim Nicholson of the Nicholson Trust; Paul O'Prey; Michael Bott at the University of Reading; Captain Norman Holme at the Royal Welch Fusiliers Museum, Caernarfon; Philip Hunter, John Kelly and Patrick Quinn at the Graves Trust, St John's College, Oxford; Mrs Elizabeth Inglis at the University of Sussex; Chris Petter at the

University of Victoria, BC; Linda O'Shaughnessy at A. P. Watt for quotations from the works of Robert Graves. I am also grateful for information provided by statisticians in the Research Department of *The Economist*.

BIBLIOGRAPHY

POETRY

Over the Brazier, The Poetry Bookshop, London, 1916; St Martin's Press, New York, 1975

Goliath and David, Chiswick Press, London, 1917

Fairies and Fusiliers, Heinemann, London, 1917; Knopf, New York, 1918

Treasure Box, Chiswick Press, London, 1920

Country Sentiment, Secker, London, 1920; Knopf, New York, 1920

The Pier-Glass, Secker, London, 1921; Knopf, New York, 1921

Whipperginny, Heinemann, London, 1923; Knopf, New York, 1923

The Feather Bed, Hogarth Press, Richmond, Surrey, 1923

Mock Beggar Hall, Hogarth Press, London, 1924

Welchman's Hose, The Fleuron, London, 1925

Poems, Benn, London, 1925

The Marmosite's Miscellany (as John Doyle), Hogarth Press, London, 1925

Poems (1914–1926), Heinemann, London, 1927; Doubleday, New York, 1929

Poems (1914–1927), Heinemann, London, 1927

Poems 1929, Seizin Press, London, 1929

Ten Poems More, Hours Press, Paris, 1930

Poems 1926–1930, Heinemann, London, 1931

To Whom Else?, Seizin Press, Deyá, Mallorca, 1931

Poems 1930–1933, Barker, London, 1933

Collected Poems, Cassell, London, 1938; Random House, New York, 1938

No More Ghosts: Selected Poems, Faber, London, 1940

Work in Hand, with Norman Cameron and Alan Hodge, Hogarth Press, London, 1942

Poems, Eyre & Spottiswoode, London, 1943

Poems 1938–1945, Cassell, London, 1945; Creative Age Press, New York, 1946

Collected Poems (1914–1947), Cassell, London, 1948

Poems and Satires, Cassell, London, 1951

Poems 1953, Cassell, London, 1953

Collected Poems 1955, Doubleday, New York, 1955

Poems Selected by Himself, Penguin, Harmondsworth, 1957; rev. 1961, 1966, 1972, 1978

The Poems of Robert Graves, Doubleday, New York, 1958

Collected Poems 1959, Cassell, London, 1959

The Penny Fiddle: Poems for Children, Cassell, London, 1960; Doubleday, New York, 1961

More Poems 1961, Cassell, London, 1961

Collected Poems, Doubleday, New York, 1961

New Poems 1962, Cassell, London, 1962; as *New Poems*, Doubleday, New York, 1963

The More Deserving Cases: Eighteen Old Poems for Reconsideration, Marlborough College Press, Marlborough, 1962

Man Does, Woman Is, Cassell, London, 1964; Doubleday, New York, 1964

Ann at Highwood Hall: Poems for Children, Cassell, London, 1964

Love Respelt, Cassell, London, 1965; Doubleday, New York, 1966

Collected Poems 1965, Cassell, London, 1965

Seventeen Poems Missing from 'Love Respelt', privately printed, 1966

Colophon to 'Love Respelt', privately printed, 1967

Poems 1965–1968, Cassell, London, 1968; Doubleday, New York, 1969

Poems About Love, Cassell, London, 1969; Doubleday, New York, 1969

Love Respelt Again, Doubleday, New York, 1969

Beyond Giving, privately printed, 1969

Poems 1968–1970, Cassell, London, 1970; Doubleday, New York, 1971

The Green-Sailed Vessel, privately printed, 1971
Poems: Abridged for Dolls and Princes, Cassell, London, 1971
Poems 1970–1972, Cassell, London, 1972; Doubleday, New York, 1973
Deyá, A Portfolio, Motif Editions, London, 1972
Timeless Meeting: Poems, privately printed, 1973
At the Gate, privately printed, London, 1974
Collected Poems 1975, Cassell, London, 1975
New Collected Poems, Doubleday, New York, 1977

PLAY

John Kemp's Wager: A Ballad Opera, Blackwell, Oxford, 1925; T. R. Edwards, New York, 1925

FICTION

My Head! My Head!, Secker, London, 1925; Knopf, New York, 1925
The Shout, Mathews & Marrot, London, 1929
No Decency Left (with Laura Riding) (as Barbara Rich), Cape, London, 1932
The Real David Copperfield, Barker, London, 1933; as *David Copperfield, by Charles Dickens, Condensed by Robert Graves*, ed. M. P. Paine, Harcourt, Brace, New York, 1934
I, Claudius, Barker, London, 1934; Smith & Haas, New York, 1934
Claudius the God and his Wife Messalina, Barker, London, 1934; Smith & Haas, New York, 1935
Antigua, Penny, Puce, Seizin Press, Deyá, Mallorca, and Constable, London, 1936; Random House, New York, 1937
Count Belisarius, Cassell, London, 1938; Random House, New York, 1938
Sergeant Lamb of the Ninth, Methuen, London, 1940; as *Sergeant Lamb's America*, Random House, New York, 1940
Proceed, Sergeant Lamb, Methuen, London, 1941; Random House, New York, 1941
The Story of Marie Powell: Wife to Mr Milton, Cassell, London, 1943; as *Wife to Mr Milton: The Story of Marie Powell*, Creative Age Press, New York, 1944
The Golden Fleece, Cassell, London, 1944; as *Hercules, My Shipmate*, Creative Age Press, New York, 1945

King Jesus, Creative Age Press, New York, 1946; Cassell, London, 1946

Watch the North Wind Rise, Creative Age Press, New York, 1949; as *Seven Days in New Crete*, Cassell, London, 1949

The Islands of Unwisdom, Doubleday, New York, 1949; as *The Isles of Unwisdom*, Cassell, London, 1950

Homer's Daughter, Cassell, London, 1955; Doubleday, New York, 1955

¡Catacrok! Mostly Stories, Mostly Funny, Cassell, London, 1956

They Hanged My Saintly Billy, Cassell, London, 1957; Doubleday, New York, 1957

Collected Short Stories, Doubleday, New York, 1964; Cassell, London, 1965

An Ancient Castle, Peter Owen, London, 1980.

OTHER

On English Poetry, Knopf, New York, 1922; Heinemann, London, 1922

The Meaning of Dreams, Cecil Palmer, London, 1924; Greenberg, New York, 1925

Poetic Unreason and Other Studies, Cecil Palmer, London, 1925.

Contemporary Techniques of Poetry: A Political Analogy, Hogarth Press, London, 1925

Another Future of Poetry, Hogarth Press, London, 1926

Impenetrability or The Proper Habit of English, Hogarth Press, London, 1927

The English Ballad: A Short Critical Survey, Benn, London, 1927; revised as *English and Scottish Ballads*, Heinemann, London, 1957; Macmillan, New York, 1957

Lars Porsena or The Future of Swearing and Improper Language, Kegan Paul, Trench, Trubner, London, 1927; Dutton, New York, 1927; revised as *The Future of Swearing and Improper Language*, Kegan Paul, Trench, Trubner, London, 1936

A Survey of Modernist Poetry (with Laura Riding), Heinemann, London, 1927; Doubleday, New York, 1928

Lawrence and the Arabs, Cape, London, 1927; as *Lawrence and the Arabian Adventure*, Doubleday, New York, 1928

A Pamphlet Against Anthologies (with Laura Riding), Cape, London 1928; as *Against Anthologies*, Doubleday, New York, 1928

Mrs Fisher or The Future of Humour, Kegan Paul, Trench, Trubner, London, 1928

Goodbye to All That: An Autobiography, Cape, London, 1929; Cape and

Smith, New York, 1930; rev., Doubleday, New York, 1957; Cassell, London, 1957; Penguin, Harmondsworth, 1960

But It Still Goes On: An Accumulation, Cape, London, 1930; Cape and Smith, New York, 1931

T. E. Lawrence to His Biographer Robert Graves, Doubleday, New York, 1938; Faber, London, 1939

The Long Weekend (with Alan Hodge), Faber, London, 1940; Macmillan, New York, 1941

The Reader Over Your Shoulder (with Alan Hodge), Cape, London, 1943; Macmillan, New York, 1943

The White Goddess, Faber, London, 1948; Creative Age Press, New York, 1948; rev., Faber, London, 1952, 1961; Knopf, New York, 1958

The Common Asphodel: Collected Essays on Poetry 1922–1949, Hamish Hamilton, London, 1949

Occupation: Writer, Creative Age Press, New York, 1950; Cassell, London, 1951

The Nazarene Gospel Restored (with Joshua Podro), Cassell, London, 1953; Doubleday, New York, 1954

The Greek Myths, Penguin, London, 1955; Penguin US, 1955

The Crowning Privilege: The Clark Lectures, 1954–5, Cassell, London, 1955; Doubleday, New York, 1956

Adam's Rib, Trianon Press, London, 1955; Yoseloff, New York, 1958

Jesus in Rome (with Joshua Podro), Cassell, London, 1957

Steps, Cassell, London, 1958

5 Pens in Hand, Doubleday, New York, 1958

Food for Centaurs, Doubleday, New York, 1960

Greek Gods and Heroes, Doubleday, New York, 1960; as *Myths of Ancient Greece*, Cassell, London, 1961

Selected Poetry and Prose (ed. James Reeves), Hutchinson, London, 1961

Oxford Addresses on Poetry, Cassell, London, 1962; Doubleday, New York, 1962

The Siege and Fall of Troy, Cassell, London, 1962; Doubleday, New York, 1963

The Big Green Book, Crowell-Collier, New York, 1962; Penguin, Harmondsworth, 1978

Hebrew Myths: The Book of Genesis (with Raphael Patai), Doubleday, New York, 1964; Cassell, London, 1964

Majorca Observed, Cassell, London, 1965; Doubleday, New York, 1965

Mammon and the Black Goddess, Cassell, London, 1965; Doubleday, New York, 1965

Two Wise Children, Harlin Quist, New York, 1966; Harlin Quist, London, 1967

Poetic Craft and Principle, Cassell, London, 1967

The Poor Boy Who Followed His Star, Cassell, London, 1968; Doubleday, New York, 1969

Greek Myths and Legends, Cassell, London, 1968

The Crane Bag, Cassell, London, 1969

On Poetry: Collected Talks and Essays, Doubleday, New York, 1969

Difficult Questions, Easy Answers, Cassell, London, 1972; Doubleday, New York, 1973

EDITOR

Oxford Poetry 1921 (with Alan Porter and Richard Hughes), Blackwell, Oxford, 1921

John Skelton (Laureate), Benn, London, 1927

The Less Familiar Nursery Rhymes, Benn, London, 1927.

The Comedies of Terence, Doubleday, New York, 1962; Cassell, London, 1963.

TRANSLATIONS

Almost Forgotten Germany by Georg Schwarz (with Laura Riding), Seizin Press, Deyá, Mallorca, and Constable, London, 1936; Random House, New York, 1936

The Transformations of Lucius, Otherwise Known as the Golden Ass by Lucius Apuleius, Penguin, London, 1950; Farrar, Straus, New York, 1951

The Cross and the Sword from *Enriquillio* by Manuel de Jesús Galván, Indiana University Press, Bloomington, 1954; Gollancz, London, 1956

The Infant with the Globe, from *El Nino de la bola* by Pedro de Alarcón, Trianon Press, London, 1955; Yoseloff, New York, 1955

Winter in Majorca by George Sand, Cassell, London, 1956

Pharsalia by Lucan, Penguin, London, 1956

The Twelve Caesars by Suetonius, Penguin, London, 1957

The Anger of Achilles: Homer's Iliad, Doubleday, New York, 1959; Cassell, London, 1960

The Rubáiyyát of Omar Khayyám (with Omar Ali-Shah), Cassell, London, 1967; Doubleday, New York, 1968

The Song of Songs, Clarkson Potter, New York, 1973; Collins, London, 1973

The only bibliography, *A Bibliography of the Writings of Robert Graves*, is by Fred H. Higginson, revised and enlarged by William Proctor Williams, St Paul's Bibliographies, London, 1966.

FURTHER READING

Robert Graves, *Collected Letters*, 2 vols, edited by Paul O'Prey (Moyer Bell, London and New York, 1984 and 1988)

Martin Seymour-Smith, *Robert Graves: His Life and Works* (Hutchinson, London, 1982; rev. edn., Bloomsbury, London, 1995)

Richard Perceval Graves, *Robert Graves: The Assault Heroic, 1895–1926* (Weidenfeld & Nicolson, London, 1986)

——*Robert Graves: The Years with Laura, 1926–40* (Weidenfeld & Nicolson, London, 1990)

——*Robert Graves and the White Goddess, 1940–85* (Weidenfeld & Nicolson, London, 1995)

Deborah Baker, *In Extremis: The Life of Laura Riding* (Grove Press, New York, 1993)

INDEX

Works by Robert Graves appear directly under title; works by others appear under authors' names